Praise for A Tramp in Africa

This tramp through Africa, on a shoestring, as sixty years of Colonial rule began to crumble, makes fascinating reading. Travel with the Tramp down jungle paths and across waterless terrain, follow his meandering into local customs and history. Enjoy his character sketches, his descriptive powers, his philosophy and colourful observations which draw his readers along in page-turning eagerness to see what lies ahead.

F.C. Lanning, MBE, FSA.
Soldier, Traveller and Administrator in Africa.

This account of a journey across Africa in the 1950's, contemporary with the travels of Wilfred Thesiger and Freya Stark, remains undimmed. Desert crossings, crocodile hunting, nights with the Masai make an indelible impression, justifying his inclusion in that august company of travel writing.

Dr. David J. Sinclair, General Practitioner.

Read this book and you feel you are accompanying David on every kilt-swinging step as he walks with innocent charm and a pioneering spirit through 1950's Africa with 'the Wind of Change' blowing at his heels.

Angus Sneddon, BBC Scotland.

A TRAMP IN AFRICA

David Lessels

Pen Press Publishers Ltd

Pen Press Publishers Ltd
The Old School
39 Chesham Road
Brighton BN2 1NB

ISBN-10: 1-905203-64-0
ISBN-13: 978-1-905203-64-2

Printed and bound in the UK

A catalogue record of this book is available from
the British Library

Cover design by Jacqueline Abromeit

Acknowledgement

My thanks to Maureen, my wife, for all her help and support to me in my writing when family life was already hectic. My pleasure at being able to present this book at last to our four daughters, who grew up with it always on the horizon. Also to Ruth, my sister, who has had to wait even longer and with regrets to my Mother and brothers, Lewis and Bill and sister Sheila, for whom sadly the waiting time was too long.

About the Author

 David Lessels was born into a mining family, the youngest of five children, in Torryburn, Fife. At the end of the war he went into the Army and was sent to Kenya where he fell in love with Africa. After his demob he returned to Africa under his own steam and travelled the long road, the length and breadth of the great continent, a journey lasting five years. 'A Tramp in Africa' describes the outward half of the journey. The second part is under way. Until retirement David was a Lecturer at Portsmouth College of Art and when not writing he and his wife enjoy spending time with their four daughters and their families.

Introduction

This Story of my journey through Africa in the mid-20th century is intended as more than a travel tale. In addition to my efforts to paint a word picture of Africa and its people at a pivotal time in history when 'The Winds of Change' were just beginning to gather momentum, I have tried to convey my own development in mind and philosophy as I went along the way. Thoughts, ideas and conclusions were hammered out to some satisfaction on the anvil of long miles of walking, often in the most arduous conditions. Indeed pitting myself against endless mental debates became the balm that dulled my mind to the savage tearing of my rucksack straps into long tired shoulders and made me forget the weariness in my legs and feet as the never-ending miles gradually crept by.

My story is as a string with many strands twisted into a tale, or, more accurately, a tapestry with interwoven threads which, I hope, blend together. There is basically the thread of my journey with the good, bad and exciting times; then there is the autobiographical thread interwoven with that of my developing psyche; and lastly there is the strong thread of history twisting and turning all the way through, from ancient times of Solomon to later Bantu Kingdoms of good and evil calibre and finally the Scramble for Africa by the Europeans.

Essentially it is a story of Africa before the door closed on colonial empires.

Author's Note

One more word, two in fact, before the music starts... Political Correctness! Anyone speaking of, and with, words of the mid-50's can be in awful trouble today. My daughter tells me that in my narrative I cannot refer to grown men, Africans, as 'boys'. If I were in Africa today I would not dream of using that term, in the same way as I would never have used my mother's generation word 'consumption' when we of my generation used the better term 'tuberculosis'. Every generation has its own words and we can tell peoples' ages by the words they use. We are all classed by the words we speak.

Therefore I would not be describing the correct scene of my story if I were to put today's connotation in the mouths of the people I met on my travels. The fact is, rightly or wrongly, in the time I was there no white person ever used any other word for African workers than 'Boy', even when the servant was in hoary old-age. Indeed, 'boy' was the genteel word used by the enlightened, in place of 'kaffir', the common word for natives of previous generations. Of these earlier times no one, not even David Livingstone, regarded 'kaffir' as too derogatory, the literal meaning of the word being 'non-believer'.

So if my words or thoughts-of-the-day grate on some modern ears I do not apologise, but beg tolerance. I was a man of my time writing of people of my time and I would be misrepresenting these people and myself if I were to write in modern jargon.

Contents

1 THE STONES ROLL   1

2 THE PARTING OF THE WAYS   13

3 RED SEA ODYSSEY   30

4 SHEBA'S CARAVANSERA   52

5 A HAPPY CHRISTMAS AND A SAD NEW YEAR   76

6 ONE HUNDRED AND ONE NIGHTS   102

7 THE LOST CITY   119

8 WHAT PRICE MY QUEEN...?   130

9 THE BLOOD DRINKERS   157

10 A GARLAND FOR A CROWN   196

11 THE LONELY ROAD TO ZANZIBAR   204

12 ZANZIBAR and 'THE TRADE OF HELL'   212

13 THE GIFT OF BREAD   232

14 MICA MINING   250

15 CROCODILE HUNTER   273

16 THE LAKE OF STORMS   327

17 FOUR YARDS OF CALICO   355

18 MOZAMBIQUE   374

19 SOUTHERN RHODESIA (ZIMBABWE)   398

20 KING SOLOMON'S MINES   424

21 ONE END OF THE RAINBOW   464

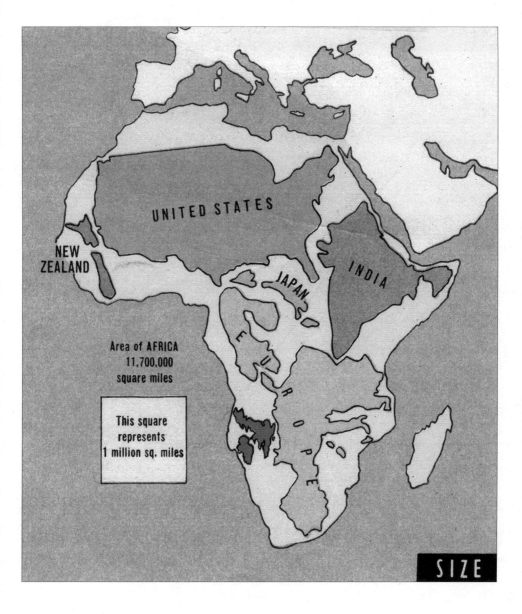

Area of AFRICA
11,700,000
square miles

This square
represents
1 million sq. miles

UNITED STATES

NEW
ZEALAND

JAPAN

INDIA

EUROPE

SIZE

A TRAMP IN AFRICA

The Outward Journey

The Homeward Journey

Chapter One

THE STONES ROLL

Wednesday 26th July 1950 – Transport Cafe, Kincardine (On Forth)
So the years of waiting have passed; so too have the past few months of
battling with the white-collared officials. We're going to have a lot of trouble
with these people before we're done, but we'll meet them as they come.

"Why do you wander as a vagabond?" asked the little man with the domed, myopic eyes that glinted in the starlight. Although the rest of his face was lost in the night I could sense his wispy hair blowing like spent dandelions in the sea breeze and his washboard brow screwed up to question-mark his words. We lay in a huddle of blanket-wrapped passengers on the deck of the Italian ship *Esperia*, three days out from Genoa, bound for Alexandria. Alec Seath, my travelling companion, was asleep and I had lain awake for a while, admiring the stars, listening to the sea, pitying the rich passengers cooped up in their cabins and wondering what lay ahead of us. But now Grasso Stellario, the Italian returning to Cairo after a holiday in his native land, had broken the spell. I pondered a while over his question wondering how best to answer it. On the surface the facts were clear.

From the time I learned joined-up letters I wanted to travel and write, to be a writer. By eight or so I was writing about cowboys riding along the dusty trail, their hands dashing to their holsters when the slightest danger threatened. By twelve I had read Richard Haliburton's *The Royal Road to Romance*, an American's trail to Andorra and other remote places of Europe, and I was hooked. I knew I had to travel. But more important: I wanted to travel and write about it, to be a journalist and send in reports from afar to newspapers and to write books about my travels when I returned.

I remember some of a little poem we had at school that fired my imagination and even now I feel the tingle, the thrill I felt when I heard it first:

I wish I lived in a caravan
with a horse to drive like the pedlar man!
Where he comes from nobody knows
Or where he goes to, but on he goes!

His caravan has windows two
and a chimney of tin that the smoke comes through…

With the pedlar man I should like to roam
and write a book when I come home.
All the people would read my book
…just like the travels of Captain Cook.

So I was a committed traveller even before I left school. All that was missing was direction. That came just before the end of World War II, when at eighteen I was called-up for the army and posted to Kenya where I fell hopelessly in love with Africa. I loved the smells and the colours. I liked the local people and their ways and attended Swahili lessons in my own time.

I took to Africa like a religious convert. From the moment the troopship docked at Mombasa and during all the way by rail up to the high plateau where Nairobi was situated I was enthralled. We arrived there in April at the height of the rainy season and we were posted to a camp on the edge of the vast Athi plain. Every day the great billowing, cumulus clouds turned into black, thunderous monsters and rain as we had never known it before turned the red earth of the camp into a quagmire and smashed in solid sheets on the wooden roofs of our mess-huts, destroying conversation. While my contemporaries described the country in good soldiers' language and lamented their ill-luck at being there, I loved it. I knew when I was demobbed I would have to come back.

I learned to drive and when the dry seasons came I would hire, borrow or purloin a vehicle for safaris across the Athi plain or up into the Ngong Hills or down into the Rift Valley to the wild Masai country. I was overcome with the sheer beauty and excitement of it all.

Africa, however, had not been kind to me. The sun aggravated a previous defect in my right eye and after a couple of years when I reported my failing sight to the Medical Officer I was rushed home on the first ship to Cowglen Military Hospital near Glasgow to have the eye removed. My other eye had been slightly contaminated and the prognosis on it was doubtful for the next four years when I would be twenty-five.

Demobbed at twenty-one, like the battered lover compulsively returning for more of the same, I immediately made plans to return to Africa. I did not mention the doubtful prognosis to family or friends. Whatever they might feel or think, however they might try to dissuade me from going, I knew I had to go. If the life of my sight was to be limited I wanted to see a great deal more of Africa before it expired.

When I left the army I made my plans to explore Africa. It was not my plan to go by ship or plane. I could never afford the fares and anyway I wanted to go overland to see the places and meet the people. While in the army in Kenya a friend from Ayrshire was called home because his brother was seriously ill. There was very little air travel then and a ship could take five weeks to make the voyage from Mombasa. So 'Movements' routed him through Uganda and down the Nile by boat and train to Cairo and after that perhaps by plane, and returned him the same way.

When he told me of his journey my mind went ethereal. Since I first heard of the Valley of the Kings when I was about fourteen I'd dreamed with all my heart of going there. And now when I was planning my return to Africa and Nairobi my army friend's journey had shown me the way.

The difference between his journey and mine of course was the simple matter of money. While he had been furnished with a Cooks' Tour-like pass I would have to fund myself. Sponsoring was not known in those days, at least I had never heard of it and even if I had I doubt if I'd have had anything to do with it. Sponsors, quite rightly, attach strings to their money. The whole essence of my future trip was freedom. Freedom to go where I liked, when I liked, at the speed I liked. The only person to manage my movements or set my direction was me.

So, without donors or assisted passage the only way left was to hitch-hike. There would be some places of course where I should almost certainly have to pay, such as crossing the Mediterranean Sea, but I hoped these places would be few.

In planning my journey I reckoned to cross Europe, sail to Egypt, go up the Nile to Uganda and Kenya, then south through Tanganyika, Northern and Southern Rhodesia and into South Africa. From Cape Town I planned to work my passage home on a ship. The whole journey I figured would take about two years. How wrong can you be! Or as Burns put it, "The best laid schemes o' mice an' men gang aft a-gley".

I went to Travel Agents, these new shops that were beginning to appear in the High Streets, to ask about visas and entry permits and regulations, but they were of little help. Their horizons were still very near. The Cote d'Azur was at the very edge of their world.

I wrote to the Consuls and Embassies in London of each country I was likely to pass through. Egypt sent me a visa, Sudan didn't reply, Northern Rhodesia was non-committal with some reference to entrants requiring proof of employment and Southern Rhodesia knocked the stuffing out of me, temporarily at least. They said all entrants must display a surety of £100 to ensure return of passage if necessary.

£100! How was I going to get that kind of money on top of what I was hurriedly saving. I had set myself a target of £50 to carry me through until I might get a job somewhere. Even that was a mighty effort for a painter and decorator earning £5 per week. Another £100 on top …! I saw my precious four years being swallowed up. Still, if that was what was required I was determined to get it. It meant my date of departure had to be pushed further away and my moonlighting efforts greatly increased. Jobbing now extended over weekends as well as evenings. Gradually the money was accrued and I was able to fix my date of departure for mid-summer 1950, two years after I had left the army. £50 would be turned into Travellers' Cheques and the £100 deposited in the Bank for which I would carry a Letter of Credit.

A month or two before I intended leaving, however, a development occurred that delayed departure a little more. Alec Seath, my lifelong pal with whom I had shared desks at school and who had often joined me in teenage hiking/climbing/ cycling weekends to the highlands, asked if he could join me on the Big One. I was delighted. To have company on the long road would be wonderful and there was no one I would rather have with me than Alec.

There was only one snag. Alec didn't have £50, let alone the crippling £100, so we delayed going for a bit so he could get as much spending money as he could together. The £100 was out of the question, we'd have to manage without it as best we could.

At last on July 26th, 1950, we swung heavy rucksacks on our backs, took our leave from our families and sauntered down Torryburn village street, Fife, on the road to Capetown. We both wore the kilt, Alec's was Argyll and Sutherland and mine the Black Watch. He wore a tartan tammy, and in my kit I had my old army bush-hat which I would don when we hit the sunshine and it would not look so incongruous with the kilt. Neighbours came to their doors to wave us off. This made us feel very proud but it also made us realise that we must prove ourselves worthy of their expectations of us. We must achieve something praiseworthy before we returned.

We had not even cleared the village when Mr Harper, who kept a little electrical shop in the village, offered to take us in his little van the first few miles along our road to the transport cafe at Kincardine. A memorable lift indeed. Not just because it was the first of many over the years to follow, but because it was nearly the last. As we entered the cafe car park a great truck backed into the van, side on. The corner of the tailboard punched a hole in the side if the van, right where we sat. As the truck continued to back up, the van tilted over and the great wheels came nearer. At what appeared to be the last moment the truck driver heard our screams and stopped.

On such a note our journey started. Was it an omen for the future? If it were, our high spirits at being finally on our way made light of it. Mr Harper waved away the damage to his van as nothing, but perhaps he was only being kind to us.

That night we knew we had not only said goodbye to kith-and-kin but to home comforts as well. We lay all night on packing crates on the back of a low-loader lorry bound for Newcastle. Our bed was hard and the night cold, but we drew some masochistic delight at this the start of our toughening-up process for the trials which were sure to come.

Two days and several lifts later we were dropped-off in the wee sma' hours in a maze of bewildering empty streets in north London. The next few hours were enough to test our metal for the on-going journey. Feeling low, cold and lost we wandered the lonely streets, looking for somewhere to spend the night. But where do you find a place at three or four o'clock in the morning? With all sense of direction lost we walked the endless streets, too cold to stop, our heavy rucksacks becoming heavier and heavier and we more and more tired.

At last, a miracle. Near an all-night café, where lots of trucks were parked, a lit-up sign in a window announced 'Rooms to Let'. With some trepidation for knocking at that time of night we tapped gently and were received with casual indifference as if what we were doing was a regular occurrence. Yes, they had a room, but it was expensive, six shillings a night each and no breakfast. It was more suited to truck-drivers on expenses than shoe-string travellers. But who argues at that time of the morning, especially people like us near out on our feet, and they knew it. The room was just a double bed which almost touched the four walls of tattered, dismal paper. But it was a haven.

In those days nobody thought twice of two men sharing a bed when travelling. There were times when sharing a bed with a stranger was not uncommon. Nowadays all manner of connotations would be taken from this and I think the world is a sadder, unhappier and infinitely more difficult place to live in now that innocence has been lost.

As soon as the door closed we both collapsed on the bed and dropped off to sleep, fully clothed. I awoke a little while later and decided to have a bath before turning in properly. Alec was still out to the world. I stripped off, got a towel, left the door off the latch and went down the corridor to the bathroom. In the meantime Alec woke up, got ready for bed, shut the door, put out the light and got into bed without ever noticing I was not there.

When I came back and saw what had happened I knocked gently and shouted his name in a stage whisper. No reply. I knocked louder, shouted louder. Still no movement from inside. In the end I'm thumping on the door and shouting my head off and every door up the corridor is open and everybody is bawling niceties to me. At last the door is opened and I get it from Alec too for wakening him up. Poor soul! Remarkably, we still remained good pals.

We took two days off to see some of the sights of London. Five years before, soon after joining the army, I was stationed for a few months at Hounslow and each weekend (I couldn't wait till they arrived) I just walked the streets of the city, a romantic-headed eighteen-year-old, enthralled at actually being in the places that I had read about and heard of in songs. The Strand where the music was so grand and where everybody went, Berkeley Square where once a nightingale sang, Baker Street where Sherlock Holmes once 'lived', Trafalgar Square where Nelson looked down in lordly fashion on the hub of the Empire over which the sun never set, Whitehall that controlled that empire, Bush House where the wartime news was beamed out to us, together with all those radio programmes our families all listened avidly to – Tommy Handley's ITMA, Quentin Reynold's weekly letter to Mr Schicklgruber (Hitler), Palm Court Orchestra with the haunting strains of Albert Sandler on the violin – and Fleet Street where as one who had dreamed from a boy of being a writer/journalist the pavement positively vibrated under my feet.

I enjoyed seeing some of it again and watching Alec see it for the first time. I should have liked to have spent longer, to have shown him more. London is quite a big place to see in two days!

But time was short. Somewhere I had acquired a shipping timetable of sorts for Genoa to Alexandria and I was aiming for a package that sailed in a little more than three weeks. This didn't seem very much time to cross Europe. We would travel 'steerage' or 'deck' and would have to pay for that. We could not afford the luxury of more public transport and were not sure how good the hitch-hiking would be. Two years before, in 1948, I'd done a circuit of France with John (Jock) Hunter, another long-time friend. We travelled from Scotland to Marseilles and along the coast to Cannes and up over the Maritime Alps to Paris. On that journey we had found that hitch-hiking in France was not easy. The French liked to keep themselves to themselves and did not appear very friendly. Now as we headed for Dover we hoped that in the intervening time things might have improved. Travellers were not uncommon nowadays and this may have helped to bring the French out of their shells.

We arrived in Dover late at night having missed the night boat. The next one was midday. It was pouring with rain but we were lucky enough to find a little cafe-cum-hostel where we slept on the floor for 4/6d (22½p). A bit pricey, but it included a cup of tea and two cakes for breakfast.

Next day we crossed to France and became foreign travellers, a notable day in the journey. On arrival at Calais, instead of going south as our course lay, we headed east towards Dunkirk. We had a mission to do and although it seemed trivial and might cause problems at Genoa we felt duty bound to fulfil it.

In the summer of the previous year, 1949, Alec and I, together with four other friends, had cycled from Scotland through England to France, Belgium and Holland and back. My idea at the time was to visit as many places where history had been made so recently during the war. On a Dunkirk beach we stood on the sand and imagined ourselves part of an orderly queue of soldiers waiting patiently to be taken off by small boat while Stuka dive-bombers screamed vertically out of the sky with blood-curdling whistling bombs and raking, lethal machine-gun fire.

At the time it all seemed so exciting and I wished I had been a year or two older so that I would have been called up earlier, rather than in the last few weeks of the war. Later in more mature mind I often wondered what might have happened had I been that year or two older. Henry Hoggan and Son, Master Painters, the firm in Dunfermline where I served my apprenticeship, usually took on two new apprentices a year. Of the few who were ahead of me by that year or two, one died in a bomber over Germany (even now I can see the haunted look on his face during his last leave; nineteen he was) one died in India of disease and one was invalided out of the army with what would have been referred to in the First World War as shell-shock and was never the same again. He had returned to his tank in Normandy after a couple of minutes to relieve himself, to find his machine had suffered a direct hit and all his mates were dead and burning. Perhaps fate did me a lucky turn when it drew the line through the list of Hoggan's boys who went to war by ending it before I had time to get involved.

When in the Dunkirk area on that cycling journey of '49 we had stayed a night at a farm near Dunkirk. We had cycled up the long path to the farm when the day was well on and asked if we could sleep in the hayloft. Neither the farmer nor his wife spoke English and none of us spoke a word of French. But by signs they made us welcome and showed us to the hay. But instead of a separate hay barn as we would expect in Britain their hayloft was part of their house, immediately above their living quarters. That night we slept uneasily with rats the size of cats, judging by the thump of their feet, running around.

In the morning the family were already working in their field before we left, so I went to take a photo of them in their picturesque peasant garb. But on seeing the camera they gesticulated wildly, threw down their rakes and pitchforks and ran into the house. With great embarrassment at the trouble I'd caused I went to the others to hurry us on our way. But as we were leading our bikes to the road all the family came running out to stop us. They were dressed in their Sunday best and immediately went into a posed group, which was not the scene I had so wanted to capture.

Anyway, I took the photo and promised to send one on and never did. So now I was determined to fulfil my promise for the sake of my self and national respect, diplomatic relations, *entente cordiale* and all that, apart from the fact that I thought it would be nice for them to have one after all the trouble they'd gone to have it taken.

The way up to the farm, walking with packs, seemed a lot further than when we cycled. Our arrival at the farm caused great consternation with the dogs racing round us barking like mad and all the family coming out to see what the commotion was all about. They didn't recognise us in kilts, packs and heavy boots as the cyclists of last year. But when I produced the photograph there were gales of delighted laughter and French exclamations. We were ushered into the house by friendly arms, fed like prodigal sons and given beds downstairs in the family quarters. We still heard the rats thumping about upstairs through the night and imagined them looking down on us through the cracks in the floorboards as we had been able to do, but we slept much easier this time.

The kindness and hospitality we received did far more than make our efforts to deliver the photo worthwhile, it did much to dispel an alien feeling that had built up in me after three journeys through France in as many years. I had come to regard the French as a distant, unfriendly people. Even asking directions in the street could be unpleasant. Aware that I was always dressed for rough travelling and my meagre list of guide book French phrases were presented in painful phonetic exactness I nevertheless did not feel I warranted the cold stare of appraisal, with eye running from head to foot, before what often seemed a reluctant answer was made. This elitist opinion the French apparently had of themselves, the belief that they had devised sophistication was all the more ridiculous when it was obvious that they and their country were so backward at that time.

In contrast to today, now that the country is as modern, and moreso in many ways, in its development as Britain, France at that time seemed to be a country in stagnation, indeed in a time warp of the 1920s or before. Perhaps the country died or had been knocked comatose by the First World War. All the towns and villages looked as if no maintenance had been done since then and all appeared very run-down. Their plumbing was a joke, their sanitation and hygiene abysmal, never enough water for a decent wash far less baths, their foot-pad squatting lavatories were always choked (at least the public ones) and positively repulsive to use. All places very grey and shabby, extensive peeling paint and second-class roads with black-clad peasant women in head-scarves carrying water buckets on yokes shuffling along them. The whole country seemed second-class; their economy was in a shambles, raging inflation (near a thousand francs to the pound) and revolving governments changing every few months.

These then were the people from whose aloof demeanour I had smarted every time I visited their country. But then, I had only spoken to the people in the streets and shops. Visiting the farm people and living with them in their home had given me new insight. Perhaps the town people, those wealthy ones who all seemed to run around on mobilettes, were different. In our short visit to the farm we had had a glimpse under the corner of the threadbare, manky carpet, which was all that transit travellers saw, and found a warm, friendly people who were a pleasant and welcome surprise.

If last year's journey to Holland was a trip through living history of World War II, the next part of this year's one was down the shell-shocked path of the Great War. As a boy I'd listened in awe to men who had been there reminiscing of the battles and terrible slaughter that had taken place in this part of France. As a fourteen-year-old apprentice during the second war I loved to hear the journeymen talking among themselves at piece (sandwich) times of their war, of life in the trenches. One in particular had a way with him. With a gesture, a look and voice inflection he painted pictures that lived; of ice-cold, knee-deep mud that froze the kilt, never designed for trench warfare, into a razor edge that cut bare knees and calves, and tangled barbed wire against a stark background of broken trees and spectre gables that had once been homes. One little, nondescript man who looked so insignificant had been a machine-gunner. He told of scything down long lines of advancing Germans and pee-ing on the barrel to hurriedly cool it down while the number-two loaded in a fresh ammunition belt before the next wave came over the hill. Such a little weedy man to have killed countless men. All for sometimes a mere hundred yards of land that would be given up in a few days with equal losses on both sides. What a war! What a terrible waste of a whole generation. And to think the next generation had had an even worse one!

And now we were passing through the places that had become all so familiar to me through living stories and reading. The following passage is from my diary of the day.

Thursday 3rd August, 1950. Amiens.

We have had fairly good lifts today. But there does not seem to be the same long distance transport there is in Britain. With the result we go from one small town to the next along the way. But of course we get to see the places that way and that is what we have come for. Cassel, Armentieres – didn't see Mademoiselle – Lille, Arras and now Amiens are a few of the towns all famous from the First World War whose streets we walked today. When I think of all the stories I've read and heard from men who were in that war it seems unreal to be here where they all happened.

Our lift to Amiens dropped us off at the Youth Hostel. What a place! Camp beds with only one blanket – thank goodness we have sleeping bags – a stove which can hardly boil a pint of water, and no lavatory. At least, we can't find one.

The next day saw us in Paris. We took a couple of days out to see the sights, walk the Champs Elysees and do the obligatory climb to the top of the Eiffel Tower.

Hitching was not so good south of Paris. Perhaps the French there are a different breed. They only slowed their cars to have a better look at the kilts then whizzed on by. We had good days and bad. The good ones usually owed their category to GB tourists who 'couldn't pass a kilt'. We slept in our sleeping bags by the side of the road, washed in the public fountains and ate bread and jam. We had a tent but rarely used it.

By the time we reached Lyon we were getting desperate. We still had a long way to go to Genoa. The route lay over the Alps to Turin and at this rate we had no chance of catching the boat. Desperate situations require desperate actions. We decided to travel by bus to Turin. The fare seemed an awful lot, 3470 francs (£3.10/-) for the two of us, but our backs were to the wall.

That journey was the most spectacular we had ever known. After Grenoble the road wound up and tumbled down gigantic mountains in great loops with nothing at the sides to stop the careless driver from going over the edge. On all sides the endless panorama of lofty peaks faded into the ragged blue horizon. In the near distance black rock faces, variegated with white snow fields in their corries, bore down with crushing beauty. And here and there were castles on pinnacles and little villages with narrow streets as steep as ski-runs where the bus had to squeeze under low overhanging roofs that were slated with thick, rough stones. Nearing the border, shops took on an Italian look with curtains of stringed beads.

Italy was so different to France. In Turin when we asked directions we would be immediately surrounded by a ring of passers-by, all eager to help or just inquisitive, all answering our queries at once. Occasionally one would push his head right between our heads, the better to hear, then talk down the person I was speaking to with his own loud suggestions. It might have been wearing had we been there longer, but for a short time it was fun.

Next day we found a place with an up-to-date shipping programme. To our surprise there was a ship leaving Genoa next day. There was nothing for it but to go by train.

The train was packed and we had to stand in the corridor all the way. But the Italians are a cheery lot and they sang while a girl played an accordion which all whiled away the hours. We arrived at midnight and passed the night in the railway waiting room playing chess on our travel set, not daring to go to sleep lest we missed the boat.

At 5 a.m. we had a wash at the public drinking pump and went to find the Adriatic Shipping Company. We inquired directions from a little man and like a miracle he asked if we were going on the *Esperia*. When we said we were, his joy overflowed. He was even more delighted when we said we were travelling 'deck' for that was how he was also travelling. This was Grasso and he took us under his wing and fussed us like a mother hen and when it was time to board he crushed his way through the throng of deck passengers to make sure he found the best corner for the three of us and was already guarding it by the time we caught up with him.

They were a mixed bag of people on deck, mostly southern Italians with dark leathery faces, the men small and lean, the women huge and carrying great bundles of food and bedding. But there were some who looked different and quite well-to-do like Grasso. Grasso said he would not like to return to Italy to live. Too much intrigue and violence, too many secret police, too many green-uniformed, jack-booted carabiniere. He had got used to British administration and liked it for its fairness, but he did not know how things were going to be now that the British had left Egypt.

Next day the ship docked at Naples and we went ashore for a few hours. A dirty, heaving, interesting city which I decided I must come back to some time. As it happened, when next I did find myself in that city a few years later I was attacked by a man with a knife at night when asleep on a bench and that could have been the end of my journey.

Now we were two days out from there with the next stop Alexandria, Africa. And Grasso Stellario had invaded my midnight reverie and was probing the innermost part of my mind, questioning motives and emotions I was not aware I had.

Why was I wandering? What was the purpose of my journey? To gather some moss, I thought of saying, but that would be too enigmatic for his English to follow. There were things I wanted to say but could not put into words. I was aware of a vague feeling, a hunch in the tangle of emotions and dreams that made up my personality at the time, but I could not explain what it was, if anything, that had set me down the road I was going.

Imbued with Rider Haggard's tales of *Allan Quartermain*, *She* and *King Solomon's Mines*, Buchan's *Prestor John* and remembering an old film I'd seen as a boy, Edgar Wallace's *Sanders of the River*, I was already an Afrophile before ever going there. Perhaps that is why I took to it so readily. To be there was to live a dream. I wanted to see the plains and the jungles, sleep under the stars, and risk my life hunting big game. I wanted so much to find adventure.

'Adventure', that was the word, that was the name of the game. I can write it now, but I could not say it to Grasso. It would sound too boyish, too immature. Instead I mumbled something about "wanderlust" and "wanting to see the world".

"Ah-a-a …" he exhaled until the sound trailed into silence. His Italian English was funny but good, his sigh eloquent of disbelief. "But," he whispered loudly, raising himself on his elbow to peer through the darkness at me, "what is it you are looking for?"

I turned my head sharply to him, my frown lost in the shadow. "I'm not looking for anything," I answered with some surprise, annoyance even.

"Oh, but you are," he insisted, "I have watched you over the last few days and I see you are a young man with a mission. You may not realise it but it is there. It governs your every move, your every thought and it has been there a

long time. You will remember my words long after you have forgotten me."
And I did. While his name reposed in my diary for all the long years ahead, his words echoed back into my thoughts for a long, long time to come.

Chapter Two

THE PARTING OF THE WAYS

Sunday 20th August 1950 – Cairo
As I climbed the pyramid and my hands grasped the rough stones, I had the strong feeling I was really making contact with the artisans who fitted them into place thousands of years ago.

Nothing in Europe can prepare anyone for their first sight of an Arab town. The noise, the ear-bending cacophony of sounds, the mad helter-skelter traffic, the mixed hysteria and somnambulism of the people, the smells, stenches, glittering colours, dirt, rags and poverty, hit you like a mad dream.

Such was Alexandria and our introduction to the Middle East. I had twice put in here with troopships and experienced the mad selling methods of the bumboats that plague every vessel that moors in the bay, but this was my first landing. I loved it. Alec too, I could see, was pleased to be in real foreign parts at last. Our pleasure was tempered however with some apprehension when we were suddenly deluged by the great wave of street hawkers trying to sell us their wares, pushing, tugging, poking their bric-a-brac under our noses and all the while pleading, wheedling, whining and sometimes bossing in very aggressive tones. Now we knew we had left all but the most elite tourists behind.

In its modern state it is hard to believe that Alexandria was once one of the greatest and most elegant cities in the world, famed as the foremost seat of learning and possessor of the largest library in the ancient world. Here once stood the great pharos or lighthouse that was included in the Seven Wonders of the World, its light multiplied by the first ever concave mirrors.

Alexandria was founded by and named after Alexander the Great nearly three and a half centuries BC. Perhaps the first city ever to be planned on the drawing board before a brick was laid. The 'drawing board' was a camp table spread with flour on which Alexander drew with his finger straight intersecting lines showing streets and this was the forerunner of modern American cities. It marked the end of his great, all-conquering, semi-circular route through the then known world starting from his Macedonian kingdom in Northern Greece.

When Alexander drew his finger through the flour he was twenty-four years of age, one year older than we were then. He had been campaigning for six years and before that had fought in the army led by his father, Philip II. At the age of sixteen he had commanded the left wing of the Macedonian army when Philip marched against Byzantium.

During his six years of fighting, Alexander won countless battles against armies sometimes four and five times greater in numbers than his own, most commanded by battle-seasoned campaigners twice his age, such as the great Darius whom he beat twice. He destroyed the might of Persia and changed history and shaped the future perhaps more than any man before or since.

Alexandria's fall from grace came when Mohammed died in 632 AD. Fired by their Prophet's edict to carry his word to the world by the sword, great armies of his followers poured out of Arabia and stormed along north Africa and into Spain, subjugating all people and forcibly converting them to the Moslem creed. Christianity died in Alexandria and elsewhere around the Mediterranean and a thousand years of Graeco-Roman culture was wiped out.

*

Grasso left Alexandria by train for Cairo, but before going he gave us his address with a warm invitation to come and stay with him while in that city. He warned us, nay, pleaded with us, not to try and hitch-hike across Egypt. So, after some time of looking around, we took his advice and caught a bus to the capital.

The journey was uneventful. I wrote little in my diary about it save to remark that although we were travelling over the Nile delta, which one would think must be the most fertile part of Egypt, the land through the window of the bus seemed nothing but desert.

Cairo in August 1950 was a city in ferment. Rioting, bombing and murder had become part of the daily life of the city and there were portents of even worse to come. Egypt was still punch-drunk after being so decisively knocked-out by Israel in 1948 when the Arabs had attacked them hoping to eliminate the Jewish nation only days after it had been formed. Egypt was still shaken and frightened and the trouble in Cairo was between the main political parties after the government had concluded a peace treaty with Israel. Woven into the internecine politics was a general hatred of Britain for its continued occupation of the Canal Zone.

Britain had had a presence in Egypt since the days of the Battle of the Nile and Trafalgar and all that, and had had total control since 1880 when she took over the 'protection' of the country. Officially the Egyptian king and his government had been allowed complete autonomy, but they were nevertheless overlorded by the British Governor who privately called the king to heel if he or Whitehall thought necessary. This covert form of governing had been particularly hard during the war when Rommel had been knocking on the door at Alamein

14

and many Egyptians would have been quite happy to have had the Germans as rulers as the British. During these moments of chastisement King Farouk had felt slighted and humiliated and after the war relations between the Egyptians and the British deteriorated. Dissension, which had always been there, ripened into open revolt. British troops had eventually been withdrawn from the main cities but they still remained along the Suez canal to preserve right-of-access for our ships going to and from the Far East. Now King Farouk was about to ask Britain to withdraw her troops from the Canal Zone as well. Such was the situation in the aftermath of terrible violence when we entered the city.

We decided to accept Grasso's invitation to stay with him and made our way across the city asking directions as we went. Language was no problem as almost everyone, even beggars in the street, spoke English, some answering in flawless Scots, even in regional dialects, when they saw the kilts. Indeed, in all my travels I never met anyone who could take off the Scots' inflection of speech better than the street Egyptian.

Grasso lived in Nasred Din el Sheikh, just off Boulac, one of the less respectable areas of the city. From windowless shops stacked high with gaudy bolts of cloth, myriad haberdashery merchants called to us to come and see their merchandise. In countless cafes, where loudspeakers blasted out noxious music, swarthy men in white linen suits and red tarbooshes lounged carelessly, sipping coffee. In the street idle men in dirty *galabeahs* – the loose fitting, ankle-length shirt which is the Egyptian national dress – wandered with aimless expressions. A man with a demijohn of red wine strapped to his back clinked some glasses and hawked his wares loudly. A veiled woman walked erect with a bundle of laundry as big as herself balanced on her head. Along Boulac rumbled rusty tramcars with people clinging on all round the outsides like shipwreck survivors. Tearaway cars with horns screaming like sirens carved their way through the crowds of sauntering jaywalkers. And over there, sedate and majestic in the whirl of frenetic humanity and deaf to the frantic horns, was a camel and rider in from the desert, unhurried and unhurriable, impervious to time and the saving of it.

Grasso had a flat in a tenement where the stairs were bare and swirling with refuse. But in contrast to the outside his home was clean and tidy. He was a widower who lived with his son, Nino, a fellow of about our own age, who seemed to spend all his time with his friends.

Grasso welcomed us like milk coming to the boil. He was so pleased we had come to stay with him. His house was ours. We were his sons. He would prepare a room. We must have showers. In next to no time the table was laid and a meal prepared. The everyday wine was replaced by a more expensive brand and complete with white apron he ladled spaghetti from the pot with a flamboyant flourish and extravagant Italian exclamations and piled our plates high again and again and replenished our glasses as soon as they were emptied, while we remonstrated wildly and wondered how long we could stand the pace. He manipulated his spaghetti with consummate ease and watched with disbelief as ours constantly tangled and fell off the fork.

"No, no, not like that," he said with amusement as a forkful slithered down my shirt front. I was inclined to agree with him. "See, let me show you." Slowly he showed us how to wind the white worms round a fork held in a spoon until we had a manageable mouthful. Later, when he felt we were proficient enough, he made us dispense with the spoon. There was no doubt our education had been sadly lacking, but now our foreign travel was paying off.

"Well, how do you like Cairo?" Grasso asked when we finally subsided into basket chairs with coffee and thumb-size glasses of grappa, the Italian firewater that Grasso assured us there was nothing quite like. Being hardly acquainted with alcohol and certainly not spirits I had, once again, to concur wholeheartedly as I struggled for breath while considering the question. From the street below the noise, the hubbub of loud talk, the hawkers, the loud piped music and the overall screaming of car-horns, was a solid thing that invaded and dominated the room.

"It's a mad city," Alec said, "but the people are very friendly."

Grasso stopped his glass half way to his lips. "When did you meet the people?" he asked. A note of alarm had crept into his voice.

"When we were walking over here," Alec answered with a note of surprise at the question.

"You walked here?" Grasso's voice had risen an octave, "in your kilts and you," (me), "in your military hat!" I had started wearing my old bush hat with pride. He let go with some Italian phrase that had something to do with God. "I thought you came in a taxi from the bus station."

"Oh no," I put in, "it was quite easy, everybody was so willing to help."

Grasso passed a hand over his face and with it wiped off his smile. Then he looked at us steadily. Gone was the little, frothy, eager-to-please man behind the jam-jar glasses. This was the sagacious man who had spoken to me on the boat, the man with the incisive mind and perceptive comments.

"You must not wear your kilts in the city, or anywhere in Egypt. People might think you are soldiers and kill you. They have taken a long time getting rid of your army and the sight of you could make them mad."

"We didn't get that impression from those we spoke to. Some even said they were sorry to see the British go," I countered.

"They would be the merchants," Grasso answered dismissively. "Yes, they miss the Tommies' money and many of them are having a hard time since the army left. But, make no mistake, there are plenty out there who hate the

British, hated the occupation of their country and would not stop at murder if they thought you might be the vanguard returning.

"As it is," he continued, "this is only a lull we are in at present. There's going to be hell to pay before you leave the Canal Zone too."

"We won't do that," I said, "the army will fight to preserve our right of passage through the canal."

"Right of passage!" Grasso scoffed, "Who ever gave you that? Britain cannot give herself rights in other people countries. You have got to believe that the colonial days are over."

"I don't think that's quite correct," I said with some feeling, remembering how the British were so well ensconced in Kenya.

"It's true. There is a new malaise that has spread through these subject countries since the war. It's called 'Freedom' or 'Independence'. They caught it from the Allies who fought for it against the Germans and they, the colonies, grew to like the idea. Egypt is like the stopper in the bottle that has been pulled out. Soon all the red ink is going to run out of the map. I give you another ten years at most. And the same goes for all the Imperialists, the French and Belgian and Dutch. The days of colonial empires are numbered.

"But let us not get too morbid about it all," he rubbed his hand over his face again and the smile came back. "This is not the time for such thoughts. I am so happy you are here and I want you to be happy too. Go out and see all the wonderful things there are to see, but wear trousers and shirts like other people. I would not like to have to send you home dead."

Here was excitement indeed! We thrilled at the danger. Here was proof at last that we had left the placid tourist zone behind. Now we were getting places! But as things were to turn out we soon began to wonder if we would get any further.

*

The next few days saw the disintegration of all our plans. My diary tells of us running hither and thither each day trying to hold on to our dream and when that proved impossible making new plans, only for these by necessity to be discarded for fresh ones.

The first blow came at the British Consulate where we were told we had little hope of getting visas for the Sudan in the time we had available and even if we did, or if we tried to approach the country and try for them on arrival, we would certainly be turned away without evidence of adequate finance to ensure we would be no burden on the country during transit or for our fares home if necessary.

If that was not enough, and even if we had been willing to try our chances at the border – a policy I found well worthwhile with later experience – the man in Jollies Travel Agency smashed us with the next blow.

"It is impossible to travel southwards by river at this time of the year," he said, "No boats can go up-river when the Nile is in flood and this year's is a particularly bad one from that point of view." Then we would hitch-hike by road despite Grasso's warnings. "No way," the man was emphatic, "the flood has broken the road up at Aswan. There will be no road traffic through there for at least a month." Besides, like Grasso, he did not recommend that we try hitch-hiking. "However," the man had a solution, "the railway is still open. I could book you through to Juba and I believe there is a bus …" but we were not listening. We could not afford that and there would still be the problem at the border anyway.

I was all for us heading for the Persian oil fields to get jobs there to work up enough money to see us through. However our friend in Jollies put the kibosh on that too. The Persian government would not let us in unless we had evidence of a job to go to.

At last we came to the conclusion that our only hope was to go to Port Said and try to get work on a ship going south passed the bottleneck. Before we went though we had to see the sights of Cairo.

*

To the traveller few cities can compare with Cairo for interest. Where else can you take a tram ride to such fabulous wonders as the pyramids and sphinx? What other museums offer for view relics to compare with those from the tombs of the ancient pharaohs, perhaps the most ancient treasures in the world? Treasures such as the solid gold coffin, inlaid with cornelian and lapis lazuli and shaped in lifelike image of the boy king Tutankhaman, whose mummy it contained; such as the boats and chariots, bows and arrows, folding camp bed, board games, vanity sets, carved chairs and other household utensils that would not look out of place in a modern Egyptian home, all used by the kings and their ladies three, four, five and more thousand years ago: treasures that were more ancient to the Romans than their ruins are to us.

Cairo loves travellers, especially of the greenhorn type which it fleeces unmercifully. It took to us with glee. At the museum a phoney dragoman offered his services for one hundred piastres (£1). But we, men-o'-the-world, beat him down to forty. Later we learned the official rate was half of that. The man insisted we pay him before the tour of the galleries since he had been caught too often by previous clients who refused to pay when the tour was finished. We didn't look that type, but … a man had to be practical! Eager to prove our integrity, we paid. No sooner were our backs turned to look at something than the man disappeared. We felt sheepish at having been taken in so easily but consoled ourselves by laying it down to experience. From now on we would be really hard and shrewd.

Immediately we left the museum a slick-talking youth in a white linen suit accosted us and, seeing we were strangers, welcomed us to his city. We had on our hard, shrewd armour now and treated him warily. No we didn't want a guide or anything. Oh, good lord no, he wasn't that kind of person. He could understand our suspicions, but he didn't want anything from us. He only wanted to help. He was a student and only wanted to be kind and friendly. Some day he hoped to come to England and he hoped he might be treated with the same kindness there. In the course of his one-sided conversation he suggested we should visit the Royal vaults, burial place of the modern kings. It was open only one day in ten years and, of all the luck, this was the decadal day. We should not miss this remarkable opportunity. He would be glad to show us the place. Admission was free and no, he insisted he did not want anything for his services. He appreciated we were not wealthy tourists, the whole thing would not cost us a bean. It did seem too good a chance to miss and while we were still swithering, he flagged down a taxi and bundled us inside.

"Pay him twenty piastres," Ali, our self-imposed guide advised us after a heated session in Arabic with the cab driver at the end of the ride, "the thief wanted forty. See, you must be very careful. There are unscrupulous people in Cairo who would prey on strangers."

Ali ushered us into a great palatial hall the floor of which was covered by one gigantic carpet, the pattern of which was an exact replica of the mosaic which covered the domed ceiling. The only light in the place came through a circular cupola glazed with thin sheets of alabaster.

At the door Ali handed us cloth over-slippers that were provided for our boots and while we were putting them on we were joined by a tall, gaunt man in a blue serge suit and red tarboosh who claimed to be the custodian. Despite his bare feet he comported himself with haughty dignity. His eyes were sunk in dark sockets in a swarthy, cadaverous face. He looked the perfect embodiment of a tomb keeper.

If indeed the place was a tomb! There was nothing to suggest the place was anything more than a mosque. Our guide kept his brief remarks to the craftsmanship of the carpet weavers, the skill of the mosaic artists who had inlaid the ceiling and to the clarity of the whispering gallery. Surprisingly, he made no mention of the crypts we had hoped to see. When asked about this he pointed to a sealed door as the one to the room in which lay the body of King Farouk's father and where Farouk would one day be interred. But there was no inscription, nothing to show we were looking at the resting place of royalty.

19

The man's bearing was aloof. His tone suggested that the whole business of conducting visitors was distasteful and beneath his dignity. His manner was so supercilious, his English so perfect it made us with our Scottish accents feel gawky so that we did not press for further information.

"That will be fifty piastres each, gentlemen," he said off-handedly as he guided us to the door, prematurely, I thought. Flabbergasted we turned to seek Ali, but he was nowhere to be seen.

"A hundred piastres!" I shouted incredulously.

"Quiet, sir, please control your voice in this sanctuary."

"But we were told admission was free."

"So it is, but you must pay for my services."

We haggled over the price. As the tempo of the bargaining increased the gaunt man forgot the sanctity he had been so anxious to preserve and raised his voice in shrill and sometimes profane shouts. It ended when the Egyptian failed to hold forty piastres Alec shoved into his grasp while the man was contemptuously refusing to accept such a paltry remuneration for his, an educated man's, services. His awesome dignity dispersed like chaff as he scrabbled for the fluttering notes in a most undignified manner. In the minor chaos we beat a retreat.

Next day we passed that way again. The gaunt man and Ali loitered by the door which was open to anyone who wished to enter. Surprising how quickly a decade can pass!

We were learning from our experience, though. We were getting the hang of dealing with these people. But at the pyramids, we came, we saw and were conquered all over again.

It is part of the price of visiting Egypt. The Egyptians have been conning tourists for thousands of years. Julius Caesar visited Cairo, or Memphis as it was called in that time, to see the pyramids and the ancient wonders of Egypt. He had an extraordinary guide in the shape of young Cleopatra who took him up the Nile in more ways than one and conned him into fighting her battles for her against her brother, the king, and having him killed so she could be queen. Visitors, or tourists, have just got to accept that the locals will use them, rob them, albeit in a most smiling and friendly way. With their skills sharpened to razor edge cutting power by daily honing, the wily Egyptian will run rings round the most astute visitor. Better to accept the inevitable gracefully and treat it all as part of the fun than get wound up miserably and not enjoy the reason for coming, that is, to see the sights.

We tried hard to be philosophical about it but it was difficult when we saw near the last of our money being stolen by sleight-of-mind. But we put it behind us and gave our attention to this experience of a lifetime.

I do not think there is anything to compare with seeing the pyramids and sphinx for the first time. The photographs and pictures in books I had studied with such longing did something in preparing for this moment but actually being there beside them was spellbinding. The pyramids look so overpowering, so huge, the recumbent sphinx so like a great indolent lion with a human head, so powerful even with its broken nose, the result, I was told, of a misplaced cannonball in Napoleon's time. What an great example they are of mankind's achievement. It is difficult to think of people of that era thinking in such dimensions, let alone building in them.

There is a presence there, a palpable awareness of the past, a feeling that one is in some contact with the people who lived and worked there to make these monuments. We climbed one of the pyramids – you could do that then, there being very few people about – and this feeling was so strong as I grasped the rough stones to pull myself up I felt I was shaking hands with the artisans who long ago had shaped them and placed them in position.

Back on the ground we went into a tomb where there was an embalmed mummy with the head exposed, a skull drawn over with thin brown leather. In a corner was a stone coffin or sarcophagus, perhaps the mummy's bed. I couldn't resist trying it out. It wasn't just my size but it was quite comfortable after a fashion and I lay there for some time trying to commune with the past and wondering how long it was since a body had lain there.

We would have liked to have gone inside a pyramid but didn't have the cash. That would have to wait until sometime in the future when we might return as proper tourists with money in our pockets for camel rides and all these things. I am still waiting.

*

When the time came to leave Cairo, Grasso arranged with a friend who owned a car to take us out of the city to a quiet place where we could catch the bus to Port Said. He wished us his fond farewell and said his house was ours any time we wished to return. Dressed once again in our kilts with our packs over our shoulders he was once again in fright. When the car arrived he held us back in the room while he looked out cautiously into the communal stairway to make sure it was empty before he would allow us out. Down at the main door he peered furtively into the street to make sure the coast was clear before he pushed us out quickly and into the car. His fear was infectious and we thrilled at the melodrama.

In retrospect I have thought that Grasso's fears may have been as much for himself and family as for us. After the past years of murder and pillage of anyone suspected of collaboration with the British he was aware far more than we were of the risks he was taking. In our naivety we thought the danger lay only with us. But then, self-centredness can be the hallmark of youth.

Our funds were now at a dangerously low level. At Port Said we booked into one of the cheapest boarding houses we could find, a warren of lice-ridden rooms leading off a dark, creaky stairway. It was obvious from the proprietor's awkward manner he was not used to European guests. We had a bed, and bread-and-egg sandwich with tea breakfast, and went hungry the rest of the day.

Daily we trawled the Shipping Agencies looking for a south-bound ship that would sign us on its crew. But few of the ships had vacancies and those that had were reluctant to sign on men who would leave the ship again at the next port. As the days passed our morale slipped lower and clerks at the agencies threw up their hands in mock horror when they saw us coming. Came the time when our fortitude dwindled to an all-time low and hunger gnawed its way into our actions. That night we held a council-of-war.

I still thought we should have a go at getting through to Basra for a job on the oilfields. If we were lucky in getting in we could make big money quickly and be back on our way down Africa in six months' time. But Alec had gone off the boil on Africa. He had just wanted to travel and for him one place was as good as another and there seemed to be an awful lot of hassle down that way. He thought he'd rather go somewhere else whereas I was committed to return to the places I'd dreamed of, worked so long to go to.

There was something else too. Perhaps I had not been entirely honest with Grasso on the boat when I'd said it was wanderlust or something of that sort that started me on this journey. There was a girl. Yes, the age old motive that has shaped history.

Oh no, she wasn't the reason for my journey. It was to Africa I was going, for Africa. Yet in all my plans, in all my daydreams of being back in Kenya there was always a face there, a lovely, smiling face with quiet, serene eyes, ringed by dark hair with a slight wave in it.

It had been a perfectly innocent friendship. Pamela Major was seventeen and I not quite nineteen when we met at the Scottish dancing at the Church of Scotland hall, Nairobi. We were regular attenders each Friday evening. I went with a bunch of fellows from the camp and she was always there with her mother and sister. Over the months that followed we danced with others but mostly we partnered each other. She accepted my request for each dance with alacrity, we laughed a lot and tongue-tied a lot, each starting to say something and never getting round to it and her mother smiled when she watched us with side glances. I never plucked up the courage to ask her out, but when I told her I was leaving, being sent home quickly, her eyes moistened and she couldn't speak when I said goodbye.

I knew then that one day I would come back to Nairobi and now as Alec said he had lost interest in Africa I knew that from that moment the partnership was doomed. Wherever else Alec might go, the route for me lay through Nairobi. We both knew then that we had to part and go our separate ways.

Alec suddenly came to a decision that knocked me sideways. Earlier that day we had met some sailors who out of interest and friendliness invited us in for some tea and buns at the Welcome Hostel. At that time British forces still occupied the Canal Zone and Port Said was a regular base for the Royal Navy. We had enjoyed our time with the sailors, not least because of the welcome food. Alec now said he thought he'd like to join the navy. He had missed conscription and now felt he'd like to experience service life.

Next day we went to the naval base, obtained entrance with an escort and Alec asked about joining up. It caused quite a stir and we had to wait a while, then someone came and said they were sorry, Alec couldn't enlist because he was too old. Too old at twenty-three! Well, it was one way of getting over the problem.

So Alec decided to join the army instead. British military presence was very visible with soldiers and trucks in the streets. We had spoken to lots of the troops and suddenly their carefree life with regular food seemed very desirable.

We went along to one of the regimental headquarters where Alec informed the surprised corporal on duty that he wished to enlist.

"You're mad," gasped the corporal.

"No, just hungry," Alec corrected him.

The request caused consternation. This kind of thing didn't happen every day. Never, in fact. We were passed along the line to the sergeant, then to a captain and finally to the lieutenant-colonel in charge. At no time was my presence questioned. The colonel pondered the question without a word. He pursed his lips, looked out the window, spread his hands and squeezed the tips of his fingers together. Ticklish problem! After much reflection he concluded the matter was too much for him and would have to be referred to the United Kingdom. There would be a few days' delay before an answer could be received and in the meantime, on hearing of our plight, he granted permission for us both to be accommodated in the military transit camp free of charge.

These next few days were like a Butlin's holiday to us. It was particularly interesting to me since I had been in this same camp while in the army on my way home from Kenya. It was Alec's introduction to army life and to me it was like coming home. I enjoyed the camaraderie, the banter, the cheery inane conversations and even the constant gratuitous swearing was like hearing an old, lost song.

With regular meals, comfortable billets and lively company our spirits soared. We swam and sunned in the camp pool and attended camp films and concerts in the evening. One night we saw Lupino Lane and company live in *Me and My Girl*.

But now Alec had a change of heart. Good food and no worry of tomorrow had laid the ghost of apathy that had crept into our spirits when we were down. When low, the idea of enlisting in the army for five-and-seven had seemed an easy way out. Now rejuvenated, that didn't seem a good idea at all. Now he had another idea and we wondered why we hadn't thought of it before.

Since ships sometimes needed crew but were reluctant to sign on men who would leave again at the next port, Alec decided to sign on the first ship available and stay with it wherever it was going. He thought we could do it together but I am a poor sailor and he was not aware how much Africa, and more, was calling me. I thought of Rudyard Kipling's maxim, "He travels the fastest who travels alone," and said it would be easier to get a ship with one vacancy than two. We both accepted the fact that we had come to the parting of our ways.

When Alec went along to say he had changed his mind he found his permission to enlist and warrant home to the recruiting base, had arrived. They received it very well, no doubt thinking he had done the wise thing, and the colonel even gave him permission to stay at the transit camp until he got a ship. There is no doubt we British travellers lost a lot when the red ink did finally run out of the map.

So Alec became a sailor. He joined a Norwegian ship bound for Calcutta and San Francisco, sailed with it for a year and became a quartermaster, before returning home with more than enough accomplished to justify his return.

I left the camp the next morning. We kept our parting brief, neither saying what we thought, but in my diary the night before, I had written, *'I leave tomorrow. It will be strange travelling without Alec. We've been good pals. It's going to be lonely.'* And it was.

*

My chances of getting on a ship to bypass Egypt and the Sudan apparently being nil I headed for Suez at the other end of the canal, just over a hundred miles away. Hitching was easy, there being plenty of British army trucks going hither and thither and none would pass someone wearing a kilt and khaki-drill bush shirt and hat, looking for all the world like a misplaced member of the 51st Highland Division. Lifts usually ended with an invitation to the mess for a good meal and perhaps the offer of a bed in the guard-room for the night.

The Suez canal is a mighty piece of engineering and a wonderful sight to behold. This great swath of water cutting dead straight across land seems incredible. If viewed from a distance the sand on either side appears unbroken and it is uncanny to see gigantic liners apparently gliding majestically over the desert. When I'd passed through it before, on the large troopships, it seemed so narrow in places you felt you could jump off either side onto land. But viewed from the road now it looked wide and huge. In its opening days some eighty years before it was a gigantic conception.

This was not the first canal linking the Mediterranean and Red Seas to be built. The Pharaoh Necho built a freshwater canal from the Nile to the Red Sea in 600 BC which operated for well over thousand years before it was finally blocked up lest it be used as a means of invasion by their eastern enemies. Egypt's history from the beginning has been a continuous saga of invasion and revolution.

The French invaded Egypt in 1798 and, although they held it for only three years until driven out by the British, the influence they cast over the land for the best part of the century was tremendous. Their prestige peaked with their greatest achievement, the building of the Suez Canal.

It was a young Napoleon Bonaparte, after celebrating his thirtieth birthday in Cairo, who conceived the idea of the modern canal. He personally rode across the isthmus with only a few soldiers, each carrying no more baggage than a loaf of bread spiked on his bayonet and a bag of water round his neck. By this way his dream to unite the Atlantic and Indian oceans was born. Unfortunately Britain turfed him out of Egypt before he had time to do anything about it and gave him other things to think about in the next few years. His dream, however, was fulfilled some seventy years later by another Frenchman.

Designed and built by Ferdinand de Lesseps, a French engineer, and opened in 1869 the Suez Canal cut nearly five thousand miles off the route from London to Bombay which hitherto had been round the Cape of Good Hope.

At the head of the canal, entering from the north, was the statue of de Lesseps. When I saw it first I was struck by the fact that his name was different from my own by only one letter. By this I felt an affinity with the man. It was many years later when researching my family history that I discovered that there was indeed a tie-up, albeit tenuous.

The name Lessels belongs to Fife. The first Lascelles or Lassals came in the 12th century, probably at the invitation of King Edgar, son of Malcolm (III) Canmore and his wife St Margaret, who introduced many Norman and Anglo-Norman settlers to the environs of his palace in Dunfermline after receiving help from the English in acquiring the crown from his uncle. These people may have come by invitation but they soon developed into colonists. They built mansions and took over the senior posts of church and state, much in the way white colonists had done in the modern Africa I was to see as I travelled.

Over the years the French names were shortened by the Scots tongue. De Bruc became Bruce, or 'the Bruce', St Clair became Sinclair, De War Dewar and Lascelles became Lessells or Lessels. Somewhere in our family history I found reference to a visit Ferdinand de Lesseps is reputed to have made to Scotland around 1850. It is said he walked into the Edinburgh office of one Lessels, an architect, to introduce himself. He had come, he said, to visit the land of his forebears and was interested to meet anyone of the family name. It would appear his grandfather or great grandfather was a Lessels who had immigrated to France from Scotland and in the course of time an 'L' of a difference had been made by the substitution of that letter by a 'P'.

It was Said Pasha, after whom Port Said is named, who in 1854 gave de Lesseps his mandate to build the Suez Canal. But it was his successor, Ismail Pasha, Viceroy of Egypt for the Ottoman Empire, who reigned during most of the time of the canal's construction. It was he who invested most of the money to build it and it was he as Ruler who stood with Napoleon III while his wife, the beautiful Empress Eugenie, cousin of de Lesseps, cut the ribbon at the opening of the Canal in 1869.

Part-educated in Paris, Ismail was more European than orientally minded. He made great efforts to drag Egypt out of the past and developed grandiose schemes to do so. Apart from Suez he built many other canals, made more than a million acres of fallow land fertile, increased the number of schools and factories and built the Cairo museum.

To finance all his schemes, and to buy from the Turkish Sultan in Constantinople, the titular overlord of Egypt, the title of Khedive, for which he paid millions, Ismail borrowed heavily from European banks. He grossly extended himself and in 1865, in order to stave off bankruptcy following poor Nile floods and a fall in cotton prices with the end of the American Civil War, he offered to sell his, by far the major, shares in the Suez Canal. He first offered them to the French who refused to buy, a costly mistake on their part as it turned out. Ismail then offered them to the British for £4,000,000. Disraeli, wily and far seeing, made no mistake. He saw the potential and personally, with the secret backing of Rothschild, bought the shares for the British government. That little dabble in stocks and shares was the shoehorn that enabled Britain to slip into control of Egypt and eventually most of Africa down to the Cape.

Within ten years of the sell-out Ismail and Egypt were again heading for bankruptcy. In order to save the shareholders of the European banks who had loaned so much, Britain and France formed a consortium and stepped in to take over the running of the Egyptian Treasury and for good measure had Ismail deposed by the Turkish Sultan and his son Tewfik installed in his place.

With Tewfik as nominal leader, Egypt was governed by the Dual Control for some years. But Britain found France a difficult partner and eventually dropped her, took over sole responsibility and declared Egypt a British Protectorate.

In 1956 the British Army withdrew from the Canal Zone at the end of their lease after having occupied Egypt or parts of it since 1880. Britain still owned the major part of the Suez Canal Company and expected to have the principle say in the administration and profits of it. But soon after their departure, in order to finance the building of the new Aswan Dam on the Nile, President Nasser, the Egyptian leader, nationalised the Canal. Britain and France were not very amused at that. Both nations had interests in the Far East and whoever controlled the Suez Canal guarded the way there. So, as in the previous century, the two nations combined to put Egypt in its place and safeguard their interests.

In a cavalier bout of gunboat politics both airforces bombed Egyptian targets and a combined military force was landed which took over and regained control of the Canal. A few days previously, Israeli forces had entered the Sinai peninsula and were fast approaching the Canal. Egypt scuppered forty ships in the Canal blocking it securely and the USA, under the banner of the United Nations, ordered the Anglo-French out. The Russians also hovered in the background. The invading Force had the humiliation of having to comply. It was one of the worst blows Britain suffered to her national pride and more than any other reduced her standing as a major world power.

More relevant to this background history, it was this act of Franco/British aggression that caused Nasser in a fit of pique to have de Lesseps' statue removed from its place at the head of the Canal he created. While writing this I enquired at the Egyptian Embassy in London of the fate of the statue and am informed it is undamaged and stored at Port Said and the possibility of it being reinstated is being discussed.

*

Arriving at Suez I found I was even less likely to find a ship there than at Port Said. After a couple of days I decided to retrace my steps to see if it were possible to get a lift on an RAF plane going to Khartoum or Nairobi. I went to the aerodromes at Fayid, Kabrite and Ismailia and at none of them was my outlandish request laughed out of court. Nevertheless, at none of them was I given a flight. At each of them I was welcomed, given hospitality and put up for a night or two while they tried to fit me in but in the end there was nothing doing.

I was now in limbo, bereft of ideas and taking lifts wherever they were going, more for the benefit of a night's accommodation than with the idea of going anywhere. When that failed I took a night at the YMCA at Ismailia and next day realised that bought accommodation was now almost beyond me. Where to sleep after this if I could not find a friendly camp was now a serious threat. In despair I could only trust in a Micawber faith that 'something might turn up'.

*

In a palm grove near the town of Fayid I dumped my heavy rucksack on the ground and thankfully sank down beside it. In the midday heat that pack weighed a ton and the kilt was like a blanket round my waist. Above, the palm fronds sighed with a slight breeze coming from the Great Bitter Lake and from nearby came the steady whining and creaking of a *sakiyeh,* the age-old water wheel; a sycamore pole driven round and round by water buffaloes or bullocks in the charge of a man who sang continually in a high-pitched falsetto. There would be no more lifts today because the army only worked in the morning and their transport stopped by midday.

I ate some dates, drank some warm water from my canteen and spread my sweat-soaked shirt out on the ground to dry. Then I dozed with one hand round my rucksack and the other grasping my shirt, for Egypt is a land of thieves.

A car passed, stopped and reversed. A voice broke into my sleepy despair.

"I say, are you all right?"

It was a bottle-green army staff car. A uniformed soldier sat at the wheel but the man who spoke wore mufti. The voice, though, had at least three pips and maybe a crown or more in it. I assured him I was fine but the telltale note of resignation in my voice made him curious. He asked if I was in the army and when I said no he thought this was all jolly interesting. He asked where I was going and I said nowhere fast. Then it all came out, my intended journey and how I had hit a blank wall and my visa would run out soon and then I'd be in real trouble.

"So what you need is a crutch, a sort of shoulder to lean on to help you along the way, what!"

"A ship would do," I commented.

"Well, hop in and we'll see what can be done." His air was light-hearted, breezy, comforting. "I'm on my way to see Sir Brian Robertson. He's a friend of mine and a fellow Scot of yours. Perhaps he'll be able to do something."

General Sir Brian Robertson, Commander-in-Chief, Middle East! Lordly company indeed for an ex-Staff-Sergeant tramp. I put on my shirt, now dry and mottled with sweat-blotches, and went off to meet the General.

At the General's residence the guards saluted my companion and we swept through the gates. Inside the court flags flew and squads of soldiers drilled in synchronised precision. The General's personal guard, no doubt.

Unfortunately Sir Brian was away in Cyprus and I had to make do with a mere Major. My affable friend introduced me like a buddy and suggested to the Major in an avuncular, 'there's-a-good-fellow' manner that perhaps he could arrange something.

"Sir Brian I'm sure would like to know that we'd helped a fellow Scot along his way, eh, what!" High commands come in so many different ways.

The Major, an early-greying man with grizzled hair and peppery moustache hid his feelings behind a sickly smile and murmured something about it being a bit out of his line but he'd see what could be done. He called in his sergeant and put him in the picture with a few terse words and an even more terse edict scribbled on a sheet of paper at which being nearest to the desk I got a fleeting glance. "Get this bod out of here," was the order.

We heard the sergeant talk to the telephone or radio operator while my affable friend kept the brittle atmosphere from cracking with lordly bonhomie. Presently the sergeant came back and laid a paper in front of the Major who read it and sat back like a man from whom a dark cloud has lifted.

"There is a ship loading army supplies at Port Tewfik," he said, "It sails tomorrow for Aden, calling at all ports en-route. Our Movements have spoken to the captain and he has agreed to take you on board, if you wish."

If I wished! Wow! I said with more outwardly calm that I'd like that very much. So it was all laid on. Army transport would take me to the port near Suez where I would be billeted the night with the RASC Water Unit and tomorrow they'd lay on a launch to take me out to the ship avoiding immigration, customs or any other irksome bureaucracy.

Just like that! A few hours ago the world was at an end and now a whole new one had opened up. I said how grateful I was to the Major but he shrugged it off as an everyday occurrence. We left the office, the Major even coming to see us off. I shook hands with my benefactor and thanked him without ever learning who or what he was. Someone who could make senior officers squirm and turn unorthodox wheels so easily had to have some clout. But he never said and I didn't like to ask.

Over the next few years there were many times when the future looked uncertain and my journey seemed finished in more ways than one, but looking back, my meeting with that man was perhaps the most important of all. Another few days at most and I'd have had to give up. His intervention was pivotal to the rest of my journey. He entered my sleep like a fairy godfather, waved his wand of magic words and my world was transformed. He wished me good luck, gave the Major a verbal slap on the back and went on his way leaving a trail of goodwill largesse behind him.

I was taken by special truck to Port Tewfik and billeted as directed by the Major and next day at early dawn transported by motor launch out into the bay where I mounted the ladder up the sheer side of the SS *Cory Freighter* a ship of some 1200 tons. Despite all the special treatment given, as I stepped onto the deck I felt more like an escaped fugitive than a Very Important Person.

Chapter Three

RED SEA ODYSSEY

Saturday 1st October 1950 – Jiddah Harbour
   "Amoud, tell me about Mecca."
   "Ah, Daaveed Sahib, you are my good ears. It all started when al'Llah made the Zemzem well to flow."

The ship had left the port and the Captain wanted to see me. I had been shown my sleeping quarters and had settled in and now this would be the call to duty. He would be a severe man with scrambled egg on his hat and gold braid and sparkling buttons on his uniform. His cabin would be all polished mahogany and shining brass. What kind of work would I be assigned to? If I looked my best perhaps he would not have me clean out the bilge or paint the crow's nest.

The Arab steward led the way to the upper deck where an enormously fat man, naked but for a pair of crumpled shorts, lay on a camp bed under an awning. This little man with the tousled hair, whose bare belly rose from the bed like a suet pudding, was the captain! I didn't know whether to feel relieved or cheated.

Captain Gresham rose, stretched and yawned me a welcome. His stomach was of such noble proportions he had to lean backwards to stand upright.

"Have a drink." He indicated a half empty bottle of gin and seemed surprised when I declined.

Now the question of working my passage. I asked him what he would like me to do. He looked at me aghast when I mentioned it.

"Work! You can't work."

"I certainly can," I boasted.

"No. No. I won't allow it. We've got a Wog crew and they will do any work that's to be done. Whatever would they think!" He gulped his gin with an air of indignation, belched loudly and lay down again. "Oh no, laddie. Remember, we have certain standards to maintain."

End of interview.

*

The ship had an Arab crew and an assorted bag of officers. Since no one ever wore anything other than a pair of shorts there had obviously been a problem as to how ranks were to be recognised, a problem which they had got round in a most bizarre manner. I was on board only a few hours when it became apparent to me that a man's insignia of rank was his stomach.

Naturally the biggest belonged to Captain Gresham. Next in importance aboard was the First Engineer, Evo Haamer, an Estonian. He was a jovial old character with many happy chins and a corporation only slightly less than that of the captain's, a great mound the colour of a ripe jaffa orange that wobbled its way further and further out of his shorts when he laughed, which was often. After him came Mr Thomas, the First Officer, from Wales, a rotund gentleman whose waistband, although adequate for his present position, had room for promotion. Next in line was the Second Officer, Felix Riart, also an Estonian, who was of the young, athletic type and in fairly good trim. It was obvious that he would have to slow up and let himself run to seed a bit if he were to advance. Lastly, there was Second Engineer Patel, of the diffident smile and uncertain manner, an Indian of the lean, stringy type that never grows fat. Poor man, there would never be advancement for him on this ship. His only hope was to transfer to a colder region where a badge of rank is worn, not grown.

*

The early days of the voyage were a new world to me. After the uncertain days of the past with money running out and the future looking blacker by the day this was a dream world. I was treated like a First Class passenger. I had my own 'cabin', a camp-bed with sheets and blanket tucked into a secluded corner of the upper deck, I dined heartily with the ship's officers – Captain Gresham ate alone – and nothing was asked of me. My time was my own to read and write as I pleased. I worked my way through the small 'library', a row of ancient looking books along a shelf in the tiny saloon. The present officers never seemed to disturb them, but they had been well used in the past. Perhaps they came that way.

There were some novels that barely held my interest and odd books of hobbies, interest, wireless, sailing – of all subjects! – and even gardening, which were lost on me. But among them all was one that beamed out to me like a lighthouse in the night ... *Trader Horn*. Written in the 1920s I had heard my father speak of it and of the film, a silent one no doubt, which I believe was made of it. I was delighted to have found it and it could not have entered my life at a more opportune time.

The story concerned an old man of flowing beard and gentle demeanour, Alfred Aloysius 'Horn' – the surname is a pseudonym – who turned up at the home of Mrs Ethelreda Lewis, a South African author, selling gridirons, toast-forks and other twisted wire utensils. While she pondered over whether or not to buy, Aloysius mentioned he had spent a lifetime from way back in the 1870s, when he was sixteen or seventeen, as a trader in West Africa. He penetrated deep into Africa along the rivers in his great sail-canoe, trading in ivory, rubber and other commodities. The upshot of the visit was that for the next six months Mrs Lewis had the old trader visit her every week from his doss-house in Johannesburg to tell her his story and to write it with pencil in exercise books which she collated into one of the finest adventure books to come out of Africa.

"Africa, Ma'am." Mrs Lewis quotes Aloysius, "Africa – as Nature meant her to be, the home of the black man and the quiet elephant. Never a sound, Ma'am, in a great landscape at noon – only the swish of the elephant grass … and me the first white man (nay, I was a lad) to pry on their happiness.

"Bound by the rites of the Egbo, Ma'am, to be blood brother to the cannibals. Look at my thumb, cut when I was eighteen in a fight with a savage and never grew again. Me? I've seen the skulls in the Josh House. Blood brother to the priests, where no white man had ever been until I came … but I was only a lad."

Well educated in a natural way, Aloysius was one of Nature's philosophers. Big-game hunters, he summed up as, an equatorial gang of cut-throats, wasting wildlife to make what they called a 'bag'. That remark was particularly *avant-garde* of the thinking in his time and mine too while I was in Africa. Nevertheless, it didn't stop him from shooting any elephant or large gorilla he saw to sell the ivory and carcass.

"There's no softness about Nature. When you're driven from the herd, it's for good. I've seen a beaten old Chief weep like a child. No wounds, mind you. But his heart broken. Aye, he knows there's no redress in a state of Nature. No newspaper talk to prop him up again. None of this so-called diplomacy. He sees '*Finis*' written all over the sunlight – same as an old elephant."

Trader Horn thrilled me. On the very threshold of my own foray into Africa I fervently hoped that I might write the best adventure story to come out of Africa of my day. And now as I write I see a similarity in our books. Aloysius told his story to the writer years after it had all happened, when his Africa had changed beyond recognition, and I write the story told to me by a young man's diaries, fifty years after the event when Africa has again changed so much from the time my story unfolded.

The only reader of the ship's complement was Captain Gresham. He introduced me to and loaned me copies of *The Saturday Evening Post*, the excellent New York magazine which he received by air-mail, a tremendous luxury in those days, considering its size and weight. I avidly devoured the short stories and marvelled at the illustrations, especially those of Norman Rockwell which formed many of the frontispieces. The Captain had me up quite often to talk and pass an hour or so and we got on very well. He seemed to have very little time for the other officers, never joining them in the saloon in the evening or at any other time except to do with the running of the ship. He chose to eat alone and really led a very solitary life. I enjoyed his company – despite our initial meeting – and I think he enjoyed mine too. We even laughed together quite a lot.

Mr Thomas, the 1st Mate and only other Briton on board, was a different character all together. A morose little man who became more morose the more he drank, which was a great deal, often. He never failed to tell me I was not welcome on board and would never have been there if the Army, one of their best customers, had not put weight on the Captain to have me. "Civilians," he would say regularly, "are bad medicine on board a cargo ship." What he meant by that I never found out.

One morning we sat waiting for breakfast in the little upholstered saloon, Evo, Felix, Patel and me. Evo had his knife and fork clasped upright in his fists as he always did, waiting to pounce on the food the moment it was placed on the table. Mr Thomas was missing. Presently unsteady footsteps were heard in the alley. Felix cocked his head, then added knowingly, "Ah huh, Mr Thomas has caught the dawn tide. Here he comes," he lowered his voice, "with a full cargo."

The First Officer entered without a word. Looking straight ahead he sat upright, rigid, manipulating his utensils with exaggerated precision when the food was served, his face impassive all the while even when Evo regaled us with one of his youthful memories, the story told with much laughter and belly-wobbling on his part.

Evo's escapade concerned an amorous wife who lured him into her boudoir and his narrow escape with his life when the husband, a great bear of a man, walked in on the clandestine scene. Evo had been chased through the street trailing his trousers under his arm while the citizens of the port, accustomed to such affairs, cheered him on his way. He only succeeded in shaking off his adversary by jumping on a bus, whereupon he waved jauntily to his chaser before throwing his clothes over his shoulder like a cloak and turning to bow graciously to the gaping passengers.

We all laughed, even Patel giggled shyly, except Mr Thomas who still sat expressionless, stuffing bacon and egg into his wooden face.

But it was not always laughter with Evo Haamer. There was sadness with him too. Like all who come from a country overrun by the Germans or Russians there are dark memories. One day he took me to his cabin and showed me a photo of his English wife. They had married recently, during his last leave, in the land he now called 'home'. She was young, in her twenties. Evo looked old. I thought there must be forty years between them, but perhaps Evo was not as ancient as he looked. When he said proudly that she was pregnant I could not help feeling sad, though I did not know why. Perhaps I had seen something in his eyes during the days we had spent together. And there it was. Even in the proud moment of showing me his young, pregnant wife, his eyes slid along the shelf to another photo of an older woman with three children of varying ages clustered round her. I flicked my eye to his and he caught my look. He hesitated a second, a moment full of emotion, so expressive, before he said in a lower voice with the hint of a catch in it, "My first wife. And my family."

When the Russians occupied Estonia and Latvia early in the war his wife and children were rounded up with countless others and taken into the wastes of Siberia and he never heard of them again. Evo had escaped, but whether before or after his family were taken he never said. But I knew by that moment between us, that infinite time of eloquent silence, I knew where his heart was and I felt sorry for that young woman in England.

Felix Riart also had his tales of occupied Estonia, but he didn't tell them. He had remained in the country for part of the war, but what he did or how he got out he didn't say. I spent more time with him, mostly playing chess, than with the others but he never spoke of his experiences except to say, referring to the fact that Estonia was occupied by both the Germans and the Russians, that the Germans, bad as they were, did seem human with at least a little sense. The Russians, it seemed, were indescribable.

Felix was perhaps five or six years older than I and we soon formed a good friendship. Most late afternoons at sea he would find me reading or writing in a camp chair by my bed on the upper for'ard deck. He would come running up the companionway and stride over to where I was sitting, stand in statuesque pose, tall, blond and Viking-like, his arm raised with lifted finger for emphasis, and announce in senatorial voice that bore the accent of his mid-eastern origin, "Now, we play the shass."

So we would play two or three games of 'shass' until it was time to shower and change for dinner. Neither of us were very great shakes at the game, each pleased to find someone bad enough to play.

This was not quite so at first, though. When we started, Felix led off with a string of runaway successes. I think I deferred to his extra years and self-confident manner and played too cannily while he, the buccaneer that he was, took full advantage of my timidity. Then I began to get the measure of him and clipped his heels a couple of times, so he fell a cropper that dented his panache. So we each reappraised the other and the scales evened up more or less. A new respect grew and the games lengthened. This mutual awareness however had its lighter side. We were both capable of making the most glaring mistakes and when it happened the other felt sure it must be all part of an ingenious master plan and was reluctant to take the exposed piece for fear of it being a decoy.

*

34

The day began a long time ago out in the bay off Port Sudan. There, half a mile off shore for safety sake, the cargo of ammunition we had brought from Port Tewfik was unloaded onto a lighter. There was cold fare for breakfast for no fires could be lit while this dangerous operation took place. This done the ship moved into the quay in the afternoon. As we slipped past the giant oil tanks, the low stone warehouses and buildings with arched doors and windows, the port had a quiet, serene air about it, unlike others we visited. Once tied-up the rest of the cargo, mostly for Khartoum, was unloaded and a new lot taken on.

The local stevedores swarmed over the ship as soon as we touched the side. They were the wildest, most fearsome men likely to be seen anywhere in the world. Black as ebony, their long, bushy, unkempt hair stood out as an inches thick mane, making their heads look enormous, and great tribal scars glistened across their black, velvet cheeks. These were the Fuzzy Wuzzies, the only men, according to Kipling, who ever broke a British square.

To them life seemed a joke. They sang while they worked, staccato songs to keep their timing as they moved or hauled, one man shouting out a phrase and everyone repeating the same words over and over again, or sometimes just one word repeated endlessly, "*Yala, yala, yala,*" "Let's go, let's go, let's go," laughing and capering all the while. The big one with the Al Jolson eyes, great white pools in the huge dark head, was the one who handled the derrick. He used it as a play-thing, swinging the loads like a pendulum, deaf to the warnings and abuse hurled at him by Mr Thomas. They laughed when the cable snapped, spilling the load higgledy-piggledy into the hold. Even the man who had his foot badly gashed showed only slight concern and barely flinched when Felix Riart stitched him up. Did these people not feel pain? Had one to be educated to know suffering? Watching their happy, irresponsible capers it seemed the price of civilisation was a high one.

The first part of the cargo to be unloaded was a seemingly endless supply of empty kerosene tins. Hour after hour the nerve-rasping rattle of the derrick, the deafening clanging of the cans and the chanting of the Fuzzy-Wuzzy stevedores blended in one awful cacophony.

It was dark by the time the cargo was loaded and the ship moved to the bunkering bay. Here fifty tons of coal were tipped into the hold by chanting natives with baskets on their heads. They filed up one gangway, emptied their baskets, and went down another in endless procession. The engines or generators could not be started because of the risk of fire or explosion from coal dust, so the work went on in lantern light. Looking down from the upper deck the scene was a Dante's hell: the pale pools of light, the endless column of chanting ant-like figures moving up, throwing their loads, and moving on down again, and the great black void of the hold swallowing all and sending up a cloud of dust that cloaked the whole scene in a nightmarish haze.

The coal dust sifted its way everywhere. Everything you touched was coated with it, the saliva you spat was black, the food you ate crunched with it. This happened in nearly every port we called on.

The bunkering completed, the hold was battened down, the motors started and the electric lights came on. But it was too late for a hot dinner and hosing down would have to wait until morning when we would sail at dawn. It was not a comfortable night.

Next morning when the first flash of pale light had barely separated land and sky the lines were slipped and the quay edged away. Pugnacious looking tugs with fierce moustaches of bumper nets fussed around their big sister, quietly but firmly pushing her round, churning the turquoise water into light green with veins of white foam across it, looking for all the world like molten marble. The propellers turned over, three short blasts were sounded on the hooter and we were off to sea again.

But not before a curious thing took place. Reminiscent of the way I joined the ship and showing that the SS *Cory Freighter* was not unfamiliar with clandestine passengers, a launch purred up to the side of the ship, a ladder was dropped over the side and a dozen or so soldiers climbed aboard, each carrying a heavy pack. They were different to any soldiers I had ever seen. Each man carried a revolver with a lanyard in a side holster. They looked rough and tough.

Once on board they kept themselves very much to themselves. They dossed down as a group on the deck and ate by themselves, drawing their food in dixies from the galley. They refused to be drawn into conversation but when I asked one if they were commandos he said no, they belonged to the Special Air Service, which meant nothing to me, not having heard of any regiment or corps of that name. The public in general had to wait over thirty years to the storming of the Iranian embassy in London to release hostages to learn exactly who the SAS really were. They left the ship at Massawa, the port for Eritrea, the former Italian colony. They did not disembark at the port though. They were put off on one of the ship's boats, somewhere along the coast. Once on the shore they quickly grouped and ran up a sand dune and disappeared into the empty interior.

"They're going after the *shifta*," Captain Gresham said later. He explained that the *shifta* were free roaming, well-armed bandits that were completely disrupting the country. No one could travel outside the towns in safety. They were the highwaymen of old, but much more ruthless, more numerous and better armed since the war had made guns much more readily available.

"Their first job is to clear the road between Massawa and Asmara, the capital up in the hills," Captain Gresham went on, "and all I can say is, heaven help the *shifta* that meet up with that lot."

After Eritrea had been wrenched from the Italians during the war Britain had been given an interim mandate to administer the country until the powers-that-be decided what to do with it. It might be declared independent or it might be incorporated into Ethiopia for that country had long wanted an outlet to the Red Sea. In the meantime Britain had the responsibility to quell the brigands and had just sent in her very best 'Dogs of War' to do so.

*

We left Massawa that night with only half the cargo loaded. The next two days were Mohammaden holidays when the port would be at a standstill. Captain Gresham obviously found it cheaper to sail than be stranded.

The reason for the holiday, I was told, was to celebrate the day Adam met Hawa (Eve). It is also the day when all pilgrims in Mecca gather round the Ka'ba shrine to kiss the holy stone. I was interested to note this reference to the ties between the religions. So we shared the Adam and Eve legend! How true is a legend? This one must be allegoric. Or is it? Eve was reputed to be buried at Jiddah, the port for Mecca, and Adam at Colombo, Ceylon (Sri Lanka).

*

It was sundown: those few fleeting moments that belong neither to day or night. I rose from my seat on the boat deck and rolled up the canvas shade now that the sting had gone out of the slanting rays of the dying sun and was struck by the beauty of the sunset. Nowhere on earth are they more vivid, more dramatic, than over the desert. As if some celestial artist had run amok with a fistful of brushes, huge streaks of red were slashed across the sky and away on the pale blue horizon he had drawn horizontal bars of red, yellow and green. The effect was unbelievable.

But the twilight is so short here. I watched it fade, or perhaps I should say change, for the beauty was still there. The reds darkened to russet brown, the blues to purple, the yellows to gold and the greens to aquamarine. The scene hung for a moment that way, then like a watercolour on a damp canvas, the colours slowly slid down to the sea. The sky was deep purple now with only a half inch of pale blue along the horizon into which all the colours had run, so that it looked like a multicoloured pencil. Then it was gone.

Sunset is a time for reflection. As the sun goes down memories can come alive.

Sunday 1st Oct. '50. At sea on the SS Cory Freighter.

This is the best time of day. Around sundown I like to reminisce. I think a chap can get closer to all the friends and happy times he used to have back home at this time of the day. I wonder how all the family are... I think a great deal about them all.

This is not to say I am overcome with nostalgia. Not for a minute. Sure I miss my home, it would be a poor one that wasn't missed, and I'll never be happier than when I see it all again. But I can't put into words the happiness I feel about going ahead and seeing all the countries.

I was reading an article in the Saturday Evening Post this afternoon where a person was asked to define happiness. Well, in my estimation, this is it. That half hour or less at twilight when a whole unknown continent lies in front of me and at the end of it one of the best homes a chap could have, a place where family and friends, and maybe an old flame or two, will welcome me back.

Maybe I shouldn't narrow it down to half-an-hour for the feeling is with me all the time. But it is in those quiet few moments at sundown when it all comes into sharpest focus and I realise the happiness of it all.

We sailed into Aden under a fat moon that bathed the rugged, barren hills in silver. The lighthouse up on the Elephant's Back beamed its light in and out and the myriad red and green signal lights of the many ships in harbour trailed dancing reflections in the water. The lights of Steamer Point town twinkled invitingly. I was eager to be ashore and on my way again. *"...this is the end of another phase of the journey,"* I wrote in my diary, but I was wrong.

Next morning an Adenese customs/immigration officer came aboard. I was all packed up, ready to go ashore with him, but it didn't work out like that. He demanded £100 returnable deposit with my passport to ensure I would be no burden to the authorities. No trouble, I produced my bankbook to prove I had just that amount in my account for immigration purposes, but he would have none of it. He had to have cash. How absurd. At that time there were severe restrictions on the amount of money anyone leaving Britain for holidays or travelling could take with them. £5 sterling and £50 in Travellers Cheques was the maximum amount allowed. And even if more were allowed how could I be expected to carry that kind of cash around with me, and in which currency? But he would not reason. I asked to come ashore where I could speak to the big animal, the Chief Immigration Officer, the white man. He would understand and make sense of it all. No good dealing with these half baked ones! My dander was up. But no, he could not allow me ashore. He would report the matter to his superior and he may come to see me.

He *may* come and see me! Surely as one Briton to another he would come and sort it out quickly. After all, inside the hard cover of my passport there was a message from Ernest Bevin, the Foreign Secretary, to all who read it, to "… allow the bearer to pass without let or hindrance …" I felt very proud of my passport and secure in the message it carried. The ship was due to sail again next day and it never occurred to me that I should not get off it.

The Adenese officer returned in a hour or so, but instead of his Chief he brought an armed policeman to guard me in case I decided to jump ship, an idea which I was seriously considering. He even insisted that I be confined to a cabin so that I could be better guarded.

All day I was shut up in Felix's cabin while every now and again the little policeman pulled himself up and craned his neck to look in through the porthole to make sure a I was still there. Although all this was a nuisance I could have done without, I drew a certain thrill from it. Any untoward happening took my journey out of the ordinary and put a new dimension to it.

Evening came and night. I was escorted to calls of nature and meals. My guards changed but there was no sign of anyone to sort out my trouble. I slept the night on the cabin floor and next morning, an hour before the ship was due to sail, the Big Man came aboard.

I have never met a more supercilious, apathetic and unhelpful person as he. My faith in my passport and expected help from fellow Brits was badly dented with the whole episode. He came aboard with a most languid air. A tall, thin man in a white suit, thick dark hair pulled straight to the side and a pained expression on his pinched face. This was all such a bore, such a waste of his good time. He threw himself into a canvas chair with a heavy resigned sigh and raised one eyebrow to me as an invitation to say what I had to say. No need to waste time or words on introduction or other preamble.

I started to tell him about the demand for a hundred pounds cash and that I had shown my bankbook to prove I had that money, but he silenced me with a cut-off gesture of his hand.

"Yes, I know all about that," he said with an air of exasperation, "but you have already been told that we need currency. Cash," the last word emphasised as if he were simplifying the crucial point for a dolt. Perhaps he was right: I was no genius on money matters. I had been in a fool's paradise, and very naive, to think my bankbook was a talisman that would carry me through all borders. As it appeared now, it was more likely to get me into hell than through the gates of heaven.

"But how can I get cash from this?" I asked desperately, waving my book.

"You must write to your bank and ask them to transfer the money to a bank in Aden where you can draw it." he said, looking aside with some agitation.

"But that will take weeks," I protested.

"Well, it'll cost you more, but you could have it wired out."

"How long will that take?"

"A day, perhaps."

"But the ship sails in an hour."

His mouth lifted slightly at one corner in a 'So what?' sneer. I was a piece of flotsom and what inconvenience or trouble he caused me was of little import. If he had taken the trouble to see me yesterday all this could have been sorted out in time for the ship sailing.

"How do I wire the money?" I asked with an air of resignation.

The man looked down and sighed before replying. I'm sure he was going to say that it was no concern of his how I did it so long as the money was there next time I arrived. Before he could speak, however, Captain Gresham came forward from where he had overheard the conversation.

"There's no need for any more of this, Brian," his annoyance was evident as he addressed the Immigration Officer by Christian name, "If the laddie has the money I'll see it's in the Cory office next time we come. As it is, I think it's a damned shame you've left a British national stranded like this. If I had the cash handy now I'd stand surety for him and let him ashore. I've lived with him these past couple of weeks and more and I know he's as straight as they come. He won't let you or me down, I'll warrant you."

Being called a laddie stung, but my goodness, my heart went out to the captain. When it was evident that I was going to have to stay aboard for another voyage my great worry was how he would react. If he were to resent my presence like Mr Thomas, the next few weeks were going to be pretty miserable. Now he had dispelled that fear and had wrapped me in such an aura of protection and character wellbeing I felt I should never be able to thank him enough. In addition he had put the pompous official down with his well chosen home-truths and had said all the things I should liked to have said myself. The man went down the gangplank with his tail down if not actually between his legs.

So for the next month I sailed the length of the Red Sea again, calling at several more ports than we had done on the first run. It had all looked so bad at one time, but in the words of an old song we sang at school,

Tho' to care we are born,
Yet the dullest morn
Often heralds in the fairest day.

Had I disembarked at the first visit to Aden I should have missed so much, particularly the two visits to Jiddha, the port for Mecca, at the height of the pilgrimage season.

As for the money, I can't quite remember the way Captain Gresham did it. I know he had me write authority for him to act on my behalf and went with this to the Cory office before we left Aden and used their wires to contact my bank. What I do know is that on arrival again at Port Sudan a message was waiting with the agent there to say the money had arrived in the Cory office in Aden and was awaiting my return.

*

The first port o' call was Djibouti, French Somaliland, a prosperous town with a light Parisian air and fine docks. At a pavement cafe with Evo and Felix I enjoyed the ambience, the soft French music and the pleasure of being free of the rolling sea and the confines of the ship. What marred the day was the sight of a beggar who came to the table and muttered the eternal word of the Middle East,

"Baksheesh?"

There had been many before, cripples, derelicts and waifs. They came and went. You have to learn to be like the bad Samaritans, not to see the hungry, the dying, let them pass, it is not your concern; otherwise you would do nothing else, give your all and be plagued by the whole pack descending on you, wanting more, tearing at you like a pack of scavengers after a wounded animal. But this one was different. He had no hands: they had both been cut off at the wrists. He was utterly helpless.

"He's from Saudi," Evo said, "They cut off the hands for stealing there," and to the boy, "From Saudi?"

"Yes," he responded in English, "from *Jidda*." How many languages did he speak? If he had been in Djibouti any time he would speak good French. So much ability wasted.

"For stealing?" Evo asked, making a slicing move with the edge of his right palm across his left wrist. The lad, he could be no more than twelve or thirteen, nodded. I had very little money, but I could not resist tucking a small note into his headcloth.

*

From Djibouti we crossed the sea to Hodeida, the main port for Yemen, a land I had heard was still locked into the time warp of the Arabian Nights, a land that refused entry to nearly all strangers, a land where the hand of Westernism had barely touched, evident from the fact that the king still had his enemies, even those of his own family, publicly beheaded by the sword in front of his palace. The more I heard of it the more I wanted to see it. Forbidden fruits are always the most desirable!

The Yemen is the most fertile corner of the whole Arabian peninsular. Even with their primitive methods of farming they exported great quantities of fruit and vegetables to southern Arabia and elsewhere. From here too come frankincense and myrrh the aromatic gum resins and almost certainly it was from this land that the Wise Mens' gifts to Christ were obtained. Their most lucrative export of all though, beating even the world famous Mocca coffee, is '*kat*' or '*ghat*', the 'gh' being pronounced in gutteral form as the Scottish 'ch' in 'loch'. Ghat is the Arabic name for Indian Hemp. The outer bark and tough fibres can be used to make ropes and sailcloth, but the soft inner fibres and tender upper stems, particularly of the female plant, are used to make narcotic drugs. When dried and powdered it is 'hashish' and if the resin the plant produces is included, a powerful hallucinatory drug is produced. When dried and smoked as tobacco or when made into a drink it is known as '*bhang*'. In Arabia and surrounding countries, however, it is used, and no doubt has been from the beginning of time, in the most natural form of chewing the green leaves. It is common for most men in these parts to have a wedge of ghat leaves in his cheek from which he digests the juices. When taken mildly, I was told, it produced mild intoxication, a feeling of wellbeing that dispersed minor troubles and tiredness and could be therapeutic on long camel caravan journeys. In extended use or abuse it could cause complete intoxication and hallucinations, much in the same way as does alcohol, which is forbidden by Moslem law.

For such a backward country it was surprising that part of the cargo delivered was a few tons of scrap iron. I could not visualise there being any large scale foundries there but perhaps the scrap was smelted on goatskin-bellows blast furnaces to make the wonderful daggers in the ornate scabbards that all the dhow owners wear.

There was no wharf or quay at Hodeida, at least if there was we never got into it. We moored in the bay and the harbourmaster came out in a dhow: no motor launch luxury for him as at other ports. Before his present appointment, we learned, he had been the court barber. In this capacity he had overheard a corrupt plot against the king which he had promptly divulged and as a reward had been given his present post. Perhaps it was the harbourmaster's head that had rolled. The barber's inexperience with nautical matters obviously had been no barrier to his promotion

The scrap iron and the rest of the cargo for the port was unloaded onto 'sambuks', small dhows with shallower draught. They were the same design as the dhows, with a short mast at an acute forward rake, or tilt, and a very long yard arm hung at 45-degrees, which set the lateen, or triangular, shape to the sails. The off-loading completed, we then took on 1700 bags of Mocha coffee, the produce of the land south of Hodieda. All the cargoes to and from were loaded into or out of sambuks amid the continual chant and banter of Arabic voices. It was all very oriental. The

Yemeni were better built and were better workers than I'd noticed elsewhere in this part of the world.

On leaving Hodieda we beat across a wild running sea to Massawa. I could not believe the Red Sea could be so rough. Although not actually sick, I did not feel good and was pleased when we glided across the calm waters of the harbour.

There was more time to spare for shore visits on this voyage than the previous one. I enjoyed the chance to wander round the towns and absorb the local scenes, especially when it meant I could miss the bunkering and all that coal dust.

I had barely enough money to buy the odd coffee and when I did I lingered over it, making it last as long as seemed decent while I talked to whomever I could. There were still a lot of Italians here, but they had a sad air, like the town. It had a run-down, forlorn look. In the present political limbo, commerce had almost stopped and no maintenance was being done. Although there were five ships in the harbour at that moment there had been none for the past ten days. People recalled the heydays when Massawa was the playground of Eritrea, when the harbour was always full of rollicking sailors and the cafes and nightclubs rang with endless gaiety and the town was alive and noisy, vibrant, as only Italian places can be. The Italians being expert builders, new shops and houses grew like mushrooms and the Moorish architecture was continually plastered and painted to look like newly iced cakes. Now, about the town there was a sad, tired air, and peeling paint and cracked, flaking stucco on the street buildings. Massawa, like its builders, had been beaten in the war.

Port Sudan, much smaller than Massawa, was distinctly different. Where Massawa had built houses right down to the harbour Port Sudan had public gardens with palm trees, all carefully nurtured and kept, that looked good from the sea. Once ashore the greenery looked much more sparse, but the town had a cared-for look, all very British, none of your cheap, fly-by-night gaiety that was so evident in the Italian province. Each town epitomised their colonial builders and overlords.

Half an hour ago the sun disappeared in a pool of blood and the night lid clamped down, tight, oppressive. It is hot. My, how it is hot! Though it is dark I still cannot wear a shirt. An oven wind blows off the desert and as I write the sweat runs down my face, courses off my body and my hands are so wet the pen keeps slipping. We lie off shore at Port Sudan for safety sake to load a cargo of benzene in jerry-cans. The bedlam finished as daylight faded but it is still not safe to start the generators so I sit in a small island of dim light from a battery lamp. The light is made dimmer by great clouds of mosquitoes that continually swirl round it. Their incessant loud whining noise is the eternal music of the tropics.

There can be no place worse for insect life than here. Myriad flies, mosquitoes, flying beetles inch-and-a-half long by inch broad, great praying-mantis and grass-hoppers that can leap five feet high make writing an ordeal. I killed one of those huge grass-hoppers that landed on my shoulder and as soon as it fell the 'undertakers' or 'refuse collectors', the ants, moved in. They covered it en-masse and now the shiny husk is left empty and transparent. Nature is very efficient.

This afternoon I witnessed a real drama of the seas. I was drawn running to the rail by a great splashing noise that sounded as if a whole crew of non-swimmers had fallen overboard and were floundering crazily in the water. Near the ship a great patch of the sea was boiling like a huge cauldron, churned up by a great shoal of fish that must have numbered millions. The shoal was being chased by a pack, or several packs, of barracuda. The little fish leapt like a solid silver streak several feet out of the water and were followed by the great marauders hurling themselves clean out of the water in amazing twists and contortions to catch them. Like a single being the shoal rose like a fountain and writhed left and right in solid mass as if governed by one brain and wherever they went they were followed by the barracuda that went through them with scything jaws. The noise was deafening. The scene made me shudder.

This area is really a wonderful place to study nature. Apart from the insects and the fish there is an amazing assortment of birds: flamingos, pelicans, eagles and hosts of others I don't know the name of. Yesterday a swallow came aboard and settled on the top of the open door of the captain's cabin. He hasn't closed it since and it's still there, asleep. It must be one of the first of the migration. What distance has it flown to make it so exhausted? Perhaps it has been blown way of course and done far more miles than is usual for the journey. I wonder where it's going? (Next morning when we woke it was gone.)

This morning while we were still tied up at the quay I had a walk along the shore and came on a enormous colony of great crabs. At first I thought they were gigantic spiders but couldn't get near enough to identify them before they disappeared down holes in the sand. These holes are about three inches in diameter and in places the shore is riddled with them.

I hurried back to the ship to borrow a pair of binoculars so I could study them at a distance. The captain informed me they were 'hermit' crabs, but why they are called that when they live in such teeming colonies seems incongruous. Back in position they were interesting to watch. There were hundreds, perhaps thousands, of them. In places the beach was heaving with crawling, carapaced bodies. Repulsive, frightening really.

Would they be so timid of an injured person, unable to move, or someone staked out by way of punishment? Ugh!

"Amoud," I addressed the ship's cook, "tell me about Mecca."
I sat on a wicker basket in which hens clucked in the ship's galley at the stern where the smells were powerful and not all good. Live goats and sheep – difficult to tell the difference between them, so different to those at home – the ship's fresh meat, clattered about the deck eating and defecating at the end of their tethers; bags of rice and sugar, boxes of curry and ghee – the Indian buffalo-milk butter that was clarified to resemble oil but which to me looked more like wagon grease – and other commodities were stacked under cover.

As a free agent with little to occupy me I roamed the ship from Evo Haamer and Patels' boiler room to the Captain's cabin and spent time everywhere, even in the crews' quarters, and spoke to everyone who could understand me. Most of all, though, I enjoyed being here in the galley where Amoud slaughtered the live goats, sheep and fowls as necessary, butchered and cooked them. With my visits we formed a close friendship and often Amoud would send me special treats and titbits with the steward when he brought my morning and afternoon tea up to my deck place.

Mr Thomas made no bones about his dislike for my maverick existence. Several times when he heard my voice at the galley – merely an area of the deck covered by an awning – he came and short of ordering me away made his annoyance known by glowering looks and mutterings. Perhaps this was the 'bad medicine' he had spoken about. But barring a direct order from Captain Gresham I chose to remain and repeat my visits.

We lay in Jiddah harbour, the main port of Saudi Arabia and nearest one to the Moslem holy city of Mecca. The ruler of the land was King Ibn Saud, a giant of a man, 6ft. 6ins., by all accounts. Prior to his gaining power at the beginning of the century the land was a collection of wild sheikhdoms. Ibn's father had been driven out to Kuwait where the son had grown through his teens. Then as a 21-year-old he returned with a handful of loyal supporters and one-by-one subdued the rabble sheikhs until in 1932 he declared himself King of Arabia. He had a reputation as a fair and wise ruler and so positively was he in charge the land was now referred to as 'Saudi's Arabia' or, as it was now officially on the map, 'Saudi Arabia'.

The pilgrimage season was at its height and sitting there I had counted over thirty ships anchored and a great armada of ocean-going dhows clustered together in a tangled forest of masts, yards and rope.

New arrivals came by the hour, in through the maze of beautiful but dangerous reefs and sandbars that lay barely awash guarding the entrance to the harbour, an entrance too dangerous to navigate at night; passed the rusting hulk of one ship that did not make it some years before and now lay as a constant warning to all who approached; passed the long, low building with small domes at each end and middle, head, middle and feet, which is said to be the tomb of Eve. If it is true that the domes indicate her size she was one hundred and eighty feet tall. But there are those who say her body does not occupy all of the building, that most of the space was to accommodate her belongings. Rather a tall story that, surely … all that space for a fig leaf!

They came with their human cargoes of pilgrims stowed into every corner of their holds and decks. Neither the shipping companies nor the pilgrims considered comfort at a time like this and indeed stoic acceptance of pain and discomfort was all part of the ethics of the pilgrimage. For many the sea journey would be the end of months, even years, of travel overland. Many would come by camel caravan and others even on foot. In contrast, planes were arriving regularly bringing in the wealthy ones, surely a new dimension to the history of the religion. Would Allah welcome the rich in the same way as he did the poor who gave so much of themselves to be there?

Jiddah was a good looking town, more prosperous than any I'd seen up and down the Red Sea and well it might with all the revenue and trade from what amounted to a vast tourist industry. In addition, the Americans had settled there since the war to explore for oil and had built a new pier and introduced many 20th century innovations, such as electricity, but I was told no telephone, radio or camera was allowed in any Moslem home.

The modern changes were limited to Jiddah and the confines of the American camps. Beyond the town this part of the world had hardly changed in the hundred years since Richard Burton, who spoke the language like a native, went to Mecca and Medina disguised as an Arab, the first white Christian to bring back a detailed account of the *hajj*, the punishment for which, had he been discovered, would have been instant death.

I sat looking out beyond the town to the long, distant range of mauve hills over which and beyond no Christian is allowed to go. Fifty miles over that hazy barrier lay the forbidden city. So intriguing. How I wished I could go there.

Amoud had done the pilgrimage some years before and warmed to his favourite subject as he sharpened his knife. I had heard the tale many times before but never tired of listening to it for each time he always managed to bring out another gem of information. I knew his journey had taken him two years to complete and what terrible years of privation they had been. I knew the details of his illness that had caused him to miss his return ship and how he had begged his way through the desert back to Yemen. But he had considered this a small price to pay for the prestige the title of *Hajji* gave and how much his chances of getting into Heaven were increased by having done the pilgrimage.

A Mohammedan from Yemen, Amoud, though lowly in the eyes of the ship's officers, was an aristocrat among his peers for he held the highly respected title of *Hajji* as one who has done the *Hajj*, the pilgrimage to Mecca which every Moslem is called on to do at least once in his lifetime, but which comparatively few ever manage to achieve. Only the *Hajji* is allowed to dye his beard with henna, a dye from the Egyptian privet. Amoud wore his little wispy red beard with pride.

"Tell me Amoud, was Mecca a holy city even before Mohammad was born?" I asked. "Ah, Daaveed Sahib, you are my good ears, you are never tired of listening. Oh yes, Mecca was a holy place long, long before the Prophet was born there. His father and his father before him were keepers of the Ka'ba and people came from the ends of the earth to worship there, just as they do now. But when Mohammed was chosen by al'Llah to be his Prophet and gave him the holy words to write in the Koran, Mohammed threw out of the building all the idols and so cleansed it of the old religion and declared that only his words would be heard there and only al'Llah would be worshipped there."

"Tell me again how it started," I prompted. I knew what he would say but was always intrigued when he told his story. It was his initial telling of his tale that had first shown me how entwined were the beginnings of the three religions, Judaism, Christianity and Islam and how much they had in common.

"It was the Zemzem well that started it all, away back in the days when we all worshipped in the same way," he said, grabbing a sheep by the snout and cutting its throat with one deft stroke, with hardly a pause in his discourse.

Unless animals are killed exactly in the manner prescribed in the Koranic law the meat is useless to Moslems. I believe the same customs and laws for the killing of edible animals are followed by the Jews, and the fact that neither eat pork, would indicate that they share common practices which must come from way back before the two peoples were separated by religion.

During the first days on board the sight of the killing, the sudden release of life, affected me deeply. Now I was hardening myself to it, pushing the ague the sight of it caused me down under the belief that such feelings were boyish. It was now a trivial part of everyday life. A sheep cost £3 including its food on board and its skin sold for four rupees (6/- or 30p). Routine stuff.

While he gutted and skinned the sheep with no more ado than he might with any little everyday task, Amoud explained that Abraham had a son, Ishmael, to Hagar, his wife Sarah's Egyptian hand-maid. For the first few years Sarah, who was thought to be barren, did not mind the child in her household, but when she became pregnant with her own child, Isaac, she bade Abraham to cast Hagar and her son into the desert. To satisfy his wife Abraham did so knowing that God would provide for them, which he did by making water gush out of the ground. This was the start of the Zemzem well, around which Mecca was built. Later Abraham, who lived to be one hundred and seventy-five, went into the desert and found Hagar and son and in thankfulness to God for preserving them he and Ishmael built a temple, a simple square affair which was called the 'Kaaba' which means 'cube'. Amoud admitted the Kaaba had been rebuilt many times since that ancient day but one stone, known as the Black Stone, had been built into every new Kaaba. Mohammad kissed the Black Stone and it is the duty of every pilgrim to touch or kiss it as the way of making contact with their Prophet and also to give thankfulness to Abraham, whose footprint is said to have been embedded in it and who is said to have been given the stone by archangel Gabriel.

Some time after Amoud first told me this story we put into Port Sudan where I was able to find a small library and do some research on Abraham. I learned that he came from the town of Ur, near the River Euphrates in modern Iraq, to the Land of Canaan (soon to be named Israel after his grandson Jacob who changed his name to Israel), about 1600 BC, after a sojourn in Egypt. So Mecca had indeed been a Holy City for over 2000 years before Mohammad came on the scene.

Amoud described the round of ceremonies and rituals he performed as a pilgrim. On arrival everyone took off their clothes, washed and put on a white garment made of a single cloth which reduced all wealth and rank to equality. In graphic detail Amoud told how with thousands of others he ran seven times round the Kaaba, the great cube-shaped building, one hundred and sixty feet high, which is all covered in black cloth embroidered with gold, each time jostling and fighting to get near to touch or kiss the Black Stone which is built into one corner and which is smooth and deeply indented from the lips and fingers of centuries. The running round the Kaaba is said to symbolise Haggar's frantic search for water when first cast into the desert.

On the eighth day he had gone the fifteen miles with the multitude to camp for a day on Mount Arafat or Jebel Er Rahmeh (Mountain of Mercy) where, it is reputed, God made his first covenant with Adam and where Adam was reunited with Eve one hundred and twenty years after being cast out of the Garden Of Eden and, even more important for Moslems, where Mohammed went to meditate and where God first spoke to him and told him to take His message to the world and where later Mohammed made his farewell Sermon on the Mount to the pilgrims before he died in 632 AD.

I noted the similarity to Christ's Sermon and other incidents and stories in the Koran to those in the Christian New Testament and was intrigued by the dual history of the Arabs and the Jews. It was incredible to think they both had a common progenitor in Abraham – the Arabs through Ishmael and the Hebrews from Isaac, a fact that might have created a close relationship between the two peoples but which instead cleft a deep schism. It is said the Jews always considered themselves superior because Isaac was the lawful son of Abraham, while the Arabs maintain that Ishmael was the first son so they hold pride of place. To me, hearing that Jews and Moslems were of one family and since Christ was a Jew, it seemed we were all tied up like monkeys' tails.

Apart from where the beginnings overlapped, Amoud could not tell me of the other religions, but his stories prompted me to research the common bonds shared by Jews, Moslems, and Christians. All three shared the Old Testament: the Torah, the Hebrew book of instruction, being in fact the first five books of the Old Testament, Genesis to Deuteronomy. When Mohammad in a feverish, trance-like state poured out the words he claimed had been told to him by God – he is said to have been illiterate – his listeners wrote them down to compile the Koran. His stories appeared to have drawn much from those in both the Old and New Testaments. All three religions worship one deity, the same deity, but each have their own name for that divine being: the Christian word is God, the Jewish word is Yahweh and the Moslems refer to Allah, or more correct, al-Llah, which means 'The God'. Moreover, the Christians and Moslems each have their own Prophet, Jesus for one and Mohammed the other, while the Jews are still waiting for theirs' to arrive. Mohammed, who was born more than six hundred years after Christ, acknowledged him as a holy man but claimed that he, Mohammed, was the only Prophet. All three religions have times of fasting: the Jews have their Passover, the Moslems have their Ramadan and the Christians have Lent.

All the names, all the tales, were so familiar I might have been at bible class back in Torryburn Kirk. I had thought that much of what I heard of Abraham and Haggar and all that pertained only to the Christian religion and here I was learning from Amoud that they belonged to all three religions. It made me ponder that if we all claimed the same roots and all prayed to the same God, even if we call Him by different names, and all hoped to arrive at His house, maybe there was more than one route to the Pearly Gates, even though each religion claimed that theirs is the only one.

Not that I was likely to choose Mohammed's way. A religion which the founder ordered to be spread by the sword was no creed to follow. The Christian religion based on love of all people, one that preached the ethics of, 'Do unto others as you would be done by,' and, 'Turn the other cheek,' was surely better than one that had its feet in the Old Testament, one that perpetuated revenge by extolling the virtue of an 'An eye for an eye and a tooth for a tooth.'

Sorting out the tangle of it all was all rather bewildering. But was it all so important anyway? Trader Horn had a word on it, "You forget the animosities of religion when you're living close to nature." It made a lot of sense. I could see myself living very close to nature in the future so perhaps there would be no problem.

Changing the subject, I asked Amoud why the Arabs cut off hands for stealing, saying it was so barbaric and did not belong to this century.

"Ah, Daaveed Sahib, it has always been so as it is written in the Koran." He began in his usual way, then hesitated, as if he were thinking how he could say an unpleasant thing without offending me, "The sahibs only see things their way. The sahibs want everybody to think and do as they do. But we are different people, we have different thoughts, we live in a different time to the sahibs.

"Cutting off the hand for stealing … it has always been so. For a time we tried to follow the sahibs' way and laid aside our own laws, but it was bad. Very bad things happened. A pilgrim goes to Mecca carrying all the money he needs to get him home again. If he loses that he may never be able to return to his family, he may live the rest of his life as a slave, or he may die trying to make his way home on foot by begging." He mentioned that last bit with great feeling.

"When the old ways were laid aside, gangs of robbers waited in the mountains to prey on the pilgrim caravans coming through, and the towns were full of unscrupulous thieves. If they had not been stopped nobody would have dared do the *hajj* and calamity would have befallen our people for not following the instructions of the Prophet.

"The old punishments were brought back and now Jiddah and all Saudi are safe again. It is so in my country, Yemen, too. Now nobody steals. If you drop your wallet in the street you can pick it up the next day. If someone even touches money which is not theirs a finger is cut off. Now pilgrims are safe and can go anywhere without the least fear. Merchants leave money, their cash boxes with lots of money in them, while they go to pray or eat and nobody touches them. Stealing hardly exists in Arabia. Can you say that of your country? Better a few thieves lose their hands than many men lose their lives, or families lose their fathers and husbands, or the country loses the wealthy trade it depends on, or our religion loses the core of its existence. Cutting off their hand is better than putting the thieves to death. If they were beheaded they would just disappear and many more would take their place. But a one-handed or no-handed beggar is a living example, a warning, to all who might think of stealing. So Daaveed Sahib, do not feel sorry for the handless ones; they are doing a good job in stopping others from stealing and ruining our lives, our country and our religion."

Of course Amoud did not speak as fluently or expressively as the way I have put the words in his mouth. His English was quite good, but hesitant and his vocabulary was limited. But he got his message across clearly in the end and it was the essence of this rather than the words that I carried with me when we finally went our different ways.

*

Life sparkled during the first few weeks on board ship. Each day brought new horizons, new ports, new experiences. But as the weeks went by the sparkle

50

faded. Amoud's tales I knew by heart and the humour had gone from Evo's after five or six times round. The 'shass' games were all-night stalemates now we knew and could anticipate each others' moves and the leisure I had taken for luxury was boredom. No port was novel now. If this was a sailor's lot, if this was all he saw of countries he visited then I was glad I was merely sampling his life.

Daily I longed to get to Aden again where I might leave the sea. But would I? Would they find something else to prevent me landing? What would I do? My Egyptian visa had now expired and if I could not leave at any port would I be condemned to sail the sea forever like the Flying Dutchman?

At last the day came when we steamed into Aden bay to pass under those barren grey rocks to tie up near Steamer Point. It was midday and, hopeful of disembarking, I said my goodbyes. Evo and Felix expressed their real sorrow at my going, Patel gave me a weak hand and a mumbled farewell and even Mr Thomas managed a smile and a few words of luck. Captain Gresham said openly that he would miss my company and gave me a bundle of his precious *Saturday Evening Post*s. I said sincerely how much I had enjoyed being on board and thanked him for all his help and for making me so welcome.

Lastly, I went to see Amoud. He seemed genuinely moved when I said I was leaving. He put his palms together on his chest as if in prayer and said, "Go in peace, friend Daaveed Sahib." I too was genuinely moved.

My disembarkation was not without a little drama. First, the Cory Agent came aboard mainly to give assurance that my money was in the office but also to present me with a bill for £11 for my time on board. This was really very reasonable considering a deck passage without food for a native for one way up or down the Red Sea was £10. So they had charged me the very minimum fare with a nominal £1 for food. There was no doubt that I had had my money's worth. However I had to tell them that apart from the immigration money I had hardly a penny to my name and asked if they could wait until I got a job and earned the amount, but to be truthful I hadn't a clue how I was going to do that. £11 represented a huge debt and I didn't even have enough money to buy food for more than a couple of days. But once again Captain Gresham came to my aid. He drew the man aside and had a few words with him, after which the agent came back and said the charge was dropped.

Next, the Immigration Officer when he arrived again refused me entry even though the Cory Agent said my money was at their office. I was taken under armed escort to the office where I drew the money and went, still under armed escort, to the Immigration Office where I handed it over and had my entry permit stamped on my passport. The guard went off and I finally left the office a free man. How sweet the pavement felt under my feet.

Chapter Four

SHEBA'S CARAVANSERAI

Wednesday 16th November 1950 – Sheba Camp, Aden.

When climbing up Sham-Shan, the highest peak on the crater rim, where local legend has it that Cain killed Able and hid his body in a cave, I was sure I was going to be the first man since Adam's son to die on that hill when the whole rock face on which I clung seemed to break and lean out.

Having said my goodbyes to the SS *Cory Freighter* at Steamer Point and now clear of Immigration I follow the Crescent road that circles the harbour. On the sea side the groves of carefully cultivated trees and gardens are cool and shaded. On the other the huddle of shops and rag-tag inhabitants are in a ferment of activity. A passenger ship has also docked and the street is busy with travellers ashore for a few hours. This is a duty free port and prices are lower than elsewhere. The bazaar traders vie with each other for your trade. Eager hands clutch at your arm and bizarre objects are thrust at you: ivory and ebony carvings, prayer mats with pyramids and other desert scenes on them, fountain pens, lighters, cameras … anything. Voices call at you: hoarse voices, shrill voices, quick voices, sly voices … all eager voices.

"Sir, look at this!"

"Sahib!"

"Johnnie!"

"Hey you, look here!"

"Come buy here, big bargain."

"See what I have."

Tomorrow when there is no passenger ship in harbour the Crescent will slip into somnolent quietness. The traders will sit talking to each other over coffee hawked by little ragged urchins who carry round great kettles and little charcoal braziers which they swing to-and-fro now and again to fan up the coals. Or they may sleep over their rugs and carpets and if you are one of the Colony's regular inhabitants and wish to buy you must wake them. Their prices will be much less than they are today when the ship is in, but even these will require pruning. Don't think you are belittling the dealer, or that he will think you mean if you make an offer half his asking price. If you give him what he asks without quibble he will think he has not asked enough and be unhappy and you will be upsetting the balance of the local economy. He is happy when you haggle, that way he feels he's squeezed the very best deal out of you. In the Orient haggling is the fun of the game for both seller and buyer.

*

I was a poor catch for any trader that day for I had barely two rupees to rub together. Impervious to their blandishments, my thoughts were on survival. I was walking, but I didn't know where, but once again the kilt and the army came to my rescue.

There had been a very strong presence of our forces in Aden since Britain landed a task force there in 1839 to put down pirates and so secure safe passage to the Far East for her ships. The force stayed on and later Britain bought land from the Sultan of Lahej and settled in on a permanent basis.

Now, at the time of my arrival, Air Force personnel from the large airfield at Kormaksor by far outnumbered the army. But it was a squaddy in a khaki forage cap with a Royal Artillery badge who leaned out the cab of a lorry and in a broad Glaswegian voice asked me who I was and what I was doing. He spoke in a machine-gun rap of words, half of which were barrack-room expletives. I explained to him what I was doing, during which time he repeatedly interjected, "'kin' 'ell", his favourite exclamation. And after many "kinell"s I found myself in the truck on my way to join the lads in the Naafi for the mid-morning cup of tea.

Later, sitting over a steaming mug of hot sweet tea and a cheese roll and swapping banter with a crowd of new friends I had cause to bless my luck. Away from the cloud of tea and bonhomie I detected an unusual smell which might have been lost to others. Looking beyond the quaffing, swearing soldiers I saw that part of the premises was not in use for service and in this area a few Arabs were painting tables and chairs. By the looks of it they were making very heavy weather of the work and I could see why. By the smell of the solvent I knew they were using cellulose paint, a very quick drying finish that was intended more for spraying cars than brushing. Applying cellulose paint by brush requires considerable skill. Above all, it must be applied with great speed using deft, sure brush strokes and never going back on the part already coated, otherwise the edge dries and the surface then resembles spat-out chewing-gum. I could see that none of the painters were skilled enough to handle the material.

Rising from the group I went over to a painter who had been ages doing half a table. The result of his labours had very much the chewing-gum effect. Without saying a word, and to his complete astonishment so that he gave no resistance, I took the brush from him and picking up his pot from the floor – a sure sign that

53

he had no idea of the craft – I finished the table in a couple of minutes, the resultant appearance being smooth and glass-like.

All the painters, including the Arab bossman, gathered round to stare in amazement and some of the soldiers came over to look too. They were all even more amazed when I said I wanted a job. The bossman said it was not becoming a white man to do such a menial job. I said it was not becoming a white man to be broke. So he took me to see the Naafi manager, a Mr Valentine, who started me on the magnificent wage of 50 rupees (£3.75p) a week. (The Arab brush hands were paid 18 rupees a week.) Moreover, he got me a bed in the billets with full board in the mess for the time I was in their employ. I had full reason now to be pleased with myself. Within an hour or so of walking into Aden I was an employed resident.

Next day at the canteen I painted many times more tables and chairs than each of the Arab workers and the Arab foreman was forever telling me to go slower as all the men would be expected to speed up their output and this would cause trouble. He hadn't grasped the fact that with cellulose paint you couldn't go slow. The following morning I was sent to the bulk warehouse at Maala where I could work more or less on my own and avoid the incongruity of having on view a white man working as an Arab in a gang, not to mention showing up the local gentry in my eagerness to work and the volume of my production. Incidentally, I did not work in my kilt, that was only for travelling. I always carried shorts and a change of clothing.

Once again I enjoyed the friendly camaraderie of army life without the discipline. But camp life in Aden was different to any I had known. There was an underlying hostility between the Adenese natives and the British forces personnel which produced a restrictive air. Life was lived in the camp except when on duty and any excursions outside the perimeter wire were done in groups or in vehicles. I was of course free to go as I pleased and constantly walked alone to and from my work and everywhere else and never felt threatened. But there were many who did not envy my freedom and were only too pleased not to go beyond the safety of the camp confines.

Night time did nothing to cheer the faint heart. As soon as darkness fell the baboons way up in the rocks all round and as far down as Cemetery Valley below the camp started a continuous round of bloodcurdling screaming and the pariah dogs that hunted in packs howled like wolves.

After a week at the RA camp, because of a coming inspection visit by a brigadier, I was transferred to an RAF establishment, Sheba Camp, for my billets. It was like being back in the Forces but being transferred from one service to another was a new experience.

Working the humdrum life of a painter after the months as a traveller could have been tedious but it never was. Everywhere I turned there were interesting things to see and working with local Arabs and watching their daily habits was the stuff of dreams that I had looked forward to for so long. Every day I watched the progress of the building of the dhows on the shore near where I worked and spent time studying in detail the methods of working.

I was thrilled to see shipwrights building the same ships on the beach at Maala in the same way and with tools, adze, auger and mallet, that had hardly changed since those early days of Sheba, 3000 years ago.

Although the Bible refers only to the great camel caravan that the Queen of Sheba came with to Solomon it is believed that she also built a fleet of ships to go there too. She may even have sailed with them, for the gifts she took and those which she received from Solomon for her return could not have been carried by camels. And at Aden it is claimed that that fleet, or at least part of it, was built at Maala, perhaps the oldest shipyard in the world, near the dhow wharf at Aden. Sitting by the dhows in construction, watching the age-old scene I felt a great affinity with these ancient times and in that muse even the fables could be true.

At weekends I roamed the area and spent time in Crater, the main town that lies in the bowl of a great volcano that blew itself to bits perhaps when the world was in the making. The town is almost completely surrounded by the mountainous, jagged rim of the crater and each weekend I climbed one or two of these peaks. Although I had done some rock climbing in Scotland I had never climbed alone, but now I was imbued with a growing confidence and gaily went into forays that I now see as foolhardy, especially as the volcanic rock was very treacherous. Once when climbing up Sham-Shan, where local legend had it that Cain killed Able and hid his body in a cave, I was sure I was going to be the first man since Adam's son to die on that hill when the whole rock face on which I clung seemed to break and lean out. I became more wary after that and prudently went down by the path that led past the stone quarry with its endless line of mules each with wood and leather side-panniers laden with boulders. Along the way too were the wonderful stone dams and water catchment works, great engineering feats, built in antiquity by Turks or other occupying forces before the British era.

Most interesting of all though were my visits to Sheikh Othman, the little town about eleven miles from Aden on the edge of the desert hinterland. This was the land port for the sand sea that stretched all the way to the north. Here strong winds blew a sand haze nine months in the year and in this dust mist the great caravanserai had a perpetual dreamlike appearance.

Here camel caravans would arrive in the mornings and others depart in the late afternoons when the sun's heat was spent, each with two to three hundred miles before or behind them. The arrivals brought coffee, skins, fruit such as mangoes, guavas, water melons and pomegranates, almonds and raisins, vegetables, firewood and charcoal, these latter items being of great value in a land that had none but ornamental trees. And of course *ghat*, the green leaves that seemed to act both as a stimulant and a balm that eased the cares of the day, depending on the mood of the chewer, the import of which the British government was trying in vain to stop, at least in Aden Colony.

Those leaving in the afternoon went laden with cans of paraffin oil, bolts of cloths and silks, battery wireless sets, gramophones with records of Arabic music, Singer sewing machines, medicines and modern drugs, colour dyes, books and stationery, tobacco and farm implements.

When I saw them arrive and depart the drovers always walked beside the camels. By their clothes and mien you could tell they were hired hands, the lorry drivers for a transport business. But occasionally a merchant who owned the string of camels he travelled with would arrive seated high and regally on his Buhrie, or riding camel, the 'ship of the desert'. These were quite different beasts to the pack variety, being bigger and more splendidly haughty, like a maiden aunt striking a superior pose while surveying the scene through her pince-nez perched on the point of her long nose.

I loved the whole aspect of the caravanserai, I loved being there, part of it, realising the likes of it might soon be lost forever. Already a few motor vehicles had been introduced on some of the regular, flat routes and while it was likely camels would still be needed on the rougher terrain for a long time to come the number of animals and drovers I was watching now would soon be a thing of the past. I was watching the end of an era that stretched back to biblical times and beyond, to the time of Solomon and Sheba a thousand years BC.

'And when the Queen of Sheba heard of the fame of Solomon ... she came to prove him with hard questions. And she came to Jerusalem with a very great train, with camels that bare spices, and very much gold, and precious stones.' 1 Kings 10

Before the arrival of the British this place was part of Yemen, and Yemen was the Land of Sheba. No doubt her main caravans went from Shabwa, her city where the more modern town of Marib stands, seventy-five miles east of San'a. But surely caravans from here where I stood would go to meet up with the main train, for the goods she took were so numerous they must have been drawn from every corner of her land.

I watched enchanted the great trains of camels grow from a puff of sand in the far distance to the reality of exotic desert travellers and fade in reverse order when they departed and each time I longed to travel into that mysterious, appealing land.

This appeared to be out of the question for no one was allowed to go beyond here without a special permit from the authorities and an armed guard. The permit, I was told, was rarely given to anyone without a very good reason for going.

Sheikh Othman was on the border between Aden Colony and 'The Protectorate'. The port area and inland as far as here was a Crown Colony and as such was administered directly from the Colonial Office, Whitehall, which might explain why I had been tied up with so much red tape. The Protectorate, the vast hinterland of the Hadramaut to the north and east, remained under the control of the local sheikhs in a feudal type system over which the British Foreign Office kept an overall watchful command.

Yemen was ever resentful of the British presence and was constantly causing trouble along the borders. It dearly would have liked to reclaim the territory, especially as the port had become one of the busiest in the world with ships refuelling on their voyages going east and west, and after Britain had built there the second largest oil refinery in the world. What seemed impossible at my time there has indeed come to pass, the British influence has gone and Aden is once again part of Yemen.

Judging by the way I was regarded as *persona non grata* when entering Aden, my chances of obtaining permission to go further afield seemed slim. Nevertheless the very fact that it was forbidden land made it all the more appealing and I resolved to try my utmost to go.

While in Sheikh Othman I visited the dye pits, the age-old industry where bolts of raw cloth were block-printed in traditional patterns. I also made acquaintance with the Church of Scotland Mission and the staff there. I liked to visit the Mission whenever I could, not so much from the religious aspect but from the fact I met so many interesting people there who knew so much about the Hadramaut and the Bedouins and I could learn from them.

The Mission, the only one of the Church of Scotland in Arabia, was founded in 1883 by The Right Honourable Ian Keith-Faulkner who was a champion penny-farthing cyclist in his day. At the Mission I met the Revd Ritchie who had only recently arrived from the UK but already spoke fluent Arabic, and Dr Smith, a most interesting man who spent most of his time travelling round the seventeen out-stations in the Hadramaut. I also met Dr Ahmed Offara, a local man, the Mission's first convert, who had graduated in medicine at Edinburgh and was a mine of information to me.

It was he who told me of the merchandise the caravans carried and their destinations. He said that the drovers would sometimes ride their camels if the loads were light, they might even sleep on them while on the move, but nearly always they preferred to walk. Thirty or forty miles a day was average.

My dream of going into the Hadramaut remained alive over the next few weeks but as the money in my pocket increased so did the itch in my feet. I was eager to be on my way into Africa. My intended route now lay over the water to

British Somaliland and south through the part of Ethiopia that juts into the Horn of Africa and thence through what was Italian Somaliland and from there into Kenya. I had applied for visas for the two non-British countries and awaited their return from Addis Ababa and Mogadishu. In the meantime I had met Commander Brodie who ran the Cowasgee Dinshaw shipping line and he promised me a free passage on the ship *Velpo*, which plied between Aden and Berbara, the main port for British Somaliland, whenever I decided to go. All things came together when I met Wing-Commander Hammerton.

Living in the RAF 'Sheba' camp gave me many unique privileges. Apart from being 'all found' I could nearly always rely on lifts from the fleet of trucks to wherever I wanted to go, so my cost of living was almost zero. My civilian status was well known but living in the camp and wearing khaki I was totally accepted within the services. I enjoyed a wonderful camaraderie with all the rank and file – there was great enthusiasm and rivalry to join me in my weekend jaunts by many who would otherwise not have left camp – and interested officers stopped or called me up to the mess or out to dine for a chat. So it was that Wing Commander Hammerton asked me to have afternoon tea with him at the Crescent Hotel, the main one in the Colony.

He was tall, distinguished looking with greying sidewings and the bearing of an officer and gentleman. He wore mufti with, despite the heat, a spotted cravat. Reserved yet easy to talk to we got on famously. During the course of the conversation I mentioned how eager I was to go into the Hadramaut.

"Yes," he said surprisingly, "I've heard about that. That's partly the reason why I asked you along." I could hardly believe I was the subject of conversation in upper echelons. Then my heart plummeted, this was a high level warning-off. But no, his next statement absolutely flabbergasted me.

"You were being discussed in the mess the other night and a couple of officers who had met you suggested we might try to do something for you. I had a word with Major Seagers on the subject and he thought I should have a chat with you and if you were all right and not a journalist he saw no reason why you shouldn't go along with the next patrol."

Major Seagers! Major Seagers had actually been discussing me! Major Seagers was the Chief Political Officer for the Protectorate, in other words, the King Pin of the Hadramaut, or at least the Western half of it. A legendary character, his status had reached mythical proportions in the services where his exploits were told and retold until now he was regarded by all with great awe. When I mentioned this back in the billets the fellas would go wild!

"And am I all right?" I asked with trepidation.

"Yes, I think I might say that," he said with a wry smile. "Mind you," he continued, "it'll be the roughest journey you'll have made in your whole life, there's no comfort up-country and you'll be in danger all the time. You'll have to sign your life away. It won't be a picnic."

"I shouldn't want to go if it were," I said, "I'm not travelling as a tourist and I will be very grateful to you if you can help me get there. I didn't realise this was by way of an interview."

"It wasn't. I wanted to meet you. We don't get a great deal of interest here, you know. On the other hand, if you hadn't measured up that would have been that. We would have had an interesting chat and gone our separate ways. As it is, I'll have a word with Seagers. Better give me a ring tomorrow. Your Flight Office will put you through, and be ready to move sharpish like if needs be."

Next day I went to 'my' Flight Office and asked the bewildered corporal to put me through to Wing-Commander Hammerton. I had come straight from work and still had paint on my hands. "You having me on?" he queried. I assured him I was not. Grudgingly he got through to the Wing-Commander's aide then, his face blank and his eyes wide with astonishment, he covered the mouthpiece and said, "He's on the line for you," and handed me the receiver.

"Ah, Lessels, there you are, I was nearly giving you up. I was just about to go but hung on hoping you'd call." The idea of the Wing-Commander hanging on for me seemed ludicrous. He really was a nice guy. "I spoke to Seagers and he has no objections to your going with the APL patrol up to Dhala. They leave on Monday morning from Sheikh Othman, which means you'll have to stay over at Lake Lines at the weekend to be ready to move off."

The Aden Protectorate Levies was the frontier force recruited from local tribesmen and commanded by British officers. The idea of going on patrol with them was something straight out of *The Boys' Own* magazine.

"Before you go, though," Hammerton added, "Major Seagers wants you to see one of his colleagues, Wing Commander Ferkard. You must listen carefully to what he has to say and do exactly what he tells you, otherwise you could land yourself in an awful lot of trouble. That's tomorrow afternoon. You'd better get them to lay on a staff car to take you up to his place. Hmmm! No, I'd better see to that. Pass me over to the Duty Officer." I mentioned this to the Corporal who went and brought a Flight Lieutenant who almost stood to attention as he introduced himself and listened to the instructions, at the end of which the Wing-Commander told him to put me back on the line which he did with an incredulous look. I'm sure they wondered who they had in me. Behind the guise of the Arab gang artisan I must be playing some kind of secret role to warrant this kind of clout. They must have been even more convinced there was more than met the eye when the Wing Commander's voice carried over to them, "Well, that's all fixed up then. You'll be taken up to see Ferkard tomorrow and on Sunday morning I'll send someone over for you. Come and have some late breakfast at Singapore Lines and then I'll run you up to Lake Lines myself." I handed the receiver back and said "Thanks" to the Flight Lieutenant and Corporal and left them in amazement.

The visit to Wing Commander Ferkard was most interesting. He lived in a large private house with cool floor slabs and shaded verandah. A houseboy in full gown and cummerbund brought us tea and biscuits. After my meeting with Hammerton I knew that despite the introductory pleasantries this was another assessment. Even at this stage a word of condemnation from Ferkard would have me back in the barracks, and perhaps out of there too, and forgotten.

An interesting man, Ferkard, he had only one arm, his left, yet he drove a car and led a full active life. Unlike Hammerton who was a RAF serving officer, Ferkard was seconded, like Major Seagers and others like them, to the Protectorate Administration as a Political Officer. As such he had to negotiate peace when trouble broke out and stave off any likely dispute by any means he could think of: a 'Troubleshooter' in modern jargon, only here the shooting could be real and to be caught in the middle of it likely to be very dicey indeed.

To start with, Ferkard reiterated Hammerton's wariness of my writing anything of what I saw in the Protectorate.

"You're not a reporter or anything like that, are you?" he asked. I assured him as I had done with Hammerton that I was not, but felt compelled to mention that I did intend writing a book of my journey some day and would like to include some reference to this journey.

"Well, you'll have to get clearance from the Foreign Office on anything you write about here," he pointed out. Now however, nearly fifty years after the event and the British influence in the area long since gone I feel I can write with impunity. "But," he went on, "we don't want anything like that tomfool article the *Illustrated* magazine" (long-time defunct) "put out about 'Bullets Rule The Desert'." I said I had read that article and thought it was very good. "Wasn't it true?" I asked

"Oh, it was true enough in a way. But we don't need all the hyperbole and sensationalism that that article carried about this corner of the world. These are very sensitive people who must not be seen to lose face. The whole place here is a tinderbox and in such a situation it is best most times not to state the obvious or even the truth. I can tell you that you will be in serious trouble if you publish anything that might prove inflammatory."

To soften the blow he refilled my cup and went on in praise of the Arabs whom he obviously liked very much.

"Now I wouldn't want you ever to be referring to these people as 'Wogs'. Remember, they had streetlights when we were still running about in woad. Up there in the Hadramaut there are cities buried in the sand that flourished a thousand years before Christ came. Real cities, not collections of primitive shacks or hovels; tenement buildings, six, seven, ten storeys high, in streets with shops and hotels and hostels for travellers."

I then listened enraptured as Ferkard told some history of Southern Arabia, or Arabia Felix (Happy) as it was known from ancient Greek times. The cities grew up at the crossroads along the ancient Spice Route to the Orient. The trade must have started just before Solomon's time, Ferkard mused, maybe a century of two before. We know from a stele with a scratched image of a man on a camel on it, that the beast-of-burden had been introduced to Arabia by the 11th century BC.

The coming of the camel had an extraordinary effect on Arabia. You could liken it to the development of the railways in the 19th and 20th centuries, especially in North and South America. Suddenly whole empty spaces were opened up. People could travel and live there. Commerce blossomed where there had been none and the countries' wealth expanded beyond belief.

The towns and cities that grew up along the Spice Route became fabulously rich from the toll money they extracted from the travellers. The tariff was a two-edged sword. Without it the cities could not have survived, and without the cities as staging posts the travellers could not have crossed the barren land. Great caravans of camels, loaded with the riches of Egypt and Canaan and Yemen, would merge along the land route of the Hadramaut that ran south of the *Rub al Khali,* the great desert that was known in English as 'The Empty Quarter'.

From my army knowledge of Swahili I knew that *Khali* was an Arabic/Indian word meaning 'cruel' or 'fierce' and I wondered how it could be translated as 'empty'. The Swahili word for empty, which may also have come from the Arabic, was *tupu* (toopoo) so why not the *Rub al Tupu.* Ferkard swept aside my smart-arse question in no uncertain terms. "Cruel it is. There is no water there. And it is hot. Nobody can live there. So it is indeed empty."

The Arabian spice route ended at a port in Dhofar where the wandering camel-merchants sold their wares to seamen who would take them to India and to the island of Serendip and the East. Serendip was the Arabic name for Ceylon (Sri Lanka) and today it lives on in the English language. It is said that when some early sailors approached the island for the first time they were so surprised and overcome by its beauty they later used the word 'serendipity' to mean the surprise of making a happy and unexpected discovery by accident when least expected. The origin of the word is given to Horace Walpole who wrote 'The Three Princes of Serendip' in the mid-18th century but Ferkard said Arab sailors were using the word a long time before that.

Having unloaded their wares the camel merchants now set about acquiring the product which was the main reason for their going there – frankincense. Second only to gold in value, it is difficult to appreciate the importance of frankincense in the ancient world. Incense was used in every place of worship throughout the known world. The gods demanded that it be burned to invoke their spirits. Without it who knows what tragedy and destruction would be vested on the people. It is said that Rameses III, Pharaoh of Egypt 200 years before King Solomon's time, had a warehouse for the sole purpose of storing frankincense for the worship of Amon, the first monotheistic God, and on one altar alone in Babylon the worshippers burned 60,000 pounds of frankincense a year to Bel, Lord of the Air.

Incense of dubious quality was commonly used in homes and with some rituals, but for the temples and other religious places only the real or 'frank' incense could be used. And the main source of this precious, aromatic gum-resin was Dhofar. Other places had it too, Yemen, Somalia and elsewhere, but none in such abundance and quality as Dhofar. By the time the Romans came to power the Arabs had got round to keeping Dhofar and its treasure product a secret. To Rome, now the biggest customer, it was said that Yemen was the land of frankincense while the majority of the gum only passed though that country en-route from Dhofar.

The Arabs had good reason to keep their source of frankincense secret. Only they with their knowledge of camel caravans could travel the Spice Route and the vast profits from that trade was theirs and they meant to keep it that way. But there was another route, much easier, quicker and cheaper. By sea.

Somehow the Romans learned the secret of the trade winds which the Phoenicians and Arabs had been using for countless centuries. It is said it was a Greek sailor, Hippalus, in the 1st century BC who made the discovery and the Romans, as the super power of the day, took it from there. They built their ships by the Red Sea and sailed to Dhofar and disastrously undercut the market. The ships by-passed the costly tariff cities and the crews went in comparative comfort to those making the long, arduous and dangerous journey by land. The Spice Route's monopoly was broken and the trade on that highway went into decline and death.

With dwindling income from the tolls, the people left the cities and the buildings crumbled from lack of maintenance. Gradually empty cities lay silent in the desert, like tombstones to a long lost world. And the winds of centuries inexorably blew sand around the gaunt buildings, lapping their sides like sea waves and filling the streets until the dunes washed over the lot and carried on rising, steadily rising, burying the cities deeper and deeper, until there was not a trace, not one iota, left of them. Now only the sighing winds that are the only sounds in that empty, cruel land know the secrets of a long forgotten, vibrant world over which their fingers drew a veil of sand, hiding them perhaps until eternity. But then, perhaps not!

"They're still there, you know," Ferkard pointed out, "those cities. The sand will have preserved them. Had it been the sea that had buried them they would have been gone forever. In the desert they built with sun-dried mud bricks which are hard as stone when kept dry, but dissolve gradually when wet. So they will be there, pretty well as they were when the towns were alive, their inscriptions on the walls still legible, the remains of their campfires fossilised, like it were only yesterday evening that a group of travellers, robe-wrapped, their heads swathed in loose turbans, their sun-wrinkled faces copper-coloured in the firelight, murmured and laughed at yarns of their journeys. All there for some enterprising archaeologists to dig and find.

"Lawrence of Arabia did just that. Did you know he was one of them, archaeologists I mean. As a young fellow straight from Oxford he went on a dig in Iraq with Flinders Petrie, one of the leading men in that game, just before the first World War. That was where he learned to speak Arabic like a native and pass himself off as one of them. They found great things in that excavation and Lawrence used to love wearing a solid gold cloak, woven with thread-like strands of gold, thousand of years old that was discovered in a tomb. Being gold and non-corrodible, it would be as good as the day it was made. Perhaps it was a flair for the theatre that made him put it on. It's said he loved having himself photographed wearing his Arab gear."

My own guess, and backed up later when I read his *Seven Pillars of Wisdom* and other biographical notes on him, was that Lawrence couldn't give a hoot for what anyone thought of him nor how he looked. If anyone wanted to photograph, let them do it. Most times, I would think, he would not be aware that they were there. He spurned all medals offered to him, and there were many from allied countries as well as Britain, and after the war he tried to lose himself from public acclaim by enlisting incognito first in the Royal Air Force as an aircraftsman, the lowest rank, and when his privacy was blown there, doing the same again in the army where he was when killed in a motor-bike accident in 1935.

As for wearing a king's cloak of solid gold, I could identify with Lawrence there. I never regarded myself as theatrical, but I would have donned that cloak in dead of night privacy with alacrity, or in a midday public square, just to feel the bond, the touch-thrill, between me and that person who wore it last, millennia before. Many years later, as a college lecturer in Painting and Decorating, when researching for an article I was writing for a trade journal on Ancient Egyptian paints and gilding, I was taken into an inner sanctum of the British Museum and was able to handle brushes and gilding tools that had last been used in a tomb in the Valley of Kings. The brushes had no handles, merely bunches of bristles bound with fibre string. But these bundles had been worn down into professional shape for cutting-in or painting. Holding one of these in my hand I experienced a thrill of the most profound nature. Once, 4000 years before, an Ancient Egyptian craftsman had carefully and expertly applied a paint made of crushed lapis-lazuli bound with gum-arabic and laid it down for the last time, the rich, blue paint still in the bristles, his thumb mark still on the worn 'handle' under mine. A touch-thrill to send a shiver down my spine. Yes I could identify with T.E. Lawrence's love of wearing his golden cloak.

"On the subject of Lawrence, there is a little aside you may find amusing," my host continued, and I did. Even moreso, I was surprised that he told his muse, for he was a singularly ascetic man. Anyway, he told me it was a charmed twist of history that Lawrence arrived in Arabia and had he not gone there the Middle-East war against the Turks might never have been won by Britain and the Great War in total could have been lost by the Allies.

Lawrence, from an Anglo-Irish family but brought up in Wales, had gone to Oxford to study the Arts, Ferkard thought, but at the end of his first year had made little inroads on his subject. Came the time of his assessment his tutor suggested that the Arts may not be for him and suggested he go for archaeology instead. This Lawrence did with time-honoured success.

It was not Lawrence, however, who was the butt of the little amusing anecdote. It was the man who was the pivotal person in his going to Arabia. This man who saw something more in his student than he was showing on his chosen path, was the clergyman, the Reverend W.A. Spooner, famous in his own right as the person who gave us 'spoonerisms'. He did this naturally and not by design, making rib-tickling gaffs that his students loved to repeat. One of his famous collection was, 'I have a half-warmed fish in my mind' for 'a half-formed wish in my mind'. Here Ferkard, with a half-formed smile on his face, remarked in a rare flash of wry humour, "I won't tell what he did with 'Friar Tuck'."

I was warming to my mentor as I was seeing a more human side in him. I too relaxed and felt he also sensed less need to be too formal. Our conversation became freer and wider ranging.

Evidence of this came when, after the mirth of his subtlety had had its moment, he said, "On the matter of archaeology, there's a big American expedition up in the Hadramaut now looking for links with the Queen of Sheba. By all accounts they've brought all of Hollywood with them. They do it in big style. We'll have to wait and see whether they'll be any more successful than lesser campaigns in the past. We can only wish them good luck for it's in all our interests to learn about the past, especially about this part, no matter who it is who finds it."

Many years later, in a second-hand bookshop I picked up Wendell Phillips' paperback, *Sheba's Buried City* and as I leafed through it I thrilled when I realised this was the man and his expedition to which Ferkard had referred. Less than six months before my arrival in Aden the Americans had started in the eastern Hadramaut at Mukulla, a town of mudbrick skyscrapers such as Ferkard had described, which proved that southern Arabian town planning and building methods had not changed in 3000 years. Phillips and team made their way along the entire Hadramaut and into Yemen. By all accounts from the book Phillips and his crew had been successful beyond their wildest dreams. To think I might have stumbled on them! That would have been beyond *my* wildest dreams.

With the mention of Sheba I was emboldened to ask, "Was this really Sheba's land and do you really believe she did exist?" half expecting to be put down again for voicing such rubbish. But no, I was not put in my place. On the contrary, I found I was in the presence of a real *aficionado* of the Queen. "Oh, she was real all right," my host replied with alacrity, warming more to our conversation I thought. "But we only have that one account of her in the Bible, in Kings, I'm sure you've heard of it, to go on." I assured him I was acquainted with that passage. "There is one other reference, I believe, quite recently found somewhere up in Palestine, a potsherd with an inscription that puts it in the 8th century BC, which could put it in the Solomon /Sheba era. It's quite exciting for it refers to thirty shekels of gold from Ophir and it's the only evidence we have outside the Bible.

"As for Sheba, the Arabs mention her in different ways, mainly in the Koran and elsewhere. They call her Bilquis, but whether she is *the* Queen, the one who went to Solomon, is hard to tell. There seems to have been many Bilquises, like Georges and Henrys in English history. In fact, there were more queens than kings in Arabia in those days. That seems strange in a country that has always demeaned women and kept them very much lower in the social scale than men. That being the case the Arabs, nevertheless, preferred queens rather than kings. Everyone knew the mother of an offspring while the father could always be doubtful. So it was safer to go down the maternal side to continue the royal line."

"Where exactly did Sheba live?" I asked enthusiastically.

"Ah, there again, like so much of that era, we can only speculate. Nothing is certain. Marib, in Yemen is reckoned to be the best guess. There they certainly built a city incomparable to anywhere else. Like many places in Arabia where the land seems to be completely arid they sometimes get heavy rain and flash floods when the river beds run wild, then just as quickly dry up again. At Marib the ancients built a great dam and caught the water so they irrigated the land and built a veritable Garden of Eden. Now that dam must have been made of stone, so we know they could work in stone, where that was available. Of course by the dam they built great buildings and commemorative pillars. It had to be someone of great importance for whom they would do the likes of that. We like to think the Queen of Sheba was the only person with the stature to command such an undertaking. Had there been anyone else of that standing we feel there would be some reference to such a person on potsherds or incised in stone.

"So you see," Ferkard ended, "these people are not Wogs. They gave the world algebra and the numbering system we use. They are an intelligent people with a long history of civilisation."

He then went on to give a long list of 'don'ts'. I was not to gaze too long at people, I must not try to photograph any group sitting chewing *ghat*. Most important of all, I must never go anywhere by myself. Wherever I went I must always take an armed escort with me. This precaution was not just for my own safety, although that was a major factor. The authorities were afraid that the tribesmen, seeing an unarmed and unescorted white man would be tempted to either shoot or hold me hostage for ransom. Either happening would lead to the RAF bombing their village. I was told later that when this had to be done, which was seldom, they always dropped leaflets warning the people to clear out – hopefully someone would be able to read – before they went in and flattened the place.

Finally my forthright but genial host wished me goodbye and said he hoped I would enjoy my journey, and by this I assumed I had passed the test.

*

In preparation for going on the journey I had to consider my work. I could have asked for a few days off which I was sure would have been granted, but I felt the time had come to move on. I had earned a little money, not much, but enough to see me through to Kenya perhaps. So that week I mounted the creaking, shoulder-width staircase that went up into the busy, cluttered office of the Cowasgee Dinshaw shipping line to see Commander Brodie. I had been introduced to him by the agent in the Cory office who had said they had given me a free passage down the Red Sea and Brodie, not to be outdone, had kindly offered me free passage to Berbera to get me on the next leg of my journey.

Brodie seemed glad to see me. He leaned back from the pile of papers on his desk and waved a boy to bring us tea. We chatted and he confirmed his offer to me of a passage to Berbera, the port for British Somaliland. The *Velpo* would sail next week and he would see I had a place on it. My visas for Ethiopia and Italian Somaliland had still not arrived but I decided to go anyway. By all accounts these could take months and I felt I couldn't wait that long.

I next went to Mr Valentine to say I would be leaving work at the end of the week. He didn't want me to go. He offered me a tempting rise in wages and asked me to stay for a few months while in the meantime he would make sure my visas were acquired. I thanked him but declined his offer.

All loose ends tied up, Sunday evening saw me at the Officers Mess, A.P.L. Lake Lines, Sheikh Othman, after Wing-Commander Hammerton had driven me over there. My diary for that day ran:

I've been given an officer's apartment to myself. It has a good room with deep comfortable chairs and the supreme luxury of bedroom with dressing

66

room and personal bathroom. Fair change from what I've been used to lately, one room shared by thirty others and the ablution block quite a stroll away through the sand.

What meals they serve in the Mess. We have just finished a fabulous one, complete with port and cigars, neither of which I wanted, but the aroma and conversation, the general atmosphere, was grand. Afterwards we sat out in the garden with the radiogram playing and the soft light of the table lamp casting a mellow glow over the green foliage ... wonderful.

Early next morning the levies paraded for inspection prior to leaving on patrol. They were a very smart bunch in starch-creased khaki shorts, shirts, puttees and turbans. They lined up in front of their vehicles, 3-ton trucks with tyres like farm tractors. I thought then that this must mark the beginning of the end of camel caravans: if the army could get about in motor vehicles the traders must soon follow. By the end of the patrol journey, however, I was not so sure. It was going to take a long time and some semblance of a road system before they swapped their camels for trucks. The reason for this is best described by a straight lift from my diary describing the journey:

Today has been one of the highlights of my journey so far. We started off in the early morning. I travelled in the truck behind the one in which the British lieutenant led. Some miles on we passed Lahej, the first of the desert 'kingdoms', a huddle of mudbrick hovels round the tall castle-like palace. I very much wanted to visit that palace but we didn't stop. Sultan Abdulkareem who is resident there is reputed to have a pipe band, complete with a kilted Scottish Pipe Major.

A few years later Sultan Fadhle Abdulkareem was suspected of killing two of his cousins and had to flee to Saudi Arabia. It is interesting to note that it was an earlier Sultan of Lahej who sold or leased the land at the coast to the British who proceeded to extend their dominion far beyond their allocated border. British rule brought a semblance of law and order to a land where there was very little before, so the landlord of Lahej had had to run from his tenant for a misdemeanour that he might have considered within his right before the meddling British came.

The road is really non-existent, just a marked track across the terrain that is unbelievably rough. How wheeled vehicles ever make the journey is hardly creditable. Sometimes the truck was slithering in loose sand, but most times it was bumping along over boulders which continually straightened the springs. I have never had such a rough ride. If I was not banging my head off the roof of the cab I was taking a dig with my shoulder at the rifle rack at my left side or taking a poke at the gear levers even though they were more than a foot away on my right. The truck ground away for miles on end in 2nd gear.

Crossing the Kotaibi Plain was a nightmare of endurance. Part of the way lay along a dried up river bed where the trucks pitched and rolled over the ruts and boulders like ships in a rough sea. But it was not just the bumping that had to be contended with. These were flat fronted vehicles so that the engine, which got blistering hot and radiated a stifling heat, was actually inside the cab. The sun heated the metal bodywork until it was untouchable and the engine made the cab into an oven. To make matters worse the windows had to be kept shut. Opening them let in clouds of dust and sand churned up by the truck in front. This dried up your mouth and eyes till it was sore even to blink and it settled into every wrinkle of your skin and clothing.

Along the entire route we occasionally came on lone tribesmen walking miles from anywhere. They had long wavy hair down to their shoulders with headbands or rough turbans and they appeared to carry nothing by way of provisions, only their long-stemmed pipe and the inevitable gun held by the muzzle over their shoulders at a careless angle. These guns ranged from ancient front-loading thunderers with half-inch calibre to modern rifles.

Going up the Khorieba Pass was a hair-raising experience. The truck careered about like a mad thing, dipping one wheel onto a deep hollow while climbing over a huge boulder with another on the opposite side, the combined action screwing the whole vehicle dangerously sideways. On the flat this made the going difficult, on the narrow ledge that served as a road that climbed up the side of the mountain in great loops, sometimes carved out of the sheer face of the precipice, this was something else. Some of the turns in the loops were so acute it was impossible for the trucks to make them in one sweep. Some manoeuvring had to be done before each one could be brought round. Each required to make a three or four point turn and each time a truck backed, its tailboard hung over space. There were the times, when tilted at precarious angles over the void, the side sliding from the huge boulders was heart stopping. At times like these, with the truck actually tilted over the void, I could look down vertically from the cabin into five hundred feet and more of space. The drivers were marvellous. Misjudging the speed when surmounting the great stones could catapult the truck, and us, into oblivion. Many times I considered getting out and walking, but I did not want to show fear to the Arabs, so stuck with it.

At the bottom of the Pass while we were waiting for our turn to go up – only one truck goes up at a time – a man leading a camel came along. We *had passed many caravans on the way and it was strange to see a lone camel drover. Anyway, after a look at the tortuous way ahead the camel turned round and lay down, bawling horribly like it was having its throat cut. It took a lot of skill, not to mention a good deal of kicking on the man's part, to get the animal up and going again.*

Dhala lies on a hill as most of these fortified towns or villages do. It was high enough for me to be cold in my sleeping bag at night. It was a wild place: rough, mud-brick houses towered over by the formidable square palace, all looking somewhat sinister against the harsh, unforgiving landscape. Wild looking, silent men watched with unfriendly eyes as we passed on our way to the camp that was some way from the town. When spoken to they adopted an obsequious attitude, but you felt they were all the more dangerous for this servile veil behind which they hid. As the first town in the Aden Protectorate on the way from San'a, the Yemen capital, Dhala was always a flashpoint ready for the touchpaper. A few weeks later the famous Major Seagers was stabbed near to death here in Dhala.

I didn't hear about the attack until some time later and could get no details. I had to wait some years until I learned how serious the affair had been. I read an account of the murderous attempt on Major Seagers life in Wendell Phillips' book on his archaeological expedition that I was so near to at the time, and to which Wing Commander Ferkard had referred. It would be to Major Seagers that Phillips would have had to apply for permission to enter the area and dig, so the two would have met on several occasions.

According to the archaeologist, while paying a visit to Dhala Major Seagers, accompanied by his wife, was walking through the streets of the town before dinner. The fact his wife was with him would indicate that they had flown up from Aden. As they walked, Seagers' sharp eyes saw a man who was not native to the area so he went over to him to ask why he was there. The man, by an incredible stroke of ill-luck, was an assassin who had come to kill the major. He had planned to make his bid later but fate had now brought his target right to him. The Yemeni had placed a large price on Seagers' head and it was not known whether the killer was motivated by the reward or by political reasons. Whatever the reason, the man pulled out his *jambiya*, the wicked, curved knife that all Arabs carried, and slashed Seagers' face from top to chin, then plunged it into the major's chest, actually touching the edge of his heart as it penetrated further. Even then the major grappled with his assailant who fell to the ground and was killed by government guards who had been following some way behind. A scuffle then occurred during which several people were shot. All this time the Major remained on his feet which showed his amazing constitution and dogged presence of mind. All this time also, Mrs Seagers watched in horror as all that happened.

Within a couple of months the bold major was back to visit Philips' site, indefatigable as ever with yet another laurel to his already towering reputation. But now he carried a side-arm which previously he had declined wearing.

Next morning I collected my escort, three levies with rifles and an Arab lieutenant who acted as guide and interpreter. I straight away went over to the town. The houses were huddled closely together, the streets narrow and filled with lounging men. Occasionally the crowd separated to allow a camel or donkey rider to pass through, otherwise there seemed to be no activity.

In the early morning sun the butcher sat chatting with some wild looking hillmen, his red meat laid out in the open completely covered in flies. His price for the best cuts, or rather 'hunks', was 12 annas the pound. There were 16 annas to the rupee (7½p) and 4 pice to the anna, which made the pice roughly the equivalent to a farthing. Europeans rarely, if ever, dealt in pice. I believe the pice had an even smaller subdivision but I never came across it even when later I actually lived with Arabs. This lesser coin must have been confined to the very lowest strata of the society.

Sitting in the butcher's group was one of the sultan's guards. In his red turban and with his rifle slung across his back by the sling and a row of bullets round his waist, he cut an exotic dash in that rather grim looking group.

There were three types of native soldiers or guards in the protectorate. First there were the levies. They were true soldiers, properly dressed and disciplined as mentioned previously. They wore smart khaki turbans and crossed bandoleers. Then there were the Government Guards whose purpose was to protect the Government Agents. They dressed in ordinary tribal gear, 'longie' – a below-the-knee wrap-round skirt or kilt of thin material – short jacket or shirt, bare legs and feet or sandals, and usually at this altitude, a blanket over their shoulder. But while the civilians wore motley coloured headdresses the Government Guards wore loose black turbans and they always had a bandolier with pouches across their front for their ammunition. Lastly, there were the Tribal Guards whose job was to protect the sultans and sheikhs and guard their forts. They were only recognisable from the ordinary tribesman by the fact they wore untidy red turbans and stuck their bullets in their cummerbunds until they had a circle of brass round their waists.

From the town we climbed the rough track up to the palace, a huge, four-storey building of sun-dried brick. A great wall, sloped up to a high battlemented crest with a watchtower pierced with loopholes at each corner, surrounded the palace. Entrance to the palace compound was through a massive carved door guarded by two red turbaned guards, one on either side. My lieutenant spoke to one who tapped on the gate and a small spyhole door was opened. After an exchange of very guttural Arabic one half of the great door creaked open.

On our entry a guard hurried to the palace and presently the son of the Emir of Dhala, Sheikh Abdullah Nasil, came to greet me. He apologised for his father's absence, saying he was away at the moment, but said he would be honoured to show me round the grounds and part of the palace. He would not be able to show me the main part, the living quarters, because there were women present and that prohibited the presence of males outside the family.

We walked the grounds and climbed the steps jutting out of the wall to the battlements, past the turret watchtowers with a guard lookout in each one. We had obviously been observed from the time we left the camp. In one turret there was a convex gong that was struck at each guard mounting.

After making the precarious descent to the yard I was then taken into the palace but was shown very little except the dungeons, but these were very interesting indeed. On the earthen floor, in pitch darkness, lay three men in leg shackles. They stirred and blinked as the door was opened. It took some time for me to see in the darkness and for the prisoners to see who had entered. When they did and saw me with my levies a look of amazement, or was it fear? spread over their faces, especially when they recognised Sheikh Abdullah Nasil.

One of the men had been confined for three years, the others for two. Every day they were taken outside to stand against the wall in the sun for two hours. The Sheikh had no objection to them being taken outside so that I could photograph them. He, nor any of the others, did not appear to have any qualms nor in any way feel that the incarceration of these men in such a barbarous fashion was in any way wrong.

The shackles were interesting, in a horrendous way. Both the two-years men had chain shackles with hoops while the three-years one had a flat bar of iron looped at either end. He could never close his legs together and could only shuffle in a most awkward and apparently painful manner that the nine or ten inch bar allowed. The hoops had no opening hinges. They had been hammered round and closed and would require sawing or levering open to release the legs.

Had these been hammered hot? The thought of red-hot metal against the skin hardly bore thinking. Hammered cold they would have required mighty blows with a heavy hammer. One badly aimed blow would have shattered the bone and rendered the man a cripple for life.

I asked how long the men were in for. When this was translated the Sheikh pulled a face and said nothing. I took this to mean he was not prepared to say or more likely that they were there 'at His Majesty's Pleasure', in other words, until his father, the Sultan, saw fit for them to go. I did not know how morally destructive this type of sentence can be until, a few weeks later, I found myself in a similar position, in prison with no exit date. With a time schedule you can mark off the days with a scratch on the wall of your cell and look forward with hope. With no date to look forward to you just stagnate.

Sadly I watched them ushered back inside and the heavy door shut again. I

71

should have liked to have taken the matter up with the Sheikh but remembering my brief from Wing Commander Ferkard that I must not cause any trouble I declined to say anything that might prove inflammatory.

On leaving the palace I met and was introduced to the Holy Man of the town, Mohammad El Maki, who was reputed to be a direct descendant of the Prophet. As well as Holy Man he was also the local judge, so I expect it would have been he who had sentenced these men to their misery.

Next day I climbed Jebel Jehaff, the rugged mountain that overlooked the camp and the whole surrounding area. With the summit at over 8000 feet and the camp at around 5000 feet it meant a fairly stiff climb of 3000 feet or so. When I asked permission to do it the Officer in Charge couldn't think why I wanted to, but saw no reason to stop me. He had obviously no conception of the climber's mentality that believed that mountains were placed there to be climbed for no other reason than the need to do so.

"I shouldn't think it's ever been climbed before," he said rather bemused, "we might rename it after you. Can't think why anybody should want to do such an outlandish thing. I'm sure no British have ever been up it and you can be sure no native would dream of doing such a thing." How wrong he was!

I left with my guard but no lieutenant today since we didn't expect to meet anyone. After 500 feet or so the guards thought that this was no way to play at soldiers and motioned for me to go on alone, while they sat down for a smoke. The going was stiff but not difficult. I marvelled at the view, the vast distances panning out before me. Almost at the top a narrow ridge of rock lead to the final pinnacle. The ridge was a sharp edge at one side and sloped to the other. It was only a few feet wide and was smooth and slippery. On both sides it fell away in sheer precipices. It looked quite daunting. However, not only did it give access to the final outspur of rock, the ledge was the one place I could photograph the landscape with the camp included at the bottom. So, cross it I must.

I decided that my hobnailed boots would be likely to slide on the smooth, sloping rock and I would be better crossing on bare feet. I sat down and was just rising after taking them off when I was suddenly startled by a shout and believed my escort had decided after all to catch up with me. But no, it was a man smoking the customary long pipe and a youth who came hurrying towards me.

Who were they? Why were they there? Had they been following me, watching me all the way? Did they live there? These were all questions that flashed through my mind, none of which I could answer. They just appeared from behind a rock at this moment of danger, in a place nobody barring a crazy person such as myself was supposed to be. The man had his pipe in one hand with the other raised signalling me to stop while the youth ran past me with sure, bare feet, his shoulder actually over the void. In the middle of the narrow causeway the youth turned and sat down, grinning, barring my way over. There being nothing else for it, I put on my boots again. We smiled and made friendly noises to each other, I took their photograph, for which the youth came off the ridge and he and the man posed delighted together, and I headed down the mountain to pick up my guards again.

I had plenty of time to reflect on the amazing coincidence of these two being up there. What were they doing there, people who, by the British officer's reckoning, never had the inclination, never saw any reason, for climbing barren mountains? Come to think about it, they couldn't have followed me up or the man – he wasn't young – would have been more out of puff than he was smoking his pipe. They had to have been up there. And their hurry to stop me crossing the narrow causeway ... was that really prompted by their regard for my safety? Could it be they were more concerned in stopping me going over for what I might find ... a hide for instance, with water and provisions. There could be no better place for one or more people to lie up. The stone slab being the only way in, they could never be surprised. The fact that they were at the point that overlooked the British camp was surely no mere coincidence. Were the British being incredibly naive in underestimating the guile or savvy of the local population? If they were spies or lookouts then every movement in or out the camp was being conveyed to someone. I felt sure the man was the observer and the boy, he would be fourteen or so, would do the running. The camp was on the very border with Yemen. When I mentioned the incident on my return the OIC voiced his surprise but did nor appear to attach any significance to it.

That evening I visited the local Political Agent at his house. It was now November and he had been there since January by himself with only his Black Guards, as I had come to call them because of their turbans, as opposed to the Red Guards of the sheikhs. A tall bony man, he had a great mane of hair and smoked a pipe continually, even while talking. When I asked him if he was lonely he said of course not, he had plenty company. He spoke and wrote Arabic like a native and no doubt thought in that language as well. Lonely or not, I wondered if he had not been there too long without a break for in that tinderbox tension of being in constant high readiness to jump into the centre of any trouble that could arise at any moment it was obvious that he was living on his nerves. As well he might: three years before, in 1947, Peter Davey, the then resident Political Agent, was shot dead by a corrupt and brutal sheikh he had gone to arrest. The sheikh died also, cut down by the Agent's guards, but that could be little solace to the present man who knew every day was tinder dry and only needed a spark to explode. His words came quick and terse, he was constantly on the move, agitated, constantly lighting his pipe, smoking matches it seemed, and talking as he did so. Not an easy man to be with, but I was pleased to have met him for it gave me an insight into the lives of some unsung people who did duty in remote corners of the Empire, as it was at that time.

We left the next day at 6 a.m., just as Jebel Jehaff was donning its morning coat of bronze. The journey back to Sheikh Othman was uneventful, an uncomfortable re-run of the way up except that the passage down the Khorieba Pass escarpment was even more hair-raising than the way up. Going up your eyes were mainly on the sky, but on the descent you looked down all the while at the drop you were likely to have if anything went wrong, and now the driver was depending more on his brakes than the gears, and too heavy a touch on the pedal could cause a skid. I was glad when we were down.

Back in the camp at Aden I wrote in my diary that I had just completed the most uncomfortable journey of my life and I didn't think I would be able to sit down for a week, but: '*I'd go through that everyday if the journey was as interesting as that one.*'

Indeed, I seriously considered delaying my departure for some time to try to get back into the Hadramaut, perhaps with the Desert Locust Survey group that I had heard was operating up there. Mainly, I wanted to get over by land or sea to Mukalla, the mysterious ancient city of mud-brick ten-storey skyscrapers and meet 'The Mad Major', Major Snell, a Scot, whom I had been hearing so much about. He was Major Seagers' equivalent in the Eastern Protectorate and by all accounts, was an even more colourful, daring, larger-than-life legend than was Seagers. But after a day or so I decided to make the break and get on with my mainstream journey.

But despite all my pre-arrangements things didn't go as easily as I thought they would due to more trouble with my old adversary, the Immigration Authorities. My visa for Italian Somaliland had arrived, but with it came a strong recommendation that I do not travel alone and should use recognised transport. I told Mr King, the Chief Officer with whom I had crossed swords on the *Cory Freighter*, I still intended to go ahead and take my chances as they came. He then floored me by telling me I needed a visa for British Somaliland. Until then nobody had said this was necessary. I think he felt guilty although he was still as aloof as ever and did not show it. He did, however, offer to radio the authorities at Hargiesa to speed things up. This he did but the visa arrived too late and I had to see the *Velpo* sail without me. I was extremely grateful to Commander Brodie for rearranging my passage. Nothing seemed too much trouble to him.

The next week's run was almost another fiasco and once again Mr King was the culprit. He seemed to be continuing his personal vendetta right up until the moment I stepped off his territory. The ship was due to sail at 2 p.m. so in the morning I went along to withdraw my immigration deposit which I intended to change into Travellers' Cheques. I had my boarding ticket to show I was a bona-fide passenger. But the clerk said Mr King had left strict instructions that my money must only be returned to me in his presence and he was "not available". It was after lunch before he arrived and by the time my business was completed

I had to run with my pack to get on board at 1.55 p.m. The trouble was, I did not have time to go to a bank and had to carry the £100 cash in rupees. Heading into wild and unknown territory with all that money in my pocket was quite a worry. It did not ease matters when the ship did not sail until 10.30 p.m.

Chapter Five

A HAPPY CHRISTMAS AND A SAD NEW YEAR

Thursday 28th December 1950 – Prison, Werdair, Ogaden Desert, Ethiopia
This morning I was turfed out of the DLS Land Rover and thrown into prison on a trumped up charge.

There were only two other passengers aboard the *Velpo* apart from the horde travelling 'deck', an Italian in 2nd class like myself and an Indian woman going 1st. We shared the same saloon for food but the Indian woman always waited until we men were finished before she ate.

The ship docked at Berbera just after dawn. I was met by Inspector D. Lloyd of the police who had been warned of my coming. In contrast to my reception at Aden he was friendly and most helpful.

I also met Dr Charles, a dapper man with slicked-down hair, gushing with friendship, who came aboard to check inoculation certificates, etc. Charles was his Christian name, though that may have been adopted as his English surname surely was. He was Austrian and spoke with quite a heavy accent. His effusive welcome was like hot honey poured over me. When he asked where I was going to stay and I said I'd be looking for a place to camp, he threw up his arms in horror and insisted I come and stay with him. He lived alone with two dachshunds and an African servant in a double-storey, government house, with the living room and bedrooms and verandah upstairs and the kitchen and bathroom, with concrete bath, downstairs. He fussed and clucked over me and in my naivety I thought of him as a most kind and generous person, which he was then.

He had a dinner invitation that evening with Mr Forrester, the customs officer and he took me along with him. The District Commissioner, Mr Lawrence and his wife were also there. I was made most welcome. Sitting at the table with the ruling dignitaries that night I could not help comparing my reception in British Somaliland with that at Aden and wondering if this was a good omen for my return to Africa.

My return to Africa! When preparing to cross from Aden I was excited about this next part of my journey. Although geographically Egypt and the Red Sea ports were part of Africa I never felt I had really returned to that continent while I was there. But now, with Somaliland I felt I would again be part of the real Africa. Even now, within a day of landing I felt at home.

Not every traveller had been as lucky as I when landing on Somaliland soil. Less than a hundred years before my arrival Richard Burton, one of the greatest explorers of all time, landed on Berbera shore to explore that piece of land known as the Horn of Africa. With him were three companions, Captain John (Jack) Speke, Sir Samual Baker, both to become renowned explorers, and one other. Unlike me, sitting comfortably on my first evening in the country, having dined and wined with the highest in the land, Burton's party was welcomed on the beach by a horde of wild savages. The unnamed man was killed, Speke was wounded in eleven places and Burton's face was slashed from cheek to cheek with a spear. The wounded party lay all night on the beach, then went home. A very short expedition.

My own expedition was to last a little while longer, but I was soon to learn that the Horn was a difficult one to crack. For the moment, however, I was pleased to enjoy my luck and the hospitality bestowed on me.

The meal over and the coffee served the men retired to the verandah to smoke and chat and me to listen and comment occasionally and enjoy the ambience of being part of the local scene. From the conversation I hoped to learn something of what makes things tick in the running of colonies. Charles remained with the women. During the meal he had been so gracious to the ladies and over-the-top with old world charm, I thought the husbands might have shown a touch of coolness, even jealousy, towards Charles. But they obviously thought him harmless and saw no reason to worry in leaving their wives to his endearments. I thought it a bit odd but at this time I had no reason to see in him anything other than a very generous person, if a little eccentric, and a very fine host. I was very grateful to him for his hospitality.

The next day I wandered around Berbera. A busy port with dhows coming and going, a population of 40,000 of which only eleven were white, it was very much a native town. The mass of houses and pokey shops huddled tightly together were intersected by narrow streets and a wide main one, all deep in sand. At corner coffee shops tall, thin Somalis in ankle length *longes* with superfluous yards of cloth wrapped round their heads and shoulders and festooned about their bodies, whiled away hours in wicker chairs under shady trees. All the men – there were no women evident – carried walking sticks which they hooked over the edge of the table where they sat and some sported sun glasses which they wore with cool panache. At all times while strolling the streets or languishing at the coffee houses they comported themselves with haughty dignity reminiscent of 18th century dandies. I could not equate these men with the Somali horde who had 'welcomed' Burton's party back in 1855.

Throughout East Africa and the Red Sea area Somalis had a poor reputation.

Lighter in colour, with finer features and often supercilious manner, they were generally thought to be lazy and deceitful people who considered themselves above work and superior to their black, Negroid neighbours. Watching them now on their home ground, seeing their vain, effete ways and mannerisms I could see how they could have earned their reputation.

Nothing moves in the heat of the day at Berbera, but a truck, a three-tonner, was leaving for Hargeisa, the capital, that evening at 6 p.m. and Dr Charles got me a place on it. It was piled high with oil drums and on top sat the police guard. By order every vehicle moving between towns in Somaliland had to carry an armed guard for whom the owner paid the government. I sat in with the native driver and how thankful I was of this as the night wore on. It was cold. My, how it was cold. The driver was wrapped in a blanket but I only had on my khaki shirt and was as cold as ever I had been in the Cairngorms or Glencoe at New Year time. I was glad I was not up with the guard who had come prepared and was cocooned in blankets.

Hargeisa lies eighty miles inland, up on the high plateau where the climate is more tolerable than at sea level. The road was a scratch of red earth that wound upwards through the forest of boswellia trees, from the bark of which frankincense is obtained. Occasionally we stopped at native villages and I was glad to join the driver in the ruddy, cosy glow of fires in the centre of the earthen floors of smoke-filled huts and drink delicious hot, smoky tea sweetened with condensed milk. Beyond the fire circle the shadows danced eerily on silent, blanket-wrapped figures smoking pipes.

White men in this country always travelled in their own Land Rovers and never used the native houses so I must have cut a strange figure to them coming in out of the night wearing my kilt, yet they never showed any surprise although the hum of conversation went low for a bit.

We arrived in Hargeisa in the early hours and I slept in the cab until the morning. I reported to the police first thing and was staggered to find they had already done a Thomas Cook job on me. A Desert Locust Survey convoy was due to leave in a week for Kenya and the police, who had a regular radio hook-up with the coast and had heard all about me, had arranged a lift with them for me. Major Fry, police 2nd in Command, even spoke about lending me a .38 revolver for the journey, the intervening territory being particularly dangerous with *shifta* and warring tribes. In the meantime the Somaliland Scouts, the local army regiment, had been forewarned and a billet was awaiting me in the sergeants' mess. It all made me feel proud, and pleased to be British and thankful that the red ink on the atlas ran all the way down to the Cape.

Of course it didn't work out as easily as that, but it was not the fault of the police that things didn't go quite according to their plan and I was indeed grateful to them for their efforts. On the day the convoy was due to leave Mr Woods, the

DSL leader, wired down to Nairobi to say they were bringing a passenger and a reply came back immediately saying that for reasons of insurance they were on no account to bring me. Dismally, I watched them go.

Major Fry was wild at Woods for saying anything about bringing me and spoiling all his arrangements, but he soon came up with another plan. An American of the Sinclair Oil Company was leaving in a couple of days for his base in the Ogaden desert and with some police persuasion had agreed to take me as far as Werdair in Ethiopia. I still had no visa for that country but Fry said I could wait till doomsday for it: he'd give me an official letter of recommendation for transit and hopefully that would do the trick. Nevertheless, once over the border I would be 'on my own' and there were lots of stories of travellers in that part of the country being confined for no apparent reason, charged for their food and detained until their money ran out. I would not be put off though and said I'd take my chances with the American. Having given the warning, the major was obviously pleased that I ignored it and said I should go along to the bar at the J.M.J. hotel that evening where the American was sure to be and introduce myself and make any arrangements necessary. He gave me the letter to the Ethiopian authorities and wished me good luck but made no mention of any firearm this time.

Glenn Fulbright was already well into his evening's entertainment by the time I got along to the J.M.J., the only hotel in Hargeisa. The place had a shabby, frontier look about it. By the entrance in a glass case was a jumble of 'goodies' on offer to weary travellers, White Hart Rum, Johnnie Walker's, 3-Star Rum, San-Izal toilet paper and tins of Nugget boot polish, all mixed up together.

I had no difficulty recognising Glenn even though we hadn't met. A rugged looking, dark skinned man – his mother was a Cherokee, he kept telling everyone – with long black hair straggled down his face, he slouched with his back against the bar and surveyed the room with a twisted grin on his face. His eyes were already hazy though the night was yet young. I said Major Fry had said he would give me a lift to Werdair. He didn't change his position nor look at me as he said, "Yup. One helluva guy, the Major, he sure twisted my arm. But, you hear, you git off ma back as soon as we're cross the border. I ain't sticking ma neck out for no bum, d'yuh hear?" I said I heard as a chill went through me. Being dropped in the desert just over the border was not something to be looked forward to. Well, it was a bridge to be crossed if it ever arose!

He offered nothing by way of conversation except to repeat "I'm just a guy," a phrase that was to fill every unforgiving minute over the next couple of days, and the silence hung heavy. I asked if he'd like another drink and still he didn't reply. Then, of a sudden he threw back the remains of his glass and swung round and actually looked at me as he spoke, "No, hobos can't buy drinks. C'mon I'll buy you dinner." His rough, candid honesty was very appealing.

He took me to the Club, the great English institution that is the centre of society in every colonial conclave, no matter how small. Where the Romans from their new tented camps first built baths before houses when pushing out their frontiers, the British when expanding their empire built 'The Club' before all else.

In the Club the atmosphere was much more stately than in the J.M.J. Here, where people stood in straight posture and handled their glasses with dignity, Glenn's slouch was distinctly antisocial. Where people ate with decorum Glenn's fork-shovelling and open-mouth chewing was looked on with disdain.

I said I had eaten at the mess but would join him for a coffee for company, but he would have none of it, so I gave in readily. He actually talked to me, and how he talked, telling me about Texas and all the wondrous things and people there. He talked as he ate, he talked between gulps of beer and as the evening wore on his voice grew louder and more slurred.

At the next table sat a group of people of the Desert Locust Survey. Included in the group was Brigadier Gibbons (ret'd), the boss of the restricted area of the country. He was a small, slight man with steel grey hair and the quiet air of command. His wife was with him and she was all that was opposite to her husband. Fiery of temperament, fierce and scathing with her tongue she rode her husband's authority roughshod over all who might dare to put forward any opinion that was in the least contrary to her own.

She was aptly known to everyone, black or white, as 'Kali Sana', which is Swahili for 'very fierce' or 'sharp', a nickname that was so appropriate she even appeared to take pleasure in it for she had great pride in her bossing ability in getting things done. She was having a new house built and she boasted how she could make the 'boys' work harder than anyone else. I wondered if she knew the derivation of her Swahili pseudonym and if so, could she really be pleased with herself?

Kali, one of the many Indian words that have been absorbed into Swahili, is the female consort of the Hindu god Siva. She represents total dynamic energy and terror and is personified as a black, naked woman (how our Kali would have hated that association) with four arms, one of which holds a sword and another a severed human head, while round her waist she wears a belt from which many human skulls dangle. She appears laughing hideously with blood-stained teeth and protruding tongue. Her many arms proclaim her absolute dominion.

I had met most of the DLS people at that table and felt desperately awkward sitting between two lots of opposing friends waiting for the spark that would set off a double reaction. It came as expected from Kali Sana who let out a sudden burst directed at Glenn. I don't know exactly what she said, I sat with my back towards her, but I was aware of the sudden electrified hush and as I turned I saw her standing with dagger eyes and red, angry face thrust forward, a veritable Kali. Glenn sat unperturbed, chewing like a ruminating ox on the cud, then he said something like, "Sit down, you silly cow, and shut your goddamned mouth." Her face was a picture, nobody had ever spoken to her like that in her life.

Immediately the Brigadier was on his feet. He threw down his napkin and said with controlled vehemence. "Sir, you have insulted my wife. If I were younger I would ask you outside. As it is I demand you leave these premises at once. You are not a member and are allowed in only on open invitation as a visitor. You have greatly abused that privilege. Go now before I call the police."

Glenn surveyed his opponent with smouldering eyes then stood up, peeling his napkin from his throat, then lurched off a few paces before coming back, reaching in his pocket and throwing an uncounted wad of notes on the table. He half staggered to the door – the booze had finally reached his legs – before calling over his shoulder, "You coming, Scottie?" I was taken aback by the sudden familiarity and giving the DLS folk a side nod and look of resignation I hurried to join him.

Outside I watched him climb unsteadily into the cab of his truck. He was staying down the road at the Sabean car park or transport depot which was run by a gang of Italians, wonderful mechanics, who serviced and repaired all the vehicles in the district and provided safe parking for vehicles and accommodation for drivers in transit. Before leaving to go back to the Scouts' billets I asked when he intended leaving in the morning and he said about seven as he revved up. I wondered what he would be like then.

I arrived at the Italian camp early next morning. Even so a few mechanics were already tinkering with engines. When I asked the whereabouts of the American one withdrew his head and shoulders from the great open jaws of a mighty articulated truck, pointed to the door of a shack and rolled his eyes in mock horror.

An unused mug of tea stood at the door and I wondered why the steward had not taken it in. My knock brought no response so I tried the handle. It gave. There was a sudden commotion inside a slurred voice said, "Come in one more step and I'll drill yu." I hurriedly closed the door. Cowboy stuff, this!

Presently he came to the door, his black hair straggled over his eyes and his face screwed up like a wet rag. He held his revolver by his side. From the state of his clothes it was obvious that he had slept in them. He gave me a bloodshot stare and said, "C'mon, let's get some cawfee," before launching himself on shaky legs towards the canteen, fumbling to stick the gun in his belt as he went.

We sat on high stools at the bar and Glenn ordered coffee and cognac. Ironi, the barman, made a strong brew and left us with the pot and the bottle while he got on with his cleaning. Glenn laced himself a strong mix. I preferred my coffee neat; it was a shame to dilute such excellent stuff.

After the fifth or sixth, Glenn forgot to put the coffee in. By 6 p.m. we had progressed from the bar to a table with a red chequered cloth on it. The Italian workmen, happy carefree men with eager smiles, had watched with amusement as they drifted in for breakfast and lunch. Now as they came for dinner they applauded Glenn's dour tenacity.

I slept the night on the floor of Glenn's room and we left early the following morning. In contrast to yesterday's performance Glenn suddenly rose and made for his truck, pee-ed against the wheel and climbed in. I caught it on the move, half-dressed and half awake. The two guards who were supposed to accompany us were left behind. When I hastily reminded Glenn of this he eloquently tapped the gun at his belt.

Away from the town the awesome loneliness of the desert settled over us cutting the truck and its occupants down to minuscule size. This was the 'restricted' area where *shifta* were thick and no one without a permit was allowed to go. At one time I had thought that my only worries lay in the capricious dealings of the Ethiopians when I met them. Now in this awful emptiness with this unpredictable man I realised that the Ethiopians might be the least of my worries.

*

The Ogaden desert covers much of the Horn of Africa. An arid, desolate area where nomads follow ancient trails feeding their animals off the scrub bush and termite ants build monolithic towers of red earth.

The British Somaliland Protectorate lay along the northern coastal belt and the Italian Somaliland Colony ran down the eastern, Indian Ocean side. Except where they touched at the tip of the Horn the two were separated by a toe of Ethiopia which jutted out into that corner of Africa and by its position, restricted all movements between the Horn and the rich East African lands.

Hour after hour the sandy miles rolled under the surging, steaming bonnet. The only things which broke the pan-flat land were the brick-red ant hills, standing like colossal sentinels of this lonely land. Broad at their base they rose nearly sheer-sided to one or several sharp-pointed towers some twelve or fifteen feet high. These were the homes of the termite ants. Entomologists do not regard them as true ants but they nevertheless follow the lifestyle of ants and nobody thinks of them as anything else. What makes them different from ants is their ability to build these colossal skyscrapers. I had seen anthills in Kenya but had been told that those of Somaliland were like no place else and what I now saw backed up that claim. They interested me and I had done some library research on their lifestyle in Aden.

Their mounds looked like inert mounds of clay, yet inside they would be alive with activity. Each could better be likened to a gigantic castle with monumental turrets which contained a great city-state within its surrounding rampart wall, all teeming with life. And what life!

*

As mankind we think we have risen above the animals because we developed a higher intellect and organised ourselves into social communities where different skills could be developed by specialist groups for the benefit of all. A civilised society, in the true sense of the word, whereby individuals give up certain personal freedoms in order to live in group harmony and accept to be governed by common civil codes or laws. We are wrong. Ants had already accomplished this millions, even hundreds of millions of years, before man ever arrived on earth. They were the first living creatures to organise themselves into civic communities and build themselves permanent homes of cemented clay.

The termite ants show a remarkable intelligence and their builders and civil engineers have developed unbelievable skills. They build high, vaulted galleries and rooms, each designed for its own purpose, food storerooms, living chambers, servants quarters, slaves quarters, etc.

When more slaves are needed the army swarms out, attacking other city-states to plunder and capture a new batch. They even capture lice and farm them at home so they can be milked by stroking them with their antennae, enticing the lice to emit their honey-dew which the ants love, and even help them to breed so they can eat their young. It all sounded remarkably similar to our own farming methods. To the best of my knowledge ants and man are the only two living species to harness other living things for their own purpose or gain.

The whole ants castle is aired and cooled by a complex and very efficient, ducted ventilation system. They even include a very practical drainage system leading into the earth below the mound.

In the ant city, as the head of state the King and Queen, who are much larger than the others, particularly Her Majesty, reside in the best rooms with walls thicker than the others, in the very heart of the building. In their society the King is vastly inferior to the Queen since it is she and only she who produces the progeny of their race. The King and Queen are the only fertile members of the community. All others in the vast, teeming population, are neuters. Only a few latent males and females gain their sexes and sexuality at the beginning of the rainy season, grow wings and go on their nuptial flight. Not so lucky for the males though, they nearly all die soon after their moment of bliss. A few females shed their wings and each go to start their own hive and be a Queen.

The Queen is always pregnant and drops her eggs at quick regular intervals and these are caught and carried away in the mouths of an army of nurses to the nursery where a special chamber will have been built for each. Since new chambers are constantly being built for the new pupa the ant hill grows in size and becomes a catacomb for the living. Break a piece off and it's like a square of Aero chocolate.

The nurses will clean, procure and feed the young larvae and if necessary even carefully carry their charges out to the surface to get the benefit of the sun or coolness. All of the community, the builders, the servants, the labourers, the slaves, work incessantly and the soldiers, who develop powerful biting jaws, watch and protect. And the whole community is governed by strict laws which, since all the inhabitants are born to do only their own job, are unlikely ever to be broken.

It is evident that a great intelligence is working there. When a new egg drops on the conveyer belt who, what, decides what it is to be? That there is some control on the births is manifest by the factory process of making only what is necessary, a new batch of workers or nurses or soldiers when a war is planned or the hive is running short of slaves. Supplant humans for ants in this story and we have Aldous Huxley's *Brave New World* and Adolf Hitler's Master Race and The Thousand Years Reich.

It appears that having been created perfect, the ants never changed. They have remained exactly the same, as in a time-warp, no development or innovations, since the beginning of time. Ants are exactly the same as they were all those millions of years ago as we know from fossilised resins.

*

Was the creation of ants God's first attempt at making a civilised community, a perfect world? What a perfectly awful world. And when he had finished did he look with horror at what he had created? The perfect mechanical world: a place for everyone and everyone to their place … for life. A complete autocratic, class-determined world. The total police-state where no one could do wrong.

And here, to escape the endless, bone-jarring monotony of the journey I began to muse, somewhere out of it all, up there, twisting, tumbling, drifting, questioning, questioning.

After his attempt with the ants did God then realise his mistake, for if no one could do wrong no one could be credited with doing good? So how could He decide who was to go to the Heaven which he had created but was still empty. And if there were no do-gooders there could be no do-baders either. So there was His arch rival the Devil, down in his basement flat he called Hell, standing beside his great fire, blazing because he hadn't had anybody to burn up since the beginning of time. If Heaven and Hell had to be occupied then there had to be creatures on Earth who were able to think beyond mere existence, creatures who had the power to reason and decide whether to do good or bad. So Humans were created.

This was a masterstroke, really, for it answered the question that all those humans would ask a million years later, "Do insects, fish, birds and animals go to Heaven?" While the unenlightened might believe that well-behaved goldfish might go there, the thinking people would realise that the entrant to either place had to have the ability to reason, which only the brain that had grown and developed in Humans could do. So, "No, one cannot expect to meet one's old pet cat in whichever place one is allocated on their demise."

It has been said that if the age since living creatures first arrived on Earth was calculated as twenty-four hours then humans stepped on the world stage at a milli-second to midnight. In doing so they became the first creatures eligible to enter Heaven and Hell at the end of their lives. That was an awful long time for these two establishments to be lying empty, waiting for their first customers. But then, hold on, that isn't right. There was another long delay in opening the doors of Heaven and Hell to the public. Have we not been told that only Christians, and only good Christians at that, can enter the Kingdom of God, primitive heathens and infidels who had never heard of Jesus being *persona non grata?* We therefore can pinpoint the year when the turnstiles of Heaven first started turning as 30 AD, or thereabouts. And does this not raise an enormous question? Where are all those lost souls of a million years or so who were good but had never heard of the Son of God? Roman Catholics would tell us that they are in Purgatory, that great waiting room where souls are kept after death while their credentials are being examined before they may be allowed into the inner Temple. And what chance have they got if they lived before the start of the main event. Anyway there they are, those lost souls, in this endless queue waiting to have their groceries checked. And even if they're lucky enough get up to the till and the things in their basket are found wanting, or if there's more than their permitted rations in there, then it's into the burning fire for them. Poor souls, after all that time! It's very worrying!

*

The long, jarring road was an open page for soliloquy and the satirical nonsense ran through my head like a gushing stream, taking my mind away from the discomfort like a balm. Perhaps there was a reason for it all. Looking back through the years, perhaps there was a place for this soul-searching. Was this the reason for my wandering? Were the answers to these unanswerable questions the reason for my quest? Was it only in nonsense that it all made sense? Was it these thoughts, unspoken and often unnoticed even by me, that Grasso Stellario had read in my face and told me was my mission in that time of my life?

Nonsense or not, looking at the anthills I was glad to be part of God's second attempt, if that's what it was, glad I had my own mind, glad that I lived by chance, that the improbable adventure could be just round the corner. And it was, only there were no corners, just a long, brown, washboard-surface road running straight as an arrow-flight into the infinite distance ahead and a great, endless cloud of dust trailing behind.

Twice we passed nomad families on the move with their camels loaded high with tents, baggage, women and children, the men striding out in front. Once the truck swerved to avoid a dead camel on which there were perched a horde of vultures, their bald heads and beaks covered in blood.

All this time Glenn hardly said a word. My early attempts at conversation were rebuffed by his monosyllabic grunts until I gave up trying. He seemed no longer human, more a kind of centaur, part man, part machine, staring fixedly ahead with unblinking eyes.

We entered Ethiopia near Awareh. There was no customs post nor frontier bar. This was the scene of many affrays, for the border was ill-defined and many tribes laid claim to the waterhole there. Here, some months later, Brigadier Gibbons was shot dead when he went to settle a dispute between rival factions. I was told many years later that the Somalis responsible for his death were terribly sorry for what they did. They claimed it was a case of mistaken identity for the Brigadier was well known, liked and respected by all the people in the area.

Glenn was remorseless. Oblivious to the heat or aching vibrations he devoured the miles with the same sullen determination he had shown with yesterday's drinking. I'll say this for the man, he could drive. While most people took two days over the two hundred and fifty miles of wash-board track, he did it in seven hours, battering the truck along at speeds few others would dare. He was no doubt making up for the lost time from yesterday's binge.

Though aching from a thwarted call of nature I restrained from asking him to stop, fearing he would go off without me. When at last I did call a halt he did just that. As I stood by the roadside, true to his word that he would not stick his "neck out for no bum", he heaved my rucksack out and drove off. Looking at the disappearing cloud of dust I felt quite desolate. For all I knew I was alone in the middle of the desert and I felt very small and insignificant.

I got a grip on myself and took stock. My water-bottle was full and I had a few tins of food the Scouts' cook had set me up with. I was all right for a day's march so I set off in the direction we had been going.

Surely he couldn't be that inhuman to leave me too far from habitation! And of course he was not. After some miles I could not describe the relief I felt when the first semblance of habitation gradually took shape out of the heat haze that shimmered on the horizon and Werdair hove into view. Glen had not wanted to be associated with me when meeting the Ethiopian officials, assuming, no doubt, that any entry trouble with a hobo would implicate him and incur their ire. His job could have been on the line and I didn't blame him for disowning me. Still, I would have welcomed a word from him at the time to let me know I was within a few hours of the fort.

I was mightily pleased when I finally walked between the straw houses, some oblong with pitched roofs like our houses, some round with conical roofs, past the village square where women sat chattering round great gourds of camels' milk which they sold; past the blacksmith shop where a boy blew up a white-hot fire with skin bellows; past two great stone ovens where bread was baked, and up to the Beau Geste fort where I reported my presence.

I met the Governor, a swarthy, grave-faced man, who surprisingly turned out to be friendly and helpful. He looked at my passport and letter from Major Fry and handed them to his interpreter who studied them closely, running his finger down each page before saying a few words in Amharic to the affect, I presumed, that although there was no visa stamp there was this official letter – which I doubted that he could read – that seemed to make it all right. The Governor lifted his chin and the interpreter handed my papers back to me. The Governor asked where I was going to stay and when I said I must camp somewhere he said through his interpreter, who spoke only broken English, that there was a Locust Survey camp nearby and I should go there. What a stroke of luck! I couldn't believe how it was all falling into place.

Outside the fort I rested a bit and took in the wild, exotic scene. Not far from the gate was the great, life-giving well around which over a great expanse were hundreds upon hundreds of camels. I had never seen so many and they were all bawling for water. The noise, the stench, the dust storm they kicked up was diabolical, yet the atmosphere was so powerful and wonderful and well worth crossing a desert to see.

The well too was a wonder. Deep, deep with a man at the bottom who filled the skin bags and others at the top who hauled them up, plump and glistening in the sunlight, and distributed their contents. So deep that when the empty bags were thrown down there was an awful long silence before the thud boomed up as they landed. So deep that the voice of the man down there singing the chant they all kept rhythm to sounded so far away, yet loud with a hollow boom like an amplified echo. This scene must have been as it always had been, unchanged for thousands of years.

I walked out to the DLS camp and received a warm welcome. There I met Messrs Selby-Lyons, Harley and Lees. They all knew of me from Wood's convoy which I should have been on and had expected me sometime. Selby-Lyons was due to leave for Jiddah in a day or two, Harley was now in charge of the area and Lees had joined them a month before. They were in tents and a space was allotted to me. I dined as their guest. Harley said he'd send a runner over to the fort in the morning to tell the people there to let us know if a south-bound vehicle should turn up. It all seemed so easy and simple.

That night we had dinner under a spreading, flat-topped acacia tree. The camp fire with the table spread with a checked cloth under a hurricane lamp hanging from a branch was the perfect camp setting. The 'boys' had their own cooking fire some distance away, far enough for their chatter not to annoy the sahibs, where they ate and from where Ali, with his head swathed in a voluminous, loosely wrapped turban, brought the food and waited at the table. Such a setting one dreamed about in later times.

Over the meal Selby-Lyons, a veteran of these parts and of the work, told me what the Desert Locust Survey was all about. Locust in great numbers devastate hot, rich, green lands and, as quoted in the Bible and written in Pharaohs' tombs, cause famine and disease every year. I had seen swarms of them in Kenya on more than one occasion, once driving in an open truck through a great black cloud of them that darkened the sky. When they land the devastation and misery they leave in their wake is appalling. Every leaf, every crop, is wiped clean from the earth. The path of the parasites is marked by miles and miles of stripped barren soil. Lifeless.

Although locusts are infamous for their destruction in lush green lands they actually breed in the desert. After their foreign travels and near the end of their life the pregnant locusts return to their birthplace to lay their eggs in the warm sand to begin the endless cycle yet again.

The eggs hatch in ten to twelve days and through their life span, from larvae to flying insect, the locusts go through five development stages as a kind of grasshopper, each lasting ten days, until they grow their wings. It is in the final stages as 'hoppers' that they must be found and exterminated. It is because locusts do not recognise geographical borders, growing in one country and giving little problem to it but plaguing another, the DLS has to be an international force operating across borders rather than being restricted within single countries.

Nowhere is the trouble and danger involved in the work better illustrated than in the Ogaden. This is not a desert in the Saharan concept. This is not a dead land of rolling sand dunes. It is a land of scrub bush, mainly devoid of water but supporting scant life. Wandering tribes have eked out a meagre living in these parts for thousands of years, staying just long enough in an area for their camels and goats to graze it to its limit then moving on to another place. This allows each grazed area to recover and be ready for their next visit. Although the rainfall is pitifully low, the fact is that, except in extreme drought years, it does rain regularly at a certain time of year. And here lies the danger for the DLS.

For generations untold the Esa tribe, like many others, has watched the locust returning to lay their eggs and a few days afterwards the rains come. To them the locusts bring the rain, not, as is the case, that the rains bring the locusts. Kill the locust and there will be no rain. It is as simple as that in the Esas' logic. During the breeding season the DLS send out scouts to look for the hopping swarms. When they are found a trench is dug across the path of the heaving army and poisoned bran is laid in it. The vanguard eat the bran, die, and the oncoming mob eat the dead so the poison goes through the lot.

"These are the simple facts of the case," as Robert Service might have said, but behind those words lies another world. Consider the enormity of the task. Despite their size locusts are extremely light insects. They rely more on their large bulk and light weight which enables them to be blown along on winds rather than by the power of their wings to cover the hundreds of miles they may fly between their birthplace and their feeding grounds. Yet light as they are, swarms can weigh as much as a hundred tons. Think then of the numbers involved. Advancing hopper armies can be half a mile wide and stretch back into the unseen distance. Baiting a large army like that is no mean feat. But that is not all.

The task becomes infinitely more difficult, not to mention dangerous, when warlike natives such as the Esa do not want the locust killed. Recently, Selby-Lyons said, they had had three scouts, who were out looking for hoppers, speared to death and frequently they had to have an armed police or army guard surrounding them when digging and laying the bait. It all sounded exciting.

A day or so later Tim Harley drove Selby-Lyons to Hargeisa where he would go on to fly from Aden to Jiddah. Tim was staying a few days and while he was away John Lees was in charge. Since my arrival John had appeared rather distant and aloof, but thrown together now he warmed and we got on well together. He was a strict disciplinarian with the natives and when the camp had to be re-sited for some reason and the boys started in lethargic, sloppy manner he soon had them jumping, army-style. The move went like clockwork while John sat as an overlord in a canvas chair like a film director.

We talked away the day with John telling me of his exploits with the SAS in North Africa and Yugoslavia where he was dropped by parachute to command groups of partisans over a large area. It was exciting stuff and I thrilled to hear it all.

The following day a scout ran into the camp carrying a dead hopper in a cloth. He said he had picked it out of a swarm, not a huge one, about six miles away. Immediately there was a sudden 'call to arms'. Bags of poisoned bran were loaded onto trucks, emissaries dispatched to recruit casual labour and a messenger sent to the fort to request a detachment of soldiers to accompany the party, but we never found the swarm.

During the following days scouts continued to come in with samples of hoppers they had found. But on each occasion when we went none were to be found. It was evident that the scouts, being paid by results, had saved a few from a previous swarm to show at a later date.

These past few days we had got the new camp better organised than previous ones, according to John. We had areas marking out for different activities. I organised the erection of a grass screen round the latrine area and had even displayed my craft skills in making a thunderbox, a luxury seldom indulged in. I thought it would be a fine thing to be remembered by long after I had gone when the user was cogitating in comfort rather than balancing precariously on his hunkers, especially after a few glasses of *anisette*, the popular local drink.

On Christmas Eve Tim Harley returned from Hargeisa bringing many goodies, including a new radio that could be run off the car battery. Now we would not be isolated in the middle of a desert, now we would be part of the great world community listening in to the seasons festivities.

To celebrate Christmas I had a shave and as good a bath as one can have in two inches of water in a canvas basin. Dinner was served in the cool of the evening under the familiar tree in the glow of the firelight under the bright yellow dome cast by a new hissing Tilley lamp, another of Tim's goodies from Hargeisa. That morning Tim had shot a lesser bustard and the cook plucked and prepared it, even to the sage and onion stuffing – thanks to Tim's foraging in Hargeisa – and roasted it in clay to perfection. All was ready when disaster struck. The radio packed in. Suddenly we were plunged back into isolation and gloom fell over the festive table.

Feverishly Tim worked on his pride and joy, switching wires, looking at valves, sandpapering plugs. Suddenly, when all seemed lost, a miracle happened. Bing Crosby came right into the firelight singing 'White Christmas'. Tim's face spoke for us all, despite the incongruity of hoping for snow in this desert.

The bird was served in traditional pose, lying on its back with its legs in the air, all nicely brown, surrounded by roast potatoes and garnished with green sprigs of something. Tim and John had foaming mugs of beer, the bottles having been a treasured part of Tim's recent buys. Afterwards, Ali proudly brought to the table a tinned Christmas pudding, topped with an acacia twig instead of holly, liberally soaked in whisky and now smothered in blue, flickering flames. What Ali, a Moslem, made of it all, is hard to imagine, but he entered into the spirit of the occasion and obviously followed the instructions he had been given to the letter. We could not have been served better had we been in the Savoy. Over coffee Tim produced some Christmas cards and we wrote them out and passed them around to each other. The first Christmas on my journey was one to be remembered.

During all this time with the DLS, no runner had come from the fort to say a vehicle would take me further on my way. I hadn't minded but now I felt the need to be on the move again. I seriously thought of buying a camel to carry my gear and water, and walking on. The price was about 100 rupees. At 1/6d to the rupee that put the price of the animal at £7.10/- (£7.50p). Maybe I'd get two, one to ride and one for my baggage. £15 was about all the money I had in the world, but perhaps I'd be able to sell the beasts at the Kenya border and recoup my funds. I pushed out of my mind the thoughts of what might happen if due to my inexperience the animal ran off and left me. Tim Harley saved me from myself.

Tim and John were leaving for Harar, the regional capital, and Diredawa, in the Eastern Highlands of Ethiopia in a couple of days and Tim invited me along. Although it was in the wrong direction, being further north, Tim said there was a British consul there and he might be able to get me a proper visa. That was very appealing as wandering around Ethiopia without a visa was very precarious. Moreover, I had heard how beautiful the country was up there, how majestic were the mountain ravines, how refreshing the crystal air. Even more attractive to me were the legends of the ancient monasteries and Coptic churches that went back untold centuries, the oldest legacy of the Christian religion in Africa and perhaps in the world. I was fascinated at the opportunity to delve into these time-capsules of antiquity. The whole aspect of Ethiopia captivated me.

For two thousand years and more, while the rest of Africa had remained static in development, this country had had an indigenous governmental structure at least equal to Egypt, and in all that time there had been only one line of kings, including, it was claimed, Prester John, all the way down to Haile Selassie, the longest dynasty the world had known. I had long known of Prester John, the legendary Christian Crusade King who swore to win back Christ's Jerusalem from the Moslems. I believe I was introduced to this character in John Buchan's book of his name. Although Buchan set his story in early South Africa it was Ethiopia that claimed Prester John as one of its early kings, even though almost every country in the Middle East as far as India and even Asia also laid claims to the legendary king and crusader as part of their heritage. I was particularly interested in a statement I had read somewhere that 'Prester' was a corruption of 'Presbyter', the name for the members of the original Church of Christ which Jesus' brother James formed, and the term taken up by the Church of Scotland for those of its ruling body and the reason why the Church is referred to as Presbyterian. Perhaps in foraging into the ancient Coptic Church I might learn more of this fascinating character who was one of the great mysteries of Africa.

I readily accepted Tim's invitation.

Next day all was made ready for the journey. A truck was loaded with gear, including my rucksack, and sent off while we three drove over to the fort in the Land Rover to pick up the two soldiers who were to escort the convoy. On entering the fort we were met by the Governor accompanied by a little, bent man whose black face was wrinkled as a prune. His match-like, scrawny legs and feet were bare and he wore a huge solar topee that seemed to lie half way down his back, and round his shoulders he hugged a blanket. The man was a Cabinet Minister, no less. The Governor asked if his 'Minister of Communications' could be given a lift to Harar, a rather strange request, I thought, in the light of the man's portfolio. Still, I could not help feeling friendly towards a fellow hitchhiker.

Permission granted the little man climbed up beside the soldiers and settled himself amongst the baggage. As he did so the Governor looked on with obvious disdain at the uncomfortable and undignified position his Minister occupied. Then he looked at me, and with a chill I could see his mind working. He suddenly remembered he had orders to hold me back for questioning.

I was ordered out of the vehicle and through an interpreter told that since I had no visa I would be taken into custody and charged with illegal entry. I protested that my rucksack had gone on ahead and I had nothing but what I stood up in. I asked that I be allowed I travel far enough to catch up with the truck and so reclaim my kit. I could then be dropped off at Awarah and be out of Ethiopian territory. But he would have none of it. The DLS men argued my case but had to give way when the Governor became angry. He was a touchy individual, Tim said, and they could not jeopardise their relations with him. Tim added he was sorry, but there was nothing he could do about it. He would inform the British Consul at Harar of my plight and hoped he might be able to do something.

I was marched off under guard and as I looked back I smarted at the sight of my fellow hitchhiker comfortably installed in my middle front seat waving his enormous hat in grateful farewell to the Governor.

*

It was Hogmanay: only a few grains of sand remained in the hour-glass of the year. This was the time, those last few breaths of the old year, when all exiled Scots feel nearer to and also further away from home. This was the time when all that takes them abroad, money, adventure or any other reason, means not a tinker's cuss if only these fleeting moments could be spent with their ain folks. The naked flame of the tiny lamp flickered as a gust of wind blew in through the little barred window. Grotesque shadows danced on the brown, mud walls.

Could it be only a week since Christmas? These past few days of solitary confinement had seemed interminable. The loss of my kit, all my personal belongings, was almost unbearable. Would I ever get them back? What would I do, how could I go on, if all was gone forever. And worse, when was I going to be charged? Would I languish in jail for years? The future seemed so bleak and the waiting, the unknown silence day after day, was intolerable.

I had no books, no writing equipment, nothing to do to while away the time. My cell was devoid of furniture except for a narrow bunk. It measured four paces one way and three-and-a-half the other and it took thirteen steps to circumnavigate it. I knew these measurements well: the numbers are tramped into my mind from hour after hour of pacing them out.

I lived for my meals – bread and tea in the morning and tough goat's meat and camel's milk in the evening – not just because I was hungry, which I was, but because they were milestones in the otherwise endless days. Boredom was my constant companion, an idiot that goaded me on to nonsensical games and violent exercise; how many press-ups, sit-ups, could I do? Could I cross the room with a single standing leap? Could I throw my hat on to a nail in the wall like they do in films? How many flies could I kill with one slap of my hand? My record for the latter was nine. Once I got seventeen, but then I had baited them with a piece of meat and waited till they had covered it in a furry mass and as I felt this could not be a legitimate claim I disqualified myself.

And now it was almost New Year. As the last minutes ticked away, a wave of nostalgia swept over me. I thought of home. There would be a cheery fire, my mother's smiling face, the family all round and a row of Christmas cards along the mantelpiece. There would be good food, good drink …

I wished I could have washed, shaved and cleaned my teeth to freshen up. At home the house would have been cleaned and tidied with extra care to welcome the New Year.

I watched the hand of my watch creep towards midnight. It hung on the mark for an instance as if in reverence to the passing year, then ticked the first seconds of the new one. I lifted the mug of brown, dirty water: this was my wine. I took the stale, sour bread I had saved: this was my shortbread, black bun and Dundee cake all in one. I toasted the folks back home. Then in a sudden moment of merry madness I burst into song:

A guid New Year to ane and aw'
and many may ye see,
And during aw' the year to come
oh, happy may ye be.

A black head swathed in a blanket suddenly appeared at the door-grill, the eyes large with wonder. I wished him a Happy New Year and invited him in. He didn't understand me but he came in nevertheless to inspect me at close quarters. He was my first-foot and by tradition he was a lucky one for he was tall, dark and he didn't come empty handed. He did not have a bottle or lump of coal as tradition demands, but he carried his rifle … at the ready.

Despite the guard's lack of New Year spirit he nevertheless proved to be a lucky first-foot. The next day a lorry from the north brought my rucksack. The DLS had dropped it at Awarah and miraculously it arrived intact. Perhaps the Ethiopian police were ruthless with thieves, especially those who might touch goods in the trust of government officials.

Later that day I was escorted to the office to witness it being searched for contraband. This provided great entertainment for a horde of soldiers, labourers and the community at large, not forgetting the Governor in person. My sleeping bag was unrolled, felt by a dozen hands and admired. The tent was unpacked and although I understood none of the comments I knew they were marvelling at its compactness. The collapsible cooking pans brought forth cries of delight. One man unearthed my first-aid kit and before I could stop him, fearing he was going to tip out the contents, uncorked the iodine bottle and took a sniff. Looking at all my belongings scattered about I malevolently wished it had been chloroform.

When he seemed about to open up my snake-bite compact I grabbed it from him and opened it myself showing him and the others that when you unscrewed one end you had a scalpel and when you did the same with the other end there was a quantity of permanganate of potash, also known as Condies crystals. I explained more by actions than words how you were meant to lance the bite and pour the crystals into the wound. I fervently hoped I would never have to put it to the test.

A week later, when I had begun to doubt I would ever be released, the door of my prison was suddenly thrown open and a soldier rushed in and grabbed my rucksack and made for the door with it. Soldier or not, I caught him and made to relieve him of his bundle. But he protested vigorously and in turn pulled me to the door and obviously was telling me to get out. I could hardly believe it but I went. Nearby a truck stood with its engine already running. The soldier heaved my rucksack up into the cab and motioned for me to get in. I wasted no time. A moment later a Somali driver came out of the Governor's office, climbed in and we were off.

I was free. The suddenness of it all was bewildering. No charges had been laid against me. I was not going to jail for keeps, I was merely being run out of the country. I doubted if the Governor had ever had any intention of prosecuting me. He had merely waited until after my rucksack had been returned and for the first truck going north to pass through. We passed the night at Awarah and next day I was back in Hargeisa.

I had a great return reception by the half dozen chaps in the Somaliland Scouts' mess and I settled in there for a day or two to consider my next move. During this time I visited the DLS camp to report my happenings with their colleagues at Werdair. While there I decided to apply for a temporary job with that group. I had liked what I had seen of the work and, who knows, I might still get my trip to the Ethiopian highlands. It was now even more imperative that I get my visa for that country and I could not think of a better way to fill in the time until it arrived.

I asked to see the Brigadier and he was very helpful. My application would have to go to Nairobi so we sat over coffee while he took down my personal notes to enable him to formulate a letter to headquarters.

"Your full name?" he asked.

"David Harrower Lessels."

"Harrower?"

"Yes. It is my mother's maiden name. I was named after an uncle."

"Is the Harrower Lessels hyphenated?"

"No."

"Oh, I think we had better hyphenate it for this purpose." I felt a sudden elevation. I had never thought of myself in the double-barrelled fraternity and while the position had a certain appeal I couldn't help feeling a little uneasy at the deception.

"What school did you go to?" the Brigadier continued.

"Torryburn Public School."

"Public school?" The Brigadier's voice had a raised note of surprise in it.

"Yes," I answered, equally surprised at his query, yet noting his obvious look of pleasure as he wrote it down. In fact, we were each unaware that we were both speaking at cross purposes. In Scotland all State schools were 'Public Schools' while fee-paying ones were 'Private Schools'. Round the semicircular top of my school's entrance was inscribed in heavy stone letters, 'Torryburn Public School'. I attended it until I was fourteen when I left to take up my apprenticeship and very proud I was, and still am, of it.

So my application for a job with the DLS went forward as from David Harrower-Lessels, ex-Public School. It was my first brush with the 'Old-Boy' network and it seemed to have worked for I was eventually offered the job. But that is jumping the gun a bit for I had to wait a fortnight before the reply arrived and much happened in between.

Apart from the frustration of not being able to get on my way I enjoyed being back in Hargiesa. There were no worries or stress here and I enjoyed the company, the camaraderie. After my self-confinement I liked the sergeants' mess banter and the conversation when I was invited to dine at the officers' mess. I went with some Scouts to the open-air cinema to see Ann Todd in *Madeline*. There were about thirty all told in the audience, each wrapped up in blankets or fleece-lined jackets, sitting in chairs they brought with them, watching mighty buildings on the screen ripple in the breeze and faces go grotesque and catching only snippets of conversation while the rest was blown away. But we all liked it. The cinema was one of the big nights, whatever was on.

Pleasant though the days were in the army mess, after a few of them I began to feel the inactivity heavy on me. I should not have liked to have been stationed there for any length of time. Frontier postings sound very romantic but there's an awful lot of boredom with them. Not having a job to do didn't help, of course, so I began to devise ways of filling my time until I heard about the job with the DLS.

*

On the horizon, looking from Hargeisa, lie identical twin mountains. They are known locally as *Lubahabalod* (Two Breasts) but to the British they are 'Sheba's Breasts'. Conical shaped, rising from the flat plateau as prominently as the name suggests they fit exactly the description of the hills of the same name between which lay the trail to the fabulous fortune in Rider Haggard's *King Solomon's Mines*. Haggard never invented the legend, he merely built on it and moved the twin peaks to southern Africa to suit his book.

We know from the Bible that the mines were real and that they lay in the Land of Ophir. But the location of Ophir was already a mystery by the time the story was written into the Old Testament, more than seven or eight hundred years after the event. In Haggard's book the way to the mines lay from the south into land that would now be called Zimbabwe. In reality, the land route to the mines would go south from King Solomon's Israel, across the Red Sea from Yemen into Africa and through the Land of Sheba where I now stood. The domain of that great queen spanned from Arabia into Ethiopia. According to ancient legend the way to King Solomon's mines lay between Sheba's Breasts and I resolved to tread that part of the golden route and perhaps climb at least one of those distant, hazy peaks.

Knowing the land to be wild with game I borrowed a panga – large machete – from the army stores and bought a spear from a native of the Midgan tribe to supplement my sheath knife.

Strange people the Midgan. They had a language different from the other Somalis which they never spoke in front of strangers. They were blacksmiths and were regarded as inferior by all the other tribes, a practice I was to find almost universal throughout Africa. Why the worker of metals, the only true artisan that existed before the coming of the European, should be despised by pastoral tribes and land cultivators is difficult to fathom. Did the class system go back to the beginning of time? In nearly all cases in Africa the smiths were the skivvies, the sweepers, the cleaners of latrines, the doers of jobs that other tribes thought as beneath them. A Masai warrior of the great tribe of East Africa who lived by the spear, would not touch anything the smith had made. He would oil his hands so he would not come in contact with surfaces prior to taking hold of the new weapon and clean it thoroughly to wipe away all trace of the smith's hands before he felt he could use it.

Reviled and ostracised, blacksmith tribes inevitably became introverted and inbred, no marriages outside the tribe being permitted. Yet it must have been different in America, for did not Hiawatha run the length of the country, over mountain and river, shooting and carrying over his shoulder a deer, to woo and marry Minnehaha, lovely Laughing Water, daughter of the old Arrow-Maker of the Dakotas. It would seem that in ancient times, before the white man set foot in America or Africa there was obviously less class distinction in the New World than was practised in the Old one.

It was early morning when I set off on the route to Solomon's Mines. Sheba's Breasts were modestly covered by a pink negligee of mist. I went up the *tug* – dry river bed – skirted the *magalla* – native town – past the abattoir where bald-headed vultures and bloated marabo storks clustered round the offal pits and lifted bloody heads as I approached.

Cross country from the *tug* the going was rough through the thorny bush. There were clear game trails which I decided to avoid, but there were times when this was not possible and as I followed them I marvelled at the profusion of varied spoor. I was not adept at identifying any but a set of large paw marks that had sharp edges and no other imprints superimposed on them sent a chill down my spine. Occasionally gazelles broke cover and bounded off in graceful arches and once a family of wild pigs crossed my path.

The morning haze lifted and the hills stood out naked in the sunlight. My throat grew parched but I rationed myself to only occasional sips from my waterbottle. Reaching the first hill I rested and ate some of the meat and bread I was supplied with at the Mess before starting the ascent. The climb was stiff but not difficult and it was gratifying to see the plain slip away below me. There was practically no vegetation now and the loose stony ground had given way to solid bare rock. My main concern now was my metal-nailed boots slipping and my ankle getting twisted or broken. I should not liked to have been rendered immobile out there.

Occasionally I heard the bark of baboons but it was not until I was near the top that I met them. I came round an outcrop of rock and there they were, quite a large troop of them. They seemed as surprised as I was and we all stopped and stared for what seemed a long time. I was unsure what to do, not knowing if they were dangerous, if they would attack or run. I didn't want to flee for I felt that might set them after me, so I started to walk slowly forward, keeping my stare as steady as I could and slowly slipping the panga from its scabbard believing it would prove a better weapon than the spear. I approached a big old man who was out in front and whom I took to be the leader. The panga was clear now and when it seemed I was going to have to clout the old fellow I swung up my arms and shouted at the pitch of my voice. The suddenness of my wild behaviour gave him quite a start. Surprise, or was it terror, appeared momentarily in his eyes and then he turned tail and went off like an arrow from a bow with the others already overtaking him. I sat on a boulder for a few minutes to savour my relief.

I did not make the top. Already the sun was beginning to slide and I thought I had to get off the mountain, get down to the plain where there was wood for a fire and I could pitch my tent and build a *zariba* – a fence of thorny branches – round it as some protection against nocturnal prowlers. Near the bottom, but still high enough to get a good span of the countryside, I spied a nomad settlement. What a stroke of luck! I hastily made my way there.

The camp comprised a few tents made of fibre mats stretched over hooped stick frames and the lot encircled by a high, thick *zariba.* When I arrived only women and children were there and they all ran off screaming and whooping. I fancied the men were all out herding the animals and though the camp was now empty I thought it prudent to make my peace with the women first before entering. They hadn't gone far and stood around watching in a mixture of fear, shyness and curiosity. I wasn't quite sure how to go about it but for a start I stuck my spear in the ground and walked away from it, hoping this would signify that I came in peace.

Gradually they filtered back to stand at a discreet distance and watch my every move. I took a piece of bread from my pack and, breaking it up, threw it to the children who crawled forward on podgy bellies and ate it ravenously. Some women became less frightened and giggled nervously into their hands. Then one did a strange thing. She scooped up a lamb that had been running about their feet and cautiously came forward. When she reached the limit of her courage she threw the animal into my lap and dashed back. Not knowing what I was supposed to do with it I ruffled the soft ears as I would a dog and let it go back bleating to its mistress. This appeared to satisfy the women for they now came forward, laughing and chattering, their fears forgotten.

Inside the main *zariba* a number of black tents were scattered. Each was high enough to stand up in and all had quite big door openings. Also inside the big *zariba* there were two smaller ones, each surrounding empty areas. I decided one of these would make an ideal place to put up my tent. They all trooped in to surround me and watch amid a great deal of chatter. When I started to erect the poles, however, they suddenly caught on to what I was doing and their chatter changed to shouts of alarm. One, braver than the others, physically intervened by pulling out my guys and throwing the canvas in a heap. I took it now that I was not welcome to spend the night with them. Perhaps like the Arabs an infidel male was not allowed to share the harem or the married quarters. So I bundled up my kit and carried it all outside, pitched my tent hard up against their *zariba* and started to build my own one round to make a little enclosure. I was so thankful I had brought the panga to do this with.

Before I had finished, the men came in with the herds led by a huge camel with a wooden bell round its neck. The camels were put in one enclosure and the goats and sheep in the other. No wonder the women had not wanted me to put up my tent in there. While the women were making the dinner the men came round to see me and offer their *"Nabad"*s (greetings). They seemed friendly enough in an impassive, inscrutable manner, showing no surprise at my being there, as seemed to be the Somali way, but none offered to help build my zariba. I tried some Swahili with them and blissfully one replied. Now that I could communicate to some extent I did not feel such an outsider. Presently they went and I pulled the high bundle of thorny branches that was my gate to close the last gap in my surrounds, lit my fire then settled down to make my own meal.

Some time later, while I still sat at my camp fire, I was surprised to hear voices approach and at my 'gate' my interpreter's voice say, *"Hodi"*, (Swahili for "Anybody at home?" or "May I come in?"). I pulled aside the branches and they came in, three of them, my friend accompanied by another man and a shy woman. The other man was offering me his wife for the night. So much for my thinking a strange man would not be welcome in the harem! I don't know whether he was angry or hurt when I thanked him but declined the offer. Perhaps he was only concerned with being hospitable and then again he maybe saw his way of making a bit on the side, but if that was his intention, and I rather fancy it was, he would be disappointed for we never got round to trading. I had no way of knowing what the lady thought, she stayed in the shadow beyond the firelight waiting for her instructions. Anyway, we parted amicably. I gave them a tin of bully beef by way of thank you and they seemed to be quite happy as they went.

Next morning my Swahili speaking friend called me out quickly, pointing to paw marks all round the *zariba*, saying excitedly, *"Simba"* (lion). I was very pleased I had not been lazy in building my defences the previous night. He said lions often came round trying to get in for the goats.

I stayed on at the camp in order to get a better glimpse of the lives of these people and all that I saw was interesting. In the morning I watched while a two-inch thorn was extracted from a camel's hoof with a knife and the wound then sealed with dung. During the day the women pounded the *jawari* (corn) in a deep wooden bowl with long poles as I had seen done in Kenya, then ground it between two stones. They were extremely amused that anyone should be interested in their daily chores. One woman sat chewing strips of bark, which I later learned was of the *galol* tree, until they were supple enough to weave into the mats that form their tents and also their pack-saddles when they are on the move. I learned also that they extracted the fibres from the *hig*, a pointed aloe plant, by beating the long leaves between stones and twisting them, the fibres, into ropes. When I eventually left I had my waterbottle filled from what they called a *karura*, a bag made from plaited fibres of roots which was made watertight by fat rubbed on the inside. I wondered why they used this method instead of making bags of skin, or hide, which would be easier and, I thought, more efficient, but my Swahili interpreter had already gone with the camels so there was no one who could tell me, and even if he had been there I doubt if my Swahili at that time was up to unravelling such technical problems and waterbottles are indeed high technology.

Consider the problem: the cooler the water in a container is kept the better it is to drink, but even more important, the hotter the water becomes the more loss there is likely to be with evaporation. Plastic or metal containers are good for water retention provided they incorporate an adequate vapour-proof cork or screw top. The water in them can get terribly hot and is horrible to drink if you are thirsty but they don't vaporise and lose their contents. Now we come to the clever stuff that desert travellers discovered at the beginning of our species.

One way to keep water, or any liquid, cool is to allow it to evaporate. The more volatile the solvent the cooler it becomes when exposed to the atmosphere. When surgical spirit is dabbed on our arm it feels, and is, cold because the rapid evaporation causes the surface temperature to drop. Skin bags are porous and allow a continuous flow of water contents to seep to the outside and evaporate which keeps the surface relatively cool and thereby the contents also.

In going over these facts I have perhaps answered the question that prompted this dissertation. When travelling, skin bags would give a degree of coolness to the water, but in the shelter of the thick matted tents coolness was not a problem and water lost by evaporation was a waste. The *karura*, fatted and waterproof would retain its contents much better. No doubt the *karura* was for use in the home and skin bags were used for travelling. The wise modern desert travellers, apart from whatever water supplies they keep in metal or plastic containers in the back of their truck, will always keep a skin bag hanging on the wing-mirror, where the flow of air and the steady evaporation ensures they always have cool water to drink. The ancient camel-men learned this a long, long time ago.

I left the nomad camp in good spirits and felt I had learned a lot about the people and their way of life in the few days I had been with them. The walk back to Hargeisa passed without incident. I saw quite a bit of wild life but nothing to bother me much.

Passing the DLS quarters I looked in to see if they had heard anything from Nairobi. A few eyes were raised at my rough, unshaven appearance, rucksack on my back, spear in my hand and panga in its scabbard hanging from my belt. Some "Oh god"s, were muttered when I said I'd been out in the bush for some time. I wondered at the tone of their reception and later I was to learn why. "Yes," a reply had been received and "yes," I had been offered a job, but only if

I signed a contract for a minimum of one year. I wasn't prepared to stay that long so I declined the offer and asked that my thanks for the time and effort spent on my behalf be passed to those involved, particularly the Brigadier who was not available at the time.

I received a much warmer welcome at the Somaliland Scouts camp. All were eager to hear of the adventure, especially one who obviously lived in awe of his surroundings and said he had not expected to ever see me again. The Officer-in-Charge gave me a friendly "Hello" and asked how things had gone on my trip. He listened with interest to my brief resume', then, reminiscent of the DLS reaction, grimaced and said the 'Old Man' wanted to see me. He had left word that I must report to him immediately I returned, *if* I returned. His tone, the officer said, had not been friendly. I had the feeling he was making an understatement, a point that was confirmed to me within the next few minutes.

The 'Old Man' was the Police Commissioner Jack Leslie, and he was decidedly not pleased when I entered his office.

"What do you mean by wandering out there on your own?" he blazed at first sight.

"I thought I'd do something more interesting than hanging around while the DLS considered my application for a job," I answered.

"Do you know I've had a dozen police with a European officer out looking for you. Only a damned fool would go out there alone and unarmed."

"But I was armed," I said. His eyebrows lifted. "I had a spear and a panga." Was that the semblance of a grin on his stern face?

"And there was all that bother when you were put inside down at Werdair, with cables flying like confetti between Harrar, London and here on your behalf. Well, it won't happen again. Until you go you are confined to the town area. If you break this order you will be repatriated to the UK at your own expense. Do you understand?"

"Yes, I understand. If it makes any difference, I'm sorry I've been a nuisance." I stood up and turned to go.

"One last thing, lad," said a different voice. I turned back and there was another man sitting there, a smiling, friendly one. "Did you enjoy your jaunt?" I too suddenly relaxed, the ordeal over.

"It was grand, sir. Really interesting."

"Tell me about it." He sounded genuinely interested. Was this really the same man who a minute before had been bringing down the wrath of Whitehall on me? I gave him a brief sketch of my outing and he even smiled when I recounted my offer of a wife for the night.

"Good man," he dismissed me with a friendly grin when I'd finished, "See Major Fry, I think he has something for you."

Chapter Six

ONE HUNDRED AND ONE NIGHTS

25th January 1951 – On Board an Arab Dhow
There is a Sindbad atmosphere about. It's fascinating to listen to the creaks of the great blocks and rigging and watch the huge lateen sail, full of trade wind, billow out against the moonlit sky and hear the guttural voices talking low all around.

"How would you like to travel by dhow to Zanzibar?" asked Major Fry, his eyes sparkling as if it were he who was adventuring. Being a poor sailor the thought of a voyage on one of those wobbling matchboxes made me heave. But apparently Fry did not notice my change of colour as he swept on, "Terrific journey. Takes around forty days and you'll probably have dysentery, smallpox and typhus all at the same time. But think of it … you'd be travelling the same way as old Sindbad the Sailor. Dhow sailing is one of the few things left unaltered by modern society. I don't know, but you would perhaps be the first white man to do that particular route by dhow. What say you? Do you fancy it?" He had sold me it.

"Thought you would," he went on enthusiastically. "Kind of thing I'd like to do myself. These dhows come from the Persian Gulf, from Basra, Oman and Muscat. They come when the wind from the north-east blows in a southerly direction starting about October and takes them down. It brings the monsoon. The Arabs call this wind the *kazkazi*. The dhows go to India or visit Aden, Berbera and all the little places down the coast to Mombasa and Zanzibar. They hole-up there for a time, careen the keel and do any repairs necessary in harbour when the tide is out, while waiting for the time when the wind does a complete about-face and swings round to blow north from the south-west. This wind blowing in a northerly direction is called the *kuzi* (pronounced 'coozy'). These two winds blowing six months south and six months north have carried the commercial sea traffic in these parts for thousands of years and of course are referred to as the Trade Winds.

"The *kazkazi* finishes in April and we may be too late to catch it. It's about the end of the season for them leaving these parts. It wouldn't do if they only got down three-quarters way and the wind turned and brought them back again. Hold on and I'll get on the blower to Berbera and see if there's anything in harbour going that way."

He came back excited. There was indeed a dhow in Berbera harbour bound for Zanzibar and due to sail in a few days. The police at Berbera had arranged with the captain that I might travel on it and Major Fry organised a lift for me on a truck down to the coast that evening. I thanked the Major for his excellent service and assured him that henceforth I would forget Cooks and do all my travel arrangements through the Somaliland Police.

Things were going well. Too well, in fact. I was on the truck heading into the night and the coast when I discovered my camera had been stolen from my rucksack while it was lying in the police station where, ironically, I had left it for safe keeping. This loss was devastating and all the moreso when I realised I would not be able to record anything of the fabulous Arabian Nights voyage I was going on.

At least this latter disappointment was solved when I arrived in Berbera and discovered the dhow captain, a little shifty-eyed rascal in a grey *galabea* about whom I instantly thought I'd have to be constantly on the alert lest he slit my throat in the night, had changed his mind about taking me. No amount of cajoling on the part of the Customs Officer, who acted as interpreter, would make him reverse his decision. Since yesterday when he agreed to take me, said the Officer, he had obviously picked up some contraband or received a commission to pick up an illicit cargo at some secluded port or beach, and didn't want a European on board who would be a witness.

There remained nothing else to do but to head back to Aden from where I would have a better chance of picking up a ship going south. My Arabian Nights escapade was partially retrieved when the Customs Officer persuaded an Omani dhow captain who was due to go to Aden in a few days to take me with him.

I now had the problem of where to stay until the dhow sailed. Camping in town was out of the question because of thieves so I decided to look up Doctor Charles who had been so overwhelming in his insistence that I must not pass his door if ever I should return to this town. And so it was that I met the other side of Dr Charles, the Mr Hyde of Dr Jekyll.

When I knocked on his door the house boy smiled warmly in recognition and went to tell his master of my return. He took a long time to come back and when he did it seemed he had been given an unusual brief about which he felt uncomfortable for his face was pained as he showed me into the bathroom downstairs, a bleak place comprising a large concrete bath and cement floor, and told me to wait. I thought it strange and wondered what order or instruction the doctor had given him. But I waited, and waited. Hours went by and no word came. In the evening I ate the piece of bread I carried with some water and unrolled my sleeping bag on the floor to sleep.

Next day there was still no welcome from the doctor. I was in the awful dilemma of not wanting to appear boorish or grasping by knocking him up and asking what all this was about and at the same time being reluctant to offend him by leaving without saying anything.

Some time after midday I went to swim at the little open air pool that was reserved for white people and there, lying sunbathing at the side of the pool was Dr Charles. I said hello and felt suddenly strange in his presence. He looked at me, through me, with cold, completely unemotional eyes and never said a word.

I swam a few lengths in the most uncomfortable bewilderment and dried myself within a few feet of my 'host'. Still he said not a word so I walked back to his house, collected my kit and left.

It took me well over thirty years and a chance meeting to have some possible light shed on Dr Charles' strange behaviour. In 1987 while in Accra, Ghana – my first visit back to Africa since my wandering days – as a representative of the British Counsel overseeing the transfer of craft examinations from the London City and Guilds Institute to a Ghanaian intercollegiate body, I sat beside a man one evening at a Consulate dinner and in conversation we found we had both been to British Somaliland about the same era, he a little later than I. We reminisced of places and people with whom we found we had mutual acquaintance.

"You knew John Fry! … well, well, it's a small world," my companion mused thoughtfully. "I took over John's house when he went home." In the course of our chat I mentioned Dr Charles and his strange behaviour.

"Ah, there we had a strange one," my informant inhaled loudly through his teeth by way of emphasising an incredible incident. He then described the possible shady side of Dr Charles.

"He was an odd bod all right, that one. Although he was German or something he always took his leave in the UK and he always made sure that the ship he went on never touched any European ports. We all used to wonder at that, but nobody knew why. Well, some years later, when I was back in the UK, I heard that someone had accused him of being a Nazi doctor in one of the concentration camps during the war. He sued this guy and won, it appeared. But the Judge awarded Charles only one penny compensation and ruled that he must personally bear the full cost of the trial which ran into thousands of pounds. It broke Charles and he died within the year."

My surprise at gleaning this information from such a chance meeting was equalled when I read in *The Times* newspaper, Nov. 6th 1996, an appendage to a report on the court case of the former Irish Prime Minister, Albert Reynolds, who had been awarded one penny for libel damages but had to pay the total cost of the litigation, estimated at more than £1 million. Among the listing of several similar cases in the past was the following report:

In 1964 a Dr Dering complained about a book, Exodus, suggesting he had performed 17,000 'experiments' without anaesthetics at Auschwitz. Counsel for the book's publishers said that if Dr Dering had no reputation requiring compensation, adequate payment might be the 'smallest coin of the realm, not a farthing but a halfpenny.' The jury agreed.

I wrote to both *The Times* and the Foreign Office to corroborate my theory and although neither would confirm nor deny the link, from the evidence I believed that Dr Charles, the man whose house I shared, and Dr Wladyslaw Dehring (the spelling changed on *The Times*' reply) were one and the same person.

In a final attempt to try and clear up the mystery I again contacted the Foreign and Commonwealth Office and while nobody there would or could cast any light on the subject I was given the name and address of Brigadier Malcolm Page, President of the Anglo-Somali Society. When I telephoned and put my question to him Brigadier Page immediately settled the issue. "Oh no, Dr Dehring and Dr Charles were different people. They both spoke German, but their accents were different. While Charles was at Berbera, Dehring was at Barao," a town further to the east, "where I was stationed. I knew Dehring well, I was at his wedding in Barao. He claimed that his wife was a refugee from the concentration camp, but we all suspected that she had been a wardress or something.

"They were two quite different characters, Charles and Dehring," Brigadier Page went on. "While Charles always made attempts to be sociable, Dehring was always morose and distant. It is true he died soon after his court case but Charles' death had nothing to do with litigation. Indeed," Page added with a chuckle, "now that you have brought it all back, I could tell you whose bed he died in." He then went on to tell a little anecdote that could be a cameo of life in the colonies for some of the few whites who lived there.

It appeared that Charles, when visiting a couple in their home, had imbibed too well and took it upon himself to undress and tuck himself up in the marital bed. The husband soon followed suit. When the wife wanted to retire and could not rouse either of the men she said when recounting the incident, "There being nothing else for it I put on three pairs of knickers and climbed in on the other side of Charles, so that he lay between us" Whether it was the surprise or the struggle that was too much for Charles he was dead in the morning.

So the mystery of Charles was cleared up. But I still believe that the doctor had a dark secret past which he tried to cover up with his frothy, social behaviour. I witnessed the two extremes of his dual personality and would say that in the wrong situation the icy one, no doubt the real one, could be frightening. With two others from the concentration camps living so near and Charles' own background in question and his desperate efforts not to set foot in Europe, is it not likely that the two doctors came together with the wardress from Nazi Germany at the end of the war in the hope of losing themselves in that remote corner of Africa? The coincidence of them arriving there separately with no previous knowledge of each other or tryst is too much to accept. In conclusion of this episode I may add I have not quoted Charles' adopted surname for obvious reasons.

On leaving Dr Charles house I headed into town to see where I could put up. On the way I met Fred Parfitt, the Public Works Department officer, and on hearing of my plight he invited me to dinner and a shakedown on his verandah. Dinner was more than two hours away and we passed the time in small-talk and nibbled nuts and things. I hadn't eaten in two days except for the piece of bread yesterday and it was difficult to be casual and handle the situation with decorum. Fred asked me how I had fared, foodwise, and I mentioned vaguely that I'd managed with something out of a tin, not liking to say I was absolutely famished and couldn't wait to sit down to eat. When the time did come and the boy brought in the steaming tray it was tantalising to eat as if this was just another meal and not wolf it down before Fred had lifted his knife and fork.

Next day I went along to the dhow and asked the captain if I could board even though it was not leaving until the following morning. The captain, a high caste Arab with fine features and aristocratic manners, welcomed me with a double handshake, in which he gripped my palm and then my thumb, before showing me to one of the four bunks on board, indicating that this would be my berth for the voyage. One of the senior members of the crew had obviously been made to give it up. I felt extremely grateful for this hospitality but looking at it I had qualms.

The bunk, like the others, consisted of a wooden frame strung with criss-cross ropes as a hammock and was suspended more than halfway out over the end of the high poop deck. Through the strings was nothing but space and far below the sea. There were no supports, no stays, nothing to stop me rolling over the side in my sleep or when the boat tilted with heavy waves. I wished they hadn't been so kind, the solid deck looked a lot more appealing. Nevertheless I accepted it gracefully, I hoped, but my look of apprehension must have been obvious for the bo'sun fixed two ropes from the outside edge of the frame across to the shrouds to inspire me with some confidence. It did, but only just.

Every member of the crew from Sala Sa'id, the captain, to the lowest deckhand made me feel welcome. I had difficulty doing anything for myself, everyone was so eager to help, to please. As I walked about the deck I was salaamed continuously until I thought I was interfering with the running of the boat, and when I sat up on the poop beside my bunk I was promptly plied with tea and coffee. How I wished then it was for Zanzibar we were heading for rather than Aden.

Sala Sa'id was a fine man, noble in features, quiet yet commanding in manner, taciturn yet not forbidding for he liked a joke. I took to him immediately and grew to like him more during the course of the voyage. As an east coast seaman he spoke fluent Kiswahili, so even with my limited up-country dialect we were able to converse to some extent.

When he went off with the manifest to the shipping office that day he was a resplendent figure. With strong face, flashing dark eye, trimmed black beard, corded headdress, ankle-length white tunic and black cummerbund into which was stuck the obligatory magnificent rhinohorn handled knife in silver sheath that was curved to an almost complete U shape, he looked the epitome of the dashing, theatrical Red Shadow. I could well see how women might swoon to be kidnapped by him.

I felt quite excited next morning when, the last of the cargo loaded, the clutch of raggle-taggle passengers settled in a huddle up by the prow, we slipped the mooring and drifted into the current and down to the sea where the long boom was hauled up, the great white lateen sail billowed and we sailed into a scene that had hardly changed since Scheherazade told her one-thousand-and-one stories to King Shahyrar, one story each night, to save herself from being beheaded in the morning as had happened to all his previous night lovers: stories of wonder, of Caliphs and cobblers, hunchbacks and harems, of jinnies and magic, of Aladdin and Sindbad, until in the end, after all her stories and three children to the King, she wins his love and her reprieve. But the magic she created lived on and spanned the years so that now I too was going on a voyage of adventure: perhaps, like Sindbad, I would meet the great Rokh bird, so big its wings darkened the sky and it fed its young on elephants. Maybe I too could tie myself to its leg and be flown to the Valley of Diamonds and discover the fabled Elephants' Graveyard.

Once at sea there was little for the crew to do. Washing and cleaning did not seem important, so apart from manhandling the sail and a few odd jobs of rope mending and the like they passed the time lying about in talkative groups while being served tea continually by the galley boy, a likeable ragamuffin with tricky, flashing eyes, who smelt of wood smoke and was as dirty as the big kettle he required two hands to carry about. Tea was drunk black and very sweet and was served in little cups without handles. I had it as often as I wished.

The galley was an open fire on a large flat stone or sometimes on a steel drum, an innovation to Sindbad's day. A kind of bread, '*Makarti ya Mova*', as told to me in Swahili, was made by sticking the dough round the inside of an Ali Baba stone jar and baking it on the fire. Sindbad would have known that one for sure.

The meal was served on an enormous platter round which all the men squatted and dug in with their hand, rolling the handful deftly into a ball before putting it, into their mouth. It was always the right hand they used. Woe betide anyone who reached in with his left. That is his dirty one, the one used for his ablutions, which gives rise to the saying, "There are no left-handers in Arabia and, nearer to home why left-handed people may be referred to as 'cack-handed'."

107

The food consisted mainly of a 'doughy stuff', as I referred to it in my diary, or rice, strongly flavoured with chillies and curry which I did not care for at the time, but I was fast learning to lose any fads and ate it heartily. The captain and myself were served on plates by ourselves, but he still ate with his hand while I used a spoon or fork.

The meal over and the group broken up, coffee was served from a great kettle to the men as they lay about the deck. It was coffee with a difference, being very strongly flavoured with ginger, so strong it seared my throat like vitriol and I tried hard not to show my dislike. But the boy noticed and afterwards served me tea.

Following the coffee came the hookah which the galleyboy lit with a live coal from the fire. When it was going fine most men took a few puffs and passed it on. The smoke, drawn through the water bowl, made that lovely hubble-bubble sound which gives it the onomatopoeic name by which the hookah is better known. This was one experience I did pass over, but I enjoyed watching. Some men preferred to make their own cigarettes which were more like cigars, being whole tobacco leafs rolled into a paper covering. I was told they bought the tobacco in Makulla, but I suspected it had more to do with hashish than orthodox tobacco.

There was only one aspect of the life of the dhow seamen which I did not enjoy sharing. The latrine. This was a wooden box, just big enough to squat in and in that position it barely came to your shoulders. You would have thought such a contraption would have been situated on the poop deck, but I was glad it was not, otherwise it would have been right by my bunk. As it was, there were two of them, one each port and starboard, slung over the sides of the ship on ropes and you had to clamber over to get into it. There were no steps to assist. You climbed over like a man or, as the women passengers did, you sat on the gunwale and swung your legs over and dropped in. Suspended over the side it didn't feel all that safe. But that was the least of your worries. The real trouble came with the performance. The hole in the floor of the box was little more than six inches wide and sometimes when the ship was rolling that ejectory was up near forty-five degrees and your head was down where your ankles should be. The laws of gravity took no heed of the laws of nature and such a situation was a recipe for disaster, not to mention an awful mess, literally. Like shooting at a moving object when you aim just ahead of your target, one had to learn to synchronise ones motions with the motion of the ship and shoot just as the hole was coming up or down to level, allowing just enough time from 'bombs away' to achieving the perpendicular. Try doing that when squatting with your head between your knees and one moment you are lying on your back and holding on like grim death to the sides of the box, and with the next roll of the boat you are ace-over-apex with your backside aiming at the sky. Trouble came at night, though, when the sea below was dark and the hole invisible. I had quite a few visits before I finally emerged with clean feet or whatever. But one learns fast in such a situation and soon, even at night with no ocular assistance, driving purely by the seat-of-one's-pants, one might say, one found one could hit the target from all angles no matter what kind of sea might be running at the time. I might say there was a bucket on a rope for lowering to the sea in case of accidents and for the normal washing.

My most precious moments of all of the voyage, those that linger still with me like a dream, were of that blissful time at the end of an interesting day and before going to sleep. Even now as I write I lie in my string bed with nothing between me and the sea, watching the stars roll back and forth through the rigging, see the great, fat-bellied lateen sail billowed out ghostly white in the pale moonlight. That vast, triangular sheet hung on its long yard at forty-five degrees from the top of the mast, the style that has not changed since the time of the Phoenicians, those wonderful sailors who dominated the sea trade before the days of Ancient Greece.

I lie listening to the sighing wind, the lapping of the water, the creaks and groans of mast and timbers, of blocks and rudder and ropes and canvas, I hear the discordant – to my ears – song the Arab quartermaster hums in a high falsetto voice as he spins the great wheel this way and that as we sail into the Arabian night. The wheel is an innovation to Sindbad's day. Then they would have had a tiller. But in all other respects we are as it always was, wind and sail, riding the tradewind.

It is generally accepted that the greatest invention of mankind was the wheel. Yet, there are those who would say that even more important was the invention of the keel. Before the keel arrived, ships could only go where wind and current would take them. Trade between countries divided by sea could only be conducted when the 'tradewinds' prevailed. Ships could cross the winds to some extent, but no vessel could beat against them without a keel. With the coming of keels, ships could tack against the wind, go where they liked, when they liked. The world was suddenly opened up.

Our dhow was a slave to the wind, going only where the sighing puppeteer would permit and I revelled in the confinement, imagining myself sailing into A-Thousand-and-One-Nights. As it turned out I didn't manage just that number and had to settle for something more like One-Hundred-and-One-Arabian-Nights.

We arrived at Aden at night and had to wait until next day for Besse's, the shipping company's, tug to tow us up to Maala. Here I ran into trouble again with my old adversary, the Immigration Authorities. When I had left Aden carrying my £100 landing deposit in cash I had tended to use that money rather than cash Travellers' Cheques, which would have been difficult to do anyway. On arrival I was again refused admission because I was short of the required amount to lay down, and I would need an armed guard to take me to the Bank and this was Saturday when none would be open. I argued some but was getting nowhere when at the height of the altercation Sala Sa'id stepped forward and, without a word, laid down the necessary amount of rupees on top of my pile. I protested. It would be Monday before I could repay him and he could be gone by that time. But he held up his hand for me to stop, and just smiled.

On Monday I hurried back to repay my debt. He was not there, though his dhow was still tied up. I left the money with something extra as a thank you with Besse's Indian clerk and returned next day to make sure he had got it. He was gone with his ship and he had received it, the clerk said. But he had taken only what was owed and returned my dash, which the Indian gave back to me. He was a fine man. They don't come any better than Sala Sa'id.

*

Returning to Aden was like coming home. On arrival at the gate of Sheba camp I was given permission to return to my old billet and was heartily welcomed by officers and other ranks alike, all wanting to know how I had faired and why had I come back. I got my painting job back with the NAAFI but only at the same pay as before. I needed money to buy a camera and my boots and watch required mending. It all seemed so cosy and secure being back in the familiar groove, surrounded by friendly people. When I walked down the Crescent traders recognised me even in shorts and shouted greetings or murmured, "Scotch", as I passed. Fishermen, walking up from the sea, clad only in loin cloths, with clusters of gaudy coloured fish dangling from the paddles they carried over their shoulders, paddles that looked like table-tennis bats with ridiculous long handles, acknowledged me, with lift of their eyes or by word.

I had only worked a few days with the NAAFI when I met Mr Scott of the Motherwell Bridge Company which had joined locally with a Middle East company to form the Anglo-Lebanese Building Company. On hearing I was in the market for a temporary job Scott put me onto his partner, a Mr Jabran from Beirut, who offered me a job in general building at the top Arab rate of £40 per month. This was roughly twice as much as I had been earning back in Scotland. Jabran's offer was a fortune to me and I promptly gave up my job with the NAAFI and started poste-haste at my new one.

I was given charge of a site where local artisans were building low-cost houses. The previous Arab foreman had just been sacked and it appeared I had come along at the right moment. The work consisted of shuttering according to the plans, filling the void between the shuttering with cement rubble to form the walls, plastering and painting, running cement floors and hanging rough doors and window-shutters, no glass. I didn't know much about the work, but neither did the raggle-taggle, so-called builders, so we got on fine. When I started I spent the first couple of hours walking about just looking, feeling a bit unsure of myself and finding my feet. The workers must have thought I was only an observer with little to do with them, or perhaps I was a spy for the big bosses looking to see who would make the next foreman. They had never had a white man working at this level before and never thought for a moment that I was that person. With the thought in mind of lifting themselves out of the ruck and into the prestigious position of foreman there were those who thought that if they shouted the loudest and bullied the others they might get the vacant job. Whatever the reason, everything was done with the maximum of noise and the minimum of production, all telling each other what to do and nobody doing very much.

I had written down a couple of pages of colloquial Arabic words, commands and instructions which I thought I might need, all written phonetically so I should get the pronunciation as near right as I could. Armed with this I called a halt to the work and had them come round, whereupon I introduced myself and split them into separate groups, cement mixers, fixers, fillers, all linked with a moving chain of wheelbarrows carting the concrete. All went along fine. Where there had been useless, non-productive shouting and bullying there was now order and even singing as they went at their work with a will. When Mr Jabran visited the site he commented on the increased speed and improved quality of the work.

After a week or two a more prestigious job was about to start. The Anglo Iranian Oil Company's Aden headquarters building, a grand four-storey affair, was to have a face-lift and I was taken off the building site and put in charge of this job. This work was beyond the local artisans' skills and a special gang of workers was flown in from Lebanon. Although they were Arabs these men were as different to the local brand as wine is to water. They regarded the locals with contempt and derided their language as foreign although the difference could only have been dialectal for they understood each other. These people seemed much more developed and certainly regarded themselves as superior. I could see in them the likelihood of their having streetlights when we were still in our goatskins which I found hard to believe of the Adenese types.

During the first few weeks of my working for the construction company I continued to stay at Sheba camp. There came a day, however, when a new, keen, young officer wanted to put me on a charge because I was not wearing a cap and I did not salute him. He told me to stand to attention and when I did not and merely smiled at him as I found the situation amusing he was rather nonplussed. I thought it would all be cleared up when the matter was taken to the office where I was known, but I was wrong. To save his face the officer had to be backed up and when it was learned that I no longer worked for the NAAFI I was asked to leave the camp and find accommodation elsewhere.

I took the matter to Jabran and he said without hesitation that I could move into the Marina Hotel, second only to the 'Crescent', at the Company's expense. I said I would rather move in with the Lebanese workers. I had come to like them and thought I'd get to know them and their ways better by living with them.

"The Pakistan Hotel?" Jabran exclaimed in horror, "You can't go there."

"Why not?" I asked, thinking there was some ban on the place for the likes of me. It couldn't be on religious grounds for I knew at least one of the Lebanese was a Christian.

"European people, white people, cannot stay at the Pakistan. It isn't nice." But when I insisted he agreed and I moved in.

Situated deep into the native area, well away from 'white' haunts, the Pakistan Hotel was 'not nice' but I never regretted my choice. We were six to a room with barely enough space between the beds to put down my kit. At night the air was fetid and the room alive with snores and grunts and muttering. It seemed the Muslims went through their prayers even in their sleep. The lavatory was a squat hole in a cubicle and the 'bathroom' was a long tiled sink set low enough on the wall of a passageway to allow feet to be washed. The three taps hung loosely from the wall some two feet higher. You shaved and washed or flannel bathed in the trickle of running water and you had to bend sort of sideways otherwise your backside stopped people who were continually passing.

There was no menu, no variety. The meal was the same every day … curry and rice. Perhaps the meat rung the changes between goat, sheep or chicken, but it was hard to tell, the curry was so strong. My taste for it grew from dislike – a dislike tempered by the days on the dhow – to liking it very much and I relished the thought of it at the end of a long day on the site. We sat at one long table and the meals were times for loud and lively conversation that often seemed more like arguments than amicable discussion. Gradually as the days went by the machine-gun rattle of the guttural sound – a sound made much deeper in the throat than the Scots' 'ch' as in 'loch', and hard r's that all seemed to run into one long 'gurr', began to separate itself into words and sentences.

I am not good at languages. Anyone with a natural bent would have been speaking fluent Arabic in no time living in those conditions. I need a lot of time to assimilate and absorb foreign conversation. Nevertheless I remember well the first time I told the group in halting Arabic of an experience I had, a tale that was acknowledged with favourable exclamations and head nodding, not for the story but for the telling of it.

It happened one weekend when we were not working. I was alone on the balcony, reading. Yusif and Abrihim were sleeping on their beds. Most of the men had gone on their weekly visit to the brothels up at Sheik Othman, sordid places that had given me the creeps when the girls sitting outside each shack laughed and called lascivious invitations to me as I walked past them on my early visits to the caravanserai. The balcony was on the first floor, overlooking the street which was solid with strolling men and a few shrouded women hurrying with great bundles on their heads. Squawking hens scampered in and out of the shuffling feet and goats and sheep ran through the throng like wild dogs. Little boys rattled handfuls of cups and shouted "Chai" in shrill voices.

Down below, on either side of the hotel were two cafes, dirty places with smoke blackened wooden chairs and tables where locals and men from the hills and desert sprawled leisurely and sipped their coffees or smoked hookahs. The cafes vied with each other for supremacy of noise from their gramophones, each with a great horn, that played loud, warbling Arabic and Indian music and songs.

Over the weeks I came to recognise the differences in the people: the light-skinned Yemeni from the hills, the darker, hawk-nosed Bedouin from the Hadramaut and the polyglot local Adenese.

This day as I sat on the balcony I propped my feet up on the balustraded rail and was absorbed in my book. Gradually I was aware of the noise of the street crowd growing in tempo but didn't bother too much about it. The noise continued to rise and now it was all too plain that the centre of the disturbance was directly below me. Just when I was thinking of seeing what it was all about but before I moved to do so, a stone came hurtling up and thudded off the wall behind me. I was definitely the target. Then another and another came even after I stood up and looked down at the angry crowd. Faces contorted with rage were turned up to me, terrible obscenities were shouted at me, fists were shaking and more stones came whistling up.

I retreated into the house and the trouble subsided, the crowd dispersed. I wondered what I had done to incur such wrath. Yusif, who spoke a little English, had been awakened by the noise and came through from the bedroom. When I told him what had happened he smiled and told me that it was my feet up on the rail that had been the trouble. Apparently, showing the soles of your feet to an Arab is one of the worst insults you can pay him, like putting your tongue out or putting your fingers to your nose at someone, but much, much worse. It seemed that I had been insulting everyone in the street. This was the tale I told in, no doubt, terrible Arabic to the others when they returned. Bad though it was, they all understood it and it marked a watershed in our relationship for they now took heed of me in their conversations knowing that I could now eavesdrop to some extent.

Indeed, once I was emboldened to break into a conversation and found I had stepped into a veritable vipers' nest. Aboica was telling someone that his wife could not conceive. He dearly wanted a son but so far she had not even produced a daughter. I broke in to ask if he had considered having fertility tests done by a doctor. Aboica, a rather stout, balding, heavy-featured man, stopped in mid sentence and stare at me pop-eyed with vehemence. I thought he was going to have apoplexy, that he was going to strangle himself or me on the spot. Then he let rip with a salvo of artillery fire, so far removed from the machine-gun rattle of general conversation that it stopped all other speech round the table.

I only got the gist of what he said but it was enough to sear the skin: something to do with his threat to kill any man, doctor or no, who would dare to look at his wife's private parts and anyone who dared to suggest such a thing … and there I was lost, luckily, I think. I thought afterwards that it was a good job he had not inferred from my remark that I might be suggesting that he too should be tested to see if he was capable of fathering a child. Had he done so that would certainly have been a strangulation job.

They were an interesting lot. Drawn from every section of Lebanon's divers people they were all so different, yet in the hotel and at work they were one homogeneous group who worked and argued and laughed together. It is hard to believe that their children would split into fundamental groups to bomb and machine-gun each other in wars that have torn apart their country, once the gem and commercial centre of the Middle East. I grew to like every one, but some I liked more than others.

There was Antoun, the Armenian, short, stocky a round, rubbery, grizzled face who nobody could dislike. With wry smile and twinkling eye he would curse anybody without their taking the slightest offence. He used to beat the drum when Aboica demonstrated his dancing skills. Aboica, the dancer, the singer, the dandy who loved to strut about in his riding breeches and shining knee-high boots and Arab headgear. At other times, such as when on a night we walked along the street to our favourite coffee house, he would swagger in his baggy Baghdad pantaloons, the ones that were so loose the crotch was down by his knees and the backside hung like an empty sack at his ankles. Sometimes he would put a stick attached to his waist down in the empty sack so that it swung like a pendulum as he walked, oh so proudly, for all to see and express their adulation.

Then there was Ami (Uncle) Ali, a thin, stringy man who looked much older than his years, hence his title, who always wore a pork-pie hat and whose brown, leathery, lugubrious face was known to crease into a smile sometimes. And Mohammad, quiet, with a ready smile, who liked to sit and watch. And Abrihim, the devout Muslim who prayed five times a day and was the best living man of them all. And Bishara, the Christian, the most Westernised, who spoke good English but went to such lengths to get his grammar right he was usually incomprehensible.

There were others who didn't feature in my diary and who don't come to mind. But I must not forget Yusif whom I liked best of all. Yusif the strong man who could lift the teenage site *chai* boy horizontal above his head at full arms stretch, yet who was so gentle in his ways. Yusif, who always remembered to do the little things that meant so much but did not occur to others. Yusif, of the deep feeling and tact, I hope you and your family have survived the hell that descended on your land.

As I write they all come to life and I see them so clearly. I see too the place and smell the smells. I live again the nightly walk along the street with Aboica always out in front, strutting splay-footed, vain as a peacock. The street at night is a magical place. Some booths are lit by naked acetylene flares that hiss as we pass, the white intense lights cast dramatic shadows that create the illusion of mystery and romance, the pungent carbide smell mingles with the rich, heavy, cloying aroma of the sweetmeats laid out for sale, some wrapped in leaves but most displayed on open trays, gaudy coloured and sticky.

The street is crowded with men, no women go out at night, but you can walk at ease. No one is in a hurry for this is promenade time. Some, like Aboica, wear their best finery such as the striped pyjama suits or gay, embroidered waistcoats which they wear with great pride, all in contrast to the ragged beggars who drag themselves on terrible misshapen limbs among the strolling feet and call pitifully for alms. Those belong to the professional beggar families who break the limbs of their children at birth to cripple and deform them in order to curry sympathy.

*

At the Anglo-Iranian office site work went along busily and, like all regular jobs after a time, rather mundanely so any source of amusement, provided it did not interfere with the running of the work, was greatly appreciated. One such incident was provided by one of the Lebanese fellows. Small, square with heavy jowls that always carried what would nowadays be termed 'designer stubble', he habitually wore a cloth round his head and tied at the back like a pirate. I mentioned this to him and he surprised me by asking with glee, "Like Tyrone Power?" I agreed he was like the famous film star and from then on he was "Tyrone", a title with which he was enormously pleased.

One day Tyrone bought a little monkey with large, intelligent eyes whose name was Sara (as Saa'ra) from a local trader and brought it to the site with him. I was amazed how quickly he took to his new master. He followed him everywhere at first but as he got bolder he scampered all over the scaffold, returning every now and again to hug Tyrone's ankle to let him know he hadn't forgotten him. Bolder still, Sara got into all sorts of minor mischiefs. One day he eyed the skipping rope of the daughter of Mr Lawson, the manager of the offices. With total disrespect for ladies Sara promptly scooted over and began a tug-o'-war and the wee girl didn't know whether to laugh or cry.

I lectured Sara daily saying that if he was going to stay on the site he was going to have to do some work, perhaps carry a bucket of cement or something, at which he would look downcast then up at me with his big, liquid pools before scampering off to hug Tyrone's leg and look over his shoulder at me as if I were a great ogre. But then we'd make up when I produced a sweet or piece of chocolate which I bought specially for him.

Apart from the Lebanese tradesmen there was quite a large force of local coolies who did the labouring. My head coolie was Abdul who taught me many Arabic words but could never quite master the English ones he continually asked of me. Though corrected until I gave up, his standard reply to any instruction or order I gave him was, "Jolly jood, Sahib."

The work on the site was not long started when I realised that I could not teach the Lebanese fellows anything about their work but I earned my keep and their respect, I think, by streamlining their methods and ensuring there were no hiccups in the supply of materials. Jabran was pleased to see the orderly site and how things were going. But there must have been something wrong with his estimate, for though work was progressing faster than normal it became evident a few weeks from the penalty clause deadline that we were not going to make it.

It was then that I came into my own and earned Jabran's gratitude. I suggested we start earlier in the morning and work weekends and that he offer a bonus to the men if we finished on time, all of which he agreed to. So all next month we worked every day and I hurried the men along as much I dared. Moreover, I designed a suspended scaffold of ropes and working platform, or 'boat', that hung over the side of the building and could be raised and lowered and could be gradually moved sideways. For this we had to remove a row of tiles from the cantilevered projection that formed the coping of the surrounding parapet to the roof to allow the ropes to fall through. None of the men had seen anything like it before and although rather a Heath Robinson affair they marvelled at it. Anyway, it worked and allowed the work to go on much faster than with the constant erection of the rough pole scaffolding that had hitherto been used.

We worked hard that month and finished the job three days before the deadline. Jabran was ecstatic. Apart from saving the fine, his reputation had been at stake. In the euphoria of the moment I think I could have asked for the moon. He offered me all kinds of inducements to make my position permanent but I settled for three days' holiday and savoured every minute of it. After those weeks starting at 5 a.m. it was wonderful to lie in and take a leisurely breakfast.

I also had time to make plans. I had earned enough to make my feet itchy again. I had bought a new camera, a better one than that stolen in Hargiesa, and my boots and watch were long since mended. It was time to move on. I used this time to go round the shipping agents to see if they had anything going to

Mombasa, having decided I had to go round the problem areas of the Somalias and Ethiopia. I asked at each office about working my passage, believing that it was the way I should travel rather than going like an ordinary tourist, but each time the clerk just shook his head.

Lastly I marched into the Hollow Shipping Company. The Indian clerk greeted me.

"Good morning, sir. Can I help you?" I asked if they had a ship going to Mombasa soon.

"Most certainly, sir," he answered with great enthusiasm. "We have very fine ship going in one week. 1st Class, sir?" he asked, already taking up his pen.

"No," I replied.

"Oh!" His brows lowered in quandary. "We have only 1st and 2nd Class sir," he added with much of the courtesy gone from his voice.

"I don't want any class," I said, "I want a job on the ship in lieu of the passage money."

"A job!" he exclaimed, the smile returning, but now it was a wry one as if he was joining in a joke. "But these ships all have only Laskar, Arab, crew." I had lost my knighthood.

"What of it. Am I not good enough?" I asked.

"But no, but yes you are," he was confused, "I mean yes indeed, plainly. But you would not like to work beside these people."

I was suffering for being white. Forty years on I could have had him for racism. I asked to see his boss who invited me into his office after the perplexed clerk had gone to tell him. Another Indian, fatter and more prosperous and ponderously heavy with the importance of his position. He thought the same as his clerk but was more suave, more diplomatic in dealing with the situation.

"No," he said slowly, his lips pursed, a faraway look in his eyes as if he was mentally running through the job lists. "No. I'm sorry. We have nothing in your line at present." I had not mentioned what my line was.

"Perhaps you could speak to the captain of the ship when it arrives, but I am sure he will not have any vacancies at this time of the year."

Did the time of the year make a difference? Perhaps. But I knew we were parrying with paper swords. Nothing would come of my request. I had gone through it all before in Egypt and Aden was no different. So I asked what the deck passage cost, whereupon all vestiges of play-acting were dropped and he asked if I would be good enough to speak to his clerk in the outer office about that and without waiting for me to rise picked up his pen to continue his business. I was dismissed with my tail between my legs.

The clerk told me the deck passage would cost 100 rupees (£7.50) which did not include food. This might seem an almost ridiculous sum at today's prices but to put it into some kind of perspective, consider that sum as a week-and-a-half of tradesman's wages in Britain at that time it would constitute say £200 to £300, or more, at present rates. He started to ask if I was sure I wanted to travel this way but stopped when I looked at him and, saying no more, sold me a ticket. In the end I was quite pleased with the outcome of the affray. I had salved my conscience by at least trying to work my passage and after these past months on the building site I was quite pleased not to be a Lascar seaman cleaning the bilges or doing whatever they did.

After the holiday I told Jabran I was leaving in a few days. He said he was sorry and that there would always be a job for me if I ever decided to return, which made me feel good. When I told the Lebanese fellows I was touched by their depth of feeling in the regrets they expressed.

On the morning I left, Yusif rose an hour before normal to make me a special Lebanese dish for my breakfast as a going away feast. It was horrible. Something swimming in olive oil. But I ate it with gusto though I was sure I was going to be sick, and smiled my thanks. Good Yusif, my special friend right to the end.

An hour later I mounted the gangway and boarded the *Diana*. Great ropes were cast off and hauled in, tugs manoeuvred her into position then, with three blasts of her horn, answered by three shrill ones from a tug, the engines turned over in a fountain of froth, and we were off. I stood by the stern rail watching the lengthening wake like a turquoise path leading straight as a die back to a fading Aden.

Chapter Seven

THE LOST CITY

Monday 30th April 1951 – Gedi, Nr Malindi,
In the haunted ruins I pitched my tent in candlelight while a myriad insects circled the flame and piled their dead in a heap round the tin the candle stood on.

The *Diana* was an Italian ship. It was run in a sloppy manner. The deck was hosed down only every two or three days and the rails and other parts never touched at all. The deck passenger area was behind the funnel and black soot fell continually. I put my sleeping bag down in a sheltered corner and claimed that niche as mine. Under an overhang I was protected from most of the soot, but there was always some and I had to continually keep shaking my gear to get rid of it.

I bought some tins of corned beef and that with bread was my staple diet during the ten days' voyage. Trouble was, my camp was directly over the dining cabin passengers and the smells coming up at meal times when I was tucking into my bully beef were tantalising.

Five days after leaving Aden the ship put in to Mogadishu for four days. 'Put in' was not quite right because there was no proper harbour there. The ship was anchored about a quarter of a mile off-shore and work was slow due to the rough seas that exist for eight months in the year. Everything, cargo and passengers had to be loaded or unloaded by the ship's derrick onto or off a barge or lighter. Unloading and loading took a long time at Mogadishu.

Going ashore was a hazardous business. It could take an hour each day for the few hardy passengers who chose to go ashore. You stood in a basket that took about half a dozen people and waited many minutes while the derrick man chose his moment, then with a sudden jerk the basket was hoisted up high in the air by the noisy, cranky derrick and swung over the side to be lowered onto the pitching, rolling deck of a little boat that looked so small and had to be continually fended off the sheer side of the big ship as it rose and fell in the enormous swell. It was amazing that there were not some serious accidents. The little boat we landed on took ages to get ashore, battling with the waves that crashed against the breakwater in mountains of spray like some North Sea harbour wall on a very windy day. Arriving back on board one afternoon I was interested to see a cargo of ivory laid out on deck. I counted over fifty tusks. None of them was really big.

Mogadishu had been a good town but it appeared to be even harder hit than the other fading Italian ports in the Red Sea. When Italy occupied Abyssinia Mogadishu had been the main port. Its past prosperity was evident in the wonderful buildings that the Italians had created with great skill. Sadly they all looked so shabby now and many of them were empty.

Italy had been given a ten-year mandate as rulers by the UN after which time it would be decided if the locals were ready for self government. On this proviso it was evident that Italy, even if it had the wherewithall, which was unlikely, was not going to invest in the country. Abyssinia, down-trodden for so long, refused to trade or even talk to their former oppressors. In this light Mogadishu, and all Italian Somaliland, seemed doomed. It is sad that the assumptions that were being drawn at the time, that the country would collapse into tribal corruption and massacre, have all come to pass. But then, the same could be said for almost all Africa.

I spoke to two Indian traders who were leaving for Kenya on the *Diana* after a lifetime in Mogadishu. They said there was no work and food was three to four times more expensive than in Mombasa.

Three days out of Mogadishu the *Diana* sailed into Kilindini harbour, Mombasa, the great natural inland waterway which Henry Morton Stanley, who was desperate for Britain to colonise East Africa, told the British Prime Minister that you could put the whole of the Royal Navy. Kenya had just had the heaviest rainfall in living memory and the land looked so green and beautiful after the months I had spent in the desert countries.

I cannot express my feelings when I was eventually ashore. The possibility of my landing and being rejected due to some immigration red tape such as no job, lack of visible means of support or not enough capital, had weighed heavily on me for months. As it was, the authorities were friendly and relaxed to the point of being ludicrous. It was after 7 p.m. and I was told the Customs were closed and would I come back in the morning to have my kit checked? I could have gone out whistling if I had had a load of contraband to get rid of before then. But even without the loot, with Africa literally at my feet, I felt in great spirits.

It was dark and wet when I disembarked and walked along the quay wondering where I would go for the night. Passing a ship I was hailed by a bearded Glaswegian merchant seaman who on spying my kilt invited me on board and where after a lot of verbal back-slapping he fixed me up with a great feed of bacon, sausages and eggs with lots of cups of tea. After ten days on bully beef out of the can that meal was delicious. Later, after discussing where I might go for the night he said his ship was sailing early in the morning so he could not offer accommodation but suggested I go to the Seamen's Mission, which I did. There I got permission to put up my tent in the grounds, use the facilities and have breakfast in the morning.

It poured rain that night and I was pleased how well my tent performed, but it did make conditions very cramped. Having no flysheet, any contact with the canvas made that area permeable and allowed the water to seep in. I therefore had to be extremely careful not to touch the sides. This was not easy in the space provided by a tent six feet long, four feet broad at the extreme low base and three feet high at the apex.

After breakfast I packed up and as directed on docking went back to the port to have my kit cleared by Customs and was able to leave my rucksack there while I wandered around the town absorbing the feeling and pleasure of being back in Kenya.

The old port of Mombasa was a wonderful place, steeped in history and oozing charm of bygone times. Here were narrow streets, dark and time honoured, and ancient buildings with elegant balconies and age-old, elaborately carved doors with great spikes in the panels, like those I had seen in Zanzibar.

In the wider Vasco de Gama street, slender palm trees leaned towards you and wagged their plumes in the breeze, fat pedlars rode tiny donkeys and tall, light brown Swahilis walked regally in the sunlight. Turbaned Arab dhowmen in exotic costumes talked in groups down by the warehouses at the sea where myriad boats were moored in a tangled flotilla waiting for the north-blowing *kuzi* tradewind that would take them back to the Persian Gulf. Here you felt you were part of a scene that had not changed since the dawn of history in these parts.

The Swahili were an interesting people. These were the people who had crossbred with Persian, Arab and other seamen who had traded in these parts since before the time of Solomon. Their tribal language had long ago taken on board so many Arabic, Indian, Persian and latterly English words, the polyglot patois became not only a full blown language in its own right but also the lingua-franca of the whole East African coast and as far inland as the Arab slaving caravans penetrated. Later, with British colonising it became solidly established throughout Kenya, Tanganyika and Uganda, the three main East African countries.

Richard Burton – we are once again in the presence of the great traveller – never had much time for the Swahilis, or Sawahilis, as he called them in his day. In his book *The Lake Regions of Central Africa,* published in 1860, he wrote a treatise on these people in which he displays the extraordinary linguistic ability and powers of observation that put him in a league of his own over other explorers. Even when seriously ill and being carried on a litter he made copious notes on the geography, flora and fauna and the most intricate details of tribal customs of everywhere he went.

After his two years expedition to Lake Tanganyika and back, 1857/59, he spoke KiSwahili and other tribal languages not only fluently but was able to explain the nuances and innuendoes that are more than words.

Having studied the coastal people of Kenya, Burton explains that, "the Sawahili are distinguished by two national peculiarities. The first is a cautiousness bordering on cowardness, derived from their wild African blood; the second is an unusual development of cunning and deceitfulness, which partially results from the grafting of the semi-civilised Semite upon the Hamite."

In his journey to the central lakes Burton travelled along the long established Arab slave routes and at times was wholly dependant and indebted to them. Although he had a certain respect for Arabs, Burton regarded the Semites as inferior to Whites. The Hamites – a Victorian reference to blacks as the children of Ham, one of Noah's four sons – he considered to be an even lower breed. The half-breed Afro/Arab, such as the WaSwahili, he held in extreme distaste and distrust.

To be fair to Burton, I must say that he was not alone in his opinion. Most whites, Arabs and Indians I came across treated half-castes with some suspicion and unfortunately with reason. Perhaps the feeling of being an outcast bred in these people a burning desire to get their own back on those who rejected them and this often came out in a work-shy, sly attitude. Burton tells us that that is how the WaSwahili got them their name.

He explains that whatever the coastal tribe's name was, it has long since been lost and that the word 'ahili' comes from the Arabic 'Msawahili' which was derived from 'Sawwa-hilah', meaning, 'He played a trick'. The people he implies were quite proud of their reputation for he says, "They boast 'are we not the WaSawahili?', that is 'artful dodgers'."

*

While in old Mombasa I visited Fort Jesus the ancient Portuguese fort which was at that time a prison. I had a letter of introduction to Superintendent Campbell from Mr Scott in Aden and was welcomed and though the place was closed to visitors I was given a personally conducted tour, which even included the women's section and an invitation to tea with the family.

Fort Jesus is a sinister looking place, formidable and forbidding. Its 400-year-old high sloping ramparts are streaked black with old rain runnels and mould and inside the walls are painted blood red. Three hundred years ago 2,500 Portuguese were besieged there by Arabs. Eighteen months later, after plague and famine had taken their toll, the defenders finally opened the gates to end the siege after a promise of clemency from the Arabs. Inside the attackers found only eleven men and two women alive and promptly put them to the sword. Terrible as that was, it was but the swing of the pendulum in the domination of this land.

The first Portuguese, indeed the first Europeans, to visit East Africa came with Vasco de Gama the navigator who left Lisbon in 1497 to look for a sea route to India. The South African Cape had been rounded ten years previously by another Portuguese navigator, Bartolomeu Dias, but no white man had penetrated so far up the east coast before. They carried trade goods for barter in the Indies, but never expected to use them in Africa. They were sure that in Africa there would be only raging jungles and black savages. Instead they found a civilised coastal land where Moors (the term used for Moslems in Europe at that time) wore rich cotton garments into which were woven designs made with gold and silver threads and women were bedecked with jewelled earrings and gold bracelets on their arms and legs. Here, at the port of Sofala, ships loaded gold from the interior where a king 'walked under a canopy supported by four staves, each surmounted by a golden bird'. In short, a land that had an abundance of wealth and a high standard of living. And so it had been for at least three thousand years perhaps, since Solomon's navy came here for the gold with which to gild his palace.

When de Gama arrived at the coast of Zinj, as this land was then known, there were thirty-seven towns from Kilwa (now Kilwa-Kivinje) in the south to Mogadishu in the north. The inhabitants must have believed their way of life was eternal, as it had been and would be forever. Little did they realise that in Vasco de Gama a deadly virus had been injected into their timeless society.

The people of Zinj did not welcome the Portuguese. The cloth and other items they had brought to trade with were generally of poorer quality than their own, but the Sultan of Milindi showed some kindness by offering to de Gama an ocean pilot who showed them the way to Calicut in India where they stayed for three months and by doing so opened up the Spice Trade that would change the world.

When Vasco de Gama returned to Portugal two years after setting out, barely a third of the one hundred and seventy men who had crewed the ships were still alive. The Portuguese soon sent out a bigger fleet with the intention of making treaties with the rulers of Zinj, but these people would have none of it. Portugal then sent an even bigger navy, once again with Vasco de Gama in command. This time they meant business. With blood red crosses emblazoned on their sails to show they intended to break the Moslem hold on the heathen natives and offer them Christianity instead, de Gama was empowered not to treaty but to use force to gain control of the land. He forced the Sheik of Kilwa to submit and pay tribute. Later, in 1505 another force under Francisco de Almeida took complete control of Kilwa and built a fort there to show they had come to stay.

The Portuguese then went on to storm and lay waste to Mombasa, leaving 1,500 of the inhabitants dead in the streets. And there the victors built Fort Jesus, in the name of Christ. The white man had arrived in East Africa.

When I visited it the evil of its past seemed to hang round Fort Jesus like an invisible but palpable shroud. As a prison it was an inhospitable place for the unfortunate inmates. Luckily a new prison was in the process of being built so now the old fort is only an empty tourist attraction.

*

Sixty-five miles to the north of Mombasa and buried in thick bush lie the ruins of Gedi, the city that was lost for six hundred years or more. Local natives say it is haunted. They tell of weird cries which come from the ruins at night and of a ghost that has been seen. There is even a story of buried treasure which is guarded by a curse.

A load of nonsense? No doubt. But though one might scoff at the folklore of Gedi no one can dispute the town's remarkable history, or the lack of it. It has been estimated that Gedi was built sometime between 1000 AD and 1350 AD. Bear this in mind in the light of the following.

In 1329 a Moorish traveller, Ibn Batata, wrote the first description of East African towns. Although he gave detailed particulars of the places he visited, he recorded no word of Gedi. Yet we know that Gedi was alive and trading far and wide at that time. Relics from as far afield as China dating from that era have been found there.

The year 1498 brought the Portuguese who fought their way along the coast crushing every town and village in their efforts to subjugate the land. They kept a garrison at Malindi for two hundred years and during that time their cartographers travelled the coast and hinterland. But although they made excellent maps which showed every little village, no mention appeared of Gedi, although the town lay only ten miles from their base. That Gedi was occupied then there is no doubt. In the ruins, on a pillar marking a grave, is inscribed the Moslem year 1011, which is equivalent to the Christian year 1601.

More than three hundred years later in 1823 history repeated itself when two British survey ships mapped the coast from the Cape to the Arabian coast. Their charts were accompanied by two volumes of description of the coast. No mention is made of Gedi although it lay only three miles from the coast and it has been estimated that Gedi's buildings and streets must have been in good condition then.

How could a bustling city grow old and die, yet never be mapped or recorded?

Was it a real life Brig o' Doon that appeared and came to life only on fleeting days throughout the centuries? Hardly, but strange! Even when it finally gave up its ruins in the 1920s Gedi still retained most of its secrets. Those skilled in reading stones could estimate when it was built. They could tell that the city had lived and died twice – the earlier period was thought to be of Persian origin while the second was distinctly Arab. In its latter days danger was introduced, as was evident from the surrounding wall with loopholes in it that had been hastily built. The architecture was Moslem. But more than that Gedi – the name is modern, the original is unknown – would not divulge.

Who were the builders? Why was Gedi built three miles inland when all other towns of that time were situated by the sea? Why did its inhabitants twice leave? Why was it never discovered through all the centuries it existed as a busy town? Why ... why ... why? all leading to the one end – mystery! Gedi had intrigued me since my army days in Nairobi when a fellow returning from leave in Mombasa said, "They say there is a lost city in the jungle down there." When I asked with enthusiasm if he tried to see it, he answered emphatically in soldiers' vernacular that no one was likely to get him to do that. Now I resolved to spend a night in the ruins to see if it was really haunted.

My plans made, I set out early one morning from Mombasa. A short lift in a truck took me a few miles and dropped me at a native village, a few thatched mud houses clustered among long slender coconut palms with notches cut in their trunks to make easy climbing. The headman warned me that walking on the roads was dangerous since the rains enabled the animals to wander far from the rivers and water-holes they congregate near during the dry weather. The area, he said, was alive with elephant and buffalo and indeed there was ample evidence of this from the fresh droppings on the road. I was greatly relieved when after I had gone a few miles a truck with an Arab driver going to Malindi came along and picked me up.

On the back of the truck, up high on the pile of goods, I joined three other passengers, two of whom were beguiling native girls. They giggled behind their hands at the sight of my kilt. One was naked from the waist up and had glossy tribal scars scored down her black, matt face. The other wore a snappy sarong. Her upper lip protruded almost horizontal and had inserted in it a black shiny spike which stuck up past her nose. I asked which tribes they belonged to but their answers were mostly lost in their giggles and all I could gather was that they came from Tanganyika. They shrank from my camera adamantly refused to allow me to take their photographs.

We crossed two ferries on barges which were pulled across on chains attached to posts on the opposite banks, hauled on by natives to the rhythm of impromptu songs. The evening shadows were long when I dropped off the truck at the track that led to Gedi. Night was falling fast: the path through the high trees became a tunnel as the darkness grew more profound. Half way there I met some native women carrying gourds of water on their heads. They fled into the forest at the sight of me. One dropped her calabash which broke with a splash. No doubt there would be another tale to add to the legends of Gedi: of the strange apparitions one may meet in its vicinity.

Rounding a turn in the track the trees gave way to an open space and the first of the ruins loomed up sudden and spectre-like against the evening sky. It was an eerie sight. Looking at the gaunt silhouette I debated with myself whether to carry on with my plan of sleeping there. I wondered if after all I was being eccentric. But it was a momentary qualm.

In the gathering darkness I wandered among the ruins of the once busy town. I picked my way through the foliage to walk down streets that had long ago rung with the hubbub of a busy town, a constant throng of oriental people going about their business, the sellers and coffee urchins loudly hawking their wares, the buyers and loungers and travellers. All gone. Now only the thump of my own boots eerily echoing in the silent ruins.

There was just enough light to see the broken masonry jutting out from dense foliage and the massive trees growing on top of high walls with their thick roots spread down the sides, as if it were the giant bird Rokh holding the masonry in its great talons. There were the remains of mosques and several tombs, one with a hexagonal pillar that pushed its way thirty feet up into the overhanging trees – this was the one, legend said, under which treasure lay buried, but death was forecast for anyone who searched for it.

Best preserved of the buildings was the Sultan's palace. Its entrance arch was in good condition though the steps to it had crumbled. Inside was a large bath, sixteen paces long by six wide. In the surrounding walls were niches which once contained lamps. This, no doubt, was the harem bath. One could conjure up the scene … the sultan in his finery, the laughter, the perfume, the splashing, the glistening bodies, the coquetry … oh, so different from today with the hungry jungle silently devouring the last morsels of the dead city.

I selected a site for my camp. It was quite dark now. There was not a breath of air. I pitched my tent by candlelight while myriad insects circled the flame, piling their dead around the tin on which the candle stood. I kindled a fire and brewed some tea and felt better for it. My world extended to the edge of the firelight: beyond was the black wall of night.

How easy it was for my imagination to cut loose here. How realistic the legends I had heard of the city now seemed: tales that had been mere fantasy during the day were grim logic now. The twisted branches that hung down into the orange dome of light were groping fingers, dipping and snatching as the flames flickered. The occasional cries of hyenas were the voices of lost souls. The muffled sounds of other nocturnal animals were the sandalled footbeats of the city's ghostly guardians, perhaps an Arab vendor or a trader from Persia returned from the dead to deal with this interloper. Could they really come back …? And over it all was the incessant drone of the insects, like some infernal machine to add a more foreboding note to the heavy, sinister atmosphere.

I crawled into my sleeping bag, debating which death would be worse; to be suffocated by some earthbound poltergeist or to be ripped by the teeth and claws of animals. Both seemed very close. I must have dozed off for I awoke abruptly. The tent was in darkness. A sixth sense warned of danger – terrible danger. I felt borne down by a heavy, evil oppression. I wanted to shout, but felt my voice catch in my throat and only an odd screech came.

Suddenly I was out of the tent and breathing deeply of the night air. I piled fresh fuel on the dull embers of the fire and blew it into a blaze. It was comforting to see the flames. I made some strong tea and passed the rest of the night dozing beside the fire: nothing would have induced me to lie down in the tent again.

With the coming of dawn, Gedi's sinister atmosphere was dispelled. I felt ashamed at harbouring the fears I had. Yet were they really groundless? Somehow I still felt my fear had been real and not just a fabrication of the mind. For one thing, I saw no birds in the trees around Gedi: was this mere coincidence? Was it just that they were not around while I was there? Or do they, like dogs, possess a sense we are only occasionally gifted with, a sixth sense that gives warning of the supernatural? That sounds daft and far-fetched, but …! Or was it just a build-up by association, by expectation. After all, I'd carried an inner fear of Gedi for five years since first hearing of it while in the army. Had I not half expected something of this kind to happen, perhaps even subconsciously wished it, hoped it, on myself just for the thrill.

These questions and ideas bumped around in my head a long time after the event but I still had no answer to them nor am I ever likely to have. It does not do to dwell too long on the subject – 'tis easier to write my fear off as the work of an over-active imagination. And yet …

A long time after my visit to Gedi I read in Richard Burton's book *The Lake Regions of Central Africa* the story of Salim bin Rashid, a merchant of Zanzibar. Africa is full of superstition and magic. The power of the *Uchawi* is infinite. The supernatural and unnatural are real entities to the primitive natives and to many who would profess to have left all that behind. So it was when Burton led his expedition of 1857 to find the source of the Nile, he happened on the little story of Salim bin Rashid.

Arabs claimed not to believe in the black Africans' magic, but many who spent long parts of their life along the slave trails came under the spell and believed. These people were referred to as having 'gone native'. Those Arabs who lived much more sophisticated lives on Zanzibar would ridicule any idea of their harbouring any suspicion of the native superstitions, as Europeans would in today's world. Nevertheless, old habits die hard! Who in Britain would not touch wood, throw salt over their shoulder when they break a mirror, walk under a ladder or step on lines even after they are ten years old.

Salim bin Rashid was a sophisticated, worldly-wise man of the mid-19th century. There was no one more sceptical of African superstitions than he. What transpired with him therefore cannot be said to have emanated from his own beliefs, or so he might have said. As a Zanzibar merchant he occasionally travelled the slave routes to the interior of mainland Africa on business. One night on the trail Salim was overtaken by a strange fit. He described later how a black mass entered his tent and he felt himself pulled and pushed. He shouted to his slaves and though they ran to his help they could not enter his tent. In desperation they pulled it down and found their master in a stupor. When I read of Salim's experience it was so like my own I went hot and cold with the memory of it.

In 1991, almost forty years later to the day when I slept there, I revisited Gedi, this time as a tourist. Big changes had been made. A good vehicle road allowed access for tourist buses and cars. While the trees standing on the walls remained, the jungle around the town had been cleared back and spacious walks made among the ruins. The area had lost much of its gruesome and forbidding atmosphere. Looking back from then I wondered how the place could have caused me such fear as I felt that night. Nevertheless, visitors my wife and I spoke to, and we spoke to a few, invariably mentioned without prompting from me that they felt the place had an air, an aura that they had not felt anywhere else. Even after the clearing of the choking jungle Gedi still has a chill about it.

Magic, superstition or nothing, be it as it may, a strange occurrence took place soon after the night I slept in Gedi. This chapter, apart from a few additions such as Salim bin Rashid's story, is almost a straight lift of an article I wrote soon after my visit to the Lost City which was published in the South African magazine *Outspan* and in the Australian *Man*.

It happened that on the day of publication in Australia my best pal in the army, Arthur Robertson, from Arbroath, was walking down a street in Melbourne. Arthur and I shared the same birthday, were called up for the army the same day, were both posted to the Black Watch barracks in Perth, did our training together, were both posted to Kenya, went through the ranks and shared a two-man room in the sergeants' quarters and remained buddies till the day we were both demobbed. Then our ways parted for Arthur soon emigrated to Australia and on the day that he walked down the Melbourne street we had not seen each other in over three years. Arthur is a very down-to-earth man, not given to fancies, yet he told me years later that when walking past a newsagent that day he suddenly felt compelled to go in and buy this magazine which he had never bought before. Thumbing through the pages as he walked along he was staggered to find my name jump out at him from my article. It was the only article I ever published in that magazine, indeed, the only one I published in Australia. Was it coincidence, telepathy or the magic of Gedi?

Chapter Eight

WHAT PRICE MY QUEEN...?

Paradise... the place of cool water at the beginning of all beauty.
(Masai derivation)

After a night of torrential rain the morning was hot and extremely humid when I left Mombasa on the three hundred miles road to Nairobi. Despite the oppressive weather my spirits were high. This was the last lap on my way to old haunts and I was looking forward so much to getting there. Although I was prepared to walk I was confident of getting some lifts even though during the rains the traffic was scarce.

Between stints of walking I got a couple of lifts that took me out of the coastal region and through the tsetse fly belt where nearly all the haulage animals, camels, horses and donkeys, that were brought in when the Mombasa-to-Uganda railway was being built at the end of the 19th century died within days. I watched the terrain change from nodding palm trees to flat-topped acacias and felt the air clear from steamy heat to a drier, cooler temperature as the road climbed higher. Sometime in the afternoon after walking a few hours I got a lift to Mackinnon Road where I decided to spend the night. There was an army camp there so I went along and asked if I could put my tent down in their perimeter, but instead I was given a night's free lodging in the guard room with meals thrown in.

Mackinnon Road, originally a staging post for caravans crossing the waterless Taru desert on their way to the interior and back, was named after the Scottish industrialist, shipping magnate and philanthropist Sir William Mackinnon who did more perhaps than anyone else to bring Kenya and Uganda under British rule.

Mackinnon was one of the few Victorians who mixed humanitarianism with commercialism, the very qualities David Livingstone called for to end the slave trade and Mackinnon was a great devotee of the famous missionary/explorer. When Livingstone emerged after years in the interior of Africa he brought back a graphic account of the horrors of the slave trading that was decimating the Dark Continent, as it was referred to in those days. On 15th December 1856 he told his story to a spellbound audience of the Royal Geographical Society, London, during a special meeting convened in his honour. He explained how the Arab slave-traders set tribe against tribe to capture each other and sell their captives to them for a pittance and when an area was cleaned out they moved on to another. In giving the details of the canker that was eating away the heart of the continent he pleaded for Britain to go and open up that unknown territory and end the vile trade in human beings. Later, in the new year of 1877, at a meeting in Cambridge, he made his famous statement, "I go back to Africa to try to make an open path for commerce and Christianity."

It is interesting to note that Livingstone, perhaps the most uncommercial and least materialistic person ever to go into Africa, should put commercialism before Christianity for his purpose. He knew that idealism alone would never succeed. Indeed, one of his most fervent pleas at the meeting was for Britain to find a way of establishing a cotton growing industry in Africa and buy from there rather than from America which was dependent on the slave trade to provide cheap labour, a fact that perpetuated the evil practice.

Livingstone's clarion call rang out like a bell, brought people to action and changed history. Throughout the land people laid aside the lives they had been following to become missionaries or laymen and businessmen entrepreneurs looked to ways best suited to invest their money in that unknown land.

Strangely, the people who paid the least heed to the great man's entreaty were those of the British government. For two hundred years Britain had declined to become officially involved in Africa and in the late 1880s when Mackinnon became involved in East Africa the last thing Gladstone, the then Prime Minister, wanted to be bothered with was the trivial matter of Africa. His concern, and the whole business of the British government, was dominated by 'the Irish problem' that had bedevilled multiple governments before his (and many more after too) and was then wearing him down into premature old age and sapping his health and political will.

The Sultan of Zanzibar, Barghash bin Said, claimed suzerainty over most of East Africa but it was a hollow claim since apart from the slave route from the coast opposite his island through what is now Tanzania as far as the great lake and up to Uganda, he had no way of governing it. He needed funding and he wanted Britain, who had had a long association with Zanzibar, to become involved but Gladstone would have none of it. Nevertheless, although it could take no official action without the backing of the government, the Foreign Office, while he was on a visit to London, put him in touch with Sir William Mackinnon.

Sir William was very familiar with Zanzibar. The ships of his British India Steam Navigation Company regularly called there for fresh water and provisions en-route to and from India. He had thought in the past of making inroads to the mainland of Africa and this gave him his opportunity. He had looked on the prospect of entering Africa with a businessman's eye but his main reason for opening up the almost unknown interior was to try and do his bit to end the slave trade. Like others he had been fired by Livingstone's plaintive call and with the Sultan's request he saw his way of getting to the heart of the problem.

What Mackinnon asked of Barghash in return for his involvement was in fact the whole of the land from the coast to the lakes, that which now comprises Kenya and Tanzania, to be leased to him for sixty-six years for which he would pay an annual rent and give to the Sultan a percentage of all taxes raised and revenue from all possible minerals mined.

In addition, and here was the crunch, Mackinnon insisted that Sultan Barghash end the slave trade in Zanzibar. This was a colossal demand. Slave trading was the main reason for his people having been there for centuries. Giving up this trade was tantamount to the Sultan giving up nearly all his state income. Zanzibar had had the biggest slave market in all East Africa and although that market had since been closed, the slave trade still functioned, even if at a lesser degree and still made up a great percentage of the economy of that country. Nevertheless the Sultan gave tacit agreement to Mackinnon's demand and signed a treaty with him.

It would seem that Mackinnon had extracted an overwhelming bargain but the Sultan was still smiling. Apart from some show of compliance he had no intention of ending his slave trade and now he had someone to develop a whole tract of land he had no more right to than anyone else, a land which he had no way of administering and which in his own words gave him 'nothing but trouble'. For very little in return Barghash, it might be said, expected a sizeable income for his realm for many years to come.

Mackinnon founded the East Africa Association, putting into it a considerable amount of his own money. He made Mombasa his headquarters base and harbour, the latter eventually overshadowing that of Zanzibar. He then set about making a road of sorts, Mackinnon Road, inland to get to the heart of the slave trouble in the interior.

A year later his Association received a Royal Charter and became The Imperial British East Africa Company (IBEA) with the right to coin its own money, print its own postage stamps and publish its own treaty documents for agreements with African chiefs. The British government was wakening up to the importance of East Africa, not for the land itself which had never been looked on as a likely investment, but as the back door to the Nile. Lord Salisbury, who had succeeded Gladstone as Prime Minister, saw that Mackinnon held the vital passageway to Uganda, a quicker and more accessible way of getting troops to the head waters of the Nile than the old way of boating and marching them up the river, a matter of dire importance at that moment, in order to stop the French who were marching from the east with their eyes on the Nile and eventual control of Egypt.

*

I knew little of all these high-flying politics and the important role Mackinnon Road had played in them, however, when I left that sleepy little town one morning and walked out on the road to Nairobi against the advice of many people at Mackinnon Road. Ahead lay many miles of waterless semi-desert teeming with game, particularly lions, rhinos and elephants. Three weeks earlier a soldier had been killed by an elephant he had tried to photograph. But to have any chance of getting a lift I had to be on the road so walked on, albeit with a wary eye though what I could do about it if I saw anything was anybody's guess. I was not likely to outstrip an elephant let alone a lion with a seventy pound pack on my back. Twice I came on steaming piles of elephant dung but luckily I didn't see any. I've got to say though, seeing these droppings so recently placed there gave me a funny feeling and I was conscious that the thump of my feet on the mud road sounded so loud I hoped the animals would not be near enough to hear me.

Five miles out I thought I heard a car coming and sure enough there was the telltale plume of dust racing towards me. But it was not a lift. Anything but. It was a police car and it had come out specially to find me. When it stopped by my side I could see that the officer was not amused at my walking. He warned me that it was extremely dangerous to walk particularly at this time of the year. During the dry season, he said, the animals stayed around the waterholes which were few and far between and well away from the road. During the rains, however, and especially this one which was much heavier than normal, they wandered all over the place. All this I knew but had to stand and listen while he read out a prepared official warning to me and had me sign it. He then turned the car and headed back to Mackinnon Road.

I was surprised but pleased he had not insisted I accompany him back to the station. Nevertheless the warning struck deep and I thought it prudent to take notice. So I dropped my pack and spread my groundsheet under a sparse tree and settled down to wait for anything that might come along. I was prepared to climb the tree if necessary but it was such a small thing I doubt if it would have done any good at all.

Luckily this was never put to the test for within a couple of hours I hit the jackpot, or so I thought at the time. Along came a car with two fellows in it. Messrs Tom Dale and Bob Sharp were driving upcountry to attend the Nakuru races next day and agreed to take me as far as Nairobi.

At Voi we stopped to have a meal at a small restaurant and the pleasant, talkative manageress told us that it would be impossible to drive the car to Nairobi as the road was blocked due to the recent abnormal rainfall. Tom and Bob decided to press on, nevertheless.

The road, like all the roads throughout East Africa, was just a dirt track. Only some town streets had tarmac surfaces. In the dry seasons the red murram soil baked like clay and made a good driving surface, except that it invariably became corrugated and rattled cars unmercifully, but in the wet times it could become a quagmire. Worse still were patches of black-cotton soil that became treacherous skid pads when wet.

Any kind of travelling in Africa had its perils which were all made worse in the rainy seasons. It was near Voi that Karen Blixin's lover, Denys Finch Hatton, hero of her book *Out of Africa*, crashed his plane and was killed.

Beyond Voi the road was quite good and we made good time. There was evidence that great herds of elephant were about in the droppings on the road and the places where the banks at the side had been broken down by their great weight when they had left the road. We expected to come on them at every turn but we only saw some at a distance.

The land was simply teeming with big game. According to a survey taken a few years later there were over 55,000 elephants in this area alone. Now less than 5000 remain. Worse still are the rhinos which, though prolific at the time of my journey, are all but wiped out now in these parts. Evidence indeed that so much of the wonderful Old Africa is gone.

We passed Tsavo without stopping, which was a pity for I wanted to experience the thrill of walking through that place to gaze on the railway bridge that spanned the river, the bridge that had been built fifty years before at terrible cost in human lives. But I had done it before on a previous visit while in the army and the memory was vivid as we passed. My pleasure at being at Tsavo was to do with living history, that by treading the earth there I could be at one with a place that, perhaps more than any other, epitomised raw, primitive Africa as it was when the white man first moved onto its stage.

*

In 1898 when the railway in the making from Mombasa to Lake Victoria was creeping through the land that would eventually be called 'Kenya', work on the track was held up for nearly a year at the Tsavo River by man-eating lions. Tsavo in KiKamba means 'slaughter' and what happened there was nothing short of that.

Lions are not naturally man-eaters. Sure they will maim and kill people if cornered or feel threatened, but they don't normally stalk humans and rarely eat them. Indeed it is said they do not like human flesh. If one does turn man-eater it is usually an old male turned out by the pride and not being fast or agile enough to hunt game finds humans much easier to run down and kill. What was extraordinary at Tsavo was that it was two young lions who teemed up together and set about systematically culling the human population.

Over a period of ten months they laid siege to the Tsavo railway camp and in that time killed twenty-eight Indian coolies and well over a hundred Africans of the surrounding tribes. The Indians had been brought in as labourers because the local population was too savage or primitive to be put to work. In common with other man-eaters the lions became incredibly cunning and bold, displaying an intelligence that was apparently beyond animal instinct. They seemed to be able to out-think their hunters, their movements and attacks never following the pattern of behaviour expected by experienced hunters. They became so arrogant and contemptuous of man's efforts to kill them the coolies and native populace came to believe that they were supernatural, ghosts that came in the night and were beyond the powers of man to destroy.

Many believed that by eating the flesh of man the lions acquired human intelligence. This belief was not uncommon throughout Africa. As late as the 1980s a white nurse was killed and partially eaten by native women in South Africa where generations of white rule and association had long removed their tribe from the primitive customs of central Africa. When questioned as to why they ate pieces of the nurse the black woman, whose tribe had no legacy of cannibalism, said that by doing so they hoped to obtain the intelligence of the white woman which they believed to be higher than their own.

The two Tsavo killers were not the only man-eaters who were abroad at that time. At Voi a lion entered the tent of a road engineer while he and his wife and two children were asleep. The lion killed the man, whose name was O'Hara, by crushing his head in its jaws and carried him off bodily without his wife, who was lying beside him, knowing anything about it.

And further up the line at Kima (Swahili for *monkey*) Superintendent of Police, Charles Ryall, was persuaded to break his train journey to Mombasa in order to shoot a lion that was terrorising the local Wakamba people. He, with two other Europeans, stood sentry into the night by the windows of his private carriage, watching to see if the lion would come. It did, and with the super cunning of the man-eater it watched the hunters inside the coach and as if knowing when to strike, when Ryall had momentarily dozed, and as if aware who its main adversary was, it leaped inside, killed the Superintendent with a single swipe of its paw to the head and bounded out again with the corpse in its jaws before the others could take in the situation and shoot.

Cool and deadly as these killers were they did not match up to the audacious cunning and intelligence displayed by the Tsavo duo over such a long period. Their tale was told in the best-selling book *The Man-Eaters of Tsavo* by Lt. Col. J.H. Patterson, an Indian Army engineer officer responsible for constructing the bridge to carry the railway over the Tsavo River. The labour force was so devastated by the lions and fever that the work was continually falling behind schedule. There were strikes and unrest and at least one planned murder of

Patterson by a gang of masons, which he put down by just talking to the mob, such was the sheer force of his personality. The completion of the bridge building, estimated to be completed in four months, took nearly a year.

Such was the terror that paralysed the camp Patterson took on the personal task of ridding the place of the serial killers. He did not know then to what a Herculean assignment he had committed himself. Night after night, month after month, after gruelling days bossing the reluctant workers, he consigned himself to torturing waits up trees and in hides, trying to catch sight of the monsters. But the killers seemed always to know where he was though he moved his station continually and would kill some way off. With complete bravado they would enter tents or wagons and carry off their victims and casually devour them within earshot of the others who listened to them purring as they crunched and chewed.

Eventually Patterson built a giant 'rat' trap, constructed of old rails, with a compartment at the back for the 'bait'. Nightly he sat in there, waiting, offering himself, always in a high state of tension, but to no avail. The animals in their uncanny way seemed to know and eventually, disillusioned with it, he gave up his trap. How he managed to cope with this strain and lack of proper nights' sleep for months is unbelievable.

Later he tried with his trap again and this time put two sepoys in the cage. Incredibly one of the lions entered it, but the soldiers were so petrified as it roared and slashed at them through the bars they could do nothing. When they did manage to get something of a grip on themselves their shooting was so wild they missed the beast entirely but did manage to hit the spring lock on the door so that it flew open and the lion escaped.

At last, nearly a year after it all began, Patterson's luck changed and from a tree he managed to hit one several times and in the morning following the blood trail they found the body. It measured nearly ten feet long. Later he managed to dispatch the other one, but only after a mighty tussle with the lion. After it had been wounded the animal actually stalked him. In its death charge he stood and fired his standard .303 British army rifle at it, a weapon considered when I was there as totally inadequate for hunting lion. That incident alone showed the man's remarkable courage and presence of mind in the face of certain death. The lion finally died barely five yards from his feet. It measured nearly the same as its partner. Their stuffed remains are today on display in Chicago's Field Museum.

Patterson's efforts and bravery in killing those killers that had been terrorising the community long before he and the railway had appeared on the scene was heroic, yet in these days of political correctness it is sad to see his deeds derided as with almost all things colonial. I recently read an account of the Tsavo man-eaters in a current well known guide book to Kenya which sets him out to be something of a bumbling fool who made useless ambushes and exaggerated and over glamorised his own part in the affair. I'm sure if the writer had even thought what it is like to hunt and be hunted at night by a man-eating killer, to stand his ground before a huge charging animal and keep his cool, knowing that if he didn't he would be dead in seconds, he/she would not have written in such supercilious and derisive vein. No bumbling fool could have hunted the Tsavo man-eaters for ten months and lived to tell the tale. The fact that he finished up victor when so many others had failed and died is indicative of his sagacity and stature. A great number of local natives owed their lives to Patterson. The lions killed well over a hundred of them and had Patterson not come along they would have gone on to kill several hundred more. The facts speak for themselves and no amount of ridicule can belittle his feat.

*

Much as I had wanted to stop at Tsavo, when we passed on I was indeed happy to be in the car. Walking through this area would not have been pleasant, so prolific were the animals and signs of them. Great herds of elephants roamed within stone throwing distance and antelopes and gazelles were so common you ceased to take account of them. In places where the road was a quagmire the mud was churned up by the spoor of great herds and we could only hope we had no mishap that might put the car out of action and leave us stranded.

At Mtito Andei we stopped at the Mack Inn (also known as 'Half-way House') and the tale was the same as at Voi, "No, you won't get through. No traffic has passed Makindu for six weeks." But we pressed on.

At 7 p.m. we reached the obstruction at Makindu. A raging torrent, twenty yards wide, in a deep worn bed ran across what had once been the road. Churned to white foam-topped waves by a fearsome current it would have carried away a tank. These were the killers of Africa in the rainy seasons, flash floods that came with battering-ram force down dry river beds across which roads passed. It was always bad but this year the floods were the worst in living memory. A few weeks later I was sad to hear that Mr Selby-Lyons of the Desert Locust Survey whom I had met in Ethiopia and who had recently returned to Nairobi from Arabia, had been caught in a flood and drowned.

By the light of the headlamps we saw there was no road at the other side. Even if we had been able to ford the river there was no way out of it. A sheer wall four feet high formed the new bank to this season's river.

After a conference Tom and Bob decided to catch the train that was due along at 2.30 a.m. and I decided to join them. There was just no way ahead on foot. So we drove back to the nearby Rest House, a crude kind of place where the proprietor hadn't been seen for days. A young chap who was staying there said that over the other side of the flash river there were two miles of mud and silt two feet deep. He worked for the Tsetse Control and his new truck had got embedded in the mud when driving up to Nairobi. He had orders to stay there until he could get it out. He had been there three weeks and it looked like he was going to be a little longer in that haven of rest.

We caught the train in the early morning and it was wonderful to slip between white sheets and feel the miles and travel woes go swinging by, and in the morning to sit in the cosy splendour of the dining car and be served delicious bacon and eggs and nectar coffee by liveried attendants while gazing out over the rolling Athi Plain stretching into the unknown distance. Herds of zebra and wildebeest grazing unconcerned as the iron monster thundered past them, giraffes in pairs and trebles looked inquisitively at the windows as if to see if they recognised anyone and Thomson's gazelles frolicked with the start of a new day.

This was a special scene to me and I let it wash over me, my mind tumbling back over the years. This was where it all started, my love of Africa. It was on the Athi plain the army camp to which I was assigned back in 1946 was situated. My first sights of Africa was as now, from the window of the troop train riding this line, taking us from Mombasa to Nairobi.

This was the railway line that was once referred to as the 'Lunatic Express', so nicknamed by Henry Labouchere in 1904 after a fierce debate in Parliament. He vehemently criticised the building of the Uganda Railway that ran 620 miles over desert, swamp and scrub bush savannah, spanned rivers and incredibly climbed 2000 feet up the almost sheer face of the great Rift Valley, at the extraordinary cost for those days of £5,000,000, nearly 50% over the original estimate. Labouchere, like most members of Parliament, could see little sense in squandering such a sum on a worthless cause that would never be any use to Britain.

How wrong can you be! The railway was the making of Kenya and repaid its investment countless times over. In fact the country as a national entity did not exist until the railway was laid down. It was the means of opening up the whole of East Africa to Britain … and me.

At the end of May, 1899, the railway reached mile 327 from Mombasa. The way ahead lay up the sheer side of the Rift Valley, at this place known as the Kikuyu escarpment. Before the start of this next, almost impossible, stage it was necessary to consolidate the position, to build workshops, stores, living-quarters, etc. The area of mile 327 was convenient and the obvious place to make a permanent depot. It was the only flat area before making the assault on the escarpment. The Masai called this place *Nakusontelon*, 'The beginning of all beauty'. Running through Nakusontelon was a river the Masai called *Uaso Nairobi*, 'Cool Water', and it was by the name Nairobi that the camp and then the town became known.

But to the railwaymen it soon became apparent that it was perhaps the worst place possible for its purpose. The flat plain that was perfect for the Masai to water their wandering herds was a Hell to the incomers with their modern ways and technology. During the rains the land became a fever-ridden swamp where trek-oxen sank up to their knees and their wagons to the axles in the black-cotton morass and living conditions became near impossible. The land swarmed with wild animals, and Indian coolies used their turban cloths as ropes to haul out herds of zebra embedded up to their haunches on the mire. Making foundations for the Permanent Way required great skill. Nevertheless Nairobi took hold, grew and mushroomed.

Within less than a year the collection of huts and tents had town status. In four years it covered forty square miles and fifty years after its birth, and a year before I arrived, when it was officially declared a city, it spanned an area of over a hundred square miles.

*

My return to Nairobi after four years was a moment of intense pleasure and anticipation. I was surprised how much it had changed during my absence. It was now a city and so much bigger. A few, great six- and seven-storey buildings graced the skyline. Walking up Delamere Avenue – so named after the doyen of the early white settlers of 'Happy Valley' – to have coffee at the Stanley Hotel was a long standing dream come true. Standing in the wide Avenue (renamed 'Kenyata Avenue' after independence) with its double carriageways separated by gardens of green grass, trees and flowers and gazing around the towering city, it was hard to believe that only five miles away lions and a host of other wild animals roamed free with no fences or boundaries to keep them at bay. Standing among those great buildings it did not seem possible that little more than fifty years before this had been all empty plain.

How charming it was that May morning in 1951 when I got off the train. The swamplands had long since been drained and the mosquito all but contained so that nets and anti-malaria tablets were necessary only at certain times of the year. Though almost on the Equator but at an altitude of over 5,500 feet it was pleasantly warm and seldom too hot. To me, after all the years of planning and effort, the endless dream of returning, the sweet anticipation, it was Paradise – the place of cool water at the beginning of all beauty.

Near the Stanley Hotel was the British Legion Club, a rather up-market affair but cheaper than the Stanley or the Norfolk hotels and I had reason not to go further down the scale and establish myself in any place to which I could not invite Pam. The Legion was full but they agreed that I could eat there and use the facilities for 9/- (45p) a day and tacitly let it be known that I could sleep in an old hut some distance away that had been part of the early site of the Legion Club before the present, rather splendid, building had been built.

This arrangement worked fine for a little while. The roof of the hut leaked badly and in these present abnormal rains the floor was more than damp, but what was this little discomfort compared to the magic of being back in Nairobi.

The resident members of the Legion Club were a miscellany of ex-service types. Some were pukka sahibs with fierce moustaches and others were Raff types with trim, debonair, Errol Flynn ones, while others sported the full pointed Navy growth and still more, like myself, had none.

All in all they were a great bunch of chaps. All had one thing in common apart from previous service time: everyone had come to start a new future here and each one was sparkling with excitement and enthusiasm at his prospects. The atmosphere was quite different to service establishments where many enlisted men languished in a mental vacuum, wishing their time away until the date came for their discharge.

The men in the Legion Club were the 'get-up-and-go'ers', people who had lifted themselves out of the ruck to carve or grab a new way of life for themselves and it showed in every face. They were bank clerks, small business entrepreneurs, salesmen and some who were in from up-country farms where they had not been long enough established to accept completely the solitude there and wanted to grab some night life and a semblance of city ways.

I soon settled in to be one of the crowd. It was fun to dress up with collar and tie for dinner in the evening, to sit at a dazzling white-clothed table with sparkling cutlery radiating in every direction from the plate and be served delicious exotic food, much of which I had never tasted before, to chat and discuss, to parry and thrust in scintillating conversation that could be profane but always subtle and seldom bawdy. There was the stand-at-the-bar half-hour before meals which I enjoyed. Although I made do with soft drinks I was heartily accepted by the beer drinkers and matched their most rumbustious spirits. On one memorable night when one of the gang was leaving I was cheered on as I climbed the great statue of Lord Delamere, sitting as he did in majestic state, gazing over the city he helped to created. In the morning the early crowd looked in amusement, I hope, at the lord in repose after the night before wearing a knotted-hanky hat and cradling in his elbow a couple of empty bottles of Tuskers beer. I hoped he enjoyed being the centre of the evening revellers, he being of the Happy Valley fraternity, but perhaps he would have preferred something less plebeian.

I soon made a special friend of a chap by the name of Frank Vernon and after a little while moved in to share his room. I slept on the floor in my sleeping bag. It wasn't long before my nocturnal presence was an open secret to which the management chose to turn a blind eye and very soon afterwards a vacancy was found for me and I moved into my own place.

Frank and I hit it off very well. We shared the same kind of daft humour and never tired of each other's company. Whimsical and light-hearted most of the time, Frank also had a dark or sad side that worried me more than I have done with anyone else. At times he would sink into quiet despondency that no amount of jesting would alter. He said he was a Nihilist, a term which I had never heard of before, and in these moods he would say that nothing mattered ... not himself, not the world, not anything, and he wondered what the purpose was in living. But these lapses were few and far between and most of the time he was an excellent companion. He taught me the rudiments of snooker and laughed with me at my ineptness at the game. But I improved a bit and my new found skill, meagre as it was, enabled me to enter and partake of that bastion of male society, the billiard room. It was some time later when I realised that playing snooker right-handed and aiming with my left eye so that I sighted across the cue instead of down it may have had something to do with my poor skill at the game.

Male bastions, if there really are such establishments, of whatever sport or pastime would be onerous places without occasional female contact. To this end there were frequent Ladies Nights when those lucky ones could escort their partners to dinner and ever so casually introduce them to their pals, while secretly chuffed to the eyebrows and desperately trying to keep their feet on the ground. But rules were rules and all females had to be off the premises by 10 p.m. – how things have changed with the new generation – except on the occasional Saturday evenings when a dance was arranged. When I walked in to the first dance after I arrived with Pam on my arm I was the proudest man in the hall though I tried in vain not to show it. Heads swivelled in disbelief and knowing winks with pulled faces were surreptitiously, and many not so subtle, flashed across the room to me. I could see my status rising by every step into the room. As one guy put it later, "How do you do it? You haven't been here five minutes and you walk in with a dream." I didn't enlighten him that the dream had been a long while in the making.

But I'm jumping the gun a bit. Meeting Pam again was not a moment to gloss over. All along my journey I had been looking forward to this moment and yet I think I had dreaded it lest it did not add up to my hopes.

On my arrival in Nairobi I desperately wanted to phone her but could not bring myself to do so. And as the days passed I kept putting off the moment, frightened of being hurt. She would be gone or married or grown away from me and not want to meet. I found all sorts of excuses to bide my time. I'd get myself established first or she might think I was approaching her for accommodation; I'd get a job so she could see I was no sponger; I'd ... I'd ...

I did get a job after several attempts. There were jobs aplenty, but nobody wanted anybody who was in transit. I felt I had to be honest and say I would only be staying a few months and at that the interviews stopped. Then I got wise. After all, who knows, perhaps I might stay. On that premise I would not be committing a sin to keep my options open and not say too much about my intentions.

The very next day after coming to that conclusion I landed a job on the East African Railways, in the workshops supervising the painting and refurbishing of those carriages I had admired so much on the last lap of the journey up from Mombasa.

When a note went up on the notice board at the Club saying there would be a dance at the weekend I could not delay any longer. I phoned and stood in a vacuum waiting for a voice. Her father answered and I hesitantly asked if I could speak to Pam without saying who I was.

"Just a minute," he said. I could hardly believe it. She was there.

"Hello." Her voice had an almost apprehensive note it seemed.

"Pam?"

"Davie!" her voice was way up the octaves. After all these years she knew me with one word! "Davie, is that really you?"

After we had both come down from the clouds and I had established she was not married or involved – I learned later that she had been engaged once but had broken it off when she realised she was not really in love with the fellow – I said where I was in town and asked if she would like to come to the dance. She accepted with alacrity. She lived in Muthaiga, a few miles out of town and I said I'd pick her up by taxi but she said her father was going into town at that time and would bring her. She had a car of her own but girls did not drive alone at night.

On Saturday evening I waited at the Legion Club door in a high state of mental delirium looking out at the wet street. The expected time of Pam's arrival had already passed and there was still no sign of her. I was already thinking that something had happened, she had changed her mind and was not going to come after all. Street lamps bent their slender necks and gazed at their reflections on the glistening pavements; cars swished by, wiping the rain from their eyes with waging fingers. Some Indians in turbans and lounge suits passed, chattering loudly. A few Africans flapped by in bare feet and inadequate clothes; one, in shredded army greatcoat and drooping, tattered bush hat, sloshed in the gutter with his foot and fished out a cigarette end that had not yet disintegrated and put it in his pocket. One or two white couples hurried along to Torrs Hotel, women with high hair-do's and men with clipped moustaches, all wrapped up in raincoats and shielded with umbrellas.

Looking at these last people I suddenly felt inadequate. The tweed sports jacket and flannels I carried as 'best', rolled up tightly in the bottom of my rucksack and newly ironed by the room 'boy', seemed shabby. I wanted to be like these people, resplendent as a fighting cock to sweep milady off her feet. But now it didn't seem to matter. She had changed her mind.

The soft music that drifted out from the dance floor now seemed odious. Forlornly I felt more drawn to the tingling strumming of an *ngoma* – the Swahili word used for dance, drum or any musical instrument – the little, hand-sized dulcimer type board with a row of sprung-steel wires that are pinged with the thumbs. The player was one of the rickshaw boys huddled round the brazier at their row of vehicles, a mode of transport that was already becoming obsolete. The weak, tinny notes brought back happy memories of army days when, after a film or a night on the town, we would hire rickshaws to take us to the big services' car park where trucks – 'passion wagons' in army jargon – waited to take men back to their various camps. When spirits were high the pulling boys would be paid extra to race their slender two-wheeled carts that took a pair of passengers to the destination and loud would be the calls and hoots as we encouraged our man to beat the others.

Despondent now and conscious of the dampness seeping through me I was about to go when a car curved into the kerb and stopped abruptly. A door opened. A shapely, nyloned leg stretched out from under a frilly orange dress and felt for the pavement. A dark head emerged and someone stood up in a flurry of colour, slammed the door as she swung a wrap round her shoulders and waved goodbye to the driver as the car pulled away. She turned and for a moment my heart dropped. This was not Pam. This person had not come for me. Pam was a long legged, doe-eyed girl with a shy smile. This was a beautiful, poised woman. I went to meet her. Her eyes smiled in recognition as she came forward in steady, measured steps, so cool, then in quick little ones as we neared each other and finally in an abandoned run and involuntary embrace. The evening was the kind that makes memories and was the start of a few wonderful, idyllic months.

*

The rains finished and endless sunny days returned and there was no better place to be than Nairobi and the then 'White Highlands' of Kenya, named as such because only white people could buy land there. At 6000 feet and over in some places the temperature is never too hot or cold. The days were warm and the nights sometimes cold enough for a log fire. And at that time there was no danger, no threatening atmosphere. You could walk anywhere at ease, through the bush country, by native *shambas* and wave to the Kikuyus as they tilled their land and have your wave returned accompanied by happy giggles, or even call at their houses and be invited in.

We didn't know it then, but this was really the beginning of the end of that era, the end of colonial rule. Even before the months I was there were up, the fingers of death were creeping through the land: there were whispers, rumours of dark happenings, a growing lawlessness, hardly noticeable at this time, but insidiously increasing; burglaries to whites' houses when only guns were stolen, bodies – only black ones then – found in clearings in the woods. The waves to the women in the fields were seldom returned and instead our greetings were met with side glances full of fear or hostility. A growing awareness crept through the European community that it was unwise to go unprotected or unarmed into isolated areas.

All this time however Pam and I were blissfully unaware of any sinister clouds that were gathering around us. We shared walks and picnics in the woods, bicycle runs in the country with lots of laughs, and trips in Pam's little car. We went to Thika to see the Falls and to Limuru that hangs on the very edge of the escarpment that forms one side of the Great Rift Valley, where the air is crystal cool and the views are magnificent beyond words. (It was there, at the turn of the century, the railway surveyors and engineers worked a miracle to take the line up the sheer face of the wall.) And, unforgettable, a trip to Naivasha, to stand by the Lake and watch the flamingoes rise in unbelievable numbers, a great, noisy, flapping, pink cloud that seemed to fill the sky from one horizon to the other.

Sometimes there were family dinners at home with her two sisters and younger brother and her mother, a lovely lady who ruled the house with firm but quiet, humorous, matriarchal authority. Father was rarely there. These were always occasions of extraordinary happiness to which I felt privileged to be welcomed. There were the visits to the theatre to watch the Donovan Maule Players, reputed to be the only resident professional artistes from Cairo to Johannesburg. And there were the dances and the candlelit dinners that helped to cast the euphoric cloud over our lives. Time went by quickly, as it does when you are happy, until John Woodward put a stop to it all.

John was Pam's elder sister Jean's fiancé. A fellow Scot, he had come as a teenager with his father to Kenya and latterly had set up his own building business, an unusual occurrence for a white person since all artisan work was normally run or controlled by Indians. Against intense, cut-throat competition his business nevertheless was prospering. So much so, he was planning to go down to Mombasa to take delivery of a new pickup van. This was much cheaper than accepting it at Nairobi and much better for the vehicle than having it hammered up the 300-mile wash-board road by an African driver who had no regard for running-in the engine, which was essential then for mechanical longevity. A person taking personal delivery at the docks therefore owned a better vehicle and gained a free holiday at the coast from the deal.

John asked me to accompany him and since I had been working for a few months and was due a few days holiday I agreed. We travelled down by train and stayed at the Nyali Beach Hotel, a semi-circular building hugging a round, open-air dance floor looking on to a row of waving palm trees and an arc of white, shimmering sand. A wonderful setting. We swam and read while sun-bathing in short spells for the sun at the coast was vicious and we sailed to the *mawe nyeupe* (white stones) coral reef and tried the new sport of goggle-fishing which was just coming in. I loved it, not for the fishing with the spear-gun which I soon found would take much more time than we had available to even hit the biggest thing we saw, but for the sheer delight of gliding over what seemed like the glass dome of a new world. I was amazed when the goggles allowed me to see so far down into the deep canyons that disappeared into terrifying black depths and then watch white hills, rich with bright coloured waving flora, gradually emerge from the deep, sinister blackness.

Another day we went to Malindi to surf the waves on belly boards and end up pell-mell on the beach, rubbed raw from sand abrasions and full of sea water and masochistic delight.

In the evenings we ate sumptuously and talked of past days in Scotland and new ones in Kenya. At one dinner an amusing incident occurred at my expense. We sat surveying the menu which to me was as clear as hieroglyphics. John, wiser in these matters, recommended the globe artichoke as an *hors-d'oeuvre* and not wishing to show my ignorance I concurred. I had never heard of the thing before. Unfortunately John decided on something else for himself. When the dish was served with a little bowl of oil beside it I had no idea how to handle it. Trying hard not to look put-out while nonchalantly in the middle of conversation, I took the oil and poured it over the plant, pulled off one of the pulpy leaves and proceeded to eat the whole thing. If I noticed John's eyes blink with amazement it did not put me off though I thought how awful the fibrous stuff was and as a so-called delicacy, I wondered what people saw in it.

I had a terrible job getting through it while all the time trying my hardest not to seem perplexed. The fact that one was supposed to nibble only the fleshy tips of the leaves after first dipping each one delicately into the tiny bowl of oil was at that time lost on me. Afterwards I watched others eating the same dish and noticed that after they had finished they had a bigger bundle of loose leaves on their plate than when they had started. The laugh came when the waiter came to clear up before the next course.

I can see him now, standing by the table looking at my empty plate. Dressed in a long white *kanzu* with red tarboosh and cummerbund he had the reserved poise of the professional waiter. His shiny black face was the picture of suppressed incredulity as he looked from the plate to me, down from my eyes to my lap to see if I'd scooped the lot down to there, then to the floor round the table and seeing nothing of the lost debris he finally turned sideways and, very discreetly, lifted a corner of the tablecloth and slid a surreptitious glance under the table before going off with an utterly baffled look on his face.

All this was of course lost on me at the time, though I did wonder at the man's strange behaviour until John could suppress his laughter no longer and explained it all. He said he could not believe his eyes when he saw me tucking in and after the moment was gone he didn't like to tell me what a bloomer I'd made. After that we both had a good laugh and so did the waiter when he returned and I explained it all and included him in the fun.

The journey back was so different to my previous one over this route. Now it was the thick red dust from passing cars rather than mud that troubled us. But overall the traffic was light, so we were not bothered too much.

We were well on our way back when John dropped his bombshell. Without preamble he said,

"How would you like to have your own business?"

It took me some time to take in what he had said and even longer to comprehend all the aspects and complications of it. He admitted he had had an ulterior motive in inviting me to join him on this journey. Although we had met off and on over the past few months we had never met without the girls around and he had wondered if we could get along together on our own. His business was going well and he felt the time was coming for him to expand and for this he needed a working partner, someone who he could rely on, someone who could push the jobs along. More than that, he offered to set me up in my own painting contracting business. He had to subcontract all his painting to Indian firms and the work was not good and he felt that not being up on that side of the business they took him to the cleaners: an odd metaphor, I thought, since his father was a partner in the 'Queens Laundry and Dry Cleaners'. Every other shop in Nairobi seemed at that time to be a dry cleaning business. Indeed, I had painted his father's place out on a nightshift basis, grabbing a couple of hours sleep each morning before going on to my railway job, and it was perhaps from this that John had conjured up the idea of getting me into full-time business.

"Mind you, you'd have to go some to make a success of it. The Indians would see to that. That's why you don't see many Europeans in the building trade businesses. The old *wahindi* are crafty, astute and completely unscrupulous. They'll gang up on you, cut their prices and even work at a loss to undercut you until they drive you out of business, or hope to anyway. They're much better suited to live on low profits than we are, the standard of living they're prepared to accept is so much lower than what we would put up with. But nobody can say they won't work if it's for their own ends. Believe me, the *hindi* will feed his wife and fourteen children on the drippings of his sweat rag. The only way to win is to beat them on expertise and be prepared to work really hard yourself."

The idea of hard work certainly didn't frighten me any more than John's lurid

146

and grossly exaggerated picture of the opposition. But much as the idea greatly appealed to me I countered that I had no money to invest in his business, far less buy the equipment to start my own. But it was obvious that John had been working on this for some time for he had all the answers.

"Look," he said with great emphasis, "you won't need a penny to start up. What supervisory work you do for me we'll do on a contractual basis and that will give you an immediate cash income. But in addition I propose to buy all the equipment and materials you need to start off with. Just give me a list and put it all to my account. For this I would want a fifty-per-cent partnership in your business. I can give you enough work to tide you over the next few months and this will allow you to hire and fire until you establish a good team of workers. In the meantime you could be pricing for other outside contracts and hopefully by the time you've done the bulk of my work you'll have built up a good book to be going on with. And of course as my building contracts come to the painting stage I'd be feeding you these on an ongoing basis. Each year I'd reduce my stake in your company by ten-per-cent until I hold only ten-per-cent, which I would retain on a permanent basis or until you buy me out. By this time I expect you will spend more time with your own work and less and less on mine. What do you think?"

I was absolutely stunned. What an offer! I had always fancied being my own boss, having a business of my own. And here it was on my lap. Made. I couldn't lose. In my dumb silence John struck again.

"I really mean this and to start the ball rolling you can have this car when we get back. Just drop me off and you can drive it away. Put it down to part of my fifty per cent."

Apart from mumbling some thanks and saying I'd think it over, I don't think I said a word for the rest of the journey. I felt I'd been hit by a typhoon that was continuing to blast me with all the implications of the offer, all the changes it would make if I accepted: more wealth than I'd ever dreamed of, being my own man, bossing my own show, and ... more than all that, there was Pam, a chance for our friendship to develop. Against all that there was my journey, the thing I had set myself to do. And there were my folks at home: I had never contemplated not going home to Scotland and settling there. I had never been so torn apart in my life.

When we arrived at Nairobi I said I needed more time to make my decision. John said he could not spare too long. A week, two at the most, then he'd have to put his outstanding work out to tender and without that cushion he doubted if I'd make it, starting up from scratch.

All that week I was in a fever of indecision. I felt I was at the cross-roads of my life. Whatever decision I made was going to shape my future. As it happened, a lot of things came about to help me make up my mind. It is strange how the end of an era can come in so many different ways all at once.

The week before, Frank Vernon had left the Club to take up a job on an up-country farm. It didn't seem a good move for him and I worried that the lonely environment of farm life would not be good for those occasional morasses of despair that occurred in his mind. The incidence of these dark patches had decreased during our time together and I hoped he would find some lasting happiness that would wipe them away for always.

About the same time another fellow entered my life briefly and his presence had a dramatic effect on my current situation. 'Entered' my life is not precisely true for I had known Windsor Duffield as a distant friend since I was in my mid teens. At that time I was doing a lot of hiking and climbing on my own in Scotland. After a short article I had published on walking I had a letter from Windsor saying he too liked hiking and having no companion he would like to join me on one or more of my outings if he may. He came from Stirling and I arranged to meet him one Saturday morning at the bus-stop at Aberfoyle and we'd do the Duke's Pass over to the Trossachs, along Lochs Achray and Venachar and down to Callander for a late bus home.

I had a surprise when we met for he was at least ten years older than I and looked anything but a country walker. He was very small, five feet or so, wore large, heavy glasses and had a pixie beaming face. During the day it became obvious he was not a long distance walker but he was a cheery companion and kept up constant light patter. Despite the disparity in ages he was happy, eager even, to defer to me on all decisions and from then and on future walks I came see him as someone in my charge rather than my elder mentor.

After I had left for Africa Windsor also got carried away with the idea of going there and to this end he somehow landed a job in the Sudan, Khartoum I think, and duly set sail for there after a big family send-off when his elder sister, whom he spoke of in terms of his matriarch, presented him with an inscribed watch in honour of the occasion. Unfortunately things hadn't gone so well for Windsor in his job, with the result he threw up his position and appeared unannounced one day in the Club. He knew I was staying there from a letter I'd written to him. To say I was surprised was – as the cliché goes – putting it mildly. Even more important, I worried what to do with him. I put him up in my room for a few nights in the same way Frank had done for me when I arrived, the only difference being that I had Windsor take the bed and I had the shake down in my sleeping bag on the floor.

During my time in Nairobi I had written an article and some letters for publication in the local newspaper, *The East African Standard*, and in doing this had become familiar with one or two of the people there. When I learned Windsor had clerical skills I introduced him there, with the result he was taken on the staff. Within days he had with the best of intentions put the skids under me. Without my knowledge he spoke to one of the writers about me and a short article appeared in the newspaper which started something like; David Lessels, who works with East African Railways, is there only temporarily. David has walked down through Africa and will soon be continuing his journey. Etc. etc.

The result was that I was summoned immediately to the Manager's Office at the railway workshops on the morning of publication. The austere man had the paper with the article folded open on his desk and stabbing with his finger asked me what I made of it. I could only say that despite some discrepancies and exaggerations there was some truth in what was there. I was at the moment pondering about going on with my journey but so far I had not quite made up my mind. He then proceeded to help me in this vexing matter. He asked if, when applying to join the Railway, I had had any intention of only remaining temporarily with the Company. I had to say that although I was undecided what to do at the moment, it was my intention at the outset to carry on travelling when I was ready to go. Whereupon he gave me the sack, told me to gather my things and any wages due and carry on my way.

There was no doubt that events were running to a crisis. Before this I had had three options: take up John's offer, carry on my journey or let things stay as they were and just continue to enjoy life. As if in anticipation of this, my easy option had been taken away, forcing me into either one of the major decisions.

My mind in turmoil and being now at a loose end in the middle of the week, I decided to take myself to the wilds to think. I had not touched my marching gear for months. My boots needed a lot of working with wax polish to lick them into shape again and I checked my tent and other equipment. I thought of going to the Ngong Hills, about twenty miles out of Nairobi, to gaze down at the fabulous Rift Valley where the scenery is breathtaking. Ngong was one of my very early memories of Africa and one of my favourite places. Back in my army days in these parts, when we could wangle a *gari* (vehicle) for a special day out it was to 'Hoppies' restaurant we went. A sprawling barn of a place with old colonial charm, it lay up the winding road, past the little group of shops we knew as 'Karen Dukas' – we didn't know then that it was named after the woman who had had her farm near there – and on to the very top of the Ngong Hills.

Ngong had its magnetism, but now I felt I wanted to break new ground. I needed complete isolation, a place that would tax me physically and strip off the town culture I had grown so used to. I knew of such a place. Where better to find it than in the Mountain of the Lost World.

In this I am being whimsically melodramatic but not entirely untrue. Down the Great Rift Valley there are several such mountains, old volcanoes where Nature had blown her top at various times in the distant past and broken through the Earth's crust at its weakest point where it had been split so deeply in the making of that valley. Any one of these so-formed mountains could be the setting for Conan Doyle's classic story *The Lost Word* in which an intrepid explorer finds a mountain, a high plateau, surrounded by savage ravines which cut it off from the rest of the world, a place where dinosaurs and other prehistoric animals still ranged.

*

Some fifty miles north of Nairobi on the Naivasha road lies the sleeping volcano called Longonot. A great 9,000ft. high, truncated cone, it dominates the drop-dead-if-you-ever-see-better landscape that strikes you speechless when the road suddenly pitches over the crest of the escarpment wall and plunges in loops to the Rift Valley floor.

Like any giant, Longonot sleeps fitfully, giving off occasional puffs of steam with just the hint of a great temper ready to burst. I had long had the desire to climb it and now it seemed this was the ideal time to do it.

I had walked only a few miles out of Nairobi when I got a lift from an Indian driving a little pickup with an African sitting up the back. He was going to Naivasha and would pass the mountain on his way. I told him what I was going to do and he was immediately interested. "I have been here nearly thirty years and looked at that mountain every morning of my life since then and I've always wondered what it was like up there," he said in sing-song English, "but I've never been there and I'm not likely to now." I thought that was fair comment. Climbing mountains was not the kind of thing Indians did in Kenya. He said there was a path of sorts from the road to the base of the mountain and when we got near he shouted out the window to the boy to tell me where the path was. The African jutted out his chin and said "*Huko.*" (Over there) On these precise directions the Indian stopped his truck and I got out and thanked him.

I had a feeling that the boy had no more idea than his master where exactly was the path and after some searching it was obvious that was the case. A little later I met two local lads and they put me on my way. 'Path-of-sorts' indeed filled the description but I covered the five miles or so to the base of the cone without too much meandering.

Looking up it was a formidable sight. Its sloping sides rose steeply and were incredibly corrugated as if they had just solidified from their molten state. With its summit at over 9,000 feet and rising out of the 5,000ft. land level I reckoned the actual climb, including going into the crater, was going to be something like doing Ben Nevis.

The upper reaches of the mountain were devoid of forestation and I had no intention to camp up there. I therefore had no desire to carry my rucksack with tent and equipment up to the summit and down into the crater and back up again so I hid it off the track a bit and covered it with branches and bracken, blazed a scar on a nearby tree with the panga I carried and piled a group of stones at the side of the path which I hoped I and no one else would recognise. The chances of anyone passing was most remote, this being such a desolate area. But, as mentioned before, there were growing rumours of gangs of natives meeting secretly in the hills and isolated woods for esoteric purposes and if this was so I didn't want any of these people finding it.

The gathering presence of these shadowy characters was now spoken of openly in Kenyan white society, but only in the confines of living rooms and then only in hushed whispers. Nobody knew what it meant but all were aware of a growing unrest among the natives, a sort of grumbling pain in the guts of their society. Everyone had faith in the police doing a surgical job to remove or contain it before it came to any kind of fruition. The idea that this unease was the first rumble of a coming storm that would actually destroy them was unthinkable then. At worst it was a growing threat that would have to be dealt with.

Had I told any of the local settlers what I was intending they would have done their utmost to dissuade me. When I told the fellows at the Club they merely said I was mad.

Carrying only my water-bottle with some sandwiches and with my panga hanging from my belt, I cleared the lower slopes and climbed onto the barren, contorted upper region. The mountain was like a great, stiff custard pudding that had been emptied from a bowl and the outer surface had dried into a deep wrinkled skin. Like a fly on the pudding you walked up the ridge of one of the wrinkles hoping the ridge would run on to another and so on, otherwise you had to go down the valley between and climb to another ridge which you hoped would carry you on and on over others. It was a game that passed the time. The going was not difficult but towards the top the altitude was beginning to have an effect and make me out of breath a bit. People coming to the highlands of Kenya always find that the rarefied atmosphere, even at Nairobi's level, makes them breathless with very little exertion. As young, fit soldiers, when I first came to Kenya, we could not understand why we all soon became out-of-puff when playing even a simply game of knock-about football. When the cause was explained to us we were able to mentally chart our progress of acclimatisation over the next few months. Nevertheless, any immunity gained at the Nairobi level seemed to have little effect at this higher region at which I was now found myself.

In addition to the rarefied air syndrome, there was another factor I realised with which I had to contend. Each time I stopped for a breather I was aware of my growing sense of loneliness and isolation. I realised this might be due to the herd life of the city to which I had become accustomed and my close friendship with Pam. If I were to go on with my journey I must grow accustomed to being without company and be totally self-reliant.

The rim was surprisingly even, only rising at one high point, and dangerously sharp, making a walk round the circumference a very risky manoeuvre since the inside wall down to the far bottom of the crater was almost perpendicular. When Joseph Thomson, the intrepid young Scots explorer sent out by the Royal Geographical Society in 1883 to explore the country now known as Kenya, climbed Longonot he was stricken with vertigo as he stood on the rim and had a great temptation to throw himself into the crater.

I fancied the crater was about half a mile wide and about 1000 feet deep. The floor looked deeply forested and I wondered what life, if any, there would be down there. Somewhere in the back of my mind, perhaps from old army days when many fellows boasted knowledge without experience, I remembered someone saying that Longonot crater was thick with snakes. Certainly, in my loneliness and looking down into the deep, wide pit so completely cut off from the outside world, it looked the perfect *Lost World* setting where one could expect to meet dinosaurs and other prehistoric reptiles.

I traversed about half way round the rim before I found a place where I could descend inside. This was no easy matter. The footing was more like clay than rock and so steep that in places I was forced to dig footholds with my panga. The clay was treacherous and often my footholds gave way and threatened to send me plummeting down. My diary entry succinctly covered a lot of ground:

However, after a hazardous journey I reached the floor of the crater.

Inside it was hot and dusty. Small scrub bushes grew close together and there were spoors of many animals including some with large hoofs, such as buffalo, but how they had managed to get there I could not guess. Had they bred for thousands of years in there, isolated from their outside cousins and if so were they now a different species? For curiosity I wanted to see some but in my heart I was glad I didn't. The feeling of being so all-alone was very heavy up there inside that locked-off piece of land. Any injury could make it impossible to climb out.

I wanted to make my way over to where sulphur jets were reputed to come up through holes in the crust, but found the going very slow through the bush and not being quite sure where they were I lost a lot of time. The sun was on the slide and I wanted to get up and off the upper slopes before it was dark: finding a way down the wrinkle ridges would have been hazardous, to say the least, and I had to find my rucksack. In the light of discretion, I gave up the attempt and headed back.

Climbing up was not as bad as coming down and I made the ridge and the descent from the top without incident, found my rucksack intact and made camp. Light was fading fast as I put three thick logs radiating like spokes with their ends nearly together to form a hob and lit a fire with small wood in the centre. When the flames had burned off I buried a few potatoes in their skins in the embers. I had a piece of steak I'd bought in Nairobi market that morning and it wasn't too bad despite being in my rucksack all day. I placed it too on the hot coals and turned it often with my sheath knife. Lastly, across the three log ends I put my billy-can, half full of water from my flask, to brew a strong making of tea, not forgetting the old habit of putting a sliver of shaved wood in the water to stop the tea tasting smoked. The 'billy' was an old syrup can with holes at the top of opposite sides and a wire laced across.

Now, sitting with my back against the bole of a tree watching my meal cooking, pleasantly tired after the day's walk, hungry enough to make the smell of the scorched steak seem delicious I was at ease with myself more than I had been since John made his offer and before that too, although I had not been fully aware of it. Of late the city life had begun to pall. The work at the railway workshop, interesting and challenging at first, had become monotonously repetitive and boring.

At the start there had been the usual contest between worker and boss to see how far the one could take the other. Any new person to the country has to pay the price for experience. The African worker will always take the person for a fool and play unscrupulously on their naivety. I had fun taking up their comments on me to each other and entering into the joke, much to their surprise and eventual, I think, respect. I also made a point of taking the brush out of the hand of someone showing some difficulty and proceed to finish the piece with ease while making sure the man saw how to improve his own dexterity. There were other supervisors there but none who were painter tradesmen, none who could teach them. From this I established a friendship and bonhomie with the African workers and life had been fun for a while.

Of late though, time at work had begun to hang heavy and the working days grew long. I needed a new challenge. So when the termination came it was almost a relief and, as things were turning out, appeared even a natural part of the developments that were culminating to change my life.

The water in the billy bubbled and broke my chain of thought. I spooned in the tea and added sugar and milk powder – called 'Klim', which was 'milk' spelt backwards – fished the potatoes out of the ashes and broke the charred crust from them and sliced them up, scraped off the worst of the burnt surface of the steak and put it with a shake of salt between two slices of bread that were only beginning to go hard after the day in my pack and settled back against the tree trunk in complete contentment. Never did tea, drunk straight from the blackened billy after the leaves had settled, and a sandwich with roasted potatoes to munch taste so good.

I felt there was an aura around me there, sitting alone in the firelight with my tent awaiting me, high up on the wooded mountainside with the darkness of the trees pressing in. Even the real threat of prowling wild animals and the possibility of even more dangerous natives stumbling on me while on their nefarious clandestine meetings combined to thrill rather than frighten.

This, I felt, was the world I thrived in and at the moment I could not think of doing anything else. City life was indeed beginning to lose many of its attractions. Life at the Club had gone a bit stale. What had seemed a blissful oasis in a hard desert was now plain routine. Always the same faces, in the same places at the same time and so often saying the same things. What had once been a haven was now something of a prison keeping me from the more interesting world.

I had recently read another of Richard Burton's books, *Pilgrimage to Al Madinah and Meccah* in which he gives to the outer world the first details of the Moslem pilgrimage to the Holy City. On this occasion, however, it was not the great traveller's epic and dangerous journey I was recalling. It was a little thing he wrote in that book in which he sums up his idea of the true traveller. The passage impressed me so much at the time I learned it by heart, and now at this cross-roads of my life's journey it seemed so pertinent I recited it to myself:

The thoroughbred wanderer's idiosyncrasy I presume to be a composition of what phrenologists call 'inhabitiveness' and 'locality' equally and largely developed. After a long and toilsome march, weary of the way, he drops into the nearest place of rest to become the most domestic of men. For a while he smokes the 'the pipe of permanence' [The long pipe an Arab uses at home in place of the shorter 'chibuk' used on the road] with an infinite zest; he delights in various siestas during the day, relishing withal deep sleep during the dark hours; he enjoys dining at a fixed dinner hour and he wonders at the demoralisation of the mind which cannot find excitement in chit-chat or small-talk, in a novel or a newspaper. But soon the passive fit has passed away; again the paroxysm of ennui comes by slow degrees, Viator loses appetite, he walks about his room all night, he yawns at conversations, and a book acts on him as a narcotic. The man wants to wander, and he must do so, or he shall die.

Burton's words summed up my present mood so well I pondered on it a while, the pendulum of the future swinging from side to side. Yes, it would be great to forget everything of the present and move on. On the other hand, would I not gain so much more if I stayed? If it were only me who was involved it would be easy. Could I forget my folks back home? But lots of people emigrated and here there was opportunity the likes of which I could not foresee in Scotland. Here there was the prospect of business success giving a prosperous future with a high standard of living with servants and all. And more than that ... there was Pam. Could I hope ...? Would I be cruel to go? Was I making too much of it all?

As one who liked, but didn't always follow, the musings of Omar Khayyam, the age old Persian poet, I remembered the gem from his *Rubaiyat*:

'Tis all a Chequer-board of Nights and Days
Where Destiny with Men for Pieces plays:
Hither and thither moves, and mates, and slays,
And one by one back in the Closet lays.

Oh Omar, you cynical old rogue, if life is but a game of chess what price mine to lose my Queen so early in the play? What chance is there for one to 'Mate without the Queen'?

Here then was the crunch: was all else of insignificant matter? Yes, as I sat in solitude by the fire in the loneliness of the forest, it seemed to me that my best interests lay in Nairobi and I should give up my journey and settle there. And there the pendulum stopped and that would have been the end of the debate had not someone, almost forgotten, whispered in my ear. Not someone in person, more a memory of words said once that even then seemed a long time ago,

"You are a man with a mission ... You will remember my words long after you have forgotten me." As clear as if he were breathing in my ear I was aware of Grasso Stellario's presence.

A man with a mission! It seemed a bit highfalutin. But was I not? I had dreamed about going the length of Africa, talked about it, told people what I was going to do. It had all been in the papers when we left. People were expecting me to do what I had said I would do. I would be letting down all who believed in me, letting myself down, if I did not at least try my best to complete my journey. I knew then, after all the debate, what I was going to do.

I came off the mountain next morning without incident, got a lift soon after hitting the road and arrived back in Nairobi for lunch, no wiser but more resolved than when I left.

*

That Saturday I took Pam to a night-club, aptly named, the 'Chez Dave'. It was an evening-suit affair and I was wearing borrowed plumes two sizes too small for me. I felt as tight as a drum, and it wasn't all the fault of the suit. When I saw her that night, when I looked at her across the table, my resolution which had been so strong on the mountain dissolved like snow in a hot oven.

Conversation was strained and unnatural. My timing was all wrong and her feet suffered. At last she could bear it no longer.

"Davie, do tell me what is the matter. I've never seen you like this before," she said with great feeling.

I told her of John's offer. Her face coloured deeply but she didn't say anything at first. I think she knew. I suppose John had mentioned it to Jean and it would have got round the family. She would not know what I intended to do for I had not contacted John yet. Whatever my intention I had decided she would be the first to know. I explained with difficulty how I had battled with my decision.

"And what have you decided?" she spoke hesitantly for the first time.

There was a long pregnant silence as we looked so earnestly at each other and I felt myself wavering.

"I'm going away, Pam. I must carry on with my journey," I said disconsolately. And then she floored me.

"Oh Davie, I'm so glad," she said in a small voice, her eyes downcast at the table.

"Glad?" I couldn't stop myself asking in disbelief.

"I've been so worried for you. I thought you were going to give in and take up John's offer. If you had you would not have been the man I thought you were."

I didn't know whether to be pleased or hurt at her reply. Perhaps she was trying to make it easy for me, another way of playing the time-honoured 'Don't bother about me' scenario. Maybe she was glad to see the back of me, but when she looked at me I had the feeling that her lips had not spoken the words that were in her eyes.

She asked when I was going and I said in a few days time, after I'd made my final preparations. I suggested that we meet again before I left but she was all up tight and said it was better that we didn't. I couldn't tell what emotion was uppermost in her mind, but when we parted on her doorstep and after she had wished me good luck, it was her cheek she offered for a goodbye kiss.

We corresponded a little for a while but her letters had no heart and the link died away. As time went by I often wondered, as one does, whether I had done the right thing. But then, is there a *right* thing to do? What is right for the time may not be right for the future. When I returned to Kenya a couple of years later the country was on a wartime footing. Building work had all but ceased. John and Jean had married and divorced. John's business had gone bust and he had left the country. Later still, much later, I heard from a friend that Pam had married happily and had had lots of children. And me? I too later found happiness and fulfilment, more than I might have dared dream.

Chapter Nine

THE BLOOD DRINKERS

Friday 28th September 1951 – Namanga River
   The rhino broke from the shade of a tree ... seeing it charge at us was like a kick in the stomach.

It was with bitter-sweet feelings that morning I headed out of Nairobi on the road to Arusha and beyond, my pack on my back, my kilt swinging and my old slouch hat pulled down to shade my eye. Maybe I'd made the greatest mistake of my life in leaving Nairobi, but this wasn't bad. This was what I'd come to Africa for and I now felt better mentally equipped to tackle the journey. I had been through the tempest of emotions and had emerged with greater confidence than I had had before. I summed it up in my diary entry of that day:

I know now that nothing short of injury will stop me from getting to South Africa. No other temptation will ever bother me.

And it was not only in the mental department that I was now better equipped. In preparation for tackling the rest of my journey I had acquired a couple of items that bolstered my confidence no end. My experiences in Somaliland and my escapade on Longonot had shown me that I would be foolish to go into these wild areas unarmed. Remembering how good it felt having a panga on my belt on my previous jaunts I acquired one from an ex-Kenya Regiment soldier and in the railway workshop ground the round end off it to form a sharp point, so it could be used to stab as well as slash, as was its intended purpose to cut cane or a way through dense undergrowth. In River Road I had an Indian *fundi* sew straps on my rucksack so that the long, broad-bladed knife could be fixed down the side of it in such a manner that allowed me draw it while my pack was still on my back.
   Also, in a little Indian gunshop near the market I stood and surveyed the weaponry there, eyeing the rifles in racks, ranging from .22 peashooters to .500 elephant guns and hand guns of all types. I had no desire for a rifle but gazed longingly at the large calibre revolvers, but these were way out of my price range. In the end the only thing I felt I could afford was a little .25 automatic Beretta pistol, small enough to be almost completely enveloped in my palm, and

twenty rounds of ammunition. The cost was 65/-. (In the three countries, Kenya, Tanganyika and Uganda, where the East African pound was common currency prices were always quoted in shillings even if the figure went into thousands.) No question of a licence was mentioned. I walked out of the shop with it like I would a bag of sweeties and thereafter when travelling carried it always in the left button-down pocket of my shirt, without ever registering it. In the end though, it was to get me into great trouble, but that was years ahead, near the end of my journey.

I was aware that the pistol would be useless against animals. It would only slightly wound a large beast and be likely to make it even more dangerous. But in the last resort, I kidded myself, fired an inch from the eye of a marauding attacker it might just give me the chance of escape. The real purpose of the gun of course was in the event of a possible attack by natives. I had no desire or intention of ever shooting to kill except as a very last resort, but a shot above the head or if necessary at the legs of an attacker bent on skewering me might dissuade him from pressing his intentions. Whatever, real or psychological, the presence of these weapons gave me a comforting confidence I would not have had without them.

I felt at this stage that I was beginning a new chapter in my journey and since it was time for major decisions I made one then that had an important bearing on my travelling life. I resolved never to pay a fare for transport, except perhaps on sea crossings, no matter how difficult my situation might be. This was not just a Scotsman's canny way of saving money, it was a challenge I now undertook. Anyone, I told myself, could travel by hired transport. From now on if I couldn't hitch a lift I would walk. If an area was impassable for any reason, I would walk round it, no matter how far. I would not pay to surmount an obstacle.

The way south to Arusha lay through the Great Rift Valley, that cataclysmic split in the early Earth's crust that goes all the way up Africa and the Red Sea. Apart from taking me south my immediate interest in coming this way was to spend some time with the Masai tribe.

Kenya is rich in the diversity of its tribes. Once upon a time there was a people in the highlands called the Athi who gave their name to the plain on which Nairobi grew and to a river. They were said to be hunters, small of stature with light brown skin. But of them now there is no trace, having been wiped out or absorbed by the invading tribes from the west and north.

From the west came the Negroes, groups of dark-skinned people whose languages owed a common origin in Aba'ntu, the tongue of a people who inhabited the Niger region, West Africa, in the distant past. Nowadays these tribes are collectively referred to as Bantu. Anthropologists generally accept that the Bantu started their migrations about the time of Christ, but later in my travels I came across information that would indicate that the drift of these people may have started to the north and then east long before the accepted date, as much as two or three thousand years before. Be that as it may, there is no doubt that Bantu tribes were installed throughout central and east Africa by the 13th or 14th centuries. Today they number nearly four hundred quite diverse tribes throughout Africa, many with quite different languages, but are still all joined by ancient linguistic links. For instance, the Swahili word *Watu*, meaning men or people, is derived from *Bantu*. The Bantus brought with them the practice of village life and a wealth of skills, notably agriculture, metal-working and wood carving.

From the north came those who used to be referred to as Hamites – the children of Ham – but today are generally known as Nilotics as denoting their place of origin, i.e. the Sudan. The Nilotics are said – though some dispute it – to have introduced kingship and government to the land. Also from the north, southern Ethiopia, came the Cushites who were shepherds and cattle herders. They brought their pastorialism with them and introduced animal husbandry to the others. They mainly occupy Kenya's arid northern territories.

Kenya then was a nomenclature of such peoples. In few other places in Africa were you likely to find such a composite group of tribes representing every stage of human development and origin in such a relatively small area. From the WaNdorobo who were pure hunters and lived in the most primitive way, building only the most simple arbours for a few nights' shelter as they followed their wanderings, through the semi-nomadic pastoral Masai to the agricultural WaKikuyu and those in between, such as the hunter/farmer Kamba tribe, you could see it all within the bounds of Kenya.

Of all the groups, and this referred to the whole of Africa, not just Kenya, the pastoral tribes tended to be the fiercest. Perhaps it was because they permanently lived with danger, guarding their flocks against wild animals they had to be prepared to do battle with lions and the like, or because herd-watching must become such a boring life they needed to liven it up with some rape and pillage, slaughter and mayhem, just to have something to talk about round the fire at night. Whatever the reason, the pastoral tribes were always the neighbours-from-hell to their surrounding tribes. And none moreso than the Masai. They arrived in the land that was to be Kenya in the 17th century, perhaps a couple of hundred years after the Bantu people. To the peaceful farmers and hunters the arrival of the cowboys could not have been more devastating if they had been hit by plague.

In all Africa there was no tribe more fearsome than the Masai. Perhaps the Zulu impis might have matched them had they met, but that never happened even though some flying squads of that wonderful fighting race in the south actually reached Lake Victoria. A few of the surrounding tribes put up some resistance, usually ineffective, against the Masai marauding armies, the largest one, the Kikuyu, even won some battles, but on the whole the Masai were left to do more or less as they pleased. For two hundred years the Arab slavers would not dare enter Masailand so the caravan route to the interior skirted it, giving it a wide berth even though it put more than a hundred miles on the journey each way. In 1895, when there were signs that the Masai were beginning to be domesticated, one imprudent Swahili caravan captain decided to cut the corner off the journey and go through Masailand. All but a very few of the compliment of 871 men were wiped out in a night attack by Masai morani warriors. Although he had never been there and knew of the Masai only by repute, H.M. Stanley, the great explorer, who had shot his way through some very ferocious tribes in his passage through the Congo, said in 1878 to an audience of the Royal Geographical Society, "If there are any ladies or gentlemen who are specially desirous of becoming martyrs, I do not know in all my list of travels where you could become martyrs so quickly as in Masailand."

These then were the people with whom I wanted to spend some time. Things had changed a lot though in the 70-odd years since Stanley's statement. British rule over the past half-century had stopped all but a trickle of inter-tribal raiding and warfare. The Masai no longer killed all strangers found on their territory. Ordinary folk of the neighbouring tribes could live in security and peace, assured that tomorrow, or today, would not bring the terror of a Masai attack when all in the camp were likely to be slaughtered and their cattle driven off.

I recently read in a book obviously meant for schools that "the Masai term of Ol Morane should be translated more as 'shepherd' than 'warrior' because the whole lifestyle of that tribe was designed as protectors of cattle," I quote: "If he is fierce toward other human beings, it is only because they threaten to deprive him of his chosen way of life." One wonders on what experience or knowledge the writer bases his/her facts for nothing could be further from the truth. How terrible to feed such misinformation to a new generation of people. The whole structure of the Masai tribe was designed towards offensive militarism on the concept that the best defence is to attack. They aimed to put such fear into their neighbours that they would never dream of rubbing the Masai up the wrong way. This way the Masai could live their lives free to steal their neighbours cattle at will and wash their spears with the blood of all who might try to stop them. Young Masai warriors earned their spurs of manhood by killing the people of other tribes. For that reason alone they would harry their neighbours. No African tribe would have dared to try to deprive the Masai of their chosen way of life.

*

The road from Nairobi was a crumbling strip of tarmac that unwound over the Athi plain. After twenty miles the surface gave out to hard, sunbaked laterite that was so corrugated the truck I had got a lift on rattled so loudly I had to shout my conversation with the driver.

The first Masai I saw were at Kagiado, the administrative centre for Kenya's part of the tribe. Back in the 1880s when Europe was dividing up Africa into colonies at the Berlin Conference, hosted by The Iron Chancellor, Bismarck, an almost straight line was drawn on the map diagonally from Lake Victoria to the coast. The top or northern part was declared British East Africa and the southern part German East Africa. The line went straight through Masailand, dividing the tribe in two. Later, after the First World War when Germany lost its colonies, Britain was given the mandate of the territory called Tanganyika. But although the whole of Masailand was now under British rule the two halves were never united, each part being administered by the separate governments. Perhaps it was thought that it was politic to divide and rule such a large, warlike tribe. That may well have had some bearing on the matter, but there were other factors by which the tribe was divided, factors which occurred before the British arrived, dissertion over which Britain had little or no influence.

At Kagiado a few *morani* lounged around the *dukas*. The terms and spelling of the singular and plural of *moran* is a matter for conjecture. Some modern guide books quote *morani* as singular and *el-moran* as plural. Tucker's *Maasai Grammar* gives *'ol-murran-i'* (singular) and *'il-murran'* (plural). Modern books do tend to follow Tucker's long 'aa' in 'Maasai' which is phonetically correct. But Tucker appears to be on his own with *'murran'* for I never heard it then nor see it quoted as such now. During my time in East Africa the terms used were mostly *'moran'* singular *and 'morani'* plural, if indeed the two were used together. Most people would use only one or the other for both or, more than likely, use the Anglicised 'moran' and 'morans'. In the name of simplicity for the reader and, more honestly, for myself, I will use those that come easiest to me, i.e. *'moran'* singular *and 'morani'* plural and spell 'Masai' as it was current in my time.

They were fierce looking people. At first sight they had a dangerous air about them. Tall, light-brown, lean men with sharp features and haughty stares, they were quite distinguishable from the Bantu people. Their skin was silky smooth, almost feminine, and all had had their ear lobes pierced and distended by bigger and bigger plugs being inserted over years until now they hung in long, skin loops down near to their shoulders. Karen Blixen, in her book *Out of Africa*, describes very well her Masai neighbours on her farm at Ngong:

"A Masai warrior is a fine sight. These young men have, to the utmost extent, that particular form of intelligence which we call chic; daring and wildly fantastical as they seem, they are still unswervingly true to their own nature, and to an immanent ideal. Their style is not an assumed manner,

nor an imitation of a foreign perfection; it has grown from the inside, and is an expression of its race and its history, and their weapons and finery are as much of their being as are a stag's antlers"; and another of her quotes, "... the Masai carriage of head, with the chin stretched forward as if he were presenting his arrogant face upon a tray."

The *morani* at the Kajiado *dukas* certainly had that look on their faces and their general appearance looked none too inviting either. Their hair had been plastered with red mud mixed with goatskin thongs so that it fell as a long pigtail at the back and as a knot on the forehead to the front. Their only attire was a mud-coloured blanket fastened over one shoulder that flapped open as they walked or with the wind revealing their genitals. At their waist each wore a *simi*, (seeme) a short sword in a red skin scabbard. In times to come I was to learn how efficient it was as a weapon. Beautifully made, with a double-edged, leaf-shaped blade, wider near the point for weight and narrowing to the handle which was made of rawhide wound round to give a good grip, it was perfectly balanced for quick wrist movement.

Most fearsome of all, each moran held a near seven-foot long spear, quite unlike any used outside Masailand. Each spear comprised three parts; a three-foot long, sword-like blade, double-edged and fluted to a high ridged spine down the centre on both sides, a short round nine-inch wooden haft, then a long round spike of equal length and balance to the fore part. These spears were made for throwing and they struck with awesome killing power. The hafts, polished with oil and smooth with handling, some made with dark wood and some with a lighter coloured type. I was to learn that the two varieties were made for a very good reason, but perhaps that would be better explained within its context.

I had first made contact with the Masai in these very same *dukas* when in the army. Hiring a truck half a dozen of us had headed down this road to see Kilimanjaro. At Kagiado the scene was exactly as it was five years later on my present travels. Indeed, until I walked on the stage on each occasion, the whole set-up could have been a stage-set left undisturbed, the characters stuck in frozen animation. On the first army jaunt, however, I was a younger, more naive person and saw the moment in sheer wonderment, oblivious of repercussions or what other people thought. In great excitement I had the truck stopped while I gaily dived inside the dark interior to meet and speak to them, a practice at which my pals were aghast, some saying they never expected me to come out again alive. No doubt ignorance is bliss, for I never saw any danger. Nor did I see any now despite the wild look of the Masai.

"Jambo morani. Habari yeke leo?" ("Hello soldiers. How are you all today?")

The faces of a few who understood my greeting lost some of their frostiness and the rest seeing their reaction looked more friendly too. Unlike most other East African tribes not many Masai spoke Swahili. Swahili, as mentioned, evolved at the coast and penetrated through the interior along the slave trails by way of conversation. Swahili was essentially the language of the slavers and nobody, but nobody, ever tried to speak to the Masai let alone make slaves of them. Sixty years later Swahili had not made great inroads into the Masai.

I chatted to them for a while, examining their spears and simis, and they in turn though reluctant to show interest asked who I was, why was I dressed like a woman and why was I carrying a heavy load also like a woman and why was I not like other *Wazungu* (White people). And perhaps because I was not like other *Wazungu* we got on very well.

But there is a limit to what you can learn as a stranger making polite noises to the local inhabitants. Like anyone spending any time in Kenya I had heard wondrous tales of the Masai; how, unlike any other tribe in Africa, they kept a standing army, how they killed lions single handed with their spear to prove their manhood, how they lived by drinking blood and how a *moran* could make love to any girl he chose. But it was all garbled army chatter, the type that most soldiers might bring back from their exciting time abroad, sensational hearsay with little detail or verification. I wanted facts and felt I could hardly go up to someone in the street and ask about their family details and intimate sex life. I had to get somewhere where I could live with the people and earn their confidence and interest so I could speak on subjects more than just passing the time of day.

I had already made a plan for this and knew exactly where I was going in order to put it into action. Fifty miles down the road from Kajiado, near the Namanga River and almost on the Tanganyikan border, was a hotel, the only European hostelry between Nairobi and Tanganyika. I had fond memories of this place and how this came to be may be worth the telling.

Back in '46 on the same safari as mentioned regarding my first meeting with the Masai at Kajiado, we eventually reached Arusha and saw Kilimanjaro. On our way back the 3-ton truck we were in had all sorts of problems. A recurrent fault had caused the engine to boil over repeatedly. Darkness found us a long way from base and in dire straits. Only one of the party could drive and knew anything about engines and he was dead beat with all his exertions and couldn't go on. We were all red raw novices in Africa and the prospect of spending the night in the wilds was frightening. We knew the place was alive with animals and the great piles of elephant droppings in the road made us feel like adding to them. The driver was drooping at the wheel and we were all in high tension when, rounding a bend, the headlights played on this long, whitewashed building with thatched roof. Obviously a European establishment we pulled in gratefully. Beside the building there was a cluster of small, round, whitewashed, thatched cottages we learned to call 'rondavels'.

The place was in darkness and there was no answer to our knocking. Someone tried the handle and to our surprise it gave to our touch. Cautiously, with bated breath, we entered. A flashlight showed that the place was set out as a hotel, but undisturbed dust lay on the furniture and cobwebs, gossamer and delicate in the light, cast their shadows. Such a place in the heart of the jungle was like a set in a spooky film. We called and whistled but no-one appeared.

Then the fellow with the torch called us to where he was. On the wall there was a typed note explaining that the proprietor was sorry he could not attend since he had gone off to the war, but travellers were welcome to use the place as they required. If they found their stay enjoyable and if they wished, they could leave such remuneration they thought fit in a box provided. The note was signed, Col. Gethin. A row of filled oil lamps and matches stood on a shelf with instructions to use the rondavel bedrooms.

Now, *there* was faith in human nature, both with travellers and the local gentry and I for one was greatly impressed with this kindness and trust. A houseboy actually turned up next morning and cooked us breakfast before we left.

A year or so later I was with another party that stayed a night at the Namanga Hotel. This time Col. Gethin was back in residence and the place was run on more orthodox lines. I was pleased to find the colonel to be the hearty, genial type I had imagined and was grateful to have the opportunity to thank him for his proxy kindness when we happened on his sanctuary during the last journey.

Once again he demonstrated his trust in people. The group of soldiers I was with drank lustily at the bar all evening. Time grew late and the bar boy left and the colonel took over. The evening grew old and eventually he too left, leaving the bar open and at our mercy. He merely asked if we would please mark down what we drank and settle up with him in the morning. This certainly brought the best out of the fellows, for what little was consumed after that was meticulously noted down.

Now on my present journey it was to the Namanga River Hotel I was heading. Not that I could afford to stay there, but it was a place I was familiar with and that gave a cosy feeling on which to start. The road was not busy, but there was enough traffic to make hitching fairly easy. On arrival in the afternoon I went in and ordered tea. How pleasant it was to enjoy the comfort of the tourist, not that there were many in those days. As I sat and drank in the ambience as well as the tea the memories rolled back and old faces, now scattered to the winds, swam in and out. It was good to be back. Although the place still retained its quiet pioneer air it now had a more prosperous feel and even sported a white girl receptionist.

I found that Col. Gethin's son was now in charge, but he had obviously inherited many of his father's caring ways for on learning that I intended to camp in the neighbourhood he suggested that I pitch my tent on the front lawn even though I was obviously poor business and would even lower the tone of the place. I was sorry not to meet the colonel, he apparently spent his time these days conducting rich tourists on big-game watching safaris. As things panned out I was later able to meet and share time with the old man and enjoy his company and stories.

I was very grateful for the comfort and feeling of safety on the hotel lawn, surrounded as it was with a six feet or more high hedge and closed gate at night. I did not realise just how lucky I was until later when in the company of Col. Gethin he told how one evening when enjoying a stroll and smoke just outside the grounds he was suddenly confronted by a rhinoceros. He remarked with a laugh that he didn't know how he did it but he cleared the hedge and though scratched he was, "… damned glad to have the thing between it and me." By the time he told me that story I already knew exactly how he felt.

I stayed a couple of nights in the hotel grounds while I looked around at the Masai camps near the place and decided where to put down roots for a little while to study them. In this I was extremely fortunate to meet Sangai. I met him at one of the Masai camps. He spoke Swahili and had done some safari work at the hotel so he was more used to white people and not so sullen and stand-offish as most of the others. When he saw that I was camping and when I told him I actually wanted to stay with his people he did not see me as a tourist and though I could promise him very little for his services he was rarely away from my side most of the time I was there.

He was a wonderful go-between and wherever we went he would introduce me to the tribe in a flow of rapid Masai. I don't know what he said but it always seemed to work. Icy stares and frosty receptions melted and I was soon invited to sit and enjoy a calabash of their curdled milk, foul tasting but very refreshing after a few hours walking through the bush in the heat. The Masai people drank considerable amounts of milk. This was taken either fresh on its own or was mixed with blood, but more often than not it was curdled then eaten. I had consumed copious quantities of this curds-and-whey, particularly after long walks with Sangai, before I learned that when empty the gourd was washed out with cows' urine so that the next lot of milk in it curdled quickly. By that time I was philosophical enough to think that if it hadn't got me by that time it must be all right and I had no wish to offend by refusing their hospitality.

In all my wanderings in Africa I never came across another tribe that lived in such filth as the Masai. Although they were tall people their houses were only about five feet high, flat-roofed rounded onto the walls with no windows. Entrance was through a low, round-topped covered passage like an igloo that ran parallel to the wall and at 90 degrees to the small doorway opening. Inside it was dark and the space was divided into two or three rooms by flimsy stick partitions.

These buildings were made with a frame of bent sticks plastered with a cement of mud and cow dung.

A village or camp comprised a dozen or so houses surrounded by a thorny fence similar to the *zeriba* of Somaliland, only here in Swahili it was called a *boma*. A man would have two, three or more wives and each would have her own house and each family would have their own opening in the fence. Into the *boma* the cattle were brought at night for protection, but unlike the Somali nomads the Masai did not fence off inner corrals so the animals invaded the living areas and also unlike the Somalis who swept out their animal pens daily the Masai never did, so that the whole camp could be covered by a carpet of dung a foot or more deep. The Masai were semi-nomadic and moved their flocks and built new camps every year or so but I never knew whether they moved to find new pastures or to get away from the dung heap when it became too overpowering. I was never with them during the rains, but I shudder to think what it must have been like.

You could tell when you were approaching a Masai settlement by the increase in the volume of flies. On entering any of these establishments I was always struck by the atmosphere of inertia, stagnation even, that was about the place. Life went on at a very leisurely pace. Since the cattle were herded by the young boys there was little more left for anyone else to do. Wars were a thing of the past and cattle raiding even if successful was a chancy business for it could lead to all sorts of trouble from the white man's government, so the *morani* stood about very much at a loose end.

The women, always the busiest members of any African community, had less to do than those of many other tribes. Since the staple diet was blood and milk the women were relieved of the chores of providing and cooking meals. They milked the cattle but they did not till the land nor gather wood for cooking fires nor pound corn nor spend hours over boiling pots.

The older men had no more to do than sit around smoking and talking desultorily with long silences, sighing over the past, lamenting the loss of the old glory days when men were allowed to be men, and deploring the waywardness of the present generation, as older men do the world over.

The young girls, finer featured than their Bantu neighbours and remarkably shiny clean despite the fact that they never washed but merely rubbed their skins with oil, helped their mothers with what work there was to do and like young women the world over occupied themselves with their appearance. You could tell the unmarried ones by the simplicity of their ornamentation: they wore only beads and small chains in their ears and iron arm- and ankle-bands, while the married ones, depending on the wealth of their husband, had profusions of wide metal neck- and ankle-bands and lots of beads sewn onto their raw-hide blanket, their only garment. A proud wife, also like those the world over, might insist that she receive a new dress frequently.

166

These hide blanket dresses of the Masai were worthy of note. In all Africa I came on only one other tribe who produced leather of equal quality as these. The material was so soft and pliable it must have been much more comfortable than any made by others. The secret of the Masai leather-workers lay in the curing and the length of time the raw hide was immersed in cows' urine and the amount of chaffing each piece received. Needlessly to say these ladies had a bouquet, a piquancy, that was quite distinctive.

Even the children in the camps seemed low-geared by lethargy. They sat playing in the dung and had long since given up trying to swipe away the flies that crawled over their faces and clustered round their eyes so that they had to squint to look at us. But despite their inertia they never failed to come running to stand beside Sangai when we arrived, whereupon he would put his hand on each shaved head in greeting. It was all such charming respect between young and old. Once a new baby boy was brought for him to see. He spat on it several times and said, as he translated for me afterwards, "This child is bad," but followed immediately under his breath with, "This child is good," because this was what he wanted to say but bad luck would certainly have befallen the child if he had praised it openly.

Sangai invited me to stay in his boma and I did so for a couple of nights but found that there was a limit to my thirst for knowledge that prevented me from availing myself of that pleasure any longer. The flies were indescribable and the stench … particularly at night! So I moved some distance away, pitched my tent and built my own boma with Songai's help.

I met Songai most days and through him gleaned as much as I could of the Masai, watching, asking, making notes. As the background filled in I became aware of the complexity of the tribal social system. On the surface they might have appeared to a pompous Victorian visitor as simple savages who lived from day to day with little structure and purpose to their lives. Contrary to any ideas of that nature I might have made, the picture, or moreso a chart, of the Masai pattern of life that gradually grew in my mind was of a strong, vibrant, intelligent people who had evolved a tribal structure which, defensibly, had put them above all others.

The Masai nation created what amounted to the finest war machine of its time and place. But though they had the means to conquer all around, the Masai had no desire to extend their boundaries once they had established them. They used their power to maraud and increase their cattle herds, to strike such fear into their neighbours that they, the neighbours, would not dream of attempting to molest them. Their frontiers were as an impregnable wall all around them. Having created the perfect Utopia they wanted no more and would not allow anything, anyone, to change it.

The following section is a *précis* of the Masai military structure that shaped and governed every entity of the tribe and tribal life. To the best of my knowledge many of these facts have not been published before and could well be the only written history of the early development of a most important and unique people of Africa. The structure was already breaking down when I was with these people and half-century on, considering all the social upheaval that has taken place in that time, it is likely that much of the anthropological and historical matter may already be lost.

Readers with less interest in history may wish to pass over this section and pick up the travel narrative after the next section break. But be warned; those who do will miss some interesting stuff!

*

The experience with the tribe I gained through Sangai was a platform for launching further studies at later times, the details of which I feel may be worthwhile recording before they may be lost with the passing of time.

From about five years of age, until they were circumcised, Masai boys herded their father's cattle and did menial jobs for the *morani*. During this phase they were known as *laiyoni*. Circumcision was the first great event in their lives and in the old tribal system this would happen any time between the ages of fifteen and twenty. The circumcision of one generation was spread over eight years and the boys fell into two groups; those who were done in the first four years were termed as 'right-hand' and those in the latter four as 'left-hand'. After this there would be no circumcision for seven years and then it would all start again. So a generation was reckoned at fifteen years.

The operation was carried out at the boys' own homes and if any sign of pain was shown by a 'patient' this was taken as a show of cowardice and resulted in loss of face, not only of the boy but of his whole family. The operators were WaNdrobo men, the tribe of hunters which is an off-shoot of the Masai

As with many other African tribes Masai girls were also 'circumcised'. Part of the clitoris was removed to reduce the sensation of love-making and so make her less likely to be attracted away from her husband. The operation was done at the her mother's house and it was no disgrace if she cried out. Immediately she recovered she was married off.

For the next three to six months while the wound was healing, the boys were known as *laibartak*. During this period they wandered about with bows and arrows shooting small birds. Each boy removed the heads of the birds he shot and attached them by the beaks to a string which he wore round his head complete with a plume of two ostrich feathers on his forehead. A boy who had shown pain while being circumcised was not allowed to make such a headdress. At the end of that period all those of an area went to a special camp which had been prepared for them where they ceremonially removed their headdresses, had their heads shaved, covered themselves with red ochre and emerged as junior *morani*.

The *morani* of each area would then go and live in a *manyatta* (barracks) away from the *enkang* (family kraal). Each manyatta contained a *Sirit* (Company) and each Sirit appointed its own *01-Aiguenani* (Company Commander) and several Sirits were commanded in battle by the *01-Aiguenani lol Poror*.

On being *morani* the men were allowed to grow their hair long and then plaster it with animal fat and red ochre and mould it with wooden weights and strips of sheep skin into the characteristic coiffeurs. When sleeping they each protected their creations with the stomachs Pin of a goat, worn as a hat or hair-net. They made shields of dried buffalo hide that could weigh up to fifty pounds and painted heraldic designs on them denoting their *Sirit*, their age-grade and district where they belonged. And proudest of all possessions, they could now carry the *simi* in its red scabbard and the long, sword-bladed warriors' spear.

The Masai did not work in metal and although they coveted spears and other weapons they looked down on those who made them. (A trait not unfamiliar in many Western societies.) In the old days there was one clan of Masai who were blacksmiths and whose members were attached to the other clans and made the weapons for the whole tribe. The members of *Il-Kunono,* the blacksmith clan, were a people apart who married only among themselves and spoke a language, or at least a dialect, of their own which the other Masai could not understand. But it is doubtful whether any of this clan still exist or if they do whether they still practise their craft, for even by the time I was there the tribe got their weapons from their hereditary enemies, the WaKikuyu and WaKamba in the north, who were famous for their crafts, and the WaHehe and WaGogo in the south. Some of the more common type spears, those carried by *laiyoni* and elders, were even stamped 'Made in Birmingham'.

Now looking like warriors and equipped and geared for war it was the duty of the *morani* to protect the tribe and to increase the cattle stock by raiding the establishments of other tribes. These raids, indeed any action of the *morani*, were never spontaneous, haphazard affairs. Permission or order for a foray into enemy territory came from the High Command and, as with the special forces during the war, every action was planned in detail before the start. This was the real strength of the Masai.

Before a raid spies were sent out and the likely resistance calculated. The *Liabon* (pronounced 'lybon' – medicine man or prophet) was consulted. He would tell if the omens were right for the attack and when the right time for it would be. Preparations for action always entailed a meat-eating feast so they could last without food for some days and the taking of herbal concoctions to build up their strength and fierceness. The warriors become particularly brave when they drank a 'medicine' made from the bark of the acacia tree.

The Masai were one of the few African tribes who indulged in night fighting and with this they gained great advantage over their adversaries. The attack was usually made at night or just before dawn. The tactician was the *Laiguenani lol Poror* who directed operations from the rear and rarely joined in the actual fighting. The fighting leaders were the *Laiguenak le Sirit* together with their *Emurrets* (Lieutenants). In attack the *morani* were remorseless and few enemies gave much resistance. Even a slave caravan with over two hundred rifles was wiped out in a sustained attack.

Raids were made on most tribes around extending as far as the coast. On return the stolen cattle were divided. First a number were set aside for the *Liabon*, then some given to those who had distinguished themselves in the raid. The rest were divided among the warriors who gave one or two to their girl-friends in the *manyatta* and handed the rest over to their own families.

If there was not enough loot to be divided 'fairly' the *morani* separated into two groups, the *il-oo-rok-kitey*, the 'black oxen' and the *il-oo-do-moy*, the 'red oxen' and fought for 'winner-takes-all'. Small raids carried out by one *sirit* were not referred to the *Liabon* who did not receive any of the spoils. As a warring nation, if they were not fighting enemies they were at it with clan disputes within the groups. Life must have become very dull and tedious when the British came along and stopped all their fun.

A *moran* who had killed in battle was allowed to wear his *Jikigisat*, the marking that denoted his deed and one who had killed many men was known as a *Laingok*. A man could earn his *Jikigisat* by killing a lion. For this he did not need to do it entirely single-handed, but he had to be the one who took the charge.

When a *moran* elected to earn his medal in this way he would set out with others to where they knew a lion to be. If the lion was in a thicket they would flush it out into the open where they would surround it and make it angry and frightened by banging in their shields. The one who was there to prove his manhood would advance and entice the lion to charge and when it did the idea was to catch the animal on his shield and as he was bowled over to thrust up with his simi into the soft underbelly. The others would then throw their spears and all being well the lion would be transfixed like a pincushion. Sounds quite simple! But in hunting big game, and especially cats, things don't always go according to the book, if ever. Anyway, if he survived the *morani* certainly deserved to wear his *Jikigisat* with pride.

There was some controversy over this exercise for I was told at another time that it was not the one who made the first hit on the lion who earned the *Jikigisat* but the one who ran forward and pulled the lion's tail and cut it off. Perhaps the custom changed in different districts so that both were true.

After about four years service in the army the warriors went through the *Eunoto* ceremony when they were promoted from junior to senior *morani*. For this ceremony a whole wild olive tree was brought into the *manyatta* and set on fire by friction. The men had their heads shaved again at this ceremony.

Junior *morani* were not allowed to marry but they were allowed free licence with the uncircumcised girls. Senior *morani* could marry but they were not allowed to keep their wives at the *manyatta*. The wife of a senior *moran* would stay at his father's *engang* where he would visit her.

With these free-range girls living in the *manyatta* each *moran* usually had his own *esindani* (girl friend) but neither partner would feel jealous if the other strayed temporarily. 'Coitus interruptus' was the firm practice and it was considered a great crime if a girl was made pregnant. If she was, she was married off straightaway to an older man who would claim the child as his.

A long time ago I corresponded with an American anthropologist who was doing research into the Masai social organisation. He wrote that he did not think my term 'lover' was an accurate translation of the Masai *'esindani'*, suggesting that 'sweetheart' would be more appropriate. "You will remember," he wrote, "that 'coitus interruptus' is practised ... so that 'lover' is less applicable; at least according to my American understanding for the word 'lover'." All this made me think of the adage that some wit coined, 'America and Britain, joined by an ocean and divided by a language.' I can imagine many elderly British people being black-affronted if they thought that you were inferring such a meaning when they spoke of old sweethearts.

Uncircumcised boys – those not yet in the army – were not allowed to have intercourse with the uncircumcised – unmarried – girls since the latter were the prerequisite of the *morani* and if a boy was found to have done so he would have been severely beaten. Considering in extreme times a 'boy' might be twenty before he was circumcised he must have felt the rule most unfair, considering what he knew was going on all around him.

The whole social structure of the Masai tribe was built round its army and the enlisted men were given entitlement to privileges and pleasures of which those in other countries could only dream. What soldier would complain of serving in such an army? Friedrich Welhelm Nietzsche, the German philosopher, on whose words Hitler built his Nazi ideals, is reputed to have said, "Man for war, and woman for a warrior's delight. All else is foolishness." It would seem that the Masai had arrived at that conclusion long before Nietzsche's day!

The *manyatta* system depended on the mothers and sisters of the *morani* living there, the mothers to do the work and the sisters, as soon as they were old enough, to be *esindani*. Some etiquette did prevail: when a *moran* came to the house to lie with his *esindani* he would take her elsewhere, away from her own place.

After the *Eunoto* ceremony the Left and Right circumcision groups, that is the two groups which comprised one generation, were united into one age group and this group, their *Il-Rika*, would be given a name such as *"Ill-Kieku"* (The Long-Bladed-Spears) or *Il-Mirishari* (Those Who Are Not Driven Back). Each *moran* would be known for the rest of his life as being one of that group, as one in Britain might be remembered as one of a certain school class.

Although amalgamated, the two halves would retain the original colour of wooden spear haft they were given on becoming junior *morani,* the first lot dark coloured and the second ones light. There was a great brotherhood bond between all the men of an age group and this continued throughout the rest of their lives. This camaraderie may best be illustrated by the custom that entitled a man when travelling, even long after leaving the army, and visiting an *engang* outside his district where he did not know anybody. He would ask where there was someone of his *el-rika* and, on being informed, he would be at liberty to enter the house of this person and make himself at home even if the owner was not there to ask. Not only was he permitted to make himself comfortable in the house of anyone of his own age grade, he was expected to avail himself of the man's wife. Indeed, if the owner were to refuse this hospitality or reprimand the traveller for having indulged himself the other members of his age grade would curse him and he would die.

The diet of the Masai was one of the most interesting features of these fascinating people. Apart from the *morani*, the tribe existed almost entirely on a diet of cows' blood and milk. Only the *morani* ate meat regularly. That is to say that once every couple of months or so they were given bullocks to feast on. These they took to hidden places in the bush before they killed and ate them. Women were not allowed to see them eat meat, although unmarried girls sometimes accompanied them. These meat-eating parties were known as *Kiroko* and I was privileged to attend one at a later date. Between the *Kiroko* parties the *morani* drank only blood and milk like the rest of the tribe. Those others not of the army ate meat only when animals died of natural causes or by accident or when animals were killed for ceremonial occasions or occasionally for a pregnant woman. Apart from those reasons the Masai would never dream of killing cattle: cattle were a man's bank balance and he would miserly refrain from drawing on it.

The blood for drinking was drawn from the live animal. Three or four men would hold a bullock still while a leather thong, was tied round its neck and twisted tight like a tourniquet until the jugular vein stood out. Into this vein an arrow, held at only a few inches distance, was shot from a bow.

The arrow was a special one of which the tip had been bound up leaving only half an inch bare so that only this part could penetrate. When the vein was punctured the blood spouted out and was caught in a gourd. When this was full the tourniquet was released and the wound was sealed with dung. The animal then ran after the herd apparently none the worse for its blood donation. The gourd was passed round for all to drink. Each one relished the drink like some others would a foaming pint of beer. When it was passed to me I went through the motions but only wet my lips so that I could wipe them clean on my arm and they could see I had joined with them. I had no stomach for the hot, thick blood.

If this method of extracting the daily meal from a living animal sounds gory and barbarous it is nothing compared with that told by James Bruce, a great 6ft.4ins. Scot with red fiery hair and a temperament to go with it, who in 1768 set out for Gondar, Ethiopia, to find the source of the Nile and did just that. But what he discovered was the start of the Blue Nile which joins the White Nile at Khartoum and was not recognised as the true source of the great river. A brilliant linguist he learned to speak and write Amharic and Ge'ez, the language of the Kushite shepherds, well enough to translate parts of the Bible into each, in preparation for his journey.

Bruce relates how he saw, when travelling with two Ethiopians who led a cow as they walked, one man cut three sides of a square through the hide of the animal's rump. The man then lifted the flap of skin and proceeded to cut off steaks for their meal. The flap was then rolled down and stuck and the cow was led on until the next meal was needed.

The time the *morani* served in the army varied according to whether they were 'Left Hand' or 'Right Hand' groups, but it would usually be around twelve to fifteen years. When it was time to leave the army the *Ngesharr* (milk drinking) ceremony took place. Then the mens' heads were again shaved and thereafter they were expected to keep them close cropped. They also at this time laid aside the warriors' accoutrement and manners and become junior elders. They were now allowed to eat salt and smoke or chew tobacco if they wished. More important, at this stage, if they had not already done so, they could marry.

When he had selected the girl of his choice the man would send an arm-ring to the girl's father and if it was retained it meant he had been accepted. He then would visit the home of the girl, taking with him three large calabashes of *pombe* (native beer). About a week later he must visit the home again with six of the same. If the girl was uncircumcised and was made pregnant by the man before they were married he had to pay to the girl's father a fine or penalty of two head of cattle and five sheep in addition to the 'bride price'. If she had been circumcised the penalty was only one cow and two sheep.

The bride-price was five head of cattle and seven of sheep and goats. The groom's father usually advanced the amount to his son to pass on to the girl's father and he might also give a few more head to his son 'to get him started'. No stated number was laid down for this, it depended on the father's means and generosity. If neither the father nor the son could afford the price, and if the bride's father was in agreement, payment could be spread out over a period, as much as five years in some cases. 'Love on the never-never' was obviously in practice with the Masai long before the hire-purchase caught on in modern society.

To the uninitiated most African marriages may appear to be merely a matter of barter, the handing over of a few animals in exchange for a girl. In some African societies or tribes it is the girl's father who pays the 'groom's father the bride-price and in others it is the other way about, the dowry going from the man to the girl's father. With the Masai, as indeed with most, but not all, East African tribes, it is the man who pays the bride-price to his future father-in-law.

Far from what might appear to be a casual affair the Masai wedding, like most African weddings, was most carefully planned and worked out in meticulous detail. As in every facet of their lives these details, laid down in times immemorial, were designed as moral and social laws to bind the people as surely as physical bonds.

Consider these details of the Masai bride-price and think what must have gone into their working out; see how they were not just a few random animals that were passed over, every one would be carefully selected for their purpose and each given a name:

Cattle – 5
1st, a cow '*NONDOYE*' = To remember the girl.
2nd, an ox '*PAKITENG*' = The father and son-in-law will address each other by this.
3rd, an ox (big) '*NGIDEDANI*' = Dowry. *This one slaughtered at the door (Check)
4th, a cow '*SOTUA*' = To confirm the agreement and to cement the family friendship.
5th, a cow No name.

*I took these details by word of mouth from an old man and wrote them on a foolscap sheet which, after lying undisturbed for over forty years, is difficult to read at the folded joints. I was obviously not sure of this one and made a note to check it, but it seems I did not. It might have been the 5th one that was slaughtered for the ceremony feast, hence it not being given a name. However, the Masai did not usually slaughter cows for eating, they being too valuable, bulls or bullocks being used for that purpose when the occasion demanded.

Sheep and Goats – 7

1st, a sheep *'ENGEENE'* = To represent the rope used to tie the first cow.

2nd, a ram *'OLE OKOYA'* = To be given to the bride's grandmother.

3rd, a ram *'OLE AGOTONYE'* = To be given to the bride's mother.

4th, a ram goat *'OLCHANI'* = Medicine for bride's father.

5th, a sheep *'OLMASALE'* = To guard the fence round the home.

6th and 7th, No names = To be slaughtered for the wedding feast.

In the case of divorce the cattle had to be paid back, but not the sheep, goats or *pombe*.

With the settlement of the bride-price and after the celebrations the man would then invite his bride to his *enkang* where they would set up home and she would be entitled to her own opening in the surrounding *boma*. Later, if the man married more wives each one would have her own separate house for herself and her children which would be placed in position within a set pattern which would denote 1st wife, 2nd and so on, and each wife would have her own 'door' in the boma.

During the next few years the man, now a Junior Elder, would sit at the *barazas* (meetings) listening to the *Ol-Piron* (Guardian Elders) as they debated on the management of the *moran*. Eventually there came the *Entalengoi Olorigha* (Ceremony of the Stool) when the Junior Elders became the *Ol-Piron* and ruled until the next group came along. After their period as Guardian Elders the group retired from public life.

During his life a Masai man distributed his herds among his wives, each one being given a certain amount to look after and milk. The cattle so distributed were said to belong to the wife's family and were recognised as the property of her sons who, however, did not assume ownership until the father's death. On the man's death his wives were inherited by his half-brothers, it being unlawful for his full brothers to take them. 'Inherited' did not mean what we might think it to be; it meant more that the widow and family came under the care or responsibility of the half-brother so there was no single-parent, unsupported family in the tribe.

In most cases Masai dead were put out to be eaten by lions. They were left on the west side of the *manyatta* and were laid on their left side so that they faced eastwards with the legs drawn up and the head supported by the left hand and the right across the chest. If hyenas took the body away it was believed the death was caused by foul means. A member of the WaNdrobo tribe was usually called in to prepare the body by rubbing it with goat or cattle fat, for which he was given a calf as payment. *Liaboni* and rich, influential men were buried and stones were placed above the grave. Whenever anyone passed the grave he had to add another stone otherwise he would be 'touched by death'.

*

"*Sikiliza bwana,*" said Sangai sitting by my fire one sundown. As the great, red orb slid out of the sky the shadows darkened. Sangai would have to go soon if he were to get inside his own *boma* before night fell. But we had a little while yet and I thrilled to hear another of his stories. "Listen and I will tell you of the great *Liaboni* who are one with *Ngai* the Great God who dwells on Karanyagga (Mount Kenya)."

Already I had learned something of the *Liaboni*. I knew that they were something more than medicine men or witch doctors. I also knew that although there were many throughout the tribe, one to each clan or group, there were two principal ones, one in Kenya and the other in Tanganyika, to whom all the others were subject. Sometime in the past there had been only one principal one for the whole tribe.

With the Masai having no Chiefs or King the *Liaboni* to a certain extent, took the place of these leaders. Practically no event could take place without the consent of the *Liabon*. It was he who decided when a circumcision period should start and when the various ceremonies denoting stages in life of the Masai should take place. In the past, permission for all raids had to be obtained from the *liabon* and they had to be given a portion of the spoils. They were the mysterious men behind every Masai activity and my interest in them had sparked off Sangai's tale.

With my interest caught he stopped while he filled his pipe made from the bone of a goat, jammed it in his mouth, took a burning brand from the fire to light it, then puffed deeply before he spoke again into the flames as if I were not there, the flickering light casting dancing shadows over his copper coloured face.

"All the principal *Liaboni* belong to the Engidong family of the Aiser clan and are descended from Ol-le-Mweiya, the Prophet who came down from heaven and was found by the Aiser clan sitting on top of Ngong. He was such a small person they thought he was a child. They took him to their *manyatta* and there they found he was a medicine man. He married and had two sons."

I was interested in Sangai's reference to God and Heaven and a Prophet. He used the Masai '*Ngai*' for God rather than the Swahili '*Mungu*', the Swahili '*Mbingu*' for Heaven and the Masai '*Liabon*' for Prophet. Interesting too that in the Masai testament God remained in Heaven and sent his Prophet down to Earth to preach and do his bidding.

Strange that the same pattern comes through Christianity, yet no Christian missionaries ever went into Masailand to pass on their tales. Were these happenings really designed in Heaven? Did God work the same scenario with all his peoples? Did he send his Prophet to all his children at different times and not only to the Jews, as we are told, for them to pass His message to the world in their words? In further travels I met many other tribesmen who made similar references of how God spoke to them. From this it has always seemed strange to me to hear people referring glibly to all non-Christians as 'heathens', in the same way as Moslems regard all who do not follow their Prophet as 'infidels', even though all may believe in God and try to follow His ways.

Sangai went on to tell of Mbatian the greatest *Liabon* of all:

[It was he who had] *prophesied the coming of the white men and told his people not to resist them for they were too strong. This is likely the reason why Joseph Thomson, the first European to penetrate Masailand, met little or no resistance.*

Thomson, the young Scot from Dumfriesshire – so young in appearance he looked like a schoolboy – was commissioned by the Royal Geographical Society in 1882 to traverse Masailand to see if that shorter way to The Great Lake and Uganda was practical. Unbelievable for the time, he lived to tell the tale, but very nearly did not. Among many adventures we find that he was charged and actually lifted by a buffalo and once he had to raise his entire camp in the middle of the night and melt into the darkness after a scout reported that the Masai were massing an army to attack them at first light. Whether the threat was real, in the light of Mbatian's instruction not to oppose the white men, will never be known, but Thomson was wise to take heed of his scout's warning.

This at the time when Stanley had said that the quickest route to martyrdom was a visit to Masailand. Thomson's book *A Walk Through Masai Land* is one of the most readable and entertaining of all those written by the Victorian explorers.

Mbatian also prophesied the great rinderpest epidemic that wiped out a large proportion of the Masai cattle during the latter quarter of the 20th century and also foretold his own death which occurred at the height of that plague.

"When Mbatian was dying," Sangai went on, "he called his eldest son Sendeyo and said, 'Come to me tomorrow for I wish to give you the medicine man's insignia.' Sendoyo replied, 'Very well' and went to lie down. He did not know that while this was taking place his brother Lenana had hidden himself near and had overheard the conversation.

"Next morning Lenana rose early and went to his father's bedside and said, 'Father, I have come.' Now Mbatian was very old and had only one eye. He did not see which of his sons stood beside him and so gave Lenana the iron club which the great *Liabon* must give to any messenger he sends out so that the people know the message has come from him. With the iron club also went the medicine-horn, the gourd and the bag with the stones which were brought from the north when the tribe came from there many years ago, the stones which no white man has ever seen. As he gave Lenana these things Mbatian said, 'Thou shalt be great amongst thy brothers and amongst all people.' Lenana took these things and went away.

"Sendeyo then went to his father and was told his brother had already been given the insignia. He was very angry and said he would fight his brother until he killed him. The tribe was divided between the two and they fought for many years until peace was concluded and both continued to practise as principal *Liabon*, Lenana at Ngong and Sendeyo at Narok. "

Once again I was enthralled by Sangai's story. It was almost identical to the Biblical account of how Jacob obtained the leadership of his people at the expense of his brother, Esau, and gave them the name we know as Israel.

There are many similarities of this nature with Christian and Moslem stories of their Prophets. Like Christ, Mohammed wandered in the desert before coming to accept God's way, and like Christ Mohammed had his Sermon on the Mount, to name but two. Since Mohammed was born 600 years after Christ those 'coincidences' could be put down as plagiarism. But how could the gospel stories of an obscure tribe of 'heathens' in Africa be culled from the Bible or Koran when we know that no Arabs or Christian missionaries ever penetrated into Masailand. Did God in his wisdom work the same switch trick with others of his people? Could it be, and here I put my credibility to the limit, that the Masai *did* meet the people of Israel and so have the opportunity to 'borrow' their tale and make it their own? Later I came to ponder this hypothesis in my mental exploration for King Solomon's Mines.

Though it was by subterfuge that Lenana gained Mbatian's prophesy that he would become the greatest Liabon of all, that fact did come to pass. In the early days of colonisation when Britain took over a country the first thing the administration had to do was to win over the tribal chiefs to their bidding, so that through them the people could more easily be governed. When the British came to East Africa in the late 1880s the authorities were at a loss when they found that the Masai did not have a chief as such. But they observed that the committees of Elders were greatly influenced by Lenana, so they made him Paramount Chief over the whole tribe. It was a great mistake. A *Liabon* could never be Chief. Although all-powerful, inasmuch as the Elders generally did his bidding, the *Liabon's* role was to prophesy and advise while the ultimate decision making remained with the Elders. When Lenana died the Masai did not appoint another Paramount Chief and the British authorities, realising their original mistake, did not enforce one.

I was intrigued by Mbatian's paraphernalia. Establishing whether the pieces were real or not would perhaps vindicate Songai's story and the thought of actually seeing the iron club and the stones the tribe had brought with them all the way from Egypt or the Sudan fascinated me. I asked if he knew where these treasures were now. He turned his face from the fire and looked directly at me and hesitated as if wondering whether or not he could trust me. After what seemed a long, loaded silence he said, "Everything is in the possession of *Liabon* Letinga, who is the son of Parit, who was the son of Lenana. Letinga lives to the south, in the mountains they call Monduli-Ju".

Monduli-Ju! (Mondooli Joo) The name had a ring about it, of mystery and adventure, like something out of a Rider Haggard novel. I very much wanted to follow up Sangai's story, to see these magical things and in particular those stones that no white man had ever seen, but I had to wait more than a couple of years before I was able to do so. I had already heard of Monduli-Ju. I knew of it as a place out-of-bounds to all but government agents although until now I did not know why. I had also heard of the Masai 'chiefs' who had been banished to the mountains, and again, I did not know why. Now the jigsaw pieces began to drop into place. The whole picture was not completed until I had the chance to visit Monduli and learn why the *Liabon* had been banished. Immediately following my time with Sangai I did not go there, partly because knowing it to be a restricted area I did not expect to get access and also because the rainy season was fast approaching and I had a lot to do before reaching the coast and felt I could not risk the time to try.

Two years later though, when returning north, I had the opportunity to go there. Although this episode belongs in another book I feel it would be breaking the rhythm to separate that part from my time with Songai and the history of the Masai.

Monduli, a little town lying in the shadow of Mount Meru, half surrounded by the lower Lengoisoiku range, the hills the Africans called Monduli Ju (heights), was the administrative centre for the Tanganyikan Masai. When I arrived there a big *baraza* was taking place between the tribal elders and the European authorities. I had heard of this important meeting from some distance and had come to witness it, especially when I remembered Sangai's words and hoped I'd get a chance to go up Monduli Ju.

Soon after my arrival I met the British District Commissioner and he invited me to stay at the Government building and also to dinner that evening. This was fortunate, for over the meal I learned the purpose and context of the meeting. Even more important, when I mentioned how much I would like to go up Monduli Ju to meet the chief *Liabon* Letinga he granted me permission and said he would arrange a guide for me when I was ready to go. This was a real *coup*, for the hills behind Monduli were still out-of-bounds to anyone other than Government

Officers. The last piece of the jigsaw, the reason why the *Liabon* had been banished, was about to drop into place.

In the early days when the British made Lenana Paramount Chief in order to simplify the administration of the tribe it did not work. Later it was found that far from making things easy the *Liabon* was passing all the wrong (from the British point of view) messages to the tribe. So it was decided to separate all *Liaboni* from the people and put them under guard in a secure place, in this case, Monduli Ju. Any messages passed from them could be censored and the government could parley with the Elders without them being under the influence of the medicine men. So at this big *baraza* which went on for several days, when the ways of the tribe as they had been for centuries could be irrevocably changed, *Liabon* Letinga was not in attendance.

Among the main items on the agenda, the DC told me over dinner that evening, was the pressing one of how to reduce the service of the *morani* and how to occupy their time in the absence of the tribal wars they thrived on. Boredom was a real problem and it was not surprising that cattle raiding with the deaths that ensued from it was a constant running sore.

As to the way of reducing the duration of army service, the idea was to make circumcision earlier and not to overlap the service of 'Right Hand' and 'Left Hand' groups for this always led to rivalry and internal fights for superiority. All this was designed to get the men through the *morani* phase and settled down earlier in life. If this proposal were to be put into progress the soldiers would serve only four years instead of fifteen, a dramatic change to an age old practice.

Moreover, something had to be done to get the *morani*, and at least the Junior Elders, gainfully employed and stop the boredom that was rotting the spirit of the tribe. But how to change the whole thinking of a nation, and even more difficult, how to make them act on it, was another matter. How to coax the Masai men to actually work, those who for centuries had done nothing but fight, those who looked on work and those who did it, especially those who tilled the land, as inferior, seemed an insurmountable task. The Masai did not even brew their own beer, the honey mead that they loved. They had the WaNdorobo do it for them. Somehow their elitist attitude must be broken down. But what a task! And if it were achieved it would be the end of the proud warrior nation as we knew it.

In addition to the matter of the corrosive boredom of the people there was on the agenda the perennial explosive issue of trying to get the tribe to cut down the number of its cattle. The land had long been overstocked and soil erosion, the dreaded land disease caused by, among other things, over-grazing, was rampant and was likely to turn the land into a desert if some control was not exerted to limit the number of animals that used it. Occasionally cattle auctions were arranged and some pressure put on the tribe to sell off parts of its herds. These auctions were never received favourably, the natives seeing no connection between soil erosion and their cattle. The suspicion was always there that the white men made them sell their cattle to impoverish the tribe, for the money received in the sale did not constitute the same status symbol as cattle.

These cattle auctions were not without their element of danger. A District Officer told me that a DC had been murdered at one a year or two before. The matter was actually being hotly discussed at the *baraza* while I was there.

Apparently on that day the cattle sales were going slow, as might be expected with reluctant salesmen. As the day wore on the District Commissioner became impatient and hurried through the crowd chivvying them up to get rid of the cattle. He came on the *moran* in question who was making no attempt to sell and ordered him to put the cattle he had brought with him into the auction ring. The *moran* said he would sell all except one, an old cow. But the District Commissioner, having given the order, made a stand and refused to listen. No doubt, in his European mind, he felt that any leniency on his part would be a sign of weakness. Such are the problems of one race of people trying to rule or administer another of a completely different culture.

What the DC did not know was that that particular cow was more than just another head of cattle to the *moran*. The Masai have great affinity with each one of their herd and none moreso than this one. Selling this cow was to him like selling his mother. The boy's real mother had died when he was only a baby and the cow, recently calved, had been put to the baby as a surrogate mother, the baby sharing the teats with the calves until weaned. By the time he was five years old the boy was looking after the herd in the wild pastures and none was nearer or dearer to him than his old nanny. Because of his intransigence the DC's order was the last one he ever gave. The *moran* greased his spear as he would before a battle, searched out the District Commissioner and by all accounts hurled it at him with such force the weapon passed clean through his body and stuck in the ground several feet in front.

Apart from the serious business that could change the tribe so drastically forever, the *baraza* was a time for feasting and dancing. On the evening and morning after the debate was finished inconclusively, further discussion being necessary before such revolutionary changes could be made, companies of *morani* came in dressed as for war. Spears shining, but with each point muffled by a ball of feathers, shields newly painted with their heraldic designs looking so like modern art, and the men with their hair freshly plastered with red mud and their blankets newly dyed brick-red ochre, they looked formidable, fearsome and very majestic. Some wore huge headdresses of ostrich feathers that hung round their faces like picture frames or lions' manes and took their height to over seven feet. Others had ochre war-paint in weird designs on their faces making them look even more frightening.

Girls came too. They wore their best finery and all had newly shaved heads, shiny with fresh oil. Without exception each wore their widest, most attractive smile and dancing eyes to charm their beaux.

Before the dancing began there was a *Kiroko* when the *morani* were given some bullocks to eat. The *sirit* I attached myself to took their animal into the bush and killed it by driving the spike end of a spear into the back of its head. Then with the animal on its side one man, working with great speed and skill while the blood still flowed, made a long slit in the skin down the side of the neck and pulled it out to form a bag. He then cut the jugular vein and the bag filled up with blood and each man in line bent and gulped it. This time, unlike the episode of the blood-letting by shooting an arrow into the vein, I demurred to even go through a semblance of the performance.

It was a most gory and chilling scene: the bullock, only minutes before a live, warm, throbbing beast, now a dead thing with its throat cut and the crowd of savages in battle array crowding round to drink its blood, each man rising with bloody face and flashing eyes, wiping his mouth with his thin hand. This finished, they skinned and cut up the carcase and partly roasted the meat over several fires. Then when they had gorged themselves of this half-raw meat they went off to dance.

For the dancing the men stood in a line and the girls in another, facing each other, a few feet apart. They sang and hopped in rhythm till they met, then they turned and went back. This was repeated over and over again for a long time, the lines turning to look at the other, bouncing, bouncing in little hops, meeting, turning, bouncing back and turning to start again, endlessly, indefatigably, and singing in rhythm all the while. Sometimes by way of a change a warrior, by himself, would start jumping up and down, his body ramrod erect, his legs hardly bending on the bounce. He would be immediately surrounded by others and when he tired another would take his place in the centre and start jumping in the same way. It did not seem violent or frenzied stuff but in fact they were indulging in the unique Masai way of working themselves up into a highly emotional state. This was evident when a man suddenly stopped his jinks and stood trembling violently and flexing all over, apparently in some kind of blind fit. Immediately several of his companions threw him to the ground and held him until the fit passed. These fits could be highly dangerous I was told since the man was quite likely to go berserk and armed for war could be lethal. During the afternoon and evening several men threw such fits.

I spent a great deal of my time at the *baraza* talking to anyone who would give me their attention, mainly the Junior Elders who were not engaged in the policy debating, quizzing them about their habits and customs. The more they found I knew of these the more they were willing, no eager, to expand on them.

The following day the DC arranged for a guide to go with me up Moduli-Ju to meet chief *Liabon* Letinga. Had I tried to go by myself I would have been soon reported to the police and been in serious trouble. As a strange European wandering through these mountains asking to meet the *Liabon* the authorities would have smelt an *agent provocateur* and I would have stood out like a black leopard on a snowfield. I counted myself extremely fortunate to make this privileged journey and was excited at the prospect of meeting this witch-doctor-cum-prophet-cum-sorcerer-cum-whatever-else who must be the very epitome of the dark, mysterious Africa that I wanted so much to find.

That morning a heavy, dramatic cloud formation hung over the Monduli mountains, unusual for that time of the year, but in keeping with the foreboding, even sinister, atmosphere that seemed to permeate my mood as I set off on my errant escapade with my native guide.

After a few hours and high up in the mountains we came to the abode of Letinga. I stood outside the *boma* while the guide called and waited until he came to meet me. At first sight he did not look impressive. I think I had expected him to have a spike through his nose and skulls and bones dangling around him. I should have known better though, because in the photographs of the time Lenana looked a very slight and even insignificant character in the commanding presence of the stern and stuffy Victorian colonisers

Letinga was a simple figure with a shaved head who wore a blanket like every other man of the tribe and as he approached he looked no different to any other native. When he came close up however there was more to him than that. For one thing, he wore a necklace of lions claws and teeth and other odds and ends. Apart from this there was something else about the man which did hold him apart. His eyes had a peculiar penetrating quality. Perhaps the fact his eyebrows had been shaved off made them look cold and stark and commanding.

He would not allow me into his *enkang*, which was not a good start. I realised that coming as I did, a stranger out of the blue, was not the way to learn the secrets the tribe had guarded for centuries. Sangai would never have told where the tribe's crown jewels were if I had walked up to him, cold, and asked where they were. It was only after he had gained confidence in me, come to like me perhaps, that he divulged their whereabouts. Who, in any country would admit a stranger who knocked at their door and asked in to see their treasures. I needed time, lots of it, but that was not possible.

Although not allowing me in he nevertheless, after much cajoling, agreed to show me his tools of trade. When he produced the items out of an old sack they looked a pitiful collection of rubbish and you could have been excused if you wondered what all the fuss was about them. But then if someone from the moon was to turn up in Britain and be shown with great reverence a tatty old bit of goatskin with funny words on it that they called the Magna Carta the moon person might smile superiorly at such naive worship of such childish trivia.

Letinga brought out a black stick with a heavy end that did not appear to be iron, decorated with beads, which was his insignia of office. I asked if this was the 'iron club' which had been Mbatian's and he nodded. He also took out a horn in which he said were all his magical things. But no amount of coaxing would induce him to display them. When I asked if the stones that were brought from the Nile were in there he showed surprise, then what looked like fear that I should know about them. A shutter dropped between us and he became taciturn, and when I repeated my question he turned almost offensive. It was evident I would get no further. So we parted on a semi-hostile note and I came away wondering if he would put an evil spell on me.

As the weeks went by I felt a change come over me. I began to feel a greater affinity with Africa, as if I were becoming part of it and it part of me. I felt my excursions with Sangai, whether they were camera hunting, visiting *enkang* and *manyatta* or conversations by the camp fire, were taking me under the surface of the great continent, down to the region where the great heart beat and I was becoming so much a part of it.

Interesting though the Masai were I came to see that there was something unwholesome about the whole scene. The tribe had a stagnant air about it. It is said that the shark is one of the only creatures on Earth that has remained unaltered since prehistoric times because it attained the perfect state of development to suit its predatory life style and nothing has altered to change the balance of its environment. Like the shark the capable Masai had developed into the highest efficient body to suit the needs of their 19th century environment. They became an invincible master race, but, unlike the shark, their world changed drastically and they had not developed with it. Like the Mandarins of China who stayed static in a changing world and so faded away, the Masai, having achieved their ultimate seemed determined not to alter their ways and were in danger of eventually being passed and left behind by their more adaptable neighbours.

The whole system had the air of a wake: the army was dead, or at least the need for it was obsolete, yet they propped it up in all its finery and pottered around it, incapable of doing anything constructive or imaginative while it was in their presence. I said as much to Sangai one day. At least I asked him why they still retained their army when the need for it was gone. His answer was full of meaning. By this time we were firm friends. "You will not always be here. We will need our army when you go." Then he said a strange thing, the significance of which did not strike me until much later when the Mau-Mau uprising was at its height. "When *Uhuru* comes," he looked straight at me when he spoke, which was unusual, "it may not be for everyone."

I pondered over that remark a great deal in later years. I knew '*uhuru*' as the Swahili for 'freedom' but at that time the word meant nothing more than a figure of speech. A couple of years later when *Uhuru* was known to all as the battle-cry of the Mau-Mau terrorists it suddenly struck me. Had Sangai been trying to tell me something, something of great importance? Had he and all the Masai known what was brewing within the Kikuyu tribe? Had it been a *liabon* prophesy or was it, when he said the word, a fact already known to all the African people? Had Sangai been desperately trying to give me a message that I could have passed on to the British authorities and so spike the guns of the WaKikuyu, their traditional enemies, believing that should the balance of power swing in the favour of their rival tribe and they took over the government of the country they would make much more oppressive rulers than the whites. Was that the reason that when the real trouble broke out the Masai never supported the uprising and any participation they made was on the side of the British against their old enemies.

But Sangai and all his people were deluded if they thought that their army would preserve them in the time vacuum in which they wished to remain. Even at its best it could not have stopped the great changes that were about to develop over all Africa. As it was, at the time I was there the tribal structure was beginning to fall apart. Although the old principles were on the whole still being maintained the *manyatta,* or soldiers barracks system was breaking down and more often than not the *morani* continued to live with the rest of the community. Even in the places where the soldiers' *manyatta* system was in vogue, as in the Namanga area, it was often difficult to see who lived apart from whom. It was certainly not the *morani* who lived by themselves, for not only did their mothers live with them to build and mend their houses, milk the cattle and generally care for them, but their lovers were also there. What soldier would complain about serving in that army? If any section of the community was kept apart it was the elders. It appeared that so long as they had sons in the army, the older men had only visiting rights to their wives in the *manyatta.*

Perhaps the Elders, sitting round their fires at night, lamenting that the *morani* of the day were not the men they had been in their day were right. The once noble Masai army was becoming something of a shambles. The soldiers still stood tall and proud reflecting the splendour of the past, but degeneration had set in, which was hardly surprising, given their lack of activities, purpose and discipline. And with their mums and girl friends there to pamper them and see to their every need, what kind of way is that to run an army? It had worked when the soldiers had gone off on the rampage to their neighbours and returned macho-like with their spoils of war. But now, with no fighting to bolster their egos, they were at a loose end with little purpose in life. The days of the proud warrior in Africa were over.

The Masai had to move on. I didn't like the idea. I wanted Africa to remain as it was, wild and adventurous, the Africa that I knew, the natives I liked to be with. But that could never be. My wish that Africa could remain in a time warp was as incongruous as an Ancient Roman returning to Britain after a couple of millennia and being disappointed to find that Boadicea's Iceni tribe had gone in an amalgam with others and that the Britons were not painted with woad, clad in skins and armed with spears.

Before concluding this chapter I wanted to confirm one or two points on the Masai wedding details and clear up a small matter to do with the *liaboni*. I rang the Tanzanian Tourist Office and spoke to a very pleasant and helpful lady from Dar es Salam who told me that contrary to the Masai custom, her father had paid her bride-price to her husband's father, as was the custom with most of the coast people. Regarding information on the Masai, however, she said I would do better by ringing the Kenya Education Office, which I did. The conversation that followed was very similar to a previous one I'd had with a Kenyan official confirmed the importance to me of making public the notes I have just written, for of a certainty anthropologists and researchers of today who are interested in Africa's past are not likely to learn very much from many modern, educated Africans.

The man I spoke to began in a civil and pleasant enough way but when I mentioned I wanted to ask about tribal customs and the Masai in particular I could hear him bridling. He could not or would not help with the past. He dismissed the written history of his country as all wrong and played down any remarks or questions referring to pre-independence days. His manner rather than his words said that reference to tribal life were not important, that Kenya was a modern country like any other, that the people thought of themselves as Kenyans and not as of different tribes, that the past was bad and finished with and I should only be concerned with the country as it is now. "Why don't you write of the Masai people as they are today and not of the past?" he asked. To any reference to the *morani* army system he said all that was finished by Law in 1967, he thought, and there was no point in discussing anything that was in existence before that time. When I mentioned the *liaboni* he sounded quite angry.

"Lybon? Lybons? Who are they?"

"But surely you must know of the Masai prophets, or medicine men as some might call them."

"Oh them," he added in a desultory tone when his bluff had been called, and then, more vehemently, "They were just people the British put in power in an attempt to dominate the Masai."

"But ..." taken aback I was at a loss for words. I wanted to say that he was wrong, that Lenana was already the *Liabon* when the British arrived; that he became a friend and offered his services willingly after being overwhelmed by British justice. This happened after a white man was killed by Masai and the British official came down in favour of the *morani* and called in no reprisal as Lenana had expected would happen. Seeing I would get nowhere in pursuing the subject and not wishing to cause any hurt or ill-will, a matter that had not inhibited my informant at the other end of the line, I let it go in favour of politeness. Had I known no other but to accept the man's explanation I might now be perpetuating biased misinformation.

The man's comments were interesting nevertheless. As said, the time had long come for radical change with the Masai military and social structure. The British Colonial administrators had pussy-footed round the problem, giving diplomatic advice and cajoling. After Kenya's independence in 1963 it did not take the Kikuyu dominated government long to perform the legal surgery on the Masia and kindred tribes' structures that Britain's diplomacy had failed to achieve over more than half a century.

On hearing of the changes that had been made in Kenya, Sangai's prophetic words echoed back to me from down the long years when we shared so many wonderful days. I remember his look when he said quietly, foreboding, "Uhuru may not be for everyone".

Now, with hind sight and sadness I have to agree that it was the right thing for the young government to do. When diverse peoples must amalgamate some personal freedoms, customs and ways of life may have given up so that the amalgam can form.

*

I had been hearing of a particularly large elephant in the neighbourhood and Sangai mentioned that it had been seen near the Namanga river barely an hour away. I was fired by the opportunity to photograph it and asked Sangai if he would track for me and he readily agreed.

Early next day he came silently out of the morning mist as my billy came to the boil for coffee, clearing his throat audibly to warn of his coming. He was passed the moran stage in life so his head was shaved and he had laid aside the long bladed spear of the warrior and carried the ordinary one with laurel leaf shaped head and long wooden shaft. He had looped his long, stretched lobes over the top of his ears so that they would not catch on the twigs as we went thought the undergrowth.

"*Jambo Bwana*," he greeted me as I pulled back a branch in my boma to allow him to enter.

"*Jambo sana, Sangai. Habari ya asubuhi?*" (Literally, "What is the news of the morning?" but colloquially, "How are you this morning?")

"*Mzuri tu, Bwana.*" ("I'm just fine.")

"*Tuta kuwa bahati leo?*" ("Are we going to be lucky today?")

"*Ndio, Bwana, kabisa,*" ("Yes, absolutely,") he said with a laugh.

I offered him some coffee but he refused. He had tasted it before and screwed up his face at the thought of it. I drank in silence, then doused my fire and we went off in search of our elephant.

As a matter of interest, during my time with the Masai I daily left my camp with impunity, knowing my belongings would be safe as the bank. I was now well known in the district and woe betide anyone who might have broken the neighbourly laws.

Soon after we left, the sun came through and dispersed the mist and on a game trail near the river Sangai read the morning news written by the feet of many animals. Eventually he pointed to what was obviously the leader column signed by the '*tembo mkubwa*', (big elephant). The trail wound through forest that varied in density from thick, clawing brushwood to open woodland and at times squeezed through long, winding passages in elephant grass, twelve feet and more high, where the air was still and thick and claustrophobic, and where the possibility of coming slap up against a waiting animal made constant companions of fear and foreboding.

As the trail became clearer Sangai sometimes picked up twigs that had recently been chewed and examined them. Presently we came to a place where soil erosion had furrowed the land into deep gorges. Here some droppings, big as great loaves of bread, were steaming and chewed twigs were still wet. After a moment's hesitation Sangai led the way forward. In the grass passages one could have at least broken the walls if one met danger, but here in these rocky canyons there was no escape route. The way was rocky and ridged. I wondered how such great beasts could have made their way through such a labyrinth of deep, narrow and rough passages. But they did, and with ease Sangai said. I was pleased when the trail led out into the forest again.

We were in an area of open forest when terror struck. Sangai indicated that the elephant herd was near. He gathered a fistful of dust and let it fall through his fingers to get the wind direction. We would go in against it so our scent would be wafted away from the animals. Suddenly he froze and cocked his ear.

"*Hatari,*" (danger) he whispered with urgency, "*sikiliza.*" (listen). I listened intently but could hear nothing that spelt danger.

"*Sikia,*" (hear!) this time sharply, as an order, "*sikia Ndege,*" (hear the bird) he gave the clue, but though I strained my ears I could not distinguish any particular bird that meant anything to me. Then suddenly,

"*Kifaro,*" Sangai screamed with startling loudness after the cathedral whispers, "*kimbia upesi,*" (Run quickly).

The rhino exploded from the deep tree shadows, where its slate-grey colour had made it almost invisible. It burst into the sunlight like an express train from a tunnel. The shock, so sudden, of seeing it charge at us was like a kick in the stomach. Sangai was off down wind, his blanket streaming out behind him like a bat out of Hades. For a brief moment that seemed like eternity I was petrified before I too was off pell-mell after him. I have a photographic vision of the great, prehistoric monster crashing down on me, its evil horn lowered with murderous intent, and feel the ground tremble as if it too was afraid.

Luckily the rhino is very short-sighted and goes mostly by smell. It charged past, stopped, cast about, its little pig eyes shining with malice, then shuffled off snuffling and snorting like a bad-tempered club bore who has seen off a noisy intruder and returns to his chair, newspaper somewhat crumpled, still in his hand. Sangai smiled, but I could see he was still keyed up. He said there were many rhinos in the area and he feared them more than any other animal. His brother had been killed by one. It was the tick bird that settles on the back of the rhino to pick the blood-sucking insects out of the cracks in the leathery skin, that Sangai had heard as a harbinger of danger.

Sangai was like a taught bowstring and was my eyes and ears as we resumed our stalking of the elephants. Two more rhinos, a mother and her calf, crossed our path and there was one blood curdling moment when Sangai, a yard or two ahead of me, entered a dense patch of shade and froze. Very slowly he turned his head. His eyes were popping and he rolled them in the direction of the nearest tree as emphatic as a stage comedian. Then raising a finger he held it across his lips. As I approached in high tension he put his lips very close to my ear and whispered softly, *"Pole, pole"* (slowly, slowly) and pointing at my boots which he regarded as too clumsy for hunting, he added, *"kwenda taratibu sana,"* (go very carefully) As my eyes grew accustomed to the dark shade I made out a rhino crouched asleep barely six feet away under the tree Sangai had indicated with his eyes. We went past very, very slowly and quietly. It did not occur to me at the moment, but it did later, that it would have made an excellent photograph. But I doubt if Sangai would have approved even if I had been stupid enough to have tried one.

Very soon after the rhino incident Sangai signalled that the elephants were just ahead. He kicked up some dust to test the wind direction. It had altered slightly since the last time so we had to change course. They were in a glade, four of them, and as they came into sight I felt sure that the noise of my thumping heart would give us away. After a last minute wind check we went in as near as we dared. They looked enormous, especially the big one that stood a shoulder above the others and whose tusks looked long and heavy. There was something very friendly, cuddly almost, about these big, ponderous creatures with rumbling tummies and loud wind-breaking, romping in their ill-fitting, rumpled, baggy skin trousers that seemed far too big for them. It made a very domestic, family scene as they went about their meal, great ears flapped back and trunks reaching up to tear down some succulent foliage and curl it down and into their mouths. They looked very contented and not in the least dangerous, but we were under no illusion on that score.

I was so busy just looking I almost forgot my camera. I took some shots but realised that they would be poor because of the deep, black shadows dappled with brilliant light. I found it so frustrating that we could go to all this trouble and have the long hunt rendered useless by the intensely contrasting light pattern. Shooting with a rifle seemed an easy matter compared with photography. Some years later I was made to reconsider that assumption.

When I eventually saw the prints I was even more disappointed. Not only were the animals so well camouflaged with the light pattern as to make them near invisible they seemed so small I could hardly believe we had been in so dangerously close to them. From this it was apparent that photographing wild animals without using telephoto lens was practically useless.

Before leaving the Namanga area I had one last episode that has lingered long in my memory. In contrast to that little walk on the wild side I had the opportunity to experience the then rich-man's motor safari to watch or photograph big game. This has become so common now with modern tourism it might seem perhaps pointless to mention it. But at that time it was quite unique for someone like me, someone without a heavy bankbook, to even contemplate. The man to whom I owed the pleasure of this experience was Bill McLaren.

Bill, a Canadian who worked at the New York office of the British Overseas Airways Corporation, was staying at the Namanga Hotel. He was a few days into his holiday when I met him on one of my forays to the little *duka* near the hotel for my supplies. Already he was beginning to feel a bit bored. He had come to see Africa but so far had not been able to venture more than a few yards from the hotel, any further being no-go land. He had a wonderful camera with, for then, a unique swivel turret with three lenses, short, medium and long. We got talking and soon found that we got on well and I asked him back to my camp where later I introduced him to Sangai. He was over the moon.

During the next few days we visited several *manyattas* and did a couple of short foot safaris when he was able to shoot some minor stuff with his long lens, but, surprisingly, no big game. Near the end of the week he told me he had booked up for a two-night safari with Colonel Gethin and said he wanted me to come along with him. I thanked him but said I couldn't afford such a thing. He insisted that I must come as his guest and when I remonstrated that I couldn't possibly accept such a gift he brushed my refusal aside, saying airily, "Think nothing of it. Look, working at BOAC I get my flight to London free and the one to Nairobi for near enough that and with the dollar as it is and the cost-of-living here being so low compared to the States the hotel doesn't cost more than a few good meals in New York. Anyway, I'd like to thank you for all you've done to make my day here. I would never have got off first base without you and even if I had, I'd never have got into those Masai camps and been able to talk to those guys without you beside me. I'd just like you to come along. I think I'd be a bit overwhelmed by myself with the old guy, just him and me out there in the jungle. Will you come?" I was delighted to accept.

Although Colonel Gethin had retired from running the Namanga River Hotel he still retained a personal interest in his Rhino Safari Lodge in what he called his 'secret place'. Forty miles away under the very shadow of Kilimanjaro lay Lake Amboseli, a dried-up lake bed which abounded with game. Gethin said he had discovered it before the war and so far no other safari agent knew of it, and this seemed to be the case for while we were there no other soul crowded us in. It was here he took wealthy tourists who wanted to view big game. Not that animals were scarce at Namanga, but there the forest was thick and animals had to be stalked on foot whereas on Lake Aboseli's dry flat pan a motor vehicle could drive round and about the great herds that roamed there.

We went down in the Colonel's battered 15 cwt., open-backed truck with two boys up the back sitting on top of the boxes and bags of stores, a fair difference to today's luxury safari wagons! I use the word 'battered' advisedly for the back of the truck was indeed badly dented and in that the vehicle may well have been unique in the world. Just how these dents were obtained we were to find out, with some surprise and not a little apprehension.

In a single morning on the lake we circled close to three great herds of elephants, countless giraffe, buffalo, zebra and innumerable antelopes and gazelles. In the afternoon we viewed motionless from spitting distance a pride of lions who seemed unconcerned by our presence. Back in the camp we sat down to sundowner drinks and a meal that would have sent an Epicurean sky-searching for the right words to describe. Served under a leafy acacia umbrella on a crisp, white tablecloth with wine glasses sparkling in the lamplight conjured up a scene which must have embellished travellers' tales throughout the length and breadth of the US of A. After dinner we sat round a huge, log fire while the colonel wove a tapestry of hunter's tales amid the tang of rich tobacco and woodsmoke.

When the tales were told and the embers were growing white we repaired to our tents, luxurious things that you could actually stand up in – a contrast to my little 3-feet high bivvy. In an enamel basin set into a folding table stand was set a large jug of warm water for washing, a fluffy, white towel folded beside it. From the tent apex there hung a hurricane lamp that you could take down and put on the little folding table beside the bed if you wished to read before going to sleep. And most luxurious of all, cool, fresh linen sheets to crawl in between; absolutely decadent. And this was roughing it! Bill would tell how he braved the arduous life under canvas in the African bush. After the weeks in the hell of the Masai environs I was sure I had entered Heaven.

Nevertheless, Bill's holiday tales would not be without some foundation: sometime in the small hours of the morning a leopard strolled through the camp and left its visiting card by way of its paw prints which were as plain to the

Colonel as the printed variety. And next day was certainly something to write home about. The Colonel, as was his style it appeared, kept an ace up his sleeve to play if the game was right in order to send his clients home in excitement.

After the usual morning of running round elephants and lions and the like, we came on a lone rhino. I think he and the Colonel were old friends, or perhaps adversaries would be more accurate. Anyway, the Colonel drove up to the great brute and circled it in ever decreasing circles.

I may add here that with no boys or stores on board Bill and I sat up the back on the benches that ran down either side of the little five-by-six open deck during all the animal spotting. The glass had been removed from the cabin window so we could converse with the Colonel. When the concentric drive had taken us to a mere ten feet or so the truck stopped with its tail-gate to the animal, breaking wind in its face with its noxious fumes, inviting it, daring it in fact, to charge. And it did.

Three tons of angry, armour-plated muscle exploded into action and came at us with frightening speed. By the time the Colonel had juggled the foot pedals the great beast was almost up beside us. At the last moment it seemed, we pulled away and kept just ahead of it. Then, incredulously, heartstoppingly, we slowed slightly, just enough to allow our irate neighbour to catch up with us and actually butt the back of the vehicle. Had we been still, the little truck would have been turned over and we three would most likely have ended up skewered like kebabs. The Colonel had obviously done this before for he kept the speed just at the boyo's optimum speed to allow it to have another go while I fervently hoped the mechanic who had serviced the vehicle had done a good job or that we wouldn't hit any pot-holes.

The Colonel was obviously a past master at this art. With consummate ease and deft skill he played the rhino as a matador would a bull, drawing it on, teasing it, and accelerating at the precise moment to deflect the force of impact. And all the time Bill and I were within touching distance of the great head and lethal horn, near enough to feel the heat of its breath, and see in its gimlet eye the anger and worse, the determination to get us. If it were a film it could not have been more dramatically orchestrated. Later, in my memory's eye, I could see the play as from above and admire the choreography and hear in my head the 'March of the Toreadors' playing in crashing *fortissimo*.

Even though the speed we were going took most of the force out of the impact of the charge, the contact nevertheless caused the truck to pitch violently and another dent medal was added to the formidable array that was already there. At last our bull's charge became laboured and the Colonel pulled away lest the animal collapsed with exhaustion, not to mention ourselves. We stopped and all got out to stretch our legs. The exhilaration had been so high that now the bubbles had settled we felt weak at the knees. I compared the two rhino charges

I had experienced lately and felt both had their memorable merits, but apart from the comparison I felt I had had my fill of rhinoceroses for a long time to come.

Before leaving Amboseli camp Colonel Gethin wrote out and presented to Bill and me illuminated certificates for each day we were there to register the animals we had seen. I wonder how the size of herds of elephants, buffalo, zebra and giraffe, the numbers of prides of lion, of cheetahs and the innumerable wildebeest, antelopes of various species, gazelles and swarms of monkeys that roamed that area then compare with now, and in a day how many safari wagons roam Lake Amboselli now it is 'secret' no more. To me Lake Amboseli was always a magic place, a place of serene solitude where you saw Africa as it always had been, undisturbed … a magic place that could conjure up the best mirages in Africa, including the Sahara, where it seemed that only yards in front of you the old lake had filled up again with sparkling water that rippled the shadows of surrounding trees, an hallucination that continually receded as you advanced, leaving the dry, savannah covered pan as the near foreground.

I wonder what changes have come about since we were there. Even in those early days of tourism Colonel Gethin was already lamenting the change in the people, the type of clients, he was beginning to have to deal with. He was becoming more and more exasperated with the increasing demands they were making.

"Do you know what the last lot, Americans they were, complained about?" he exploded that last night by the fire, "The lavatory paper," he exclaimed incredulously, "Out here in the bush, they said they didn't like the bog paper I provided." When asked "why", he said they didn't like what was then standard British issue, the shiny, brown, strong, non-absorbent 'San Izal' type.

"I felt like telling them not to bother with it then, but held my tongue and asked them what they did want and they said they preferred that damned crepe stuff, soft and bloody dangerous. The Yanks go on about all this Western stuff, rawhide riding and all that, but I reckon the Brits are harder arsed than they are. Now I suppose I'll have to have two rolls hanging side-by-side to suit all customers." He then fell into silence, no doubt pondering this cataclysmic innovation he was going to have to make. Fifty years on I'm sure 'we Brits' are grateful for the paper revolution the Yanks forced on us.

I suppose successive waves of modern tourists will have demanded more than a new brand of toilet paper for their comfort and well-being. Perhaps the safety factors of clients on open-backed vehicles may have tightened up a bit! There is little doubt that today's safari operators work under far greater restrictions, demands and stress than did Colonel Gethin in his day.

The safari ended my time at Namanga River. When Bill went home I moved on to my next goal, Kilimanjaro, the highest mountain in Africa and indeed, the highest single mountain rising direct from the ground, in the world. Since my army days I had longed to climb it and at last the time had come to try to fulfil that dream.

From Namanga I crossed into Tanganyika without trouble and headed south, past Mount Meru and on to Arusha. There was a special pleasure in being in Arusha, apart from recapturing memories of visits there while in the army. Arusha marks the halfway mark between Cairo and Capetown, being roughly 3500 miles north and south from each, and as a matter of interest and almost the same from Timbuctoo to the west.

On the last lap of the road to Arusha I was given a lift by the Police Commissioner of the district and his wife who were returning from Nairobi. They invited me for dinner that evening and dropped me off at the New Arusha Hotel, assuming no doubt that I would be booking in there. I went in and ordered some tea and was hailed by a voice rich with alcoholic beverage. Turning, I was just in time to see an old Locust Officer I'd met in the past, who had now moved into this area, practically falling off his stool at the bar in his hurry to come over and greet me. Rakish thin, with lantern jaws and watery, colourless eyes he implored me come up to the bar and have a drink. I said I'd stick with my tea but later joined him for a chat until I said I had to go to find a place to camp, whereupon he insisted I come over for a shakedown at his place. And shakedown it was. We went to his house nearby and as I unrolled my sleeping bag on his concrete verandah he said to make myself at home before setting out unsteadily to take up his duty again at the bar. I didn't see him again until morning when we passed the time of day as he burst hurriedly out of the mosquito-gauze verandah door on his way back once again to the hub of Arusha's social life, the New Arusha Hotel, without even pausing to think of breakfast. A likeable chap, running fast through his years, and looking it.

The previous evening, before bedding down for the night on my friend's comfortable verandah, I went along to the Police Commissioner's house to accept the kind invitation to dinner and passed a most enjoyable evening with the couple over an excellent meal. In the course of conversation I mentioned I was interested in studying the various tribes and making notes of their tribal habits and history. In the morning the Commissioner sent out a runner to bring in an old man who he said was an authority on the local tribes and put him at my disposal for a day or two. It would appear the man had been connected to the police office in the past, perhaps in some clerical way, for he turned out to be reasonably well educated and spoke quite good English. I rather suspected he might have been a spy of sorts or at least some kind of observer for the police.

Whatever his past, he was indeed a mine of information to me. He belonged, he said, to the WaRusa tribe, who were very closely allied to the WaMasai and their language was KiMasai. Arusa, or Arusha as it had become, comes from the Masai *'Larusa',* meaning 'of mixed blood', the WaRusa obviously having intermarried to some extent with neighbouring tribes. Nevertheless, he said, they, the WaRusa, followed exactly the Masai pattern of life, from the *laiyoni* stage through to the *Ol-Piron* and they recognised Letinga as their chief *Liabon*. He was a wonderful old character with a regal, almost haughty air in his toga-like wrap-round blanket, who took his teacher's status very seriously and I was indeed pleased and grateful to be his pupil. Some of the material he passed on to me has been included in this chapter.

Chapter Ten

A GARLAND FOR A CROWN

Sunday 6th October 1951 – On the way to climb Kilimanjaro
I'm somewhere between Arusha and Moshi. I've walked all day and
now I've pitched my tent. The ground is hard. It was like driving the pegs
into concrete. There's a hyena hooting not far away. I hope he isn't following
a lion.

On a clear day you can see Kilimanjaro from Nairobi. One hundred and twenty-five miles away as the crow flies it pokes its head over the horizon and beckons you, challenging you to pit yourself against it. That's how it had appeared to me when I first saw it from the Athi plain during Army service there and when I left Africa I took the challenge with me, feeling in my bones that some day I would return to take it up. Now that time had arrived. From my camp in the bush near Moshi (Smoke) I gazed at the mountain as it reared, copper-coloured, nearly 20,000 feet into the sunset sky. The wood-smoke pillared straight upwards in the stillness that precedes the rains. There was not much time left. Already storms would be playing around the snow-capped dome and I did not feel happy about my prospects of success. My greatest asset in the matter was a deep-rooted determination to stand on the top of the mountain I had heard described as 'The Crown of Africa'.

The first white man to set eyes on Kilimanjaro was Johann Rebmann, a missionary – only the second to go to the coastal area of East Africa, the first being another German, Dr Johann Ludwig Krapf, both of the Anglican 'Church Missionary Society' – who on 11th May 1848 saw the great mountain with two peaks of which he wrote, "I fancied I saw the summit of one of them covered with a dazzling white cloud ... which ... was perfectly clear to me ... could be nothing else but snow." When the message got back to London the scientific fraternity ridiculed Rebmann's claim. "Snow on the Equator! Whatever next?" they scoffed. Soon afterwards Dr Krapf confirmed his assistant's words, he himself having by then seen the snow on Mount Kenya and knew that it was very likely to be on Kilimanjaro too.

Most record books give credit to the German geographer Hans Meyer as the first man to climb Kilimanjaro in 1889. However, an English Methodist missionary, Charles New, wrote about climbing it in 1871, but perhaps he is not given credence of reaching the summit because he did it alone with no one to verify his claim. The local Chagga people thought it absurd that any man should think that he could climb their mighty mountain because white water demons protected it and drove anyone out of their mind who was stupid enough to go up there. And here we may have the reason why the mountain has the name by which it is known today and I contend the popular belief in the origin of the word is wrong.

There is considerable mystery about the word *Kilimanjaro*. I have often seen it explained as *Kilima Njaro* – Mountain of Snow. But when analysed it doesn't add up. To start with, in KiSwahili *Kilima* means 'hill' and the word for mountain is *Mlima,* although that in itself is not conclusive for the two words are often used freely for either.

Regarding the word *Njaro* meaning 'snow', this cannot be true for the simple reason that there is no word for 'snow' in Swahili, which is not surprising. Arabic has fifty words for 'camel' because the animal features so much in the life of Arabs: the East African natives don't see a great deal of snow so they've never had to invent a word for it. Neither does *'Njaro'* feature in Masai or Chagga. But there is a word in Chagga, *'Kilemieiro'*, meaning 'that which is difficult to climb'. So it is possible that when the missionary Rebmann asked, 'What is that?" referring to the mountain, a Chagga might have said, "That is *Kilemieiro"* and that has come down to us as 'Kilimanjaro'.

But back to Charles Newman gazing up at *'Kilemieiro'*; if the Chagga thought their mountain could not be climbed he proved them wrong. He hired porters and a guide but they dropped off one-by-one as they gained height and the cold and rarefied air hit them so that eventually he had to go on alone. Only one who has climbed the mountain can realise what that means. And to be the first, going into the unknown, that must have taken rare courage and fortitude.

On my climb I was not going alone, nor was I going into the unknown, yet I felt apprehensive. Above all other difficulties to be overcome, if I were to reach the summit, were the high-altitude effects that would be experienced near the top. Once over 13,000ft., the rarity of oxygen is apt to cause a temporary reduction of willpower and initiative and lower one's resistance against headaches, fever, frostbite, and many other maladies that are rampant at that height. With the Kaiser Wilhelm Spitz, the highest point, at 19,565ft., that leaves a long way to go in these conditions. I had heard tales of people who on attempting the climb had temporarily lost their minds, and it is not always the physically strong who are least affected. It is said women are less upset by the altitude than men. It is a question of acclimatisation. If one were able to remain at each successive level for a few days before proceeding to the next one the effects would be considerably reduced and in many cases eliminated. But each additional day, because of the extra food and wages of the guide and porters, would push up the cost of the safari so that luxury was beyond my shoestring budget.

There are also the grimmer stories of the people who have died in Kilimanjaro's snow. These tales go far back in history. One legend has the mystery of 'King Solomon's Mines' about it. In Abyssinia it is said that the Menelik, the son of the Queen of Sheba and King Solomon, died while climbing the mountain on his way back to Ethiopia from his father's mines at Sofala. He was buried with all his treasures in Kilimanjaro's snow. Even today it is said that the belief lingers in Ethiopia that one day a new King of Kings will sweep south and reconquer the long-lost Ethiopian empire, and that day will come when the Menelik's scarab ring is returned from its resting place on Kilimanjaro.

Nonsense of course, but it is strange how these legends of King Solomon's mines turn up all over eastern and southern Africa. Why the prince should decide to climb this great mountain rather than go round it is anybody's guess. After all, climbing mountains just to get to the top is a modern phenomenon. But then, that's the stuff that legends are made of.

I found myself ill-equipped for this expedition. However, at the 'Marangu Hotel', a wonderful little place on the foot slopes of the mountain, the Czech manageress and her daughter turned up trumps. I stayed there two nights and they loaned me balaclava helmet, sun goggles, alpenstock, and a pair of heavyweight trousers that had to be mended before I got them. And they prepared all the food I'd need and arranged to recruit my guide and four porters from the Chagga tribe, who inhabit the lower slopes of the mountain. By law this is the least complement with which one is allowed to make an attempt on the mountain. Anyway, there was no way I could have carried all my needs and climbed to that altitude.

Kilimanjaro has two peaks, Kibo and Mawenzi. Mawenzi is much more rugged than its neighbour, its jagged outline standing out like a row of broken teeth against the sky. But Kibo is the higher of the two and is permanently snow-covered. So it was Kibo I must aim for if I were to sit on the Crown of Africa.

The first day's march was along shady paths in the forest. A stream of ice-cold water from the mountain gurgled at our feet. Rich wild flowers grew in profusion and a little white waterfall bounced into a black pool. Further on the forest grew into dense jungle. The branches overhead were knitted into an almost solid ceiling. Here lichen-covered creepers dangled and elephants roamed. We didn't see any of the latter, but their presence was evident in the trail of broken branches and half-chewed twigs that lay along the track.

There were three huts on Kilimanjaro, all built by the Germans during their tenure of office: Bismarck Hut situated at approximately 9000ft., Peters at 12,000ft. and Kibo at 16,000ft. We reached the first, without much difficulty. It was made of stone, all of which must have been carried up to the site. Quite a feat.

Torrential rain fell all through the night and late into the morning. We hung on until there was a break in the storm before setting out on the next pitch. When the rain stopped, the steam rose from the ground and permeated the forest like a laundry.

Shortly after leaving the Bismarck Hut we broke through the forest and entered more open, scrub bush country. The rain started again, and all the way up to Peters' Hut visibility was reduced to a few yards. I was amazed at the toughness of the porters. They carried the 50 lb. chop boxes on their heads with ease, while I staggered along behind carrying only a light pack of personal kit. About an hour away from Peters' Hut we left the vegetation level. Before we did so the porters all downed their loads and dashed in unison into the last of the bushes. Thinking it was unanimous calls of nature I marvelled at such co-ordination. Perhaps the tribe had a discreet side to their nature and this was their last chance of some privacy in this delicate matter. But no, they all emerged with huge bundles of firewood which they added to their already gargantuan packs. All fuel had to be carried now. With their elephantine loads on their heads these mountain men went on and on, tireless, climbing over the roughest terrain in their bare feet without a quiver to shake their bundles.

Although born on the mountain the Chagga people do suffer from the effect of the altitude when they go into the higher regions. When one wants to become a guide he often has to have several attempts before becoming acclimatised sufficiently to reach the top. With more climbs the altitude affects become less and less.

Peters' Hut was made of corrugated iron. Inside it was lined with plywood, mellowed with age and brown with smoke. Names, with dates as far back as 1920, were still discernible. In each hut there was a book in which climbers sign their names and add some remarks. At Bismarck hut the remarks had been effervescent: "Kibo, here we come!"; "It's a piece of cake!"; "Leaving now, the Whitsun special for Kaiser Wilhelm Spitz, calling at Peter's Hut, Kibo Hut and Gillman's Point"; and one that smacked of my own countrymen, "It's a dawdle!" Here at Peters' Hut the names were fewer and remarks more sober.

This hut was named after Carl Peters, the man known to the Africans as *Mkono-wa- Damu,* literally 'Hands of Blood' or 'The Man-With-Blood-On-His-Hands'. Peters was the explorer/adventurer who did more than anyone else to make Tanganyika into German East Africa. He thought of himself as Nietsche's *Ubermensch,* (Superman) who by his 'will to power' could 'create his own law' and boasted of the trail of devastation he left behind him and the thrill he got when he shot any African who opposed his word.

Peters was appointed Imperial Commissioner in German East Africa by Chancellor Bismarck in 1891, but there were many people in high places who, knowing his terrible ways, were appalled at him being given such a position. With total authority Peters went on to fulfil every dissident's expectation of him.

His last act was to have his African houseboy hanged from a tree because he suspected him of having an affair with his, Peters', young African mistress. The girl was flogged until her back was raw then she was also hanged. Later Peters was recalled to the colonial court at Potsdam where he was tried and convicted of 'indiscipline' – no mention of murder for these and all the others he had personally killed – and dismissed the service without a pension. Later, however, the Kaiser was persuaded to restore him to the position of Imperial Commissioner.

I found it hard to sleep at that altitude although I was tired. The boys had difficulty in making a fire and food took a long time to cook. The air was getting thin. Next day we climbed on to the 'Saddle', the seven mile long neck or ridge that connects Kibo and Mawensi. Once on top, we swung left and headed for Kibo.

On the Saddle it is flat. Although the sun shone, a biting, icy wind blew. It was unusual to have to combat the two extremes in climatic conditions at the same time. My old army bush hat, which I had always found sufficient protection against sunstroke on the veldt, was hardly enough up here because the rare atmosphere made the sun's rays twice as dangerous. I lined my hat with several layers of brown paper for added protection, not knowing if this would prove effective but feeling at least it was a thicker insulation between my head and the sun. At the same time I applied a thick layer of Vaseline to my face to prevent frostbite.

By this time I was really feeling the effects of the altitude. My head ached, and I had difficulty in curbing a desire to sit down and rest every few yards. I did not know until some thirty years later that an illness I suffered as a very small baby had left one of my lungs working to little more than half capacity, so all through my life I have had to make up the difference between me and the average person with extra effort. Never had my weakness shown up more than at this moment. Of course not knowing then the reason for my debility, and believing it was all in the mind, I chided myself for weak thoughts and drove my tired self on to greater efforts.

Towards afternoon snow began to fall. The wind increased in force until we were bent almost double into a piercing blizzard. About 5 p.m. we arrived at Kibo Hut. Once inside, with the stove lit, the world seemed a bit more friendly. I felt sluggish and although I had lost my appetite I forced myself to eat the food the cook prepared. Outside the wind howled and fairly danced with temper, and in spasms worked itself into screaming tantrums in its endeavour to lift the roof off the hut.

The dwindled amount of names in the book here told their own tale of thwarted enthusiasm. Apprehension had crept into the remarks. "Hope we make it"; "Not feeling so good now, but determined to last as long as possible"; "Why do we do this?"

Next day was zero day. I was wakened in the very small hours and had an attack of mountain sickness immediately on rising, but took the porridge and tea the cook made although I didn't feel hungry. Also I hadn't got used to sleeping at that altitude yet, so I wasn't feeling very frisky. This was the day for the final assault on Kibo. Only Kimitani, the guide, accompanied me now. We set out at 3 a.m., dressed like men in the Arctic, Kimitani carrying a hurricane lamp. He had even donned boots for this last lap.

Yesterday's storm had blown itself out. But a hard frost put a razor edge on the slight breeze that blew. Crisp moonlight added to the intensity of the cold. 4 a.m. at 17,000ft. is no joke, even though almost on the equator.

As the time dragged on I fully realised that as a first-timer to Kilimanjaro I was fighting the full effect of the lack of oxygen. My head was splitting, and I was compelled to sit down and rest at very short intervals. I forced myself to breathe through my nose, although my chest was burning and shouting for more air; breathing the icy air through my mouth might have had lasting repercussions.

While resting I was struck by the beauty of the moonlit landscape. It seemed almost unreal. A thousand feet below, a sea of cloud looked solid enough to walk on. Through this sea Mawenzi had stuck its rugged head. The snow lying in its deep crevices and gullies reflected the blue moonlight so that it glowed with a faint luminosity like a fairy island in a Hans Andersen world.

But soon a thin, misty veil crept across the moon and the swinging lantern in Kimitani's hand became an eerie glow in a nightmare world. The icy wind cut through the layer of Vaseline and made my face stiff and immobile. When I spoke to the guide my speech was inarticulate. Perspiration froze on the outside of my balaclava and formed a crust that crackled as I moved. I stumbled along after Kimitani, slipping on the ice and levering myself over huge boulders with my long, spiked alpenstock, all the time trying to keep within the circle of lantern light. Kimitani, veteran of many climbs and long since acclimatised to the high altitude, climbed with effortless ease.

Just before 6 a.m. a red flame split the firmament along the horizon and Mawenzi dug its broken teeth into the sky and bit out its silhouette. Kibo's snow-capped peak was a raspberry-flavoured ice cream cone. About this time we reached the caves, half-way mark in this last pitch and starting point of the scree. This is a stretch of almost 2000ft. of volcanic ash, stretching up nearly to the top of the mountain. The most exhausting part of the whole climb, it is encountered when the altitude effects are at their highest and resistance is at its lowest. This is where most spirits break and dreams of conquest fade.

After a brief rest at the caves we attacked the scree. With each step our boots sank ankle deep into the rubble before finding a solid base to take the strain. With heartbreaking slowness I edged my way up, slowly putting one foot in front of the other, and all the time trying to make each movement a smooth motion for now my head banged like a gong and I was forced to sit down and rest every few paces. The air was so thin that even breathing was a heavy task.

Gradually the caves receded into the haze and the top came into view and grew so clear I felt I could run towards it in a few minutes. But one must allow for the rare atmosphere when judging distances on high mountains.

I asked Kimitani how much further we had to go.

"Mbili na nusu sa, Bwana," he answered.

Two and a half hours yet! Surely he was wrong? The top seemed so near, and also I couldn't endure the climb for that length of time more.

I tried to keep my mind off my troubles. I thought of places I had been to, of people I had met, of the various countries I had passed through on my travels, of books I had read – anything to keep my mind off that great bell I had for a head.

I can hardly remember pulling myself up the last rock on to the rim of the crater at Gillman's Point. Kimitani had been wrong, of course, when he said two and a half hours. It had taken three!

There followed the sweet satisfaction of signing my name in the book that was kept in a tin box up there. Funny how the pen kept slipping from my fingers when I tried to write. The names here were a select few, the remarks graphic in their brevity. *"Sheer hell!"* I wrote.

How delicious the hot, sweet tea from the flask Kimitani carried tasted up there. After a rest, when I recovered my composure, we set off round the crater rim and climbed the Kaiser Wilhelm Spitz, the true top of Kilimanjaro and highest point in Africa. You don't climb Kilimanjaro for the view. Though the scene was crystal clear a bank of cloud wiped out the distance below. But up there I was an eagle in the sky, on top of the world and the moment was sheer ecstasy.

Kilimanjaro is an extinct volcano. Inside the crater the crust is wrinkled and rugged. In the centre is the 'Ash Can', the actual hole of the volcano, around which lie large sulphur deposits. Perhaps it isn't so extinct!

It had taken nine hours from Kibo hut to the top, six of these on the scree alone; the journey back was done in two. I stayed at the hut only long enough to get something to eat, my appetite then returning fast, and pressed on the ten miles down to Peters Hut arriving there at 5.30 p.m. It had been a long, long day.

Next day we left Peters Hut at 7 a.m. and did the twenty-two miles back to the hotel at a brisk pace, arriving at 1 p.m. in time for lunch. A remarkable effort considering the porters were still carrying their loads. The distance from the hotel to Kibo top was about forty miles, so the safari amounted to some eighty miles in five days, plus the climb. But how can distance be measured in miles when it takes an hour to do a hundred feet near the top.

When we were once again down to the vegetation level Kimitani called a halt while the boys picked and wove a garland of everlasting flowers for my hat. This is the prize they gave only to those people who reached the top. How proud I felt when, at the end of the five-day safari, I walked into the hotel wearing my crown!

Chapter Eleven

THE LONELY ROAD TO ZANZIBAR

He was a man with the devil on his back. The witch doctor had put a curse on his head that he would die within seven days.

On the map the road to Tanga looked impressive; a thick red line that curled its way down through Tanganyika past imposing place names to the coast. In reality it was a dirt track that meandered through thick forests and endless bush country. The places named were in fact small groups of Indian-owned corrugated-iron shops; little huddles of humanity so isolated you wondered why anybody settled there.

At Himo, the nearest place on the main road coming from Kilimanjaro, I loaded up with supplies: tinned corned beef, potatoes, tea, sugar and enough bread to last me three or four days. My rucksack weighed well over seventy pounds; that was in the morning – by evening it had increased to at least a ton.

Most places in East Africa have two rainy spells in the year, one long, the other short. The short rains were due any day in this area, consequently there was practically no traffic on the roads, for when the rains come the mud roads become impassable. So now the accent was on 'hike' rather than 'hitch'. I had hardly turned the fork of the road to Tanga when a car came in the opposite direction and stopped and the European driver asked what I was doing. When I told him he said I would be most foolish to carry on. He told what I already knew, that nobody would be starting out for the coast now, and suggested it would be better that I come back with him to Moshi and wait there for anything that might come along. I thanked him but said I would take my luck and carry on my way. He muttered something not very flattering, wound up his window and sped off. Seeing him disappear in the dust made the road seem even lonelier than before and dented my confidence.

Despite my previous forays in the wilds and life with the Masai I was still raw to solitary bush life and felt my position more than I realised. Often while walking I became aware of being keyed-up. I would slacken off then the tension would unconsciously build up again. Loneliness was a positive thing that bore down with crushing force and smothered me into admitted insignificance. The cathedral silence was a megaphone for every sound. It emphasised the creak of trees, the coarse cries of birds – in Africa they don't sing like thrushes back home – or the clump of my boots on the hard mud. For miles on end sometimes the road was a tunnel through deep, heavy jungle where animals might lurk within feet of me.

Occasionally the stillness would be shattered by the scurry of a hidden presence that had left it late before beating a retreat, then the silence would fall again more sinister than before. Drawing my panga, which was fixed down the side of my rucksack, was an awkward business while on the move. So, in case of emergency I practised the draw while I walked until I became quite fast at it. The pistol I carried in my shirt pocket. Possessing it inspired more confidence that its value as a weapon warranted.

Few animals put in an appearance. Sometimes a troop, twenty or more in number, of black-and-white Colobus monkeys, lovely creatures with sable black bodies and long, white furry tails, would come as a wave through the trees, stop in comic surprise when they saw me, then go on with added haste, swinging through the branches and leaping incredible distances as if they were flying between trees. Here and there packs of baboons sat in the road and watched my approach. But I had the measure of them now and scattered them by clapping my hands and shouting. Nevertheless, I was aware that they posed a serious threat and though they cleared off the road and out of sight I was aware that they were watching me and as I passed by the place where they had been I was always in a high state of tension and I'm sure the hairs on the back of my neck stood up like a ruff. Every pack was in the charge of a huge, sinister looking male who was always out in front facing the danger and all the others watched him to do his bidding, presumably to attack or run. I would only have gone thirty yards or so when the bull would come cautiously back on the road followed by the others and they'd sit and stare malevolently until I'd gone out of sight.

With the approach of night and into the darkness the sounds changed. As the sun went down and the shadows deepened the loud, unforgettable calls of the tree hyrax often burst with startling suddenness from the empty blackness and the long, pleading, pitiful cries of the bush-babies came with extraordinary volume for one so small to tear at your heart-strings and leave a hiatus of chilly silence afterwards. In the darkness myriad fireflies danced like showers of electric-blue sparks among the bushes and the high-pitched whine of mosquitoes and the loud racket of crickets were continuous. Occasionally the hoot and chilling laugh of hyenas came from far and sometimes very near. In the loneliness you knew the land had come to life.

But although danger increased after dark the overwhelming solitude was mitigated when I had made camp and the firelight pushed back the solid black walls of night to form an orange dome that was my home. And in my home I was not lonely. The camp-fire was an assuring and talkative ally. Its friendly glow lulled one into a sense of security and its conversation was in the stories, the ideas, the dreams, the memories it conjured up in its flames. And it is strange how one can feel a companionship with such inanimate things as a pair of worn boots, a shabby rucksack and blackened camping equipment. This was my home and looking round I had a wonderful feeling of possession and wellbeing. This was my world: a world of cramped conditions in the small tent, eye-watering wood smoke, tinned food and bread rock hard with carrying it a while in the sun, where everything that crawled and flew in the night bit and bit hard. But with the tent pitched, an ample supply of firewood cut and stacked for the night and a meal cooked and eaten I was comfortable. The day's gruelling march was forgotten and sleep was an appreciable gift that awaited. I was content with my world.

*

Suddenly I was awake. What had disturbed me? Was it the rain that pattered on the tent? No, I had been expecting it for that night the moon had come up with a blue ring close round it and I had slackened the tent guy ropes in preparation for it. Yet something had disturbed me. My every muscle was tensed and ready to act. It was not the tension that came with the daytime caution. This came from that inner sense that warns of danger which Nature breeds into those who live close to her and which had been growing in me of late. I knew I was in danger although there was nothing, no sound, nor smell to prove it. I was so sure of it my hand went automatically to the pistol in one of my boots which with my shirt over them served as a pillow.

Yes, there it was, the soft but heavy pad of paws on some twigs outside. A hyena perhaps, extra bold, come to pick up any scraps lying around. Or a leopard! In my mind I waited for the spine-chilling saw noise a leopard makes in its throat, petrifying when heard close at hand. For ageless, excruciating moments I listened as it walked round the tent. It was uneasy. The twang of a guy-rope it touched sent it leaping back with a snarl. But it returned and continued its inspection. I wondered how long it would be before it plucked up courage to rip the canvas with its claws. What could I do? The pistol was worse than useless for it would only wound and make the animal even more ferocious. But to sit and wait and hope it would go away was to sit on the defensive with nothing to deal with the attack if it came. I had to take the initiative now while it lay in the balance waiting for the first one to act.

When the stalker seemed almost in front of the tent I rummaged for my little torch with as much clatter as possible. It sounded as if it stopped, puzzled. Quickly I loosened the door-flap ties and thrust my arm out and flashed the beam, at the same time shouting as loudly as I could and firing off a couple of shots from the pistol, aiming too high to hit anything. The combined effect was devastating – to me, at least. My torch was small and the battery weak but in the feeble beam I caught sight of a tawny form dappled with dark patches, mostly hidden by bushes, belting off into the night, but what it was, leopard or hyena, I could not say. The loud, ringing silence hung with me for what seemed an eternity. I lay listening for a long time, hardly daring to breathe lest the sound dulled my hearing, until sleep claimed me once again.

*

The rains had come. The tent was wet and heavy when struck and rolled. The road was like melting butter. The mud clung in great clods to my boots and made walking difficult. From then on the nights were a hell where volumes of whining mosquitoes bit sleep away and left large, itching lumps on any exposed flesh. I had no mosquito net and cursed my greenhorn negligence.

The mosquito bites worried me. I knew it took ten days from the time one contracted it for malaria to show and I wondered if in that time I would be laid low and if so would it be in some remote place where no help could be expected. Apart from no net, I did not carry any of the various brands of anti-malaria tablets which were in general use.

Those days were not good for my physical wellbeing nor my mental outlook. I was therefore quite pleased that damp afternoon, to put rather a fine point on it, to hear the sound of a motor vehicle coming in my direction. When it came into view I saw it was a Public Works Department truck and hoped it would stop for me. It did, but not along the road for some distance and ended with its nearside front wheel axle deep in the mud at the edge of the road.

Half a dozen native workmen with shovels piled out of the back, obviously well drilled through plenty of practice in the matter of getting the vehicle moving again.

"*Matata gani, Bwana?*" (What's the trouble?) the driver and leader asked with great concern, while they all goggled at the muddy, kilt-clad European who carried a pack and walked during the rainy season.

I assured them that except for the elements and a slight touch of madness nothing troubled me. I tried to explain why I was there in such a state but it was hopeless. To them a white man travelled only by car and if he did go on a walking safari he always had servants to carry his loads. I had to be some kind of *pumbavu* (idiot) sun-struck or something and all the more reason for treating me gently and looking after me.

While they dug a way into the wheels and laid tracks of grass and twigs behind the rear ones so that they might grip, the driver explained they were a road gang heading for the PWD camp near Gonja which was about twenty miles away. He readily agreed to take me with them and even though I protested he told the native who had been travelling beside him in the cab to give up his seat for me.

The preparations made, the driver set the gears in reverse and revved the engine. The wheels raced in the mud, suddenly caught and the truck shot back and skidded once more to a halt in the deep mud at the other side of the road. Despite the boss-boy telling me not to get involved I joined the gang at the rear to push the truck into forward motion, but unfortunately placed myself immediately behind a wheel so that when the engine started I was showered from head to foot in mud. A very muddy European wiped his face and jumped sheepishly into the cab, philosophically laying his stupidity down to experience. Before reaching Tanga I was very much experienced at digging and pushing vehicles out of mud.

But I was not at Tanga yet and there were times on this one section of the road when I wondered if I would ever reach there. The truck skidded so often into the deep mud and had to be dug out it seemed we were getting nowhere fast. Eventually the driver had chains fitted on the wheels and for a time we made good progress. But the chains brought their own troubles and we had two punctures, one after the other, in both back tyres. The spare was fitted to the first one, but when the second one went he said he had neither pump nor repair kit so we would have to make a dash for Gonja, still some miles away, before the tyre went completely flat.

That ride was a memorable one. When I first met the driver I could see he was strained. Who wouldn't be, being in charge of a vehicle and men in those conditions? But when we started on this last lap he seemed terror-struck and his face, despite the pigmentation, was positively ashen. He drove like a maniac, as if he had the very devil after him and though I did not know it then that was indeed the case. Despite, or perhaps because of his advanced state of nerves, he handled the truck like a virtuoso, throwing caution to the wind, skidding into corners so that the back slewed round, then accelerating out of the turn before the wheels stuck, bouncing over or through ruts that only the speed carried the vehicle through and taking a thousand chances he would never have done before. I braced myself strongly between the back of the seat and the front panel, otherwise I'd have rattled about like Quassimodo's bell clapper. Goodness knows how the men up the back fared, but they were all there when we arrived which was quite surprising, though some of them were visibly shaken and decidedly stirred. We were just in time, the tyre pancaking as soon as we arrived in the work camp. Later, not only did the tyres have to be repaired but it was found that there was a broken spring as well to be mended.

There was a white district overseer there when we arrived, but he didn't stay. Before he went, however, he filled me in with some of the background of the scene I'd just experienced. The driver indeed had the devil on his back.

He was of the Chagga tribe, an intelligent, forward-looking and industrious people who even in those days had organised themselves and others who inhabited the lower slopes of Kilimanjaro into a Farmers' Co-operative Society. He married a woman of the Kamba tribe who had left him. The driver then went to the WaKamba to demand his dowry back.

When the driver confronted his erstwhile father-in-law regarding the said dowry a fracas occurred which led to the aforesaid father-in-law going to the witch-doctor and having a curse put on the head of the plaintiff. The curse was that the man would die within seven days by illness, a lion or his lorry overturning.

It was well known in Africa that when a curse of this nature was made the recipient nearly always died, the cause of death no doubt being psychosomatic. Education is normally the most effective talisman against these spells, but even in European society after a few hundred years of education nobody likes to offend the Devil by breaking mirrors or walking under ladders and so invoke his bad luck. We call it superstition; to the African it was real.

It was only the day previously that the curse had been made so that explained the tension mounting in the man when he was caught in 'the horns of a dilemma' between the possibility of being benighted by the punctures and so be exposed to a possible lion attack or getting back to the camp before the tyre went flat even though the mad dash might bring about the last of the trio of death causes.

The overseer had gone when I suddenly wished I had given him my poste restante address so that he might drop me a note to let me know the outcome of the affair. It was a Thursday when I was with him and the seven days were up the next Tuesday. I even thought of staying on to see what happened, but then thought that would be rather macabre, standing around to watch him die. So I never did know if the man lived or not.

Oh yes! and I almost forgot; before he left, the overseer also said that the area where I camped the night before was notorious for rhinos. Truly, ignorance is bliss.

By quite a bit of walking and a series of local lifts I finally made it to Tanga. I arrived late in the evening and camped in the rough of the golf course. Believing the club members would not appreciate me making a fire on their hallowed ground I bundled up my kit in the morning and walked into town to give myself the luxury of a hotel breakfast.

Tanga had the reputation of being a very hospitable town and the moment I entered it I found that the reports had not been exaggerated. I suppose my appearance as I walked down the street caused murmurings to fly round the place. With no facilities for washing and brush-up on my particular part of the of the golf course I would look rather an unkempt figure with a few days growth of beard, torn shirt, muddy kilt and clods of mud for boots.

I dumped my kit at the entrance to 'The Park Hotel' and went into the dining room for breakfast. Hardly had I sat down before the African waiter, tall and thin with a great round head and beaming smile that lit his face up like a Belisha beacon, came over and said the *bwana* would like me to be his guest and would I please order anything I wanted. I considered this rash offer and asked for egg, bacon and coffee. It came piled up high on a plate as big as an aschet*, the biggest breakfast I'd ever seen, and was accompanied by the manager who welcomed me to Tanga and asked whatever was I doing. I said I had come from the north through Kenya on my way to South Africa, but I had deviated to the east to visit Zanzibar. But more important than going to that island, I had come to meet the people of Tanga whom I had heard were grand folk and within half-an-hour of getting here I found that it was all true. Well, a bit of flattery doesn't go amiss.

In a trice the manager had phoned up the President and Past-President of the local Caledonian Society, Mr Bain and Mr McEwan respectively, who left their offices to join me at the breakfast table. Mr McEwan insisted that I come and stay with him during my time in Tanga. They each took me round to meet their friends and fellow members of the Calley Society, a small, tight and very active group of people, and in no time I felt I knew all Tanga and was familiar with everything and everybody. What a welcome!

There is tale, oft' told, that describes the characters of the different races that inhabit the British Isles. It so happened that eight men were shipwrecked on a desert island. Strangely the group comprised two Englishmen, two Scots, two Welshmen and two Irishmen. Being very reserved, the Englishmen never said a word to each other because there was no one there to introduce them. The two Scots immediately clanned-up and formed a Caledonian Society. The Welshmen started to argue and the two Irishmen began to fight.

But just to show it was not all a clannish affair it was a Norwegian, a Mr Christiansen who dealt in shipping, who, after a wonderful few days of social whirl, introduced me to an Indian dhow master who offered me free passage on one of his boats to Zanzibar. He was a queer little chap with large, buck teeth and a squint in one eye who looked as if he might have been a sweeper instead of quite a rich man who ran a fleet of dhows. He was, despite his appearance, a jovial, likeable chap and kind. All he asked in return for my passage was that I mention him in my book if I ever wrote one. I am really sorry to have been so long in making my payment to him.

Tanga's kindness continued right up to the moment I left the town and beyond. Just as I was leaving to go to the dhow a servant came and handed me a sealed letter-of-introduction from his *bwana,* whose name I never got to know, which I should present to the proprietress of the Zanzibar Hotel on arrival.

---

* A serving plate. A common word in Scotland. During the France/Scotland (The Auld Alliance) alliance, many French words were incorporated into the Scottish language.

The dhow, smaller than the one I had been on before, lay in deep water ready to go in the morning. I embarked the evening before, but first had great difficulty in raising the attention of a reluctant crew to send in a small boat to pick me up. But eventually one pulled away from the ship and came to the wharf. It was quite a hair-raising business clambering down the flimsy, vertical ladder from the pier and into the very wobbly shell of a boat with my heavy pack on my back.

Things were even worse, much worse, when they had rowed me out to the dhow and I had to climb up the rope ladder that hung down from the stern. As I climbed, the weight of my rucksack on my back swung me backwards under the bulge of the hull, creating an overhang which was, to say the least, difficult to clamber over. I heaved a sigh of relief when I felt the boards of the deck under my feet.

I was not so fortunate on this dhow voyage as to be offered a bed. Nevertheless, I was thankful to curl up in my sleeping-bag on the deck and look forward to sailing with the tide in the morning.

Chapter Twelve

ZANZIBAR and 'THE TRADE OF HELL'

Friday 9th November 1951 – Zanzibar
I am sitting in the sand with my back against the bole of a great palm tree. I have just had another swim and feel grand. There is a slight breeze which is rustling the fronds above and the surf is rolling white and cool barely a yard from my feet.

Zanzibar Island lies off the coast of East Africa some eighty miles south east of Tanga. The voyage took over twenty-four hours and the passage was rough. Food was not provided so I carried my own but ate very little due to the heaving seas. I cannot say I enjoyed that trip but as a traveller I was pleased to have experienced making the passage from the mainland in this mode of transport for this was the way, in ships exactly the same as this one, that the slaves travelled and that was the main reason for my coming to Zanzibar, to see at first hand this, the very hub of what was the East African slave trade. On this trip the dhow carried a cargo of ivory, white ivory, while less than a century before the merchandise stowed in the hold would have been 'black ivory', as the slaves were known. And 'stowed' was the operative word, as we will see.

In those days the slaves were brought to Bagamoyo, a town about half way between the present day towns of Tanga and Dar-es-Salem. I really wanted to follow the slave route to Bagamoyo where all the caravans to and from the interior began and ended in days gone by. But since the once major town on the coast had slipped into almost complete disuse I had fancied, rightly, that I stood a better chance of getting a passage to Zanzibar from Tanga.

Bagamoyo, named by the natives 'The Place Where You Lay Down Your Load', must have been a welcome sight for those who had survived the journey. They may have been walking for three months under the most arduous conditions and those who arrived may have represented only a small proportion of the number that had started the journey. General Rigby, one time H.M. Political Agent and Consul at Zanzibar, wrote, 'Taking the Shire Valley as an average we would say not one-tenth arrive at their destination.' Travellers of that time said you could follow the path of a slave caravan by the bones and corpses left in its wake, or from a distance by the circling vultures who knew the value of following these long lines of pitiful people.

The sight of these caravans appalled Livingstone and he painted graphic word pictures of them. He told of the long lines of wretched people, the males yoked with cruel forked sticks back and front that chaffed their necks raw, each one bowed down with a heavy bundle, an elephant's tusk weighing sixty pounds or more, or other merchandise of equal weight. The women in addition carried their babies. If a woman slowed up the caravan a Swahili ganger would take the baby and dash its brains out against a tree. Any slave who became ill or was injured was killed or at best unshackled and left by the side of the path to die or be taken by wild animals. One Arab slaver boastfully telling of his slave journeys said they always killed any slave who showed signs of weakness in carrying the load or slowing the march. They had to, he said, otherwise others would feign sickness or weakness and the caravan would never get along. The fork-stick halters the slaves were forced to wear were never removed from the day they were captured until they were handed over to the shipper. At night time they were staked to the ground to prevent escape.

David Livingstone wrote in his journals, 'No man can estimate the amount of good that will be done if this awful Slave Trade be abolished. This will be something to live for.' 'All I can say in my solitude is, may Heaven's blessing come to everyone – American, English, Turk – who will help to heal this open sore of the world. To overdraw its evils is a simple impossibility. The sights I have seen through common incidents of the traffic are so nauseous that I always strive to drive them from memory.' But he cannot, 'The slaving scenes come back unbidden and make me start up at dead of night, horrified by their vividness.'

To those slaves who survived the awful march to the coast and 'laid down their loads' at Bagamoyo it must have seemed that their tribulations had come to an end. Far from it. The worst was yet to come. There was the sea passage to the island of Zanzibar and on that a high proportion of them were likely to die in the most horrible way.

The dhow that would take them would be like the one I went on, but there would be a big difference between the two; a terrible, even fatal difference. The slave dhow would have its hold empty when the slaves were brought for shipment. Some of the slaves were made to sit on the very bottom of the dhow. When there were children they were squeezed between two adults or sat on the legs of one which added to the subsequent discomfort. Then a bamboo deck was built a few inches above their heads, whereupon another layer of slaves sat down and a further deck was built on top of them until the ship was packed solid. No provision was made for sanitation. Many people died of suffocation and cramp. The voyage was expected to take twelve to sixteen hours, but if the ship was becalmed, as it sometimes was, and the voyage took two or even three days, the death rate could be very high.

At Zanzibar one Marie Theresa dollar Duty had to be paid for every slave brought through the Customs gates. When a slave ship arrived, the dead were thrown in the sea and any slave who looked like dying was not taken through the gates but was laid out on the beach and left to recover or die. Eye witness accounts tell of rows of dying and dead, as many as fifty at a time, lying along the beach in the sun with dogs tearing at them. If anyone of those slaves revived enough they would try to stagger or crawl to the entrance gate where they might be taken in, provided their master would pay the dollar for them.

In an attempt to put some figures to this 'Trade of Hell', as he called it, General Rigby said 19,000 slaves from this Nyasa country alone passed annually through the Custom House at the island (Zanzibar). This was exclusive of those sent to Portuguese ports. This figure was also exclusive of about 15,000 per annum imported by relatives of the Sultan. These did not pass through the Customs House and no duty was paid on them. He added that these numbers that arrived represented perhaps only 1/10th of the number that started, the rest having died en route

This then was the Zanzibar of sixty years or so before I arrived, little more than the time lapse between then and now as I write.

*

The importance of Zanzibar to the sea-going fraternity goes back a long way. There is little doubt that early Egyptians, Phoenicians, and others of the lands we refer to as 'the Middle East', called here from thousands of years ago. But it did not obtain its 'modern' importance until 1840 when Seyyid Said, Sultan of Oman, who, in the natural way of ascendancy practised by Arab gentry, had gained his title at fifteen when he stabbed his predecessor in the stomach, and moved his capital from Muskat, one of the hottest places in the world, to the comparatively cool, lush island of Zanzibar. The Omani Arabs had long been settled in Zanzibar, which at that time included part of the coastal area of mainland Africa, and Said (pronounced Sa-eed) already regarded himself as Sultan of Zanzibar. The move could be likened to Queen Victoria moving lock, stock and Parliament to Delhi to govern both Britain and India from there.

Richard Burton, with his incisive linguistic abilities gives a very in-depth explanation of the origin of 'Zanzibar'. "Zanzibar," he writes, "signifying Nigritia or Blackland, is clearly derived from 'Zang' (Persian) in Arabic 'Zanj', a Negro, and 'bar' a region. This Zangbar was changed by the Arabs who ignore the hard g, into Zanjibar. They ... consider it synonymous with ... an expression, 'Mulk el Zunuj', or 'The Land of the Blacks'."

David Livingstone, however, had another name for it. He called it 'Stinkibar'. People who were resident there, such as Sir John Kirk, The British Agent and later Consul of Zanzibar, became immune to the malodorous fumes that came from the rotting bodies on the shore and general filth that filled every corner of the streets. The tall, quiet Scot had accompanied Livingstone as doctor/botanist for six years on an early expedition and stayed on in Zanzibar to become one of the, or *the*, most able anti-slavery and territory negotiators during this most crucial transitional period of history.

The evil smelling atmosphere was not the only odorous thing about the Zanzibar of Livingstone's time. After dark the streets rung with wild carousing and fighting and good people did not go out and kept careful watch on their children for it was not unknown for people to disappear and be sold into slavery.

British interest in Zanzibar went back deep into the 19th century and although the Sultan was the nominal Ruler, and did rule, the British Consul, with increasing efforts to make the Arabs agree to end the slave trade, became more and more the power behind the throne. As time went by, succeeding Sultans came to know that the velvet-gloved hand at his back could very quickly turn into a mailed fist at his face.

When Chancellor Bismarck in Berlin, at the end of a Conference which included Britain, France and others in 1886, apportioned Tanganyika as German East Africa he included Zanzibar within its boundaries. Germany had long envied Britain's power there and a German naval squadron had actually sailed into Zanzibar harbour in an effort to tilt the balance in their favour. Sultan Barghash, incidentally, was not invited to the Conference that carved up his domain.

Britain however had no intention of losing Zanzibar. The island was the lynch-pin for control of the East African coastline and penetration of the interior for commerce, Christianity and the snuffing-out of the slave trade. In 1890, in exchange for Germany's recognition of British interests in Zanzibar, Britain gave to Germany the little North Sea island of Heligoland, which lies just off the German coast, which she had captured from Denmark in 1807.

*

When I landed in Zanzibar I was pleased to find that it could no longer be called Stinkibar. All the gore of the slave-trade had long since gone and in place of the stink the air had a delightful faint scent of cloves, which was even more evident after a shower of rain of which there were many during my stay there. The fragrance of the cloves lingered with me long after I left the island.

After the voyage from Tanga, which had not been an easy passage, I was glad to be on dry land but berated myself for even thinking of my petty discomfort when walking on the very street the surviving slaves had trod after their voyage and all that had gone before it.

I walked to the Zanzibar Hotel, presented the letter-of-introduction that I had been given at Tanga to the proprietress, Mrs Kibo-White, and asked if I might pitch my tent in her grounds so that it could be left safely unattended while I went about the island. She read the letter and with no more ado invited me to be her non-paying guest in the hotel. She never said who the letter was from, no doubt assuming that I knew, and I didn't like to ask. After treading the road to Zanzibar and the voyage I was only too pleased to settle into my comfortable room, spread out my things to blow away the tight confines of camping, wallow in deep baths and cold showers and bless my luck and wish the best of health and wealth to my unknown benefactor who sent the letter when succulent, nose twitching meals were placed in front of me.

The hotel was a lovely old Arab mansion with a magnificent, brass-studded front door. It had the quaint atmosphere of a steadfast, respectable house that had lived through and seen all the horrors of evil times and come out with its honour intact and was determined to keep it so. Outside, all down one side of the street, Baghdad-like merchants sat cross-legged beside Ali Baba baskets and jars, wonderful, gleaming copper ware, flame-red in the sun, and cloying sweet-meats whose clinging aromas wafted before and aft in the stillness as you passed. In such atmosphere I would not have been surprised to have seen a flying carpet come over the roof tops, its fringe flapping back against the wind, a fat, turbaned merchant with exotic curled moustaches sitting amidships on a flight of great import and secrecy.

Zanzibar was a treasure trove of interest. I enjoyed ferreting about its dark alleyways where the few beams of sunlight that managed to penetrate the close, overhanging buildings festooned with ornamented balconies, some low enough to graze a tall man's head, made the shadows more intense. The streets were filled with a great mixture of Arabs and Indians, bearded Mohammedans followed sometimes by their women shrouded by black sheets over their heads like ghosts with just an eye peephole to go by and clean-shaven Hindus with their women barefaced in exotic saris, bible-like characters in long-flowing robes of blue or white, many regally embroidered with gold and silver, some with little black or white caps, others with big shaggy turbans and one or two in splendid neat golden ones, and sometimes a man on a donkey with side panniers practically touching each wall crushing past amid a following crescendo of guttural complaints. And always the constant barter banter, the occasional shrill calls of some market vendor, high and piercing, cutting through the loud fugue of noise like a woman's scream, the hawking and spitting, the hubbub of the daily commerce. I was in my element here.

I even crossed the little bridge over the creek where few people other than the inhabitants dared to go and ventured into The African Quarter, the place they called Ngambo (The Other Side) where even locals were warned not to enter without a guide or at least a compass. Here over 30,000 people – the descendants of the freed slaves – huddled into an area barely three-quarters-of-a-mile square creating what must have been one of the most closely packed communities in the world. There was one small street where a few *dukas* and grim coffee-shops flourished, but away from there was a maze of unbelievable complexity. In there dense clusters of mud-and-wattle houses with palm-thatched roofs, so close together there was barely room to squeeze through, had grown to no pattern or direction at all. Twisting paths between the hap-hazard houses meandered in a most convoluted labyrinth that lost you within yards. Occasionally you came across little open spaces of sandy soil that were like gems, lung areas where you could actually breathe. There was a lot of filth as would be expected in such congestion, but the surprise was that there was not more of it. Indeed, generally the place was tidy, with the spaces between the houses being swept clean and all the houses were not of the slum type. Occasionally you could come on quite a comparatively grand mansion, showing that not all the inhabitants were impoverished, that some who might have afforded better chose to live there.

Judging my direction from a few glimpses of the sky I blundered about, at times being completely lost, asking my way of the few people I met, who were always friendly, but with no roads or direct paths to point out they could merely show the direction to go, often by merely lifting their chin and jutting it towards a path and muttering, *"Huko."* (Over there. That way.) The path would soon convolute in mad, dervish twists and leave me bewildered in no time. The inhabitants obviously navigated by an inbred memory of the paths imprinted by generations of life there. Without that I was a lost sheep, but nevertheless managed with great relief to emerge into the sunlight at the other side of the warren after a couple hours or so.

The government at that time had embarked on quite an extensive building and re-housing scheme and if this development survived the departure of the British administration and the Communist coup of 1964 then no doubt Ngambo as it was will be no more.

To walk through the streets of Zanzibar was to walk through the history of modern Africa. Zanzibar in the 19th century was the door to all the east and central regions of the great continent. Nearly all the names who made history there began their expeditions here walking through these narrow streets. Where they had walked one felt in close company with these hardy, intrepid men. Here is the house where David Livingstone stayed. There is the place where Richard Burton and John Hanning Speke lived while putting together their caravan before pushing into the unexplored interior in search of what was then the mythical Central African Lakes and the possible source of the Nile. Henry Morton Stanley put up here before setting out on the 21st March 1871 into 'The Dark Continent' on perhaps the most famous of all expeditions, the one that coined the immortal words, "Doctor Livingstone, I presume?" They all came here: Cameron, the

217

first European to cross tropical Africa from east to west; Grant, who joined Speke to discover the source of the Nile; Thomson, the first white man to walk across Masailand, and many more, most of whom, apart from Burton, Speke and Stanley, who was Welsh, were Scots.

But if these so named represented the famous and the good, there was one door that was the hallmark of evil, the epitome of the infamous. The wonderfully carved and brass-studded door with black and white marble step was the home of one Hamed bin Mohammed el-Marjebi, better known as Tippu Tib, the greatest slave-trader of them all. Some say his nickname meant 'He-Who-Blinks' and that he gained it because of a nervous twitch. This may or not be true, although a nervous twitch does not altogether go along with Stanley's description of the man, '... a tall, straight man, in the prime of life, a picture of energy and strength ... the air of a well-bred Arab, (he was in fact a Swahili with Negroid complexion) courtier-like in his manner ... a remarkable man.' A fitness-fanatic he could outrun any man he raced. Not, it would seem, the nervous type. He did, however, have red-rimmed eyes and locals said he owed his pseudonym to the bird named scientifically *Centropus superciliosus,* but known commonly as the Tippu Tib bird.

Stanley had full reason think highly of Tippu Tib, for deep in the interior while on his search for Livingstone the slaver gave him much needed supplies and agreed to lend him a guide who would take him to the sick white doctor. Livingstone too was therefore indebted to the slavetrader, the very epitome of the evil he had spent most of his life combating, and not for the first time for he, as well as other white explorers, had also been helped by the trader in the past.

Burton and Speke, credited with being the first white men to penetrate the uncharted interior to the great lakes, nevertheless followed well defined Arab trader trails, staying sometimes at Arab camps and established towns ruled by Sultans who were permanent, or semi-permanent, residents and often received much needed help from them.

My trail in the future several times crossed that of Tippu Tib and the legends of him were as alive then as when he had passed a century before.

It rained quite a lot during the time I was ferreting the bazaars but I didn't mind. The daily showers came at fairly regular times and I soon found the public reference library which was part of the museum and gladly spent those times trawling the books on Zanzibar's wicked but colourful past which was also the modern history of all East and Central Africa.

I hired a bicycle and ranged far and wide in solitary bliss, the breeze in my face, drinking in the serene and very friendly island. Everyone rode bicycles on Zanzibar particularly in the town and environs, though I was perhaps the only white person who did so. It was interesting to see the local gentry in their long white *kanzu* robes cycling sedately through the streets in the rain holding up their umbrellas with one hand as they rolled along. When the showers passed, the umbrellas would be rolled up and hung down the backs of the riders with the handles hooked into the back of their collars.

One day I cycled to Chwaka, a little place on the Indian ocean side of the island. Near there lay the ruins of Dunga Palace where once lived a long dynasty of African chiefs of Shirazian descent who ruled Zanzibar before Omani Arabs occupied it in the early 18th century and deposed the African chieftain line. The name of the African tribe to which the early rulers belonged has been lost in the mists of time. It was the Omanis who referred to them as *Shirazis*, their early term given to non-Arab people of the East African coast, as *Swahili* refers to those of mixed Arab blood.

While the *Shirazis* were not of Arabic blood they would not have been wholly African either. The name by which they were known comes from the Persian *Sheraz* and would indicate they had mixed with these people since the Persians founded their Zenj Empire (Burton would have called it the 'Zang' Empire) along this coast in the 10th century. Since the *Shirazis* built in stone and their chiefs lived in great style in grand palaces it is obvious that as a people they had moved away from the indigenous Bantu stock.

Slaves were said to have been buried in the palace walls and in 1914 when some clearing work was done on the site, human bones were found at the bottom of a dried-up well. The palace ruins were reputed to be haunted and there was even a legend of buried treasure. Not having brought my spade with me I wasn't able to clear up that mystery. Earlier diggers were more successful when they found the sacred Swahili drums and horns of carved wood which were now in the Zanzibar Museum.

Fri. 9th November, '51 Zanzibar
The rain had stopped and the sun was shining when I awoke this morning. I decided to take the bike and go over to Chwaka on the other side of the island about 22 miles away. It has been a grand day. I am writing this at Chwaka. It's about 4pm and I'm just going to get started back for Zanzibar town.
The journey here was fine, through lanes of coconut palms and clove trees. I passed houses with the cloves selected in different groups laid out to dry on great square concrete yards.
Chwaka is just a little native fishing village with a few houses occupied by Indians, I think. (Although only a cluster of native huts at the time of my visit Chwaka, in its heyday a century before, had been a celebrated country retreat for wealthy slave-traders. Here on the eastern coast facing the endless Indian ocean there was always a cool breeze blowing and the stench and clamour and evil doings of Zanzibar town were far away.)

I cycled along the beach north of the village but was cut off by the tide and was forced to take a path parallel with the shore. It was hardly a path. The trees were growing so close together it was hardly possible to pass. It was so rough with coral rock there were long stretches where I had to carry the bicycle. When I became hot and sweating I went in for a dip. Oh! that was grand.

Eventually I made the road and came back near Chwaka. Now I am sitting in the sand with my back against the bole of a great palm tree. I have just had another swim and feel grand. There is a slight breeze that is rustling the fronds above and the surf is rolling white and cool barely a yard from my feet. My lunch consisted of fruit today. A whole lot of bananas and oranges bought for 20 cents (2d). Less than 1p.

Reading my diary entry for the first time since I wrote it how well I remember that day and others like it. Zanzibar was a dream island where long slender palm trees hung over empty, golden beaches, simply posing for travel brochures. Its tranquil, serene atmosphere belied its bloody past. Now it made a respectable living by growing coconuts and in conjunction with the neighbouring island of Pemba produced nearly the whole of the world's supply of cloves.

Cycling along, one hand in my pocket sometimes, through groves of tall palms and shorter, beautifully coloured and aromatic clove trees conjured up such an exotic, serendipitous experience I kept wondering what new romance lay round each corner and why I was so lucky to be part of it. Whatever hardships had gone into getting there were more than worth it.

It was Sultan Seyyid who was given the credit for starting the cloves industry in Zanzibar, although, as we shall see, cloves were already being grown there when he arrived. But it was Seyyid, during his early visits to the ends of his domain, before he upped sticks at his Muscat camp and moved permanently to the island, who saw the export potential and expanded the business by having many more of the plants imported from the Seychelles and Mauritius islands where in earlier times they had been brought from their indigenous roots in the Moluccas islands. By mid-19th century, Zanzibar was well established in the trade.

The buds of the clove tree, which is allied to the myrtle family, were all picked by hand and, after being separated, were left to dry in the sun for a few days on the concrete platforms (*sakafu*) or on coconut matting. Afterwards they would be sold as an aromatic spice for flavouring in food and even in some eastern cigarettes, and would also be used in medicine and perfume.

Cloves and coconuts do not grow together. Although both grew in great profusion in Zanzibar, the areas that were good for one were unsuitable for the other. When I first saw the coconut fruit brought from the tree I did not recognise these large pumpkin-like things as the hairy nut we used try to knock off their pedestals at coconut shys at fairs. It was only when I watched them being split in half by being impaled on a 3-foot wooden spike driven into the ground in the yards of houses I passed on my cycling perambulations, that I realised the complexity of the fruit. The splitting of the great pod required rare skill. As I watched a man raise the large object high above his head with both hands and bring it down with great force onto the spike I shuddered to think what injury he could do to himself if his aim wandered even slightly just once. Inside the large outer skin was packed with a fibrous matting known as 'coir' and in the middle was the kernel or nut that I could recognise.

Coconut production took second place to cloves in foreign exports returns but the tree and its fruit have long been the mainstay of existence of the inhabitants. In a land where good water is not always readily available the milky liquid, *madafu*, inside the nut provided a welcome drink. The white fleshy kernel meat provided the staple diet and when it was dried and became known as 'copra', oil was extracted from it which was used in soaps, hair-oils, edible oils, margarine and later, synthetic rubber. The residues were used in animal feeding-cake. The hairy coat of the nut as we know it was used to make coconut matting and the fibrous coir packing was made into mattresses and used to make ropes and cordage. Being resistant to salt water there was always a great demand for Zanzibar ropes from dhow seamen and in the Fungani Quarter, on a long peninsula where fishermen lived, you could watch those ropes being made as they had been since time immemorial.

Since that time too the hard shells of the nut have been used as fuel in a land where firewood is scarce. Some were cut and polished to make cups, ladles and other eating utensils. The tree trunks have been used to build houses, boats, bridges, etc. The tree fronds were used to thatch the houses and also to make fish-traps, baskets, brooms, mats and other useful household articles. From the stalks of the plant a whitish liquor called *toddy* – not to be confused with the whisky variety, though the name may have come from there – is obtained. In its original state it is a very popular, refreshing drink, but after a few hours fermentation when it develops into a very potent liquor, which the natives call *tembo* and others refer to as palm wine, its popularity increases. From distilled palm wine a type of *arack* is made.

Nothing of the palm tree is lost. Even the tree root contributes its share to the well-being of the community. The coconut palm root has long been known to have narcotic properties and locals were often chewing a quid of it.

The coconut palm bark is corrugated with raised circular rings, which denote past frond and fruit crowns. The pickers use these crustaceans to shin up the trunk, which they do with great agility and speed using a thong some eighteen inches in length that is tied to each ankle at the back of the trunk. Taking a grip round the tree with their hands they lift their knees and place the thong into one of the round hollows between the ridges and brace it taught with their bare feet. They then push up from their knees, reach higher with their hands and raise their knees again to repeat the process. The action is done in a swift, flowing motion and in this way they seem to bound up the tree.

Each tree produces about thirty nuts a year and their average life runs to about sixty or seventy years. Clove trees can go another ten years or so. In 1872 a great hurricane destroyed two-thirds of the cloves and coconut trees on the island, so that when I was there the trees I saw were those planted after the hurricane and were coming to the end of their lives. Soon, they would be cut for their timber.

*

To me Zanzibar was an isle of serene enchantment. I loved the peace and tranquillity I felt as I cycled round. But mostly it was in Zanzibar town that my interest lay. My reason for coming was to follow the slave trail and this was where the African part of it ended. Zanzibar was the big clearing house for central and east Africa. It was here that the future of each slave was decided. This was the place that so appalled Livingstone that he launched his special appeal for the Christian Church's intervention to try and stop this 'Trade of Hell'. Even he perhaps could not have dreamed just how successful that intervention would be.

If Livingstone's Stinkibar had gone there was one place more than any other that was a poignant reminder of all the evils that were an intrinsic part of the life at that time and how these evils were vanquished. Like a war memorial whose purpose it is to remind future generations of not just the names of the fallen but to impress the horrors of war and evil on those who look on it so that they may do all in their power to prevent anything like it ever happening again, the Anglican Universities Mission to Central Africa (UMCA) Church of Zanzibar stands like a St. George's statue with the slayed dragon of slavery at his feet.

The UMCA was formed as a direct response to Livingstone's great call for help in ending slavery in Africa made at that memorable meeting in the Senate House at Cambridge on December 4, 1857. In winding up his speech Livingstone said, 'I go back to Africa to try to make an open path for commerce and Christianity. Do you carry on the work which I have begun. I leave it with you.' The Universities of Oxford and Cambridge soon took up the challenge and a year or so later were joined by those of Dublin and Durham. Two years after Livingstone's call, in the same Senate House where he had spoken the now time-honoured words, Charles Frederick Mackenzie, aged thirty-four, was chosen to lead the Mission into Central Africa.

They sailed from Plymouth in October 1860 for Cape Town and eventually round to East Africa from where they went inland in an attempt to establish their first Mission station by Lake Nyasa. But like so many of the early missionaries Bishop Mackenzie died of fever after the canoe overturned in which he and a companion, the Revd H. de W. Burrup, were travelling down the Shire (pronounced Sheree) River in incessant rain.

The UMCA band, now under the direction of Bishop Tozer, arrived in Zanzibar in August 1864, having decided to withdraw from the Zambezi valley due to the high incidence of malaria and because it was too dangerous to live there due to wild tribes. The missionaries had decided not to retaliate if attacked even if it meant losing their own lives for it seemed wrong to kill any of the people they had come to convert. The move from Lake Nyasa to Zanzibar was not popular with everyone, least of all Dr Livingstone. But it made sense. Zanzibar was the hub of all the traffic and industry to and from the interior and it was here that the man who controlled the slave trade lived. If Sultan Seyyid Said could be made or persuaded, in any way, to have a change of mind or heart regarding slavery a great blow would be struck towards its final demise.

Some inroads in that direction had already been made over the years, but those had been brought about more by the shadowy mailed-fist-in-a-velvet-glove advisory influence Britain held over the Sultan rather than by any religious or humane persuasion. Since the beginning of the 19th century after Britain's withdrawal from the West Africa/Americas slave trade, Britain's anti-slavery crusade had been broadened to include East Africa.

In 1822 Seyyid Said had signed an ineffectual treaty with Britain to which the Sultan had paid little heed unless it suited him. Such as the time he confiscated Mtoni (*Mto-ni* – the place of the River) Palace, the biggest building on the island which was owned by an Arab by the name of Saleh, who it was had first introduced the clove trees to Zanzibar from Mauritius. Seyyid charged Saleh with dealing in the slave-trade in contravention of the treaty he, Seyyid, had concluded with Great Britain. The irony of the situation when nearly everyone on the island, including the Sultan, was doing the same did not appear to enter Seyyid's conscience.

At that time Seyyid was still resident in Oman and if the thought of moving was growing in his mind he must have viewed Mtoni with avaricious eyes. It was a most desirable residence, fit for a King or even a Sultan. Water to it was conveyed along a stone aqueduct from the Chem-Chem well and tame flamingos, peacocks, gazelles and ostriches roamed the gardens. Little wonder he forsook Oman for permanent residence in Zanzibar. So, not only did he dispossess the man of his house he took over his clove business, expanded it and claimed the introduction of the tree to the island as his own. Only the ruins of the palace remained when I was there.

The transportation of slaves to America was begun by the Spanish when they sent the first shipment to their colonies there in 1517. The Portuguese were soon into the trade and they were followed by many other Europeans, Germans, French, Swedes and Danes. England's participation began with a foray in 1562 by the merchant privateer Captain John Hawkins. But another hundred years were to pass before she entered the trade in a big way.

It was King Charles II who took England into the slave trade. In 1663 he chartered the Company of Royal Adventurers of England Trading in Africa. To commemorate the start of the Company's trading he ordered the Royal Mint to strike a new coin made of the purest gold, worth the odd figure of 21 shillings, which he called a 'guinea', named after that part of Africa from whence the precious metal came.

Although coming late into the game the English and later the British became most proficient. They devised the 'triangular trade' – West Africa to England with slaves, gold and ivory; England to America with slaves and other merchandise; and America to West Africa with cotton cloth, etc to barter for slaves; each side of the triangular voyage being rich in trade in its own right. The 'Middle Passage', that leg across the Atlantic to the Americas, was the most infamous due to the terrible cramped conditions, poor food and other inhuman privations to which the slaves were subjected for so long.

The 'Black Ivory' trade must always be a stigma that every nation which was involved in it must carry with shame. None moreso than Britain. Without trying to minimise Britain's guilt it can be said, however, that it was there that the first rumblings of a national conscience against the evil practice were to be heard. This conception was gradually orchestrated by people such as William Wilberforce, who entered Parliament in1784 at the age of twenty-one, and swelled in volume to thunderous level until 1807 when an Act of Parliament was passed prohibiting slavery and making all dealings with it unlawful. That marked the beginning of the end of the West African slave trade.

But if it was ending in the West, the trade was only just beginning in East Africa. There had always been some slave taking in the east, going back to the time of the Phoenicians and beyond perhaps, but it had always taken hind place to gold and ivory as trading merchandise from the interior. It was not until the arrival of Sultan Seyyid Said in 1804 that the slave trade really hit the big time here in East Africa. Seyyid was the ultimate entrepreneur, the far-sighted merchant adventurer who could see the potential of a small running business and turn it into a mega money-maker. As he did later with cloves he did first with slaves.

Prior to this time, few of the visiting seamen ever penetrated inland. They purchased slaves at the coast from the more dominant tribes who preyed on weaker ones. Seyyid did things differently. He sent his own men in to harvest the crop at the source. At first they did not need to go far, but they cleared the land as they went and gradually, gradually they had to go in deeper and deeper. By the time the explorers Burton and Speke came along some fifty years later in their attempt to penetrate the interior and try to find the fabled Great Lakes, of which garbled references had come down in history since Roman times, Seyyid's red flag was already flying there. The two explorers followed along the Arabs' trails and saw the evidence of the carnage and inhumanity that had gone before them, the scale of which must rank among the worst the world had ever seen.

The Royal Navy having been successful in blockading the West Coast of Africa had more difficulty in patrolling the East Coast because of the long route round the Cape and even when they got there they had no rights at the beginning to apprehend slave ships. Nevertheless a few Royal Navy ships were kept in East African waters in the hope of effecting a brake on the slave trade and also to forestall any French claims to East Africa during the Napoleonic wars. Although they had little success with slaving ships in these early days their presence did wonders for British diplomacy with the Sultan.

Throughout the 19th century Zanzibar grew in wealth and importance due to its expanding clove exports and booming slave market. The latter reached its zenith around the middle years due to increasing demands from the French colonies of Mauritius and Seychelles where industry was expanding. Zanzibar was therefore a fat, rich plum, very ripe for a takeover.

In 1861, after the death of Seyyid Said and a confrontation between two of his sons, Thuwaini, who ruled in Oman and claimed that that seat was the principal one, and Majid who had taken over from his father in Zanzibar, the two parts of the dominion broke. With British aid – indeed it was Lord Canning, Governor General of India, who declared that the two parts must separate – Zanzibar became independent from Muscat. A state of loggerheads remained between the two Arab countries and Oman now posed a threat, as did other Arab states, not to forget the Portuguese, Indians, Persians, etc., for which the Sultan's little navy was inadequate. It was therefore to Britain and her resident navy that the Sultans of Zanzibar looked for protection and received it. However, protection rarely comes cheaply as Zanzibar was to learn to its cost.

In 1873 Sir Bartle Frere arrived in Zanzibar under special commission from the British government to try and stop the slave trade. He put his proposal to the ruling sultan, Seyyid Barghash, second son of Seyyid Said, and his men. They let it be known that they broached no interference to their way of life. At the beginning of their history Abraham and Ishmael had owned slaves, so why should they not continue to do likewise as had always been the way of their people. That, as far as they were concerned, was the end of the matter. Not so for Frere, although he gave no sign other than a courteous acceptance of their answer. But in private he slipped the velvet glove from the mailed fist.

A little later, nine men-of-war, six British, two French and one American, under the command of a British admiral, sailed into Zanzibar waters. Strangely enough, Sultan Seyyid Barghash had a sudden change of heart and agreed to sign a treaty with Great Britain to prohibit the export of slaves from East Africa and to close all slave markets in his domain. One has to admit that gunboat politics were not all bad.

It was a great moment in history, a momentous victory for British diplomacy. At last the treaties were beginning to bite but unfortunately not to kill. A great step forward, yes, but so far it did not end slavery in this part of Africa. Barghash had not abolished slavery, only prohibited the export of slaves and closed the markets. A great deal would continue in the background and it may be remembered that slavery was still the biggest bargaining issue when Sir William Mackinnon parlayed with Barghash fourteen years later and the Sultan handed over the administration of the mainland territories to the British East African Association.

Although slavery still existed in less obvious ways than before the Sultan's prohibition, one very obvious sight marked the end of that era. The great Mkunazini ('The Place of the *Munazi*', a tree whose leaves could be pounded to make soap) Slave Market was now empty. That rectangle of bare earth, fifty by thirty yards, lay derelict, abandoned. Here, in its hey-day, every afternoon dealers led their strings of slaves around the viewing area where they would be handled and pummelled and scrutinised indecently, particularly the girls, by prospective buyers. Some of the slaves would be sold straight from the boats at knock down prices, but most would have been kept for some time in the slavers' special camps to recover from the horror of the march and be fattened up like cattle. In 1868 prices had fallen but girls still brought in 11–15 dollars a head, adult men 12 dollars, women 9–10 dollars and boys from 7–8 dollars. Shipped on to Muscat they would fetch four or five times the price paid at The Great Slave Market of Zanzibar. Back in the interior of Africa, at the very source of the trade, three or four slaves might have been exchanged for a bullock.

During my browsing in the Zanzibar library I came across the following extract from a book in which a naval Captain Smee gives a graphic account of a day in the life of The Mkunkazini or Great Slave Market:

"The show commences about four o'clock in the afternoon. The slaves, set off to their best advantage by having their skins cleaned and burnished with coconut oil, their faces painted with red and white stripes as is here esteemed elegant, and their hands, noses, ears and feet ornamented with a profusion of bracelets of gold, silver and jewels, arranged in a line commencing with the youngest and increasing to the rear according to their size and age. At the head of the file, which is composed of all sexes and ages of six to sixty, walks the person who owns them. Behind and at

each side two or three of his domestic servants armed with swords and spears serve as a guard. Thus ordered the procession begins and passes through the market place and principal streets, the owner holding forth in a kind of song the good qualities of his slaves and the high prices that have been offered for them.

When any of them strikes a spectator's fancy the line immediately stops and a process of examination ensues which for minuteness is unequalled in any cattle market in Europe. The intended purchaser having ascertained that there is no defect in the faculties of speech, hearing, etc., that there are no diseases present and that the slave does not snore in his sleep, which is counted a very great fault, next proceeds to examine the person. The mouth and teeth are first inspected and afterwards every part of the body in succession, not even excepting the breasts of the girls many of them whom I have seen handled in the most indecent manner in the public place by the purchasers; indeed, there is every reason to believe that the slave dealers almost universally force the young females to submit to their lust previous to being disposed of. The slave is then made to walk or run a little to show there is no defect in their feet, after which the price is agreed. They are then stripped of their finery and delivered over to their future master. I have frequently counted between twenty and thirty of these files in the market at one time, some of which contained about thirty slaves. Women with children newly born hanging at their breasts and others so old they can scarcely walk are sometimes seen dragged about in this manner. I observed they had in general a very dejected look, some groups so ill fed that their bones appeared as if ready to penetrate the skin."

After the selling, for the slaves who remained in Zanzibar, the worst of their lot was over, for Arabs, apart from the dealers, were generally kind to their slaves. But even so, the average remaining life in slavery was only from seven to eleven years so a constant fresh supply was needed.

For those who were transported to Arabia and elsewhere across the sea, their main troubles could just be beginning. When the dhows were pursued by a British ship many or all would drop the cargo overboard, chains and all. The dhow was always considered to be worth far more than the slaves. When one dhow with two hundred and forty slaves on board was pursued, the throats of all were cut separately before they were thrown away. That every one was cut showed that this had to be done in a methodical manner. In a panic some might have been done, but many or most would have merely been pushed overboard. And the only methodical way would have been to have them in lines moving forward while the men with the knives took them one at a time. Those in the lines would have watched those in front being disposed of while waiting their turn, an indication of how broken in spirit they were, how the terror and harsh treatment on the long trail and confinement had reduced them to being utterly incapable of making the slightest protest.

In horror I visualised myself as one of the slaves. In my imagination I stood in line and felt the whip across my shoulder, heard the sharp order, "*Upesi, upesi,*" (Quick, hurry) and watched those in front shuffle forward and step up on the bulwark and lift their heads in dumb obedience to expose their throats to the wild faced Arab or Swahili in ragged turban and blood-soaked robes. I counted … 3, 2, 1, …

One dhow boarded by Rigby only a few hours after it had left the harbour had over a hundred girls on board, all of whom had been selected for their good looks. A fatigue party was sent to take over the provisions and every sailor fainted as soon as he went into the hold, so unbearable was the stench. The surgeon of the *Hydra*, the British ship, ordered the immediate destruction of the vessel and said that if the dhow had got away to sea there would be no doubt that not one of the slaves would have survived the voyage. The passage to Muscat took thirty to thirty-five days but often they were delayed by weather.

*

Now, with the Great Market empty and unused, we again take up the thread of the UMCA that was steadily being woven into the tapestry of Zanzibar and Africa of these times. After some nine years in Zanzibar, and only twelve since Livingstone made his famous call, the Anglican missionaries decided it was time that a church of permanent structure should be built. The task fell to Dr Edward Steere, the new incumbent leader of the community, a remarkable man in so many ways, and his name will always be connected to the cathedral and the building a fitting tribute to him.

There is however one other name which has an intrinsic and most important connection with this church, one that may now be lost in time for this person lived less than two years after his arrival as a new, eager recruit to the Mission before death cut him down as it did to so many early arrivals in Africa where life-expectancy was so short. When the Reverend A.N. West, a Buckinghamshire man, arrived in Zanzibar the great Mkunazini slave market place was lying empty. There was talk of building a permanent church and it was West's brilliant idea that the Mission should build on the site of the old slave market. To put substance to his proposal West, a man of considerable means, bought a part of the area which had a large house on it and presented it to the Mission. A bizarre gift followed when a rich Hindu merchant, Jairam Senji, gave to the Mission the whipping post at which countless slaves had suffered over the years. The foundation stone was laid by Capt. Prideaux, Acting Consul-General, on Christmas

Day, 1873, appropriately the same year as David Livingstone died. Below the stone was put a parchment record in Arabic and English of the object of the building, together with some coins. But building work did not start properly until 1874 after Steere returned from England where he had been consecrated at Westminster Abbey as the third Bishop of the Mission. The new Bishop proved to be a very able designer, architect and hands-on builder showing the unqualified labour force how it should be done, from building scaffolds, mixing mortar, even drawing straight lines which at first they seemed unable to grasp, to turning window arches and forming fine roof tracery. The building was completed in 1879, a remarkable achievement considering all the difficulties that had to be overcome. The clock in the tower was presented by Sultan Seyyid Barghash in 1880, a nice example of religious tolerance on the part of a Moslem.

A man of so many talents, Steere was first and foremost an outstanding linguist. He spoke German and Portuguese fluently and soon preached in perfect, idiomatic Swahili. His Swahili grammar handbook became a classic – it was the Course text book for the Swahili lessons I attended in the Army at Nairobi in 1946 – and he translated most of the Bible before he died in 1882, having refused to go home to England though very weak in order to carry on his translating until the last. The work was completed by Archdeacon Hodgson who had collaborated with Bishop Steere since its inception.

Dr Edward Steere was a great man. So much achieved in so short a lifespan and in the final few years he was only half the man he had been after a near fatal bout of malaria that kept him in chronic poor health.

I had read quite a bit about the UMCA church before I visited it but even so I was still overcome by the sheer size of the cathedral building. Perhaps it was because I had learned so much about it, the work that had gone into Steere's colossal efforts on top of all his missionary work, that made it all the more impressive. His building could take its place in any city and no one would imagine it had not been built by master masons. Only local materials were used in its construction.

The great, carved entrance doors were an excellent example of native craftsmanship. A stained-glass window, given in memory of British sailors who died in action while engaged in anti-slavery duty, cast its soft coloured light over the interior. High above, sixty feet or more, the vaulted ceiling gave the building an authentic cathedral appearance.

The roof had given Steere particular problems. Copper would have been too expensive. Corrugated-iron sheeting did not seem appropriate and would have been too hot in the sun and too noisy in the rain. He overcame the difficulty with a brilliant idea to span the area by means of a concrete vaulted roof formed with a mixture of crushed coral and cement.

Above the pulpit hung a wooden crucifix made from a branch of the tree under which David Livingstone's heart had been buried after being removed from his body where he died at Chitambo (Northern Rhodesia at the time of my visit, now Zaire). The story of how Chuma and Susi, Livingstone's faithful servants, after removing his heart carried the body six hundred miles to the to the coast for onward transportation to Westminster Abbey where it is interred, is a thrilling saga in its own rights. Livingstone had written in his diary that he wanted to 'be buried in the still, still forest' but Chuma and Susi, with or without knowing their master's dying wish, decided that his body must go back to his own people. The Great Missionary's heart, however, will forever be where for the greatest part of his life it had always been, in the still, still forest of Africa.

The altar of the magnificent Cathedral of Zanzibar had a special significance. It was situated on the very spot where once stood the whipping-post, surely the epitome of the metamorphosis that this site and Zanzibar, and indeed all Africa, had undergone.

Wonderful as these changes were, slavery had not yet been eliminated. That did not happen until 1889 when, with further 'persuasion' from Britain, Sultan Khalifa bin Said declared that the purchase and sale of slaves should be prohibited within his dominion. Even so, it was not until 1928, however, that the legal status of slavery was finally abolished. Or was it? Even in the 1950s as I travelled Africa there were rumours and whispers of the trade still being active, if in much smaller ways, especially of caravans through the Sahara desert.

*

The time came all too soon when I knew I had to get back on the road. The rains were not yet over and the road inland was perhaps going to be even worse than the one to Tanga. Zanzibar had been a quiet interlude and long would I carry the memories. In the weeks ahead I would long for the comfort and tranquillity I had known on the island and always I would carry with me memories of blissful walks and bicycle rides and cool sundowners sitting in glorious technicolour while passing that quiet half hour in musing conversation.

In the hotel I had met Jock Slater, a Scot from Banff, who came for the evening meal. Jock, in his late thirties or so, was a shipwright *par excellence* who was there on contract to repair the Sultan's barge and build another. Loquacious on his own subject, Jock was full of stories of boats ... and boats ... and boats ... and we usually passed the last hour of the day watching the sun go down, he with a pint or two and me with something else. I see now red sunsets fringed with palm fronds and watch the darkening silhouettes of the returning fishermen standing in their *ungulawas* grow in size as they draw into land, hear the long rasping noise of the sand and surf as they beach in the gathering gloaming.

The *ungulawa,* the dugout canoe with stabilising outriggers on either side is, as far as I know, unique to Zanzibar and is surely the original catamaran and trimaran. Did this unusual craft for this part of the world mean that the Polynesians once came here?

I crossed from Zanzibar to Dar-es-Salaam in a small, motorised schooner owned and run by a Mr Grundy and his wife, a lovely friendly couple, both past middle age, who had promised me a passage whenever I decided to leave. The craft was comfortable but cramped and at the time I thought it said a lot for the couple at their time of life that they both lived on board. The sea was like glass, the voyage delightful and I slept on board before landing.

Alec in Cairo wearing his 'solar-topee'
(sun-helmet)

Dhow building at Maala, Aden

A caravan ready to go from Sheik Othman, Aden

A Tribal Guard at the Sultan's Palace, Dhala

A street scene in Dhala. The man is smoking the long-stemmed pipe used at home as opposed to the short *chibuk* he would carry on a journey

John Lees stands by an ant hill in the Ogaden desert

The water wagon comes to the building site. Note the difference with the Lebanese arabs, in white, to the local Adenese people.

Yusif, the strong man, lifts the *chai* boy.   Aboica stands to the left.

An Arab dhow similar to the one on which I travelled to Aden. Note the latrine box hanging over the side beside the main mast.

The Palace entrance, Gedi

The harem pool in the Sultan's palace

The ruins of Gedi. Walls gripped by great talons.

Masai warriors shoot an arrow into cow's jugular vein to draw off blood to drink.

Young rich Masai woman standing by her house made of mud, blood, sticks and dung.

Masai playing 'bao', a game found all over Africa

FROM NAMANGA RIVER HOTEL TO			
← SOUTH	**MILEAGES**	**NORTH →**	
ARUSHA.	73	NAIROBI.	103
MOSHI.	126	KAMPALA.	547
VOI.	226	M†² OF THE MOON.	747
MOMBASA.	327	JUBA.	874
DODOMA.	336	KHARTOUM.	1816
MBEYA.	755	CAIRO.	3015
BLANTYRE.	1521	KANO.	3256
BROKEN HILL.	1401	TIMBUCTOO.	4418
ELIZABETHVILLE.	1602	ALGIERS.	5612
LOBITO BAY.	2774	LAGOS.	4131
VICTORIA FALLS.	1815	PARIS.	7169
JOHANNESBURG.	2635	LONDON.	7395
DURBAN.	3251	JOHN O'GROATS.	7954
CAPE TOWN.	3605		

NEW YORK. 10535½ . HOLLYWOOD. 13219.

Masai warrior in full war regalia

Mileage radiating from the hotel near
where I stayed with the Masai tribe

A Garland for a Crown

Zanzibar street scene. Note the parasol to shade the traffic policeman

UMCA Church of Zanzibar

Slave Gate - Zanzibar

Ungulawa canoe- Zanzibar beach

Chapter Thirteen

THE GIFT OF BREAD

Wednesday 12th December 1951 – On the road to Iringa.
I heard a lion roar last night. Now that is a sound to shake anyone to the marrow, especially when camping alone with no rifle.

Dar-es-Salaam did not add up to its name. After Zanzibar it seemed noisy, very busy and dirty. To its founder, Sultan Majid bin Said (*Sa'eed*), who it may be remembered took over Zanzibar and the coastal area from his father, Seyyid, in 1856, it was indeed a quiet Haven. Despite waging bits of war, with British help, against his two brothers, Thuwaini in Oman and Barghash in Zanzibar, Majid was not a fighting man. Anything but. His great pleasure was his harem. So much so, he had built a Pleasure Dome in the quiet seclusion of the mainland, away from the hurly-burly on Zanzibar, where he could grab himself a quiet couple of days or so and relax among his most choice, hand-picked maidens. He called his love nest his Haven of Peace, or in Arabic, *Dar-es-Saleem*.

By the time I arrived things had changed a bit. The Pleasure Dome was no more and the name Haven of Peace had been passed on to the great town that had grown in its place. Dar was now the capital of Tanganyika and its biggest city.

A mile or so out of town was the local army camp of the King's African Rifles. I went and made my usual request to pitch my tent in their compound and was pleased when this was granted. This time, though, they took me at my word and no bed or meals were included in the invite.

After settling in I had the great joy of going to the post office to collect my mail. I always chose a place a month or so along my intended route and put my address as poste restante there. Sometimes it was two or three months and even more before I got to the place and the joy of receiving the letters was then even more enhanced. This time, apart from those from home, there was a letter from Frank Vernon saying he had given up his job on the up-country farm in Kenya and was heading my way and hoping to meet up with me. I was really pleased and looked forward to seeing him again and sharing some laughter and fun. But there was a down side to the idea of him coming that made me worry. Did he really want to travel or was he just setting out to try and find me. His letter was a couple or so weeks old and I wondered how he was making out. If he was travelling by car or by public transport he should have been here by now. Frank wasn't my kind of traveller and any idea of us teaming up would have been quite impractical. Maybe he didn't think of it that way. Perhaps he needed help. I had never thought it was good for him to go to that lonely farm. I felt I had to wait in case he needed a shoulder to lean on.

I went down to the post office at the same time every day and left a message for him to say I'd meet him there at that time. After a couple of days I had done everything I wanted to do in Dar and was eager to be on my way but hung on. It was still raining and there was little comfort in my little tent to while away the days. The total entry for one day in my diary of the time was succinct and descriptive:

Wed. 21st Nov. '51, Dar-es-Salaam
  No mail, no Frank, plenty rain, plenty insects.

I answered all my letters and wrote some more and then the time really did hang. After a miserable week I felt I had to make a move. One last try at the post office then I packed up and hit the road. I felt mean, but days without doing anything but eating were not good for me nor my budget. We never did meet again and I often wonder what happened to Frank. I left a letter for him with my next poste restante address but there was no reply. I thought about him a lot after that and worried about the downcast side of his make-up and wondered how he took it when he got there, if he ever did, and found me gone.

Before leaving the KAR camp the quartermaster issued me with a little green, army mosquito-net which was more practical to me than any I could buy in the shops. It was just over six feet long and a couple wide and its sides were just a foot and a half or so high so that when I turned on my side my shoulder almost touched the top. It weighed only a few ounces and suited the close confines of my tent admirably, but as often as not I didn't bother to pitch the tent and just pegged the net down on its own and slept under that so I could look through at the stars. I used it for years until … But that is another story a long way down the trail and will have to bide its time until we get there.

The way inland towards Morogoro and Iringa was not easy. Going west and south-west I was following the rains. Further north they had finished, but going as I did I seemed to be continually in them. The road was churned and rutted as a ploughed field and in places was quite impassable until the Public Works gangs had worked on them. In places such as these a barrier would be placed across the road with an *askari* or two guarding it to stop large vehicles going through, because of the damage their large wheels could do before the road surface could be made up. Cars were allowed to travel but there were very few of those and practically no through traffic. So even when I did get a lift it seldom went far. Nevertheless I was always grateful.

You have to walk in the mud, soaked to the skin, feel your clotted boots grow heavy as lead and try and forget the discomfort of your pack straps chaffing deeper and deeper into your shoulders to appreciate the ecstasy of being lifted out of it for even a short while.

With the short lifts too I had the opportunity to meet a great cross section of people. With few Europeans about my travelling companions, when they took me aboard, were mostly African, Indian or Arab and it was good to talk to them about the country, their families and habits and all that made up their way of life. Sometimes too their kindness did not stop with the lift but extended to inviting me to eat with them or even to spend the night in their homes.

I spoke to Africans of family and tribal ways and of things they were surprised at anyone, particularly a white person, knowing, and with each conversation I became more and more aware how complicated and sophisticated was their social structure. I learned that with coastal people inheritance did not pass down through the father's family. All his wealth, his cattle and possessions, passed to his sister's eldest son and in the old days before the white men came and stopped slavery, an uncle had the right to sell his nieces and nephews. When I asked if an uncle still had rights over his sister's children they covered their faces with their hands, giggled and said, *"siyo"* (No) with too much emphasis, I thought. Their embarrassment appeared to be that of one who had been found out and I sensed that avuncular rights were still very, very strong. I was developing a growing conviction that there was a whole underlying strata of tribal rites and activities, many of which would be regarded as criminal or morally corrupt by European standards, that existed deep down where white man's laws did not reach.

I was not many days out from Dar when after a particularly heavy shower that had soaked me even though I'd sheltered under some trees during some of it, a native policeman came running after me to ask what I was doing. Unable to understand my ways though I explained carefully what I was up to, he went away but returned very soon to tell me that I must accompany him to the *Boma* (Government Office). When I reported to the District Commissioner he was very good about it though astonished that I should be trying to make my way during the rains. He made no move to stop me, but, over a welcome cup of coffee, he warned me against walking in these parts because of the game. This was lion country and there were elephants and leopards as well. He obviously did not overstate the case for my diary entry for later that day says:

The DC was right about the animals. I got a bit of a scare when a leopard crossed the road about a hundred yards in front of me; it went into the bush. There was also some fresh spoor of elephants.

The road was really in a shocking condition. The black cotton patches were unbelievable quagmires. I knew this part of the road was closed until something was done about it, so was surprised to hear a truck in the distance coming towards me. I had stopped for a rest so did not have my pack on. I thought it must be the PWD gang come to work on the road, but when it hove into sight I saw it was a trader's wagon. Before it arrived I knew it was an Indian's for they always vastly overloaded their vehicles and this one was certainly well over the top.

As it drew near I stepped into the road and raised my hand. The truck slithered to a halt. In deference to the Indian driver who I was sure would resent being spoken to in Swahili I asked in English where he was going. He looked vacantly at me and mumbled, "No understand." I then explained in Swahili what I was doing and asked if he would be good enough to give me a lift. Immediately his sullen face broke into a huge smile and, miraculously, he remembered he could speak English perfectly, albeit with a heavy accent. "Yes, yes," he said eagerly in his clipped, sing-song way, "I am going to Morogoro and I am so happy for you to accompany me." I realised then the reason for his lapse of memory. He had obviously bribed the *askari* at the road stop to allow him to pass and when he saw me without my pack standing in the road in my kilt and khaki shirt and bush hat he took me for some kind of soldier or policeman and assumed he could be in trouble.

Despite my protests he ousted the African from the seat in the cab and had him clamber up beside half a dozen others perched precariously on top of the mountain of goods at the back and bade me to sit in with him. What followed was a memorable journey. Steering the overloaded vehicle on a good road would have been difficult: on this one it was near impossible. Times without number we skidded and bogged down. Down would come the natives from the back to dig us out – the reason for their being there – and off we'd go again for another mile or so, leaving behind the deep ruts the heavy-loaded wheels created and the great holes in the road that had been dug to get down to the sunken wheels. If these holes were not repaired and the road surface not graded smooth before the sun eventually baked the surface dry and hard as concrete they would pose a dangerous hazard to traffic This was the reason why at times heavy vehicles were generally banned from passing certain parts at the height of the rains.

At the Ruvu River there was a small ferry that could not take the loaded truck. The stores had to be unloaded and two journeys made to ferry everything across. Once again the load was piled high and lashed down and on we went. My diary takes up the story:

About 9pm last night we struck a particularly bad patch of black-cotton soil, slewed round and bogged down past the axles. The load had all to be dismantled again for the truck was in danger of going over on its side. The boys dug, and laid down branches as usual, but when the driver started up the truck only ground itself deeper. Hour after hour they tried and tried. (The Indian had positively forbidden me to work with the boys, deeming physical labour beneath Indians and Europeans and it was bad for discipline for a white man to be seen working shoulder-to-shoulder with the natives.) *Some boys were directed to keep fires alight for this is lion country. The mosquitoes hummed, the bullfrogs croaked loudly, the crickets droned and the fireflies flitted in their millions, their darting little blue lights forming fluorescent clouds round the bushes. About 2am I curled up in my sleeping bag at the side of the road and slept. I was badly bitten by mosquitoes.*

Morning found the truck deeper in the mud. The boys were nearly all-in, but the old Indian kept them going. Towards noon a PWD Road Supervisor drove up. He was a Goan about my own age and was exceedingly friendly. I expected trouble for the Indian for being on the road, but whatever passed between them, a good dash from the Indian no doubt, their meeting appeared very amicable.

The Goan, de Silva by name, was going back to his house and invited me to come with him. I was pleased to accept and after thanking the Indian was glad to be on the move again.

The Goanese people, of whom there were many, held a peculiar position in the class structure of East Africa. Although originating from Goa, the Portuguese colony in the Indian sub-continent, they did not regard themselves as Indian. In the layered class society of those days the Goans, as they were referred to, being mostly Roman Catholics and carrying Portuguese names, liked to consider themselves as Europeans. The Europeans however did not accept them as such. They therefore tended to hover somewhere between the White society and the Indian one. The Africans occupied the lower strata of the unwritten pecking order of East African society. The upper echelons of the Indian strata however did not regard the Goans in any way superior to them and indeed often employed them in minor capacities. Goans would not be found in the Club, except perhaps as senior barman or junior manager; they would not be eligible to 'member' status. Goans did no manual work. They were clerks or as in the case of de Silva, supervisors of African labour. On the whole they tended to be rather obsequious and not always trustworthy in what they said.

Despite my misgivings I was grateful to Mr de Silva's invitation to stay the night with him.

De Silva lived in a lonely, little cottage on the edge of an African village at about the centre of the stretch of road for which he was responsible. An African girl who looked at home in the house drifted away and wasn't seen again after a few, hurried, undertone words from my host as we entered. Conditions were rather primitive but de Silva tried so hard to make me feel welcome and comfortable it was almost embarrassing. I was most grateful and felt sorry I was putting him to so much trouble He made me feel a king in the way he fussed to make sure I had hot water and a clean towel, hustled his servant to clear a place where a bed could be made up for me and sent him running to the *duka* for provisions which he obviously never used himself. I was sure I was the first European who had ever entered his house and certainly the first he had ever entertained as a guest.

The meal that night was touching if somewhat embarrassing. De Silva, greatly over-playing his ideas of European ways, was obviously awkward in handling a knife and fork and yet persisted in using them for the most unusual tasks, such as taking the paper off the butter and cutting the loaf of bread like it was a side of roast beef. He even fished biscuits out of a tin with them and tried to pass one across the table to me with them. But here he became unstuck when the utensils slipped and the biscuit flew into the air and I caught it with no ado as if it were all perfectly natural table manners.

As he grappled with the eating irons, de Silva talked with great airs and exaggerated casualness. His English was quite good and without the clipped manner of the Indians whom he referred to as 'them'. I was surprised that having established his European ways, his natural subservient mien had dropped from his shoulders like a cloak and now he was the over patronising host. There was nothing he hadn't done from shooting all manner of big game to winning a waltz competition at a grand ball.

When we reclined with a cup of coffee so that I stretched my shirt across my chest he saw the outline of the pistol in my breast pocket. He asked what it was and I said it was a .25 Beretta automatic. Oh yes, he had had one but dispensed with it because it was too small. I said it was difficult getting ammunition of that calibre. No trouble, he still had plenty. How many packets would I want to carry? Well, one packet would more than replace those I had used to frighten away animals, thank you. I couldn't believe my luck, that calibre of bullet was not easy to come by. Point 22 was common, available nearly everywhere, but .25 bullets were like gold dust. Languidly, as if he did this all the time, he called his houseboy and told him to fetch a packet of the *risasi kidogo* (little bullets). The boy was to his back and in my view, de Silva talking over his shoulder. The African's face wrinkled into a question mark, obviously bewildered. But perhaps used to his master's ways he decided to play along and went off shaking his head when he thought he was out of sight, returning in a few minutes to say they were all finished. De Silva, face-saved, remembered he had had good cause to use them.

Next day the roads Area Inspector, an Englishman, came by and was surprised to find me there and even moreso to learn that I had actually stayed the night in the Goan's house. He offered to take me to Morogoro to where he lived. Road Inspector Tim Chisholm, a fellow not much older than myself, drove a Citroen car which he claimed was the best vehicle for the African roads. It rode high out of the ruts when raised to the full height of its hydraulics and with its front-wheel-drive cornered at speed round the most mean bends without skidding even on wet black cotton soil. The logo of two inverted V's that all Citroens carried across their radiators was Monsieur Citroen's way of cocking-a-snook at the officers' class who retained their ranks after demobilisation at the end of the first World War. Monsieur Citroen was a corporal and proud of it so he made sure his badge of rank would remain long after the officers were forgotten. It's wonderful what gems one picks up along the way!

Chisholm was an easy and cheerful companion. He laughingly called himself a 'nutter' as all were known who had come out on the disastrous Groundnut Scheme and stayed on in Africa after its collapse. He referred to the grandiose scheme dreamed up with all good intentions by the Government in London in 1947 and put into operation through The Overseas Development Organisation. The aim of the scheme was to turn a great part of southern Tanganyika into a groundnut prairie and so create a vast export commodity. To this end the British Government invested untold millions of pounds, built a new harbour – which I believe has since gone derelict – on the coast in anticipation of an export bonanza and persuaded the local farmers to forsake their traditional crops and plant groundnuts instead.

Unfortunately the whole thing went terribly awry for the simple reason that the nuts did not grow. Groundnuts, or peanuts or monkeynuts as they are more commonly known, grow on the ends of long stalks which have a peculiar way of bending down after flowering and pushing the fruit under the ground to ripen. The product is rich in oil. Needless to say the plant requires a very special type of soil which was not there in the place chosen for the Scheme. Local farmers said the area was not good for growing *karanga,* but what do natives know in comparison to soil analysts with letters after their names? At the time I was travelling that part of the country the whole thing had just come to an end and there were an awful lot of red, egg-splattered faces about. The only way for those caught up and thrown out by the disaster was, in Chisholm's way, to laugh at it.

He drove me to Morogoro, a pleasant town which had a wonderful fruit market. To the south of the town rose the majestic Uluguru Mountains which against a dramatic sky looked magnificent. I thought that if I had to live in this country this would do me very well. As it was, I only spent a day or so there before pushing on for Iringa, a part of the way that was not the easiest, but had its moments of supreme interest.

Mon. 10th Dec. '51, On the Road to Iringa
Got on the road this morning and walked all day. How lonely the road is, not a thing, just miles and miles of nothing.

Tues. 11th Dec. '51, On the Road
More endless miles today. If I don't catch pneumonia soon I deserve to. I get soaked to the skin with showers of torrential rain – oh how it rains – then the sun comes out and my clothes dry on me. Then I sweat till my clothes are saturated and the sweat drops off the end of my kilt. I have a rest and my clothes dry on me again leaving salt stains from the sweat. When I start again the sweat or the rain soaks me again. I wonder how I would have taken all this a year ago! Walking all day on my own, always on the alert in case of a sudden attack from animals.

Then there are the nights of pitching my tent in the rain, looking about for dry sticks and trying to coax them to light while I arch my body over them and hold up my ground sheet to keep the rain off till they blaze up.

Many nights the ground is sodden where I lie and even my sleeping bag is invariably damp since my pack gets soaked as I walk. Still it is all in the day's work! Can't have it all fine.

Wed. 12th Dec. '51, On the road
I heard a lion roar last night. Now that is a sound to shake anyone to the marrow, especially when camping on your own with no rifle. They say that when a lion roars there is no danger, (because he roars after he has eaten) but it is a nerve wracking experience to hear one so near under those conditions. But I must admit it is a wonderful noise.

Tonight I am staying with a Greek family. About 5 p.m. I came across a little farm miles from anywhere and decided I had gone far enough for one day. I asked permission to camp near them so that I could get water easily. But they brought me in, invited me to dinner and gave me a bed.

There is the old man and his wife and daughter. The daughter is in her early twenties and it seems a sin to bury her away up here in the wilderness. She is the only one who speaks English. The old Greek is trying to scratch a living off the land here but is finding it difficult due to the animals. He has had to clear the forest before planting. Then the buffaloes come along and trample the plants. He is growing sisal and sunflower and paw-paw. The wild hogs tear up the plants too and don't even to bother to eat them. The worst offenders are the monkeys.

"Oh, if only no animals", exclaimed the Pioneer in his broken English, and he sighed as if his life would be a picnic if that were the case. I wondered how some of the farmers back home would do if they had to start clearing their ground of forest and were confronted with bigger pests than rabbits and rats.

The daughter was telling me that only two weeks ago a leopard came and took two of her dogs. Big Alsations they were and only a few feet from the door. What grand company they are. What a lonely life they lead. Kilosa is their nearest place and that is almost 70 miles away.

I am averaging twenty to twenty five miles a day. The daughter was telling me also that there are man-eating lions further back. I must have walked right through that district. Ignorance is bliss! She warned me against walking in this district. It is one of the wildest parts in Africa. There are places where even the denseness of the forest is frightening. Still, I am so far in now and I am not going to turn back.

Thurs. 13th Dec. '51, On the road

Well, against all the warning of the Greeks I came away and continued to walk. The old man pleaded with me to stay with them until some motor came along. "You no go, ple-ase" he kept saying, his outstretched hands gesticulating. His concern for a total stranger was touching. But as luck would have it I encountered no danger. There was just dead quiet and the odd gazelle and occasional monkeys.

Towards evening I came on a little village, just the usual kind of a few grass huts and a corrugated iron duka or shop. It is an Arab who runs the shop. When I dropped in he brought a chair for me and had tea and chapatis ready for me in no time. When I asked if I could put my tent down near he said I needn't bother, he would put a bed out on the verandah for me. After that he brought rice and curry. He wouldn't take any payment. He says I am his guest.

The bed is the usual string affair and the verandah is just the overhang of the corrugated iron sheets. But it's a luxury and I appreciate it as it is the best the Arab can offer. It is night time now and the lamps have been lit. Small hurricane lamps. But I have just a home made effort of a tin with a hole in the lid and a piece of string as a wick. The naked light casts a smoky glow round my string bed. The word has long gone round the village of my presence and there is the odd inquisitive face – an Arab shaven head or an African's woolly mop occasionally popped into the light to have a look at this strange white man who has come to stay for the night.

240

My food is certainly varied. On my own I do all right on eggs and bread and jam, tinned meat when I have it or an occasional chicken and potatoes roasted in the fire or boiled if I have enough water. In African huts I get posho (maize meal porridge). Then last night with the Greek family when I had their type of food and tonight an Arab curry and rice and chapatis.

After leaving the Greeks this morning, my route lay over a range of mountains. The route coiled itself in great loops up the escarpment. How tiring it was to see a point only a few hundred yards away yet to reach it I had to do about a mile in great curves. It was impossible to cut off any of the curves as the valley between was too deep and quite sheer in places.

Somewhere on the way up I came on a little work party of Africans mending the road. I had seen them for a while, standing agog, watching the lone, kilted Mzungu on foot approach from way down below. When I arrived and was pleased to ease the rucksack from my back and sit in their little thatched shelter they crowded round plying me with questions. I asked for water and they brought me that and some cold posho (very stoggy maise meal porridge, stiff enough to be like a loaf of bread) which at normal times I would have abhorred, but now tasted delicious. It was all that they had and they had given it freely. I was very grateful.

After the top the road tumbled down in a great series of loops to the valley floor. The country isn't so wild now.

Fri. 14th Dec. '51, Near Sourhill.

Today was my lucky day. I have got a lift right down to Mufalira in Northern Rhodesia. It was the CopperBelt I was heading for in the hope of getting a job on one of the mines there and be settled for a while and enjoy Christmas and New Year in something like home comforts.

This morning, just as I was finishing my breakfast of chapatis and strong, sweet tea that the Arabs like, two of the oldest cars that I have ever seen stopped outside the duka. One of the drivers came in to see if he could get some motor oil. The duka didn't stock that but imagine his surprise when he saw me sitting there in my kilt. Imagine my surprise when he said he and his wife came from Kingseat (on the outskirts of Dunfermline) about six miles or seven from where I live. It's a small world! He said he hadn't even expected to find an Arab shop out in the blue, far less a Scotsman in a kilt staying there. He agreed to take me to Mufalira.

Dick and Margaret Bernard had come to Africa a few years before when Dick had decided to swap coal mining in Fife for copper mining in Northern Rhodesia. They were a lovely, friendly couple to be with and to be able to lapse into our broad Fife tongue together was like a breath of home. They, with their little girl and I, travelled in one car while their friends, a South African family, were in the other. They had all been on holiday to Dar-es-Salaam and it was a wonder how they had got there and back. Both cars were in a very dilapidated condition. Apart from the need for oil, one car had a leaking radiator, so we had to fill jerricans whenever we passed a stream, and apart from those peccadilloes both cars suffered from a multitude of minor to serious ailments.

So followed several days of wonderful chaos. The cars broke down sometimes twenty times a day and the men worked manfully over them – not me for I knew nothing about engines – while the women grew fretful and the children bawled from hunger, tiredness and boredom. I helped particularly in the evening when we may have gone too far for the day and needed to make camp in the dark when everybody was tired and at their lowest ebb, and sometimes I even tried my hand at the cooking and that was not all that easy as an entry in my diary describes:

This morning I had half-a-dozen eggs fried when Ken's (the father of the other family) youngest bairn, about eighteen months old, calmly put a handful of sand over them and mashed them up. He and his three year old brother both have diarrhoea and it seems to get everywhere.

But it was great fun, great company and far better and quicker than walking on my own. But that stopped after we passed through Mbeya and arrived at Tunduma on the border with Northern Rhodesia. What followed there fills three or four pages of my diary with wild invective over the iniquities of the conduct of the British authorities to poor travellers as opposed to rich ones. I poured out my vexed heart over the pages but on re-reading it makes very poor and boring copy. What it does show is the value the diary was to me: a constant, private companion to whom I could confide my prejudices, my anger, my weaknesses and my fears with complete trust and by absorbing all allowed me to present a more sane and level-headed exterior to the world, since without it I might have had to vent it all on the world at large.

The trouble had begun in Mbeya when I presented myself at the Boma and asked if my £100 immigration deposit was there for me to pick up. It was not and no one knew anything about me. When I had given the money to the official on arrival at Mombasa I was told I was free to travel anywhere within Kenya, Uganda and Tanganyika, the three British administered East African countries. When I was due to leave I was told to tell the authorities in Nairobi my intended point of exit and the money would be forwarded there for me to pick up. I had nominated Mbeya, but now it appeared nothing had been done. It might be at the border post at Tunduma, someone said, so I went there with Dick and his companions in high anticipation.

But once again I met bitter disappointment and in the end I had to make my farewells to my Rhodesian-based friends and sadly watch them disappear in a cloud of dust, smoke, clanking metal and greetin' bairns and sorry I was not to be with them.

*

That night I camped near the Tanganyikan border post. The next day I was due to make my return to Mbeya to make a formal request to Nairobi to have my immigration money forwarded. As if to compound my misery at losing my lift to the Copper Belt it rained that night. Rain like I had never seen before with thunder and lightning like I have never seen since. Salvo after salvo of thunder rolled across the sky, rising in volume until it reached its crescendo with an ear-splitting crack that ripped the sky apart, all illuminated by continuous, fearful lightning. For hours the wildfire had warned of its approach and when it came it arrived like a great express train hitting a tiny station and I felt I was lying between the rails. For hour after hour the sky was rent asunder with gigantic, multi-forked flashes of intense, electric-blue light. I kept telling myself there was nothing to worry about; it was all happening up there. But I had no words to calm myself with when, perhaps due to copper and other minerals lying close to the surface and therefore acting as a conductor, the lightning danced across the sodden ground barely yards from my tent. Not once, but many times and I wondered when I must be hit.

Blessed relief came when an *askari* policeman, backlit by the most dramatic stage-lighting effects, came with a shiny oilskin held over his head and shoulders, showing only his big, luminous, frightened eyes, to tell me he had been sent to bring me into the station for safety. I was given a cell, complete with iron bars, all to myself. I wallowed in relief. So safe, dry and comfortable! No lifer could have wished for better.

Next day a police officer who was going that way took me to Mbeya where I sent a cable to the authorities in Nairobi to forward my immigration money to this point of exit from the three territories. This could take a few weeks I was told. To fill in the time and a little more – a great deal more as it happened – I resolved to try and hunt down a man Dick Barnard had told me about during the journey. The man in question had worked at Mufilira copper mine with Dick some time before. A hard, Afrikaans man, who nobody would cross, he was by nature a hunter. At weekends he would head for the open bush to hunt antelopes and the like, or most often to the rivers to shoot crocodiles. He was known to everyone as Crocodile Pete. Dick never knew, or certainly never mentioned, his real name. Some of the men from the mine often accompanied Pete on his hunting forages and his name was legend throughout the mine. There came the day, though, when Pete had to leave the mining community in something of a cloud of low spoken references after some fracas in a pub. Once again Dick never knew or chose not to mention the details, but I gathered between the lines that Hunter Pete had a fight with a man and knocked him about pretty badly. Whatever the reasons it seemed that Pete had left the mine and gone to hunt crocodiles full-time for a living. Dick had heard he was somewhere near the top end of Lake Nyasa. So on these flimsiest of details I set out to search a thousand square miles of wild, mountainous, riverine African bush country for a man I knew of only by a past pseudonym in the hope that I might join him, and even if I were lucky enough to come up with him he would be most unlikely to want anything to do with me.

I headed down the road to the lake and up some of the rivers, always asking the natives if they knew of a *mzungu* who was hunting *mambas* (crocodiles) and always the answer was '*siyo'* (no) or '*hakuna'*. (there is none). The answers highlighted the differences in the Swahili spoken in Kenya and Tanganyika, something I had had to contend with since I crossed from the one country to the other. Swahili, as previously mentioned, evolved at the coast and passed along the trade routes into the interior. Since the main arterial passageways to the early gold mines and slave harvesting areas lay through Tanganyika it followed that these places got first-hand contact with pure coastal KiSwahili whereas places away from the trade routes, such as Kenya, received the language many hands over as it percolated further afield. I spoke the Kenya or 'up-country' dialect that was less refined or articulate than the coastal or Tanganyika tongue. As an example, *siyo* was rarely heard north of the border. There, *hapana or hakuna* were used for all negative answers i.e. 'no', 'there is none', 'not', 'none' etc. As I travelled it always made for interest when new regional or dialectal words were introduced in a conversation.

*

Sunday 23rd December, '51, On the Road to Lake Nyasa
I am sitting in the corner of a native hut writing my diary by candlelight. It has been a hard day, all uphill and pouring rain. My old boots are lying there, their crinkled uppers separated from the soles, grinning at me. Good old pals, your days are numbered. At the other end of the hut are a couple of cows and some hens. The place is heavy with their smells.

In the centre of the earthen floor a woman cooks over an open fire. Her shaved head shines in the firelight and her flat breasts swing as she stirs the pot. She has arms with bulging biceps like a man. A naked child straddles her back, fast asleep. When it is ready she will bring me a bowl of posho and pumpkin leaves and a gourd of water to drink and will pour some off to wash my hands, for I will eat with my fingers as they do. It will be gluey, insipid food but I will enjoy it. Only a short time ago I watched her pound the maize corn in a stick and log pestle-and-mortar to make the flour for the meal.

This hut is one of a little settlement of the WaSafa tribe that I came on when the light was fading. Like all African huts there is no chimney and the place is filled with smoke. It makes eyes water but keeps down the mosquitoes. Children of various ages are running about. The WaSafa, until a few years ago, were cannibals and even today they still file their teeth to points, an old cannibal custom. There are still dark rumours that they sometimes eat their dead, which is a change from the old days when they only ate their enemies

When I arrived I was welcomed by all. An early-teenage boy talked excitedly to me and sitting on a stool somewhat on her own sat a young woman stirring something in a bowl in preparation for the meal. I took her to be the eldest of the children, but when the youth, who appeared to be only a year or two younger than she, referred to her as his 'mama kidogo' (little mother) I looked surprised until he explained that this was his father's second wife.

When the father came in just before dark after walking miles from his work on the road it was plain who was master in the house. When they heard him coming the boy stopped talking and the young wife rose from the stool she was sitting on and sat on the floor. No matter how little he is thought of at work he is king in his own castle. He has grey hair and wears a thick, ivory bangle round his wrist. He was surprised but affable to find me here.

The meal over the old man now lies over in the shadows with his young wife. He removes the cap from a hard skin phial he wears on a leather thong round his neck, tips out some tobacco snuff onto his thumb and screws it up his nose. As an afterthought he pulls the thong over his head and gives the container to the girl to bring to me. I take my time to open the phial, and by way of courtesy take out a pinch and nod my thanks over to the old man. In the candlelight the girl has a silky, delicate beauty. She has a fancy hair-do with six partings in it and her only garment is a skin skirt. It hardly seems fair that she should be married to an old man and that in a few years she will be like the older wife, as tough and leathery as a worn strap. She drops her head to smile shyly as she takes the skin bottle at arm's length and hurries back to her husband, with the timid smile still on her lips. The snuff tickles my nose and makes me sneeze and the old man laughs wheezily and nods his head vigorously in appreciation.

It was not always lecherous old men who took second or third young wives. Sometimes the man would be content with his lot and have no wish to rustle up the means for another dowry when his wife would say, "This house and garden and cooking and the children are all getting too much for me. You'll have to get yourself another young wife who can share the chores and make life a bit easier for me." She knew that no matter how many wives came along she would always be Number 1, the boss of the houschold and hold sway over all. As it was, in that house the young girl/wife must have been in her honeymoon phase and the older one of sympathetic nature for her to be beating the corn by herself while the girl sat talking to her son. It would not be long before the young newly-wed would be expected to be in there swinging with her new mother/matriarch, and told in no uncertain terms if she were unwilling or slothful.

Next morning I was awakened by fluttering hens and the loud chewing of cattle. I got on the road and was embarrassed when a European in a private car stopped and offered me a lift. I would have preferred some old truck for I felt sure I smelled heavily of cow-dung and wood smoke.

Shortly after being dropped from that lift I was picked up by a battered old freight truck. The African driver had a bevy of beauties in with him so I climbed up in the back where there was an untidy load of bags, baskets and people, and selected a seat on a basket of mangoes. The edges were ragged and jabbed into my legs, but I was thankful to be there – one lift so soon after the other marked my lucky day.

But my thankfulness dissipated as the hours wore by. The journey was a paroxysm of stops and starts. Every now and again the vehicle stopped beside some huts. Bags of 'mealies' (corn on the cob), mahogo, pineapples or flour of various types were unloaded and a stalk of bananas or oranges in split-cane containers put on. At each stop the driver and passengers alighted and chattered for ages until the driver suddenly leapt back into his cab, blew the horn and drove off. The passengers hastily clambered on the moving vehicle and I was trampled under at each stampede.

Once on the move the pace could be so slow that some young boys jumped off the back, ran up front and climbed onto the bonnet and over the cab into the back again. On other stretches the driver would take it on himself to show his admirers what he could do. Then we charged along pell-mell, swinging recklessly round corners; while boxes, baskets and people bounced high and dangerously, until the inevitable group of traders waiting by the roadside appeared and we halted abruptly. The products of each district were distinctly divided. Rarely would different types of produce be loaded at one place.

The people in one district were more primitive than in others. They wore only strips of hide as loin cloths and were clearly hungry and had nothing to trade for food. The natives on the truck looked down on them and blatantly teased and taunted them with great delight. As the truck went past them slowly, those on board would hold out bananas and leer at the wretched people running till their hearts were near bursting trying to get hold of the fruit. Just when the eager fingers were touching the fruit the bait would be snatched away from them amid gales of jeering laughter. Sometimes the person holding the banana would throw it and that would result in a pell-mell scramble of the primitives and all aboard would howl with great delight, back-slap and snap their hands from the wrists like cracking a whip so that the fingers slapped together noisily, as only Africans can do.

A bright moon shone by the time we trundled into the little town of Tukuyu. In six hours we had covered forty miles. I lowered myself stiffly, thanked the driver, and hurried down the street looking for a place where I could bivouac. Near the end of the town, amid the last of the ramshackle, corrugated-iron shops I met a man who gave me a lesson in travelling that was to make a substantial change in my life.

*

He was an old native with a face like a hideous rubber mask and a twisted and deformed leg that trailed out of his ragged cloak like a withered stick. There was a gaping empty socket where an eye should have been and for a mouth he had a twisted gash guarded by a few askew, yellowed teeth. He hobbled out of the shadows between two shops, levering himself along heavily with a stick, calling to me, "*Effendi, ngoja kidogo, baksheesh, effendi.*"

He took me by surprise, but it was his dialect that first caught my attention before he emerged from the deep shadows. Away from the coast or large towns travellers were rarely bothered by beggars. He pleaded he was no ordinary beggar and indeed I knew he was out of place. The fact he used the Arabic *baksheesh* which had not been incorporated into Upcountry Swahili showed he belonged, or had spent much time, by the coast. Inland, if any up-country native had asked for money they would be more likely to say, "*Nipa shillingi*" (Give me money). Moreover, from his words I knew him to be an old soldier. He used the military term '*Effendi*' (Sir) rather than '*Bwana*' (Master) the more common African civilian address to the white man. Also, at one time he had had some kind of command, an NCO in the army or a bosun on a ship. Otherwise he would not have told me to '*ngoja kidogo*' (Wait a bit).

When more in view I could see what a pathetic creature he was. As I dug into my pocket and handed him some change I glanced over his shoulder and saw a cosy fire burning in the darkness behind with his pitiful few possessions beside it. There was nothing wrong with his perception. He must have seen the look in my eye for he wagged his head towards his fire and invited me to his hearth. Like a man proud to show me his home he motioned for me to sit and with no more ado placed the pan with the *posho* he had cooked between us and indicated to me to join him, which I did. We both dug into the pan with our fingers, rolled the handful into a ball to clean our hand, and popped the dollop into our mouth. Then I shared the fruit I carried.

As we ate the firelight glowed and the shadows flickered round this travesty of a man, this ragged bag of bones with the Frankenstein face whose world I was sharing. He was indescribably ugly and yet I could not help feeling compassion for him. We had a lot in common and I wondered what had maimed him so. When I asked him he merely stared. Perhaps that spot was a blank in his mind. But he told me he had been to South Africa and had worked on the gold mines. Perhaps it was a mine accident that had done it. There were no life pensions for disabled itinerant workers there. He had also been a sailor and had seen the Persian Gulf. Apart from his appearance he was an unusual character for most Africans know little or nothing of the world beyond their own area.

When we had eaten and talked we curled up on either side of the fire to sleep. Something akin to friendship had sprung up with the sharing of a few simple things, a bowl of mealie meal porridge, some fruit and a fire, and tonight we were brothers of the road with the stars as our ceiling.

It was in the morning that I learned something so worthwhile from this strange character. He showed me how to make bread. From a dirty cloth bag he produced some flour which he mixed with a little water and added some baking soda and a couple of pinches of salt. He next pushed some of the fire to one side with a stick, then scooped a hole in the earth where it had been. He patted the dough into a fairly flat pancake and put it into the warm hollow where the fire had been, covered it with the hot earth he had removed, then raked some red embers back over the lot. In twenty minutes or so, by which time I had made some coffee, he uncovered a beautiful loaf that only required the earth and ash dusted off it before we ate it. Delicious! I had never met any native who baked bread. He must have learned his skill in South Africa where, later, I learned that the old Boers used that method.

By this time the village was awake and a few passers-by stopped to look and wonder at us. That anyone, least of all a *mzungu*, should associate with a *maskini* (very poor person) was beyond their belief. Yet, how glad I was to have shared a night with this scarecrow of a man. With his lesson he gave me the gift of bread and that was to help me so much through my wandering years.

But it was not just bread he gave me. Thinking it over I began to see how the idea could be extended, widened to encompass the whole of my 'kitchen'. I was carrying mostly tinned stuff which was heavy, bulky, expensive and wasteful, for what could not be eaten at one meal could not always be kept until the next. Now, I reckoned, if I carried dried foods in cloth bags, such as flour, rice, porridge oats and banana meal, this would be lighter, cheaper and I would be much more mobile. Banana meal was made by sun-drying green bananas and pounding the fruit into flour. In the very early, green phase the fruit has no sugar content and tastes like potatoes. I could always pick up some fresh meat occasionally along the way, chickens from the natives or venison if I were hunting. My wise and most unlikely tutor had presented me with a new threshold that I was grateful to pass over, a step into the world of the fully-fledged tramp. He taught me something else, even more important – no man should be discarded for his looks and appearance.

After our breakfast I packed up. Before leaving I put a five shilling note – East African currency ran to notes even of that denomination – in his hand for my board and lodgings, far more than I would normally give, but he had more than earned it. He stared at it. He had probably never had so much as that in his hand at once since the days he worked at the mines. Then he wrapped his chicken-bone fingers round the note, screwed it up into a ball and raised his hand to his twisted gap of a mouth and kissed his fist, while above it his one eye gleamed with a diamond sparkle, all the world like the Hollywood GI throwing dice. Where he had learned that gesture was not in the wilds of East Africa. And in that moment, behind the shambles of his exterior, I saw a man, a man of the world, a man of spirit.

Chapter Fourteen

MICA MINING

Monday 28th January 1952 – Mica Mining
   There must have been a death yesterday in the little village below us. All through the night the inhabitants were chanting and wailing, the women's high pitched keening, trilling their awful dirge... and the death drum continuously tolling its single mournful beat.

It was Christmas-eve morning when I walked away from my friend-of-a-night intending to get to the head of Lake Nyasa where I hoped I might find the crocodile hunter. But I didn't get very far. Not far out of Tukuyu, as I was passing a large house by the name of 'Kyiambili', a man with his arm in a sling who happened to be crossing the garden did a double-take in my direction then came to the gate to hail me and ask what the devil I was doing walking about the country like that. I turned and met one of the finest men I was privileged to meet in all my travels. In his mid-fifties perhaps, with dark, thinning hair combed straight back from a thin, deeply lined and rather severe face that nevertheless had creased into the merest semblance of a smile, there were eyes that were warm and friendly. I gave him a thumbnail résumé of my life and added that my immediate concern was to locate a guy who I heard was hunting crocodiles somewhere in these parts. To this he replied in so off-hand a manner I hardly took it in at first, "Oh that'll be the Martin fellow. His place is about fifteen miles down the road. Off the beaten track a bit. Can't go there tonight. The chap's hardly ever there and it might be a bit embarrassing for his wife, you know."

   I'd found him! Just like that. I could hardly believe my luck. I said I'd camp some place and look them up next day. He was bound to be home for Christmas. But Major Strickland, as I soon got to know him, would have none of it. "You'd better come in," he said, opening the gate and leading me into the house that was more like a minor baronial mansion.

   On entering, an elderly gentleman with snow-white hair and moustache rose rather startled from a huge winged chair, his newspaper still in his hand. Mr Parks – or Daddy Parks to all his friends – was tall and thin with an aristocratic bearing who, nevertheless, I learned was most approachable and friendly. In no time the Major had his houseboy prepare a room and draw me a bath in an open tub.

Both men had an invitation to a dinner-party that evening and insisted I come along. I protested that I was not invited and I'd feel out of place but they would hear nothing of it. "Oh, don't worry, Lady Pringle won't mind." My goodness! The ups and downs of life! Two nights ago I slept with cannibals in a mud hut, last night I dossed down with a native tramp between shacks, and tonight ...! Tonight I would dine in high society.

The dear old Lady, one of the celebrities in these parts, lived in a large house set into a hill with wonderful panoramic views from the windows and verandah. She lived with her son who managed the tea estate. There was quite a crowd there, everybody was very friendly and I enjoyed myself immensely. I even ended up with a large box of cigarettes from the pile under the Christmas tree which Lady Pringle had hastily wrapped up and labelled for me. I was really grateful and was pleased later to hand them over to Major Strickland as a little 'thank you' for his hospitality.

Next day, Christmas, Mr Parks would not hear of me going away over the festive season so I was pleased to spend one or two days in excellent company and comfort. The men had had colourful pasts and regaled me with wonderful anecdotes. The best were from the Lupa goldfields that lay about fifty miles north of Mbeya and where the two men had each worked their separate claims. Mbeya in fact started its existence in the late '20s as a supply point for the gold-fields. An early missionary writer said that there were about three score miners working on the diggings in the mountains by the Lupa River in 1925. By the start of the war in 1945 there were over a thousand there. But then many of the mines had begun to run out and by '41 or '42 most men had joined up or gone to other work and, by the time the war ended, higher wages and the decline in the price of gold made the mines uneconomical. They were still there, the mines and the gold, but Chunya the little town that was life's centre to the miners was now all but empty, ghost-like, with the dust blowing through it, doors swinging on single hinges, a tombstone to a past era.

Once it all throbbed with excitement. Hard working, hard living men with the gold lust in their eyes would hurry at the end of the day to the town's saloon for booze and company. A set of scales was set on the bar where men weighed their poke or nugget and drank its value in an evening. In the end, as always, the bar proved to be the best gold mine in the field. Supplies came up to the claims once a fortnight and men partied together on the site during the first few days and half starved till the next lot came in.

Looking at my two hosts I could hardly imagine them, each so gentlemanly, as hard-bitten, raw miners. But then, most men who had settled in East Africa for any time had hard, tough backgrounds to draw on. I wish I had written down their stories. They would have made an excellent book in themselves. I can just see it, *Tales From The Lupa Gold Field.*

Funnily enough, although nearly all the tales they told have slipped from my memory one little comment of Daddy Parks comes back loud and clear and it had nothing to do with the Lupa, more a sign of the times, a milestone in history. I can see him now, looking up with an air of incredulity from reading a letter from his daughter in London. "Do you know," he said in almost disbelief, "a fellow can't take a girl out on the town these days, to dinner and a show and taxis, for under five pounds. Imagine that!" However shocked Daddy was, I was moreso. That seemed an awful lot of money to spend on one evening out. Then I had the mental image of a Lupa miner bursting into the bar, full of swank and big talk, throwing on to the scales a nugget worth perhaps £150, as both Daddy and the Major assured me was not uncommon, and calling for, "Drinks for the house." With luck it could last all evening. So how did a night-on-the-town for two in London, for the incredible sum of a fiver, compare with £150 for a night-on-the-tiles in the wilds of Tanganyika? The apt words of Robert Service in his *The Shooting of Dan MacGrew* ran through my head:

'A half dead thing in a stark dead world,
Clean mad for that muck called gold.'

'Kyiambili' was a grand, old, rambling house with terraced gardens lying at the base of Mount Rungwe, a dormant volcano to the north, with the vast Poroto Mountains behind. In every direction the views were magnificent. To the south-east lay a forty-mile vista over the misty plains to Lake Nyasa and the blue Livingstone Mountains beyond. South-west lay the valley-riven Bundali Hills where powder-puff clouds played on the winds that raced through the many time-worn glens. At an altitude of five thousand feet with a very high annual rainfall the land was so fertile it could produce two crops a year. It was always much cooler up on this high plateau than it was down by Lake Nyasa where it was hot and steamy and palms trees grew.

What tales, I wondered, could these blackened old timbers up there in the gloom of the high ceiling tell. The house was built as a mission station at the beginning of the century when Tanganyika was still German East Africa. With the demise of the Germans after the First World War the League of Nations gave the mandate of Tanganyika Territory to Britain, Kyiambili then became a Station of the Scottish Churches Mission and started a new life as a school, the African Girls High School. The remains of a long dormitory building, mostly demolished, was still there. After the Second World War the Mission closed and the land was sold to the Brooke Bond tea company on condition that the church in the grounds must be allowed to remain in service. Messrs Parks and Strickland rented the house from the tea company.

Now the old house bore a new air. There were record slabs of mica on the wall and other mementos of past mining days and hunting. The furniture, all locally made by African craftsmen, was in a class of its own. There were no symmetric lines in it. The legs of the settee, the table and the chairs stuck out, or in, at acute angles. When I first arrived I was a bit wary when offered a seat and sat down gingerly, testing it before giving it my full weight. It was as solid as a Jacobean masterpiece. The legs of my bed and my wash stand stuck inwards at threatening angles but they were as solid as any furniture with orthodox lines. Somehow they didn't look out of place or topsy-turvy.

Outside on the verandah there was a constant drone of bore-bees. These were large bees with armour-plated heads with a spike sticking out. They bored holes half inch in diameter in the rafters and made their nests in them. I was told they had a sting like a scorpion. The garden was a battleground. Through shortage of labour there was very little maintenance. The weeds were high and rambling, but in a clearing there was a fair crop of vegetables and even some brave, gaily-coloured flowers. The monkeys were the chief enemies. They stole the avocado pears from the trees and tore up the young plants, just for devilment.

Over the next few months I was to return time and again to Kyiambili for a day or two at a time. These were always times of such peaceful bliss after hard weeks of mining and crocodile hunting that I came to look back and forward to them with true longing. Kyiambili became my very own Dar es Salaam – my Haven of Peace and Rest.

To choose a book from the shelf that constituted the Kyiambili library and sit on the rustic seat by the great avocado tree in the still of the early morning was a delight. With a stick I knocked off a plump, pendant fruit, split it open, and savoured the soft, creamy meat. Spread out before me the land round about was coming to life, smoke beginning to rise from the houses, each set in its own little banana plantation. People were emerging sleepily to follow the calls of nature, and further out, my gaze ranging over the great valley basin, watching the blue, rolling forest ocean change gradually to green, was my moment in paradise.

*

But it had not always been so serene. The dirt road outside the gate was once one of the slave-routes from the interior. In those days within living memory of elder Konde people it would have been a path broadened by the tramp of many feet and down it would come the wretched columns of the most pathetic humanity, all yoked together in lines by heavy forked branches round their necks, all driven on by the lashes of the Arab and Swahili drovers. They would have already walked for weeks and would still have another four hundred miles to go before reaching the coast. Many more would have started the journey, many less than those that passed by would finish.

It was sights such as those I saw in my imagination, only a few yards from where I sat in the garden of Kyiambili, which so enraged and tormented David Livingstone that he jerked awake at nights, sweating with horror, and cried out loud, one lone voice in the vast blackness of this great continent that would ring round the world to sound the death knell of that evil practice.

I read most of the books on the shelf at Kyiambili but there was one I returned to again and again each time I went there. Written by a missionary, Dunlop Ross Mackenzie, it was entitled *The Spirit-Ridden Konde* and I was thrilled when I first saw he signed off at the end of his preface with the words 'D.R. Mackenzie. Kyiambili, Tanganyika Territory, February, 1925'. I learned recently from the Mission archives of the Scottish National Library, Edinburgh, that Revd Mackenzie was minister at Pluscarden, Moray, and from 1901 served thirty years as a missionary at Livingstonia and Karonga. As his book would imply he was an authority on the Konde people and their language.

As I sat reading his book a time-bridge suddenly leapt across from this man to me. He had sat right here where I was sitting, to when I read, 'As I write there is a church being erected at Kyiambili to seat about seven hundred and fifty people. It has fifteen windows, each with three Gothic arches, and six doors each with its own Gothic arch.' He went on to describe how the whole was done by native workmen with only amateur supervision, only one of whom had had any kind of craft training.

The church was still there, just over from the house a bit, and was very much alive, as was intended when the covenant was made at the time the house was sold. Its mournful bell tolled every day for something or other. On Sunday the African locals rolled up in droves dressed in their best finery, many of the men in fine suits and perhaps sporting umbrellas, large spectacles or sun glasses and white topees; their ladies a riot of colour in their once-a-week dresses. Watching them I was reminded that it was not so long ago at home that people spoke about wearing their 'Sunday Best'.

The people of this area call themselves Nyakyusa, but are by origin and language part of the greater Konde tribe (also known as Wa-n-Konde and Ngonde) whose territory stretches from slightly north of Tukuyu to nearly two hundred miles south, down the western side of Lake Nyasa to Karonga and on to Livingstonia.

The Nyakyusa were thieves and burglars and proud of it. They would boast that they could cut a hole through the wattle-and-daub wall of a house, lead out the cattle which were penned in with the owners and even remove the blankets off the sleepers should they have any, without disturbing them. Blankets were not always universal; sometimes only the man of the house would have one while the mother and children slept nearly naked with their feet to the fire. The first thing the burglars did was to hand out any weapon in the house, spears and the like, so that the residents would be unarmed should they wake. When the burglars made a hole in the wall, just big enough for one person, the first man in would go in feet first on the assumption that it is better to be stabbed or clubbed on the feet than the head should the owner be awake.

Not all Nyakyusa were burglars, of course, but there were enough of them to give the sub-tribe a bad reputation. In the days when caravans were the only method of travelling from the coast to the interior, the guards at a caravanserai would be doubled when it was known that Nyakyusa bearers were due in with the next 'train'. The high rise in thieving was the one thing that honest natives lamented about the British administration following the Germans. It appeared that the Germans had 'vays' of ensuring that thieves did not steal again.

*

Like so many other tribes in this region, the Konde life and tribeland were shaped by the slave trade. They were a peaceful people and when a great number of the Henga tribe, driven out of their own land by the savage, warlike Angoni who were pushing up from the south, arrived among them, the Konde took them in and settled them as part of their own. The Henga, by necessity were a more aggressive tribe than the Konde, but they were no match for the stronger, wilder Angoni. Later, despite the kindness and hospitality shown to them, the Henga treacherously did a deal with Arab slave traders and sold many Konde people into their hands.

Not that the Arabs needed intermediaries between themselves and the potential slaves. They were quite prepared to grab the merchandise themselves and cut out the middleman. One of their methods of doing this was their own wooden-horse scenario. A few Arabs, apparently weary of the way, would appear at a village and ask for shelter which the natives invariably gave. Once among the community the Arabs would keep themselves to themselves and erect a strong stockade which they would say was to protect them from wild animals. Their hosts would no doubt smile with silent derision at the newcomers' fears since they lived quite satisfactorily without such fortifications. Little did they realise that the strong barricade was not to keep the animals out, but, to keep the Africans in.

When all was ready the Arabs would start shooting all the men and when this was done they would herd all the women, children and young lads into the stockade to be kept there until more were gathered elsewhere.

With their enclosure in operation the Arabs' methods of collecting their victims from the surrounding villages were less subtle than the 'please take me in so that I may rest' ploy. They, with their Swahili hirelings, would walk up boldly to a village and without preamble or warning start shooting.

When enough of the local population was harvested to make a payload caravan the prisoners would start their long walk into slavery, manacled and forced to carry the mandatory 70 lb load or tusk on their heads; babies were not accountable, mothers had to carry them as well. Only those lucky and tough enough to survive the journey and the sea passage would 'enjoy' the comparative luxury of their new lives.

Another early missionary's report on the massacre by the Arabs of the Wan-Konde in order to take prisoners at a place near Karonga, tells more about their methods. Dr James Stewart, of whom we will hear more later, describes in his book *Dawn in the Dark Continent, 1905*, how in the incident he described, those who could get away ran and hid in the dry reeds of a nearby lagoon. The Arabs set fire to the reeds and those who survived were forced to give themselves up.

This incident actually started a two-year war between the Arabs and the few British people who were in Nyasaland at that time. There was no British military or administration presence there then, the nearest being the consul at Zanzibar. A volunteer force was recruited under the leadership of Captain, later Sir, F. Lugard who fortuitously happened on the scene at the time. Lugard was severely wounded during his service there. Had he not survived, the later history of Uganda and West Africa, where he made his name, might have been different. That little war – not little for those involved – finally broke the Arabs' hold over Nyasaland and started events that eventually ended their slave trade.

*

Over the next few months of close contact with the Konde people I learned that some of the practices mentioned in Missionary MacKenzie's book were still in vogue, albeit mostly under the surface. Only those very closely associated with the Konde might get an inkling of what went on and only then if they happened to be at the place at the time or if they became friendly enough with a native who might talk or hint. The Konde were indeed a tribe who, perhaps more than most others, were bound by iron-strong superstitions and deep, deep, ancient rituals, many of them evil and decadent as any practised in the basest black-magic circles. Yet on the surface they were the gentle people, polite and friendly and much given to merriment and dancing.

It was in their dancing that their dark habits materialised. In the light of day the dances appeared little more than one saw all over Africa, although it could be said there was more body contact with some Konde dances than with most other tribes where the dancers nearly always moved separately in lines or capered individually. In his book Mackenzie gave good descriptions of the Konde dances.

The *Ikimbimbi*, like so many African dances, where two lines were formed, one male, the other female, advancing to almost touch then retiring, repeating this over and over again, while the onlookers tramped their feet in time to the drums.

The *Ikindundulu* when no drums were used and the rhythm was kept by loud shouting and singing: two men advanced to the women's line, one of whom came out to meet them, selected the one of her fancy and retired with him to her own line where all the women danced round him with mocking songs. Two more men faced the ordeal until all had been through it.

The *Ikisepe*. Each dancer had a piece of cloth or bark rope tied at the waist, one in front, one at the rear, and a reed in the hand: the dance consisted of heaves of the body which caused the streamers to be thrown out fore and aft, while the drums beat and the songs went on as each couple filled the centre for a moment.

These were some of the dances of the daytime. The change came on moonlight nights when the dancing took on an entirely different character. That was when they danced the *Ikikweta*. Then the four drums that always accompanied this dance beat a wild tattoo, way beyond the norm, accelerating the tempo of the dancers to a madness-making pitch that would last all night. In this frenzy more than wild dancing took place to the rhythm of the drums. Missionaries described the proceedings as 'indescribable'. Mackenzie called it 'a highly objectionable dance, better not too minutely described'. Others, more blatant, used words such as 'wanton' and 'wild abandon', 'depraved, physically and mentally', 'uncontrollable lust' and even 'incest' and 'sodomy'. And the *Ikikweta* was not the only one of its kind. Mackenzie said, '… and there are other very evil dances which no decent people would have anything to do with.'

This kind of dancing did not happen all the time, not every moonlight night. The 'evil' dancing came like an epidemic at no particular time, without warning or prediction, ran its course and died away until the next plague struck.

When tackled on the subject of these dances some Konde would say that these dances did not exist before the white man came. They would postulate that since the white man had stopped their wars and fears of wars and slavery they now found life was so dull and uneventful that they needed some stimulation to make the adrenaline flow, otherwise they would go mad. They would not, of course, use such words as 'adrenaline' and their colloquial euphemism for madness would be more like today's 'bonkers'. But these were the words mainly of the young and not-so-young, mindless trend-setters. The older and more serious minded people who knew how terrible their lives had been before those peaceful days under British administration, would tell you that the dances were always part of life and that decent folk shut their doors and tried to sleep through the wild nights. And if they could not sleep they would never dare complain to the revellers otherwise they might end up with a broken head. Sounds like our modern society.

What was true, the older Konde would tell you to put the record straight, was that the dances and other lewd behaviour had increased since the British had taken over the administration of their country. Before then strong Chiefs who abhorred the dances meted out strong punishments, so those who would risk their lives to participate had to go to secret places to indulge and that way did not bother decent people. But now that the British had taken away the power of the Chiefs and the British administration laws were much less fearsome than their tribal ones the dancers had free rein to do almost as they pleased. So the wild revelry had come back into the villages and 'decent folk' could only shut their doors and tut at such behaviour.

Societies of all types, it appears, have followed the same patterns of behaviour since the beginning of time. The young demand some kind of action in long times of peace and elders say, as I heard with the Masai, that every generation needs a war to make the boys grow into responsible men – those that survive, presumably. Each generation believes that as the modern one they can do it all better, more wisely, than their less-informed forebears. So nations rise and fall. In the early and mid-20th century, the period of which I write, the Konde customs and behaviour would be regarded in Britain as evidence of the complete degradation of a society. Now at the end of that century morals and behavioural trends within our own society have changed so much the Konde lifestyle does not seem so out of place after all. If we believe that we now live in a more enlightened society, free of the moral maze and religious and community society inhibitions that bound our people in the first half of the 20th century, might we infer from this that the Konde with their free society were further along the road in development than we were at that time? If that really was the case then it could be said that by the end of the century we had caught up.

Whatever their secret lifestyle might be the Konde people, to any passing traveller who had neither the time nor the will to scratch below the top-soil, appeared to be a perfectly ordinary, peace-loving people. They tilled their gardens and socialised round a brew of *pombe* while their children played games, some of which were very similar to those I played as a boy.

Games such as the *Eya Kalenda* where the children form a circle with one, the leader, in the middle. The leader turns his head to the right, the others do the same. He does the same to the left and the others follow and so on, saying or singing a few words that each must repeat. All very like 'follow my leader'.

There was also the *Ikyula* (the frog) which was very akin to one we used to play. Two sides in rows face each other some distance apart. Squatting and hopping like frogs they went to meet and circled round each other. Those that fell from tiredness or lost balance were 'captured' and had to join the other side until all were on one side. As boys we played a very similar game, but instead of squatting (we would have said going down on our 'hunkers') we hopped on one leg with our arms folded across our chests, and, perhaps because we were more boisterous than the Konde, we were allowed to knock an opponent with our shoulder to help him lose balance. If he did and put his other foot down, he was 'out'. This game was called 'Cocky-Dunty'. The Konde adults too played guessing games and conundrums similar to those in vogue at home. MacKenzie gives a few:

'My house has no doors?' An egg.

'I hoed a large garden, but when I gathered the crop it did not fill my hand?' Haircutting.

'It has neither feet to walk with, nor hands to seize with, but it devours everything?' Fire.

Proverbs too. 'A familiar road needs no signposts.' 'If one fish in a basket rots, they all rot.' (Beware of evil company.) 'A liar has only a short way to go.' (Your sin will find you out.)

From such little, everyday things it was evident that at the grass roots people are the same the world over. So similar are those sayings to these we all knew it might seem obvious that the Africans must have learned them from the white people. But this is not so. Indeed, it is likely that it was we who learned them from the Africans for they were telling folk tales perhaps long before we were. There is strong belief that the Uncle Remus and Brer Rabbit stories came out of Africa with the slaves from the west. Mackenzie relates the old Konde story of 'The Tortoise and the Hare'. This being so it is likely the Bantus, who originated in West Africa, were telling each other stories like these all the way across the continent as they migrated to East and South Africa.

The Konde were indeed people who liked their life and loved their homes. So much so, they took great pride in painting their houses, the like of which was never seen in the rest of primitive Africa. The Konde decorative skills and decor appreciation went beyond painting. A Konde woman would put a large pot in a prominent place on the floor, just on view, as someone elsewhere might place a choice vase or arrange a bowl of flowers to set off a room. I never saw this practice anywhere else in East Africa.

There is little doubt that it was the Konde grace and politeness and their flair with their house decoration that moved Joseph Thomson, the young explorer, to refer to this place as 'the perfect Arcadia'. The encyclopaedias tell us that Arcadia was the mountainous region of Peloponnesus in Ancient Greece. The pastoral inhabitants were celebrated throughout the Hellenic world for their simplicity of character, manners and politeness. Those attributes, together with their way of life and their attitude to it, combined to make a Utopia. Thomson, on an expedition for the Royal Geographical Society in the late 1870s, made his remark while on his way – no doubt right past this tree where I sat – to be the first white man to reach Lake Nyasa from the north.

As a person whose life's work circled round paint I was intrigued at the practice of natives decorating their mud huts with paint long before the white men came to Africa, so there could be no question of it being due to European influence. Later, when travelling down Lake Nyasa I came on a little cameo of history that showed just how much the people of these parts valued paint.

In 1888, at the very dawn of British presence in the land, Mr Buchanan, the British Consul at Zanzibar, came on a tour of inspection round Lake Nyasa in order to deal with the Arab slave-traders. He was accompanied by Dr W.P. Johnson, a renowned missionary who spent more than half a century working in these parts. At Makanjila, just on the border of Portuguese territory, they were set upon by a party of wild natives and only narrowly escaped with their lives. The natives stripped them both and treated them with great indignity. Buchanan made a grab for his revolver but had difficulty getting it out. Johnson appealed to him to be calm and not to resist. He said later had Buchanan fired, both of them would surely have been killed. Matters did calm down. The natives kept the two travellers prisoner for the night. By then their passions had died down and instead of killing their prisoners, they demanded a ransom of two kegs of paint for them, a price that was gladly settled from the stores of the SS *Charles Janson*, the little steam ship on which they were travelling. I do not know if this represented the low value the natives put on life or the great value they put on paint. All I know is that when I heard the story first I found it incredible that raging savages of that era could even know what paint was, far less put such value on it.

Although this episode ended in almost farcical style there is no doubt that the two men were in deadly danger. The evidence of this came a few years later, 1895, when a young man, George William Atlay, the son of a Bishop, was out on a day's hunting expedition with his bearers on the shores of Lake Nyasa. They were taking an afternoon siesta beside a stream that flowed into the lake when they were suddenly confronted by an Angoni war party. Atlay rose quickly and faced up to the warriors, his Winchester repeater rifle levelled at them. What followed next was described by one of Atlay's bearers who escaped.

Whether the Angoni had no idea of the deadliness of fire-arms or because they were primed up for battle and felt themselves immune to harm, the natives took no heed of Atlay's challenge and crowded round him, one clubbing him on the head. Atlay then appeared to kneel in prayer while the clubs rained on him. Badly injured, he ran to the water where he was speared and his head held under water by a pointed bamboo. His body was found with the loaded rifle beside it, the savages obviously having no use for the weapon. The Angoni did not know how lucky they were that the man they attacked, who could easily have cut them down with his repeater rifle, was one who would rather die than take a human life.

All this, of course, happened before British administration put an end to the wild side of life in this country. There are interesting stories that abound all over Africa of native soothsayers who predicted the coming of the white man long before he actually appeared. The Konde were no exception. According to their folk tales Mwakipesire of Masoko, a famous prophet, climbed a hill with a great number of people and there pronounced;

A man will come out of the lake, white of body, and he will be lord of the whole country. War he will bring to an end, Angoni he will conquer, the Arab he will expel. He will bring us cloth and we shall throw away our garments of leaves ... but he will not come until all who are here today have gone to the Spirits.

Another Konde prophet, Maseke of Karonga, said that the white man would come in a canoe that sent out smoke and that the peace would be so great that none would carry a spear and that the world would be filled with wonders that no man had ever heard.

But though the white man had banished war among the natives and made illegal nearly all customs that did not fall within the European general code-of-practice he had not managed to completely eradicated these old habits. Beneath the surface of the mid-20th century British law much of the old superstitions and tribal ways still held sway. Soon I was to go into the hills and find strong rumours that the old Africa was not quite dead, that practices even worse than dirty dancing were still in vogue.

*

The closing of the Lupa goldfield had not ended Messrs Park and Stricklands' interest in mining. In association with one other man, a Mr Lawson, an old prospector, they owned and ran a mica mine that lay in the upper reaches of a tributary to the Songwe River, high up in the Bundali Hills, two days' march south near the Nyasaland border. I gathered that Lawson had discovered the mica deposit some years before but being penniless had needed his two partners to invest in it in order to finance the mining of it. Lawson lived up there to work the mine and sent the mica down to Kyiambili by a string of porters and the other two members of the syndicate arranged the onward transportation and sale of the precious material.

I asked if I might go to the mine and the Major, although amused that I should want to suffer the journey and the rigours of living up in the mountains, readily agreed to my going. The porters arrived one day about noon carrying the flat, square, wooden boxes about six or eight inches deep and each weighing fifty pounds. They rested a while and were fed by the cook. After the paid they then went to the *duka* to buy what stores they required. The Major had had a special pack of provisions prepared for Mr Lawson. Sometime in the afternoon we started off. I left most of my kit, including my kilt which I only wore on my main travels, at Kyiambili. I took my sleeping bag and a few personal things and, after being warned by Major Strickland, my jersey which I rarely wore but was extremely grateful for when up at the mine.

The path to the mine corkscrewed its way over mountains and down into valleys where, from the crests tiny white threads at the bottom eventually grew to be raging torrents which were crossed by narrow, creaking, suspension bridges without side ropes so you had to get into the rhythm of the swaying planks very quickly, hold your breath and try and look as nonchalant as the porters who crossed them regularly.

That night we stopped at a village that clung to the steep side of a mountain, the only one on the way to the mine, a few thatch-and-mud huts, pitifully lonely. No *duka* or any such vestiges of an outside world graces their presence on this little place. The porters slept in a hut, but I had heard that the habitations were bad for ticks and since it was too high for mosquitoes I made a bed of dried banana leaves outside and unrolled my sleeping bag on that. I did not have a good night.

First, I was overrun by an army of red ants. I was lucky not to be at the centre of their line, but even the outriders and the stragglers were enough. I was suddenly aware that they were all over me, covering my face, in my hair, biting me all over, running wild in my sleeping bag and, in good British understatement, making rather a nuisance of themselves. I shot out of my bag, stood on a rock and sluiced a gourd of water over myself, washing them away. I shook my bag, turned it inside out and minutely picked it clean. All this in the thin starlight. I made myself a new bed well out of the way of the ants' path and lay down again and fell asleep.

I was wakened again that night with something scurrying and scraping at my side and when I looked my blood froze. In the dim starlight I saw the form of a rat rummaging in the leaves of my bed. I could not tell whether it was the vermin type or an edible one which the natives favour. Whatever kind it was it gave me a very creepy feeling. A slap on the ground and a low shout sent it scampering out of sight. I don't know why a rat should make my flesh creep when there was an even greater chance of meeting a much bigger and more dangerous night prowler, but it did. Perhaps we have an inborn, atavistic abhorrence of these loathsome creatures, maybe because they have carried so many plagues to mankind.

The next day we crossed three mountain ridges. Down 2000 feet, up 3000. In places the path was only feet wide round the cliff wall with a sheer drop on the outer side, for all the world like the melodramatic drawings in Victorian adventure magazines. In places where the soil was wet clay and a slide could have been disastrous I took off my tattered sandshoes and went barefoot.

I had left my boots at Kyiambili. They were far gone and I had to eke out their last days by using them only when I carried my heavy pack. I knew I had to find a good, inspired cobbler very soon along the way.

Towards late afternoon we entered the valley where from the floor the porters pointed out the mine high up near the opposite crest. The sight was quite remarkable. The mine huts were out of view and all I saw was what appeared to be a strange phenomenon. Out of a cave or tunnel in the mountainside a waterfall spouted and flowed, glistening and sparkling, down the steep slope. Then it stopped. Strange! It must run underground again, I thought. But I was wrong.

We wound ourselves up the steep, tortuous path and at last the whole scene of the mine came into close view. What I had taken to be water was in fact waste mica, the unwanted slag that spewed from the mine and lay grey and placid like a glacier in the shadows now that the sun had gone behind the ridge.

Mr Lawson greeted me as I came up the steep path on to the flat where the mine huts were built. A runner had gone ahead to tell him of my coming and a hut had been prepared for me. I think I had expected a hard, old prospector/miner, forged tough and taciturn by a lonely lifetime of hopeful foraging in remote areas. He was nothing like that. Tough he surely was, but taciturn and forbidding, he was not. He had a round moon face with a warm, friendly smile. In his later years he had run to a bit of stoutness, no doubt due to his contracting asthma a few years previously so that now he did not walk very far. He welcomed me most pleasantly in rather a shy manner as befitting one who saw few visitors in his life.

He had lived here nine years with only two boys and his woman housekeeper, a lovely, chubby lady with polished walnut cheeks and eyes that sparkled and jolly chins that wobbled with mirth. She wore a European dress and white apron, but her feet were shoeless. Whatever arrangements they had when on their own was anybody's guess, but while I was there they kept their separate ways and stations.

During all his years at the mine Lawson had gone down to Kyiambili and perhaps as far as Mbeya about two or three times a year. Up to about three years before my visit he had always done the journey on foot, down and up the switchback path and sleeping in a tent at the village. When his asthma made the journey too much for him he remained at the mine over a year without going down. Then Major Strickland pioneered a rough route, some seventy miles each way, that allowed him to drive his car within a few miles of the mine and those were over fairly level but boggy terrain that allowed fairly easy walking, but were impassable for wheels. This route could only be attempted in very dry spells which were not often in this area. Tukuyu, with an average of 120 inches a year, had one of the highest rainfalls in Tanganyika. Here in the Bundali Hills it was nearer 150 inches. Consider that when the annual average for Edinburgh and London is about 26 inches. Mr Lawson sent a message down with the porters when he wanted to go down, together with a note on local weather conditions, and the Major came up and got him. He had only been down once in the year that I met him.

The mine lay at 9000 feet and in the evenings I was glad I had brought my jersey. Looking down and over the way we had come you could see the path coiling its way down past the little huddle of workers' huts, where the women prepared the meal and children played in the dust. Down, down, hugging the side of the mountain, running into a ravine and reappearing thinner on the other side and on down to be lost in the veil of blue mist that was drifting in on the cool evening air. Our position seemed very lonely, yet in a mystic, faraway sense, quite sublime.

*

"Hodi", the boy said as he rattled the door to dislodge the stone I had put against it when going to bed.

Morning tea, what luxury! *"Karibu,"* ('I am near', the greeting for 'come in') I answer. Rising from bed I took care not to touch the low rafters with my head that would bring down a deluge of dust and dry rot. I walked over the earthen floor and opened the shutter that filled the foot-square aperture-window. The mountains were propping up a lid of clouds that would soon be levered open by the sun. A few feet from the window the ground fell away so that I could see right down into the valley. The village was wakening and some huts were oozing smoke and cattle were being turned out, their bells jangling musically.

These were the people, another sub-tribe of the Konde, but as mountain residents they were tougher, more hardy than the Nyakyusa who lived in the Kiambili area. Like all the Konde they shared some dark practices, with a few even darker ones of their own thrown in.

There must have been a death yesterday in the little village below us. All through the night the inhabitants were chanting and wailing, the womens' high-pitched keening trilled their awful dirge. The men would be running back and forward sticking their spears in the ground at the door of the hut where the body lay to drive away the evil spirits. It would all go on for three days while the grave was being dug and the death drum continuously tolling its single, mournful beat.

The grave would be dug four or five feet down as a shaft, then a hollow or chamber would be opened to the side, big enough to take the body.

At the end of the three days friends and relatives would come to offer their condolences to the next-of-kin. The body would be taken and placed in the chamber, the opening closed with a wicker frame, and the grave filled in. After the solemn rhetoric that would accompany the burial everyone, as if released, would laugh and jest and drink. As the day wears on the language and gestures would become more obscene, all with the same end in mind, all leading up to the 'Death Dance'. That would start in daylight and go on into the night. As emotions rose so would more free rein be taken until, as Dr MacKenzie reports, '... more definite evil follows in the darkness.'

Some months later, after the 'obscene' would come the 'gruesome'. When it was estimated that the flesh of the deceased would have rotted away the grave would be re-dug, the side chamber opened and the body disinterred. The bones would then be taken into the forest and placed against a tree. Or, as an alternative among the Bandala, the bones might be wrapped in banana leaves and kept under the roof overhang of the next-of kin's house.

Even more gruesome and evil were the stories that still lingered in these hills of a special rain-making ceremony that involved a human sacrifice. After a long drought a victim, usually a young boy about ten years old, would be secretly selected by a gathering of chiefs. The victim would be forced to drink beer till he died. His parents were not allowed to mourn their son's death in public as this would solve the mystery of his disappearance. The boy's body would then be burned and the flesh pounded to powder that would be distributed for consumption as a sure talisman for rain. Since the coming of the white man this practice was prohibited and a cow substituted. But old habits lived long in the hills and Lawson said strong rumours and innuendoes of such goings on still arose occasionally.

*

The working day started with the arrival of the miners, some having done more than an hour's tramp across the hills. Their numbers varied daily, but there were usually about fifty. They were a motley lot. Some wore ragged shorts which long ago had stood up to military demands for smartness, others were clad only in loin cloths, while a few squared their shoulders a bit more than the rest and held themselves slightly aloof because they owned the remnants of jackets. They all wore head cloths tied with a knot at the back over which they clamped down their safety helmets as far as they would go.

They reminded me of home. Of the coal mine near my village and the loud hooter heralding the end of a shift that preceded the stream of black-faced miners coming down the street in the days before pit-head baths were installed. After that innovation only their pallid faces and silky skins from lack of sun and wind, their hair soft and woolly through daily washing and blue scars like tattoos where cuts had healed with coal dust in them, told that they spent their working days in the earth's bowels.

My father was a miner and his father before him. Coal mining in Fife went back to monastic times. Since then, generations on generations of families depended on the industry for their living. Meagre it may have been and hard, very hard, for parents to bring up big families, but we never considered ourselves poor. As children we never knew what a struggle our parents had. These were iniquitous times for workers, and especially miners. The one-week annual 'holiday' was unpaid so there was hardly money for food that week let alone to actually go away somewhere or even have a rest.

And there was always danger. My maternal grandfather, William Harrower, whom I never knew, died from injuries in the mine when the roof of a tunnel he was in collapsed. Others died beside him. A man renowned in the district for his great strength, it was said that he staggered out of the shaft with ribs and collar-bone broken, dragging with him two other men, one with his good arm and another with his teeth. He never survived his injuries and died soon afterwards.

In my own time, as a boy I remembered that awful Saturday morning in 1938 when we woke to the news that there had been a terrible explosion at Valleyfield colliery at the head of the village. My father worked at Blairhall, the neighbouring mine three miles away. He was on permanent 'back' shift, going out at lunch time and returning late at night, so was at home in the forenoons. As soon as he heard the news my father hurried to the Valleyfield pithead to offer his services for rescue work. Thirty-five men were killed in that disaster. Thirty-five husbands, dads, sons, brothers uncles, and cousins, all gone at a stroke from a little village. Classmates at my school wept at their desks. The sorrow still lay across the village like a heavy shadow.

Six years after that disaster, when I was sixteen, my own father was killed in a road accident while walking on his way to work at Blairhall colliery. After a bus journey from home he had to walk two miles to the mine-head and the same underground to get to his work face, and then the same back at night in the blackout darkness of the war when he finished work.

All this background was the reason I had wanted so much to come to this mine when I heard of its existence. My father never wanted any of his sons to go into the 'pits', as the mines were referred to, even though it was often the only job available. "You must get a trade," he had insisted and I certainly never had any desire to be a miner. Even so, I had not realised how much mining was

---

*Saltpetre, also known as potassium nitrate or nitre, can be seen as efflorescence, a white, crystalline salt, on new or damp walls. Saltpetre is used in medicine and it is the basis of gunpowder.

in my blood after generations on both sides of the family had come down that path. I now felt an urge to experience the work. This wasn't deep mining by any means, but it had to be something like it.

Years later, when I had finished my Africa travels I purposely worked a year in Valleyfield colliery because I felt I wanted to experience the life that had coursed through my family for so long in the hope I might capture the atmosphere, the feel of it all and one day breathe its life on to paper in writing and preserve it for eternity. Alas, in that I failed. The story never came and now the opportunity for anyone with like intentions is gone for ever for nearly all the Fife mines are no more. Not the slightest vestige of Valleyfield or Blairhall collieries remain. The great hoisting gantries that crowned the pitheads for decades were no longer the first fingers that broke the dawn horizon, the huge, spidery wheels that became almost invisible as they whirled when lowering the miners into the depths and drawing up the hard-won, black-diamond coal, the metamorphic remains of the prehistoric forests that once grew there when Fife had an equatorial climate, turned no more. Even the great bings (slag heaps) have disappeared, levelled without trace.

Is it a good thing they are gone? Perhaps. Coal mining was an awful, inhuman and unhealthy environment in which any person should be obliged to spend their life's work. And yet ... it provided a living when there might not have been one and around the mines grew wonderful, warm and supportive communities, villages that produced people of great compassion and spirit. I count myself privileged to have grown up in such an environment and I regret not one moment spent in the local mine.

The work was hard at Valleyfield colliery but the company was worth it all. So many characters, all gentle men. They were rough, as work shapes the person, but seldom coarse. As in any walk-of-life there were some who had foul mouths and few inhibitions, but to portray miners in general as uncouth morons would be wrong, wrong, wrong. These were warm-hearted, thinking people, full of dry humour, rib-tickling mirth and droll ways and seldom given to gratuitous cursing. In all my life I never heard my father swear nor say an unkind word. And so it was here in Africa. The three men I had recently met, all miners, were each gentlemen to the core.

Here at this little mine the shaft went into the side of the mountain rather than down. Some way back different chambers led off from the main tunnel. In these the men dug with hand tools, crow-bars, picks and shovels, careful not to destroy the mica when it was found encased in the rock. In the main tunnel others continued to drive further into the mountain. We dug out the rock, sluiced away the rubble and timbered the passages.

As a boy I remember my father saying he did not like the new steel beams that were being introduced into his mine. Pit-props were his job. He shored up the new tunnels and repaired the old. There was no job more important in the mine. If he and his gang did a bad job, men would die as sure as fate … and I use that phrase pointedly, not as a cliché. The new, curved steel beams were much stronger than the pine props and made runways twelve feet high and wide. More space to work, to breathe in and improve the working conditions beyond belief. But the old miners did not like them. My father said that wood spoke to the miners, creaking and groaning all the while, petrifying, I should think, to all newcomers. But the seasoned miners learned the language of wood and they knew when the props were saying, "This is very heavy, I'll have to ease my position a bit. Don't be frightened if I groan a little, I'm all right, just settling to be more comfortable." But there were times when a more anxious note would come from the wood and the miners would perhaps hesitate in what they were doing and cock their ears to pay more attention to what the props were saying. "Quick, you must help me. The rock load above me has moved and I don't think I can hold it. Put in more props immediately." Or, the last shout of warning, a higher, louder, splitting note, terrifying to hear, "I'm going. I'll give you a few seconds, maybe a minute, even two, but no more. GET OUT."

Always the last, friendly warning. Never would the wooden props die or allow the men whom they guarded to die without that note which told them to escape if they could. The new steel props, though stronger and allowing so much better conditions for the miners, could collapse without a note of warning when the load became too much. Just fold up. Instant eclipse.

*

In the Bundali mica mine things were not quite so dramatic. Still, the danger was there and I paid particular attention to the props and could almost feel my father looking over my shoulder and nodding with satisfaction. Now and again a 'book' of mica appeared and was dug out carefully.

Mica is a laminated, crystalline rock which has a shiny, pearly, metallic lustre, shot through with multi colours. In the cutting 'room' – an open sided erection of a corrugated-iron roof shielding a heavy, rough table – the 'book' was split between the laminates and separated into 'leaves'. When thick with many leaves the mica is translucent and transparent when separated into thin, single plates. In some parts of the world, Russia for instance, these were sometimes used as window glass. In the more modern world sheets of mica were used as insulating plates in electric irons and other electrical appliances.

After separation the leaves were then sent to the cutters who removed the cracks and other flaws. When cut most of the pieces measured from four inches up to a foot across, but down at Kyiambili, displayed on the walls there were some record pieces twenty-eight inches or so in breadth. These were nothing like the gigantic plates measuring many feet across that were mined in Canada and elsewhere, but even so the Bundali mica was still a very marketable product. From the cutters the mica was packed into fifty pound boxes for the porters to take to Tukuyu and the outer world. This was 'green' mica. I learned that 'ruby' mica was the highest grade, then came 'brown' and then green'.

All over the mine there were slag heaps of the waste that looked like piles of glass. Had the mine been more accessible, by truck for instance, all that would have been saleable too for mica dust was used in the manufacture of lustre wallpaper and other products. As it was, where every piece had to be carried manually, only the best was worth transporting.

Mica dust was everywhere: it got into your shoes, in the texture of your clothes, in your mouth, in the grooves of your skin, it covered your hands so that they looked like mail gauntlets and when you combed your hair it fell like sparkling dandruff. In retrospect, I would have little doubt that Lawson's asthma had been brought on by the mica dust but in those days few people had heard of industrial diseases.

The signal to stop work was given about 3 p.m. Immediately a change came over the miners. The lethargic mood which had governed their movements since the morning dropped from them like a cloak and down the hill they went, laughing and capering to stack their picks and shovels at the hut. Even the ragged jacketed aristocrats got caught up in the effervescent mood and joined in the mad rush, their proud rags streaming out behind them.

After a bath in half a 40-gallon drum cut longways and steadied from rolling by bricks under each side, dinner was served on the rough-hewn table that rocked unsteadily on the uneven floor. The ever radiant Kamina, pearly white teeth sparkling and fat, high cheekbones glistening in the lamplight, fussed her charges like a mother hen, puffing a little in her portly gait, courteous and friendly with me, but oh, so gentle and loving to her own man, making sure his chair was just so for comfort, seeing that a cushion was placed at his back and that he had everything that he required, then retiring into the shadows where she remained, ever watchful for anything, that little something, that we, but particularly Lawson, might need.

Then we yarned or read away the evening while the temperamental old pressure lamp hissed and spluttered through its broken mantle and Lawson wheezed and sometimes hacked with coughing at the phlegm on his chest. At times we listened to the radio, a big galleon of a thing with round corners and sloping sides and a front of faded fabric behind an Art Deco plywood fretwork. It was very temperamental and oscillated and whistled alarmingly until the turning knob of black Bakelite caught on to a station and teased it out of the crackling ether and into our little mud hut on top of a wilderness mountain. The reception was not always very clear, especially when the battery began to fade. The first voice to emerge from the crackle and static made a memory for me that has haunted me all down the years. It was a new, young singer, Jimmy Young, rendering the song he had just made all the rage, 'They Tried To Tell Us We're Too Young'.

Music was not limited to the radio though. In a corner of the room was Lawson's pride and joy, a wind-up gramophone with his store of precious records in a tin box beside it. That I grew to like more than anything. He had records that conveyed me right back home as a boy listening to the same tunes played by my father on his little portable gramophone 'ben the room' (in the parlour) with the fire lit some Sunday evenings. John McCormack singing 'I'll Walk Beside You' and 'The Garden Where the Praities Grow', Richard Tauber with 'You Are My Heart's Delight' and 'Vienna, City of Dreams', Nelson Eddy's 'There's a Little Brown Road Winding Over the Hill' from 'Smiling Through' and many more. Some of my mother's favourites from 'The Maid of the Mountains' were there too, such as 'If I Could Find (or was it 'Hold') the Key To Your Heart' and 'Love Will Find a Way'. As the lilting notes hung in the air I glanced across at Kamina, our own maid of the mountains, sitting so quiet and faithful in the dark corner of the whitewashed, mud walls, her dark face serene, her thoughts lost in the music and words that must have been so foreign to her. Although she understood not a word, were these the thoughts, the wishes, she held in her heart? If they were, then the magic of love did eventually find a way. Many years later I heard that Lawson had retired from the mine a year or two after my visit and had taken Kamina south with him to Northern Rhodesia where they were married, a very, very unusual thing for a white man of those days to do, and, as far as I know, they lived happily ever after.

Instrumentalists too featured in our evening soirees. The magic strings of Albert Sandler's violin made the roof tingle and turned your heart over with haunting, pleading melodies from the Palm Court. 'Song of Songs' and many more.

Two that he played made me go quiet in reverie, 'The Nun's Chorus' from *Casanova* and 'Invitation to the Dance' which less than a couple of years before Alex Seath and I had sung with others in a Youth Fellowship concert directed by the Reverend Thoms Webster, minister of Torryburn parish and Fellowship leader. Already that time seemed long, long ago in a different life.

One record I particularly remember came out of Lawson's special wallet containing the complete set from *La Boheme*. He played 'Your Tiny Hand Is Frozen', sung by someone unknown. I was truly moved. "You liked that?" he asked. I didn't need to speak. "In that case, listen to this." He then put the same aria on the turntable, but this time sung in Italian, 'Che Gelida Manila' by Beniamino Gigli. Whatever I felt before was as nothing to this. I was lifted somewhere up into the rafters, transported. It was magnificent. But moving though it was there was something else that made the moment sublime for me. It was the first time I had heard Gigli, but I knew of him. As the music, the voice, filled that lonely room I was again a little boy, seven or eight maybe, sitting on the long, wooden fender-stool in front of the glowing range in the house of my best friend, Jim Fitzsimmons, three doors up from my home.

Jim's elder brother, Willie, was something of an anachronism. A miner's son, like all of us, brought up in the same homespun environment, Willie was sophisticated, cultured. Where, how he had acquired this was a mystery, for both his parents had come off the land and were plain, honest, couthie people. But at eighteen or nineteen Willie appeared to have a classical background. Not that I knew anything about that, but I saw him as someone different to anyone I had ever met before. There were those in the village who did not take kindly to Willie's pretensions, but I saw him with a child's uncritical eye, accepting what I saw and heard. And I liked what I heard.

Willie played the violin wonderfully, to me at least. And he sang songs different to anyone else. Songs like 'La Donna et Mobile' and 'Che Gelida Manila' in Italian. He liked to perform and he would announce to his audience, his mum and dad, Jim and me, what he was going to do, 'The Londonderry Air', a violin arrangement in the style of Fritz Kriesler, or he would sing 'O Sole Mio', explaining in his announcement, "English translation, 'Beneath Thy Window'. I will sing it in the Italian as of a piece by that wonderful Italian tenor, Beniamino Gigli." In later life when recounting to someone these moments when Willie would announce a 'piece by Gigli' I might add in whimsical mood, or in Scots' idiom, 'A Jeelly Piece'. Willie would not have been amused.

At weekends I scoured the mountains for more minerals, panning the mountain streams for gold dust, but never finding any, and collecting rocks, carefully noting the district where they were found. At first Lawson came with me to show me what to do and what to look for, then I widened the radius on my own. The rocks were knapped and splinters examined under the microscope, but nothing I found proved of value. How beautiful though were the rock fragments under the glass, worth gathering for that alone, many of them sparkling like precious gems, vivid coloured with the various metals and other minerals they contained.

Lawson was a keen photographer and the proud possessor of two Leicas. There was developing and printing to be done. And he had built a plant to distil perfume from the mountain flowers, so these had to be gathered and processed. Altogether life seemed full up there on the roof of the world.

At length the time came when I decided, reluctantly, to move on. A band of porters were leaving next day for 'Kyiambili' and I would go down with them. That night I think we were both sad, lost for words and the records seemed particularly poignant. Lawson tried several times to say something but the words drifted and he couldn't continue. I think I knew what he wanted to say but I could not help him. I too was feeling the moment.

In the grey light of early morning the porters were loaded and we made to start the journey. Mr Lawson stood on the edge of the flat clearing as I stepped onto the steep path that ran down the side of the cliff like a staircase. We said our goodbyes and I quickly dropped some twenty feet or more then turned to look back. My heart went out to this lonely old man with the warm, moist eyes, standing there in battered hat and long, shabby shorts, waving rather wistfully with a little twirl of his fingers at waist height. I waved too without saying a word but I wanted to shout back, "Please don't be lonely now that I've gone, old friend. I'll come back soon and we'll talk and laugh and play the gramophone and pick the wild flowers and make scent for Kamina. I'll come and see you again and again because I want to," but I knew I never would.

The main arterial road from Dar-es-Salaam to the interior during the monsoon

Ferry over the Ruvu River

Wasafa children showing the filed teeth of cannibals

Sluicing at the mine

My first crocodile

The wounded hippo we hunted for days

Under the Livingstone Mountains. The start of the canoe journey down Lake Nyasa

Church of Scotland, Blantyre

Captain Aires de Abren, Ann Santos and Peggy

A Baobab tree

Goodbye, old friends

I arrive at Tete on the Zambezi River in boots tied with rope

A mighty boulder typical of the landscape

Great Zimbabwe – Note the quality of the dry stone walling

Later development – Note poor quality of the masonry work

An ancient Phoenician coin showing a conical tower similar to that in Great Zimbabwe

With William and Mrs. Nagle at the dam

A Zulu girl

Family with whom I shared the cave – Swartzberg Pass

Man in the cave smoking dagga

Statue of Jan van Riebeck with Tablemountain in the background.

Chapter Fifteen

CROCODILE HUNTER

Thursday 3rd January 1952 – Crocodile hunting on the Songwe River
   *This morning one of the boys saw me take out my glass eye and clean it.
The word got round like wildfire. I heard one whisper, "Muchawi"
(Magician) and others refer to me as Bwana Macho Uchawi." (Magic
Eye).*

He was an odd looking character. His beard was bushy and his hair curled out
from under his stained and battered bush hat. His shirt and shorts were incredibly
mended, with barely anything left of the original material. His bare legs were
scratched and dotted with veldt sores, some weeping. On his feet were the
remnants of sandshoes, only now the canvas had nearly all gone and the soles
were tied on with bark thongs. Over his shoulder he carried a rifle. I could
hardly imagine that this person with his hand stretched out towards mine was
me as I reached down into the glassy pool to scoop up a handful of water to
splash over my sweaty face.

   Three months ago Major Strickland had said, "If you're going to shoot
crocodiles, you're going to need this," as he handed me his 6.5 Mannlicher
Schoener rifle with a couple of cartons of ammunition. I looked in disbelief. A
man in Africa was never separated from his rifle. It was a very personal thing.
To offer it to an almost unknown stranger – at this time I had only known him for
three or four days – was the most generous gesture I could think of, especially
since, as he would know far better than I at the time, crocodile hunting is like no
other hunting, being dirty, messy and always carrying the danger of the weapon
being submerged in mud or water, just about the worst scenario that any rifle
owner could envisage. He shooed aside my remonstrations of not possibly being
able to accept such an offer with the excuse, "Well I'm not likely to be using it
for a while, so you might as well have it."

   He was referring to his arm in the sling. He had told me before how he had
been on safari only a week or so before I arrived when his wagon had skidded
on wet mud and gone over the side of an embankment, rolled a few times and
ended in a small river with his African driver killed and he with a broken collar
bone and arm.

   It was a beautiful, well-balanced rifle, with tapered barrel and I could hardly imagine myself possessing it, even if only on a temporary basis. I had wanted to meet up with the crocodile hunter but I had never really thought of actually taking part in the shooting, other than perhaps being allowed a potshot or two. Without a rifle I knew that at best I must be a reporter of the action rather than a participant and in that I would have been content, knowing that at least I had experienced it. Now, with the potential of joining as a combatant, I set off with renewed vigour and anticipation to find the man I knew as Crocodile Pete.

His camp was some fifteen miles down the road towards Lake Nyasa. It lay off the road some way, near (but not too near because of the crocodiles) the bank of the Kibira river. I only found it by asking the natives. By this time every one I spoke to knew 'Bwana Mamba' (Mr Crocodile) and where he lived. Indeed, the nearer I came to his place the more the natives expressed their knowledge of him. Some openly rolled their eyes and I sensed their apprehension, and even fear. Others drew in their breath and shook their hand loosely from the wrist, as only African natives can do, and one or two accompanied this gesture with the expression, "*Huyu kali sana.*" (He is very fierce.")

I walked into his camp three days after Christmas and found him at home with his wife, Iris, and their two children, girls around nine and eleven, on holiday from school. They all sat at a rough table set alfresco under a huge mango tree that shaded the large square, thatched, wattle-and-daub house. A hesitation fell over all as I emerged from the thick bush into their clearing. A single stranger suddenly walking uninvited into your home deep in the bush must always be regarded as slightly suspect, especially when he carries a rifle over his shoulder, and I could feel their apprehension. Having a kilted Scot arrive among them was not their everyday occurrence. But the kilt worked its magic again. Nobody with sinister intentions would ever make themselves so conspicuous as a kilty in outback Africa.

After their initial surprise they received me with considerable excitement and obvious pleasure, especially the girls. But though I say I was well received, this was only partially true. While the woman and children bubbled their welcome the man I took to be the one I had looked so long and hard for remained stern-faced and greeted me with a curt word or two. I offered my hand rather gingerly and introduced myself.

As he rose to shake my hand I could see he was a powerful man in his thirties. Although almost as tall as I he looked stocky because of his great barrel chest, fat calves and heavy, hairy forearms. He looked the epitome of the hunter. He exuded a presence of total fearlessness, towering strength and complete self-confidence within his chosen field.

Thawing somewhat he introduced himself as Pieter Martin, his wife Iris and the children, Alice and Rose. In terse, but not too unfriendly terms, he invited me to sit with them and over coffee I said I wanted to learn the ropes of hunting and asked if I might join him for a time. The temporary thaw suddenly froze again and with it an awful silence fell as he looked steadily at me with his cold, pale blue eyes and I sensed hostility. I refused to be put down and met his stare with a steady but friendly look, hoping he would not read the caution and wariness that was going through my head.

Major Strickland's quiet warning as I left flashed through my mind, "Be very careful how you deal with that man," he had said, "there's a lot of mystery about him and more than a hint of violence in his past. He keeps himself very much to himself, as if he has something to hide. He has made no effort to meet the local whites and, frankly, there are those who would not welcome his advances if he did," were his parting words.

From the first time I'd heard of Crocodile Pete I'd known he had had to leave the Copper Belt because of his brawling and I could well see now how easily he might have nearly killed the man with his fists as he was reputed to have done.

"Why should I teach you how to hunt for you to set up shop and do me out of business?" he asked, full of malice. I explained uncomfortably that I had no intention of being a professional hunter nor of wanting to take away any of his livelihood. My main purpose, I said, was to feel the thrill of hunting and gain experience of it so I could write authoritatively on it in a book I intended writing. I told him of my journey and of my intention to make my way slowly down to the Cape and then return to Scotland. He looked at me unswervingly and said, "You're young." I wondered what that had to do with it. That, had I known it, had everything to do with it. "Not that young," I said, "and I'm no stranger to the bush." He went on as if I had never spoken. "This is no game. No little adventure for you to write home about. It's hard out there. It's hard work and I must keep up my quota. It's how we live. I have no time to nurse you." With his last words he turned away dismissively. But I had come too far to go without a fight. I assured him I would not prove a burden to him, but if ever I fell back he only needed to say so and I'd be on my way and not bother him anymore.

He turned back to stare at me, still undecided. Suddenly, into the cold, fragile vacuum I had an ally in Iris. "Piet darling, David would be a good companion to you, even if it was only for a short while. You know how I worry about you, we all do," indicating the children, "while you're doing such dangerous work." She spoke in a sweety-pie, best English voice I could not imagine her using had I not been there. Both she and Pieter spoke English with heavy Africaans accents, Pieter particularly. The girls gave their mother queer looks and Piet threw her one that was decidedly hostile, as if to say, 'You keep out of this.' But the girls jumped in with childish glee, saying mummy was right and pleading with Pieter to let me stay. Iris, not put off by the wild look she had received, waded in with her rabbit punch. "Grandfather Martin would not be pleased if you turned David away."

With that opposition Pieter capitulated grudgingly and agreed to take me on.

It was not the best atmosphere to start a new job and I knew I would have to gain his respect quickly if I was going to stay around. As it was I was deeply indebted to Grandfather Martin and was interested to learn where he came into the equation. I gathered later that Pieter's grandfather had been a Scot in a Highland regiment that fought in the Boer war. At the end of hostilities he chose to settle in with the enemy and married a Boer, or Africaans, girl. That's how it was told, but I reckoned it was more likely to be the other way round; he fell for an Africaans lass and at the end of the war took local demob and moved in with her folks.

Whatever, Grandfather Martin had played a towering role in Pieter's growing-up years, more than his father it would seem since I hardly heard Pieter mention him. Certainly at this moment I was really grateful to my late, elder countryman who, through Iris, had topped Pieter's highest card with an ace. Over the next few months together Piet, as I grew to know him, drew heavily on his Scottish ancestry in our conversation.

Despite his manly bearing and tough exterior I found Piet, during our very close association, to be in many ways a simple soul who could be thrown by a remark, as with Iris on that crucial occasion. At all times he cut a comic figure. Even at the table he wore a sun-helmet without the crown so that his bald head stuck out through the top with only the brim resting round his brow like a halo. His round face was severe – but could crease into smiles too, as I later found out – and his large pale blue eyes had a merciless look. It would have been a foolish man who laughed at him. I learned later that someone had told him that the sun playing on his head would restore his hair, so he had torn off the top but retained the brim to protect his neck and eyes. A rather eccentric use of headgear, that was designed primarily to protect, of all places, the top of the head.

There was something odd about the whole set-up. When I set out to find him I imagined he would be a Robinson Crusoe character, alone in a sea of bush, apart from a Man Friday or two. I could never have encompassed a man taking his wife and children deep into the jungle, cut off from all of their kind and way of life, and subject them to the dangers that went with their castaway type existence. They were indeed quite a remarkable family.

The girls went to a school, perhaps a mission one – for sure Piet could not have afforded expensive education for his family – over in Northern Rhodesia and either boarded at school or lodged with a friend from his Copper Belt days. I wondered how many of the girls' peers could boast of such an exotic, Swiss Family Robertson existence. Perhaps, they did not boast of it, did not even speak of it, or, if they did, transform it into a mansion for the sake of their prestige. If so it would have been a great shame, for I'm sure any child they might have invited home would have been thrilled. But then again, children can be brutally, cuttingly, snobbish and afterwards the visitors might have made the girls' lives a misery.

After my initial introduction Piet welcomed me in a more friendly though taciturn way, pleasant but less overt than Iris' obvious pleasure or the squeals of joy from the children as they ran to meet me in the days that followed when I appeared out of the bush – in shorts now – and into the clearing, each wondering noisily what game we could play.

They had a little pet monkey, Jimpy by name, who ran free about the place and ruled the roost. The girls loved dressing him up in blue trousers and a checked shirt that Iris had run up on her Singer sewing machine. Jimpy seemed to like getting toffed up and acted like the little gentleman he was meant to be for a short while, then he would forget he was a swell and scamper off and be his usual mischievous self, chasing the hens, pulling the cats' tails and stealing their milk, standing on the dogs and pulling their ears when they were asleep and even climbing on the head of the visitor to search in his hair for fleas. Quite a character was Jimpy, and no end of a source of interest and mirth. The expressions on his face were almost human and it was easy to tell his emotions by them.

Iris was perhaps the most remarkable one of the family. Living in the bush, in a native style hut with absolutely no mod. cons., she looked as if she were the young mother in her house in Johannesburg. On that day and in all the future months, even when we came back unexpectedly, she was always neat and tidy in town clothes, with even a little make-up on. When the children were at school and Piet was off hunting she lived entirely alone in the bush with only a couple of casual houseboys who came and went more or less when they were needed. Although she did not like to be alone at night there were times when Piet's work kept him away for days on end. Like Piet, she spoke fluent Swahili and she used it like a whip at times with the boys, cracking it like a lash over their heads so that they jumped as if cut by its thongs.

*

While the children were home Piet and Iris could not offer me accommodation. Their native style house had only two rooms divided by a flimsy stick partition. Three miles down the road towards Kyela though there was a soap factory where arrangements had already been made for me to stay when required. It was owned by the two entrepreneurs, Messrs Park and Strickland and run by an elderly manager, Mr Williamson, another old Lupa goldminer.

It was there I had stayed overnight before that morning I walked into Piet and Iris' camp. Over my time in these parts I grew to like old man Williamson who always maintained with a wry smile that his greatest delight in being in Africa was that it kept him and his wife apart. If there was the slightest truth in his statement she must have been some harridan for his life as I saw it was one of abysmal rustication and inactivity. He paid little attention to his attire or personal appearance and did not move much as he bossed his senior boys as they ran the business.

The factory was a small, bare, brick building. Local gatherers, mainly women, brought in great bundles of wood and roots which were burned to collect the alkaline ash, or potash salt, that would be used to saponify the oil that was extracted from the leaves of the Munazi tree and other special vegetation and nuts that came in great, head-carried piles. Some palm-oil extracted from the trees down at the lower level by the lake was also used.

The method of obtaining salt from the ash of burnt wood was used all over Africa wherever bed-salt, rock-salt or sea-salt was not available. To the natives it was an essential part of their diet. David Livingstone, in his Missionary Travels, 1857, tells how as a doctor he cured poor natives who could nor afford to barter for meat and so were prone to acute indigestion brought on by an exclusively vegetable diet by giving them each a spoonful of salt.

The soap at the factory finally appeared as long bars, about two inches wide by one inch thick, which were cut up into six-inch long cakes. It was grey in colour, mottled with white, and some of the more expensive stuff was scented by Lawson's perfume brought down from the mica mine. Anyone who ever imagined that African natives cared little about personal hygiene or perfumed soap should have seen the queues that formed in the early morning when a batch of soap, hardened from yesterday, was due to be sold. I don't know if the Soap Masters exported their product to other districts but from what I saw I would say all the production could hardly supply local demand. 'Local' covered a very wide area, the women walking miles and miles, some distant ones even camping the night or begging the floor of a friend or relative, so they could be early for the 'Sale' in the morning.

Over the next few months I occasionally spent a night or more at the soap factory, sometimes creeping in very late after hunting and returning early in the morning to Piet's place where I enjoyed the family life there. After a long morning on the river and a twenty miles' slog back to the family home, and sometimes a late hour's hunting, these last three miles from Piet's place to the factory, always in the dark when I carried my rifle in the crook of my arm ready for predators, were long, long miles.

*

During our first conversation Piet examined my rifle with admiration but said it was not the best type for this kind of hunting. The Mannlicher Schoener was an extremely accurate rifle. It had very high muzzle-velocity which gave it a low trajectory, or in other words, a straighter flight-path. A bullet from any gun does not go in a straight line. It rises and falls in a shallow parabola before reaching its target, some rising more than others. This is why a marksman, knowing his gun might aim slightly low of his target, especially at near distances. It follows that the higher the speed that a bullet leaves the muzzle, the lower the trajectory and more accurate the rifle. High muzzle-velocity also has a bearing on penetration, which in a way was good for killing hard skinned animals, but at 6.5mm its calibre was rather light for the armour-plated hide and bone of crocodiles.

I had always found the calibration of guns rather confusing. All were rated in decimal terms, but those of British and American manufacture, such as the standard .303 British Army rifle of the time, with which I was familiar, were geared to the inch or 'Imperial Measure' while those of the Continent, the German, Italian, French and Czechoslovakian, etc. were graded to the metre or more accurately, the millimetre. At this time, long before Britain accepted metrication and me being locked into fractions of an inch, I could only comprehend the comparisons by remembering that 25 millimetres were roughly equivalent to one inch and make rough conversions from that inadequate benchmark. To confuse the issue, my little Beretta automatic pistol, although an Italian job, was graded by Imperial measure and at .25 calibre I likened it to quarter of an inch. My crude comparisons would have appalled any mathematician or ballistics expert and brought a heavy calibre retort down on my head. But in a clumsy way it suited me.

The calibre, however, was only one part of the equation, the charge behind the bullet was even more important. A bullet with a greater cartridge behind it is more lethal than one of the same calibre with less propulsion. For instance the impact of a .45 revolver bullet is nothing like that of a .450 rifle. In addition there are the 'magnum' guns, in both rifles and small arms. These have an even greater charge than the normal and this increases their killing power. For instance, it was illegal to hunt elephant with a standard .375mm rifle, but a .375mm magnum was permissible.

One more item completed the hunters' trilogy; hard-nosed or soft-nosed bullets? Hard-nosed, those cased in nickel, were reckoned to be best for hard skinned animals, crocodiles, elephants, rhinos etc., while soft-nosed, those made of lead, were suited to soft hides, antelope, lion, etc. The reason being that lead bullets would flatten on impact with hard hide and not penetrate enough to do more than wound the animal, while nickel-nosed bullets could pass right through a soft skinned animal, unless it hit bone, and again wound rather than kill. The whole essence of hunting is to kill the prey stone dead, preferably with one shot, and so eliminate or minimise pain or trauma to the victim.

There can be, of course, many cross threads in that simple treatise, the varying likes and dislikes of weaponry emanating mainly from the experience, skill and assurance of the hunter. A completely self-assured person, cool and accurate in the face of a charging lion, might prefer a nickel bullet that would penetrate the skull for a brain shot and result in instant death, where most others are likely to prefer to rely on the stopping power of a soft bullet, which needs less accuracy, but which would blunt the charge and allow time for more shots to finish the business. It should be unnecessary to add that anyone who is not ice-cold and confident in the face of a lion charge would be most unlikely to get a second, hard-nosed shot in if the first bullet passed through the skull without hitting the brain.

Piet did not lecture me on guns. What I have written here is my drawing together of snippets that dropped out of our conversation, and in doing so I may be drawing on many other conversations over the next few months and not just on that first day. This is my interpretation of what he said, and while the meanings are his, many of the words are mine. Piet was not a man of letters. Words such as 'muzzle-velocity' and 'trajectory' were not in his vocabulary. Inevitably too, much of what I have written here includes knowledge I picked up from a great deal of hunting in which I participated over the years I wandered Africa.

*

The first morning after my introduction I arrived back at Piet's place early, but not early enough. He had already been out on a dawn hunt and shot a waterbuck and a wild pig. Piet came back for some breakfast and I returned with him and some boys to butcher the animals and bring back the meat. The buck seemed huge and the pig, an evil looking beast in life, almost sad in death. When the carcasses were cut up the pieces were loaded into baskets and carried on the heads of a procession of *bibis* (native married women) back to Piet's camp. There, under the great mango tree, the yard became a market place.

Word had got round with the speed that only happens in Africa and even by the time we got back the place was crowded with women with their wares to barter for the meat. We had heard the loud clamour of their shrill voices and laughter over the last half mile as we approached. Before trading started Piet laid aside his own choice cuts, then the action began. This was the way that Piet lived. This was his bank, his currency. No money changed hands. With a quick eye Piet judged the size of piece of meat to exchange for the produce that was offered. When the meat and the women were all gone the yard was full of baskets of maize flour, mahogo (a long white vegetable) flour, hens, eggs, milk, pumpkins, nuts, rice and lots more. Not a bad morning's shopping for the price of two or three bullets, I thought, surveying all the produce, and it wasn't even midday yet.

When the din and dust had died away the fresh meat Piet had kept for their own use was preserved in a mixture of half-a-cup of saltpetre* and five cups of salt to two gallons of water. The meat would be kept in that for four or five days, then hung up to dry. A few tender steaks had been kept aside and we all enjoyed an excellent lunch before Piet and I prepared to go hunt crocodiles.

*Saltpetre, also known as potassium nitrate or nitre, can be seen as efflorescence, a white, crystalline salt, on new or damp walls. Saltpetre is used in medicine and it is the basis of gunpowder.

I now began to see into Piet's life and realise what a shrewd operator he was. In a few hours he had provided sumptuously for his family and now he was off to get the hard currency required for ammunition, the girls' schooling, clothes and the little extras that made Iris happy and lifted their lives from that of the natives.

*

The day already seemed old when noon had barely gone and we were ready to set off for the Songwe River, some twenty miles away over difficult terrain, to catch us a crocodile or two. The three boys behind us carried the loads. The route led through a paradise of mango trees, the small type which are much sweeter than the more common variety. We feasted on them as we walked, filling our pockets when they became empty. We crossed the swirling torrents of the Kabira river by dugout canoe. Piet advised me to take off my boots and socks in case the boat overturned. Later we crossed the Songwe river by the same method and again I had to remove my footwear.

The native boatmen were experts. They took the canoes across sideways, always keeping the head of the boat into the current, never letting the force of the water hit it broadside on. In each river the water was a dark-brown, boiling cauldron.

We came up on the Nyasaland side of the river and reached our destination just before dark. The Songwe river is the dividing line between Tanganyika and Nyasaland. Immediately over the river I saw a change in the villages in the form of sanitation. In Nyasaland each hut had to have a latrine, in Tanganyika there was no such law.

Our destination was a native village where Piet had stayed before. On our arrival we were greeted by the Head Man who said how honoured the village was with our presence. Piet declined the offer of a hut which did not look all that clean and as such carried the risk of ticks, the bites of which could bring on their own type of virulent fever. Beds of banana leaves were made for us out in the open and baskets of fruit were brought to us, paw-paws, mangoes, oranges, grenadillos. We feasted on the pork of a wild pig – how succulent it was!

The next day I won my spurs. I shot a crocodile. I tried to look casual about it, but inside I was chuffed to bits at having made my mark with my first shot so early in the business. *"Yesterday the boys addressed me as 'Bwana'. Today I am 'Bwana Mkubwa'* (Big or Great Master)," I wrote in my diary. Actually, it was not quite my crocodile.

Since early morning we had stalked the reptiles along the bank. The undergrowth was so thick that in places we had to get down on our bellies and slither under it, just like the crocodiles we were hunting. This on my first real day at the game made me feel very vulnerable. I kept wondering what was going to happen when – not 'if' – we came face-to-face with one. But that never happened.

Later in the day we came to a place where the river was fairly narrow and the *meteti* reeds receded from the bank some way leaving a small stony beach. On the opposite side a fair sized crocodile lay asleep, its head, as always, facing the river. I watched in fascination as Piet went through a little pre-shooting drill which he did on every occasion before using his rifle. Over the following months I came to know this practice so well though I never adopted it. He drew his rifle close to himself, perpendicular, as if presenting-arms, reached down, lifted the bolt and slid it back to make sure the breach was open, thereby ensuring the gun would not go off. He then put the muzzle to his lips and blew down the barrel, all the while never taking his eyes off his target. Satisfied there was no obstruction, he then shot the bolt home, raised the gun to his shoulder and squinted along the sights.

He told me afterwards that he had seen a man take his rifle from his gun-bearer who carelessly had allowed the barrel to stab in the ground and become jammed with earth and stones. When the hunter fired the gun exploded in his face. He lost his eye and was horribly scarred for life and indeed was lucky to have survived the accident. Since then this little ritual he went through had become second nature to Piet.

I came to know Piet as a remarkable marksman, but on this occasion – doesn't it always happen when you have a stranger with you whom you want to impress – shooting from the slightly elevated opposite bank, his shot was slightly high and hit behind the crocodile's head. It was badly hurt and threw its head up and back, showing the white underside of its throat. But it would have made the water and been lost before Piet had time for another shot. He didn't blow down the barrel when he repeated shooting, only at the start of any action. Nevertheless he would not have had time to work the bolt this time.

I had my rifle primed with one up the spout and the safety-catch off and more by gut-reaction than thought or even proper sighting, let fly almost immediately after Piet, so that the two shots sounded like a double-barrelled gun going off. My bullet must have gone up through the soft underpart and found the brain, for the crocodile's head dropped forward again like a well oiled hinge and it lay stone dead. There was an instant lull where everyone stood perfectly still until Piet said in an undertone, "Where did you learn to shoot like that?"

Where did I learn to shoot! Apart from the firing range in the army, where I won a small prize as best shot of the day up to 300 yards, that was the first shot I had ever fired in earnest and it was obviously an extremely lucky one. Still, some practice a long time ago might have gone into making it lucky. I think it was on my twelfth birthday that my father gave me an airgun on my promise that I would not shoot any birds. It was the kind you broke in the middle of the barrel to compress the air, put in a pellet – we called them 'slugs', it sounded so much better – and snapped it shut again.

Running home from school at four o'clock I felt that my feet were made of lead. I wanted to fly and they were holding me on the ground. I could hardly wait to drink the tea that my mother had ready for us coming in, before grabbing my rifle and rushing into our long garden to practise with it. I put a can on the clothes post and banged away at that until it posed no problem. I put smaller objects further away until that too became boring with lack of challenge. As time went by I worked up all manner of innovations to keep spicing up my interest.

I remembered my dad telling me many years before about a cowboy he had seen or read about who was in Buffalo Bill's Circus when that show came over from America, who held up a mirror in one hand and shot backwards over his shoulder to hit targets with unerring skill. So I tried this too, imagining myself in one of Bill Cody's great arenas. It was terribly difficult. Everything was back to front. When you wanted to correct to the left you had to move the barrel to the right and so on. But after some time I mastered it fairly well and could ring the bell most times.

As a variation I stood with my back to the target, then bent over double and shot backwards through my splayed legs. Compared to mirror shooting that seems comparatively easy but that too has its own unique idiosyncrasies. Even then, without knowing anything about ballistics or muzzle-velocities, I had learned that in straight shooting if you didn't aim slightly low of your target you did not hit where you wanted to hit. Shooting upside down made a whole lot of difference with gravity increasing the rise, or now the drop, of the flight curve.

To hit a moving target I tied a can on a string to the clothes-line and had another, longer one also tied to the line which I held in my hand. By pulling this long string the line jerked and the can hanging from it swung and danced a wild jig. And when the simple stuff began to pall I did them all again, but this time with snap-shooting, taking no time for prolonged aiming. Just up and bang.

But things had changed a lot since then. With the loss of my right eye I now had to shoot from my left shoulder. This was not one of the stunts I had worked into my repertoire in my airgun days. Even if I had, it is unlikely it would have done me any good with a real rifle. Like golf-clubs, bolt-action rifles are made for right-handed and right-eyed people. The bolt is on the right-hand side for easy handling. They are designed for sighting with the right eye. There may be some specially made left-handed ones, but I never saw one. Shooting from the left shoulder meant that I had to awkwardly reach over the stock with my left hand to work the bolt. Not an easy thing to do for a right-handed person, but with practice I got quite slick at it. Moreover, sighting with my left eye meant I had to lean my head well over the stock so I could get my left eye aligned with the sights. Altogether a cack-handed posture for hunter whose life or livelihood might depend on quick, accurate shooting.

Anyway, on that first day, with my first shot, some of my airgun games half a lifetime ago must have come through to make me lucky for I never had a better one all the time I was hunting crocodiles. What was even more important to me than his accolade was the fact that I felt a marked change in Piet's attitude to me. With his new respect we had drawn closer together and from then on he spoke more freely and man-to-man with me.

*

The next few days were a real baptism of fire. From early morning through most of the day we slogged up and down the rivers recording some successes and a great deal of hard, empty miles. My boots were worse than useless for the game. Apart from being burst and hopelessly worn out they were constantly soaked and heavy as lead. Even more annoying than the weight was the awful job of taking them off and putting them on again every time we crossed a river by canoe which we did often. Fighting to get on wet socks and lacing up sodden boots each time we landed was wearing for me and a nuisance to the others who were held up. Piet wore rubber sandals on his bare feet and I had to get something similar, something quieter than the boots for stalking.

On the last day of the year we did some miles down the Songwe before heading back the twenty rough miles to Piet's home. He said the Africaans people honoured the New Year like the Scots and I looked forward to a quiet celebration of Hogmanay with them at midnight. But after a dinner prepared by Iris, Piet surprised me by saying we'd go out in the dark after buck. I thought they had all the food they'd need for ages after the great market a few days ago. But Piet said while they had plenty of salted meat and biltong*, they needed a constant supply of fresh meat for themselves and the boys, that being part of their promised wages and indeed in most cases the only reason for the natives of these parts accepting to work with crocodiles.

At the outset of his hunting there Piet told me he had had great difficulty recruiting labour. The natives there were steeped in anti-crocodile folklore and it said a lot for them and a great deal about the pulling power of fresh meat to people who wanted it for their families but can rarely procure it themselves, that they would lay aside their prejudices and superstitions and work with these

---

* Biltong - strips of fresh meat dried in the sun until it is almost black and very, very tough but also nutritious. Biltong was very important to the Boers during the South African War. With bundles of biltong in their saddlebags a Boer commando - where the word was coined - could be an extremely mobile unit. With no need to forage for food nor be lumbered by slow, horse-drawn, kitchen vehicles as the British Army was, the commando could range far and wide and be gone from danger before the British troops could muster.

creatures that they feared and abhorred. In later times I heard of people who ate crocodile flesh but I never fancied it myself. I can only think that the people who might eat crocodile steaks had never lived by rivers infested by them. I often thought in the months ahead what a terrible waste it was when people all around were hungry for protein to roll a great body back into the water, after stripping off a piece of its hide, where it would be food for other crocodiles and scavengers. But to have even suggested to the local natives they eat it would have been in the worst possible taste. These reptiles had a long history of eating the natives' nearest and dearest and their ancestors that even to taste the flesh would have seemed like cannibalism.

So on the last night of 1951, after having already done that day more than twenty-five miles over difficult terrain, we went out at night from Piet's house to hunt with the lamp. The world changes after dark. The paths through the grass were narrow corridors with solid walls, trees came to life in the form of ghostly apparitions and a banana plantation was a nightmare land. Now and again twin balls of fire lit up in the beam, but mostly they were owls and other nocturnal hunters like ourselves. Once a wild cat was hypnotised by the light but never a buck came into our world. We came back empty-handed. But I enjoyed it just to see at night the fantastic land we live in.

The children being at home, at the end of that long day I had to do the few miles down to the soap factory in the dark without a lamp, hoping all the time that I wouldn't meet anything on the road for there would be no warning. I'd be on it, or vice-versa, before I knew it. Piet had made no mention of keeping Hogmanay and I was glad. Little wonder that for the first time since I could remember I slept my way into the New Year and was very pleased to do so.

Before dropping-off in my makeshift bed on the bare concrete corner of the factory floor I sleepily wished my folks back home a Guid New Year, but didn't sing my song this time. I dreamily mused over the two New Years I'd experienced since leaving home; last year in prison in the wilds of the Ogaden desert of Ethiopia and here now on the threshold of the open door of 1952 I was buried deep in the Tanganyikan bush, experiencing the toughest, most interesting time in my whole life.

Piet had declared New Year's Day a holiday and spent it with his family. But the day was no holiday for me. I had to do something about my boots which were falling apart. So on this New Years day I walked the ten miles to Kyela to try and find someone who might work a miracle with them and to see if I could buy new, soft shoes. Hardly a mile down the road my boots gave up the ghost. The sole of one literally separated from the upper and even though I bound it round with string it was no use. So I took them off and carried them like I was sorry for them and did the rest of the way barefoot.

At Kyela I managed to find a shop open where I bought a new pair of sandshoes and with some difficulty I found the home of an Indian boot *fundi*.

The cobbler hefted each boot, one after the other, scrutinising them this way and that, shaking his head in disbelief and, I thought, pessimism, while I waited timorously for him to pronounce them dead. But to my great relief he announced he would try 'damn hard' to make 'damn good job' of them and he did. The finished job, as I saw a few weeks later, was not Saville Row, but considering what he started with he produced a fair retread that would add some more mileage to the footwear I depended on for heavy, pack-carrying slogging.

Next day Piet and I walked the twenty miles cross-country to the Songwe River. We arrived in the tail-end of the afternoon and immediately started the 'day's' work. We were not long there when Piet hit a smallish one on the bank. We were sitting near while the boys skinned it when a woman came along in an excited state, clapping her hands and saying "Oh Bwana, Bwana, there is a crocodile up there as big as an elephant, whose teeth are as long as my legs".

Off we went with the woman. Piet, with uncharacteristic humour and wry smile, said that we would hunt this croc for its ivories alone. However, we passed some natives and the woman related her story to them. This time the giant had shrunk to the size of a cow.

The croc was there all right, a big 14-footer. Just the knobs of its head were visible above the water. Piet planted a filed (dum-dum) 9.3 bullet clean between its eyes. Now it was the work of Dinya, one of Piet's boys. He was the bravest man I ever knew. He volunteered to do this work and got a few extra shillings for it. He was stripped off in a second and dived in after the croc. The water was only about 4ft deep at this bit and he went tramping about looking for the reptile, slapping the water with a stick in case there were any others in the vicinity. Eventually he went into the water and came up covered in blood but gripping the crocodile's tail.

Then we were into the water, the two boys and myself, with Piet covering us on the bank. We hauled the croc to the side hoping it was dead and that there were no more to come in revenge. I knew what it was like to be covered in blood, to taste the stuff as it ran with the water down my face.

When the great, repulsive body was clear of the water we set to skin it. Darkness was near and we all got into the job – it was the first time I had done that. I dug my knife in and ripped along just under the knobs on its back. In my inexperience I dug too deep and the cold blood ran down my arm. Underneath the skin was an inch thick layer of fat which the others, more skilled than I, never penetrated. The flesh was cold and clammy.

It was a heavy skin. The boys wound it round a pole and carried it between them. Back at the camp the skin was rolled up and tied to the carrier of one of two bicycles owned by boys who had the job of ferrying the skins to Piet's house where Iris saw that they salted them properly. Sometimes they would wind a smaller skin round the bar of the bicycle as well as one on the carrier and that would make a tremendous load to be ridden and pushed through fifteen to

286

twenty miles of rough territory including crossing two or three rivers by canoe. When I mentioned my admiration of the carriers, Piet played it down and said it wasn't too bad when you stuck to the main paths. But later when I did the bike-run myself I found his statement less than accurate. The following day Piet received a note from Iris, brought by one of the bicycle couriers, saying that she had had trouble with an African servant and sacked him. She wanted Piet to come home for the next few nights because she didn't want to stay by herself in case he came back for vengeance. She also wanted Piet to see about hiring another boy. Piet commandeered the bicycle and left straight away. I noted that he did not take a skin with him though there were several waiting to go, nor did he on any of the many occasions he rode home during my sojourn with him. Perhaps he felt it was *infra dig* for the boss to be seen doing such a menial task.

So within a few days of the start of my crocodile hunting career I found myself not a bystander, nor a reporter or companion, but the one in charge of the outfit, even if only for a short period and many more to come. I took it as a compliment that Piet apparently had no qualms at leaving me alone. Nevertheless I paid by repute and he by material loss for my inexperience.

Piet had a few 'safe houses' scattered about his hunting territory where he stayed regularly. These were usually in small villages or family groups of huts where he and his entourage would be given accommodation. This was always given freely and a welcome bestowed on the party for the villagers knew that in return they would be supplied with fresh meat, a rare and much desired commodity since the average tribesmen were seldom hunters. At each 'station' we left a bag of salt to be used for dusting the skins lightly for primary preservation until they arrived at Piet's house where they were washed and properly salted and so preserved until enough skins had been acquired to make a payload. Then Piet made contact with an Indian trader in Mbeya who came out with his truck and took them away and paid cash for the assignment.

Salt was an expensive and highly desirable product for Africans and what happened when I was in charge of operations while Piet went home was an insight into the African psyche of that time.

I got to the African village that the boys said Bwana Mamba used. I introduced myself to the headman and Piet's personal boy, Dinya, explained what had happened and why Piet was not with us. In good African measure another of the boys who had without invitation or instruction attached himself to me as my personal factotum, told the chief and all who had gathered to see and greet us, that I too was a famous hunter who could shoot the eye of a *mamba* at a hundred paces and would do daring deeds while I was there. It was an awful burden to hang round the neck of a novice such as I felt at that moment.

The boy who attached himself to me went by the wonderful nickname of *Boro Mrifu* (literary 'long penis'). I never knew his real name for nobody ever referred to him as anything other than that. In literary fashion it seemed rather obscene to be shouting this name out in public but after a time it became quite natural. It was his name, all he had.

It reminded me of a fellow in the Club at Nairobi whose name was George but who was introduced to me as Dick and was called that by everyone. Some time passed before I learned that Dick was short for Hickery Dick because his surname was Woodcock.

After Boro Mrifu's hyperbolic introduction I was given a bamboo hut to stay in while the others of our entourage were placed in another of lesser distinction. The natives brought me eggs, milk and bananas, free, but the headman let it be known that he hoped I could provide them with meat.

Now heavy with responsibility I went out just before sundown to look for a buck. It was very difficult to walk over the plains there. The grass was of a particularly tangled type that had several roots and loops between them which formed snares that tripped you up and, being bare-legged, tore the skin off your insteps. It was almost dark when I spotted a bushbuck. I tested the wind with a kick at a dust patch between grass clumps and went in against it. As I drew near it became suspicious and threw up its head and listened. How graceful he looked, every nerve alert, his nose in the air, his every muscle tensed for that leap that would begin his race for freedom. He leapt in the air as I hit him and went off in great bounds. My second shot broke his spine and he cartwheeled over and over. The boys cut the carcass in half and carried the pieces on poles between them into the village where they were met with great hooping, trilling and hand-clapping as Africans do.

The mosquitoes were bad that night. There were a few holes in my net and I itched all over in the morning. Boro Mrifu (pronouced Ma'ref'oo) brought me a bowl of water to wash in and one of the boys saw me take out my glass eye and clean it. I heard him gasp, "*Macho Moja*" (One eye). The word got round like wildfire. I caught a few of them gaping at my face in wonder and before long I heard one whisper "*Muchawi*" (magician) and others to whisper "*Bwana Macho Uchawi*" (Bwana Magic Eye).

I was never quite sure how to take this nickname. *Uchawi* basically meant 'Magic' or more precisely 'Black Magic' and one who practised it was a '*Muchawi*' (Witchdoctor) while a *Mganga* (Doctor) was one who practised 'White Magic', medicine, water-divining, rain-making etc. In Swahili, particularly 'Up Country Swahili', however a word could often have a wide range and I hoped they saw me as a 'goodie' rather than a 'badie'. Black or White Magic though, I fancied my status went up a notch or two and I caught one or two looking at me with some awe.

Piet was away a day or two sorting out his domestic affairs and when he returned one morning soon after 8 a.m., having left his house by bicycle before

5 a.m., I was just preparing to go up-river with the boys. They told him in glowing terms about the buck I'd shot and how well they had all eaten. I could see he was impressed although his face remained inscrutable and he said very little. A sudden light in his eye showed he was even more pleased when he saw the two croc skins I had acquired in his absence. But here came my naive fall from grace and with it an example of how natives would exploit any weakness or inexperience in any person who came amongst them with an air of authority. I had a feeling Piet was not too put out about his loss since it set me back a bit in my place.

The bag of salt was always a temptation to the headman in charge of it. It was equivalent to asking a pauper to guard gold bullion. During the past couple of days I had supervised the salting of the skins we had brought in and knowing how much the stuff was desired I belaboured the custodian that I had tied the bags with a very special knot and I would know if it had been tampered with as soon as I returned and woe betide him if any had been stolen. By the second day I knew it was being pilfered but could see no way how the bag could have been opened and tied up again exactly as I had left it.

When Piet returned I had to report the loss of some salt. Yet, I added that I was sure the bag had never been opened. Piet's eyes indeed sparkled when he told me that he knew exactly how they had done it. We went to the bag where it was lying on the floor of the hut and he rolled it over to look at the bottom of it that was dirty with the red earth. Roughly with his hand he wiped the base clean and pointed to the twine that sewed up the seam. I had to look very closely at a place where the binding had been neatly cut and the end drawn through to make a hole. When they had poured off as much as they thought would not be noticed immediately the thread had been fed back through the existing holes in the canvas material and the two severed ends stuck together with a strong gum. When rubbed along the earthen floor the incision was invisible. It was a very, very neat and crafty job and I had to admire the ingenuity and skill that had gone into it.

Piet collared the headman and laid into him verbally, and no man did it better than he. The man cringed and wrung his hands and said that the Bwana could flay him with a *kiboko* (long leather whip made from the hide of a hippopotamus) and he would not complain if it ever happened again. Piet put on a face that was the devil incarnate and asked the wretch why he had dared to steal from his bag when everyone in the village knew he had laid a curse on anyone other than his own workers who even touched it. The man, strangely, became quite lucid over this. He said he had discussed the matter with the elders of the village and they had come to the conclusion that the curse could only be invoked by Bwana Mkubwa Mamba and since the bag had been brought by the *bwana mpya* (new master) Bwana Macho Uchawi it would be all right to take some. It was a big bag and a little would not be missed. He said they had lived in great fear the first day, but when nobody died or fell into fever they took it as an omen that it would be all right to have a little more.

Piet put his brutal mask to within a couple of inches of the man's face and spoke in a low, lethal voice. He addressed the whimpering man as *chura* (frog or toad) and told him that he and all his elders were very lucky that it was Bwana Macho Moja they had dealt with. He told them that I was indeed a magician, an even greater magician than he, and if I had wanted to I could have turned him into a frog to live the rest of his life hopping around the swamps, croaking his heart out, or a dirty *fisi* (hyena) and be a scavenger, or worse, a *nyoka* (snake) to live for ever crawling on his belly. But because I was a kind magician, a stranger to the area, and a guest in his house I had deferred punishment until he, Bwana Mamba, had arrived.

So now, Piet went on, it was not the *uchawi rafiki* (friendly magician) he was dealing with, but Bwana Mamba and his magic was evil when he wanted to punish people who stole his property. He said he invoked an even greater curse on any thief who even laid a finger on any of his possessions, even if he was not there when they were brought.

And now his voice rose to thunderous volume bringing the wrath of justice down on the heads of all who would break his curse. In words that spat as fire, or curled slowly out of his twisted lips as if tortured, he warned any culprit that his fingers would wither and twist like fire-blackened twigs; his testicles would rot like last year's fruit; his wives would go barren: and if that didn't happen his sons would be born effete and never continue his line or name. There was more, much more, for Piet had a gift at this kind of oratory, all the punishment twists being worse than death.

The wonderful thing about all this was that the word went out all over his territory and nobody would dare try to see if it might not happen as they did with me. The wrath of demons hung around Piet like a wraith and nobody dared call his bluff.

*

Once again back in harness after his days away, Piet was like a man possessed, determined to make up his lost time, driving the boys and me near to exhaustion, yet appearing to be indestructible himself. But despite terrible tiredness at times I determined never to show it and when all was finished for the day, I'd do that little extra on my own, just to show I had more in me. I had been taken on because of my boast that I would never hold him back and I was determined to keep my word and bottled my fatigue under an eager exterior that said I was always ready for the extra mile. There were times when I thought we were playing the same game, that Piet the wily campaigner, had set off to break me to prove his superiority. And there were times when he nearly did, but never did land the knock-out punch. In retrospect I realised he never could, for if I was feeling blasted, he was even moreso. We were like two sluggers in a ring, weight-for-weight and punch-for-punch equal, but he with a lifetime's experience that enabled him to hide his state of mind and how he felt and the guile that let him parry and dance away from the killer punches, while I, new to the ring, had only raw heart and a fistful of years in my favour. Had I known it then, I would have been more confident with my taskmaster. Like the ageing boxer, Piet began to realise that those ten and more years between us were going to decide the match. There were times when I saw his footwork falter, his footsteps show signs of lead in them, but in my inexperience I could not put it down to his tiredness, for I thought, as he intended me to think, that he was indefatigable.

Later, gradually, I began to realise that I was Piet's equal physically and, with youth on my side, perhaps a little more. About this time I think he came to accept this too. I believe he had expected to drive me into the ground as he had done every man who had gone hunting with him on the Copper Belt, as he had told me several times. That was in the beginning and it helped to build up the awe I held him in, as it was intended to do. It was not empty boasting for I knew from what I had heard before meeting him that he had left a legend in Rhodesia as the Iron Man.

As time wore on though and he came to see that I was not going to buckle, a change came over him and our relationship. He became less harsh, less distant, less taciturn, more friendly, more human. We continued to work hard, but he no longer drove us all, himself included, to the limit.

But that was some time in the future. Meanwhile, that morning we continued the silent contest to beat each other when we set out down the Songwe river heading for Lake Nyasa. Twenty miles down narrow jungle paths and over the plain, wading waist deep across tributaries that run into the Songwe, squelching ankle-deep through mud and forcing our way through solid walls of ten feet high rushes and all the time feeding on mangoes.

Presently we came to a village where a crowd of people were gathered under the shade of a huge tree watching two men playing a game like draughts, called *bao* (board) in east Africa. It is played all over Africa and I came to the conclusion that the Bantus must have played it on their migration all the way from West Africa two thousand years ago. It is played on a board in which rows of shallow hollows have been scooped out, with small stones as 'men' that are dropped at great speed from the hand of the player into the hollows. I watched it played so often from the Indian to the Atlantic Oceans but never got the hang of it. When I asked for it to be explained it was always demonstrated so fast that it was incomprehensible to me. Perhaps the exponents treasured their secrets and it amused them to bamboozle the dim-witted white man.

On this occasion we had no time to watch and left the players to their game. Most onlookers departed the contest to give us a welcome. They brought us stools and water to wash and more to drink. The villagers told us there were crocodiles in the vicinity and they were frightened in case they came into the village at night. I was surprised at this. I thought crocs never left their river habitat. Piet said it was rare from them to do so, but it did happen. There had been occasions when the odd one had been found more than half-a-mile from water. So we went with a couple of the locals to show us where they were.

A few hundred yards away there was a small island in the smooth water on the other side of the main stream. The mound barely rose above the surface but there was a patch of fairly dense *meteti* in the middle. Lying dozing on the spit of sand, partially in the water, was a good sized croc. Piet hit it on the side of the head but though badly wounded it was still alive enough to know it had no chance in the water. Instead it darted, wobbling, into the thick *meteti* out of sight.

With the report of Piet's shot another, smaller croc hidden by the reeds suddenly dashed for the water. It was almost there when I hit it with a snap shot. It made it to the river but was wobbling from side to side as it swam and was obviously in a bad way and remained only partially submerged just off the island. What followed next could have come straight out of *Boys Own* magazine, only this was not fiction. This was real. Very, very real, and was one of the greatest highlights of my crocodile hunting saga and a stirring memory I have carried with me ever since.

With a word from Piet, Dinya went in after the wounded crocodile in the water. Powerful swimmer that he was, he had to battle manfully against the midstream current that threatened to take him away. That alone, to voluntarily dive into such a raging torrent that could be seen to be crocodile infested, was an act of great bravery. What followed next was unbelievable.

Dinya swam directly towards the crocodile which was watching him coming, swinging its tail from side to side. It had to be badly wounded or it would have gone into deep water or come for Dinya. Perhaps there was an element of surprise, even bewilderment, because this was completely against the natural order, and it did not know how best to react to it. Whatever, before it could do anything Dinya dived right under the beast and came up with his arms wrapped round the base of its tail where it could neither get round to bite him or lash him. Then ensued a wrestling match which I doubt if any man has seen the like.

The croc twisted and turned but Dinya held on, letting it have its way like playing a fish as it turned and rolled, but never letting go. I could hardly believe what I was seeing. Never had I watched such a display of sheer guts. He was shouting for us to put another bullet in it, but it was a long shot across the river and we couldn't fire for fear of hitting him.

"Piga, piga," (Hit, hit) he screamed desperately and it was terrible not to able to help him.

Piet stood and shouted and cursed him, which I thought was a callous and stupid thing to do. Perhaps this was his way of encouragement.

Gradually the crocodile's struggles became more feeble and Dinya began to make way towards the bank. But there was still some fight left in it when he rolled it onto the sandbank at the edge of the water. It seemed unable to move but its great jaws were snapping hideously only inches away from Dinya as he finally released his grip and staggered up the bank a step or two to seize a branch that was lying near, and with his last ounces of strength he smashed its head with it, then collapsed beside it.

Piet's tirade at the hero increased in pitch and vocabulary. He cursed him for a lazy, good-for-nothing, telling him to get to his feet. It was, Piet said, the only language Dinya knew and he had to whip him into life, to get him to rise from that spit of sand before the other croc, which we knew was still only feet away in the reeds, came and took him. Like a boxer fighting the knock-out mist that swam in front of his eyes Dinya hauled himself off the floor and stumbled to higher ground before crumpling up again. Then Piet turned to me and said with unusual feeling, "Man, I would never do that." It was the first time I had ever heard him show admiration for an African. Nevertheless, in admiration or not, he gave Dinya only the briefest of respite before he was at him again, lashing him with his thundering tongue, blasting through the miasma that clouded the braveheart's punch-drunk brain. And once again Dinya pulled himself up from the floor to make one last stand to finish the fight.

Piet shouted for him to beat the rushes and it was a moment before I realised he was calling for Dinya to go after the other croc in the reeds. It was then I realised how tough, brutal and absolutely right Piet was. He had to make sure the other croc was dead before he allowed Dinya to rest. It was the act of a true leader. Compassion now could be a weakness and cost the man his life. What he was asking Dinya to do was in itself was an act of the bravest of the brave.

On shaky legs Dinya retrieved his club of wood and staggered towards the place where the wounded croc had gone in to escape the bullets. With wild swings he beat the tangled reeds and somehow found his voice to shout. The crocodile, either so badly wounded it had no fight left in it or so bewildered at such behaviour by a man, turned tail and ran. It came out the way it had gone in and exposed itself to us. As it wobbled out into view Piet made no mistake with his second shot.

Piet shouted to Dinya to stay where he was and they'd come for him by canoe. So while we all went back to the village Man Friday sat alone on his little island, marooned with his grisly, erstwhile opponents. He really was a remarkable person. With the heart of a lion he obeyed Piet's every command with a slow, dog-like obedience. He was a constant target for Piet's scathing tongue and the only thanks he got, barring the few extra shillings per month, for doing what any hero would flinch at, was a good cursing. I often felt sorry for him. During the time I was with Piet Dinya performed so many acts of bravery it is hard to know how he had survived so long or how much longer he would continue to do so. Had it been in war he would have been plastered with medals. Here it was all in the day's work and he was hardly recognised for his valour. Piet said he was too stupid to know fear. But behind his abusive attitude towards Dinya Piet held a deep respect if not affection for him. Many times he told me "He is the best boy I have ever had – I'll never get another like him. But it doesn't do to tell him so." My heart went out to the brave, simple soul. All that and never a word of praise. And, as it was, when we returned to the village it was Piet who received the accolade.

The news of the killing had gone ahead and pandemonium broke loose among the people when we entered. The fear that had hung over the village for weeks had lifted now. Word was sent ahead and the rest of the inhabitants were waiting to greet us. Stools were placed under the shade of a mango tree. We sat in state while more fruit, eggs and even a live hen, was brought by a woman who, in true Konde fashion, went down on her knees before giving it to us. When a woman passes a native man she curtsies low till her knee touches the ground even though she is carrying a load on her head.

A canoe had been provided for the boys to go over to skin the crocs and bring the hides and Dinya back with them. Under the mango tree where we sat waiting for them to return no king could have been held in greater respect than Piet. It was amusing to see the people sitting staring with such awe and him sitting nonchalantly with one plump leg crossed over the other and the crown of his head sticking ridiculously through his battered hat.

After Piet left for home I went with a couple of boys to hunt meat and bagged a gazelle and a smallish wild pig, so all was merry in our little community that night. We were offered a house and I accepted gladly. The area was bad for ticks but the house looked clean enough. I decided it was worth the risk of tick fever to sleep inside with the place filled with fire smoke that dispersed the mosquitoes than lie outside and be at their mercy.

The house, a rondavel hut, was divided into two rooms by a head-high, woven reed partition so suited the him-and-them state of the class system. Actually in times like this I liked to sit round the fire with 'them' rather than on my own. That evening I enjoyed the ambience as I wrote up my diary by firelight in the boys' half while the shadows from the flickering flames danced weirdly all around and the boys squatted on their hunkers in a circle murmuring as they cooked the food. This was the Africa I came to find.

But I had to admit I enjoyed too the little bit of privacy the screen gave and

I think they preferred it too. Without the boss sitting among them they could be more at ease, and being by themselves they could speak Konde and know I could not eavesdrop. When I was beside them etiquette bade them speak Swahili, which was a second language to them.

Later, near sundown, I surprised the boys by saying I was going down to the river to see if I could see anything there. Actually, being on my own with nothing much to do, my diary was written up, time for once lay heavy on my hands and a wave of nostalgia passed over me. Not wishing to succumb to that I decided to take my rifle and mosquito net and go down by the river to see if there was a twilight croc that was tired of living. Boro Mrifu insisted on coming with me but I told him to stay. If I got anything I said I'd come and get them.

Down by the river's edge was a crocodile carcass that had been skinned up-river some days ago and put back in the water. Now it had surfaced and been carried downstream to be caught by an overhanging branch and swung into the side to lie half submerged in the mud. I had seen this carcass earlier in the day and the idea to come back to it must have then formed in the back of my mind. I wanted to be there if or when another croc came along to sample the easy meat. They liked putrid flesh and didn't seem to mind cannibalism.

When I arrived I hid myself in the rushes and covered myself with my mosquito net and lay in wait, prepared to be there some time. This was why I had turned aside Boro Mrifu's offer to accompany me. It would not have been fair to subject him to this. He would not have liked it.

It grew dark and there was only the sound of the rushing water. A hyena hooted nearby. The night prowlers were out and I was one of them, but in the darkness I was at the mercy of everything. While I relied on sight to catch my prey they only needed their nose and could pounce in the dark. From the village came the sound of singing, a man had taken himself another wife. I was waiting for the moon to rise and when it did so it spread its silver mantle. How lovely it looked through the green veil of the mosquito net. How utterly ghastly was the corpse I was guarding.

It was an awful sight. Lying belly up, stripped of its hide, bloated with inner gases, grotesque, the blubbery white body blue in the moonlight. Even then, long before public revulsion produced such reactionary groups as the Animal Protection League, I wondered if those women who bought crocodile leather shoes and handbags in the fancy, elegant shops could see what I was looking at, would they still like to wear those articles. But business, enterprise, is spawned, nurtured and thrives by public demand and we were thirty or forty years before animal rights and all that came about. This was not sophisticated London, Milan or New York. This was raw, primitive Africa where life lived off life, one animal (including the human type) killed another in order to survive and the ants cleaned up the last crumbs.

I lay for hours but eventually, stiff, damp and very tired gave up and returned to the hut. As I quietly pushed the creaky door open Boro Mrifu's wide eyes glinted over the partition. Faithful partner. He had waited awake for me.

"*Jambo Bwana. Mzuri tu, saa.*" (All is just right now) he whispered. His eyes disappeared and by the sound of his breathing he was asleep before I had my clothes off. The strain of the day had its way with me too and I followed my friend within minutes.

Next day the corpse was gone. Whether taken by the current or another croc there was no way of telling. So it was all for nothing, the risk, the discomfort, the boredom! Or was it? To this day I have the memory of that night and it reminds me so much of the Africa I knew.

*

Piet's time away was bad for business and I knew he worried about that. Not only did it keep him out of money making, it also took a bicycle out of action for ferrying the skins. The couriers were used to travelling in pairs for company and safety and although in theory one boy went with Piet he was soon left far behind and on his own, which he dreaded, because carrying no skins Piet went much faster. Not only that, but the bike Piet used was far superior to the other, as I discovered to my discomfort some time later.

While he was away I carried on by myself but I could not operate on the scale he did. My ammunition was running down and I worried about that for I had no means of getting more since I earned no money from Piet. What I shot I was content to give for my keep and experience. While at the beginning I had been prepared to operate solely as an observer, now having experienced the full life of the hunter I had no wish to continue on any other level.

Perhaps Piet could see my growing confidence and tended to arrive later and leave earlier in the afternoon to be back before dark. Nevertheless, he put in a hard working day by any standard. In order to reach our camp by 11 a.m. he would have to leave his house by 7.30 to 8 a.m., cycle twenty miles along rough paths, ford two rivers by canoe, and push the bike through several extensive marshy areas. During the four hours or so he was on-site he worked us all at fever pitch, then got on the bike again to do the twenty miles home again. Not exactly your nine-to-five job with time out for lunch and snacks. Then after dinner he would probably go out with the head lamp to bag some fresh meat. I don't think he would have any difficulty in getting to sleep. Come to think of it, neither did I.

Eventually Piet returned full-time, his domestic affairs settled at least for a time. While I was growing easier in my position of part-time in charge, I welcomed the stability of his return. Even I was getting worried at the build up of skins at the various houses and the need to get them down to Piet's place for proper salting.

Every day was exciting, but gradually even the exciting became common place and the time passed in a haze of days. But there were those days that, had we been making a graph of the daily activity, would have made high pinnacles in the jumpy line. Such as the day that started like so many with the call-to-arms in the shape of a mug of coffee and whatever was left from last night's meal eaten cold. Rolling out of the sleeping bag, donning shirt, shorts and sandshoes, doing the needful behind a tree, slunging the face from a pan of water, and we could be off down the trail within minutes, eating the last of the breakfast on-the-hoof before the sleep was properly out of our eyes and the sun only half awake.

Before getting to the operational area there was nearly always a long slog along narrow tracks through dark banana plantations and forest, stopping now and again for a drink of water. The people would bring the water and always offered something to eat too such as ripe bananas.

This was river water and against all the 'Travel Mandarins' advice to visitors to Africa never to drink unboiled water we did that all the time. Indeed in all my wanderings throughout Africa, a great deal of it living with and as the natives, I never boiled water for drinking. How I never suffered bilharzia, the scourge of people in Africa, I'll never know. Bilharzia is caused by flatworm larvae that passes through snails into fresh water and then into any bodies swimming in or drinking the water. The larvae passes into the intestines and bladder and can grow into half to one inch-long (12 to 25 mm) worms that cause inflammation, dysentery, blood in the urine and anaemia. If not treated early the disease can prove fatal. Bilharzia is essentially caused through snails and in this case the rivers being fast flowing, perhaps did not allow snails to live in them. Perhaps Piet, with antecedents going back two hundred years in Africa, had an inbred resistance to the parasite and I, living close to the ground, perhaps developed some, or maybe I was just incredibly lucky.

On this day we were heading down the Kabira, pausing at each village to ask if they knew of any crocs in the neighbourhood. Eventually, in a village on the bank of the river we were welcomed like white knights. The welcome was more exuberant than usual and we knew they had a problem. As at other places there was a particular man-eater in the vicinity and from the description it had to be the daddy-of-them-all. For once they didn't exaggerate. It had taken two women over the last month and lately it had walked boldly to the edge of the village and eaten two dogs, at different times, who had gone on their guard duties to warn it off. It sounded so like the previous killer escapade that I hoped Dinya would not be called to do a repeat performance.

Piet had an idea and I shuddered when he mentioned it. It was still fairly early in the morning and he hoped the killer would still be looking for his breakfast and not sleeping it up in some hidden sunspot. Now here was the horrible bit I dreaded witnessing. Since the croc had developed a taste for dogs Piet sent two natives of the small party that followed us back to the village to bring one. While they were gone we cut a straight branch from a tree to make the staking pole and drove it into ground, clear of the water. When the natives returned with the unlucky dog, a little mongrel, we tied it on a leash to the pole and retired to hide in the bushes nearby.

We lay in the brushwood waiting while a native threw lumps of mud at the unfortunate dog to make it yelp. This was a bit callous, I thought, but Piet said we were dealing with a man-eater so it was worth the sacrifice. Furthermore, if all went well the dog would come out of it unscathed.

I lost track of the time we waited. The dog yelped pitifully and pulled at the rope while I desperately wanted this nightmare to end. Presently, from the other side of the river, a pair of eyes appeared on the water, making towards the dog, leaving a trail of 'V' ripples as it came. Tension mounted in the bushes where we lay. Could the beast be enticed out of the water? Would it see or smell us? Would the natives keep quiet enough at the crucial time? Apprehension throbbed.

When its feet touched land it looked about then began slowly to climb out of the water on to the bank. It was huge and must have stood four feet at the shoulders and its tail was still in the water when its head was more than a long room's length up on the beach. What a repulsive sight! To make it more grotesque, more fearsome, out of its back grew half a wide spearhead. It had been stuck a long time ago for the shaft had broken off and the visible part of the blade was deeply rusted and corroded. To make the wound more hideous the thick, knobbly, horny skin had grown round the blade so that it appeared as a mound on the creature's back, topped by the rusting iron. It was obviously old, very old and perhaps past hunting, too slow to swipe an animal drinking and at its mercy into the water with its tail. Maybe that was why it had turned man-eater, made it go for the weak, slow humans: or was it intelligent enough to go in revenge for the kind of animal that had speared it and caused it so much pain? Whatever the reason or cause it now looked a terribly dangerous, repulsive and yet a sorry creature.

But as soon as I thought that, I knew any sympathy was misplaced. I mused as I waited that an African would not attack a crocodile with a spear unless he really had to. Africans do not hunt for sport. They only kill if they feel it is necessary. And they did not eat crocodile. There is only one time the average native would go that close to a crocodile and that is if the reptile had grabbed his wife or one of his family. So now, that spear head conjured up a horrific picture of a woman in the crocodile's jaws and her husband, throwing caution for himself to the wind, leaping onto the creature's back and plunging his spear into it. It had to be that. A thrown spear would have gone in at an angle and not so far in. This one had gone straight down as a lunge into its back in an attempt to make the creature drop its prize. Any sympathy or doubt I had harboured was dissolved by a cold, avenger's passion.

The dog's yelping was now reduced to a whimper and for a moment I put myself into its position watching this monster reptile lumbering up to me heaving one short, bow leg in front of the other, its two saucer eyes cold, hypnotic and merciless. The crocodile has not changed one bit since the dinosaur era. This really was a prehistoric monster lumbering up the beach towards us.

I shook my head to get rid of the vision and raised my rifle. We were both waiting until it was completely clear of the water. Piet was placed for a side shot while I had a full frontal position. We dare not miss. I remembered Boro Mrifu bragging that I could shoot out a crocodile's eye at a hundred paces; could I now be sure of doing that at half that distance. Slowly, slowly, nearer, nearer. We held our breath.

Suddenly, within feet of the dog, now silent and wetting itself, the great beast stopped and we saw it stiffen. It was wary, on its guard. Had it caught our scent? Had it spotted one of the natives in the bush behind us, they had become restive from the growing fear or excitement, for it suddenly made to whip round and scamper for the water. A croc can move fast on land despite its awkward bulk. But before it could move we both fired together. Piet went for a heart shot while I indeed hit it through the eye for a brain shot and saw splinters from the back of its head splatter about. The combined firepower stopped the beast dead in its tracks. My first impulse was to go and release the dog. At first it was too frightened, mesmerised even, to move. But I smacked its rump and it scampered off.

When skinning a croc usually only the belly hide was stripped but with this one we decided to have a look at its back where the spear blade had entered. We were surprised to find that there was practically no metal showing inside. The stomach acids had almost completely eroded it away. The upper half of the spearhead was now held in place by the mound of carapaced growth that had grown up round it. Such were the natural healing powers of nature.

Having gone so far, Piet decided to have a look inside the stomach. When we cut it open we found quite a number of articles that marked the man-eater's long life as a serial killer. There were some bangles, ivory and silver, buttons and even the blade of a knife, partially dissolved by the stomach juices. Only the noble metal articles remained intact. No doubt a long list of ferrous metal articles of apparel and weapons had long since disappeared. Quite a number of human bodies had been processed and passed through this chamber. In this case we felt we had been agents of justice rather than mere hunters. The villagers certainly looked to us as such and gratefully paid their thanks in kind, far more than we could take with us. The place was stunned with a sudden air of euphoria. There would be great dancing and merrymaking tonight.

The day was still young and if the events so far had raised the peaks of the memory graph above the norm, more was to come to push the summits even higher. We crossed the Kabira by canoe ferry and made our way upriver, trawling the banks, asking at the villages until we were well up where the river was running fast and wild. Piet shot two sizeable ones and I nailed a smallish fat one.

Piet said it was the fattest one he had ever seen which was a great bonus, for the skins were priced by measuring across the body. Small, wide skins were therefore likely to be more valuable than longer, narrower ones. In addition, these small stout crocs, like people, being less active were less likely to be aggressive, so usually bore less scar callouses from fighting – known as 'buttons' – than the larger ones often had. In the cordwainer business these scar marks had to be cut out and so lessened the skin's value. Piet was paid two shillings and sixpence per inch for good skins and the average was about thirty inches wide (£3.75p new pence). Looking back, especially from today's prices, it was not very much for the danger and hardship by which the merchandise was won. All the way up the marketing tree, each one who handled the article earned more and more for less and less.

Within the next hour I was to learn just how much these skins could cost and how dangerous was this trade we were following.

The afternoon was wearing on when we arrived at one of the regular canoe ferry points and Piet decided to call it a day and go over and make the way back to our base. We had a fair load of skins and Piet sent the boys over with these and told the ferryman to come back for us. As an afterthought, and most unusually, he put the rifles in with the skins. The canoe went off and returned for us some time later.

The canoe was none too big, barely enough room to squeeze your buttocks between the concave rims of the sides and once seated you felt you were padlocked in round the waist. All went well until we got out to midstream where the current was a mad cascade of swirling, white-crested brown water, rutted like a deeply ploughed field. I don't think the ferryman was all that experienced. He was young and we had not seen him before. Perhaps he was nervous of having white men in his boat, no doubt the first he had ever had in his charge. Whatever the reason, he chose an awful moment to make his first mistake.

He must have misjudged his timing and put too much of the nose into the current. We developed a wobble which the more we tried to rectify the worse it got. The canoe tilted to a frightening angle and then capsized. For a terrifying moment I thought I was jammed in, suspended upside down. Then I felt the current tear at me like giant, clutching fingers, clawing me out of the cockleshell trap and pulling me down into its dark, wildly turbulent depths. I struck out with panicked strength, fighting the downward force, and suddenly the rush of water was in my ears and I came to the surface. I called to Piet and his answer was faint above the noise of the water way upstream. The current had borne me quite a way down. I struck out for the bank hoping no crocodiles were near. The bushes on the bank were passing by like the scenery from the windows of a train. I seemed to be making slow progress. Further downstream I saw a huge tree with its branches stretched over the water and I used all my strength in a bid to make up the leeway. I thought I was going to be swept past but the outer branches were just within my reach and I made a wild grab to reach one. My fingers gripped and that nightmare journey ended.

Still in the water I worked my way along the branch with my hands. There were a lot of bushes along the water's edge that seemed a natural place for crocodile and I prayed there were none as I dangled in the water. I managed to swing myself onto the branch and climbed along it and jumped to safety on the bank.

I quickly made my way back to Piet. He had come up near enough to the canoe to make a grab at it. The ferryman had also been near and he still held on to the paddle, so between them they managed to make their way to the bank. So apart from a bit of a shake-up it seemed we were all back to normal again. I was thankful we had sent the rifles over on the first canoe. Had they gone down I did not know how I would have approached the major to tell him I had lost his rifle.

I did have a worry about my camera though. I always carried it in its case attached to my belt. Wherever I went it always went with me, including swimming in the river, unfortunately. I tried it and it didn't work but I thought it might be all right when it dried out. I was more concerned with the film in it and feared it would be ruined. This was a terrible disappointment. As a 36-shot 35mm reel it had all my crocodile hunting photographs on it. Weeks and weeks, months, of wonderful stuff ruined. The loss was a blow I can hardly describe.

I didn't have much time to dwell on my bereavement for quite a lot happened in a short time just then. We were making our way down the path towards the tree where I climbed out of the river when Piet's eagle eyes spotted a large crocodile carcass, bellyside up, coming down with the current. Piet shouted to Dinya who grabbed a rope, ran along the branch on which I had come ashore, and dived in. He swam strongly out to the where the corpse was coming down to him and as it passed he looped the rope round the head and swam back, pulling the body with him. What a man!

While all this was going on, however, dire things were happening here on the bank beside us. When Dinya dived into the water there was a rustling in the undergrowth not twenty yards from this tree where I had pulled myself out of the water and a crocodile, which must have been there then, slid out and made to enter the river. Instinct told Piet what it was and though facing the wrong way while watching Dinya he was already swinging his rifle up to his shoulder while on the turn. In doing this he struck a branch with the rifle muzzle and was thrown off balance. Without taking time to steady himself he fired on the way down, rolled over and hit the croc again with a shot while spread out on the ground. It was a fine demonstration of automatic reaction and it may well have saved Dinya's life for there was little wonder what the beast had in its mind.

Oblivious to the drama that had gone on in his absence Dinya swam in and pulled himself out of the water, still holding the rope. He gave the dead croc at the water's edge no more than a cursory glance with eyes that had seen it all so often while he tied the rope to a branch. We hauled the bloated corpse into the shore and set about skinning it. It would have been shot a day or maybe two before and would have sunk and remained submerged until the internal gases blew it up and it would then have risen like a balloon, perhaps the night before, and come floating downstream. If left too long the scales lift with heat of the sun. But if caught in time the skin could be worth having even if sold as second quality. In their blown-up state they are not a very nice sight but they skin easier because their hide is tight and cuts easily. But you had to be careful not to cut too deep and puncture the inner skin and allow the gasses to escape. You paid dearly for that mistake, as I knew at the beginning, for the stench is a bit overpowering. More truthfully, it is absolutely awful and the smell hangs about you for days even if you bathe in the river, which we did often, so long as one of us was standing by the side with his rifle cocked. Where crocodiles have risen like this one the skin must be salted immediately or else the scales come off.

There were now two crocs to skin and Piet chivvied the boys to be quick. I went to help with the one that had just been shot when I heard Piet explode with a strong Africaans expletive, which surprised me. I was used to his strong, brutal even, language to the boys in KiSwahili and Konde but he was not usually given to blaspheme in Africaans or English. This time he had good reason. He had just noticed he had lost the foresight of his rifle. The knock on the tree as he was going after the crocodile must have loosened it and now it had dropped off. I went to help him look for it. On hands and knees we separated grass and leaves and twigs and, miraculously, found it.

Fixing the sight on again was now a real problem and from this crisis an interesting little example of native life emerged. Seeing Piet's consternation one of the boys said for him not to worry, he would fix it. So saying, he disappeared into the bush and returned with a little branch of tree. It was green and looked like a holly branch. He quickly gathered some dried grass and leaves and small twigs, laid them in a pile and asked Piet to light the gathering. This done he held the branch he had brought over the flame, turning it so it didn't catch fire, warming it until the sap oozed out through the bark. Then he broke a stick to form a flat side and edge of new wood which he used as a spatula to scrape off some of the sap from the heated stick and spread the thick residue on the rifle barrel and stuck the foresight on again. The mark of where the sight had lain before was plainly visible so placing it accurately was not difficult. We laughed at the well-meaning effort but placed no confidence in the repair. Plant adhesives, such as gum-arabic, had been around since the beginning of time, but everyone knew they were only used for sticking paper and theatre moustaches and the like. But what was required here was heavy-duty stuff, way out of the gum league.

By the time we arrived back at camp Piet had made up his mind to go home and solder the sight on properly. The day was already well worn but if he put on a spurt he reckoned he would make it before dark.

Left on my own I could now look at my own troubles with my camera. I felt absolutely lost without it. Having tried it again and finding it still not working I carefully wound back the film into its cassette and opened the back. There was still some dampness so placing it on a large leaf I left it outside to gather the last couple of hours of sunshine. After the evening meal and the fall of darkness I took the camera indoors and left it near the fire, partially closed to avoid smoke dust entering it, and willed it to work in the morning. When this did not happen I decided I must do as Piet had done and go down to the big, wide world of Tukuyu to see if I could get the camera repaired.

Piet arrived back before midday next day with his rifle sight properly fixed with metal solder. I admired the workmanlike job he had done and reflected that a man in the wilderness has to be a Jack-of-all-trades and master of every one. Regarding the repair of the previous day he had an interesting comment to make that was, as mentioned previously, an insight into African native life. Piet told me that when he tried to take the rifle sight off to allow him to use solder, it wouldn't budge. Even a tap from a hammer refused to shift it. He had to heat it up again before it would come off. It is a remarkable glue that sticks metal to metal as efficiently as that. This was long before modern glues such as Epoxy were discovered or invented. Had it been exported to Europe it would have out-performed anything on the market then. Afterwards I regretted that I never learned the name of the tree. We didn't go back to that area during the rest of my time with Piet and the incident was soon lost in the hurly-burly of a busy life.

When I mentioned to Piet my decision to go away for a day or two to try and get my camera working again I could see he was not pleased, which I took as a compliment, remembering how reluctant he was in taking me on. But he could see my mind was made up and asked where I would go. I said I'd go down to the soap factory for the night and go to Kyiambili tomorrow. My friends there might know someone who could have a look at it. I said I'd take the bloated skin with me so it could be properly salted but Piet said it was better I didn't, I'd have enough to cope with just cycling. But I insisted, saying it was the least I could do when I was taking time off. What I did not say was that I had to prove a point to myself that I would not do as Piet did by going empty-handed each time he went down and I'd show the natives that I did not consider myself above that kind of work. I have got to say though there were times on the way I wished I had taken Piet's advice and not been so idealistic. We shared a bite of lunch together then I got on my way.

It was quite a journey and made worse by being nearly all uphill. The bike was rather old and decrepit and the more I travelled on it the more my respect grew for the native who owned and rode it. To do a 40-mile round trip on it daily over such rough terrain was really Herculean work. Sometimes he would do one-and-half round journeys in a day, staying at the opposite end to the previous night. This would mean 50 or 60 miles in a day, depending on where in the river country we were working, and the further I got along the way the more I realised what that meant.

In its own way it was quite an ingenious machine, a masterpiece of improvisation. There was no front spindle, merely a six-inch nail with the prongs at the end of the forks squeezed to keep it in place. It had no fancy gadgets such as brakes, seat, mudguards or rubber pedals. For a seat there was an old sack wound round the prong where once a comfortable, leather gadget had been fixed. And as a minor irritant the chain was slack and kept coming off. I carried three skins, two at the back on the shaky remnants of a carrier and one wound round the bar so that I had to peddle with my knees splayed out like a Sumu wrestler.

It creaked and groaned up hills and with no brakes and the load of skins putting weight behind it, plummeted down them with me completely at its mercy. In some places where the land was waterlogged due to the heavy rain the bike had to be pushed and sometimes carried for a mile or more until I got onto the main path. Carrying it with skins attached was no joke. Where I could see that portage was going to be some distance I took the skins off, carried the bike over, then went back for the skins. The time lost in untying the load, making the double journey and reloading, tore shreds off the remainder of the day.

It was not until I had a puncture that I learned the full extent of the machine's ingenuity. On taking out the inner tube I found there had been many previous punctures, but no sticky patches had been used. Instead, the rubber round the hole had been gathered up and tied with string. Who said the African was backward? It took a nimble mind to think that one up. Oh! mine was a fine bike! I could see now why the boys liked to travel in pairs.

Once on the main path there was some traffic of people. Not many, the odd couple of women with baskets or bundles on their heads and occasionally a man or two, some on bicycles. Women never rode these fangled machines.

Everyone I met was very courteous to me and to each other. When they passed they never failed to greet each other in Konde.

"Wanile."

"Ndaga, Wanile."

"Ndagio."

Always *Ndaga* (Thank you).

Joseph Thomson was right, politeness and manners was indeed the natural way with these hill people. In a land more noted for its savagery, of man's inhumanity to man, this was indeed an Arcadia, perhaps even a Utopia. It was strange and rather moving to see natives flashing past on their bikes and taking their eyes off the pot-holed path to lift their hats or raise their hand to show their palm in salute to me and to others. One or two actually stopped their bicycles and got off just to do this when they saw me coming. At the time I wondered if the over show of politeness was a legacy of the German iron rule from the time when they were in charge of the country but later, when I read of Thomson's remarks on these people at a time before foreign domination, I accepted that this was their natural way.

Crossing the rivers by canoe ferry was not an experience for the faint hearted. The skins had to be unloaded and put in the belly of the canoe and the bicycle laid crossways with the wheels dangling over each side. The rifle I kept strapped to my back even though it was awkward sitting with it that way. After the previous incident I was wary of losing it to the bottom of the river. On my back, if I had to swim, it went with me. A wetting would not damage it. I was certainly more aware of the crossings now. Prior to the tumble I had put my complete faith in the skill of the native paddler and crossed light-heartedly. Now I watched his every move.

I had another puncture; the tyres were as smooth as a balloon and nearly as thin. With each one I had to release some rope from the skins on the carrier, fray the end and tease out a strand thin and strong enough to tie up the tube, put it all back and pump up the tyre. I felt sorry for the owner trying to keep his transport business going with a machine like this. On top of this, Piet made use of either bike at will. I couldn't bring myself to ask him if he paid the owners for his personal use but I very much doubted that he did.

With the punctures and all it was nearly dark when I wheeled into Piet's place and unloaded the skins. Iris bustled out and halted in her tracks, obviously expecting to see Piet. When she took in the situation she greeted me like a long lost friend, even giving me a kiss on the cheek, and was full of questions and comments.

"Why have you come? You've been in the *bundu* for weeks! Let me look at you. My, you look awful. That great beard you've grown, I wouldn't have recognised you in the street. And look at your legs, all these veldt sores. Oh I must give you some ointment for those. Pieter never said anything about them or how you were. And your shoes, in tatters and all tied up with riems. What a mess you're in." She followed me as I picked up a skin under each arm and made my way to the salting shed and watched as I unrolled them on the pile already there. Then she added with a funny smile on her face, "But that hard work and the outdoors has obviously been good for you. You look so big and strong," and as she spoke she laid her hand on my shoulder and squeezed tightly.

I took up the shovel and went over to the salt barrel, but she would have none of it. No, no, the boys did that job, and I must be famished for a cup of tea and, I had to admit, I was. Over the tea she found out all my news, such as it was for all the days seemed to have run into one, and about my camera being the reason for my coming in from the bush. She asked me what I intended doing and I told her.

"Go down to the soap factory! You'll do nothing of the kind. There will no comfort for you there, and if old man Williamson is not expecting you he won't have a bite to eat for you." I knew this to be true and had no expectations in that direction. "Anyway," she prattled on, "it's almost dark. You never know what you could meet on the way down there." She seemed to have forgotten that I had walked that road several times on pitch dark and starbright nights. She went on without a pause in case, perhaps, I might remind her, "There's no reason why you can't stay here tonight. The girls are away at school so there's the spare room you can have and you can catch the bus up to Tukuyu tomorrow. You look as if you could do with a good bath and put your feet up for the evening. I'll get the boys to fill up the bath in the outhouse with lovely hot water and give them soap and a big soft towel to take in for you. While you're bathing I'll make a little dinner for us."

Her words fell over me like a balm, dulling my senses as a narcotic. The sheer pleasure of being looked after by a woman, the tenderness, the comfort, the bliss was the antithesis of what my life had been for what seemed an awfully long time. To turn down all that she had said for the dark, concrete floor of the soap factory and a chew of biltong that I carried in my pocket seemed the height of madness. I smiled my acceptance and went and put my small pack and rifle in her spare room. In the heady euphoria I inarticulately mumbled my thanks, for naïve, young, bumpkin fool that I was, I believed she was doing it all through kindness.

But if inexperience had not sharpened my perception of the older, predatory woman I was under no illusions when I went into dinner after bathing, combing my hair and trying valiantly to untangle my hayrick beard. Anytime I had eaten here the meal was always wholesome but very much plain fare. Little attempt was made at refinements, but this time a square of cloth laid diamond fashion decorated the table and cutlery was laid out rather than handed out with each dish. Even more atmospheric, in place of the universal tin lamps that always graced the night, two candles, usually kept for emergency in the event of the oil running out, lit up each end of the table.

Further and even more alarming to me, Iris was dressed to kill, literally. She had on her war paint; her lips were more red than usual, her eyes outlined with mascara and her cheeks heightened with rouge. More dangerous still, she was wearing a dress that was not intended to be off-the-shoulder but she had made it so by not doing up enough buttons, so revealing her bronzed shoulders and a deep, startling cleavage. Iris was a Joan-of-Arc, encased in armour with her banner flying for all to see her intent, her whole aura trumpeted her fanfare, heralding her charge to battle.

Tonight the boys had been dismissed and Iris had done the cooking and serving herself. When she filled my plate she stood so close she brushed my cheek with her hand, said, "Sorry," and did the same on the way back. When she served herself at the other end of the table she faced me directly and bent so low I might have seen her shoes down her cleavage if the table hadn't been in the way.

Now all the alarm bells were ringing and I felt trapped and way out my depth. Any girls I'd known had all been rather shy and reticent. I'd never been drawn to the forward, brassy types and in their company was always tongue-tied and awkward. Now, having a female tigress literally breathing down my neck I was in a panic, though I tried not to show it. In my monastic life I should have been climbing up the wall, and in my mind I was, but this was a married woman, my boss, my mentor, the wife of my friend – yes we had developed a close bond – and I had no wish to cuckold any man, least of all him. And, apart from moral grounds, I knew it would be only a suicidal, hari-kari idiot who would even try it.

Suddenly, I was struck by a bolt of lightning and clear perspicacity. This was what it had been all about. This was what had happened over and over again during their time on the Copper Belt. There, where all the men were digging copper, Iris had struck a gold mine of young, womanless men, each willing to risk his life for one of her gold nuggets. This explained all the mystery about their being here, why a man brings his wife and children and buries them in the *bundu,* as lost to civilisation as on a desert island. It made sense of their not making any attempt to socialise with the few whites in the district. The last thing Piet wanted was for Iris to have any contact with other men and she would never have wanted to invite the wives to her native-style abode. How Iris must have missed the company. It lifted the lid off Piet's pub brawling for I could never understand that. You get to know someone you've been as close as I'd been to Piet in the past months and despite his rough play-acting with the natives he never seemed to me to be a mindless, boozy, violent man. Oh yes, he could dish it out if needs be, as was proven, but he was not a drinker, not a man who craved liquor. Apart from an occasional bowl of palm wine down by the lake sometimes after a long walk, which I enjoyed too, I never saw him touch alcohol nor hear him mention it. Now I could see why he sought out those men in pubs whom he believed had meddled with his wife. And knowing Iris he knew that some day he would go too far in his rage and be had up for a killing.

It was his way of escaping a very likely tragedy in their future. And it made clear every word that was said when I walked into their lives. Piet must have looked at me in horror, seeing in me all the ramparts he had built between Iris and men being destroyed; knowing I would be as a bottle of whisky left in front of a dried-out alcoholic. It explained why he kept me out hunting till last thing at night and whipped me off into the bush the very next day, out of harm's way, and kept me there. And yesterday why he did not want me to bring down the skin because it meant I had to go to his house with it and, knowing Iris, he knew she would not let me out of her clutches until she had her way with me. No one knows better than the hunter the animal actions and interaction, and that includes the human species.

As the dinner wore on Iris went from coquetry to innuendo and onto plain, brazen 'come and get it'. She was standing sideways toying with the buttons on her dress and flashing me a look when she said, "What would you like for sweet … Me?" Before I had time to think of a reply the door swung open and Piet stood there, his bulk filling the doorway, rifle slung from his shoulder, bald pate sticking through his comic, tattered hat, just looking. There had been no warning, no footsteps. Piet had approached with a hunter's stealth.

Luckily Iris had her back to the door with her long hair covering her shoulders, and as she glanced round she suddenly doubled in a paroxysm of coughs and sneezes. By the time her spasm had subsided and she was able to straighten up she had somehow managed to wipe most her make-up off and pull her dress back into place and do up some buttons. She said, "Sorry darling, it must have been the door swinging open that startled me and made me catch my breath," and went over and kissed him.

Piet walked in and never said a word, but his eyes were fires burning into both of us, taking in the set table, missing nothing. Iris prattled at high speed to fill the unforgiving minute, saying what a wonderful surprise 'to see you back, darling' and busied herself laying another place at the table. Piet remained silent but I could see he hadn't missed a trick. He had the hunter's eye for detail and atmosphere and could read a situation in a glance. Where I expected his hostility and anger he gave me a nod of welcome and settled down in the chair. Not a word of why I was not down at the soap factory. Had his eagle eye seen that the look on my face, even behind the matted beard, had been one of intense relief rather than fear or anger and frustration when he arrived. He put his elbow on the table and rested his head on his fist thoughtfully, his eyes following Iris's back as she high-heeled into the kitchen – so ludicrously inappropriate in the bush – still filling the room with nervous chatter. When she disappeared through the doorway his eyes slid round to me and did the corners of his mouth lift almost imperceptibly in the merest hint of a conspiratorial smile?

After a cup of coffee I said I would be on my way to the soap factory but Piet said not to be crazy, now he was home there was no reason for me not to stay in the spare room. On the pretext that it had been a long day I retired blissfully and went to sleep to the low babble of conversation, or was it recriminations, and the sound of sobbing and tears coming from the other room.

*

Piet said that after I left and was likely to be away for a few days he decided that he would take the time off too and use the break to arrange to have his stock of skins taken into his buyer in Mbeya. He was running short of ammunition too and with cash in hand from the sale of the skins he would be able to buy some more and even allow Iris to do a little shopping, which was the highlight of her life. It was all necessary stuff for their lifestyle, but we all three knew that he was plastering over the cracks and were each aware of the real reason for his actions. This allowed our lives to carry on as normal but I was sure they both, like me, had horrific images of what the scene might have been like today if Piet had walked into a situation that had gone too far.

Piet had left instructions with the boys to bring in all the outlying skins over the next day or so. He sent a note with the driver of the daily bus to his buyer in Mbeya to send out a truck and driver to collect his consignment of skins. He intended Iris and he to travel in on the truck, see his sale through, and for both to return by bus.

I left them and got on the road to Kyiambili and did not walk far before getting a lift to the door. I received a warm welcome from Messrs Park and Strickland and enjoyed a few days of blissful relaxation and reading in the warm, tranquil ambience of the wonderful old house. Rather than lament my appearance as Iris had, the men warmed to me even more when they saw the authenticity of bush life in my appearance and apparel. No doubt I reminded them of their own bygone days and in a way were reliving them through my association with them. The Major had a woman take away my clothes to launder and mend as best as she could and loaned me clean shorts and shirt until my own were returned. Unbeknown to me he sent a boy into Tukuyu to buy me a new pair of sandshoes after he had established my size and would take no payment for them. It was all like coming home and being fussed and pampered and appreciated.

The camera problem was beyond them though. There was nowhere near where I was likely to get any repairs done. Major Strickland scoffed at any idea of getting camera repairs done in Tukuyu and was quite sure I would not find anywhere even in Mbeya. For things like that, he said, you had to go or send to Dar or Nairobi.

So saying, he left the room and to my surprise returned with his own camera which, without hesitation, he offered to me. It was a folding 120 (now known as 'medium format') job similar to my own, so I could use my own films that I had in my rucksack at the soap factory. As with the rifle I protested profusely, but he would have none of it. "You can't go home without a photo record of what you've been up to in Darkest Africa. What about this book you're going to write?" Knowing how my own camera had been ruined and how easily his could follow suit, his act was one of extraordinary generosity. He even threw in another carton of rifle ammunition to keep me going in the same off-hand manner and just waved his hand when I protested.

After talking around the camera situation with various residents, it was obvious I was not going to get any repairs done until I got into Southern Africa, so I decided on a bold, cheeky move. I had had a couple of articles published in the Johannesburg *Sunday Times* and on this slender connection I parcelled up my camera and sent it by post to the editor, explaining my predicament, and asked if he would have it mended and send it to poste restante Blantyre, Nyasaland, and I would settle all accounts when I arrived in South Africa in a few months' time. Surprisingly it worked like a charm and the whole procedure was an example of the excellent postal communications and trust that existed in Africa in those days.

Piet and Iris arrived back from Mbeya and we immediately made plans to return to the fray. Piet had had a hippopotamus added to his hunting licence and had purchased a couple of dozen great meat hooks used by butchers for hanging full beef carcasses. Many times we had discussed a great idea of his while down at the lake, but I had never thought I would ever see it put into action. It transpired that it was because I was with him that he now decided the time was opportune to try it.

With this and in many other ways I felt I had crossed a watershed with Piet following the fiasco with Iris. When we returned to the bush after that incident there was an openness between us that had not been there before. There was no doubt that Piet had read the scene accurately, had seen my reluctance, despair even, and knew exactly where the danger lay. He now gave a trust to our relationship that had not been there before. Iris's attitude to me also changed, but in the other direction. Whereas before she had been sweet and warm, she was now rather distant and cold. Whether through embarrassment or realisation that the future in that direction was now bleak, I was too ignorant or inexperienced in the wiles of women to know.

Piet's great wheeze was the idea of catching crocodiles like fish, but on land rather than in the water. I had already passed it off as hairbrained, but who was I to doubt the master. We set off as close as two schoolboys on a new adventure.

We followed our usual course south-west, keeping to the highlands, comparable with the lie of Tukuyu, until we came to the river Piet had decided to follow down to the lake. On the approach to the lake, the rivers tended to run into each other by way of a web of tributaries and marshlands. I was always amazed how quickly the terrain changed over the thirty miles or so of, to use South African jargon, high and low veldt over which we ranged. In one day's tramp you could walk through wide grassland studded with sparse, flat-topped acacia trees, where the air was dry and the breeze could be cool. You could go for miles by the river without hardly seeing the sun except through the forest roof formed of great branches and big leaves of tall trees, and nearer the lake where the air grew steadily more hot and humid, drop into a native village and slake your thirst with a cupful of fresh, unfermented palm wine.

On this day when crossing a savannah plain between the Kibera and Songwe Rivers we spotted a small herd of buffalo and Piet decided to go after them and bag one or two for trading. On the open plain they would be difficult to approach, but further on the open land gave way to the belt of river forest. On the left the land rose sharply and on the right it dropped steeply towards the river bed. If driven, the herd would most likely keep to the flat stretch that ran into the trees and shelter. The only thing against that for them would be that we would be there, waiting.

The plan made, Piet and I set off on a wide circle that would bring us, hidden, in front of the herd. I was a bit apprehensive about the hunt since I had heard that the buffalo is one of the most dangerous animals to hunt. It was said that the buffalo would charge on sight and had the cunning of a maniac to wait and ambush the stalker or to double back and take him from the rear. And if a buffalo is wounded but still on its feet, then woe betide the hunter. In Africa they don't say 'as crafty as a fox', they say 'as cunning as a wounded buffalo'.

Mad attackers they may be as individuals, but in a herd they can be stampeded by beaters and that was what Piet intended. Near the river the grass was high and the undergrowth thick. From this tangle we emerged near the outer edge of the forest line and climbed a tree that was far enough back to hide us but near enough the front to allow us to look out to the plain and watch the herd approach. Piet gave a long, high-pitched whistle that could have been a bird. Dinya, Boro Mrifu and the others caught the whistle signal and the hunt began.

The boys moved forward in a wide line shouting as loud as they could. As they drew nearer the herd became restless, some throwing up their heads and others just staring as buffalo do. At last they got on the move and without hurry approached the way we hoped they would take. They all stopped at once and milled around, edgy but not in panic.

The boys drew closer, the tension rose. Which way would the beasts go, to us or turn and charge the line? The beaters slowed their pace. We knew how frightened they must feel. It was a toss-up as to who was going to break and run first. The animals cracked a split second before the men seemed as if they would. As if orchestrated by a leader the herd charged forward, but not along the way we had expected. Instead they broke to the side, preferring to go down the steep slope in the shortest line to the forest and were lost from view in seconds. Once buried in the bush they stopped as if knowing their sound of movement would show their position, showing once again, it seemed, that they were led by a wily old campaigner.

The beaters followed them in, and now they would be scared. They could see practically nothing in front of them and if the herd chose not to move the men would stumble on them and have no time to run.

Up in the branches of the tree we waited, tensed. A long time passed. There was not a sound except the "Whaugh" "Whaugh" of the beaters. There was not a sign of the buffalo and for a time we thought the boys had made a mistake in their place. The buffalo, unlike antelopes, held their silence and position. The tree in which we sat was not very big and I seemed to be awfully near the ground. Was there room for a buffalo to pass under me? Would a passing one be able to catch me with a lift of its horns? The tension mounted as the beaters drew near.

It happened in a flash. The air was suddenly filled with snorts and bellows and the whole area seemed to come to life. A herd of about twenty in wild stampede bore down on us. The big knot in my stomach was gone with the sudden action. I remember only feeling immensely pleased with myself at seeing them coming, the great heaving mass of animal power, jam-packed, steaming with exertion, heads down, pounding, pounding, death to all caught up in front of them, the earth vibrating, trees shaking and the thrill of the hunt was like electric currents running through me. I was waiting for Piet to shoot but he didn't. They came right under us, so close, a mere couple of feet, that the steam and heat and thick smell of their sweat engulfed us in a heavy cloud that clawed at your throat and stopped your breath. But suddenly they swerved to the right and were gone in thick bush before we could get a shot in.

It would have been easy just to shoot into the herd and hoped some dropped, but a professional hunter would not do that. His is the quick kill or not at all. Later, Piet said he had not wanted to drop one at the front that might have caused panic in the herd. That way the felled one might have been trampled and had its hide and horns, both saleable items, damaged. He wanted to get one near the back of the herd but the sudden change of direction wrong-footed him.

We cursed our luck and went after them but that was the only time we got near them. Three more times we tried to encircle them but they were wary now and before we could get into position we heard them crashing away from us until, beaten, we gave up the chase. My feelings were quite ambivalent. I was sorry we had not succeeded in the hunt, for the sake of the experience of it all and for Piet's sake. But I had had the thrill of the chase and I would have been sorry to have seen one of those magnificent animals as beef.

Apart from that, this would not have been a good place to have done major meat trading for all the barter produce would have had to be portered a long way and across the Kibira and Mbaka rivers to be taken to Piet's place for preserving and storage. Better to do that kind of business on the north side of the Mbaka so the transportation would not involve crossing rivers.

*

Towards evening that day we dropped into a native hut where we were given a meal of cassava, bananas and ground nuts. The natives still grew these nuts successfully despite the British fiasco of trying to do so. Piet decided to stay there that night and we were given accommodation. Hospitality was never refused. Over the next couple of days we made our way down to the lake. Piet shot a few crocs en route, of which I had a hand in some. It was at the lake Piet had mind to put his idea into practice.

Nearing the area Piet made his way to a little village where he had a 'salt station'. We were given a great welcome and settled in. The place was just before reaching the delta and high enough for the land not to be marsh. But it was near enough the lake for the mosquitoes to be thunderous in their night song and murderous in their intentions.

It's a hard life this, I thought as I turned in. You go on from first thing in the morning to last thing at night, walking, walking, wading across tributary rivers, forcing through bushes, sliding and sometimes crawling through mud. You must get an evening meal over before dark and, just when you are feeling all in and want to sleep, the mosquitoes find their way into your net and make sleep impossible. You scratch and tear at the itchy lumps they leave until the blood runs. Next day the flies get at those scratches and turn them into septic sores. You scratch and tear and curse and sweat until through sheer exhaustion from the day's exertions you find blissful sleep.

Once by the lake Piet put into action his idea of hooking crocodiles. The lake ones were usually much bigger than those in the rivers but hunting them was different game to getting the river ones. You had to have a good boat, not a canoe, on the lake and hunt at night with search beam and gaff, all of which was beyond Piet's pocket. He hoped to hook the crocs on the shore.

Just getting to the shore from up river was not easy and quite dangerous. The delta formed by the rivers was a wide waterlogged area tufted by little meteti-covered islands. You had to wade through from island to island. It was a not all that deep, knee to thigh mostly, but there were times it was shoulder high and we carried the rifles and camera overhead with raised arms and measured every step to make sure we were not going deeper. You couldn't see far between the islets and all the time you knew there could be a crocodile just round the corner.

Once on the shore we cut three stout branches from trees and dug holes and hammered these into the ground as sharpened staves some distance apart, topped up the holes again and hammered the ground tight. Round the posts we tied multiple strands of rope and fixed a hook to each. On the way down Piet had shot three monkeys to bait the hooks, he said crocs were particularly fond of them.

After all this was done we waded back through the nightmare delta and made our way to our camp. That evening Piet, never loquacious, said less than normal. I could see he couldn't wait to see the outcome of his experiment. This could be the start of big things. If it worked it meant the end of the slogging up and down the rivers. It meant working in one area with the advantages of centralisation, a permanent hut and established a transportation route and the comparatively easy work of baiting the hooks and harvesting the captured crocodiles next day.

Next morning we retraced our steps to the beach. The whole thing had worked very well. The crocs had come all right and taken the hooks and bait. The only thing that was wrong was that they had gone away again leaving three straightened hooks and taking with them very sore mouths. Hooks attached to poles having proved useless, Piet had another good idea.

He had us all build three cages in the form of tunnels of bamboo posts driven well into the ground and roofed over, each big enough to accommodate a sixteen foot crocodile but not big enough to allow any manoeuvres. Three long days we worked hard on them, returning to our camp up-river each night. Conditions at the lake level were very hot and sultry and any exertion was much more trying than on the higher ground further up the rivers.

On the last evening when the traps were finished each tunnel was baited at the farthest end with a great hunk of high-smelling meat. To get at the bait the beast had to knock down a thin post set precariously in the middle of the run. This pulled away a prop that had kept the door open and when it dropped it induced a bar to fall across it to keep it shut, so preventing the reptile from backing out. Ingenious contraptions and each worked beautifully, exactly as planned.

The crocodiles came stealthily out of the lake in the dark of the night – I wish I could have watched – sniffed at the putrid meat and wormed their way up the tunnels, knocked over the fall-posts and imprisoned themselves as the gates slammed down and locked. There was only one flaw. Not one was still there when we arrived. From each tunnel the bait was gone and every enclosure had been thrashed to bits. If we needed any proof of the power of the trapped reptiles this was it. Surveying the scene of devastation Piet finally concluded that to try and catch crocodiles alive was not worth the candle.

*

We had now been out more than a week and Piet felt that he should go back to Iris for a couple of days. He was keen to go after a hippo to do some household trading. Iris's larder, it seemed, was wearing low. So I said I'd do a reconnaissance down at the mouth of the Mbaka river and he would find me there when he came back. All three rivers we hunted on ran on a south-eastern course into the lake and I said I'd make camp on the north or east bank of the Mbaka so there would be no need to cross the river on their way there from home. There was never a problem finding each other even though separated for a few days. So long as we knew the area the other was in we only needed to ask around and we'd find him. I ceased to be amazed at the way our presence became common knowledge wherever we were. Bush telegraph or whatever, people always had prior knowledge of our arrival or where we were. Any fugitive white man who thought he might lose himself in the bush or jungle could think again. He would do better knocking on the door of the constabulary and asking for a bed.

Getting a hippo was not as easy as it might seem. There were lots on the lake but we had no boat or equipment to hunt them there. Occasionally one might come up the mouth of the river as far as it could swim and even rarer was the one that might walk further inland.

Piet welcomed my suggestion and went off. The rest of the boys followed him on foot, taking with them the skins we had collected through the week. They would have a couple of days at home before returning. Boro Mrifu said he would stay with me and though I could offer him no pay and said he should take advantage of the break he insisted and I was glad he did. It was not until they had been gone some time, too far to catch up with them, that I realised that in clearing the camp because they would not be returning to that place, they had taken with them my sleeping bag and all personal goods apart from rifle and camera. I was now in the bush for a few days with what I stood in.

We crossed the Kibira River in a decrepit old canoe that had only a couple of inches of freeboard. I hoped for the sake of the Major's rifle and camera that we wouldn't tip over. Luckily all went well.

On some maps I have seen this river spelt 'Kiwira' and I'm not sure which is correct. I knew it as the 'Kibira', Piet called it that and missionary Dr Mackenzie, thirty years before me, wrote it in his map as Kibira. It may be that 'w' and 'b' are interchangeable in Bantu languages as are 'l' and 'r'.

If the canoe over the Kibira was scary, the one over the Mbaka was positively alarming. It had a bend in it like a stretched boomerang and the ferryman had to fight to keep it from drifting in a circle in fast current. I chose to cross high enough up the river so the nights would be cooler than if we stayed down by the lake. I reckoned the walk to and from the hot lake shore would be worth it. I was really quite enjoying being on my own with Boro, making the decisions, feeling confident, at home in the bush. Travelling as companions gave me the opportunity to talk on a level with Boro, something that was not possible when Piet was there for he maintained the strict Boer code of superiority which forbade such informality.

Over the Mbaka Boro let it be known that I needed accommodation and it was not long before a man came and invited us to stay at his house, a tidy, well appointed, clean place that looked as if it had been prepared for me coming. On arrival Boro was taken into the household and I was shown into a separate area of my own. I was given a bowl of guavas and oranges with a gourd of sour milk, not something I would have liked normally but wonderful after a long day on foot in the heat.

Boro must have told my host that I had no equipment with me for without a word he laid a blanket on the string bed he had provided and even fixed up a mosquito net. I had noticed that quite a lot of Africans used them now. No wife was evident but I was pampered by his two young daughters, Amansi and Euesti, who cooked and waited on me shyly but eagerly, I think. They blushed and positively died when I asked each their name. They brought me a bowl containing rice and spinach made from the leaves of a pumpkin and then some *ugali* porridge (a thinner, paste-type posho) with meat and beans.

Food was plentiful down here. The mangoes were finished now but in their place there were oranges, guavas, monkey-nuts and pawpaw for the picking and of course bananas and sugar cane. With such an abundance of fresh food I was surprised to be served meat for the natives rarely rose to that although they loved it. In its scarcity it was treated as a great delicacy so I treated it as a great favour and compliment to be served it. I asked them what it was and Amansi said shyly it was *nyama ya mbuzi* (goat meat) and I was certain they had killed the animal specially for me and I was touched by their hospitality. I resolved that I'd replace the meat three-fold at least before I left and I did so. They were a lovely family.

I noticed while staying anywhere without Piet I was given much more kindness and friendship than when we were together. Piet, known far and wide over his hunting territory, was held in great respect and awe, but also with great fear. I too was becoming known and I felt, perhaps erroneously, that I was welcomed in friendship.

It was the following day that I learned about the mother. The previous night, as I sat on a stool he had provided for me and he squatted low with the firelight on his face, I had asked the father what had become of her. He scratched his cheek and pulled a face and just stared at the flames as if he hadn't heard and I did not press him. Next evening when Boro and I had returned from the day's work I asked the girls as they fussed me. Amansi didn't speak and her eyes moistened. It was Euesti, the younger, who spoke up and surprisingly, her voice was firm, "She was taken and eaten by a crocodile two months ago as she washed clothes by the river."

I was overwhelmed by a sudden wave of sadness and didn't speak. Instead I put out my hand and touched each on the cheek with the back of my fingers and I think they appreciated that more than words. Looking at them I knew that it would be Euesti, young as she was, who would pull them through.

Was this the reason why the man had come to invite me to his home? When he heard that the crocodile hunter was in the area, did he feel by helping me he was in some way avenging the loss of his wife and his daughters' mother? There are not many good points in hunting but if my being with them gave the family some solace then I had no regrets about the work I was following.

The morning after we arrived Boro and I got a canoe to ourselves and with it searched among the thick rushes where the river runs into the lake. It was useless to use the paddle, we moved by just pulling on the rushes. The canoe made a swishing sound as we ploughed a furrow hither and thither. I saw one huge croc that went past us like a great submerged log before it sank like a submarine. I could have easily hit it but the water was too deep here to get the body out, and hoping to retrieve it when it would rise in two or three days was useless. The lake was rich with crocodiles and any carcasses would be gone before we saw them.

Once a hippo surfaced at the edge of the rushes. It looked towards us and opened its cavernous jaws in a great yawn. I held the rifle at the ready in case it should come for us but it turned away and sank from view. I hoped it had no idea of coming up under the craft and tipping us out, as they are known to do, and once in the water …! Since my mission at this stage was purely exploratory as far as hippos were concerned I noted its position and decided I'd check on it the next day and see if this was its regular patch. I didn't think this was a good place to shoot one because of the difficulty of landing it, but I'd let Piet be the judge of that. It was a sick, evil place in that swamp and relief showed on Boro's face when I said we'd had enough of the delta swamp with all its mosquitoes and lurking dangers for one day.

We did go back the next day and the hippo was still there. This time it did not yawn sleepily like yesterday. It was almost totally submerged with only its little pig eyes showing and it watched us steadily with a malevolent stare. I was quite sure this was no place to take it on.

We hauled ourselves about that awful place for a while that day but the more I saw of it the less I liked it. There were plenty of crocodiles in the water between the *meteti* groves, great lake ones as big as our canoe, that swam past us alarmingly close. I kept my rifle poised, covering any near one in case it took a turn towards us. In the end I confirmed my view of yesterday, the difficulty of landing anything in there, croc or hippo, was too great to risk any shooting.

Pleased to be done with the canoe I walked the bank of the swollen river for a while just to see what I could see. Then a lot of things happened at once. In the afternoon a runner came up to me panting to tell me that a hippo was coming nightly to eat the rice in his village *shambas* (tilled land) and asked if I would come and shoot it. A few nights before some natives had tried to kill it – they were allowed to kill any animal that damaged their crops – but the first spear had missed and the hippo had charged the thrower and he was lucky to escape with a trampled, crushed leg. The others had thrown their spears and at least two had gone in. They had all fled and since then they had left it alone although it was returning nightly. They were sad that all their rice was being eaten up.

It seemed a prime opportunity, to actually find a hippo on land. What a stroke of luck after considering going into the marsh for one. What was surprising was that the man had run from near Mwaya, almost ten miles away on the lake, and even as far as that they already knew I was operating in the area though I'd only been there three days.

About the same time I got word that Piet and entourage were on their way and would be with me soon. Also at that time Boro pointed out a crocodile to me. It was lying in mud almost the colour of its hide so that it was almost invisible. I was lucky enough to nail it stone dead with my first shot. I told Boro to go up the trail to meet Bwana Mamba and bring him here with the boys and to take the hippo messenger with him so the Bwana could be considering what he wanted to do about it. I'd wait there beside the croc until they arrived to skin it.

When they were gone I considered getting on with skinning the beast but felt lazy and thought I'd enjoy the last little while before the circus caught up with me again and lay back and dozed. It is not easy for one person to skin a big crocodile. The body has to be turned over on its back and that can mean cutting poles for leverage, and the thought of all that was suddenly too much.

I was brought back to reality with the sound of the boys approaching. I stood up and slung my rifle, but the noise had done more than waken me. At the same time as I rose a crocodile lifted its head and slithered down into the water only a few feet from me, so close that I could see the two big teeth that jutted out from its lower jaw and overlap the top. It must have been just behind me all the time I was lying there. I upbraided myself for having been so lax and careless, but in the days to come I was to remember that incident and think less harshly of myself. I realised that day was the beginning of the end of my hunting episode.

Piet was keen to go after the *shamba* raider and decided to make camp nearby and go over to Mwaya next day. One thing about having only what you stand up in is that you don't need to go back to your previous camp to pick up anything. Nevertheless I was sorry on this particular occasion not to say goodbye and thanks in person to the family I'd enjoyed staying with. I was glad I had left them well stocked with enough buck meat that they could share and trade some with their neighbours.

Piet shot a couple of crocs on the way to the hunting field next day. Once there we established camp, had an early meal and a few hours' sleep before rising in the dour, sma' hours and going into the inky darkness for a killing, hopefully. We did not know what we were letting ourselves in for. Two of the villagers came with us to show the area the hippo usually came to. Before the sleep was right out of my eyes I was soaked to the skin with drizzling rain and wet grass.

We didn't have far to go before we heard the hippo grunting in the rice shamba. Piet, as usual at night, had the lamp strapped to his head. The animal looked huge when the beam first picked it out. Piet was the only one who could shoot as he had the light. As he raised his rifle the hippo turned to face us and let out a terrific bellow. Mlanga (queer name – it means 'door') one of the boys with us took fright and started to run and crashed into Piet just as he fired. The shot had been intended for the brain but, as we discovered later, hit the animal in the mouth. It ran to the side, bellowing loudly and shaking its head from side to side it went off into the night before Piet could get another shot in.

Then began a nightmare chase that I will never forget. Through the shambas we ran and stumbled, Piet in front, flashing his torch to pick up the trail of drops of blood, me at the back running as hard as the darkness permitted. In the blackness we blundered against thorny bushes and splashing through the marshy rice paddocks.

At the Mbaka river we thought we could hear the hippo at the other side but were not sure. At the time we didn't know how badly it had been hit. We had to make sure. There was no way of finding a canoe at this time of night so there was only one thing for it – to swim across. To swim it at night when the crocodiles hunt … !!! Piet cut a banana tree stock into short lengths with a panga to make a small raft. It is easy to cut and floats well. We wrapped the rifles, ammunition, batteries for the torch and camera in an oilskin and tied the bundle down on the raft. At all costs we had to keep these things dry. Piet told the boys to make their way back to the camp and we'd come and get them when necessary. Then pushing the raft in front of us we stepped into the coal black water.

It was not all that deep and in most places we could touch bottom, but there was a strong current and, where it was too deep to wade, we had to kick out as the water clawed at us like eager, grasping hands. We thought we were cutting a diagonal course but at night you don't know. It seemed as if we were making little headway against the current and at times there was the cold horror of a floating branch brushing against my body that felt awfully like the scaly hide of a crocodile or the hunted hippo turned hunter. Hippos have been known to break a canoe in half with one bite. What could they do a man? Fears hallucinate in times like this.

Will we ever reach the other side? What a stupid idea this was. I am getting tired and I can hear Piet gasping rather than breathing. Was a bundle of meat worth all this?

Then the wild joy of the bump against solid ground and the feathery touch of the grass on the bank as our outstretched hands groped madly for a handhold and the delicious feeling of pulling yourself out of the broiling rapids. Piet, seasoned as hard as a hickory pick-shaft with this life, summed up both our feelings when he breathed involuntarily, no thought at this moment of hiding his feelings, "Thank God that is over." I knew his words were in true thanksgiving and not in blasphemy.

After a few minutes stretched out on the bank to regain our breath we continued the chase. The blood trail had stopped, but we picked up a spoor, but whether it was new or a couple of hours old was hard to tell in the torch light. More running through *shambas* and tangled undergrowth, then the spoor was lost in a tangled mass of *meteti*.

About half past four, cold, wet and heavy with failure, we coaxed some damp sticks into a fire and sat and waited till the dawn. How friendly was that campfire in the wee sma' hours of the morning when the trees were dripping with dew and the grass was wet and the mosquitoes were biting hard. Gradually the sky paled to grey and the fire lost its intimacy as the dark, damp walls of the night retreated.

In daylight we got a canoe and searched among the rushes and *meteti*, but found no trace of any hippo, wounded or not. Reluctantly Piet called the hunt off and it was with great relief that we crossed back over the river, this time in a canoe, and made our way to the camp for a welcome meal and blissful rest.

Next morning we had two reports by runners. The first from the place where the hippo had regularly plundered the *shambas* that said the hippo had not returned last night and that a tooth had been found where it had been shot. So maybe it wasn't badly wounded after all, but sore or frightened enough not to go back to these haunts. The second message said that there was a hippo hanging about in a little bay near the Customs shed at Mwaya on the lake. Could this be the same chap? Very likely. There were only a couple of miles between its home bay and the killing field. So we hurried to renew the hunt.

At this part of the lake the surface of the water at the side was completely overgrown with a mass of tangled reeds and *meteti*, a solid carpet that undulated with the movement of the water. And below this carpet of grass the hippo swam. Yes, it was there, restricting itself to a 50 yards square area and only poking its nose up in the middle of the floating islands to snort and inhale another bellyful of air. We could catch its movements sometimes as the carpet rippled with its passage as it swam underneath. But it was cunning and never showed itself for more than a few seconds and nearly always well away from us.

We each got a canoe and all through the afternoon till sundown we waited for a chance to shoot. It was like sailing on dry land, at least that was when we were in the canoes. In some places where the grass over the water was too high and tangled to pass over we had to get out and push or pull the canoe through it. Walking over the treacherous carpet was like walking and balancing on a trapeze artist's safety net. The net stretched with our weight and we sank up to our waists. And with every step you felt as if you could sink through a hole and be trapped under it, like going through ice.

But walking on the grass net was not the only hazard when in the water. While doing my acrobatics, submerged up to the waist, I got many blood-sucker leeches on me, five at one go, some in the most inconvenient places. They were like black, slimy worms. They buried their heads in the skin and grew fat on the blood. When I pulled at them they stretched like elastic and left a bleeding hole when they finally detached.

Watching the ripple swell as the hippo swam about it would have been easy to have scored a body hit but the risk of only wounding and losing it was too great. This time we must make sure. It was tantalising yet exhilarating because of the danger, seeing the ripple pass a few feet from the canoe and even to feel the canoe lifting slightly as it swam underneath, perhaps only inches from my feet, and not be able to shoot.

Very occasionally it would surface in a bunch of *meteti* only a few feet from the canoe and let out a frightening snort and it would seem that it was ready to charge the canoe. But if we tried to get into the *meteti* it always sank before we got there. It was these rare occasions that we prayed for, hoping that just once we would be able to get a shot in.

Towards evening the mosquitoes became unbearable, the worst I have ever experienced. You could see them passing in clouds. So we gave it up and hurried back to our camp, tired, miserable knowing we had another day and maybe more in that cesspit and more than half eaten alive by the mozzies.

It took another day in that gruelling place before our luck changed. We began in the morning again with the two canoes. All day we listened to its snorting and watched the ripple as it swam around and under us. The flies and the heat were terrible. But about 5 p.m. the hippo made its one and only error in the two days we had hunted it. It lifted its eyes out of the water a couple of feet from Piet's canoe to have a look at him. Piet's unerring rifle did the rest and ended that awful hunt.

I paddled over to Piet and was in time to see the mass of bubbles break the surface. Now began the task of getting it out. We had already estimated with poles that the water was about eight feet deep. We cut a clearing in the grass above it and the boys dived and put ropes round it. We recruited a battalion of local natives and, after some struggle, the dead hippo was rolled up onto the bank.

It was our hippo all right. The wounds from the spears were evident as was the broken tooth in its mouth. So! Piet's bullet hadn't wounded it much after all, apart from giving it a bit of toothache. What was much worse though was that one hoof was almost severed and pussy with the remains of a native wire trap still embedded in it. This was the reason why it was on its own away from its herd in the lake and why it had chosen to hide up in its own little creek and only come out at night. It could not have survived long there. Knowing that made me feel better when I looked at it dead on the bank. Better a quick death than a long lingering, painful starvation that would certainly have followed had we not come on the scene.

We slept beside the hippo that night, ringed with fires. There was no way we were going to allow other predators, crocs, big cats, hyenas or humans, to help themselves to a free meal. By dawn the meat was cut into lumps that could be carried. Piet enlisted an army of porters and by the time it was transported to his house the meat was beginning to smell a bit in the heat.

When we arrived the whole business of bartering began again. As always the news had spread like lightning among the natives. Already some were waiting with baskets of flour, rice, maize, etc., to trade for meat. Within an hour the place was like a fairground. Hundreds of *bibis* were shouting and squeezing towards us where we hacked away at the meat with pangas, cutting it into sizeable lumps. The din was incredible. Darkness fell and brought the show to a halt.

The fun began with the dawn. If yesterday was a fair day, today put it in the shade. The meat, even in the shade, was smelling very high and turning a decided green. But that did not deter the hundreds of women, many with their babies slung on their backs, carrying their baskets on their heads, jostling each other to get near it. The natives brought all kinds, maize, beans, flour, banana meal, mahogo, oranges, tangerines, hens and eggs, rice and many other varieties. Piet must have enough food to last him for six months if it could keep that long, I thought.

Late into the second day the meat was positively green and smelling like an open grave, but still they clamoured for it. As the supply began to grow noticeably less, the pushing and shouting increased and began to get out of hand until, towards the end, the noise had worked up to such a crescendo we had to shout in each other's ear to be heard. We were pushed into an area where it was almost impossible to swing the panga.

But finally it was finished. It took a long time for the disappointed ones to realise there was no more. Slowly they broke up and eventually the last ones reluctantly went away.

As the crowd dispersed I felt absolutely shattered. When the last had gone I realised I was just standing there, lashing with sweat, the bloody panga still in my hand hanging languidly at my side. During these last few days the tiredness that had been creeping over me had become worse. I had had to be continually chiding myself for being lazy and forcing myself on. Now I was prepared at last to give Piet best.

"You all right?" Piet's voice had a softer edge on it than I had ever heard before. He was in the process of bossing the boys in getting the place cleaned up and all the produce stored away when, it seemed, he had just noticed me still standing there.

"Oh yes, I'm fine," I answered, startled, and jerkily hurried to help. Piet eyed me shrewdly then came over and grabbed my arm. "You're running a temperature, man. Better pack it in for today and have a cold bath and stay here tonight. If you're no better in the morning you'd better get down to Kyela. It's the doctor's day at the dressing station tomorrow." So saying he called for a couple of boys to fill up the bath in the outhouse. Even now I can feel that moment, the wonderful luxury of letting it all go, feel the cooling water wash over me and relax into a dreamy oblivion.

Next morning I felt better for the rest but Piet advised me to see the doctor. So I set out the ten miles on foot. It was a mark of the way of life that there seemed nothing wrong or odd in their seeing me off by myself, obviously ill, in burst sandshoes and with no transport. I thought I might rest at the soap factory for a bit, but I was lucky enough to get a lift in a truck that took me quite a way past it and I only had the last three or four miles to do.

"You look pretty fit," the doctor said to me airily, "What brings you here?"

I said I thought I had a touch of malaria. He asked if I was taking any prophylactic and I said that I usually took Paludrine in likely infected places when I could afford it but recently I'd got some Mepacrine, but those had run out some days ago.

"Ah yes, that explains it. I thought your pallor was a little yellow when I saw you first. It'll be the Mepacrine, it turns you a bit that colour, you know. I'll give you some and you start taking them again straight away. You'll be as right as rain in a few days, you'll see."

I didn't get any lifts on the way back and those miles, all uphill, were the longest I've ever tramped. I thought I was never going to get back to Piet's place. I passed the soap factory and resisted the great temptation to go in. I knew if I did I would go no further and the thought of being bogged down there was not an option. I hardly remember the last miles on leaden legs. I vaguely remember Piet lifting me onto the bed and Iris being so concerned and solicitous. Whatever had happened, or not happened between us in the past was forgotten. All *that* belonged to life's theatre, the froth of interplay. This was real and both Piet and Iris could not have been kinder or more helpful.

I learned later that Piet cycled over to Kyiambili to enlist the help of Major Strickland. That in itself was no mean thing for Piet to do, knowing how much a pariah he was considered by all the whites. I believe it was the first time the two men had met and from the meeting a mutual respect was born.

The Major, his arm now healed, drove over to Piet's place and took me back to Kiyambili where he laid me up before going in haste to the doctor who came with a speed stoked by a feeling of guilt or failure. My pallor, which he had casually put down to the effects of anti-malarial tablets, was now obviously the symptoms of jaundice. With that, combined with raging malaria, the danger was now black-water fever, from which few survived. His diagnosis in a quarter of Tanganyika renowned as one of worst malarial areas in all Africa, was, to say the least, ill-considered. He personally drove me the 70 miles to the hospital in Mbeya, a journey of which my only very vague recollection was urinating with great relief and distress into a pot that overflowed.

*

If I were an ardent believer I would discount chance and put all serendipitous meetings down to a predestined manipulation with the grand puppet-master pulling the strings. And if I were an ardent disbeliever I would begin to have doubts and wonder, after all, if there really was someone up there meshing my cogs with wonderful synchronisation. Was my contracting malaria and jaundice not all part of the grand design? How else would I have met Padre Cann?

Padre Stanley Cann was a young missionary of the UMCA, the Anglican Church order whose wonderful Cathedral I had admired at their headquarters in Zanzibar. Two or three days after I had broken surface he came on a pastoral visit to the hospital and although I was not of his church he came to visit me. A quiet, lean, energetic man in his mid-thirties, we immediately set up a mutual rapport.

I was surprised to learn that he had come from the other end of his parish a hundred miles down the lake. When I asked him and he told me how he travelled I almost leapt out of bed. He said he came by canoe, a wonderful, huge, lake-going, dug-out canoe. Visions of *Trader Horne*, *Sanders of the River* and Conrad's *Heart of Darkness* danced in my mind. In answer to my flood of questions he said the canoe was his common mode of transport in these parts and, yes, he would be returning in it to his mission station. When I asked him if he would take me along with him he seemed pleased but surprised. "I don't see how that's possible. I'm leaving from the Customs shed by Mwaya on Thursday morning." This was Tuesday. I said, if I could get permission to leave the hospital would he take me. He said he would be delighted as long as the doctor thought I was up to the journey. I thereupon asked him if he would go to ask the doctor to come to me and I'd put it to him in his presence.

The two came to my room a little while later, the doctor in brusque mood asking what all this nonsense was about me leaving the hospital. I outlined the wonderful opportunity I had to continue my journey south with Padre Cann and how devastated I'd be if I missed the chance. "I don't know," pondered the doctor, weighing up my condition with the danger of premature exposure to the rigours of a lake safari. "You've been very ill, you know, more than you perhaps think. You've only just come round and are in no fit state to take on the world yet." I argued that a canoe journey was surely a wonderful way to recuperate. I saw the Padre grimace but he said nothing. The doctor understood the Padre's concern and said I should not underestimate that kind of journey. I said whatever it was like it could not be more strenuous than the life I had been leading, particularly during the past three months. "Yes indeed that may be so," the doctor warmed slightly, "you were remarkably fit. That in fact is what pulled you through. We thought we had lost you at one stage. It was your fitness that saved you."

A vibrant hiatus dropped over us. Neither of us spoke, the doctor thoughtfully sizing up the situation, tapping his teeth with his spectacles and me bursting with anticipation and showing it despite my bushy beard and matted hair that made me look more than ten years older than my twenty-four years.

"All right. I can see what this means to you. If you think you can do it I won't step in your way. All the same, I can't give you a clean bill of health. You will have to sign a form of indemnity accepting your discharge as your own responsibility. And remember you will be very weak. Don't overdo things or you'll land yourself back in care, that is if you're lucky enough to find it where ever you are."

I could have whooped with joy and perhaps my whole being did just that for the doctor looked at me and smiled for the first time. "If you're happy about it, then," he said softly, "that could be more powerful medicine than anything I can give you. I think you're going to be all right. Good luck."

Padre Cann had other business to attend to and went on his way. Within the hour I had discharged myself and was on the road, hitchhiking my way back to

Tukuyu. I had no kit with me and it was just as well for I doubt if I could have carried it. My legs felt like rubber and walking fifty yards brought the sweat of tiredness out on me. I'd lost nearly two stones in weight, from 13st. 2lbs. to 11st. 4lbs. My shirt and shorts hung on me, flapping.

The doctor's 'good luck' wish must have gone with me for I was extremely lucky to get good lifts and arrived back at Kiyambili before sundown. I was met by my two benefactors with great surprise and concern for my foolhardiness in coming out of hospital so soon. Nevertheless they made me welcome and comfortable.

As things had turned out it was the right time for me to be moving on. Everything seemed to be coming together as in a well-planned scheme. My cogs were indeed meshing smoothly. The crocodile hunting was finished for the next month or two. There had been a phenomenal rainfall over the weekend. Tukuyu at any time had the highest average rainfall in Tanganyika, but this time it exceeded all living memory – 22 inches fell in three days. Consider this against London's total annual rainfall of 20 inches. The Kabira burst its banks and hundreds of African huts were flooded. The river was like a sea and it was impossible to get near it due to a deep swamp on each side. I knew that the Songwe river must be the same as its banks were not very high.

When I went to say goodbye to Piet and Iris I could now see the wisdom of their building their house on high ground not too near the river. I was just in time to catch Piet. The crocodile hunting season over, he was just leaving to hunt elephant (he had three on his licence) on the outer fringe of the Selous area and prospect for minerals in the Poroto Mountains which formed the wonderful backdrop to Tukuyu and its area.

When we shook hands in goodbye and I looked into his eyes I knew I would never meet another character just like Piet. He was a man of remarkable contrasts; a hard, tough man with, yes, a soft heart; a man who thought himself a Christian but whose thoughts and actions belonged to the old testament; a man who said grace before meals even in the bush and read his bible at bedtime, yet believed in the divine right of whites over the blacks and administered it with an iron hand; a man with a Scottish grandfather yet called himself a Dutchman; a man difficult to get to know, but when you did penetrate that place into which he allowed very few people to enter, you found a wealth of good points that belied his iron exterior and nefarious reputation.

Chapter Sixteen

THE LAKE OF STORMS

Tuesday 22nd April 1952 – Canoeing on Lake Nyasa
I could see their head-plumes riffling with the breeze and their coloured rawhide shields slung over the side of the canoe. We were off to war and the hooting and singing were as stirring as distant bagpipes.

The canoe was a great, fat-bellied monster. A huge tree-trunk, almost 30 feet long, that had been dug out and hollowed to a thin shell. It sat high in the water despite being loaded with the great assortment of stores Padre Stanley Cann was to take back to his mission station at Manda, nearly a hundred miles down the lake. The six paddlers stood by the craft to steady it as the padre and I climbed aboard. They were lake men with broad, well developed shoulders and powerful arms. You could see they spent their lives in canoes.

As the last man pushed off and jumped in I thrilled at the start of this new adventure. Six paddles plunged into the water in unison and the canoe surged into the lake leaving the Customs shed and Kyela receding in the distance. I almost felt sorry to be leaving Tanganyika. The months spent there had all been hard and sometimes brutal, but in a masochistic way I looked back with pleasure and satisfaction. Tanganyika had shown me so much of the Africa I had wanted to know and I felt better equipped to tackle whatever lay ahead.

But I was not finished with that country yet. We were in fact heading north a few miles to Mwaya, the padre's last port of call before turning south and at the end of the canoe journey there would be Manda, the Padre's station, on the east side of the lake and still in Tanganyika. But this was the end of my wandering in that country.

Mwaya used to be the main German port on the lake when they governed Tanganyika. Now there was hardly anything left of it bar a little mission station comprising a school, church and dispensary. Nevertheless, some shades of grandeur still remained. Like a scene from a Hollywood movie we paddled up a majestic avenue of tall palm trees that used to be a street but was now submerged by the recent flood, the mirror image of the trees waving gently in the smooth lake water. In my mind I named it 'Lake Avenue'. Any other time we would have had to tie up the canoe at the lakeshore and carry all the belongings and cargo up for safekeeping. But now, just like in Venice, we paddled right up to the very door of the dispensary where we were to disembark and spend the night.

Early next day we crossed to the east side of the lake and turned south under the towering, sheer face of the Livingstone Mountains. The scenery was breathtaking, absolutely crushingly awe-inspiring in every sense of the words. High overhead, as high as we could see, the massive, perpendicular rock wall plunged sheer into the water and carried on down 300 fathoms and more. 2000 feet deep under our canoe! A long way down if we overturned. David Livingstone was the first European to see Lake Nyasa which he discovered in 1859, although it had been known to the Arabs for hundreds of years The lake is some 350 miles long and 15 to 60 miles wide. It is the second deepest lake in Africa – Lake Tanganyika claiming first – and is part of the Great Rift Valley that runs from the Mediterranean Sea all the way down to the Zambezi River. It is also one of Africa's wildest and most unpredictable lakes, where storms and raging seas can spring up as sudden and violent as epileptic fits. Three or four years earlier the lake ferry steamer went down in a storm with the loss of many lives including seven Europeans. In the crushing black shadow of the Livingstone massif the possibility of our canoe capsizing was not beyond the realms of conjecture. Ere the day was over and on the next that possibility had gone beyond conjecture.

Later that morning when the sun came up over the mountains and dispersed the black shadows, we fried in its heat. We sat on bags of provisions in the deep belly of the canoe and did our best to partially shelter behind other bags and boxes. The paddlers kept up their easy stroke for hour after hour and now, out of the shadows, sang their rhythmic songs that helped them keep in unison.

The endless rock wall provided few places for landing and it was 3 p.m. before we rounded a corner to find a tiny triangle of pebbly beach in a little fold of the sheer cliff onto which the paddlers drove the nose of the canoe, two men having jumped overboard at the last second to hold it steady.

In this pitifully small clearing, crushingly hemmed in on three sides by the sky-high granite face and by the ocean lake on the forth, people lived their lives. A few huts only with tiny, tiny *shambas,* one huge tree and two or three palms and the lake to harvest fish. The few residents seemed quite content. A very steep, corkscrew path climbed precariously out of the back of the clearing showing there was access to the lofty plateau.

Before these mountains were named the 'Livingstone Range', by Dr Laws of the Livingstonia Mission, they were the 'Kinga Mountains', named after the people who lived there. The Kinga, closely related to the Konde but like the Bandali, had developed into tough, rugged hill people.

I was told that the land on the roof of the mountains was unbelievably hilly but fertile and in places the Kinga had cultivated gardens that hung on the steep slopes like blankets out to dry while their homesteads clung desperately beside them. It was intensely cold up there at nights for much of the year and the people had taken to digging shallow trenches in which they burned fires to heat the soil and shovelled out the embers before crawling in to sleep. The practice I believe was dying out by the time I was there and no doubt is now gone for ever.

As part of the Konde group, the Kinga were peace-loving people and like their kinsmen they hid dark secrets in their hearts. The last recorded rain-making ritual child sacrifice happened up there on the high plateau.

By the time we were finished our late lunch and were preparing to be on our way again the paddlers said a storm was brewing. The weather was calm. There was not the slightest sign to indicate a change and the lake looked quite inviting after even a short while in the claustrophobic confines of our stop-off place. Had I been on my own I should have suspected the boys of malingering, of feeling they had had enough for one day, as is not uncommon among Africans, or workers of any creed or colour for that matter. The Padre, however, said it paid to listen to the boys in this respect and sure enough, within the hour the sky greyed, the wind rose and the waves crashed on the tiny beach with North Sea gale force. I should have hated to be out on the lake then. Livingstone called Nyasa 'The Lake of Storms'

An example of the tragic consequences that can occur when the lake men are over-ruled happened about 50 years before this time. The newly appointed Bishop Chauncy Maples, just two months after his consecration in St. Paul's Cathedral, London, and keen to get to the UMCA headquarters to take up his new position, was in no mood to delay his journey when travelling up the lake on a little sailing boat. When Ibrahim, the native captain, called for the boat to put into shore because of an approaching storm the Bishop countermanded the decision. He should have known better for he had already spent twenty years by the lake before his promotion. The storm blew up as predicted, the boat capsized and the new Bishop and his companion, Joseph Williams, were drowned. The mission steamer which the Padre hoped to meet at Manda had been named the SS *Chauncy Maples* after the hapless bishop.

So we passed the rest of the day under the huge tree with the enormous spread and when night approached put our mosquito nets up on the sand and fell asleep to the sound of the storm concerto.

Next morning about 3.00 a.m. Emmanuel, the padre's personal boy, said the lake was fine and it would be better to get on our way. The canoe was loaded in lantern light and we pushed off with only the starlight to guide us. On our left the black hulks of the mountains cut sinister silhouettes in the faintly luminous sky. Everything was very still. The lake was as sleepy as a kitten that had played itself out and what we could see of the water was as smooth as glass. Even the boys were silent which was unusual. There was only the splash of six paddles dipping in unison and the swish of the water slipping past. The padre and I lay on top of a pile of cargo, pulled a tarpaulin over us to screen the biting breeze and tried to continue our interrupted sleep. I awoke with the sound of the canoe grating on sand and pebbles to find that the boys had taken the opportunity of a small bay to put into for breakfast. Emmanuel soon had a fire going and porridge, tea and sardines on toast prepared for us. The crew gathered round a big pot of sticky, gooey mohogo porridge, which they scooped up with their hands, smacked their lips and licked their fingers clean.

By the time we were prepared to go again the sun was almost at its zenith. Warned by yesterday's scorching when we just lay and baked, we had some huge banana leaves cut and erected a kind of shelter. We had hardly been going an hour when, without warning, the water became very choppy. The canoe see-sawed over huge waves that were higher than our heads when we were deep in the troughs. The situation became anxious when we couldn't find a place to run ashore. The precipitous side of a mountain appeared to be unbroken for miles. However, as we rounded a spur of rock that jutted out into the lake we saw a small beach. But on closing in we found that the surf was too wild. To have attempted a landing would have been risking being piled up in a broken heap by the angry foam-covered rollers that crashed on the high, pebble beach.

The anxiety of the paddlers had now visibly increased to fear and before long developed into more than a slight panic. Those who are brought up on the lake obviously have a healthy respect for it in all its various moods. As for me, I was in a fool's paradise, quite enjoying the thrill of it all. I was worried, frightened really, like everyone else, yet confident that this must be a common occurrence for the Padre during his lake meanderings and it was just a case of holding on until we were through it as he must have done countless times. It was not until nearly half a century later when I again met Stanley Cann in retirement in Sussex that I learned the truth of it all.

In his own book, *Into Africa*, Stanley describes that day and only then did I learn that this was by far the worst storm he ever encountered on the lake. To those who knew it, our plight that day was indeed fearful. My companions must have thought me remarkably composed in the light of our danger, but in truth I was the epitome of the parody on Kipling's words, 'If you can keep your head when all around are losing theirs, it may be that you are not fully aware of the facts.'

Writing his book many years after the incident, the Padre had long since forgotten my name and I was referred to as 'the hitchhiker'. It amused me to think that there can be few, if any, hitchhikers who ever thumbed such an exotic, wonderful lift as I did the day I met Stanley Cann.

For an hour the crew battled with the elements. Sometimes the canoe would balance precariously on the crest of a wave from where the bottom of the troughs seemed far below, next instant we would be in the depth of a tunnel-like trough with white-topped waves bending over it, soaking us with spray, like some arched-back demon dripping saliva. Just when it seemed that the wave would crash down and swamp us the canoe would lift its nose and climb onto the back of the next wave while the previous one slapped down just behind us.

Finally we saw a little stretch of sand the boys thought might be safe enough to attempt a landing. They skilfully rode the waves as we approached. Just before we touched bottom they jumped over the side and steadied the craft and held it back from driving into the steep bank of pebbles. Hastily and with great difficulty they unloaded the cargo and beached the canoe high and dry to save it from being pounded to destruction by the merciless waves.

Luckily this was a little mission station. There was no school, only a small, dilapidated church built into the side of the steep mountain. A few huts and some banana groves made up the settlement. As the rain began to pour we found sanctuary in the church.

Again the weather showed no sign of abating so we had to stay put and hope that the lake's temper calmed down by the morrow. But although there was a slight improvement by breakfast time that looked promising to us the boys said it was only a lull and it would blow up again. So we sat and watched the day slip by. The padre held a service, the strangest one I ever attended.

The church was built with mud and had a scraggy, leaking thatched roof. There were no seats, the congregation sat on the earthen floor or stood leaning against the stick walls that were so perforated you could see what was going on outside at every glance. All our kit was stacked in the corner; bags of rice, flour, boxes, crates and even a turkey in a wicker basket that the padre was taking back to the mission, and two or three hens in another basket. Fishing nets hung drying on the walls. The church 'bell' was the blade of an old *jemby* (native hoe) that a boy rattled with another piece of metal. The few people slowly assembled, the women brought their babies on their backs, the men piled their spears outside before entering.

As the service went on children began crying, hens screeched their heads off, dogs ran in and barked and snarled at each other and then went out howling after getting a kick. Even the old turkey took it into its head to start gobbling and all the time the rain teemed down and dripped in pools through the leaking roof. The weather prophets were quite right – it did come down pretty badly.

The water was calm enough to put out next morning but we only managed a couple of hours progress. In that time we arrived at another little mission station locked in a fold of the rock face. While we were there the lake rose again and we were weather-bound for all that day and the next. We found accommodation in a little room off the classroom.

These were long days cooped up in our little island-like patch. But it was interesting to be there, to see at first hand life in such isolation. So primitive, yet so self-sufficient with such limited resources. And the wonder of it all – a school! We listened to the native teacher talking in Kiswahili to the wide-eyed children, who squatted on the earthen floor, taking them through the 3 R's and I marvelled at the intensity of the children's response. Locked in their little world that was so small they could run in a minute or two from one end to the other in any direction, they might have believed they were the only people on Earth. And even if they knew there were others out there they must have had little hope of ever seeing another human in all their lives. Yet in spite of this terrible isolation they were keen to learn to read and write.

But there was more than 'riting and 'rithmetic in their curriculum. The teacher finished the afternoon session with a lecture on, "What to do to prevent hook-worm." We had to smile, however, when he finished his lesson with the reassuring remark he had "had it seven times".

After another day in the postage-stamp refuge the delay was becoming serious. Padre Cann desperately wanted to get to Manda where he was the Priest-in-Charge. It was imperative that he be there in time to see the Bishop who was sailing round the Lake on his farewell voyage and was due to call within the next few day. In addition, we were running very short of food. There were plenty of bags of meal and livestock but these made up the cargo for delivery. It was the rations for the journey that were now nearly out. I had given my carrying food, maize and banana flour and what ever else I had in my pack, to Emmanuel to eke out the store but even with that we all now faced short fare.

Here I will let Stanley take up the tale from his own book *Into Africa*.

We travelled for a day and a half and all seemed to be going well, but my crew warned me that a wind was getting up. We were very close to land as we came up to a certain point, but as we breasted the point I realised we were not making any progress: in fact we were travelling backwards! We got ashore as soon as we could and did our best to make the canoe secure (we could not afford to lose that!). There seemed to be little prospect of rain so we did not bother about a shelter; we just camped out on the beach and waited for the wind to abate. It was a long wait – seven days. (There is a slight variation between Stanley's memory and my diary on the number of days here.) *My food supplies began to run low, but the hitch-hiker had obtained a supply of banana flour and we handed this over to Emmanuel who concocted some meal for us. There were one or two African huts near us so we were not quite marooned. We sat and watched the waves roll in – longer and longer. There was little chance of getting away as yet. One small child from a neighbouring house was having the time of his life. He had a diminutive canoe, about six or seven feet long and so narrow that he could kneel in it but not sit in it. He made his way out through the waves, turned his craft and then came roaring in on the crest of a wave. Bondi Beach here we come! As he got into the shallow water by the beach he very skilfully turned his canoe, fell out of it into the water, climbed in again and then retraced his route through the waves until he was able to catch another wave to bring him in. I envied him his skill! Eventually we did get away.*

At sundown that evening the whispers of a calm fanned our anxious faces as we gazed out over the endless sea, mentally pleading with the lake for a window in its wild, angry mood. Padre Cann explained to the boys that it was very important that he should reach Manda as soon as possible. They said they would make an all out effort if there was the slightest chance.

About 4 a.m. they woke us to say it was all right to start, but they did not think the break in the weather would last for long. They'd just have to do their best while the going lasted. By the yellow light of lanterns and the silver glow of the Southern Cross and other stars the canoe was loaded and pushed off. Daylight found the crew still going strong. There was no question of stopping for breakfast this morning, the time was too precious.

Slowly the great, buttress wall of the Livingstone Mountains slipped by. Gradually the top began to slope down and eventually even show the green vegetation of the plateau. But for long hours the range still presented a sheer precipice of flat rock of formidable height rising out of the water. Still a complete barrier. Occasionally there were the little bays and semi-circular folds in the wall where a few huts and banana groves signified habitation, but we didn't stop now.

The sun rose from behind the mountains in a savage blaze. Our banana leaves were soon limp and dry but they still provided a modest shelter from the sting of the rays. With the sun the crew's spirits began to rise and with them, so it seemed, came the prospect of the good spell of weather extending its duration. At Makonde, a bigger place than any we had seen up till now, we pulled in for a late bite and the opportunity for Padre Cann to make his official visit. Built on a rock ledge some twenty feet above the water level, this was quite a thriving station with a church, a school and a small dispensary.

As we were about to leave Makonde a young African hurried up to Padre Cann and said he wanted to go to Manda. Another hitchhiker! But unlike the other one he brought his own paddle to work-his-passage and joined the crew. That made six men up in the front and one at the back who used his paddle to steer like a rudder.

The paddlers seemed tireless. The leader at intervals would start up a chant to keep the rhythm of their strokes. This worked like putting a car into overdrive, you could feel the canoe surge forward. The leader would sing a few words, then all the men would shout "A-ow-owhoop", ending in a high pitched "hoop" as they plunged the paddles in up to the hilt in perfect unison and their big muscles would ripple across their backs as they gave an extra push. As the tempo quickened they became even more excited and some would start trilling and hooting in high, girlish voices. That put the last touch to the atmosphere. It was easy to imagine that we were in a war canoe. I could almost feel my pulse rise with the thought of battle. I could see their head plumes riffling with the breeze and their coloured rawhide shields slung over the side of the canoe. Occasionally the sun glinted on their forest of spears or an unsheathed knife or shiny, heavy knobkerry. We were off to war and the hooting and singing were as stirring as distant bagpipes! But I don't think Stanley Cann, had he been able to read my thoughts, would have been pleased to know that I was likening his fine UMCA canoe to a man-of-war.

About noon we stopped at the Roman Catholic mission at Lupingu. Here the mountains receded to allow a large area big enough for farming. The RCs had a grand station with fine buildings and were self-supporting. We had a lunch of their own-cured boiled ham and a tremendous variety of fruit and excellent home-produced wines were offered. Whatever difference in the interpretation of the Christian religion the two factions had, and there were real bitter feelings between the RCs and the C of E's, I have to say the Roman Catholics were excellent hosts and as far as I could see also first-class colonisers. But later when I expressed those opinions Padre Cann said I must not allow myself to be won over by their fine hospitality and lavish lifestyle. He blamed them for being unscrupulous in their methods in attracting Africans to their religion. "Their religion?" Were they not all preaching the Christian religion? This was all getting 'curiouser and curiouser'

It appeared that the 'Romans', as the RCs were referred to, were too high-handed. They built their Mission stations outside and away from native communities, in places where they could get plenty land to farm, grow vines, and be self supporting. They enticed the local population to come to them. The UMCA missionaries, on the other hand, went to the people and built their churches in the midst of the communities, thereby limiting their own freedom and resources but creating no barriers between them and their flock. I was to learn later that the Church of Scotland missions followed this same principle.

There was of course far more than where-to-live-within-the-community that divided the branches of the Christian religion. Feelings indeed ran high whenever the matter was raised. I found it very strange to hear such antithetical comments and views expressed regarding two principle factions of the same religion. I found the matter quite disturbing and yet deeply interesting. I suddenly felt that somewhere in this conundrum lay a kernel of knowledge that I hoped to find or unravel to my own satisfaction, and the hope of finding some answer was part of my reason for wandering the world. At that moment and later over the years I travelled, I listened avidly to comments and opinions on the subject when in the company of people more learned and knowledgeable than myself, hoping that by listening I might piece together the answer I sought. For the moment, at the end of that day on the canoe I wrote in my diary, *'I must learn more about those two factions of the Christian religion before I make comment.'*

Having tucked this morsel into my memory bag there was little time for further discussion. Within the hour we were on our way again and the sea did nothing for my cogitation. During the afternoon the waves became very choppy and splashed over the side of the canoe, soaking us to the skin. However, it wasn't bad enough to stop us.

About five o'clock we put into one of those little clefts in the granite rockface where there were a few huts and a decrepit old church. After the meal we all crowded into the little church to grab a little sleep. There were still six hours more travelling to go and the padre wanted to arrive in the forenoon. With all the kit, the seven members of crew and our own two selves it was a tight squeeze in that wee place. It began to rain. The grass roof offered as much protection as a sieve. The floor was damp and cold before, and now with the rain it had become a mud bed.

The boys had us up at 3.00 a.m. The canoe was loaded and we went on our way again. The lake wore its usual nocturnal serenity. The crew was indefatigable. Although they had already put in long hours of this hard work they plied the paddles with the same vigour as if they were fresh men. Like automatons they bent and dipped their paddles to a steady rhythm, one deep thrust, one shallow one, one deep thrust, one shallow. Again I was thankful to put the tarpaulin over me and go to sleep.

We arrived at Manda at 9.30 a.m., the boys having done the six hours paddling without a break. That on top of almost twenty-four hours before. A truly remarkable effort. Truly remarkable people.

Stanley's final words on our journey reads, *"It took us nine days whereas I had previously done it in three. We arrived just in time, for there, as we crossed from Nsungu to Manda, lay the CHAUNCY MAPLES, our Mission steamer, and the hitch-hiker's chance to get down to Nyasaland. Fortunately Captain Hayward was a keen Scout, and he readily gave the man a lift. How he fared subsequently I do not know."*

The canoe journey was a memorable experience and I consider myself extremely fortunate in having had the opportunity to do it, especially in the company of Stanley Cann who was an excellent host, companion and conversationalist. My one regret was that since my camera was ruined in the Kabira River, I had no photographic record of the people and places of this episode in my journey, nor for those ahead too. Even with a detailed diary, memory alone can be a sad substitute at times. Even so, sights do etch engravings on the memory plate that jump into focus when my diaries switch on the mental video tape of the events, no matter how old that tape may be.

Interesting times apart, the canoe journey had been the ideal convalescence after my illness. Even with the restricted rations at times I had put on weight and felt much stronger. I don't know how I would have coped had I been required to paddle my own canoe from the start. As it was, I could not have wished for better than my days of travelling in lordly manner with very little physical activity. The doctor at Mbeya hospital had been right, the adventure of the journey had been far better medicine than anything he could have given me.

*

Manda, known in the days of German occupation as Wiedhafen, was Tanganyika's main, indeed only, port on the eastern side of Lake Nyasa. Situated beyond the end of the Livingstone Mountains where the land was now flat and fertile it had a natural little harbour that could accommodate the few small steam-ships that plied the lake. The Mission here was quite big and in fact the Mission Station *was* Manda. The church was large and there was a hospital and a sizeable school.

While Manda was fairly easily accessible on the lake side this was not so by land. On that side it was extremely remote and isolated. Just how isolated could be gathered from the fact that the mail from there was carried for five days by relays of runners to Njombe, away in the north, from where it was then sent by bus to Mbeya before the airmail ever saw a plane. No doubt things have changed since then.

As Stanley mentioned in his book, the UMCA steamer, the SS *Chauncy Maples*, lay in the bay with the Bishop's flag flying at the masthead. Bishop Frank Thorne was travelling on it, making his farewell journey round the lake. The diocese was being divided and a new Bishop was due to take over this territory. On hearing I was going south, Bishop Thorne invited me aboard as his guest. I had hoped to travel on the ship and had wondered if I might be so bold as to ask the captain for a lift. But to be invited was so much better and this being a Mission ship the Bishop's word was final on the matter.

My day at Manda was spent among the few missionaries and staff, all of whom, black and white, gave Padre Cann a most warm welcome back and received me as a friend, and willingly showed me with pride round their Mission. They were all very dedicated and enthusiastic about their work and remarkably cheery considering the hardships and frustrations they all had to live with. On the day I was there I saw two hardy women missionaries who were not young, accompanied by a padre, all newly out from home, setting out in heavy boots and safari clothes to start a four-day climb to a lonely hill station 6,000ft. up on the Livingstone Plateau. This station was called Milo I think, where Padre Cann also started his work in Africa some sixteen years before. That was just after a weekend's record rainfall and the going would be extremely tough. Despite the austerity and trials of their lives they were eager to be getting on with it.

Dinner at the Mission that evening was a happy occasion, full of lively discussion and teasing, verbal swipes at each other. The warm bonhomie atmosphere round the table surprised me considering the Bishop was seated at the head. I was to learn over the next couple of weeks or so that Bishop Frank Thorne was not one for stuffy formalities. He was a man who wore the dignity of his position easily and was a friend to everyone.

The *Chauncy Maples* was due to sail at 4 a.m. next morning so I went on board that evening and was delighted to be allocated a cabin to myself. The ship was going all the way down the lake to Mponda at the most southerly point of the lake and I could stay aboard all the way if I wished. I did indeed wish. Mponda was only a few miles from my next poste restante pick-up point at Blantyre. It was now nearly four months since I had received any mail and I was desperate to hear from home.

The SS *Chauncy Maples* (affectionately known as '*CM*') was a wonderful old, wood-burning puffer. She had celebrated her 50th anniversary on the lake just over a year before. Built in porter-weight pieces at Glasgow and shipped out as 3,500 parcels to East Africa, taken on barges up the Zambezi and Shire Rivers as far as the Murchison Falls and carried to the shore of Lake Nyasa where she was assembled. The boiler, which could not be dismantled, was sent out whole and rolled the last sixty-five miles from the cataract by 450 Angoni natives, through the bush, up hills and over river beds and arrived intact.

It is interesting to note that it was the wild Angoni who did the hard work in moving the boiler. It might have been expected that one of the less aggressive tribes would have been more likely to be chosen for such a task. But it is a fact, as Dr MacKenzie of Livingstonia wrote, that the warlike tribes such as the Angoni and Yao, both of Zulu extraction, made far better workers than the people of the peaceful tribes. Once befriended the Angoni were loyal and would work with a will and fulfil their contract. The Kondi were not loyal, resented work and would malinger and drift if given the slightest chance. From this it might be taken that fearless people with spirit are likely to be more industrious people in peace as well as in war.

When launched on the lake in 1902 The SS *Chauncy Maples* was welcomed as a great improvement on its predecessor, the SS *Charles Janson*, which in its day had done valiant service but had become too small and cramped for current needs. The *CM* was 43 paces long by my measure, so that made it nearly 130 feet. Initially, apart from moving people between stations, it was intended as a floating school and originally on the main deck there was a class-room with thirty desks. But that did not work for very long. Lessons were hard to hear above the noise of the engines and many students (and teachers) were very sea-sick and could not give of their best. As time went by, the extra space without the school on board proved invaluable in accommodating the growing number of peripatetic missionary staff.

For over half a century the *CM* had gone about her business like an old, clucking hen, puffing and wheezing round her run, each circumference of the lake taking one month, keeping all her brood in touch and making sure they were all right. And like any self-respecting, genteel hen, she never travelled after dark.

During the war the *CM* was 'called up' for government service and was badly missed by the mission personnel. She served the military valiantly for three years until, in 1943, her boiler blew beyond repair. With no hope of getting a replacement until after the war she lay idle and forlorn until a new boiler was shipped out from the UK in 1946, only five years before I sailed on her.

The grand old Dame burned wood for her boiler and couldn't go far without restocking. So every few hours of sailing time she had to put into shore to collect firewood. These were regular stops and the natives at each of these places had a contract to have a stockpile ready. They had been given a stick one-yard long and they cut the logs to that length and piled them to that height and each pile was ten stick-lengths long – ten cubic yards. Captain Haywood, the doughty old skipper who had been running the *CM* for the past thirty-five years, said as the years go by it was getting more and more difficult to get the wood for the boilers as the trees along the lake shore were rapidly disappearing. He told me how he used to pay one yard of calico (4d. a yard) for one cubic yard of wood. Now the price was around 2s.6d. per cubic yard, 6½ times its original price.

With the wood all kinds of parasites came on board, the most dangerous being scorpions and snakes. Two snakes, each about eighteen inches long, were killed the first day I was aboard which made me think the voyage was likely to be very interesting in more ways than one, but I never saw any more during the rest of the journey.

At all the firewood stops and to those of the many Mission stations, large and small, on both sides of the lake I went ashore to see the places and talk to the natives. The Bishop, knowing my interests, made a point of including me in all the landing parties.

Bishop Thorpe was an extremely interesting and friendly person. A remarkable man, he could speak three or four tribal languages as well as Portuguese and Swahili and he had a flair for crossword puzzles for which he could get meanings from the most subtle clues. He would say with a laugh that his dog, Socrates, (surely few dogs have been honoured by so noble a name) was a 'Daniel', being a cross between a dachshund and a spaniel.

The *CM* was flying the Bishop's flag and no doubt the natives had been warned that this was his farewell tour. Everywhere he went crowds gathered to sing a welcome to him. When he landed they would kneel in front of him while he passed a blessing over them. He would have a walk round the place talking to this one and that, changing his language effortlessly to suit. Then when we were leaving the people would start singing their farewell and would keep it up while we were rowed back to the *CM*. They all seemed very reverent. The years of missionary work had obviously made their mark. The songs were all so musical and the sincerity was touching.

On one occasion when we had arrived back on board after a particularly moving scene, we stood at the rail and watched the crowd still standing singing on the beach. I did not know what the words were but the Bishop did. They must have been very poignant. As the *CM* weighed anchor and slowly slipped away the crowd became an indistinct blur on the receding shore and their singing grew faint until the words were indistinguishable and only the lilt of the song was audible. Still they sang their farewell. I turned to speak to the Bishop. He was still waving goodbye although he must have been quite invisible to them now, the tears running down his cheeks. Suddenly I felt ashamed to be there. It was as if I had barged into the privacy of a father's farewell to his children. Diplomatically I turned and walked silently away. The Bishop never noticed my absence. For a long time he stood watching the shore with shiny eyes.

The two senior members of the ship's crew, Captain Bertram Haywood and Engineer Harry Thomas were both interesting characters. The Captain, with his short, stumpy stature, severe, deeply sunburned countenance and short pipe sticking out of the corner of his mouth, was the personification of the typical seadog, or, perhaps more appropriately, 'lakedog'. He was nearing retirement but was still a stickler for discipline. But he held more of a fatherly hand over the ship than that of a strict disciplinarian. He just let everyone know, from the Bishop down to the lowest deck hand, that everything on board had to be done properly. One of the African crew writing in a short article to the UMCA magazine published in England, spoke about the 'Father Captain', a term that was most apt.

We struck up quite a rapport, the Captain and I, and had long conversations during which he showed a side of himself that might have surprised most who knew him. Inside the rather severe looking exterior was a young, adventurous man ready to leap out. Perhaps that is why we got on so well. He said he had always had a hankering to do the thing that I was doing and having met me he was giving serious thought to what he might do after his retirement in a few months' time.

Summing-up the captain in my diary I wrote, '*he is a Boy Scout at heart, dreaming of weekend camps and open air cooking,*' without knowing how accurate the words were. Much later I learned that unknowingly I had been in the company of the Chief Scout of the whole area and that honour had been laid on his shoulders by none other than the grand master of Scouting himself, Lord Rowallan. Two years earlier, in January 1950, his Lordship had paid a visit to Mponda and presented Bertram Haywood with a warrant that constituted him Commissioner of Scouts on the Lake Shore.

He must have travelled the world over and over again by the medium of his pipe and armchair. From what he said I could see that all his life his great pastime had been, and still was, to think up pipe dream inventions, some of them ingenious but impractical, most of them quite ridiculous. For instance a bicycle on which he would travel Africa and other places, as I was doing. But a bicycle with a difference. A bicycle built on the lines of a grocery delivery bike with a box in the front. The box would be equipped with two drawers. The top one would pull out flush with the top of the box to form a bed, the bottom one devised for carrying his equipment. Of course this might prove a bit heavy to pedal so he would fix up a kind of sail to blow him along. I thought of the still forests where there was no wind and the roads of deep mud I had walked through and I thought he might have some difficulty with his bike.

But a better idea had been in his mind lately. If he could equip a single-decker bus to his use, that would be the thing. He had evidently spent a lot of time and tobacco over that one for he had it thought out to the smallest detail as to how he would fit it up. But the bus would have had to be at least 60 feet long to accommodate all the gadgets he wanted to build into it.

Most of his pipe-smoke ideas were so funny a horse would have had difficulty keeping a straight face, but they were told with such earnest enthusiasm I could not show the slightest scepticism for fear of hurting him. Well, nobody grudges an old man his dreams and I liked him so much for them.

Harry Thomas, the Engineer, kept himself mostly to himself. Apart from meals he rarely joined the company. Yet, on his own, I found him talkative and friendly and very interesting. He told me with great enthusiasm of the journey he had done in the '30s on the Trans-Siberian railway from Moscow to Vladivostock. Such a long overland journey for a sailor! He described the great expanse of empty country, the people he saw at the stations and met on the train, the thrill of it all and I envied him, desperately.

The Bishop and I were the only two travelling the full length of the lake, but other mission personnel joined the ship for a day or two between stations. Most had walked for days to catch the ship and would do the same when they left it. Some, perhaps most, were rather straight-laced in their ways as became their vocation, but all were very pleasant, interesting, extremely intelligent and well read and everyone was a character. The women, I thought, were particularly tough and determined, even in their pleasure, but were gentle and feminine with it. They were schoolteachers mostly, but also nurses and one was a doctor.

In the evening, after dinner, there was always a foursome at bridge and I played chess with any odd one out. I held my own mostly until, that is, Canon Cox, an old, semi-retired missionary, came on board. He wiped the floor with me, but with great grace and gentleness.

Most of all, though, it was the conversation that I remember as the stimulant of the journey. Bishop Thorpe had spent some time in his early years as a missionary on the Lupa goldfield and, like the gentlemen at Kyiambili, he had many interesting yarns to tell of that place. His tales from around Lake Nyasa, however, would have eclipsed even those of the goldfield epic. Here were stories of derring-do, of incredible courage and fortitude that surpassed fiction, tales of brave people who placidly accepted death in the course of their duty and some who had miraculous escapes from it.

Take for example the massacre of the priests and nuns at the Roman Catholic mission at Nyangao and the incredible escape of others during the Maji-Maji native uprising against the Germans in eastern Tanganyika in 1905. The revolt was the culmination of the natives' resentment at the Germans policy of forced labour, compelling them to cultivate cotton under the whips of Swahili overseers. The first spark of revolt came from a spirit-medium or witch-doctor named Kinjikitile, who claimed he had devised a magic potion – a concoction of millet seeds mixed with castor-oil and water – which would turn the German bullets to water. Hence the name given to the uprising, Maji-Maji (water water).

At first Kinjikitile's prophesy appeared to come true. A band of rebels attacked a German post. They fired flaming arrows into the thatched roof and the soldiers were burned to death. The blackened head of an NCO was spiked on the flagpole as a grim warning. The rebellion spread like wildfire, down the coast and south-west as far as Songea, the Ngoni capital, and to the shores of Lake Nyasa. The Ingoni involvement marked the deadliest challenge to the Germans, for while the other tribes that had risen fought as rabble the Ingoni fielded 5000 disciplined warriors.

At the beginning of the rising, after the slaughter of the Germans at their outpost, the rebels poured down on the Roman Catholic Benedictine Mission at Nyangao and killed the Bishop, two Nuns and two Brothers. And now, here comes the miracle.

As the rebels ran through the Mission, killing and raising mayhem, Father Leo with several nuns prepared to meet their doom. As the nuns knelt and the Father stood over them to give them absolution a band of frenzied rebels burst upon them. Unabashed, Father Leo continuing with his dedication made the sign of the Cross. Immediately the natives stopped and believing that the Sign was a potent spell, which in this case it obviously was, they fled followed by the entire murderous band.

The Maji-Maji affair lasted over two years. Matters took much longer to evolve and resolve in those days than in modern times. While it lasted the times were desperate for all whites and coastal non-blacks. Eventually, marines were landed from ships in the vicinity and reinforcements were sent from Germany. The rising was crushed. Kinjikitile was caught and hanged. The rebel armies soon learned that the Magic Water was no match for machine-gun bullets. Even the Ngoni threw away their Maji bottles and fled. Their chief in the north, Mptua, was hanged, while Chabruma, chief in the south, fled to Portuguese territory but was murdered there.

Thereafter the Germans exacted terrible retribution. The lands of the three main tribes who had started the rebellion were laid waste. Houses were burned and the crops ruined. The famine that ensued killed ten times more people than were lost in the fighting, the total running from half to three-quarters of the total population. The havoc was so great the tribes never again cultivated their land. That went back to nature. Wild animals moved in and eventually the whole area was incorporated into a gigantic game reserve.

*

On the Saturday we arrived at Likoma island, one of the strangest set-ups in all Africa. On this island was the headquarters of the United Mission to Central Africa, cut off from all the stations on the mainland. The reason for this was really the history of Nyasaland (Malawai). It had all begun some sixty years before I arrived.

When David Livingstone made his call at Cambridge for people to go to Africa to stop the slave-trade, it was to the Lake Nyasa area in particular he directed those brave enough to take up the challenge. When the United Universities sent their Mission to Africa it was to this region that they came in 1861 after terrible travail en route. But those early missionaries found the land too hostile from warring natives and killing diseases to establish a bridgehead, so were forced to leave and set up shop in Zanzibar instead.

The hostile natives were the wild Angoni. As previously mentioned, they came up from South Africa as a breakaway Zulu impi which split into three parts near the bottom of Lake Nyasa. One section under its chief Mombera, came to the north of the lake and plundered and displaced the local tribes there. The slave trading was at its height then and it did not take the Angoni long to see the business attractions in it. They captured the local people and sold them to the Arabs. So serious became the ravaging that the local tribes fled en masse.

Now it appears that the Angoni had one weakness; they would not cross water. They had of course crossed the Limpopo and Zambezi rivers on their way, but that was by necessity and these rivers, mighty as they are, were not the open waters of the sea-like lake. The local people took advantage of the Angoni phobia and fled to Likoma island.

Although the UMCA had put down permanent stakes in Zanzibar they had not forgotten Livingstone's call and their pledge to establish a Mission on Lake Nyasa. When the missionaries returned for their second attempt in 1885 they found the mainland sparsely populated by the warlike Angoni tribe and the bulk of the population settled on Likoma island. So in 1885 they started their Mission on the island and built a large, fine cathedral, the like of which was incredible to find on an island far out on the lake. When the Mission eventually spread to the mainland and the rash of little Stations, such as we had visited, began appearing all along the lakeshore, the HQ remained on Likoma island.

A strange place indeed to find in the open lake with its huge cathedral, school, hospital and printing press. The Cathedral Church of St. Peter on Likoma island was indeed a marvel. It was built to replace an earlier church that was destroyed by fire in 1892. With that fire went the library, with the loss of 1,400 books, and nearly all the dwelling houses; just one of the disasters the early missionaries had to overcome.

The foundation stone of the new church was laid in 1903. Built in cruciform shape of local granite with arches formed with fired, ant-hill clay bricks. The roof was corrugated-iron covered with thatch for sound and heat insulation. It was somewhat smaller than the UMCA monumental one at Zanzibar, but with its colonnades and soaring arches it was still in grand style. But while the builders at Zanzibar had the benefit of being by the sea and therefore had greater facilities to hand, those by Lake Nyasa in the deep interior had very little. As Zanzibar Cathedral was built over the old slave-market so Likoma Cathedral was sited almost on the spot where witches were once burned.

*

We stayed on Likoma for three days over the weekend. It was pleasant there and I enjoyed strolling about the island. What a lovely place it was. It was bare except for a few enormous baobab trees, so big that you could have cut an arch in some of them and driven a car through. But the bareness had its beauty. Low, undulating hills made the walks interesting and the light breeze from the lake was refreshing. A few miles away the mainland looked blue and hazy.

On the Sunday I attended a service in the Cathedral. I found it a strange and rather disturbing experience. So foreign. Not African foreign. Foreign to me – a different religion. So different to the Church of Scotland services I had grown up with in Torryburn Kirk.

In conversation with the missionaries when travelling down the lake, I was hit with such a welter of new words on religion I began to think of them as of another language which I was expected to know and didn't, and that made me feel gawky and inferior. Words such as Eucharist and Matins and Canonical and Mass, some of which I had heard before but didn't know what they really meant. So, even though it showed my ignorance, I decided to ask and to read anything on the subject I could lay my hands on, first at Likoma where they had a good library, and wherever possible along my way.

It was easy to look up the words in a dictionary and when I did I was so disappointed. To find that 'Eucharist' and 'Mass' referred to the celebration of the Lord's Supper, the breaking of bread, those Latin terms seemed a travesty of words. 'Communion' was so much better, warmer, more descriptive and meaningful. And 'Matins' was 'Morning Prayers'! … oh dear, oh dear. I suppose it would be all right if you grew up with such things, and there was a certain advantage in having universal Latin terms which allowed a person to join in church services anywhere throughout the lands that once formed the old Roman empire, but in British environs it seemed such a shame not to use the beautiful English words for these events. I was pleased that my Church had left those Latin terms in the 'long, long ago'.

In describing the scene of the service in Likoma Cathedral I wrote in my diary that night, *'Of course the UMCA is very High English and as far as I can see, it is near being Roman Catholic, although they would not hear that said since there is a fairly bitter feeling between them. But I can't say I go with candles, tinkling bells, kneeling and chants. How different from the Church of Scotland'.*

I print the excerpt raw as I spoke to my diary at that time. Perhaps some judicious editing might save offence, and if taken I apologise. Quoting it in its original however carries the force and perplexity of a young man trying to grasp the imponderable. Here on Likoma I reiterated my decision made on the canoe journey with Padre Cann that I must find out more about the factions within the Christian religion.

What were the differences between the Roman Catholics of Lupingu Mission and the High English of Likoma? Their churches and their services were so much alike and their missionaries were all priests, yet they abhorred each other's ways. I had to sort out, if I could, a great number of conflicting thoughts and part-beliefs that confused my mind when I thought of them.

Really, the whole ethos of religion and religions was bewildering. Could one really accept the presence of an omnipotent God in the sky, all powerful, all-pervading, who could, and did, watch over every single soul on Earth and know, every minute of the day, what each one is doing and even thinking? And if one could accept that Presence, could one believe there is only one religion, and more incredibly, one faction of that religion that is acceptable to God, and that He would forsake all others even though the followers of those religions are praying equally piously to Him, albeit by different names of address, as the so called 'chosen ones'? It was all so baffling.

There was also the scientific side of the matter! With the great strides that were made in the last century, scientists could explain how the earth was made and eventually, no doubt, how we and all living creatures appeared, without, seemingly, all the hocus-pocus magic. A person could go mad thinking about it.

I did ponder over it as I travelled and what I write now is the product of assimilation over years, but which I believe is better included here while on the subject. I listened to those whom I thought might know the answers, as I did with the missionaries on the lake, and read all I could lay my hands on. I unravelled some threads to my satisfaction but mainly I was still baffled and perplexed.

The next section of my narrative deals with the complexities of religion which were very real and bewildering to me at the time in my life when I was travelling. To many readers, what I say may seem to be out-of-place or irrelevant in a book of travel. Nevertheless, since my story is part autobiographical as well as travel, I feel I must include my developing psyche and the soul-searching that went to make it. Indeed, without knowing at the time, this seeking for knowledge was partially the reason for my wanderings.

Some references and opinions I make may cause displeasure to some and if this is so, I apologise. I can only hope that some tolerance may be allowed a young man who thinks and dares to talk about what has become almost an unmentionable subject as religion. I hope that many may find my discourse interesting and even informative.

Those readers who have no interest in the subject or no desire to consider it in this context, may turn the pages to the section where the *Chancey Maples* steams away from Likoma Island.

*

First I had to sort out this question of 'Catholic'. Meeting the Romans with Padre Cann and attending the UMCA service at Lupingu had made me think deeply on the subject. On this 'Catholic question', it was with great surprise that I read that David Livingstone came to Africa as a missionary of the London Mission Society and not of The Church of Scotland. That, disconcerting as it was, was not the surprise I refer to here. It was his reason for choosing the LMS that I found strange. He made his approach to the LMS because of, as he wrote, its 'Catholicity'. He wrote that the LMS aimed, 'not to send

Presbyterianism, Independency, Episcopacy or any other form of church order, but only the glorious gospel to the heathen.' At the time I read that I knew only of Roman Catholicism and I could not equate that with Livingstone.

There is an interesting comparison with my religious quest and that of David Livingstone. It seems we not only shared initials but also an early desire to sort things out for ourselves rather than accept willy-nilly what we were expected to believe.

Neil Livingstone, his father, was a Calvinist zealot who abhorred even the mention of alcohol and believed that all non-religious literature was trash. David idolised his father but did not always see eye-to-eye with him, particularly on religion. Indeed it was a matter which drove a wedge between them. There is no record of David ever imbibing but he did disagree with his father in what he read.

"In reading," he wrote, "everything that I could lay my hands on was devoured except novels. Scientific works and books of travel were my especial delight; though my father, believing ... that the former were inimical to religion ... Our difference of opinion reached the point of open rebellion on my part, and his last application of the rod was on my refusal to peruse Wilderforce's *Practical Christianity*."

The great argument between science and theology seems to have worn better than the ways that fathers dealt with their teenage sons and their daft, modern ideas. 'Spare the rod and spoil the child' apparently did not end with childhood in those days but went on into the late teens. David did not sort out the ambivalence in his beliefs until his early twenties. Following his last experience of his father laying down his law by the rod, Livingstone wrote, "This dislike for religious reading continued for years." His rebellion ceased however when he devoured a special book, "The admirable *Philosophy of a Future State*," by the nonconformist minister, Dr Thomas Dick, a verbose writer whose monotonous style did not stop David from ploughing through it. "It was gratifying to find my own ideas, that religion and science are not hostile, but friendly to each other."

It says something of David's character that having read and been carried away with the book he beat a path to the author's door in Broughty Ferry, not far from Dundee. Dick, a rather strange character who had built his house on a self-made hillock – 8000 barrow loads of earth and a year to make – in order to study astronomy. David and the old eccentric appeared to hit it off well together and David came away with the peace of mind from Dick's wisdom that implied that, far from denying God, science, by proving the utter complexity of the world, made it obvious that there had to be a Maker.

David's parental turmoil ended on a happy note, I was pleased to learn. Neil Livingstone mellowed and turned away from the severest side of Calvinism and thereafter he and his son grew ever closer together.

Later I learned that 'Catholic' meant 'universal'. From that, the term used at the beginning of Christianity and for the next three hundred years afterwards, in reference to the whole body of true followers of Jesus Christ, was simply the 'Catholic' or 'Universal' Church.

*

This state of affairs ended in 325 AD at Nicaea, Asia Minor (now Iznik, Turkey) at the first Christian World Council under the patronage of Emperor Constantine the Great, who had a fine palace in Nicaea. At that conference Rome accepted Christianity and made it its own.

But before Emperor Constantine would make Christianity the official religion of the Roman Empire he insisted that certain changes be made to the existent doctrine. The Immaculate Conception had to be included and made official, a matter that caused great consternation among the Jerusalem Christians.

On a personal level, the idea of the Immaculate Conception had bothered me from my early teens. In the village where I grew up people didn't talk about religion other than in the church. Maybe that was just as well, for with people of all denominations living cheek by jowl discussions or arguments of that nature would have affected neighbourly relations. Since time immemorial communities have learned not to bring such subjects to the surface and it is when this policy is forgotten that civil order crumbles and wars break out. But while the 'don't mention religion' ethos was good for social relations it did not help an enquiring mind to develop.

It was my call-up to the army at eighteen that gave me an opportunity to mix freely with Catholics and others in a partially jocular, irreverent manner and thereby widen my parameters on God. In Nairobi on some Sunday mornings a few of us would go to the church that gave the best tea-and-buns after the service and the RC Chapel was high on the list. We non-Catholics did not attend the service, but shared in the laughs and ribaldry round the table afterwards on who got what, Hail Mary's and the like, by way of punishments after their Confession.

It was all light-hearted and froth-on-the-surface stuff and soon forgotten, except, that is, if you had a mind to dig deeper. I got to wondering how the RC's could do whatever they liked during the week and go and get absolution on Sunday in return for a few incantations, while we non-Catholics had to live with our sins till we died. Surely God had never intended to create such an unfair world. Even more bewildering to me then was hearing my Catholic pals appear to direct all their prayers for forgiveness and help to Holy Mary, while that deity was hardly spoken of in the Protestant Church. It appeared that in the Catholic Church Mary was placed on a higher plane than Jesus.

I tackled a Protestant Parish Minister about this, albeit in a very diffident way, and he said in a low, confidential manner so as not to be heard by others who were there, "In The Church Of Scotland you don't have to believe in the Immaculate Conception." That remark gave me great peace of mind.

Further research began to make sense of it all. I learned that Romans had no trouble believing in man-made gods. Indeed, it was common practice to make the high-and-mighty of the land into gods to raise them above the common man, a custom they inherited from the Greeks before them. Had not Emperor Augustus paid a great deal to have himself made a god in his own lifetime and Constantine fully expected to be made one when he died. And did not the mother of Alexander the Great say that his earthly father, Phillip II, was not the real father of her son, but that she had been visited by the great god Zeus and by that Divine Being she had had an immaculate conception? So Virgin Births were not unique by the time Jesus came along. However, neither Hebrews nor Christians made any claims to Mary's conception being anything other than natural. The matter of Jesus' divinity was not raised until the time of the Council of Nicaea in 325 AD.

At that meeting, in modern day Turkey, Roman Bishops, under the influence of Emperor Constantine, insisted that the Immaculate Conception be made Christian dogma against the creed and wishes of the Antiochene party Bishops from Christ's homeland. These two Bishops represented a long line of Christians, going back over 300 years, and they and their flock believed Jesus' mother Mary was no more than a good woman who had had a natural conception.

Without the aegis of the Immaculate Conception the Romans could never have worshipped a Jew, one of an inferior, subjugate people and especially one whose legitimacy was in question. If there were any doubts as to the value of the Virgin Birth to the Romans' need to dissimulate Jesus from his people or race, it is a fact that less than a century later Emperor Augustine proclaimed that Jews would be allowed to exist in the Christian empire, but with inferior status. Christians had emerged from the shadow of persecution and were now a world power.

More changes to the Christian religion were required by Emperor Constantine before it could be adopted by the Romans. Perhaps even more controversial than the original Creed being adjusted to accommodate the Virgin Birth, was the insistence of Constantine that the Bishop of Rome be made Pope in perpetuity and that only he could commune with God and interpret His words. These changes appalled the bishops who represented Antioch. That Romans should claim total ascendancy of the religion they had had no part in forming, seemed more to do with the Glory of Rome than the word of the Lord. Moreover, that even the Emperor, the most powerful person in the world, could claim to speak for God in nominating His supreme envoy on earth was surely totally absurd. Three bishops actually plucked up enough courage to write a letter to Emperor Constantine saying, 'We committed an impious act ... by subscribing to a blasphemy from fear of you.' With the changed ethos of the Christian Church the religion was now, rightly, called *Roman* Catholicism.

So Roman Catholicism and the Papacy were born and Roman dogma dominated Christianity for the next twelve hundred years.

During the 16th century a great social and religious upheaval developed throughout Europe. People such as Martin Luther and John Calvin protested against the ways of the Pope and Rome. They wanted the Church to be reformed back to the way it was in the beginning. After much upheaval the Reformation was brought about. Gone from the Protestants' churches were the Roman Catholic theatrical ceremonies, effigies and ostentation. There were those who said that the pantomime was all part and parcel of the old pagan religions that the Romans carried with them when they accepted Christianity.

Protestantism broke the link with Rome and the cult of Mary was minimised. Latin was dropped in favour of the language of the country. In Britain King James VI of Scotland and I of England had the Bible translated into English so that all, not just those academics skilled in Latin, could understand what the 'Word' was all about.

Two hundred years before King James' time Henry VIII broke from Rome when the Pope refused him permission to divorce Catherine in order to marry Anne Boleyn. He set up his own Church of England with himself as head, but changed little else. The priests, the ceremony and the church décor remained much as it had always been. Eventually the majority of the Church of England did follow more in the ways of Protestantism but a small elite, though distancing themselves from Rome, still retained the ceremony and rituals of the Roman church. Such then was the High English Church.

All this finally explained to me how the 'Romans' of Lupingu on the Lake and the High English UMCA priests of Likoma Island differed, although to the uninformed appeared to be of the same.

*

On the Monday the *Chauncy Maples* steamed away from Likoma and headed eastward across the relatively short passage to the coast of Mozambique. A short distance it may be, but no travel on Lake Nyasa is without possible hazards. In that narrow strait a water-spout, one of many likely to occur suddenly on the lake, may rise from the primeval bowels of the earth with the speed of an express train to burst from the surface with a force that can knock over a steamer. Ten years before this time the *Ousel* of Likoma was sunk by a water-spout here with the loss of two lives. And in 1945 the *Chikulupi* suffered the same fate, luckily near enough the shore to ensure no loss of life. Many canoes with their occupants have been mangled in this fashion. It was not for nothing Livingstone called Nyasa 'the Lake of Storms'.

The *Chauncy Maples'* destination on this occasion was the UMCA Teacher Training College at Kango, directly opposite Likoma. Here I enjoyed my first steps in Portuguese East Africa. Kango was quite a big Mission station where teachers of both sexes were trained for work here and in Tanganyika. Apart from a little school somewhere it was the only UMCA mission on Portuguese territory. There had been others, many others, all up the eastern side of the lake to Tanganyika. These had been established before the territory was divided into political units.

Although the Portuguese were in East Africa centuries before any other European nation and laid claims to suzerainty over great tracks of land, they never tried to penetrate the interior more than a few miles from the coastal areas. It was only when the British missionaries with a few commercial pioneers settled in what was then the far interior that the Portuguese, as represented by a Major Serpa Pinto, ventured out in 1888 to claim what they had assumed to be their rightful territory. Sir Harry Johnson, representing British interests, went and parleyed with the Major and between the two they settled the division of the land amicably. Thus was history made. All the land from the lake to the coast would be Portuguese territory and that which became known as Nyasaland, and later Malawi, would be recognised as British administered land.

This way all the mission stations on the eastern side of the lake were now under the rule of the Portuguese who became very difficult and belligerent to the British missionaries on their land. The matter came to a head in November 1911, when a UMCA missionary, Padre Arthur Douglas, whose brother was later to become Bishop of Nyasaland, was shot dead by a Portuguese officer. There was no record of the Portuguese official ever being charged and as time went by matters with the Portuguese bureaucracy became so difficult the Mission gradually closed down the stations in Mozambique until only Kango and the little school somewhere were left. I was told the story of Douglas' murder while standing on the very spot where it had happened, which made it all the more poignant.

From Kango the *Chauncy Maples* crossed the lake again to the eastern, Nyasaland, side to visit stations there. I hoped we would visit Livingstonia, 'the Scotch Mission,' as it was generally referred to. The term 'Scotch' was in current use in Scotland when I was a boy. We thought of ourselves as Scotch and spoke about Scotchmen. But Scotch seemed to go out of fashion and Scot and Scotsman, which had been less used before, came into more common use.

Livingstonia was the mission of the Free Church of Scotland and here I had to sort out another conundrum like that of the priests, for Scotland had two Churches, both Protestant, but fearfully independent. In my home village,

Torryburn, our kirk was Church of Scotland while the next one, Newmills, had the Free Church. I doubt if a handful of people, if that, knew the difference. The services in both were the same and to all intents and purposes they were the same. But the villagers who went to one did not enter the other. We children at school sat together and played together but we never knew why our parents attended different kirks. Alec Seath, who started the journey with me, shared a desk with me in every class was a Free Kirker, but we never got round to knowing why we were different in that respect. It was not until I ran into the Missions of the two 'Scotch' Churches that I set myself to find out.

The National Church of Scotland was founded in 1690 very much on the Protestant faith of John Knox and the doctrine of John Calvin. The Church is presided over by The Moderator who is elected each year at the General Assembly at Edinburgh

The Free Church of Scotland was a breakaway unit from the National Church of Scotland. Similar in most ways to the national church the 'Free Kirk' was adamant in having no truck with Episcopalianism, or Government Patronage. The break came in1843 when the Presbytery of Auchterarder, Fife, was required by government rule to induct a Minister not of the choice of the Parish. At that year's General Assembly the Revd Dr David Welsh, who had been the Moderator of the last Assembly, did not convene the meeting, but rose and asserting the rights of the protesters, marched out of the hall and convened another meeting in the Tanfield Hall, constituting those attending as the Free Church of Scotland. Although broken from the Establishment the Free Church still maintained the Confession of Faith and the Standards of the Church of Scotland. The protesters maintained that the Free Church, known locally as the 'Wee Kirk', was the true National Church of the Reformation and many parishes went over to the Free Kirk'. Torryburn Church has on record that a certain minister of that time stood down from the pulpit one Sunday morning and walked down the aisle and out of the church, followed by half the congregation, and set up a Free Kirk in the neighbouring village.

The sentiments of David Livingstone, a most apolitical man, would appear to lie with the Free Kirk. As a boy, before the breakaway from the National Church, he must have listened to adult conversation in his house and been carried away by angry comments and references to 'patronage'. To show his feelings he carved on a tree the slogan, 'No State Church'. This seems a most unusual thing for an undemonstrative person like Livingstone to do, but I had another personal experience of him doing that again, which I will relate when we get there, further down the trail.

Livingstonia was the Mission of the Free Church of Scotland. Unfortunately not being a UMCA church, it was not on the Bishop's itinerary, although from what he said I gathered that had the Mission been more easily accessible he would have gladly called in to say his goodbyes for courtesy sake for there was apparently good feeling between the churches. But Livingstonia was situated some distance from the lake, on the rising uplands leading to the Nyika escarpment that barred the way to the fertile plateau on top.

It was obvious that Bishop Thorne had the highest regard for the Scotch Mission. He described to me Livingstonia's wonderful church, the excellent workshops that turned out skilled craftsmen and most of all, in his interest, the first-rate hospital. Apparently several missionaries of all denominations had been grateful for the medical skills and facilities at Livingstonia. One early UMCA missionary of great note, Dr W.P. Johnson, recuperated from illnesses there on more than one occasion. He is reported to have said, "Should Dr Samuel Johnson have visited there, he certainly would have lost all prejudice against the Scotch." Had that happened, despite the time difference, perhaps the great man of letters might not have made his celebrated remark that 'oats are only good for horses and Scotchmen.'

It was not only the white missionaries who were grateful for the medical skills available at Livingstonia. The hospital was designed and intended for the natives and to them the early medics, Drs Law and Stewart and others, practised the very latest surgery and medical care. There is on record a case before the turn of the 20th century when one doctor from Livingstonia administered mouth-to-mouth resuscitation on a native far gone with fever, surely one of the earliest mentions of this type of first-aid. There is no record of how the native faired, but the doctor, through his efforts, was smitten with the disease and died.

I already knew that the Scottish Missions in general and Free Kirk in particular, put the emphasis of their mission work on teaching practical skills, in contrast to most other denominations who see reading and writing as most important so that the students are able to read the Bible. Perhaps this was the Scottish hard-working and hard-headed ethos that Livingstone echoed when he put commercialism before Christianity in his call for help in Africa. An early Livingstonia timetable showed there was little time for dallying for both students and staff throughout a working day. Hard work, and lots of it, was rated at least as high as time spent in the classroom and church.

Livingstone knew all about that. As a boy of thirteen, like most others in the little town of Blantyre, his day, summer and winter, started, with the clanging of the mill bell at 5.30 a.m. After a rushed bowl of porridge he ran to the tall, gaunt, gabled factory and worked at the spinning jenny, with only breaks for meals, until 8 p.m. An oddball, he worked with his Latin-grammar book and others propped up in front of him while his nimble fingers worked mechanically, and mill lassies with glee pitched bobbins to try and knock his book down. After 8pm, with other lads, he attended night school for two hours, followed by a special Latin class and then at home continued his 'dictionary work', as he called it, until his mother chased him to bed at midnight.

The importance with which night schools, often financed and run by benevolent industrialists, were held in Scotland was emphasised by Livingstone in his first book, *Missionary Travels*. There he writes of his night school where his teacher was moderate in his charges, '… *and some of my school-fellows now rank in positions far above what they appeared ever likely to come to when in the village school. If such a system were established in England, it would prove a never-ending blessing to the poor.*'

From Livingstonia the *CM* puffed her way down the coast to the UMCA mission at Kota-Kota. This is where Bishop Chauncy Maples, who was drowned in the lake, is buried. Here there was a good brick hospital and surgery that almost rivalled Likoma. Changed days from half a century or so before when Kota-Kota was a bustling Arab town with 10,000 mixed population and the biggest slave depot in central Africa.

Twice more we crossed and re-crossed the lake to visit other stations before finally we steamed into Monkey Bay where Bishop Thorne disembarked and we made our farewells. A most unforgettable man, warm and friendly yet possessing great dignity.

The *Chauncy Maples* had one more stop before I reached the end of my voyage. Next day at the most southerly point of the lake the *CM* steamed up the mouth of the Shire River. Gradually the banks on either side grew nearer until we stopped at Mponda where I disembarked. I offered to pay Captain Haywood something towards my fare but he sternly refused with the remark, "Away with you, you're going to need all you've got where you're going and I wish I was coming with you." Grand old man, I mused, I hope I have your imagination and zest for life if I'm lucky enough to get to your age.

Looking back over Lake Nyasa I realised how privileged I was to have been given such a journey. The canoe run with Padre Cann and the voyage on the *Chauncy Maples* with the opportunity to share time with the bishop and all the missionaries and the crew of the wonderful old puffer. A memorable journey for a very lucky and appreciative hitch-hiker.

Regrettably, I must end this chapter on a sad note. While writing of this episode in my journey I contacted the UMCA offices in London to ask about Padre Cann and learned he had retired some time before and now lived at Bexill-on-Sea, Sussex. It was a wonderful moment to talk to him on the telephone and hear his surprise and later I had the delight of visiting him at his home. He was not a well man, but we spent a wonderful afternoon reminiscing about old times. He showed me his book *Into Africa* and particularly the part that included me, and proud I was to have a place there. I said I should like a copy and asked if he had one for sale. He looked taken aback, apologetic even, "But they cost

£10," he said with some discomfort, and then by way of explanation, "All proceeds are going towards putting a new roof on the school at Manda." My heart went out to him. In his last days he was still the missionary. "For that," I said, "I will willingly pay double."

Not long after that I received a letter from Evelyn, his wife, to say that Stanley had died. How thankful and pleased I was that we had renewed our friendship after all those years.

Chapter Seventeen

FOUR YARDS OF CALICO
And A Pile Of Rotting Skulls

"Let the head grow wise but keep the heart always young and playful."
(David Livingstone)

If conception may be said to start with a twinkle in an eye, the town of Blantyre, Nyasaland (Malawi), could owe its birth to the crusading glint in a very special man's eye. The story begins late on a night in May, 1874, when a charismatic man of towering inner strength and composure rose to address the Scottish Free Church General Assembly, in Edinburgh. The evening was far gone and the assembly had sat through a long and particularly boring speech. Minds and bodies were longing to up-and-away. Indeed, many people had already left and great deserts of space mottled the audience. 10 p.m. is a late hour for men who had risen early and done a long, hard day's work before they arrived. Nevertheless, those who remained were the backbone of the organisation, and as in any other, those to whom the decision making nearly always fell. But even those people sat with lack-lustre eyes.

Yet when Dr James Stewart stood to his full height and bold stature and paused to survey his audience with those steady, compelling eyes that blazed with sincerity, a galvanic charge ran through the room and even the dullest eyes snapped awake and everyone listened eagerly before even a word was spoken.

The motion which Dr Stewart was about to propose was that The Free Church of Scotland should establish a Mission by Lake Nyasa to fulfil the request made by David Livingstone in concluding his speech at Cambridge in 1857.

This was not the first time Stewart had addressed this august body on such a matter. Fourteen years before, in 1860, as a young medical student, he had put forward a proposal that he, with a band of similar minded colleagues whom he had drawn to himself, be allowed to go to that place to establish a Mission. On that occasion the array of balding, grey heads with hoary faces contrasted dramatically with Stewart's boyish looks. Almost to a man the meeting saw Stewart as a callow boy and thought his idea was so fantastic it was not even put before the committee.

The Free Church was strong on foreign missions and had them in India, China, and South Africa, etc., but to put one in Central Africa where no white person other than Livingstone had ever been seemed too wild a prospect, especially in the hands of such young and inexperienced people. Perhaps they were right. The early history of Missions which eventually settled in that area showed that 60% of all missionaries sent there died within the first five years of their service, mainly from malaria and blackwater fever.

Although Stewart's early attempt to go to Nyasaland was laughed out of court the Assembly was impressed by his youthful zeal and character. So much so that the following year, 1861, when the Free Church Foreign Mission Committee decided to send an envoy to meet Dr Livingstone on the Zambezi River and discuss the feasibility of establishing a Mission by Lake Nyasa it was the young Dr Stewart whom they sent.

That was a momentous journey. On board the ship was Mary Moffat, Mrs Livingstone, who was looking forward to being reunited with her husband whom she had not seen since his return to Africa four years before. One can imagine the thrilling anticipation of young Stewart on his way to meet his hero and to witness the reunion of the now world famous husband and wife. Alas the whole episode was to prove an unmitigated tragedy.

A few months earlier a party of UMCA missionaries, headed by Bishop Mackenzie, had joined Livingstone by the Zambezi on the same premise as Dr Stewart, to see about setting up a mission on the lake. Mackenzie had expected Livingstone to put himself and his boat, the *Pioneer*, at their disposal to get them to the lake. After all, they had come at Livingstone's suggestion to start missionary work there. But Livingstone was at that time set on exploring the course of the Ruvuma River which runs into the Indian Ocean some six hundred miles to the north of the Zambezi, as an alternative to the Shire River which only he knew, being the only white person to have reached its source, gave access to Lake Nyasa. The Shire unfortunately was blocked by awful cataracts no boat could pass. At that time Livingstone had no way of knowing that the Ruvuma did not flow out of the lake, its source being in mountains further east and therefore useless as a means of access. Never one to alter plans already made nor be diverted from a path once started, he was not disposed to abandon his own work at the arrival of the UMCA people. They had to wait three months until Livingstone would be ready to lead them to the lake.

While waiting, Bishop Mackenzie, lacking Livingstone's long experience with the natives, became embroiled in tribal politics and squabbles which in Livingston's view would undermine the Bishop's missionary work in future when he would have to be seen by all tribes to be unbiased. Mackenzie made his way inland to a small Mission that had already been established to settle slaves who Livingstone and Mackenzie had released from their Arab captors before the explorer had left to complete his present task.

Later, in appalling wet weather Mackenzie, accompanied by a younger assistant, the Revd Henry Burrup, set off on a journey of several days in a canoe down the Luo River to meet up with Livingstone on his return. The Luo, also known as the Ruo, from the Portuguese *Rio* is a tributary of the Shire which is a tributary of the Zambezi. Well behind time and desperate to keep his rendezvous with Livingstone whom he feared would not wait for him and almost driven mad by hordes of mosquitoes, he and Burrup attempted to make a night run to avoid camping. The pale moonlight for once was not blotted out by rain and all went well until the canoe hit a sandbar and overturned. Although they all struggled onto the sand island and managed to retrieve most of their sodden belongings, their case containing their life-saving quinine was lost. Bishop Mackenzie, well under par in health at the start of their journey, died first and three weeks later the younger Burrup, after a horrendous journey on foot back to the little mission station, followed him.

Meanwhile at the rendezvous by the mouth of the Luabo River a boat had arrived bringing with it, on the last arduous leg of their journey from Cape Town, an elderly Miss Mackenzie, the Bishop's sister, and the young, lively Mrs Burrup, a bride of less than a year. Instead of the glad meeting, so looked forward to, they were given the sad news that both their men had died. Heartbroken the women were taken back down to the sea for the journey home, in the care of John Kirk (later Sir, British Consul, Zanzibar) out of the place that Kirk called "hell on earth, if ever I saw one," and Kirk had seen many such places in his five years with Livingstone.

It was all a sad ending to a beginning filled with so many high hopes and brave crusading spirit. Blame would be levied at this one and that and on reasons beyond anyone's control. There was little doubt that differences in personalities had had their effect. Before the frost set in, and despite Livingstone's abhorrence of bishops, he and Mackenzie had got on very well, each respecting the other, the Bishop's warm, jovial personality contrasted with the Doctor's dour reticence with flashes of mirth.

But the sunny lining to the dark cloud did fade away and there was little cohesion towards the end. Did Livingstone renege on that which was expected of him? Did the UMCA expect too much by not coming fully prepared, and did they presume too much by taking it for granted that the Doctor would lay aside his own work and give their mission his full time and attention? Had Livingstone become more explorer than missionary and did he put his dream of establishing a white colony in the Shire highlands before his evangelical work? Did he, weighed down with trying to be all things to all men, become just too cantankerous to deal with? Did his brother Charles, a pernicious, impossible man by all accounts, who was in his party and who lacked David's reticence, let his hate of the Episcopal High English Church run raw and foul up any attempts of harmony? Whatever the causes, the differences between the UMCA and David Livingstone rendered further co-operation impossible.

As to the question why Livingstone did not give the UMCA mission the immediate support that was expected of him, my own view is that, pragmatist that he was, he held the ending of the slave trade and the slaughter of countless thousands of natives that ensued from it at the very top of his priorities, even before missionary work. It was no slip of the tongue that he called for Commerce and Christianity to be established in the Lake Nyasa region, the epicentre of this awful blight on humanity as he saw it and described so vividly.

Ever in his mind, as I recorded in Zanzibar, were the sights of no-hope chain-gangs, weighed down with tusks and other exports, in abject misery, lashed and abused pitilessly by their drovers, leaving behind them a trail of corpses that marked their passage and stank from far off. The Reverend A. Hatherwick, an early Church of Scotland missionary, in his book *The Romance of Blantyre* quotes some prices at which slaves would be sold further along the line;

A young, strong man	*58*	*yards*	*of*	*calico*
A young, unmarried woman	*56*	"	"	"
A young mother	*36*	"	"	"
The child extra	*4*	"	"	"
Elderly man or woman	*4*	"	"	"
Toothless old man	*2*	"	"	"

Calico was 4 pence or 6 pence. (approx. 1½ to 2½ new pence) per yard. There was not a chief or a headman who had not his hands red with the slave trade.

Pitiful as these prices were in representing the value placed on human beings there were other quotes of prices in some places being as low as four yards of calico for each man, three for a woman and two for a child. The pile of rotting skulls that went with each live slave handed over was included in the price, free.

The Arab slave-traders had to be stopped and the wild, aggressive tribes pacified. A war had to be fought and that was not the job for Christian missionaries who had to be seen always as people of peace. Unlike Muslims who, it is said, were told by Mohammed to spread their religion by the sword, white settlers were required to bring peace to the land. That was Livingstone's abiding passion and he would go to the utmost lengths to try and bring it about. He saw the need for a steam boat to counter the Arab dhows ferrying the slaves across the lake from Kota-Kota and for that he was willing to put up £2000 – a fortune in those days – of his own money, raised by the sale of his book, *Missionary Travels*.

At the time of the UMCA Mission's arrival Livingstone was desperately looking for an alternative river route to Lake Nyasa to allow settlers easier passage than up the Shire River. This then was his reason for not laying aside his exploration of the Ruvuma River at the arrival of the UMCA mission. Every day away from his task meant thousands of natives lost on the treadmill of slavery. Better a thousand native lives preserved, he may have thought, than perhaps one or two souls saved. What good a Mission in an empty land? More lives saved today meant more souls to save later. The establishment of a white colony was imperative for the ultimate benefit of the Africans.

Livingstone, Missionary or Explorer? Hard to say, but he certainly accomplished more by his exploration than his missionary work. But who can separate the two for all his exploration was directed to saving the natives in body and soul. He was almost certainly a disappointment to his parents-in-law, especially Mary who it would appear believed that their son-in-law was more interested in self-aggrandisement by wandering in the wilds than in mission work. She felt he could be more useful doing what was expected of him when he was brought out, i.e. helping in the mission where everyone was overworked, rather than traipsing round the jungle, more interested it seemed in the geography of the country than the people.

My own view, from gathered legends that still lingered in areas where I crossed his old paths and afterwards by a great deal of research on the man, is that he never ceased being God's man. From the time he went to Broughty Ferry his faith never wandered. What did alter after he went to Africa was the direction he believed God wanted him to go, and the purpose of his efforts to do God's will. I believe he realised from what he saw in East Africa that saving lives by stopping the slave trade was of more immediate importance than trying to teach them Christianity. Indeed, he was short-tempered with some missionaries – as with Bishop Mackenzie – when they put the setting up of missions before the terrible slaughter of the natives and the plight of those that survived. Nevertheless, throughout all his wanderings he never forgot his initial mission to spread Christianity. He makes many references to preaching to the locals, usually in their own language, of which he spoke many, when he was long enough in an area to do so. Even the most primitive natives usually recognise a God. He may not have converted many but he was recognised far and wide as a non-violent, holy man and as such made many influential friends and always left behind him a legacy of goodwill which benefited white men who followed him in later years. And far from exploring for self-engrandisement, I have the impression that the man could not care less what people thought of him. Everything he did by way of exploration was directed to find ways into the interior from east or west to allow the introduction of white commerce in order to eradicate slavery. In the end, who did the more good, he or his colleagues? Where they counted on their fingers the souls they saved at enormous cost of white lives, he saved hundreds of thousands of lives, millions perhaps, and averted colossal untold misery.

Missionary or Explorer? The values? Souls or life? 'Souls' defined by virtue of the native stating his/her acceptance of Christ and showing they are leading their life in accordance with Christian principles. 'Lives' measured by thriving communities going about their daily lives in areas that would have been empty. Which is more important? It depends on whose scales you use.

The UMCA sent out the new Bishop Tozer to lead the mission by the Zambezi, but soon he declared the Lake Nyasa region was not yet ripe for mission work and, as previously mentioned, withdrew all their personnel to Zanzibar. Nearly twenty years were to go by before they returned.

All the events leading to the deaths of Bishop Mackenzie and Henry Burrup had happened while the young Dr James Stewart was on the high seas on the same errand as the tragic bishop had been. So it was into an atmosphere of real doom and gloom that he arrived. The only gleam of light was in the happiness that was so apparent in the united Dr and Mrs Livingstone. But even that light was soon to be extinguished.

Within three months, on 27th April 1862, Mary Moffat was also dead from malaria and buried under a great baobab tree at Shupanga, near the banks of the Zambezi. She was forty-one. Even the sadness of her death was overlaid with David Livingstone's acrimony, directed at, of all people, Dr James Stewart. It seems that Mrs Livingstone and the young doctor formed a strong friendship during their many weeks voyaging from the UK, and spurious rumours were rife. If those who spread the gossip had only known the secrets the pair shared they would have been even more surprised than that of the time-honoured assumption they made that they had witnessed assignations between the young man and the woman twice his age. And indeed they were right, for notes had gone from the woman inviting the young man to her cabin at all times of the night. Alas, it was not his sexual prowess she wished him to display but his medical skills. Yet, strangely, she was not ill. At least not in medical terms.

The Mary Moffat who arrived with James Stewart was not the wife David Livingstone had left at home four years before. Approaching forty, with a three-year-old child and others growing up, so tired of managing on her own with no real home for the past ten years, she 'hit the bottle' and cursed the stupidity of missionaries who ruined their lives and those about them in a useless cause. Never the quiet, genteel, suffering one that one is led to believe, she had now become loud and coarse in her condemnation. In the night, wild with the frustrations of her life, riven with guilt that she, the daughter and wife of missionaries, should condemn their work, all fired up with liquor and unable to sleep, she would send for Dr Stewart to come and administer laudanum to her so she could find escape in sleep.

A strong bond of friendship had grown between them, but it was not that that Livingstone criticised. Indeed it was because of this friendship and the help that Stewart had given his wife that David asked James to say the last rites at her funeral. What made the missionary angry with the young doctor, that which he would always hold against him, was the fact that James had told Mary, perhaps in a jocular way, that people were suspecting them of having an affair. Mary was appalled at the idea that anyone should think of her in this way. So-much-so she raved of it in her delirium and her husband would have it that she might have survived if she had not been worried out of her mind with the shame she would have to live with in the future.

But what worried David even moreso was his belief that Mary had lost her faith and had gone to her maker an unbeliever and as such be condemned to everlasting darkness. He took some heart from the fact that when in her last moments, too far gone to speak, he asked her if she believed in God she had looked up skywards, an act which he took to be affirmative.

A little story ends this sad tale, one that runs against all the disparaging things that have been written about Mary's ways and behaviour and her husband's tough, uncompromising exterior. The words are David's own to Mary as recorded in his diary:

"I said to her a few days before her fatal illness, 'We old bodies must be more sober and not play so much.' 'Oh, no,' she said. 'You must always be playful as you have always been. I would not like you to be grave as some folk I have seen.' This led me to feel what I have always believed to be true, to let the head grow wise but keep the heart always young and playful."

This history of the early missionary days in the Lake Nyasa area was made all the more poignant when told to me only three or four weeks after my own encounter with malaria and I realised how lucky I was to be living in an age of modern drugs and knowledge. In Livingstone's time the basic fact that malaria is carried by mosquitoes was not known. Had I done my wandering in those days I would almost certainly have died from the bout.

After Mary's death, heart broken but still indomitable, Livingstone carried on with his exploration, more pertinacious than ever, much to the chagrin of those who accompanied him. His brother Charles together with Kirk became so depressed and ill they had to be sent home.

Like those of the UMCA, James Stewart also came to the conclusion that it was useless to consider the setting up of a Mission station in this region at that time. He had been greatly saddened and disillusioned by the whole business and the people involved. It is said he even threw his copy of Livingstone's book, *Missionary Travels* into the Zambezi. On his homeward journey he arrived back in Zanzibar ragged as a beggar, in poor health and more than a little demoralised. The report he gave to the Free Church Foreign Missions Committee on his return was despondent and dispirited.

But here he was, fourteen years later, back in the same hall, addressing the same Assembly, older, more mature and purposeful, putting forward the same motion he had done as a callow student. That time he had been inspired by Livingstone's cry for help. This time he was fired by the awesome tragedy of the Great Missionary's death. He had attended the burial in Westminster Abbey on Saturday 18th April 1874, and regained all his earlier fervour for taking up the challenge that Livingstone had set. He now looked back with a more adult view at his encounter with the man who had thrown the entire nation into mourning and was proud of have actually met that man. He now viewed with compassion the peccadilloes of behaviour under extreme hardship and sorrow that he had witnessed and saw them now as human. Livingstone's work and achievements were too great to be cast aside because of some minor personal differences. He decided then and there to give his life to furthering the work to which Dr Livingstone had given his life. This time, when Stewart put forward his motion it was carried unanimously.

*

On the morning of 12th October 1875, something happened that had never happened before in Central Africa, something after which nothing would be quite the same again for the people who lived there. Under a sun-burnished sky from out of the head-waters of the Shire River and into the calm of Lake Nyasa the little SS *Ilala*- named after the place where David Livingstone had died – completed her maiden voyage. It was the first steam ship ever to sail on any Central African waterway.

Those natives who were near the lake shore drew back in fear and astonishment, wondering how a boat could move without sail or paddles, and seeing smoke belching from the funnel, they called it the 'fire ship'. Their fears were unfounded for unlike the dhows this boat had come to save rather than enslave them.

After the engine was silenced and the anchor lowered the sound of singing floated across the water and may have allayed the fears of the locals even though they would not understand the words.

All people that on Earth do dwell,
Sing to the Lord with cheerful voice.

Seventeen months after James Stewart's proposal the first people of the Free Church of Scotland Mission by Lake Nyasa were singing their praise and thanksgiving for their deliverance at the end of their long, arduous and often dangerous journey from home.

In charge of the party was Lieutenant James Young, a most remarkable man in many ways. He it was who had led the earlier expedition with Mrs Livingstone and Dr Stewart to meet Dr Livingstone on the Zambezi in 1861. Apart from his great qualities as a leader Young had already passed into history in a completely different field. Starting with his father as a joiner in Glasgow he soon went on to study chemistry at Anderson's College and later became a leader in that field. Following his experiments between 1847–50 he discovered how to distil oil from shale in Scotland and founded a great industry in Midlothian producing liquid and solid paraffin. He later became known as Young of Kelly. David Livingstone, a life-long friend, called him Sir Paraffin. Having acquired wealth, Young gave generously to fund Livingstone's expeditions and later gave his time and energies to the Free Church causes following his great friend's call for volunteers to end the slave trade.

It was an enormous task of the day to put the Mission on the lake. Young had made sure they did not make the same mistake the UMCA had done fifteen years earlier by arriving without having their own boat. The SS *Ilala* was designed and built in Scotland and was the forerunner of all other steam ships that would sail on the lake, including the SS *Chauncy Maples.* She was made in portable units that could be bolted together and dissembled and assembled when necessary, with a boiler that could be rolled or sledged across difficult terrain. Transported by large ship from builder's yard to Africa, up the navigable Zambesi to the mouth of the Shire River, assembled there, sailed by its own steam to the foot of the cataracts, dissembled and carried, the boiler rolled, to the top, reassembled and sailed serenely onto the lake. A remarkable achievement for everyone concerned.

Young was sixty-four when he arrived on the *Ilala* and only stayed a year before returning to Scotland. In that time he saw the Mission put down roots by a bay at the south end of the lake where the water was crystal clear, a place that would be named Cape Maclear after Sir Thomas Maclear, Astronomer Royal at the Cape, a lifelong friend of Livingstone's and to whom the explorer sent copious reports and map readings. As a navigator Livingstone had few peers. Sir Thomas said you could plot your way through Africa by David's readings and know at all times exactly where you were. The established Mission was named Livingstonia. James Young died seven years later in 1883.

When he left, Young handed over the leadership of the Mission to his second-in-command, Dr Robert Laws who held that position for over fifty years and became famously known as Laws of Livingstonia.

Laws' presence in the Free Church Mission was something of an anachronism for he belonged to the National or Established Church of Scotland and at that period the schism between the two Churches, each claiming to represent Scotland, was wide and deep. Having a National in charge of a Free Church mission may seem strange even today. Having it happen in 1875 must have been incredible. Yet there it was.

When the Free Church took up Stewart's proposal to send a Mission to Nyasaland the National Church was not prepared to join with them. But they did offer the Free a golden present in the shape of Dr Robert Laws, a recognised most capable man, to help in any way possible. That said a great deal for the Established C of S because within a year they were to send out their own Mission, and Laws would have been the very likely choice as leader. Perhaps this was the beginning of the end of the separation but it took nearly another seventy-five years before the two factions were reunited.

Unfortunately the original siting of the Free Church Mission proved disastrous. The clear, sparkling water of Cape Maclear beguiled to deceive. The whole area proved to be an extremely unhealthy, malarial place, which resulted in six missionaries dying in the five years it was there. Some price for just one convert in all that time!

Dr Laws eventually abandoned Cape Maclear and resited the Mission three-quarters way up the lake at a place called Bandawe, which was in turn abandoned when the Mission was moved to a higher, more healthy place nearer the Nyika plateau, where it was when I passed by on the *Chauncy Maples*.

Dr James Stewart, the prime mover in the Mission coming to Lake Nyasa, ironically was not there at its inception. He did not arrive until the following year after the return of Lieutenant Young. He was there only a year or two before he was recalled to Scotland, then sent to a Mission in South Africa where he remained for many years and earned himself the title by which he was afterwards known, Stewart of Lovedale. Later he was posted back to Livingstonia where he remained during his active life and where he wrote his book *Dawn in the Dark Continent*. In that book he tells of the day he made the remark that may have spelled the beginning of Blantyre town.

As mentioned, within a year of arrival of the Free Church of Scotland's Mission in Nyasaland the Established Church had also sent its own one. Stewart's arrival and that of the C of S Mission coincided. Stewart tells of a time in those first few months when he with one other, possibly someone of the C of S group, were exploring the Shire uplands. They camped on a high plateau. The air was cool with few mosquitoes, the scenery breathtaking. Sitting by their campfire Stewart remarked to his companion, "This would make a good place for a Mission."

It would appear that in his assessment he was not just thinking of the welfare of the white missionaries, but in the fact that this area was right at the source of the slave industry. Only the day previous they had come on the smoking remains of a large native village, the roof ribs of some houses lying like spoked wheels where they had once covered houses and families, and the whole area

Four Yards of Calico

littered with human skulls and bones, broken and stripped of their meat by hyenas.

General Rigby of Zanzibar had written, *'The Nyasa area used to be well populated. Later it was necessary to travel perhaps eighteen days inland before finding a village. The passage would be through miles of ruined towns and villages.'* Here at the heart of the matter his estimate of an 80% to 90% death rate on the march was a likely conclusion. Only that small, 10% proportion of the total number of the population ever lived to 'enjoy' a continued life as a slave. Here, on the high Shire uplands, Stewart could see why Livingstone woke stark in the night with the memory of scenes he had witnessed when passing through areas immediately after a slave caravan had gone.

Whether it was from Stewart's remark or not, that was the place the National Church of Scotland's party chose to build their Mission. They called it 'Blantyre' after Livingstone's birthplace in Scotland.

At first there was only the Mission, but soon afterwards, to complete Livingstone's equation, commerce arrived in the shape of the brothers John and Frederick Moir whose name would become synonymous with the rise and growth of the country that would be known as Nyasaland, and later Malawi.

They opened up their first store near the mission in 1878. The natives referred to the store as 'Mandala', the word in the local language for 'spectacles' which the older brother wore. The word was more of a simile of water than a translation, for until then spectacles were unknown in the land. However the word came about the name stuck and in my time there Mandala was a great corporation with shops all over Nyasaland. The Moir brothers were everything Livingstone had hoped for in commerce. They soon earned a name for fair trading with the natives and all.

Later, when many more settlers had arrived and the inevitable war against the Arab slave traders took place, both brothers were wounded in battle, as was Sir F. Lugard who led the British. That war lasted two years and ended the Arabs' hold on the land and the vile trade they had perpetrated there for a century and more. The presence of the white settlers also stopped the Yaos and the Angonis from preying on the weaker tribes and peace came to the land. For the first time in living memory and long before, native people could live, grow old and die in the villages where they were born without the threat of violence, slaughter and slavery always on their shoulders. Livingstone's dream had become reality.

*

Although the commercial centre of Nyasaland, Blantyre was not the capital. That honour had been invested on Zomba, a third of the way nearer the lake. Up on the Shire highlands, situated in an area of breathtaking views, Zomba had been described as 'the British Empire's most beautiful capital.'

I was lucky with lifts and soon arrived in Zomba where, as officially my first place of entry into the country, I reported to the police. The officer appeared interested in my travels and without hesitation grabbed a rubber stamp and banged it on my passport, saying, "Mustn't hold up these wanderbugs," I wished his views were common in all the realms of officialdom.

I did not linger in Zomba. Having walked out of the town and on to the open road I soon got a lift to Blantyre. It was dark by the time I arrived on the outskirts of the town where I camped the night in the municipal site. A comfortable place this, but not convenient for leaving my kit and tent unattended when I went into town. So in the morning I went in search of some cheap lodgings.

Walking into Blantyre was quite like finding myself, dreamlike, in a little town in Scotland. The Scots tongue was very prominent everywhere, which was not surprising, as I soon learned, for Blantyre grew up round the Scottish mission there. But it was not only the accent that made me feel so much at home. After collecting my poste restante mail, my first for over four months, I went into a shop to buy notepaper and the Scots woman behind the counter remarked about the weather in an accent that would have been at home in Edinburgh, "Good morning. Fine morning isn't it, but I think there's a haar coming." So homely, and having a white woman serve me was way out of Africa. She was the first white shop assistant I had seen since leaving Europe.

There is nowhere in all East and Central Africa more suited to Scots than the Shire highlands. With the towns lying at between 3000–4000 feet above sea level the days are always temperate and the nights cold enough to make a fire welcome. But that is not all. In Scots' lexicon a 'sma' haar', or the 'haar' to which the lady referred, means a chill, drizzly mist which Sassanachs call 'Scotch mist,' and in Blantyre, Nyasaland, they have a great deal of haar. But there it is given another name. There the local mist that rolls in so often is called a *'Chiperoni'*. This name is taken from the Chiperoni mountain that lies to the east of Blantyre in Mozambique. Great, heavy clouds hang permanently around that lofty peak and when the wind blows from that direction and passes over that mountain it tears great lumps off and carries them with it and deposits them over the Shire uplands. It is the ever changeable climate that the Chiperonis produce that make the Blantyre folk as daily weather-minded as any Scot back home.

Blantyre was not an inspiring town to see, but it had a warm, friendly feeling about it, brought on by the instant welcome shown to me by everyone I met. Perhaps my talisman, the kilt, had something to do with it but I like to think that the welcome and immediate hospitality shown to a passing stranger was genuine. People stopped me with ready greeting and asked from where I had come and how long was I staying. One of the first people to whom I was introduced was Mrs Green, wife of the Minister of the Church of Scotland Mission, who immediately invited me to stay a few days at the manse. There I met the Reverend Green and felt instantly at home.

*

Blantyre's Established Church of Scotland Mission Building was magnificent. Second only in size to the UMCA Cathedral in Zanzibar it was a most outstanding building. I spent considerable time exploring it and valued every minute. The architecture was a gem of ingenuity. It was no classic masterpiece but nevertheless it was a work of art and also a magnificent achievement considering the designer and builder had no knowledge of architecture and had never seen a brick laid. The man was David Clement Scott, one of the leading missionaries ever to come to Blantyre.

The building was a mixture of Gothic, Byzantine, Moorish and Norman. But it was no patchwork. Scott moulded the lot into a fine looking building which is renowned throughout the cleric world. The ceiling tracery, the window mullions and decorations were truly wonderful. The wood carving too was of a very high standard and a delight to the eye.

All these mission buildings round the lake, Roman Catholic, UMCA and C of S and Free Church were made from bricks made from ant heaps. It was found that the ant heap soil could be burned into a perfect brick, far superior to those made from ordinary sun-dried mud clay. The ant heaps were broken down, mixed with water and poured into moulds. They were then dried in the sun for several days before being stacked into a pile the shape of a kiln and fired for a week. When finished they had the ring of the proper brick as used back home.

I had marvelled at the buildings of all denominations I had seen. All were wonderful, especially considering they were built by amateurs in the wilds of Africa, with African materials and with no modern building aids. Of those I had seen I thought that Blantyre church put the lot in the shade.

Scott had no drawn plans, the building grew as it shaped in his head. His native builders had never seen a brick, far less use one. Each day he had them build a section with loose bricks for him to view. If this suited his idea, he would have them dismantle it and rebuild the piece again, this time using cement mortar.

There was a time, in the beginning, when the Mission stood in majestic solitude, owner of all the land to the horizon in every direction, for the Shire Highlands was granted in entirety to it by the local chief. As more and more people, mostly Scots, came to Nyasaland and settled near the mission it became necessary to form some sort of administration. The mission granted a site to build a township about a mile from the mission thinking that was ample room for the small community and far enough away from them not to have any interference with the mission work.

As the years went and the population grew rapidly it became necessary to continually extend the town boundaries until it had engulfed the Church and marched even further afield. When I arrived the Church stood well within the municipality and the minister was complaining bitterly that the Mission was being charged exorbitant town rates. Such is the march of time.

Living with the Reverend Stephen Green and his wife Marion it was natural that I attend his service on Sunday morning and glad I was that I had the opportunity to do so. The minister came from Aberdour and listening to his soft, educated Fife accent was like being at home in Torryburn Kirk as I grew up. The pattern of service was the same as I had known. As I listened I could have been sitting as a boy in our regular pew with the weak sunbeams slanting in through the tall, leaded, gothic window and hear the Reverend Pitcairn Craig, our resident minister who had christened me as a child, talking in similar voice to that of Reverend Green.

I saw him then, a little, stoutish figure with round, happy face and fair fringe circling a bald crown, with eyes that twinkled behind steel-framed glasses. He always had something to say to the young people. Not childish stuff, but stuff that appealed to people of all ages, and always with an inner message wrapped in an interesting story, messages you could carry through life.

After a hymn, while the congregation settled Revd Craig would lapse into reflective mood as if conjuring up an impromptu story, then laying aside formality, put his elbows on the pulpit lectern and pause to gather his audience while beaming at one young face and another, so all knew who he was talking to. Always he was talking to me personally, or so I felt. Now in Africa I mused, this is how Jesus preached. Not in rhetoric, but in stories about the unlikelihood of camels going through the eye of a needle and wild sons returning home and a kind man who tended the wounded while all others passed him by. They called them parables in those days and as parables they would have hidden meanings which were no doubt lost on me. I heard the stories as not necessarily of worship, but incidents that directed the way people might think and behave. To this day I still carry some of Mr Craig's stories and think of their meanings. One which illustrates what I mean jumps into mind as I write and may be worth the telling.

Two knights in armour stood on either side of a swinging tavern sign. One knight in white said, "Look how the sun glints on that gold sign". "Nonsense," answered the black knight, "that sign is not made of gold. It's of lead, I tell you." "You're blind," said the white knight, "can't you tell the difference between lead and gold?" "Call me blind, you stupid oaf. I see better than you and I say it is made of lead." So they argued and then started fighting. When they had fought themselves to a standstill, each wounded and blooded, they called a truce and both crawled to the sign to establish the truth and found it was made of lead and one side was gilded. *Message, look at both sides of an argument before passing judgement or taking up arms.*

*

One of the wonders of travelling through Africa in the mid-20th century was that in the wild tribal lands that had existed unchanged for millennia, nearly all of the developments that make up the modern world – the great brick towns, motor cars and commerce – had taken place during the previous seventy years or less, all within living memory. This being so you could always find someone who could remember those 'unspoiled' days and take you back to the wild past and make you see it as in real life.

One night I was invited out to dinner by a Mr and Mrs Smith, both old missionaries, now retired. Both came to Africa in 1900 and married a year later. It was wonderful to hear Mr Smith reminisce of the Africa he knew then when there were no towns in Nyasaland. He told me of the time when money was not in vogue with the Africans and all trading was done with cloth. However, even in ancient Babylon they had discovered that organised government requires taxes to fulfil its duties and those taxes are best collected as coin of the realm. Also, a developing, civilised society requires its inhabitants to work for their living and the only way to acquire coins for taxes is to work for more than a person's immediate food. So trading in hard money replaced barter when acquiring the necessities and goodies of life.

On one of the first occasions when Mr Smith was prepared to pay in cash for goods received by the mission he had about £10 (a fortune) in pennies and halfpennies in canvas bags beside him. When a woman brought her wares he pushed the whole lot over to her by way of a joke. The woman looked at the bags and pushed them back saying she wanted back her goods as she had no use for his iron.

Mrs Smith was as broad spoken as anyone at home despite her fifty odd years in Nyasaland. When I remarked at her not losing her Scots tongue she said she had made up her mind coming out on the ship that she would always hold on to that. She too could tell many interesting tales of old Africa. She told me of the late Reverend Heatherwick, one of the very early pioneer missionaries, who came to Blantyre in the 1880s and was the author of *The Romance of Blantyre* (previously mentioned). He told how he had sat on the very verandah where we sat at that moment and watched a hand-to-hand battle between Angoni and the Yao warriors just down the hill. The local Yao, warlike fighters in their own right, were no match for the Angoni Zulus. The missionaries could only watch the dead strewn on the battlefield and listen to the dying moans of the wounded, unable to intervene in any way.

*

About fifty miles east of Blantyre, near the border with Mozambique, stands the mountain called Mlanje. Nearly 10,000ft. high it is one of the strangest mountains in Africa. Rising straight out of the ground without foothills, its lower sides almost sheer in most places with few places of access, it is a mountain that wraps stories and mysteries around itself like the mist shroud it nearly always wears. It was the setting for Rider Haggard's *People of the Mist* and only a year before I arrived, Laurens Van Der Post's *Venture to the Interior*.

Post's book had only recently been published and at the time of my arrival it was the Book Society Choice but not the favourite of Blantyre residents. Everyone had read it and it was the number one topic of the day. From the vehement comments expressed it was obvious Mr Post would not have been welcome had he decided to revisit the country.

The book deals with a journey by the author at the behest of the British Government to explore the unknown part of Mlanje summit and an unmapped plateau further north. The general opinion was that the writer overplayed the 'unexplored' and 'unmapped' stuff and that his mission was 'secret'. Mlanje, they said, was hardly 'interior' for there was a logging camp and thriving farming up on top – which Post acknowledges – and the 'unmapped' Nyika Plateau was in the Livingstonia area and missionaries and traders had been living there and criss-crossing it for half a century. The residents' main resentment, however, was not so much levied at the book, but more as to why he made the journey at the time when he did, for due to torrential rain a young forestry officer who accompanied him, whose name he thinly veiled, was swept away and drowned in a swollen river, leaving a wife and two young children. The cloud of mourning still hung heavily over the town.

I borrowed a copy of the book and hastily devoured it. Glossing over the pages it was evident why the writer did not endear himself to the residents of Blantyre, irrespective of the tragedy that occurred on his visit.

I quote from his book:

'Blantyre is a small, ugly, commercial town. ... sixty years ago the government dealt it an unkind blow by setting Zomba as the official capital and so robbed Blantyre of its dignity and respect. ... it looks today rather ashamed of itself. I do not know what I expected (when I arrived) but obviously nothing quite so drab and insignificant as these hunched, perfunctory buildings dumped by the side of the road full of dust. In the

main street itself we had to go very slowly to avoid breaking the springs of our fat American car in the pot-holes. ... The houses gave on to gardens of a marked similarity. Each tried to have the same neat, level hedge round the inevitable lawn. I say 'inevitable' because I believe, in Africa, the vision of an English lawn flies over the exiled British imagination like colours nailed to the mast of an out-gunned, sinking ship of the line. The lawns impinged on borders that grew European flowers of a sickly and outrageous appearance. There were more Orientals than Europeans in the street. Most of the few Europeans were in some kind of khaki, with set, sallow, lifeless, disillusioned faces under wide-brimmed hats. They climb in and out of their cars with a listless, predetermined air. I had the impression that they all longed for nightfall so that darkness and drink would help them to imagine themselves to be somewhere else.'

Blantyre must have caught Mr Post on an off day, perhaps a little bilious after a long journey in his fat American car. Strange though for a man who often tells us how his ancestors travelled Africa in ox-wagons and that trekking was in his blood. Conversely, I found Blantyre a warm, friendly town with an exciting, pioneer air about it, the epitome of a town rising raw out of nothing, a place with interesting people leading interesting lives, all making the best of their situation away from European comforts and conveniences.

Hearing and reading of Mlanje piqued my interest in this strange mountain and I decided I must climb it. However on the day I had set to go we awoke to the land blanketed with a thick Chiperoni mist. In those conditions the safari would be useless, and considering these wipe-outs last for multiples of five days I had to call the whole thing off. I could not abuse the Revd and Mrs Green's hospitality by hanging on for even five days, let alone perhaps ten or fifteen, waiting for it to clear. Also I was keen to be on the road again.

Secretly, even to myself, I was not sorry to abort my Mlanje climb. It was less than a month since I had left hospital and having travelled by canoe and ship I had had very little exercise, so within me I knew that I was not ready for a strenuous climb. As it was, the road ahead by itself appeared a big enough challenge. By all accounts I could not expect many lifts. I was told there was very little traffic through Mozambique. To compound this problem I could not get a map of Portuguese East Africa for love or money. Not even a road map of the place at the AA office. Everyone advised me to go west through Northern Rhodesia (Zambia) but I had already been turned away from that country. Anyway I fancied seeing something of Mozambique. When I mentioned that desire I was warned that there were no proper roads there and long stretches with no population, and plenty of big game wandering loose. Well, I had experienced all that in Tanganyika and it seemed that most of the warnings were based on rumour rather than experience.

Indeed I was surprised how little the Blantyre residents knew about their neighbouring country. On top of all this lack of information I was worried about my boots. The repairs that the Indian cobbler had made at Kyela were already beginning to give way. This was not his fault. The boots were rotten and the stitches he had put in were tearing the leather. I had tried to buy new in Blantyre, but could only find fancy ones with thin, comfortable leather, not intended for foot-slogging. It was all a bit grim, but though a wee bit apprehensive about my prospects I was all the more determined to go there. Matters were made worse because I could not get any information about immigration into South Africa. It was a dark shadow that lay on my future. All the official information the police could give me was that, "it is difficult down there now", the 'now' meaning since Malan's Africaans political party had very recently taken over power from the long standing English-speaking one and had formed an anti-British government. I began to feel that after all the effort getting there I would be denied entry and be unable to complete my set task. The future was very much in the dark as I wrote in my diary:

Wed. 7th May, 1952. Blantyre

I'll get on the road tomorrow. I have no idea what lies ahead of me and only a very hazy idea of the country. I always like to carry in my head a map of the country ahead of me, but this time I have none. I'll head for Tete, the first town in Mozambique. It seems away out of my line to the west, but as far as I can see it's my only route. After that ... well, that's tomorrow's or next week's worry.

But I didn't get away the next day. When I mentioned to Mrs Green my intention she said I couldn't go because she had invited one or two people along for tea-time to meet me. And that was a brilliant stroke of luck and made me wonder if I did have a guiding hand on my shoulder. That next day when I went to the Post Office to see if there was any last minute mail I found my camera had arrived back from South Africa in working order. Had I gone the previous day when I intended I would have missed it.

If Mr Van Der Post saw his venture into the well-trod interior of Mount Mlanje and the Nyika Plateau, with guide and porters, worthy of derring-do mystery, then I too felt in similar vein as I set off, ill-prepared, for my next stretch of road through what would appear to be from local information, Darkest Africa. As with most build-ups of this nature, not all was well founded. All the same, a great deal of it was out of the ordinary and part of the way did go through some of the darkest areas of Africa I ever came across.

From Blantyre I headed west on the road to Tete, the main town over the border in Mozambique. At Tete I hoped to get a road going south, but even of that I was not sure. The road was in a terrible condition, the Chiperoni having changed to a pouring rain. I walked a while then got a lift in a car that skidded sideways for yards on the soft buttery road on more than one occasion. Twice we were held up by trucks stuck right across the road and had to wait while they were dug out.

On arrival at the outgoing customs office about 4.30 p.m. I decided to go no further that day. The Customs Officer was very interested and helpful and told me I could pass the night in the office. In the morning after a farewell handshake with the Customs Officer I set off on this momentous moment in my journey, for it was at Tete I would cross the Zambezi River. A milestone indeed.

Chapter Eighteen

MOZAMBIQUE

Monday 19th May 1952 – Portuguese East Africa
  I am in a really serious position. If I don't get water tomorrow, then…

It was gold that brought the Portuguese to Mozambique. They had been plundering and trading in gold on the West African coast for more than half a century and by 1450 they were minting coins with African gold in Lisbon. Tales came to them on the Senegal coast of a land rich in gold far into the interior of Africa. When the Portuguese finally rounded the most southerly tip of Africa and sailed up the east coast in 1498 they once again heard of rich gold lands deep in the interior. They may well have thought the same mines supplied both east and west of the continent.

Over the next fifty years they built several town bases along the coast. It was at Sofala they found the centuries-old outlet, the trading port, for the gold brought by porters from deep in the interior. Even at that time legends among the resident Arabs said that the gold arriving at the port came from the mines of King Solomon or the Queen of Sheba or Prester John, in a place known as Manicaland and the keeper of the mines was a man named Munhu Mutapa.

To reach this land they made their way slowly up the Zambezi, building forts at Sena and Tete. Their explorers ranged far into the hinterland. Francisco Barreto claimed to have reached Munhu Mutapa, or Monomatapa, as the name was more commonly spelled, and managed to persuade him to expel his Arab advisers, but no gold was found. Mines they found in plenty, but even by then they had all been worked out. Gasper Bocarra, it is said, crossed Lake Nyasa in 1620 and if this is true it qualifies Portuguese claims that David Livingstone was not the first white man to see that lake.

They were great men these early Portuguese. Thereafter the administration grew corrupt and after 1700 moral and social decay became consuming. It was said that, 'intermarriage reduced the Portuguese … to a race of spineless half-castes.' The ruins of their once proud fortifications at Zumbo and Jesuit missions and stone buildings dotted deep inland, long since cocooned by jungle or half buried with time, bears testament to the ancient decline. Whether the slur was warranted or not it was a fact that throughout Africa Portuguese people with a lineage in Africa, the *assimilados,* were never acknowledged nor accepted as

374

'European' (even by those Portuguese new out from their homeland) never seen as members of clubs, always confined to the shadows of outcasts at the level of *duka* traders.

By the early 1700s the country was stagnant and remained so for the next hundred and fifty years. In the latter part of the 19th century after the British Charter Company had moved into the lands that had become known as the Rhodesias, the Portuguese colonies on either side of the territories, Mozambique and Angola (the latter also indolent due to the motherland's own poverty and lack of drive) began to enjoy a gathering spin-off prosperity from the boom economy developing in the British occupied territories. Both Northern and Southern Rhodesia were land-locked and both Portuguese territories had seaboards. All imports and export to and from the British occupied countries had to pass through Portuguese-held land and, from the tariffs involved, Mozambique gradually awakened from her long slumber.

Such was the state of Mozambique as the history books described it at the time I walked into the country.

*

On leaving Nyasaland I walked the few miles to the Portuguese border Customs Post and there I met a madman and got no further. The Portuguese official, a large man with a wine-blotched face and great, bushy moustache, threw a fit when I walked up to the barrier and presented myself. He asked where my car was. Had I broken down? When I said I had no vehicle and I travelled on foot he went into a paroxysm of disbelief. In spartan English that came out in explosive bursts he wanted to know why I was doing such a thing, and more importantly, as far as I could gather, why was I doing such a thing to him.

I presented a new problem for him. It was the first time he had encountered anybody coming into his country to travel on foot and he didn't know what to do with me. The trouble was due to me carrying a pistol and a camera. The normal custom was to register anything like that with a car, but since I had no car he had no security that I would not sell these things in Mozambique. He explained to me at great length that in Nyasaland and Tanganyka it was not uncommon for people to arrive on foot. But in Mozambique it was different. The Portuguese had never thought that anyone would attempt to travel their colony on foot so no provision had been made for such an event. Now this official was at a loss – he had no special form for my case and without the appropriate form he was as good as a soldier going to battle without a rifle. I would have to wait until he received instructions from his headquarters in Tete to see what to do with me.

As he spoke he flailed the air with wild, gesticulating hands as if he were a demon conductor taking some phantom orchestra through a stormy concerto, while the room reverberated with his thunderous voice. I had to stand more than an arm's length away from him in order to avoid a thrashing from these lethal, exaggerating hands. But with all his dynamic performance he was not angry. It was only – as I wrote in my diary – his Continental, excited way.

All day he tried to get through to Tete by telephone but could make no contact. He thought that a pole must be down with the rain and I began to worry how long I was going to be held up. I hung about all day. It was cold and wet and miserable. I cooked myself a couple of meals and ate them surrounded by a group of gaping natives. At night I slept on some bags of maize on the verandah of a ramshackle Portuguese store near the barrier. As I cuddled down into my sleeping bag the mist came rolling in, damp and cold.

In the morning the official called me into his office. He said he had decided to let me go on. But he would give me a letter with which I must report to the police at Tete. When his phone was in order he would get through to confirm that I had reported. If I failed to report a general warrant would be sent out to have me pulled in. He explained over and over again every little detail of why he had had to hold me back. He hoped the senor was not angry since he was only doing his duty. He wished me "*Boa Viagen*" and warned me to be careful since there were many lions about and rumours of man-eaters about forty miles on.

The sun shone that morning, but the first couple of hours before the road dried up it was heavy going. The mud clung to my boots in great heavy clods and squeezed inside where the uppers were separated from the sole. I grew tired of scraping them for in minutes they were like weights again and each step was an exercise.

About noon, as was my usual practice when on the march all day, I 'drummed up' and had an hour's rest. Stimulated by the tea and strengthened by the rest I found that the forenoon's exertions always seemed far away and I began the afternoon almost fresh.

By about 4 p.m. I estimated that I had covered 18 or 19 miles and decided to call it a day. I estimated my distances on my average walking pace of three miles per hour, depending on the terrain. Seven hours walking gave me 20–21 miles, but I knocked off a few miles because of the difficulty of the early walking in the mud. With a few 10-minute rests when I would not take off my 70lbs. pack but savour the relief of lying back and resting it on the ground, and a longer break for lunch, I generally put in a 9-hour day on the road.

I was just planning to pitch my tent when a small van came along and picked me up. It took me another 20 miles and dropped me off before it turned into a side track to go to some lonely residence. I was thankful for the lift since it put me another day on my journey, but it left me in a most uneasy position. I always liked to make camp by daylight and get a stock of firewood in for the evening, especially in wild country. Now it was dark when I arrived and it was dangerous to move about looking for firewood and especially since I was on the edge of the area the Portuguese official said man-eaters were rumoured.

I gathered enough firewood to cook some rice. When I finished my chores and wrote up my diary I crawled into my tent and sleeping bag and, like the ostrich, buried my head in the down to escape from the heavy, sinister feeling of imminent danger into the oblivion of sleep – grand companion! No danger came my way during the night and apart from the usual nocturnal sounds I heard nothing to justify my fear.

However, after the first few miles in the morning I began to feel there was something in these rumours of man-eaters since the country was almost entirely empty of population and where there were signs of native life the houses were on long stilts, high off the ground. In the twenty miles I covered the next day I saw only two settlements of this kind, each with only three or four huts. None of them inhabited. I concluded these were mere hunting lodges, not used for permanent living.

It was a lonely walk. Apart from a few monkeys I saw no game, but I was aware that that did not alter the fact that the place was alive. Daytime was bedtime for the animal world. It was during the night those warriors roamed.

That night I took the precaution of erecting a boma of thorn branches round my tent; small protection against the lion man-eaters for they had been known to break down the door of a house or scrape through the solid mud wall to get at the humans inside. Still, it added some confidence and made the atmosphere at bit more tolerable. At Blantyre I had not been able to get any ammunition for my pistol and I had only two rounds left. Still, I knew that even if danger did arise it would have been worse than useless.

I wrote in my diary:

'At the moment the monkeys are making a terrible row, some bush babies are crying pathetically and the inevitable hyena hoots at intervals. If I could make a record of the nightlife at the moment how strange it would sound playing it back home. There are lots of snags in this life but even at this moment I wouldn't exchange it for a sheltered, daily routine. The gypsy freedom of going where you like and doing what you like is worth all the risks it includes. It has its lonely moments such as now, but as I look around and see my tent, my rucksack and especially my old burst boots, I feel I have friends with me; and of course the camp fire is a warm, friendly companion. Does all that sound silly? ... Tete is another 30 miles on yet.'

Next day I had walked a good part of the forenoon and covered about 10 miles when I got a lift from a truck run by the Rhodesian government for transporting labour recruits from Nyasaland. It brought me to Tete, or at least to the compound outside the town where the recruits were concentrated before being transported to Salisbury. I crossed the Zambezi in a small sailing boat like an Egyptian felucca. A momentous milestone indeed.

Like the Rubicon, on crossing the Zambezi many things change. There are some marked differences in the topography as you go south from there and, less noticeable to the fast traveller, there are changes in the peoples' ways too. For instance, north of the great river most tribes' ancestries follow the mother's line while to the south patriarchal lineage is more common.

But to me, crossing the Zambezi meant something more, much more than these little points of interest. I was now in Southern Africa.

*

Tete was like a Red Sea port, arid, hot and sandy. How different from the country further north in Tanganyika and Nyasaland. The houses were scattered haphazardly and there was no main street. Shops were tucked away in the oddest corners, very few of them having signboards, making them extremely difficult to run to earth. Although the Portuguese had been in this part of Africa for four hundred years and claimed dominion over vast tracts of land further west which they had never seen, Tete was the farthest inland they had colonised. They came in from the coast by way of the great highway of the Zambezi River hoping to penetrate the deep interior. They made many stations further west but found the natives beyond here too fierce and were driven back. Compared to the British colonies, what I had seen of Mozambique seemed backward and primitive. Over the next few weeks, however, I was to change many of the ideas I formed then.

I reported to the 'Administrador' who read my letter and put me into the hands of a Customs officer. In his turn, he read the letter and seemed quite apathetic about the articles I carried and, since he couldn't speak English, he waved me away.

Without maps or a knowledge of the country I was at a loss as to my next move and I decided to try the local hotel to see if anyone spoke English. All down Lake Nyasa and through Nyasaland I had been told that the Portuguese were extremely anti-British and I could only look forward to coldness or open resentment from them in my intrusion of their colony. But the treatment I got at the hotel proved otherwise. The few residents were anything but cold. On the contrary, in their Latin way they were almost childlike in their eagerness to converse and learn of my journey once they got to know how I travelled. I suppose it wasn't their everyday occasion that a bearded traveller in kilt, floppy bush-hat and boots bound up with string walked into their midst. Two or three of them could speak fairly good English. The local doctor happened to be there and when he learned that I had been unable to obtain a map of the country he hurried home and returned with a sketch one of Mozambique which he said he never used. It was a very, very basic, small-scale drawing, but I cherished it like a life-line thrown to me in a maelstrom. It saw me through, though, I must add, not without some difficulty. I still have it today, rather tattered, and it lies beside me as I write these words. One resident wanted to buy me a pair of shoes after looking at my old boots. I thanked him kindly, but although extremely touched by the gesture I declined the offer. The proprietor insisted that I stay for lunch "on the house". When I left he pressed on me enough bread to keep me a couple of days and refused payment.

It was late afternoon when I left the hotel to look for a place to camp and all the residents and the proprietor came to the door to wave goodbye. On the bank of the Zambezi I found a small water-house which I thought would be ideal to stay in and leave my kit while in town. The door to the hut was locked and on enquiring from a group of natives working near, one who could speak a little English (I was now out of Swahili country) I learned that the local PWD man held the key. The one who could speak English said he would take me to the custodian. The keeper of the key, a half-caste, said he was sorry he could not give me permission to sleep in the water-house, which was government property, but if I liked I could spend the night in his tool shed. I gratefully accepted his offer, whereupon he invited me to eat with his wife and family that evening.

The man's offer of accommodation and invitation to dine was one of the finest examples I could get of the difference in life-styles between the British and Portuguese colonies. In British-run territory a half-caste would be extremely embarrassed and diffident to have a white man stay with him. As to offering the white tramp his tool shed, he would be more likely to move in there himself with his wife and offer the white man his own bedroom. Here, in Mozambique, my host showed no embarrassment, and certainly no malice, in offering me his shed. And how I liked him for it! I cleared an area among the pile of tools and other junk that accumulates in a garden shed and felt well settled in.

The meal was real proof that I had entered foreign territory. There was wine on the table and Lisbon sausages that contained everything from lumps of fat to peas. The man was fairly light skinned, his wife was black and their children were in-betweens. I pondered, was this the product of the less stringent outlook on interracial marriages found away from British colonies? But unlike the half-castes I had met in the British colonies they were much more European in their mode of life. The house was European style, the furniture beyond anything I'd seen in any African's house and his wife was obviously house proud. The place was clean and very tidy. The table was well laid with the correct cutlery in its proper place. The children, three girls and two boys, were extremely well mannered and table-wise, the parents easy and warm with the stranger at their table. This was not a European show put on for my benefit. This was their regular way of life.

I did not know it then but I was witnessing one of the strange facts of colonial Africa. This was my first forage outside British rule and there seemed to be contrasting patterns running through the lives of the indigenous people of the different countries. I later learned of the fundamental variations in approach to governing the African people that each colonial power followed.

The Portuguese, Belgian and Spanish, although all having some differing individual trends, all followed the main 2-tier social system, the making or acceptance of a first- and second-class citizen policy. Baldly, the natives could elect to live as Africans or Europeans. Those who continued by desire or necessity to live in the tribal way would be classed as second rate. As such they would not be able to enter first-class accommodation and other places and would not be eligible to apply for a passport even if they had the means to travel overseas for education or interest. In Portuguese territory, should the native reach a certain level of education, learn to live as a European, forsake all tribal religions and accept Christianity, he could apply and possibly be granted first-class citizenship. There were very, very few first class native citizens and it would seem that in my hosts at Tete I had met one of those rare families.

In a census of about that time the Portuguese structured the population into 'tribalised Africans', 'civilised' and 'westernised'. Of the 6½ million people there were only 4,000 'Westernised'. The granting of so-called first-class citizenship to a few natives did not appear to have much effect in assimilating the indigenous people to Portuguese rule. In the north of the country where the majority of the population lived, the land was in ferment and would soon break into open war against the Portuguese who, it was rumoured, retaliated with extreme ruthlessness and cruelty.

But none of that was evident to me during my sojourn in Mozambique. Indeed, my impression was that there was a great deal of *laissez-faire* in the attitude of the authorities, which perhaps accounted for the fact that in four hundred years the Portuguese had hardly explored the country they governed, far less developed it.

In contrast to the freedom and status granted to the Europeanised-natives I gathered that those of the second-rate tribal variety were treated by the authorities much more inhumanly than their counterparts in British run territories. But to the best of my knowledge only in the British colonies was there no official designated class system. Officially a Masai or Kikuyu in stark tribal dress could walk into Torr's Hotel in Nairobi, stand at the bar and order a drink. Unofficially it would never happen. The hotel would have rules on 'proper dress' or some other criteria whereby the visitor would be asked to leave.

On the other hand there was no reason, should he have the means, why a native in British-run territory should not apply for a passport and be granted it, and enter a British university or live as a British citizen in the United Kingdom if he should choose to do so, an option that would be denied all black people in other European administered African countries.

This basic difference in the governing systems was to be the one open door which allowed a very special black man to enter the colonial fortress that caged Africa from Cape to Cairo and from Dar es Salam to Dakar, and by his efforts start the events that would eventually bring the whole edifice crashing down. But that story must wait until we arrive at that milestone nearly two years later.

Next morning I had a stroll round town and did a bit of shopping. The price of food was exceptionally high and made worse by a low rate of exchange; only 16 shillings to the pound. It was not too bad buying plain food such as rice, potatoes, bread etc., but as soon as you touched on luxuries it was terrible – if bully-beef at 7s.6d. a tin may be called a luxury. As always I stuck to plain food.

Later I returned to my tool-shed home, collected my gear, thanked my hosts and got on the road. Not far outside the town as I passed an army camp, a grand affair with a castellated wall and watch tower, I was thunderstruck by a woman's voice with a faint Scottish accent hailing me from the grand portal of the fortress, "What's a kiltie doing walking these parts?" So I met Mrs Ann Santos from Morayshire, "Come away in and we'll have a good cup of tea," she said. Just like that, in the wilds of foreign Africa, the first home grown voice I'd heard since leaving Blantyre. She had seen me at a distance from an upstairs window and had hurried to the gate to catch me before I passed. Many years before that day she had gone to Portugal as a young woman and married Senhor Santos, who had died, and their daughter, Peggy, had married Captain Aires de Abren who was the army commandant in the fort. The Portuguese army, I gathered, did not believe in splitting up families and while it did not apply to the ranks, an officer could have his mother, or even his mother-in-law, as in this case, beside him if he wished when posted abroad. The army even paid a small allowance, about 30/- per month, towards her keep. Ann had not been back to Scotland for many, many years, and yet she still retained that soft lilt in her voice, so distant that it may only have been perceptible to another Scot.

I found the whole family very hospitable and extremely friendly. The cup of tea extended to lunch, then Captain de Abren said he was going down town and if I waited till he came back he might be able to fix up a lift for me. When he did return he said there was a truck going about 100 miles south in a few days' time and if I liked to stay in the 'Quartelle' (army quarters or barracks) until then I would be most welcome. He fixed me up in the officers' quarters where there was only one officer staying, a Lieutenant Chichero, who could not speak a word of English, but we got along quite well with sign language and the Latin derivative words common in all European languages, and lots of laughter, the common denominator in every language in the world. So there I was – *'rather a long cup of tea!'* I wrote in my diary.

Those days in the Quartelle were a wonderful interlude. Ann Santos was keen to talk about Scotland and I noticed as the days went by that her native tongue became more and more apparent, whether by longing or association, it was hard to tell. Even Peggy laughingly remarked of the growing change in her mother as we conversed.

I was not familiar with Morayshire but I spoke of the Grampians that I knew well and which would be her rugged horizon when she was young. I told of sunrise on Ben Nevis and moonlight in the Lairig Gru, the great glen that cleaves the Cairngorms, and of the 'The Big Grey Man of Ben MacDhui,' the huge mist ghost that lurks at Lurchers Crag and possesses climbers and lures them to their doom from that lofty precipice. I spoke from experience for as seventeen-year-olds, a small group of us were sure we were in his presence one mid-summer midnight.

And not just mountains. I reminisced of my Scotland as a boy which she would remember: of a fireside warm and cosy, of sweety shops where the bell clanged as you opened the door and the woman rolled a paper square into a cone and screwed up the bottom and put your penny-worth into it: of grocer shops with sawdust on the floor, where the man in white apron displayed his cold meats in glass cases on the counter and sliced off the number of ounces you wanted with knife or ham machine, while passing the time of the day and the state of the weather in couthy (coothy) chit-chat. And as I talked her eyes sparkled and danced like a Highland burn in summer, and like the burn moistened a little sometimes.

Peggy, her daughter liked to listen too. Fluently bilingual she laughed without prompting at my Scottish nuances and even she seemed to roll her r's moreso as the days passed. She was a ravishing beauty with blue-black hair and the flashing eyes of a flamenco dancer without the haughty stare.

The working day in the Quartelle seemed very short and the men had a lot of time to indulge in volleyball, soccer and other sports. I joined in as much as I could, making up for my lack of skill with wild enthusiasm, at which all the men laughed and backslapped until we were all firm friends though we could hardly say two words to each other.

One afternoon some NCOs invited me to go hunting with them. There were five of them with three service rifles between them. They each drew about themselves a mantle of bravado, all full of verve and swagger, rolling along in a cloud of tough talk and cigarette smoke, flicking their stubs in high arcs into the bush with macho nonchalance. I could not conceive a less likely band of hunters.

In such close proximity to Tete and 400 years of Portuguese habitation the land was not overpopulated with animals. Still, there were odd little groups of gazelle about, but few and far between. The landscape was open savannah, dotted with lonesome baobabs, those mighty, grotesque, ugly ducklings of the arborescent species, and clumps of acacia and some ironwood trees.

'Ironwood' is the name given colloquially throughout Africa for the exceptionally hard woods that grow in a particular area. There was some ebony here and that was sometimes referred to as ironwood, but the real ironwoods are much harder. The most prolific ironwood along the Zambezi was the mopane tree that produces a most remarkable wood, and not just for its hardness. For one thing, the mopane is useless for shade at noon. Against all the apparent laws of nature it folds its leaves together and turns them edge-on to the sun so only the slimmest shadow is cast on the ground. A particular flying-insect is attracted to the leaves and spreads a sweet, sticky secretion over the surfaces which in turn attracts the 3-inch long lopane caterpillars. The natives, who loved both the sticky leaves and the caterpillars, ate the lot.

Even stranger than the mopane's trick with its leaves was the natives' claim that these trees were struck by lightning more often than any other type of tree and warned travellers never to shelter under them in a storm. In contrast, another tree, the morala, had never been known to be struck by lightning. Branches of this tree were put on Portuguese houses to ward off or to act as a conductor to a strike. Even stranger, many claimed that anyone in the shade of a morala tree was safe from a charging elephant as the animal would never enter the field of the tree.

The morala tree is a type of baobab and in contrast to the hardness of the mopane its heartwood is soft and spongy. From the baobab, also known as the 'monkey-bread tree' and the 'ginger-bread tree' from the taste of its long pod fruit, the natives extract a sticky gum and a soothing emollient. This tree is one of Africa's freaks of nature. Although well used to its weird shape, which looks more vegetable than tree, the sheer size of one on the plain we crossed drew me up to gaze in wonder at it. Over thirty feet in diameter and a hundred in girth it stood like a fortress defying time. Some say these are the oldest living things on earth. Adanson, from whom its Latin name, *Adansonia digitata,* is derived, believed that some standing today were growing in the time of the flood. David Livingstone scoffed at this, but there is little doubt that they rival the Californian Redwoods for longevity. Livingstone believed that apart from some fungus attack these trees are practically indestructible. Fire cannot harm them, they stand unscathed after the worst forest conflagrations. The natives strip off the bark as high as they can reach to make cloth and strong ropes from the fibres between bark and wood, a process that would kill any other tree, but the baobab grows another bark and gets on with its life. In some places the natives dig into the spongy innards of large trees to form a room or more and live in them. The tree goes on living and growing.

But now, on with the hunt! After some time we came on a scattered group of gazelles. Long before the soldiers were at a suitable range for shooting they grouped together and unslung their rifles. A somewhat heated discussion followed, which without understanding the words, I could see was to do with who were to get the first shots. The sergeant stood on his rank and the two other rifles were taken by the most vociferous pair. I believed they were now ready for the stalking approach. But no. To my horror the trio lined up in slack, standing postures and proceeded to let fly a few potshots at the animals. In a flash the herd flew into flight and no dead or dying animals were left behind. But it grieved me badly to think there might be some wounded victims in the herd in great pain.

By international law army bullets are nickel-plated and, as such, hard-nosed so they do least damage after entering a body. The idea being that a soldier may be wounded and put out of action but not be maimed too much if he survives. Soft-nosed lead bullets are the most humane ammunition for hunting soft-skin animals. The sheer force of impact, when the missile flattens out, will knock the animal over and the terrible internal damage caused is more likely to ensure a quick kill. Hard-nosed bullets are likely to pass right through the body and exit if they do not strike a bone. The animal may long survive the wound, but hit in the intestines will have a lingering, painful death. Moreover, when shooting into a herd a hard bullet is likely to go through a body and wound another, so causing needless pain and suffering. Much more skill and accuracy is required with hard ammunition. Only brain, heart or vertebrae hits are likely to drop an animal in death or be rendered immobile long enough to allow the *coup-de-grace* to be rendered at close quarters.

I was so appalled at what they had done and no doubt had repeated often in the past, I hurried forward without thought of etiquette or over-stepping my place and took the rifle off the first one I came to, put on the safety-catch, and remonstrated in actions to them. They deferred to my assumed authority and when we were ready to move on even the sergeant waited for me to lead. When I started in the opposite direction to the lost herd, however, one was bold enough to say in very fractured English that we should be going the way the animals had run. I said more in actions than words that there was little chance of us getting near them again. They would be in a high pitch of fear and very alert. Better leave them and try for some others.

Now ready to go I realised I had, foolishly perhaps, put myself into an unwanted position of authority and responsibility. Nevertheless, after the months of crocodile hunting, with the rifle slung from my shoulder, I slipped comfortably into the mould. After the past days of shared sport when I was the goof among the skilled, I was now on my home ground. Confidence came naturally. So much so I did not find it awkward to lay down some rules of play, and in my game I was not tongue-tied with foreign words. In hunting, communication is done in sign language and that is universal.

First, a finger across the lips: no talking, the animals would hear from afar. Next, a pantomime of inhaling a cigarette and a wagged finger: no smoking, the smell would carry. Lastly, walk in file to reduce our image.

So off we went. Not so much fun as their slapstick Ned Karno's Army capers, but much more efficient. Presently we came in sight of a small scattering of antelopes. Testing the wind, I took the party in a wide curve to go in against it. Using the cover of bushes and small trees, even though it meant zigzagging, we finally made it to a position much less than half the distance that the shooting took place on the previous occasion. I could see the nearest ones were becoming restive. Now was the time.

I pumped my hand up and down, fingers splayed, palm down, for all to hunker-down, while I lay down prone in front and motioning for the sergeant to crawl up to me. I had him take up the standard, army rifle-range position, lying flat with legs apart, elbows solidly set on the ground and rifle tucked firmly into the shoulder. Indicating the animal I thought best to go for I bade him wait until I got into position. I crawled to a little tree nearby and stood up behind it. The trunk divided at about the right height for me to use as a prop. I fancied I might need the mobility the tree would give me rather than the ground posture. Once in position I whispered, "OK", figuring that that was known to all. A second later the sergeant fired. The beast was hit badly at the rear end, partially collapsed, but then leaped forward to join in the general stampede following the explosion. I was glad I had anticipated what might happen. With my elbow on the fork of the tree I was able to swivel instantly and caught the wounded creature with a heart shot in the middle of its first, high parabola. It collapsed on landing and lay still.

All the soldiers rushed forward, the rules of secrecy and quietness forgotten. Everyone seemed to be talking at once, the sergeant over casually pleased as Punch. They were all for leaving the animal lying, hunting to them meant only shooting. But I tried to explain we must take something back to justify the killing.

I had my sheath-knife and they all had army knives. So I set about gutting and carving up the carcass while involving the others as much as possible. We set off on the homeward journey in manly style, two men each with a rear leg and haunch over their shoulder and others with choice cuts wrapped in leaves under their arms. I no longer curbed their exuberance. The hunt was over. The noisy babble rose and would stampede herds a mile off. The tobacco cloud hung in the stillness and trailed our party like smoke from a steam engine. The return of the hunters was being heralded far and wide.

I brought the party round and back up the trail of the first group we had encountered to see if there were any wounded or dead that had dropped out of the fleeing mob, but saw nothing. It was likely that with their kind of shooting the animals were quite safe from soldiers.

The days at the Quartelle passed as if it were an interlude on a desert oasis before setting out into the unknown sand-sea. When the word came that my lift would leave next day I could not help feeling some sadness and I think Ann Santos and family felt that too.

On the morning of my departure Captain de Abren called me into his office. I was surprised to see all the sergeants and corporals there, about eight in all gathered together. On a table was pile of groceries and other goods. In his broken English the Captain said the men wished me luck on my travels and had bought a few things to help me on my way. I was completely taken aback by this generous gift. A tin of powdered milk, a pound of tea, two kilos of sugar, half a kilo of very salt bacon, two big, high smelling Lisbon sausages, a large tube of toothpaste, four bars toilet soap and a large whisky bottle full of malted syrup. From my forage in the Tete shops I knew all this was expensive stuff, much of what I fancied but knew was beyond my reach.

Two other items were placed at the side and at these my eyes danced. A bush-hat to replace my old battered one and, wonder of wonders, a pair of reconditioned army boots, all purchased from the army stores and carefully, secretly, matched to my size. I didn't know what to say. How could I thank these men who spoke no English and I no Portuguese. To the Captain I stammered out some words of thanks which I asked him to translate. To the men I said the one word I had learned in Portuguese "*Obrigato*" (Thank you) and turned away, choked.

The value of the boots to me was immeasurable. Feeling my old ones literally disintegrate about my feet had been a terrible worry to me. Now with sadness I silently said goodbye to my pair of old pals who had carried me many a mile and interred them in the bin. The men no doubt thought my battered old bush-hat had also seen its day, but losing another old friend all at the same time was too much to bear. The new one was a soft, foldable type and though I wore it for all to see as I left I put it away in my rucksack and returned my old felt one to its honourable place on my head when out of sight.

All the groceries were really too much for me to carry but I felt that refusal of any would look like lack of appreciation. So I gathered them all up with enthusiasm, but before I left I made a parcel of the heaviest items and gave it to Peggy. I thought the bottle of malted syrup would be good for her baby. She protested but thanked me with a kiss when I insisted. We were all sad when we waved our goodbyes as the truck went out through the high portal and I felt a strange chill as I looked back and saw the great doors close and shut me out of the security and friendly warmth of the fort.

The truck was going to Mungari, about 75 miles south of Tete. The journey down was uneventful except to impress on me the lonely, wild country I was passing through and the unlikelihood of getting any lifts along the way. We saw no other vehicle throughout the journey. At Mandi, a small cluster of thatched huts round a cluttered *duka,* we left the 'main' road, which on the map was marked red, a crime for which in modern times could have had the cartographers in chains on a galley ship for gross misrepresentation. We crossed the River Luenha, a tributary of the Zambezi, on a pontoon raft where the men hauled on chains to pull us over. The road we now followed was hatched in modest brown as 'secondary', but even that was a claim beyond its station for it was merely a track marked by the wheels of very infrequent trucks. The farther we went the more desolate became the land.

It was nearly sundown when we arrived at Mungari, a little, isolated clutch of houses surprisingly neatly arrayed with an army post to which the truck had brought supplies. I camped in the post that night and started out on the road next morning. The first fifteen miles were on the 'brown' road before I rejoined the mighty 'red'. I was breaking-in my new boots and so far we hadn't slipped into the easy partnership I'd had with my old ones, so I decided to call an early halt. Also, buoyed up with striking the autobahn and seeing it stretching out before me my foolish hopes carried me away in thinking I might be lucky in having a lift come along.

I made camp a little distance from the road, near enough to hear any vehicle approaching, but far enough away that any nocturnal prowlers or walkers, such as elephants, who all liked to use roads as easy game trails, might not find out I was there. From the next day I will let my diary take up the story.

Saturday,17th May 1952. Portuguese East Africa.

Walked all day without a lift. I don't expect to get any transport until I reach Vila Gouveia, 80-odd miles away from Mungari. What desolate country! Only saw one native village. It's a wee bit lonely.

Sunday, 18th May 1952. Portuguese East Africa

Well, that is another 19 or 20 miles nearer my destination. With the heavier pack with the extra food I'm carrying (over 80 lbs.) that is far enough.

My, this is lonely country. I never saw any sign of life today. Just dead country. Last night the hyenas kicked up a terrible din with their hooting and came very close. I have been told many times, and especially just before I started this stretch, that it is sheer nonsense to venture over these lonely stretches without a rifle and I am beginning to agree now. I really don't know what I would do if an emergency did arise.

I hope I come to water tomorrow. I don't see any marked on the map.

There is a thin scratch-line that crosses the road with no name which I hope is a river or stream and which I might be near. I really hope so. My map is such a small scale one. All day I have cut my ration just in case there is none. Tonight I cooked some rice in so little water it was almost dry. I allowed myself just a few sips to wash it and the bread down.

Monday, 19th May 1952. Portuguese East Africa
Today I have known what thirst is. As I write my tongue seems to fill my mouth. I am in a really serious position. If I don't get water tomorrow then -! I still have a few drops left in my water bottle but I must keep that for the heat of the day tomorrow. Tonight I ate some dry rice and sardines from the Quartelle and drank the olive oil from the tin. Normally that would make me blanch but how delicious it was to feel it running down my throat – I never tasted it. Funny how your taste disappears when necessity makes it and you eat or drink for the sake of the food or liquid.
Never saw any animals, but there are plenty spoors including elephant.

Tuesday 20th May 1952. Portuguese East Africa
What a day! I set out this morning feeling really weak from lack of water. Funny when you really crave for something sleep is no escape, for you dream about it and even on the move it keeps nagging, nagging at your brain until you become oblivious of everything else and you become an automaton driven on by that gnawing desire.
About 10 o'clock I drank the last dregs from my bottle. I realised then I had to do something, and quick or it really would be kismet. The roof of my mouth felt like sandpaper. I left my kit at the side of the road and set off light. I reached the river about noon. How good it felt. I took my clothes off and lay in it and then drank and drank and drank. Then I lay at the side until I felt refreshed.
I filled my bottle and headed back for my kit. Now everything seemed fine, my mouth was no longer full of tongue and it was lubricated by saliva and I could spit.

Going back I saw the first animal since leaving Mungari, other than the hordes of monkeys, that are always around. A leopard. I came round a thick cluster of trees and there it was, hardly a dozen paces away coming in the opposite direction. But it must have got as big a fright as I did for it only looked for a second and then bounded off into the bush. But for that second I have an indelible picture of it halted in its tracks in surprise with its paw raised in the middle of a step. I can still see its lithe shape and long tail as it turned off the road. I hope I never meet another one of these again unless I have a rifle in my hand. I got my kit and came onto the river before camping. As usual I have built a fairly strong boma round my tent, but tonight I will have to be doubly careful since animals are sure to come to the river to drink.

While I travelled I wrote up my diary in an assortment of notebooks which I acquired when necessary and posted home when full and I had access to a post office. As I read the relevant part prior to writing this narrative it gives me a very strange feeling. At times I felt almost as much a stranger to the writer as the present reader must be. Then the evocative words, to me at least, clear away the mists of time and I am there seeing, feeling, smelling, fearing, loving a whole world wrapped up in a few terse words. My nerves tingle. I am there, living it and every sense in my body is strung to snapping pitch. I had heard that leopards, unlike lions, rarely attack face-to-face. They are more stealthy, preferring to circle and charge from the rear. Although I did not mention it in my diary I remember so well those couple of miles or so after our meeting when my flesh crept each time I looked to the front as I walked. I had my head jammed to the side so I could swivel my eye forward and back with every few steps. My neck ached with keeping it permanently twisted. I remember feeling pleased I was not wearing my rucksack as the load would have made my half-sideways step much more difficult. But I missed my panga with which I had practised long and hard to acquire the quick-draw for just such an occasion.

Later on in my journey, in Northern Rhodesia (Zambia) I stayed on a wild farm where a leopard was caged in a large, wire-netted compound. We stared eye-to-eye and I could see the malevolence in its look, perhaps because it was a prisoner. To test the theory of its mode of attack, I stood within a foot of the wire surround and turned my back to it. In an instant the brute thudded against the netting with such force it bent the wall so far it almost touched me. It hung there for a second or two, long enough for me to turn and look again at it face-to-face, but now only inches apart, and this time its eyes were not malevolent, but wild and killer-like and the claws hooked over the wire, evil and terribly threatening. The experience proved a point and many times after that, when walking alone in wild places, the image came back so vividly in my mind and I saw again those burning eyes and smelled the guff of its hot breath so close to my face.

I reached the town of Vila Gouveia the next day and now as I write I again feel the intense relief, the exhilaration of walking into the town and safety. I recorded the moment in my diary, *'Well, that was a bad stretch and I am glad it's over. I think I should manage a lift for a bit from here.'* And I did. A day later I got a lift on a truck to Vonduzi, almost as far as I had walked in the past six days. A tiny place of neat houses, this town was of great importance to me, for this little gem was on the railway that came out of Southern Rhodesia on its way down to the coast at Beira. By reaching here I hoped I had left the desolated area to the north behind me.

It was not until later I came to know just how empty of people that land I walked through really was. In a population survey of the time that area was estimated at less than 5 (probably nearer 2 or 3) to the square mile. Considering those few who were there would live in family groups of a dozen or more, that would mean their surrounding square-miles would be empty.

I made camp by invitation in the back yard of an Indian shop, one of only three that served the 'town'. It was late, near 11 p.m., and I had already settled down, when the Indian, whose yard I was in and who spoke quite good English, came and said there was a van going to Villa Pery and I could go if I liked. 'If I liked!' He said it almost apologetically and I wondered if there was a catch to the offer. A man had to be mad or drunk to start out on any journey, no matter how small, in this country at this hour of night. He was drunk.

I had noticed a slight stagger in mine host's step but had put it down to the late hour and tiredness. There was no doubt about his companion, also Indian, when he greeted me. He was gloriously, uproariously drunk. Drunk Indians are a rarity in Africa. They are usually too poor, too religious or too keen watching the pennies to imbibe. But these two cronies had had a skinful that evening, especially my driver.

At that moment it was premature to call him 'my driver' for I had yet to make up my mind. The land had changed dramatically on the run down from Vila Gouveia. In complete contrast to the desolate, barren land I had walked through we were now in the fringes of the Amantongas Jungle, one of the densest forestation in all Africa. No sane or sober person would contemplate starting into the jungle at this time of night, especially with a drunken maniac for a driver. I wasn't drunk, but neither was I entirely sane, otherwise I wouldn't have got myself into this predicament in the first place. It hadn't been easy rousing myself out of my cosy sleeping bag and the thought of packing up camp now wasn't exactly pleasant. But neither was the thought of losing a lift and the alternative of walking all day tomorrow. So I decided to chance it and rolled up my kit.

My driver, now I can say it, spoke even better English than the shopkeeper and protested in lordly fashion with some out-of-the-ordinary language when I had to help him into the driving seat. He was perfectly capable of getting into his own colourful car and he'd show me just how he could drive when we got going.

We went off with a burn-up of the tyres, taking in both sides of the road as the car careered into the night. Luckily there was no other traffic. He insisting that although he had had a drink he was in complete command of his vehicle. To prove it he would take both hands off the wheel and wait till the car was almost leaving the road before grabbing it again and pulling the car back into line. With the dense forest walls all round and over us in the lamplights, this was not funny. Luckily he was no speed maniac. Still, the way he had to fumble for the gear stick when he needed to change didn't instil confidence in him. Despite all the run of play however, we arrived in Vila Pery in one piece. I slept in the back of the van.

In the morning I had a stroll round the little town and was very impressed, as I had been with all the little places I had seen on my way down. In contrast to Tete which was a 400-year-old tangled muddle of a town, these places I had passed through were delightful. Of Vila Gouveia I wrote:

'I'm particularly struck by these little towns in Portuguese territory. They are so clean and well laid out and look so neat with their whitewashed stones along the roadside and all seem to have street lighting. Although there are many Indians here in Mozambique who own shops, etc., there is no squalor and no rows of filthy, little, poky shops that one finds in the British territories.' And of Vila Pery, *'What a grand little place it is. I think it is the nicest I have ever seen. Wide, red mud streets lined with green trees. All the houses are of the villa type or bungalows and everything seems so quiet and peaceful. To be truthful, any town after these past few days would look the best I had ever seen!'*

Later, I came to the conclusion that I did the British territories an injustice in comparing some squalid conditions there to the pristine look of these townships I now saw in Mozambique. I realised from later conversations and observations the Portuguese authorities applied stricter control over their native and Indian population, with much more heavy-handed enforcement to comply, than was the way of the British administration.

During the next few days I walked through the great Amatonga jungle on my way to Beira. The walking was fitful, interspersed with short lifts. The road was quite dark in places where it burrowed under close-knitted branches of the huge trees. Great creepers as thick as my wrist dangled down from the branches overhead like lurking snakes. It was impossible to see more than a few yards on either side of the road, the undergrowth was so dense and the trees so close together. The sun's rays never penetrated the great roof of foliage overhead. Everything was silent. Heavy sinister silence. Nothing but the clump of my boots on the hard mud road and the occasional creak of a branch or tree. Suddenly a bird or animal would start up in a nerve-wracking burst of noise and dash off. Then everything would fall silent again – a silence you could feel.

This was the jungle that claimed so many lives when the railway was built through it at the beginning of the century. It was said that for every sleeper laid on the way through the Amatongas a man died either from fever or attacking animals or snakes.

When the big lift came it seemed a most unlikely one. A little pickup piled high at the back with household goods came flying round a bend, going far too fast for the road and load. It went past me with no hint of stopping but pulled up gradually further on. When I caught up with it a white face gingerly looked up from under a wide-brimmed hat and murmured something in Portuguese which I smiled at and held up my hands, then pointed in the direction and said "Beira." Crammed into the tiny cabin was a Portuguese farmer, his half-cast wife and three coffee-coloured children. I gathered that it was the wife who had bade her husband stop for he did not seem all that friendly. After we had established that I wasn't going to eat the children or chop off his head he jerked his head to the back and said something that I presumed to be 'climb up', which I did without taking my pack off first in case he changed his mind. On top of the high pile of luggage I quickly slipped off my rucksack, settled it and put my foot through one of the straps in fear of it rolling off, and hung on grimly to the cab roof as the little truck swung round the sweeping bends. The driver was either in a great hurry or frightened of the jungle. As it turned out he was probably both. I did not know how far he was going and expected him to stop at any small lead off from the road and tip me off. I did not know how lucky I was for he was going all the way to Beira. So he was driving like a maniac to get there before it was dark, having no wish for he and his family to be benighted in the jungle.

But glad as I was to be going with him it was a most uncomfortable ride for me. There was only one small place where I could sit and hold onto my rucksack and the cab roof, no way I could change hands for a grip or ease my position from cramp. As the afternoon grew old we emerged from the jungle into drizzling rain. By sundown it was bitterly cold. I was soaked to the skin and so frozen I could barely keep a grip on the side with my numb hands. The rain seemed to go right through me.

It was well into the evening when we entered Beira. Thankful in every way I was dropped off in a fairly dark backway and walked the streets aimlessly for a time looking for the bright lights, but thankful for the movement to thaw out my bones. Guided by the rising noise and better lighting I eventually arrived at the town centre. It was a great feeling to be there, seeing modern shops and mingling with city people. Blantyre seemed a long way back and I was pleased I had completed this part of my journey.

Drawn like a fly to an extra bright window I saw it was a café. Strange really, I hadn't seen a real café since Dar-es-Salaam and looking in the window it looked so inviting and warm I went in for some tea. My arrival caused a bit of a stir. A kilted tramp with great beard, battered hat and mountainous back-pack, sitting with the steam rising off my shirt, was not the ordinary run of clientele. I ordered tea and when that caused some doubts, changed it to coffee with some bread and butter. I would have asked for jam, but thought that would have caused just too much eye-rolling. As it was I got neither. Instead, a steaming plate of spaghetti-bolognese, or something like that, and a glass of wine was set before me. I tried to say I had got the wrong order, worried at the price the mistake might cost, but the black waiter took no notice, said something I didn't understand and walked away. I sat bamboozled, at a loss from the futile conversation, until another diner rose and came over and said in good English, "The manager wishes you to be his guest. The meal is gratis." I thanked my interpreter and looked across at the kitchen where the chef, oiled hair centre-parted, waxed moustaches perfectly curled, cheeks rosy red, beamed at me. I nodded my thanks and set-to in good trencherman style, the aromas suddenly reminding me how hungry I was, and trying hard not to show how embarrassed I was with the crowd who gazed at me in childlike wonder.

The drizzle was coming in sweeping shoals when I left and I decided to make for the beach to camp. Down there the wind was a gale and the drizzle had changed to driving rain. I had quite a job pitching the tent. It kept billowing out like a sail and I had to dig deep holes in the sand before the pegs could get a grip. I scooped out a comfortable hollow in the wet sand before spreading my groundsheet, tied up the door tapes and soon crawled into my sleeping bag and lay warm as a pie, although it was more of a steamy heat rather than a comfortable warmth. I wrote up my diary by candlelight while the old tent strained on the guys. It was taking a good pounding with the wind-driven rain and I wondered how often I would have to get up in the night to drive in the pegs. I went to sleep with the thunderous crashing of the Indian Ocean surf on the beach, like a gargantuan 1812 Overture in my ears.

I spent a few nights in like circumstances while staying in Beira, enjoying the city, speaking to people who could understand me, and preparing for my next step of the journey. My intention was to carry on down through Mozambique to Lourenzo Marques (Maputo), from where it was only a step to enter South Africa. But I was told that it is virtually impossible for me to go to Lourenzo Marques by land. Only a few cars ever attempted the journey and then only in the dry season, so there would not be the slightest hope of getting a lift, and there were long stretches of over a hundred miles without water or habitation. In the light of my last stretch from Tete I decided to exert discretion, change my plans and head east, back through the Amatongas to Southern Rhodesia (Zimbabwe).

I left Beira on a sunny morning, but some pewter clouds on the horizon heralded more foul weather later. And that came to pass, though it wasn't just rain that was the problem. Not far out I got a lift from the manager of an asbestos cement factory situated near Donda, twenty miles from Beira. He took me into lunch and showed me over the factory, the only one of its kind in Mozambique and only recently built.

Soon after leaving the factory I passed the Chef du Posto, equivalent to the District Commissioner Office in British territory, and a native policeman ran after me to say I must report to the office. The Chef du Posto was a short fat man. He couldn't speak English, but brought in a Goanese Indian who had spent time in Kenya to translate. He demanded my passport and examined it with the air of one looking at an article he knows is not genuine, good imitation though it may be. Then a barrage of questions came my way. Where had I come from? Where was I going? Why was I in Portuguese territory? And many more that I passed with the semblance of a smile. When he saw the stamp of the Portuguese customs at Zobue where I entered from Nyasaland he couldn't understand why I was coming from Beira, and no amount of explaining on my part could convince him. He asked why I had not reported to the British Consulate in Beira. I told him I didn't need to when my passport was in order and wasn't in any trouble. I let him rave on. At times they, that is the Officer and the Goan, would go into long sessions of Portuguese, their arms flayed the air. After a particularly long burst the *Chef du Posto* threw up his arms in a gesture of defeat, then sank back in his chair like a deflated balloon. Then, with a broad beaming smile as if it had all been a game, he handed me my passport and wished me *"Boa Viagen."*

Outside, the Goan explained to me that the whole trouble arose when the Chef du Posto saw me in kilt, khaki shirt and bush-hat he got the fixed idea that I was a deserter from the British Army who had escaped into Mozambique. We got talking, this Goan and I, and I learned that during the war he had served in the British army near Nairobi and was actually attached to the RAOC depot where later I served. So he said, but I was sceptical. The army in Kenya employed civilian Goanese and others as secretaries and clerks and I thought he must have been one of those. Sikhs and other Punjabies were soldier men. Goans, those indigenes of Portuguese India, were not.

The biggest export of all the countries round the British administered countries was men. From Angola and Mozambique a constant flow of voluntary black manpower was carried to and fro from the areas of comparatively high wages and prosperity. At Dondo there was a camp where all those who sought work in Southern Rhodesia were kept, ready for transportation to Salisbury. The return journey would bring those migrant workers back with their wealth. I had read or been told that migrant labour with all that it entailed in transportation and imported wages, accounted for over half of Mozambique's national revenue.

Before these times a man would be an elder before he could afford a dowry to obtain a wife, thereby perpetuating the age-old system where young girls attaining puberty were married off to men twice and three times their age while the young men languished as warriors or watched the herds. Now young men returned with wealth unknown to their fathers, and maidens' eyes danced with the thrill and anticipation of the near future, as did those of the returning young men, while elders smoked their pipes round their fires and lamented the changing tribal ways.

It was the job of de Vesta, my new-found friend, to check the migrants onto the train. He said if I waited until tomorrow night he would be able to put me on the train with a batch of natives and I would get a lift right to the Rhodesian border. No trouble, he was in charge, a good man to know. He lived in a native mud hut with his African woman. So I slept there too that night, on a string bed under the overhang and cooked my own food.

I did not get on the train that night. De Vesta said it was a particularly big batch that went through and I would have had to be crammed in with the mob where it would be stifling. Better that I wait till the next night when he was sure he could fix me up with an empty compartment to myself. The icy touch of doubt dropped into our relationship. But I waited, and sure enough about noon of the following day he came sheepishly and said the train was gone and there would be no more for some time. He said the station master had come to him earlier that morning without warning and made him couple his carriages to a goods train, so he couldn't put me on it. But, he said, his carriages were only being shunted to a siding at Mafambesi, ten miles away, and were to be coupled up to the mail train for Rhodesia that night at 7 p.m. If I walked there I would still manage to get in with the recruits and get a lift.

Trusting him, despite my qualms, I set off into the Amatongas jungle again and arrived at Mafambesi late in the afternoon. The siding was off the main road a mile or so and it was only by luck I managed to find the track to it through the forest. There were no carriages and no labour recruits there. I should have known, I scolded myself. De Vesta had proved to be as shallow and untrustworthy as all his race, I noted in my diary. To be fair, I pondered later after the initial sting had gone, his heart had been in the right place and he no doubt really intended to get me on the train and thought he could do it. Where he deceived was to imply he had far greater authority in the matter than he possessed and the story of catching the train at Mafambesi was a lie to get rid of me. Ah well, Goans will be Goans!

But I should not knock de Vesta too much for by a strange quirk of fate, and completely unintentionally by him, his lie sent me to the one man who could do for me what he had hoped to do, but failed.

Nearby was a private siding for a lumber camp. I heard the great saws going and went round to ask if they knew if the labour train had arrived. On entering their compound I watched the boys rolling huge tree trunks weighing several tons up and onto wagons. It was marvellous to see them manhandling them, accompanied by the usual singing and chanting to keep the rhythm. But none of the Africans knew anything about my train. Later, the Portuguese fellow who owned the sawmill came on the scene and took me up to his house. I explained to him the reason why I had come to Mafambesi. He said that no labour trains ever stopped there. However, the mail trains did come to his siding to couple up his timber wagons and as luck would have it, one was due that evening. Even more important, he said he was friendly with the ticket collector and he would ask if I could get a lift.

Before leaving he loaded me up with nearly half a hundred weight of oranges from his orchard nearby. When the train arrived he spoke quietly to the ticket collector while I waited in high anticipation nearby. The train was already on the move and my heart had dropped in sorrow when the collector waved for me to climb aboard, which I did with alacrity after wishing my benefactor a quick thank-you and goodbye. The ticket collector said I must get off at Vila Machado, the next station, but I asked if I could go as far Vila Manica, the last town in Mozambique, three times as far, and he agreed. But he added emphatically that I must make sure I got off there and make my own way to the border, which I readily agreed to do. Once under way he told me to stay in the corridor where I was and wait until he returned. When he did he took me to an empty compartment, which he had obviously gone to find, and pulled down the blinds and told me not to leave there until I arrived at Vila Manica early the next morning. With the whole compartment to myself I lay full-stretch along one side of seats and soon fell fast asleep while the train hurtled all night through the jungle, a fair change from my journey in the opposite direction down to Beira.

The new day started with excitement at 5 a.m. At that time I was rudely awakened when the door of my compartment slammed open and another ticket collector entered demanding to see my ticket. Still half asleep I told him I had none. He asked me where I was going. I told him Villa Manica. He said we were just leaving there. Now wide awake I saw the platform lights of a station slide past the window. Also I made a quick sum up of my position. My friendly ticket collector must have handed over to this man at the previous station. I could see a lot of trouble ahead for me in his demand for the fare and at the border if the police were called in. I had already been refused entry into Northern Rhodesia from Tanganyika and if the two Rhodesias shared data I would be known as persona non grata. If I didn't get into Southern Rhodesia now I would be faced with that impossible journey down to Lourenzo Marques on foot, which I could hardly contemplate. No doubt if I landed in the soup for travelling without a ticket the other ticket collector would deny all knowledge of me to save himself and I wouldn't blame him. All in all, I didn't think much of my chances of talking my way out of this lot.

On the spur of the moment I pushed this Collector out of the way and before he could regain his balance I thrust open an outside door that luckily was almost opposite my compartment and threw out my rucksack, then my bag of oranges and jumped. The train was going at a fair speed now and I stumbled to my knees. As I looked round I had a last look at the ticket collector, his startled face pushed out of the open door, before he was carried away into the darkness. I gathered my gear together, climbed the embankment and made my way to the town of Machipanda on the border. I watched the dawn light up the mountains. A wonderful sight.

At 7 a.m. I went up to the main local hotel and swapped my bag of oranges with the proprietor for a breakfast. After that I got on the road for the border. I didn't want to delay since that ticket collector might get on to the police and I didn't want to get caught up by them. I hadn't gone far when I got a lift. It was the first time I had to run out of a country! Contrary to all my fears about getting into Southern Rhodesia I had no trouble. They gave me a transit visa for the country and never asked for any cash deposit. How different to Northern Rhodesia where I had been turned away. I was to learn that, despite the similarity in names, the two countries were quite different in character with completely different immigration laws.

Chapter Nineteen

SOUTHERN RHODESIA
(ZIMBABWE)

Deep into the lonely Matopos Hills, not far south of Bulawayo, on the edge of the eerie Mount Injelele (the Hill of Slippery Sides) there is a secret cave approached by a sheer-sided, winding ravine, where once lived the Umlimo Oracle, a timeless old witch, strung with a kilt of skulls, bones, beads and sundry gruesome artefacts, who could smell out evil, cast spells and tell the future.

Southern Rhodesia was like no other country in Africa I had seen. You noticed it as soon as you crossed the border. Mozambique so torpid, lying half-asleep for centuries, and Southern Rhodesia so alive, throbbing, as if it was going somewhere. Fast. In little more than sixty years a land had flowered from nothing and grown to a modern metropolis comparable with many in Europe. Brick and tile villages, towns and cities had risen out of the open veldt to change the horizons forever and asphalt streets and roads had rolled over grass and bushland to wipe out nature's growth. I had thought that Kenya, and Nairobi in particular, had had a rapid rise from nothing to modern commercial status, but in comparison the rise of Southern Rhodesia in a similar space of time was phenomenal.

The difference between the two countries lay in the varied immigration laws that existed for each. Southern Rhodesia grew out of South Africa where there had never been any restrictions on white immigrants. In its early days pioneers from the south had followed Cecil Rhodes' band across the Limpopo River into the land they had 'acquired' from Lobengula, king of the Matabele, the land which Rhodes' Company now administered. Later, when the administration passed to direct control of the Colonial Office in London, Southern Rhodesia was declared a Self Governing Crown Colony with more autonomy that any other British governed colony in Africa. White immigration was allowed to continue freely as in South Africa.

Entry to Whites in other British administered countries north of the Zambezi had always been restricted. In these places entry permits were granted to those with administrative and commercial business and only very few early settlers were permitted land ownership, except in the relatively small area known as the 'White Highlands' of Kenya.

Here in Southern Rhodesia there were practically no restrictions and the migrants came in their thousands. The greatest influx arrived in great waves after the two World Wars. I arrived on the crest of the mightiest one in the aftermath of WWII. Migrants from the UK were pouring in by air and sea. Many came by ship to Biera, Mozambique, then by rail, as I had done. Some even made the long haul from Britain overland on wheels. Lately too, there had been a rapidly rising flow from South Africa, following the success of Malan's Afrikaans party in the elections in that country.

In the past five years the whole country had mushroomed. New villages had appeared out in the blue, the old ones had swept up to the size of towns and the towns had become cities. People said that Gwelo was like Bulawayo was at the start of the war. Now Bulawayo had grown almost as large as Salisbury (Harare). Gwelo, still growing rapidly, was vying with Umtali for the place of the colony's third city after Salisbury and Bulawayo. Que-Que and Gatooma were rushing to catch up. You could feel the boom in the air, the mad fever to build and expand. The country was thriving and wages were high. Even black wages, low as they were in comparison to white, were better than could be earned by natives in most surrounding countries and drew in hordes of hopeful workers. The politicians were negotiating a neighbourly tri-part Federation for the benefit of all, black and white, encompassing the man-power of Nyasaland, the wealth of Northern Rhodesia and the know-how of Southern Rhodesia.

There was certainly a buoyant air abroad in the people I met that early May morning when I walked the few miles from the border and down the wide street, lined with gorgeously coloured flowering trees. I had arrived in Umtali (Mutare) the main town of Manicaland Province, the nearest town to Portuguese territory. The place had an early colonial look and atmosphere about it with its mass of low buildings sprawled up the sides of Christmas Pass. It stood in a setting of unimaginable beauty with backdrops of the Vumba Mountains receding into blue mist to the south, while to the north rose the green and pleasant Nyanga Highlands where lay the many buried ruins of chiselled ashlar stone buildings of a long lost civilisation.

I had hardly gone halfway down the main street when a police motorcyclist drew up beside me to ask what I was doing and who I was. But this was no police-state action. Constable James Burns, a Scot from Rosyth, six miles from my home, was merely curious and after getting a sketch of my story he went off with a welcome smile and wave. I even remembered having met him before at home. He must have written to tell of our meeting for later a report of it appeared in my hometown newspaper *The Dunfermline Press*. Perhaps it was he who passed on the information to the local press for within minutes I was again accosted, this time by a friendly reporter from the *Umtali Post* which ran his story the next day, together with a Leyden cartoon – the 'Giles' of Rhodesia –

of which I was particularly proud. From then on I was a known character and people stopped and talked and I felt part of the community and among friends.

I felt good being back in English-speaking country again. But it was not just the easy-speak aspect that made me feel at home here, there was more to it than that. That day, and moreso in the months to follow, I grew in amazement at what was being achieved here in Rhodesia and I felt proud to be part of it, if only for a little while.

Here was the breadbasket of central-southern Africa exporting food to the surrounding countries on a scale never before imagined, a veritable Utopia, a land of opportunity and new wealth for both white migrants and black, the latter mainly returning in short cycles in order to spend their earnings at home and then replenish their fortunes, all of which was good for the economy of their homelands.

There was a comparison here to my own, wide family group, a similarity of events that was before my time but was always current conversation as I grew up. In the 1920s America was the Eldorado that drew young, aspiring fortune-seekers with the light of gold in their eyes from all over Europe and particularly from Britain. Four of my mother's brothers, all coal miners, went as a group to the coal-fields of Colorado and returned after three years richer beyond their dreams than would have been possible had they stayed at home where the wages barely stretched from one week to another. All did very well and they and their families benefited enormously. Two did better than others. Each built a fine new house, almost unheard of in mining communities, and enhanced their way of life for the rest of their days.

From this background I was able to identify with the Southern Rhodesia boom and the hope and happiness it engendered. Here in the 1950s was the universal dream of better living for all, black and white, that reached out to hungry masses far beyond the borders, in the same way as America had called to those across an ocean in the '20s, a generation before my time.

It was like nothing else I had encountered in all Africa. One of my first surprises was to see white men doing manual labour. All the artisans were European here. Nowhere else in Africa had I seen this. I was to learn as I became more familiar with Southern Rhodesia that black Africans were not allowed to practise their trades in towns. They could work as builders, carpenters, painters, etc. in the country places and in the reserves, but the towns were white territory. Blacks could be house-servants or do labouring and some menial jobs in the town, but they were not allowed to follow a trade there. The whites had built the towns and regarded those places as theirs. There could be no competition between the races for the blacks' wage rates were far below that of the whites. This demarcation of labour, even when both races were engaged on the same type of work, was a practice that had been imported from South Africa where it had long been the rule. Apart from seeing more white faces in the street than in any other town in Africa that I had so far visited, the sight of white men engaged in manual labour made Southern Rhodesia feel so European and different to all the other countries to the north.

How did all this come about?

*

To discover the making of Southern Rhodesia (Zimbabwe) we must wipe away the mists of time, grope back through the shadows of almost a century and a half and enter a Zulu regimental parade ground nearly a thousand miles south. It is a bright, sunny morning with the first chill edge of early winter in the light breeze. The year is 1822.

The parade ground is a vast round open area of bare earth beaten cement-hard by thousands of bare, stamping feet. Outside the surrounding palisade lies the town of beehive shaped Zulu huts, honey coloured in the sunlight, all placed in orderly, evenly spaced, circular rows. Before us is a scene archetypal of the Africa of legends of Haggard and Buchan and others, the epitome of the warrior tribes at their height and very best, before all that was swept away by the coming of the white man and lost in the mist we passed through.

On parade in orderly ranks, almost unknown in native armies, are thousands of Zulu warriors divided into named regiments, each under their own clan chief. There are many clans and even different tribes that all belong to the Nguni nation of which the Zulu clan is only one, and all the clan groups speak derivatives of the Uguni language. The assembled impis are about to spread the shadow of their great chief, Chaka, further and further beyond its present extensive boundaries. Since Chaka (also spelled Tshaka, Shaka and others) took over the Zulu chieftaincy in 1816 he has drilled the clan into the war machine it is today and extended its borders in every direction and absorbed the conquered people as Zulus. One day the miscellany of family groups will all form part of the great Zulu nation that today is in the making. From this day forward history will be made.

The great army stands remarkably silent, the head-plumes ruffled by the breeze, the long, throwing assegais and short stabbing ones with the lethal wide heads glint in the sun. It was Chaka's personal invention of the short sword and the introduction of it to all his troops that has made the Zulu armies invincible. At close quarters Chaka's ranks press forward when in close combat, screened in front by their solid wall of overlapping shields, through which the deadly short assegai can stab from behind when the long spears of the enemy are useless in the crush. This way they roll over rabble armies as an armoured tank will a century later.

It is interesting to note that three armies in history, the Romans, the Masai and the Zulus, who, without co-relation, each invented the short, stabbing spear or sword in conjunction with the testudo moving wall of shields, became the invincible and dominant nation of their time.

But the short assegai is not the only reason for the Zulus success. With it goes rigorous training, iron parade-ground discipline in the face of battle and ruthless punishment for defeat. Together, these have made the Zulu nation what it is, the greatest native war machine in all Africa prior to the introduction of bullets and cannon. Well-trained Zulu soldiers are indefatigable. Daily training may include 50- or 60-mile jog-trots carrying heavy shield and assegais that finish with parade-ground manoeuvres and mock battles with padded spears. Any man who falls out on the route-march/runs is instantly killed with his own spear by the induna (headman) who brings up the rear.

The atmosphere is brittle with expectancy when on to the scene strides a great figure of a man in splendid native war attire, animal tail kilt, feathered ruffles at the knees and head-dress like no other on the parade ground, consisting of a single blue crane's feather, eighteen inches long, rising from a band of small feathers of the red lourie bird. The King's crown. Chaka the mighty Chief has come to send his armies to do his will. A boom like a heavy, dull explosion bursts from the ranks as thousands of right feet thump the ground and a mighty cry as a single voice like the crash of a mighty wave on rock echoes far and wide as every throat shouts *'Bayete!'* (Thy will be done). Chaka acknowledges the accolade then strides to his second-in-command, the great general, Mdlaka, and gives him a division of the army made up of seven regiments with orders to go south into Natal and restore order in those places where dissident clans were making trouble. Chaka then goes over to a tall, well-proportioned young warrior, the deposed chief of the Kumalos clan, who recently threw in his lot with the Zulus. Chaka gives him his first full command, that of two regiments, with orders to go north on a cattle gathering, or rustling, expedition. Chaka, like all Nguni chiefs, is always ready to increase stocks. The young officer to whom he speaks is Mzilikazi Kumalos and this is where the history of Rhodesia as I knew it in the 1950s begins.

Mzilikazi, to whom Chaka had taken a particular liking, is twenty-two years of age and although Chaka is only seven years older he looks on the younger man with almost a paternal air. Later while sharing some beer and snuff at Chaka's request the Chief said, "I will miss you sorely, my son." But at this moment on the parade ground the Chief turns to Mbopa, his major-domo, head of the royal kraal, *Bulawayo* (The Place of Killing) and as such the keeper of the most rigorous etiquette of ceremony. Mbopa had been following Chaka and takes from him several accoutrements of war he has had prepared for his new commander. A resplendent head-dress of white ostrich feathers; a great, glossy white, raw-hide war-shield of standard Zulu regimental length that must reach from lips to toes; a stabbing assegai with an extra large head; and most treasured of all, an ivory-handled axe which Chaka had won in mortal combat with a crazed giant even bigger than he. Gifting the axe, a very personal possession shows the extent of the Chief's high regard and affection for Mzilikazi. Being able to know the future, we travellers of time, it is sad to see that the prodigy does not live up to his 'father's' expectations. With his new attire and weapons Mzilikazi looked every inch the perfect impi commander. The ostrich plume enhanced his size, but even with these he is still inches short of Chaka who stands taller and broader than all, a splendid figure of a man whose high single feather on his head makes him appear even taller, a colossus looking down from a height at his minions. To Mzilikazi he says, "By conquering the north become my right hand there." *"Bayete! Ndabezita."* (Thy Will be Done, Great Sir) answers Mzilikazi and his regiments thunder their foot stamp and boom out, *"Ba-ye-te."*

So we return to the present time and look back on the consequences of that day. Mzilikazi led his impi north and ravaged the tribes there and stole their cattle. While he had been away Zwide, who had deposed him of the Kumalo clan chieftaincy, had himself been deposed and Mzilikazi reinstated. The return journey to Chaka's kraal passed by the Kumalo kraal, so when Mzilikazi learned he was chief again of his clan he decided to leave Chaka's army and remain with his own people. He therefore sent the stolen cattle on ahead to his past commander. However, so successful had he been, the number of cattle so great, he assumed Chaka would not notice if he kept a few – quite a lot really – to himself.

But Chaka's spies were everywhere and he sent a group of messengers to the Kumalo chief's kraal to ask for an explanation. Mzilikazi sent no word but in eloquent action he had the plumes that waved above the messengers' heads cut off and sent the runners back like decapitated chickens. Whereupon the sorrowful Zulu Chief mused, "The young cockerel … must have his comb clipped," and sent his veteran Belebele Brigade after his wayward protégé. Mzilikazi's regiments repulsed the first attack, but due to treachery lost the second and he escaped with only three hundred of his men together with quite a number of woman and children.

Now there was no going back. Only death awaited anyone who disobeyed Chaka Zulu. If he were lucky because the Zulu chief still retained some affection for him, he might be condemned to a quick death by strangulation or be thrown over a high cliff to be smashed on the rocks below. Even the method of strangulation could carry a quality of mercy.

For this method of mercy-killing, the middle of a length of rope would be wound round the condemned man's neck and two slayers would take the ends to their extremities on either side of him and haul the rope tight. If Chaka was feeling really humane towards his erstwhile protégé he might, while the condemned man was in the early throes of strangulation, engage a strong man with a great club to smash down a heavy blow on the rope, the sudden jerk causing the neck to break. In the same manner, a condemned man on the gallows dies instantly when he drops to the extent of the rope after the trapdoor is sprung, as opposed to the slow, agonising death of one who is lynched.

There are many worse ways of killing people than hanging and Chaka knew them all ... and used them. Mzilikazi had no intention of sampling any of his past master's favourites.

The die cast, he led his people west beyond the Drakensberg Mountains and north, conquering all before him, press-ganging all fit male survivors into his army. In a few years he held sway over a vast track of land stretching from the Vaal River in the south to the Limpopo in the north, and from Portuguese Mozambique in the east to the land of the Bechwana in the west, an area many times larger than Chaka's Zululand He made a great kraal by the banks of the Vaal River and lived there for some years, then went north and built a King's kraal to rival Chaka's near the Crocodile River at a place where one day a city called Pretoria would flourish.

If Chaka had been disappointed with his protégé when he was in his command he would have been proud and flattered with him now, for everything he did he modelled on Chaka's teachings and example. His kraals were the same, his army drilled and fought in the Chaka fashion and his control and punishment methods with offenders and dissidents were in the style of the Master. And by the example of Chaka he was always warring, warring, always warring with all other tribes around him and winning. Like the Masai arrival in East Africa, the cowboy neighbours-from-hell had arrived, smashed all the local people and gone off with their cattle and were now the strongest, wealthiest and most feared in the land.

It said something for Mzilikazi that he was able to incorporate so many 'inferior' people into his army and bring their standard up to equal the Zulu best. This was proved when Dingane, Chaka's half-brother, murderer and successor, sent the full force of the Zulu nation against Mzilikazi in a punitive expedition and the battle was a draw, both sides losing many men and Dingane going away licking his wounds, but managing before he left to grab a great deal of Mzilikazi's cattle to take back to his OK corral.

Although Mzilikazi's army had given a good account of itself the battle taught him a lesson. He was still too near Zululand for comfort. So he led his people away further west where he met Robert Moffat, the great early missionary and David Livingstone's father-in-law. Though diametrically opposed to each other's beliefs and way-of-life they each formed a great respect and liking for each other that lasted all their days.

By this time with all the influx of different peoples into his original little band Mzilikazi's people had changed enormously since leaving Zululand. Even their language was not the Uguni as spoken by the Kumalo and Zulu clans. So changed indeed, Mzilikazi's tribe was now known as the Matabele and the language they spoke was Ndebele.

On the subject of names, the spelling of Mzilikazi comes in different forms over the years. David Livingstone and Robert Moffat spelled it Mosilikatzi, with a 't', which is probably the better phonetical pronunciation.

Though the Matabele were a much-changed people from Mzilikazi's original tribe the roots and customs were preserved by way of a 3-tier class system he designed. The top level, from which the indunas and all governing personnel were drawn, were all of the King's Kumalos clan. They set the rules and saw they were kept. A middle tier comprised other Uguni clans. They could hold positions of lesser rank or importance, but would never serve in the King's bodyguard or other high places. Lastly, the lowest tier was made up of the motley non-Uguni people who had been absorbed as fighting men but who, by way of training and forced following of Uguni ways and customs, would have every appearance of good Zulu stock.

In modern times the word or term Matabele has tended to be dropped and Ndebele used for both the people and the language. But at the time I was there they were the Matabele and that name has its place in history. When Mzilikazi's impis were ravishing the land that would later be called Transvaal they were named the 'Tebele', meaning 'Uguni strangers', by the Sotho tribe. 'Strangers' may have been a polite or less accurate interpretation for the Sotho meaning of their word! To Tebele was added the Bantu prefix 'Ma', meaning 'people'. The name stuck and forever after the Uguni invaders were known as the MaTabele. So much so, they began to call themselves by that name, but by a strange twist the Uguni interpretation came as Ndebele, by which they are known today. But I will continue to call the tribe the Matabele which is familiar to me and appropriate for the time.

Established in the territory that would eventually become known as northern Transvaal, the Matabele ruled all the land beyond many horizons. No other people would dare oppose them. But that state of affairs ended when the White Tribe arrived. In 1837 the vanguard of the Voortrekkers entered the land Mzilikazi claimed as his own. These were the Cape Dutch people, more commonly called Boers at that time but since the war of that name have been known as Africaners who speak Africaans. These pioneers had started an exodus in 1834 that went on for twenty years and became known in South African history as the Great Trek. They set out in groups of several families in ox-wagon trains to escape the British taxes and civil rules. Most of all they hated laws that enforced them to pay their African servants and treat them humanely, thus overturning their way of life that had been unchanged for centuries.

Like the Israelites who left Egypt and crossed the wild desert looking for the Promised Land, or the American wagon trains heading for a dream life in the Wild West yonder, the Voortrekkers ventured further and further north into what was then the wild, unknown interior of Africa in search of the fabled land of milk and honey where they could live in peace, free from 'redneck' laws and constraints. They wanted to continue their lives as their forebears had lived, and as Dutch Reform Churchers, heavy on Old Testament value, they brooked no interference in their using the natives as slaves, as they had always done. They believed the black people to be the Children of Ham who were, in old biblical terms, condemned forever to be Hewers of Wood and Carriers of Water.

The Boers were hard people, as different from the British and modern Dutch (whom the Boers called Hollanders) as the natives were. The Boer forebears in Africa went back centuries. Africa was their country. They had been in Southern Africa longer than the Zulus. They broached no truck with blacks and regarded any land they wanted as theirs to have and to hold, and assumed the divine right to take what natives they wanted as domestic and agricultural servants.

And woebetide any press-ganged servant who misbehaved or did not work fast enough or up to the standards demanded by his master. One favourite punishment in extremis was to lash the wretched native to one of the 5 foot-plus diameter wagon-wheels, spread-eagled, arms and legs wide apart tied to the great spokes, while the wagon trundled along for miles, bumping over rough ground, the poor devil revolving like a Catherine wheel.

Mzilikazi set his forces on the first lot of trekkers when they arrived and had one or two initial successes when they butchered some families. But more Boers arrived as reinforcements and the tide turned. The Matabele had overwhelming numerical superiority. The sight of their ranked legions surrounding their laagered camp, when the wagons were drawn into a circular formation with the people and animals on the inside, must have been a fearsome sight for the beleaguered Voortrekkers. But the Boers were not the raggle-taggle rabble the Matabele were used to scattering. They were tough, fearless and disciplined in battle and always led by a wise, resourceful trail-commander. And they had guns and knew how to use them. The men, all crackshots, fired at the advancing enemy from between or under the wagons and passed their empty weapons to their woman-folk to reload. And if necessary the women took up the guns and used them like the men with deadly accuracy.

After many affrays Mzilikazi knew his warriors were no match for the white invaders. And now he had reports that there was a steady stream of Voortrekkers on their way up from the south who would swell the ranks of those he had already met. Fifteen years had elapsed since that day we saw him given his first command by Chaka on that Zulu parade ground and now the time had come to move on once again. The only way to go for safety was north, and to do that he had to take his Matabele across the Limpopo River. And here we have the dawn of Southern Rhodesia as it was in the mid-20th century.

On crossing the river Mzilikazi divided his people into two groups. He kept his own group as a rearguard and sent the other under Gundwane, his generalissimo, ahead. With that group went his sons and other members of the Royal household. They found little resistance from the less warlike Shona people who were resident in the land north of the Limpopo. The Mashona had already been hit by the Zulu Angoni migrants when they passed through on their way to the Lake Nyasa region. But the Matabele did not pass away and later the Mashona were to rue the day the 'strangers' entered their territory for they were to be ravished by the Matabele as all other tribes had been in their wake.

For some reason the two Matabele groups went their own ways once into Mashonaland, Gundwane's one to the north-west and Mzilikazi's to the north-east. The two together numbered 15,000 people and that was perhaps too large a number to move easily and live off the land until they found the place where they would set down their roots. Nearly two years were to pass before they met up again at the place Mzilikazi decided to make his King's kraal, which he called 'Bulawayo' after Chaka's one. As 'the place of killing' it was aptly named for now there was trouble in the camp. Big trouble.

While on the move Gundwane, worried because there was no Royal leader in his group to command the 'first fruits' ceremony, had appointed Mzilikazi's eldest son, Nkulumane, as Chief. When they met up, Mzilikazi regarded that act as treason and had both Gundwane and Nkulumane put to death. And following that there was a scene so typical of the ancient classics and raw, old Africa. Mzilikazi ordered all his sons to be killed so there would be no one to usurp him. This act was played out to the letter of the old legends, for one son was to survive the slaughter by the subterfuge of his mother. Fulathi, daughter of a Swazi chief, hid her son LoBengula so he survived to take his father's crown when Mzilikazi died nearly thirty years later in 1868.

During his reign Mzilikazi carved out his territory that would become known and be written on maps and in geography books as Matabeleland. Mashonaland had shrunk to less than half its former size and the Shona people paid homage to Mzilikazi and lived in constant fear of his impis falling on their villages to 'wash their spears' and carry off their cattle and womenfolk. Mzilikazi had a wicked way of impressing his stamp on his subjugate neighbours. He had the Chief of the Mashona, the Mambo of the Rozwi tribe, skinned alive.

Life for the Matabele was less turbulent and dangerous than it had been in the Transvaal as Mzilikazi lived on into ripe old age. It was his son, Lobengula, who had to face the next wave of white insurgents, the British. They were different to the Boers who had driven his father from the land south of the Limpopo River. Their leaders were more friendly, suave, articulate, persuasive and twice as deadly.

*

Cecil John Rhodes, who was responsible for the British going into Matabeleland in force, was a most remarkable man. He came to South Africa with his brother in 1871 as an eighteen-year-old when the diamond rush to Kimberley was at its height. By the time he was nineteen he was a multi-millionaire. Over the next few years, despite his tender age, he became one of the most influential men in the country and wrote his name more indelibly over the sub-continent than any other man – and there were many men of great stature and drive, trying to carve the country to their design and benefit during that era. From the modern point of view he is mainly vilified as the unacceptable face of colonialism. In his day many saw him as the most brilliant, perspicacious man that ever entered South Africa.

Soon after his arrival in South Africa Cecil Rhodes had a dream and very much by his own efforts he made that dream come true. His dream, his fervent wish, was to see the map of Africa from the Cape to Cairo painted in red that denoted the British Empire and Commonwealth and by the 1950s when I travelled down Africa that had become fact. Had I been able to have gone up the Nile, and had I not been stopped from entering Northern Rhodesia, I would have travelled the whole way under the British flag and English would have been the *lingua-franca* at every customs-post. I remember vividly sitting in school, enthralled by the geography teacher enthusiastically running the pointer up and down the big, roll-down map of Africa, emphasising the red swathe that joined the whole eastern side of the continent from north to south and swelling with national pride at the achievement. Perhaps that was the seed that grew and made me want to travel that land.

In Rhodes' early days Egypt and the Sudan were well under British domination. East Africa was becoming more and more under British influence though the Germans were strong in Tanganyika. The land south from there to the Limpopo, apart from Portuguese territory, was ruled only by some wild, savage chiefs and so was up for grabs. Rhodes' problem was to get round the Transvaal that by now was an established Boer country.

Immediately north of British South Africa territory lay Bechuanaland with a long history of British friendship fostered mainly by Robert Moffat and his son-in-law, David Livingstone. The Bechuanas feared both the Boers and the Matabele. True or false there were rumours abroad that the Boers were planning to move into Bechuanaland. If this happened Rhodes' dream of the British Empire marching north in Africa would have been blocked. The rumours were conveyed to the Foreign Office in London and mainly through Rhodes' efforts Britain offered the Bechuanas protection from their Boer and Matabele neighbours and this offer was accepted. British administrators moved in and Bechuanaland became an official British Protectorate over which fluttered the Union Jack and red ink crept one step more over the map of Africa. Matabeleland now lay immediately in Rhodes' path.

Rhodes' opportunity came when gold was discovered in Manicaland. Perhaps 'again' should be added to that past sentence, for gold had been discovered in that land many times going back into distant history. It was not a big strike but it was enough to show the country's potential. In South Africa Rhodes pondered over the situation. The way to the gold lay through Matabeleland and Mashonaland. No easy course.

In the early days, after Lobengula had taken over as King after the death of his father Mzilikazi in 1868, many hopeful prospectors and ivory hunters had drifted into the country. Like his father while he was in Transvaal, Lobengula had allowed a few who took his fancy to follow their ways. This led to a very ragged situation with wandering prospectors and small-time miners scattered throughout the land. Rhodes had his eye on bringing Lobengula's domain under the British flag, thereby preventing the Transvaal Boers from annexing Matabeleland and so cutting off his way north.

The possibility of the subjects of a foreign power hitting the gold jackpot was the last thing Rhodes wanted to happen. Due to his inspiration, drive and foresight the British South African Company was founded and he applied to Lobengula for the company to be given the sole rights to prospect and mine all minerals over all land under the rule of the Chief and that went well into Mashonaland as well as Matabeleland. Also in the application was the condition that all Boer activities be prohibited. At the time there was a lot of squabbling and intrigue going on between British and Boer factions in his domain and Lobengula believed that by giving the British company the sole rights he would have more peace and order in his land. He was helped towards his decision by a shrewd offer from Rhodes: £100 a month for the king, a riverboat and 1000 rifles with 10,000 rounds of ammunition. Some called it a bribe and there were those who said it was a swindle because, they claimed, the wording of the request was misinterpreted to Lobengula. Right or wrong, it was the sale of the century for with the mining grant eventually came the country.

In 1889 Rhodes acquired for the British South African Company from the British Government in London a Charter granting the Company the right to represent Great Britain, to make treaties and in all matters deemed necessary to further her interests. With this backing Rhodes raised the BSAC's own troops in South Africa and in 1890 the 'Pioneer Column', a force of 500 men led by

Frederic Courtney Selous, skirted Lobengula's territory and set up fortified camps in Mashonaland and Manicaland to protect the mines and British interests throughout those lands. The first to be built was Fort Victoria, named after the Queen, the second one they called Fort Salisbury, after Lord Salisbury the then Prime Minister of Britain. These two were in Mashonaland. The third in the same year was Fort Umtali in Manicaland where the latest gold discovery had been made.

Although he did not command the Pioneer Column it was on Selous, as scout and advisor, that the commander relied to get them through the dangerous land and difficult terrain to their destination. It was Selous who found the pass up the ravine that blocked their passage onwards from Fort Victoria and it was on his shoulders the success of the party constantly lay.

Frederick Courtney Selous was a most remarkable man of his day and any other, the archetype of the early white hunter/explorer and the role model for at least one modern author's multi-series of Africa fiction. Born in London in 1851 and schooled at Rugby, Selous went to South Africa when he was nineteen and from then led a life that defied fiction, one that boys/men of his era, and of at least a century later, could only dream. Before his employment by the Chartered Company in 1890 he had spent eighteen years big-game hunting and exploring the land north of the Transvaal as far as the Congo basin. With a keen, natural, microscopic interest in all flora, fauna and ethnology he added a great deal to the knowledge of the day and brought back many specimens and samples of natural history, much of which rests in museums and private collections throughout the world.

A quarter of a century after leading the Pioneer Column to Manicaland, at the age of sixty-two, during the First World War, he enlisted in the legion of Frontiersmen as a subaltern, was promoted to captain while in service in Tanganyika, then German East Africa, and was killed on 4th January 1917 at Beho-Beho, where he was buried. He rests in the area that was declared a game reserve in his name, which was, at that time and probably still is, the largest, least known and most densely populated by large animals, in the world. Selous was a legendary character, even in his own time, and on his demise the commander of the opposing German forces, General von Lettow-Vorbeck sent a letter to the British military HQ expressing his deep sorrow on learning of his death in action.

But back to the 1890s; the Pioneer Column included several men who would ripple the waters of history in the future. None moreso than a fiery Scot from Edinburgh with the grand handle of Leander Starr Jameson, later Sir but usually referred to throughout his life in Southern Africa as 'Dr Jim'. He graduated in medicine in London and, due to delicate health, went to South Africa and set up practice in Kimberly where he met and doctored Rhodes and for the rest of his life became friend, advisor and acolyte to the man who made countries and uncountable wealth. It was Dr Jim who had negotiated the deal with Lobengula that paved the way for the Pioneer Column's entry into Mashonaland and it was Dr Jim who later lit the touch-paper that destroyed the Matabele and laid the country open for a British takeover. Later still, after the death of Rhodes and out from under his shadow Jameson became Prime Minister of the Cape and afterwards Chairman of the Chartered Company even though he had served a prison sentence for his misdemeanours.

But that is jumping ahead over too much important ground that made up the jigsaw of Africa as I knew it that day in June 1952 when I walked into Salisbury (Harari). Although not officially named 'Rhodesia' until 1895 the country started when The Pioneer Column marched into Mashonaland, set up their forts and ran the Union Jack up their flagpole. A great deal of history-making stuff had happened in those five years since the Column set up shop. In the wake of the troops had come an influx of pioneers, traders, settlers, miners, hunters, etc., many bringing their woman with them for the beginning of a new life, all knowing they were protected by the umbrella of the British Government, albeit under the aegis of The British South African Company.

It was said that Lobengula did not like it, that he had not intended settlers and other permanent-stay personnel to be included in the mining rights. The official history says that in 1893 he mobilised his impis and sent a force against the British. But that is only one of many reports of the start of what was to become known as the 'Matabele Wars'. But as in all wars, depending on the bias of the reporter, there are always many conflicting reports or reasons for the outbreak of hostilities. Another account says the Matabele *indunas* rose against Lobengula because he was too lenient towards the British 'invasion'. There were other reasons they might have thought but never voiced, for fear of instant death at the hands of the royal slayers. Accusations for instance that their chief did not want to lose his King's Pension from the British. And there was more that could not be mentioned in the King's presence or that of his spies.

Lobengula was not the man he had been. In fear and dread those around him had watched his failing health and growing dissipation due to the white mans' liquor which was freely given. In matters of state he was slow to rouse, but in dispensing punishment his verdict was quickly given and now almost always was the death sentence.

But, as already mentioned, death by itself could be a lenient sentence. Take for example the incident described by Colonel Marshall, a contemporary of Lobengula who wrote a book on the African king. One of the King's subjects was brought before him charged with drinking the royal beer. The King was furious.

"Cut off those lips," he screamed, his voice high falsetto in anger, "for they have drunk the King's beer." The deed is done immediately with two slices from a sharp spearhead.

"Cut off that nose, for it has smelt the King's beer. And cover his eyes with the skin of his brow, for he has beheld the King's beer." The nose is sliced off and the skin of the brow is flayed and darkens the eyes. Finally, in relief, the screaming man is led outside and mercifully slain.

Such was the man at the hub of events that were to change the country forever. Did he, or did he not, give the order for his armies to rise against the Pioneers? There is another account that says that the whole thing was a mistake, that Lobengula actually sent his warriors to *help* the British by attacking the Mashona who were sabotaging the visitor's property, i.e. cutting down their telegraph poles, and it was our Leander Starr Jamison, who had been appointed as Administrator, who misread the signs and, believing the Matabele were coming to attack the BSAC, sent his forces to oppose them.

At the same time the British High Commissioner in South Africa, Sir Henry Loch, ordered the invasion of Matabeleland in November 1893. One can only presume that this action was taken to aid the British who were being attacked by the Matabele, or to assist the British personnel of the BSAC to attack the Matabele when the Matabele were coming to attack the Mashona who were attacking British property. The reasons for and the convolutions of events at the start of the first Matabele war are very confusing but the outcome was quite clear. The Matabele were smashed as a fighting force. Rhodes' troops destroyed Bulawayo, the King's kraal being once again the Place of Killing, but not before Lobengula had escaped with all his possessions in several wagons and headed north. A troop of British soldiers, under the command of Major Alan Wilson, chased after him. The King's bodyguard allowed the horsemen to pass then encircled them and at the Shangani River, though the British troops fought valiantly, they were slaughtered to a man, as most official reports state. But there is one account of an eyewitness who claims that three soldiers survived. Lobengula died the following year.

The BSAC now took over the complete administration of the country which was opened up to British and South African immigration, areas of high ground being designated as 'white' and the Africans allocated their own tribal lands. In 1895 the country was officially named Southern Rhodesia. The following year, 1896, the Matabele tried again and rose under the command of Lobengula's son, Nyamande. But it was a forlorn hope and ended with Cecil Rhodes, alone and unarmed, walking into an arranged *indaba* with the King and parleying peace.

The site of this meeting was a place nearly thirty miles south of Buluwayo, in the bare, bald-headed Matopo Hills known to the natives as *'Malindidzima'* (The Place of Benevolent Spirits) which Rhodes renamed for himself as 'World's View'. It became his favourite retreat, his refuge where he would come alone to meditate and recharge his batteries. And it was here where he chose to be buried, and when the time came in 1902, his body was interred in a grave cut down into the solid rock. Nearby too, but later, 1917, Sir Leander Starr Jameson was also laid to rest in similar style. Close friends in death as in life.

The Matabele Wars, as they were referred to, happened a little more than half a century before I arrived in the country. For the first half of that time the British South African Company administered the country, but the gold that had attracted them to it had never materialised in any quantity worth the trouble. Instead, the real gold was found in the Transvaal, the land of the Boers, and it was to there that Rhodes and Dr Jim and Co. turned their attention and that culminated in the Boer War in 1899. The BSAC administered Southern Rhodesia until 1923 when the Colonial Office in London took direct control. Since then the country's development had galloped along at breakneck speed.

*

Early travellers loved to bring home grotesque tales that heightened their image to gasping audiences. Today's listeners would not be so credulous. Nevertheless there are many wonderful stories that come out of Africa that even today beggar belief but cannot be caste aside as fantasy. Most popular of all perhaps are those relating to secret wealth just waiting to be tapped. Forlorn trails of lost and hidden treasure criss-cross the African continent like a lace curtain laid over the map. Wherever you go there are tales of wealth untold waiting to be found. Most never get known beyond the local borders. Others, such as those of *King Solomon's Mines* and *The Elephants Graveyard*, are known the world over. Most have the stuff of fables surrounding them. But even fables have a kernel of truth in their beginning, before the embellishments of time dulled their authenticity. There can be little doubt that some, such as that of Solomon's Mines, (which we have touched on and will do so again), are based on fact, while others, as that of *The Elephants Graveyard*, cannot be.

The graveyard tale tells us that when elephants know they are dying they make their way to a secret place and there lie down and die. If a traveller or hunter were to discover this elephants' hallowed ground they would find wealth beyond dreams in centuries of accumulated ivory. The truth is that at the time from whence this story came elephants were in such profusion of numbers that if they had all made their last atavistic journey to one place the converging, well-worn trails of millennia would lead anyone with half an eye to the graveyard. The fact is that ivory left on the African plains would fall foul of the sun, hyenas and termite ants and would not remain to be found decades, never mind centuries, later.

There are, however, some lesser-known treasure trove tales which do carry the seal of authenticity. Take for example the legend of Lobengula's lost millions, the treasure of diamonds, gold and coins the vanquished Matabele king took with him when he fled from Bulawayo and has never been found. This tale has more mystery, mystic and drama than any writer of African adventure could ever have concocted.

It was well known that Lobengula had a fortune. He had a horde of ivory tusks stashed away and he purchased two safes to keep his gold, diamonds and sovereigns in. He had long possessed a quantity of gold from old Manicaland mines that had now run out. But when the gold and diamond mines were opened in South Africa he obtained a regular supply from them. Many of his subjects went to work in these mines and on their return it was the custom, nay, the royal command, that they each bring to their King something of what they had stolen, a diamond or nugget or gold sovereign and so the horde grew. An eye-witness maintained there were three boxes of diamonds in one of the safes.

Who was this witness? A very reliable one, it would appear. His name was John Jacobs, a Cape half-caste, educated at Lovedale and Scotland, who was fluent in Ndebele, English and Cape-Dutch. He joined Lobengula in 1888 as a young man just when the African King needed a linguist to parley with the British and Boer insurgents. It was Jacobs who translated for Lobengula when Leander Starr Jameson treated with the King to give his prospecting concession to the BSAC. He was the King's secretary and advisor in all matters dealing with the whites. And more than that: he was the King's most trusted confidante.

Jacobs lived on into the 1930s and was the complete authority on the private life of Lobengula. He told of the African King's most intimate fears and fantasies. How, sometimes in the night his master would bade him bring his treasure to him from the safes. Then, in traditional miser fashion, he would delve his hands into the boxes and let his wealth pour through his fingers. Sometimes the King would have Jacobs cover his oiled body with sovereigns so that he lay like an Ancient Egyptian golden sarcophagus. Jacobs estimated the safes' contents exceeded £2,000,000.

There were the times when the King plummeted into the depth of the occult in true Rider Haggard fashion. Deep into the lonely Matopos Hills, not far south of Bulawayo, on the edge of the eerie Mount Injelele (the Hill of Slippery Sides) there is a secret cave, approached by a sheer-sided, winding ravine, where once lived the Umlimo Oracle, a timeless old, hairless witch, hideous as sin, with brown parchment skin stretched tight over her gaunt skull, who would dance a chilling jig to the rhythm of her kilt of strung skulls, bones, beads and sundry, gruesome artefacts, and who could smell out evil, cast spells and tell the future.

No native would enter that cave. But Lobengula did, frequently, as did his father, Mzilikazi, before him. And before these invaders the Mashona hierarchy had come too to be told their fortunes, and, who knows, maybe before the Mashona the San Bushmen came too for the Oracle was timeless.

Casting her spell, the Oracle, surrounded by her priests, told Lobengula of the coming of the white man and nothing he could do would prevent them inheriting the country. Perhaps this was the reason why the Chief had done so little to oppose the British until it was too late. Was he fatalistic and saw the end was inevitable? That could be the reason why he buried his treasure.

Following a visit to the Umlimo Oracle, before the outbreak of the Matabele War, Lobengula in great agitation gave Jacobs and four *Indunas* secret orders to load all his treasure onto several ox-wagons and with them he went to a secret place in the the bush where all the trove was buried.

Many years later, in 1930, when quizzed by a fortune-hunter, Jacobs remembered that they travelled north then eastwards for many days before crossing the Zambezi River, which would put the site in what became Northern Rhodesia and later Zambia. Finally they arrived at the very remote place, deep in the forest that had been selected to bury the cache. As well as the four *indunas* they had brought with them fourteen Matabele warriors to do the digging and move the treasure. Two great holes were excavated in the side of a cliff. In one went the safes and in the other, each piece wrapped in sheets, went the ivory. The openings were walled up with stones and disguised. A few nights after the burial the warriors were murdered by the *indunas*, assegaied in their sleep, by order of Lobengula.

Shortly afterwards the first Matabele war broke out in 1893, the King's kraal, Bulawayo, was sacked and Lobengula went in retreat to the north in his ox-wagons loaded with the considerable fortune the chief had kept for his daily use. On the fateful morning, December 3rd, when Major Wilson's patrol approached Lobengula's caravan, Jacobs said the King gave him £1000 to take to the white officer to call off his men. But Wilson would have nothing of it and ordered the charge in which all but three of the white soldiers died.

Six months later Lobengula was also dead and nothing more was heard of his lost treasure. The *Bulawayo Chronicle* of August 5th, 1923, carried the message that 'John Jacobs, the grey-haired Cape man, who alone today is said to know the whereabouts of Lobengula's buried millions ...' And though he accompanied at least one treasure-hunt safari from Johannesburg thirty years after the event they never found the burial place. Did Jacobs memory fail him after all that time, or did he choose not to reveal his past master's secret? Perhaps Lobengula's ghost lay too heavily across the old African's shoulders and the awful sight of that mutilated face with nose and lips sliced off and the skin flapped over the eyes, together with the agonised, blood-curdling screams and whimpering, was too vivid a warning to him of what might await him in the next world if he gave away the secret.

There have been many reports of excursions to find Lobengula's lost treasure but not a whisper of any having been found. The story remains as one of the many lost trails of Africa.

*

By the early '50s when I came along it was an experience in itself to see Salisbury, realising that most of what you saw was what had been made in the last thirty years: the square miles of city, all carefully planned, the buildings, shops, offices, industry, and streets. Streets! Rushing rivers of flowing metal with mad whirlpools at every crossroads. That was where the life-blood of the city ran. That was where you could feel the pulse beat, see the vitality of the city, the will to get on with life, fast, the urge to expand, build an even greater country. It was said that the country had more cars per head of population than any other country in the world, the ratio being one car to every three persons – white, presumably!

Not all residents were pleased though. Those older ones who had known the country between the wars were wary of the new immigrants, sure that the settlers from Britain were not the type that had made the country, fearful that the sudden rush of South Africans would alter the British life-style of the colony. The veterans said it could not last and prophesied boom-and-gloom. How right they were. But even these old-timers did not dream that within a decade of my arrival the bubble would burst. Already the machinations of an overpowering native discontent were rumbling on the horizon like distant thunder.

The wheel of destiny turns inexorably and what appears to be irresistible is resisted and kings and tyrants have their day. People displace people, country borders are redrawn or made anew and history is shaped as it has been since the beginning of mankind. Long, long ago the Bantu came from the north and wiped out or drove into the south-western desert the gentle San bushmen people who had occupied the land since time was lost. In latter years the Mashona were displaced and subjugated by the Matabele who in turn were vanquished by the British who, when the wheel had turned full circle, were toppled by the Shona.

There is an interesting point of note in that cycle of events. When the British came to the land they eventually called Southern Rhodesia they stopped the Matabele massacring the Mashona who lived in fearful misery, constantly waiting for the next attack. But when the British rule was broken some seventy years later it was the Shona who rose and emerged as the most politically adept people and who eventually became leaders of government. But for British intervention the Ndebele might still be washing their spears in Shona blood and those people would still be second-class citizens living their lives in constant fear of death and privation. So did the weak, or meek, inherit the earth.

416

*

Umtali (Mutare) town developed from Fort Umtali, the third of its kind built in 1890 by the Pioneer Column. The site was moved to be on the Salisbury-Beira railway which reached the town in 1898 and repair workshops and sidings were built. The name Umtali was derived from a people of long ago meaning 'metal', which is not surprising for it was known from times of antiquity that gold, silver, lead and copper have been mined here. This was Manicaland which, before the political lines were drawn on the map, extended well into the territory that the Portuguese regarded as theirs but which they only visited on long and infrequent safaris in ancient times to try and make contact with the famed, mysterious Monomatapa whom they believed was the keeper of the King Solomon's Mines.

On my arrival I soon found and established myself in the camping site about a mile out of the town. It was the best one I had ever come across, with firewood and barrels of hot and cold water laid on and guards to make sure it was safe to leave your gear and go down town. There were a couple of overlander families encamped there while they looked for permanent quarters and work and it was great to swop our stories. They had come in convoy by the overland trail from England across France and Spain to cross into Africa from Gibraltar, traverse the Algerian mountains and navigate the trans-Saharan passage from Columb Bechar to Niameg and on to the Niger River and through the Congo to Northern Rhodesia (Zambia) and into Southern Rhodesia. A dream-journey of three or four months for families to do in search of new and better lives and I admired their courage and loved their stories, those iridescent threads that were being woven into the tapestry of Africa.

After a few days of meeting the people and wandering up Christmas Pass and the surrounding hills I got on the road and had no difficulty in getting lifts to Salisbury, something less than 200 miles into the country. The road, like all others outside town limits, was two strips of tarmac, like rails, with grass or mud in between. This was fine so long as only one car was using the road and a big improvement on the bare mud tracks elsewhere in Africa north of Rhodesia. But when another vehicle came along, or if one car was overtaking another, then it could be tricky, especially at high speeds. Both cars had to get off the rails and bump along on the mud, then rise up on to tarmac after passing. In wet weather this could get a bit hazardous. After a few lifts mixed with some walking I was dropped off in Salisbury about 9 p.m.

I walked round the streets for a while. I had a scout around the back of some buildings to find a place to doss down for the night. Then I struck on the idea to go the station to sleep in the waiting room. While making my way there I was attracted like a fly to the bright lights of the Jacaranda Café and went in for some tea. It so happened the proprietor and his wife came from the Isle of

Arran and came over to talk when they saw the kilt. On learning of my plan to go to the station waiting room they offered a spare room for the night. My diary entry for that day, Friday 6th June 1952, ended with the words, *'So once again I have landed lucky.'*

Next day I met Nelson Gregory who had come to town for some provisions. He owned a brickfield about seven miles out into the *bundu* (typical Rhodesian word). When we were talking I mentioned I would be looking for a job for a month or two. He said he knew a lot of builders in town and was sure he could get me fixed up the following week. In the meantime he invited me along to stay with him over the weekend. An interesting and friendly person, Nelson showed me with pride over his brick works during my time with him. He had come to Rhodesia some years before with no trade or profession and on seeing the building boom at its height had hit on the idea that the one commodity that was in great demand was bricks. He had only a hazy idea how they were made, but nevertheless acquired this piece of land and set about making his product by trial and error. Along with a few mishaps he gained knowledge and confidence and now his bricks were highly sought after by local builders. He fired the bricks in open stacks, each pyre carefully and eventually expertly laid with the right amount and type of wood, all equally layered and spaced to allow even burning. In the beginning he had overburned those in the middle while those at the sides were underdone.

On Monday Nelson was as good as his word. He took me to a builder who saw me as manna from heaven, though by the man's canny approach he gave nothing away of his relief that I had appeared on that special day. A craggy Scot and dour in his appraisal – I learned later that the sun could shine on his face when we had a laugh together – he asked what I could do. I said I was a fully apprenticed and experienced painter with City and Guilds certificates. He looked at me hard, studying. I matched his eye. He ran his finger round his mouth, speculatively and gripped his chin. Pondering. Had I had experience of managing jobs? he asked. Yes, I replied, I had no worries in that respect. How long did I intend staying? Oh, a couple or months or so. The sun slowly lit up his face when he smiled.

"You can start right away if you like," he grinned.

I started next day and worked exactly two months. 'Sixty days' was the sentence that had been passed on his Africaans painter-foreman on Friday, the day I arrived in Salisbury, for stealing a motorbike. I finished my time the day after the prisoner was released and took back his job. I was taking a chance accepting the job for I had only a transit visa with no working permit. And what was the job in which I was now involved? The completion of the new Central Police Station!

That same day I managed to get 'digs' with a Mrs Wilson who took in boarders in Baker Avenue, near the centre of the city and moved in straight away. She had two sons, one married, and another who was about my own age, who all lived in. I still wore my beard from my croc-hunting days and perhaps appeared older than I was. I shared a room, and the bed, with a complete stranger who was nearly always drunk, or part way so. He had just broken with his wife and the reason seemed obvious. He left at the end of the month – there were mumbles of not paying his rent – and I then had the room to myself until I left.

I started work the next day. The wages and conditions were exceptionally good compared to UK standards, 7s.2d. (36p approx.) per hour, nearly three times that in Scotland when I left. We worked a 42-hour, 5-day week. Money galore and a long weekend every week. What luxury! From the time I had started in the trade I had done a 44-hour, 5½ day week, ending twelve o'clock on Saturday. The 5-day week did not come to Britain for some years later.

There were half-dozen white painters and some black labourers. We all met rather warily, they wondering who I was and where I'd come from, one or two at least having expected to have been upgraded to foreman. I, for my part as a newcomer to the country, not wanting to tread on any toes but determined to get a grip on the job and make it go.

As it was, we all had nothing to worry about. Determined not to be a standing foreman, I worked in the thick of it all and soon found I had nothing to fear from the competition and they knew why I had been given the position and accepted me in it. It was obvious they were used to easier working conditions than I had been brought up to accept as normal. Later they openly stated they were glad to see the back of the Africaans fellow. It appeared he was a surly curmudgeon with a wicked and profane tongue, though these are not the words they used in reference to him. I gathered they were not going to be glad when he walked in again and jumped up on his old pedestal.

If the whites were glad he was gone, the blacks were ecstatic, and showed it. One got the slightest impression the South African had not been too kind to them! Now they had smiles on their faces that made their teeth sparkle white against their shiny, black cheeks. We joked. But they also learned I was no easy touch for sloppy work or slack behaviour. That went for all, whatever the colour of their skins. The job went along fine.

After two years in black Africa it was strange to be working with and bossing white, manual workers. It was stranger still to see white men behave in the free, natural, uninhibited style of site workers back home, especially in front of Africans. Like workers the world over the painters sang loud and clear all day long. It was the time when songs had words that could be sung and made you want to sing. This was before the days of 'ghetto-blasters' and potted music so workers had to make their own entertainment or distractions. So people sang and whistled. When did you last hear someone whistle a tune? What a loss to society has been the demise of that simple pleasure.

One fellow in particular was very vocal with a voice like a chain-saw. 'Mac the Knife' was the current rage and as a singer my man was far more blood-thirsty than the character of the ballad for he murdered that song day after day with continuous relish. He is singing, loud and raucously, in my ear now as I write.

Saturday of my first week was particularly precious. When not working I always had the feeling I had to use every minute of my time gainfully employed, finding out this, looking at that, talking to this person and noting down every iota of interest. Now as a working man on his first day off I could relax in lovely, idle, earned comfort; saunter down the street, wander into a café for coffee, watch the world go by. My diary entry summed it all up: *'Sat.14th June 1952. Lazy day.'* It was my 25th birthday. It was not until Sunday that I found half my wage packet was gone. Not the best of presents! I was only 99.9% sure my drunken bedmate was the culprit and so said nothing to upset the household so soon after moving in, but I made sure everything I had was battened down or close to my chest.

Salisbury was a wonderful town to be in. Everyone seemed relaxed and happy. Business was good. The tobacco industry, of which it was the centre, was one of the best and most prolific in the world. There was money about. The main government buildings and many others in town were built low and airy in a kind of Spanish colonial style and the streets were lined with a riot of flowering, exotic trees. Blazing flamboyants and azure-blue jacarandas carpeted the pavements with petals that scattered with the breeze like drifting blue snow. Situated at nearly 5000ft., the days, even in the cool season when I was there, were pleasantly warm and the nights cold enough to welcome a fire. It was hard to believe that only sixty years before all this had been open plain where lion and elephant roamed. The old, 1893 fort on top of The Kopje that stands sentinel over the city it spawned was the only reminder of those early pioneer days.

During the months I worked in the city life went on in fairly humdrum style after the initial novelty. In social life I became a son in Mrs Wilson's family and was drawn into a group of friends that usually met most weekends and some evenings. Time passed. One weekend was memorable. It was a long one, Monday and Tuesday being holidays to commemorate Rhodes and Founders. I went with a group of local climbers, who jokingly called themselves 'The Glee Club', to the Chimanimani Mountains, back along the road over which I had entered the country. The Chimanimanis lay on the border of Rhodesia and Mozambique and rose to over 10,000ft. I was told that literally translated, Chimanimani meant 'The Gap between the Table and the Chair', but I wondered about that. 'The Gap', yes, but would the early natives who coined the name know about tables and chairs?

We were in two cars and left on Friday night after work. We motored down to Umtali and on to the mountain road to Malsetter. That night we slept under the trees at Junction. On again on Saturday morning with breakfast at the Black Mountain Inn. A couple of hours later we arrived at a friend's farm at the foot of the mountains where the cars were left. From there we did a five-hour tramp into the hills and camped in a glen with an icy stream running through it.

There were nine of us in the party. One of the party was a professional photographer who intended to make a 16 mm film of the journey to sell to the tourist trade. He wanted an exciting photo of someone on a rock face or exposed buttress for the front page of some magazine. He got his film all right and his magazine photo too, but he could have done better if he had been more accustomed to walking and been a climber himself for there were places where the going got very hairy and he could not follow.

On Sunday morning we came out of the glen and established a base camp on a small plateau sheltered by hills on three sides. Then the party split into two, half doing some rock climbing near the camp and the other half of us doing a long distance bash over into Portuguese territory. It was an interesting tramp that day. Rugged mountains and ghost valleys with mighty finger rocks standing out like the columns of some ancient Grecian ruins; many carved by the winds into fantastic shapes, others eroded at the base to mere pinpoints, forming natural miracles of balance.

Another member of the group and myself had a swim in a river. It was only a few minutes' dip for the water was ice cold, but how it rejuvenated me! After it, my whole skin tingled and the fatigue from the tramp was lost.

Next day, as a contrast to the foot-slogging of Sunday, we went out to do a bit of rock climbing. We went up a peak that rose sheer on all sides. There was no easy way down after reaching the summit and we had to abseil. Pity Jeff, the photographer hadn't managed it up with us. He could have had all the spectacular photos he desired, provided he had had the ability to hang on with his teeth while he worked his cameras. Some bits were a bit tricky and it would have been a long way down if any of us had come off.

It was fun in these mountains and even more interesting considering that that area had never been accurately mapped. Most of the peaks had never been named, far less climbed.

The evenings were marked and remembered for the tea and singsongs round great campfires in true Scout jamboree fashion. Here I was introduced to two fatal adversaries, Ivan Skivinsky Skivar and Abdul Abulbul Emir, not to forget 'Those philogolistic blokes who seldom crack jokes', who have stayed with me all my life and make me smile inwardly when they break into my thoughts, sometimes at most inappropriate moments.

So the weeks flew by with work and weekend socialising and forays in and around the countryside. Came the day when I received my last pay packet to which the builder added a small bonus to show his appreciation, as he said, for moving the job along as I had done. The work fellows said all the right things in their farewells and the Africans did not need to say anything. It was all in their faces as they each gave me a double handshake and a little bow as they murmured their goodbyes.

The Wilson family made me feel sad to be leaving. Mrs Wilson insisted on giving me a little memento to remember them by. I remonstrated weakly and then agreed that I would treasure a book. She had me off in a jiffy to the bookshop to buy any one I wanted. Never mind the price! I went off in high elation. I knew exactly the book I wanted. I had browsed and fondled it many times over the weeks, trying to coax myself to buy it. Now I walked from the shop highly delighted. The book I carried with me was a hardback edition of *The Seven Pillars of Wisdom* by T. E. Lawrence (Lawrence of Arabia). I carried it with me for a while, reading and rereading it, each time pleased to see Mrs Wilson's parting words 'To Jock' on the flyleaf. She was a very fine lady.

But now, with my kilt wrapped round me, beard trimmed (hacked) to be less bushy, boots polished, bushjacket laundered, all tears and rents drawn together with my ham-fisted stitching, and rucksack on my back feeling much heavier than I remember after my two months' holiday, I left friends and city behind and swung along the last lap of the road going south.

It was fairly late in the forenoon when I left and I had walked only a few miles when I was given a lift by a farmer returning after selling his tobacco at the market in the city. The tobacco auction! That was something to experience. I can still see the great bundles of tobacco leaves in the huge shed, feel the high tension of the sellers and buyers and hear the utterly incomprehensible rap of the auctioneer and marvel at the speed at which the whole business was done. The auctioneer rattled his figures so fast it was not English, but a completely different language. Yet the farmers and buyers easily understood the state of play. It must take generations to learn.

My lift took me all the way to Elkerdown where I dossed down, and next day I made it to Umvuma with quite a bit of walking in stages. I made camp just out of town intending to spend a couple of nights to view an old mine I had heard of here, the only one I was told that produced both gold and copper. It was exhausted and derelict, ghostlike, but it was interesting going over all the old workings.

My camp was near the village's water reservoir, two huge corrugated tanks buried in the ground with the asbestos cement roofs almost flush with the ground. The natives had conveniently removed one of the sheets for their own use, so I found it handy for getting my water. On the second evening I dipped my pan in and filled it with water. When I brought it over to the light of the fire

I found I had scooped up a dead rat, half decomposed. Not a sight to give one an appetite, especially when it is in the cooking pot!

Next day I walked a few miles then got an easy run into Fort Victoria (Masvingo). It was dark when I arrived so, with some money in my pocket after working in Salisbury, I went into the local cafe for a meal. As had happened before, the manageress, hearing my accent, came over and chatted and I found she came from Aberdour, a village in Fife only a few miles from my own, and had been lifelong friends with an older cousin of mine. How small the world is! Next, the proprietor, Mrs Cobban, came on the scene and was very chatty. She and her husband, both Scots, also owned and ran a small bakery. Mrs Cobban said I must stay the night and be her guest, which I thought was very decent of her. We Scots do stick together when abroad!

That night was a very special time for me on my journey and I tingled with the excitement of what the morrow would bring. Only twelve miles from Fort Victoria, a 4-hour walk, lay the ruins of Great Zimbabwe. Legend had it that long, long ago this area of Africa was the biblical 'Land of Ophir' and that these old ruins were the remains of King Solomon's Mines ... and I was going to see them!

On leaving Fort Victoria next day I had little difficulty reaching the Great Zimbabwe ruins. I walked an hour or so then got a lift that took me the rest of the way. I pitied Theodore Bent, the first professional archaeologist to conduct a dig at these ruins in 1893. His party, including his wife, took seven days 'of excessive weariness' to do that same journey with their horse and oxen wagons. In his book, *The Ruined Cities of Mashonaland*, published in 1895, he tells us that in his time there was only a 'Kaffir path' and they had to skirt swamps and cut paths down to and up from streams which they crossed by cutting down trees to make 'corduroy bridges'. At one river, the M'shagashi, crocodiles basked on the banks, so they 'resisted the temptation to bathe'. Worse still, the area was 'sick' and nearly everybody went down with fever and horses died from 'horse sickness' which was thought to come from grazing in the early dew, and oxen expired from lung sickness which was called 'drunk sickness'. One man of Bent's acquaintance brought in eighty-seven horses of which eight-six died. In the fort a row of one-hundred-and-fifty empty saddles once belonging to the early pioneers told their own melancholy tale. Even Bent's own animals, which he had been assured were 'salted' when he bought them, went sick but survived. Such was the lifestyle of travellers and pioneers of this land some sixty years before me.

Luckily for me, times had changed since those wild, pioneer days.

Chapter Twenty

KING SOLOMON'S MINES?

Saturday 10th August 1952 – Zimbabwe Ruins
  What a place this is! What a mystery! Anybody with half an imagination could dream for days in speculation. One's imagination could run riot and yet still be in the boundaries of possibility. Am I in the fabulous land of King Solomon's Mines? I may be wrong, but I like to think I am.

In mid-20th century Rhodesia you had to watch how you dealt with the tales and legends of King Solomon's Mines. To show too much enthusiasm in spearing into them could incur peoples' doubts in you, make them feel you were childish. Like time-served soldiers to a rookie, those who had been in the country any time might smile benignly at a new person eager to believe the fables that were ingrown there. Like knowledgeable parents gently weaning their bright-eyed children into the grown-up world, their smiles would remark, "These are all just fairy tales. They only exist in the land of make-believe. They are nice stories, but not real, you know."

If you persisted with your ideas someone more in-the-know would tell you that a great archaeologist back at the beginning of the century had examined the ruins and confirmed beyond doubt that the ruins were the work of Africans around 500 years ago. This was some 1500 years after Solomon's time, so the ruins definitely had nothing to do with any mythical goldmines. Some years after this, another eminent archaeologist did another survey and she also concluded that Great Zimbabwe was the work of Bantu Africans about time of the 14th century. Surely two world renowned experts could not be wrong! Or could they ...?

So I kept my own council to a great extent and delved into the places where few of these knowledgeable people went, into the books and references libraries that did not scoff. I told myself it was essential to go in as an interested sceptic and be prepared if encouraged to cross the chamber to the side of the believers.

I read everything with the merest reference to the mines and engaged in conversation anyone who showed the slightest academic interest or knowledge in the biblical references. Gradually a picture, a map of time, grew and formed in my mind.

*

Great Zimbabwe is one of the greatest enigmas of all Africa. Its discovery by a German hunter/explorer, Karl Mauch on 11th September 1871, must rank among the most interesting, mind-blowing and imagination-spinning events in history, akin to Hiram Bingham's discovery in 1911 of Machu Picchu, the mysterious ancient Inca city, high up in the Andes of Peru. The difference, however, between Machu Picchu and Zimbabwe is that when it was discovered the South American city was almost immediately placed in the framework of ancient Inca history. Not so Zimbabwe. Since the African ruins were discovered no one had been able to put it in any known slot in time nor know who or what kind of people built it.

Although Mauch claimed to have discovered Zimbabwe and is given the credit for it in books, he was not really the first white man to see it. Indeed he did not find the ruined city, he was taken there by another white man who had stumbled on the site some time before. His name was Adam Renders, an American elephant-hunter who had 'gone native'. Renders hoped that Mauch would make a fortune from the publicity of the find and only agreed to take the German to the ruins on agreement that he would have a 50/50 deal on the profits. In this the hunter must have been disappointed for apart from the fame of finding King Solomon's mines, as he and all the public would have it, Mauch made no capital out of the discovery. He returned to his fatherland and obscurity and an early death.

Long before the Zimbabwe ruins were discovered, rumour and legend had it that somewhere north of the Limpopo River lay the Biblical Land of Ophir, from whence came the gold that gilded King Solomon's throne and much else. From the Bible, I Kings, 9, we have the story;

And king Solomon made a navy of ships at Ezion-geber ... and Hiram sent in the navy his servants and seamen ... and they came to Ophir, and fetched from thence gold, four hundred and twenty talents, and brought it to king Solomon. ... the king made a great throne of ivory, and overlaid it with the best gold. The throne had six steps and the top of the throne was round behind: and there were stays on either side ... of the seat, and two lions stood beside the stays. And twelve lions stood there, one the one side and one the other upon the six steps: there was not the like made in any kingdom. And all king Solomon's drinking vessels were of pure gold; none were of silver; ... for the king had at sea a navy; ... once in three years came the navy ... bringing gold, and silver, ivory and apes, and peacocks.

There is one thing wrong with that quotation when we place Ophir in Africa. There are no peacocks in Africa. This has strengthened other claims that Ophir lay in the east, in India or Malaysia or other unlikely places. But I do not believe that one reference to something unAfrican can preclude Zimbabwe from having been Ophir. The problem could lie in translation since that story must have passed through several languages before it was written by Hebrew scribes. For 'peacock' the word might be 'parrot' or 'parakeet' as gaudy-coloured birds in some local dialect. In Bechuanaland I heard some old Afrikaner men refer to leopards as tigers and in South Africa wild dogs are commonly referred to as wolves. There are no tigers or wolves in Africa. There are no buffaloes in the USA but the Americans call their bison buffaloes, which could cause a visitor from Mars to take back to his fellow aliens completely misleading information.

Long after I had written that statement in a note for later use I was pleased to have some confirmation of my assumption by one no less than the eminent American archaeologist Professor W.F. Albright who accompanied Wendell Phillips in his 1950 expedition to the Hadramaut and Yemen to which I came so near when I went to Dhala. Professor Albright, a biblical scholar, was, among other appointments, the director of the American School of Oriental Research in Jerusalem and excavated many sites in Palestine. Way back in the 1930s he pointed out that 'apes' and 'peacocks' are the same Egyptian words as the names of two different kinds of monkey brought from Punt by the Egyptians. Therefore one reference to peacocks can hardly be sufficient evidence to put beyond all reasonable doubt that Ophir was in India rather than Africa.

There is good reason to expect some discrepancies in the written word of the Bible. The Israelite scribes who committed their tribal history to paper, and that of Solomon's gold in particular, did so some six hundred years after the event. The reason being, the Israelites could not write until that time. Prior to learning the written word their clerks recorded their history by the spoken word, relying entirely on memory.

One cannot decry oral history: many advanced African tribes have their specialist historians who start as apprentices and must learn to recite word-perfect the lineage and deeds of their people since their time began as an organised community, and the Bible proves that the Jews were past masters at that before they learned to write. Before writing was invented, histories of heroes and heroic times were often committed to verse as an aid to memory and a method of passing the stories down through generations. How often do we recall the long lost words of a story-ballad when we hear the rhythm or tune played. Conversation words are easily lost, song words never. The reason why much of the Bible is written in words that flow, beautiful writing to which few modern writers ever aspire, is because the Hebrew writers wrote in the poetic way they had been taught to remember.

But even accepting the accuracy of oral history, an awful lot happened to the Hebrews between Solomon's time and the writing of the Bible to muddy the waters of memory. After Solomon's death they fought among themselves and weakened by this were smashed in 586 BC by Nebuchadnezzar of Babylon who sacked Jerusalem, destroyed the David/Solomon temple, and led the Chosen People into captivity in Babylon, where they remained for three generations or so.

The Hebrews learned many things by the waters of Babylon. They were introduced to the 12-hour unit by which time was measured from midnight to midday and vice-versa. From the Babylonian mathematicians and astronomers they learned to use the 60-ratio in calculations. All these practices came through to the Western world. Some 2500 years after the Hebrews' sojourn in Babylon we still use the 12-unit, which we call 'a dozen', and when clocks were invented, an hour was divided into 60 minutes and a minute into 60 seconds.

It was in Babylon too the Hebrews were introduced to the week of six-working-days-and-one-day-rest. Most important of all when researching Solomon's Mines, it was in Babylon, the modern-day Iraq, that the Hebrews learned to write. It was in this period of their captivity that the majority of their rote history was converted into the written word, so many centuries after the Solomon era. The writers then would be third generation Babylonians whose grandfathers, and only those who were in their seventies, could possibly have seen the Promised Land.

I highlight the Jewish history to show that it is little wonder if some omissions and even discrepancies occur in the Biblical accounts that have come down to us. The vital point in the story of *I Kings, 9,* the matter of where lay the land of King Solomon's Mines, is vague. Although the poems and rote history carried so many details of his Palace and navy it would appear that no historian of the day went with the ships to record where the Land of Ophir really was. And for nearly three thousand years adventurers have been trying to find it.

*

Through all the old legends of Solomon's gold one mysterious group of people keeps cropping up – the Phoenicians. Who were they? Where did they come from? There's mystery here, for there never was a country called Phoenicia. True, it appears on some maps but that is more informative than accurate for there never was a people of that name. Unknown people, yet so important to us because they were the forerunners of so much that makes up our history. It would not be wrong to say that Ancient Greece, which is acknowledged as the cradle of European civilisation, developed out of Phoenician culture. They gave us our writing and much more, yet there appears little trace of them. Where did they go? What happened to them?

When the Israelites were still nomads in the desert the Phoenicians had built themselves cities of stone and were living as an organised society, trading with the world. Only, they were not known as Phoenicians, that was their nickname. They called themselves Canaanites, as mentioned in the Bible.

No one really knows where the Canaanites came from before they arrived in the land to which they gave their name, but learned speculation says it was from southern Arabia, possibly Yemen, the land that was within the empire of Sheba. Wherever their beginnings had been, by 3000 BC they were living along the western seaboard of the Mediterranean, from Egypt northwards as far as, and including part of, Syria.

Although farmers and great builders in stone, the Canaanites were, above all, boat builders and seamen. The forests on the Lebanese mountains provided an endless supply of fine cedar wood and being good craftsmen they learned how to make excellent ships and fine harbours. They built different types of ships, fat-bellied merchants and long, lean, fast ones for carrying marines to guard the big ships. They travelled the ocean and traded with Egypt and the Minoan empire and from those civilisations they had imported many of their ways and building styles.

As the first real maritime nation the Canaanites brought to the world navigation by sun and stars – although they never sailed by night – and, perhaps even more important, invented or developed international trade. Yet it was for something much less significant they became known and remembered by the world. And it was from this that they got the nickname by which they are remembered to this day.

Somewhere in that early time the inhabitants of Tyre learned how to manufacture a vivid purple dye from the *murex* mollusc that thrived in the sea near their city. Until the present day of synthetic dyes, purple was always a difficult colour to produce. At best it was rather a muddy colour with no brilliance. But that produced by the Tyrian people from their shellfish was more vivid than any other in the world. With that one product alone the Canaanites were welcomed by Egyptian pharaohs and kings all over the known world.

So scarce and expensive was the dye that only the highest in the land could wear a purple cloak. Lesser aristocrats had to make do with a purple edge to their garments while ordinary mortals were banned from wearing it at all, even if they could have afforded it, which would be most unlikely. In Roman times it was a capital offence for anyone other than the Caesars to wear the royal colour. Not for nothing was there coined the saying, 'born in the purple'. It was also said that the Tyrians produced a vivid Cardinal-red dye from shellfish for which garments and carpets were coloured at enormous cost. So scarce and expensive were carpets dyed with this colour that they would only be rolled out for the feet of kings or the most highly honoured guests.

So famous did the Canaanites become with their dyes that people all over their known world referred to them as Phoenicians, the Greek name for 'colour' or 'people of the colour'.

But it was not just shellfish dye for which the world clamoured from the Phoenicians. From Tyre was exported the finest, diaphanous, coloured silks that Cleopatra was known to wear 500 years later. Glass from Sidon was no less famous, also articles of gold and silver and brass ... they were skilled artists in every medium. And not just in the arts. Centuries later Homer was to report that the Phoenicians *were skilled in architecture and mining.* Bear that in mind when we come to see if they have a link with Solomon's mines.

Such, then, was The Land of Milk and Honey that Moses and his Israelites gazed on and took for granted as their God-given own, their prize for enduring the long journey from the pharaohs' Egypt, past the Red Sea and over the terrible Sinai desert

If you look at a modern map and follow the eastern coast of the Mediterranean Sea, up past Tel Aviv and Haifa you will see the ports of Tyre and Sidon. These were the ancient ports of the Phoenicians. Further up, slightly north of Beirut, you will see, if you look very closely, a little place called Jubeil. There is nothing much there but some old temple ruins where once the followers of Baal and Astarte worshipped. Once it was a bustling port full of ships coming and going, boat builders' yards and all the commerce of a busy city. But when the town was so alive it was not called Jubeil. This, in its day was Byblos the busiest port in Phoenicia and the world. Here too they made and exported the finest paper, or papyrus, in the world. There are those who say that the art was invented here and not in Egypt. Whether or not that is true it is a fact that a scroll of papyrus became known as a *byblos*, after the port from whence it came, and from which we get the word *Bible.* Byblos will crop up again, but it is to Tyre we must go to follow the trail of King Solomon and his dreams of grandeur.

Before going there though, there are a few pieces of jigsaw that must be put in their places to show that speculation on Zimbabwe being the site of Ophir is based on some facts rather than pure fantasy. Four pieces representing three different peoples or nations, and the forth an event of cataclysmic proportions. Two of the nations have already been mentioned: the Israelites and Phoenicians or Canaanites. Solomon was an Israelite and without him there would be no case to question. The Phoenicians are important because it was they who built the ships and sailed to Ophir, and also because Solomon's mother was one of a sub-group of those people, and more important, it is likely that it was from her Solomon got his gold lust that sparked off all this mystery.

The third people in the jigsaw are also well known from the Bible. They are the Philistines who play a minor role in the set-up, but provide a compelling clue to the authenticity to my claim that Zimbabwe is, or was, the Land of Ophir.

The forth jigsaw piece represents perhaps the greatest catastrophe that has occurred in the world since humans first fell off the trees. An event that changed the geography of the planet and shaped history as we know it today. Without that pivotal event there would have been no Solomon, no goldmines in his name, perhaps no Bible and no mystery to unravel.

*

In the autumn of the year 1628 BC, in the Aegean Sea, the island of Thera (now Santorini) was blown to smithereens by a volcanic eruption of unbelievable proportions. The gigantic pall of volcanic ash and dust that issued forth from the explosion encircled the globe and shut out the sun for a year and more and poisoned the earth. Nothing could grow. Famine and pestilence gripped the world as described in the Bible. We only know of the conditions in Egypt because that is where the Israelites were at that time and so recorded it in their history. Other places must have suffered just as badly but there were no master historians there like the Hebrews who compiled their tribal past in the most wonderful history book in the world, that which we call the Bible.

It is from this dust cloud that the exact date of the catastrophe can be calculated. The annual ring for that year of the bristlecone pines of California, reputedly the oldest trees in the world, alive then and now, showed no summer growth. No sunshine had penetrated the dust pall that year. The same date result, a yearlong winter, was also recorded in China where similar trees grow.

How the precise time of the year when Thera – or 'Atlantis' as Plato would have it – exploded, is based on the trade winds that blow through that part of the world and down the East African coast, as I had encountered on my dhow journey. In the spring and summer the wind blows north-west and in the later part of the year it turns round and blows south-east. The fact that only the eastern part of Crete, some seventy miles from the epicentre, was devastated while the western half was left untouched, showed that the wind that was driven with incredible velocity and carrying volcanic debris and searing gases that cindered tongues and vaporised lungs, was travelling in a south-eastern direction. Adding proof to this is the fact that the eastern part Egypt, including the delta, was struck while the land to the west was hardly affected.

Houses on Thera that were not totally destroyed were buried under 200 feet of volcanic ash. Others were covered much more thinly and that layer was washed thinner and thinner over the next 4000 years.

On a day in 1961 a Santorini farmer by the name of Arvinitis was travelling over his land on his donkey when the ground literally opened up and swallowed both rider and animal. Neither were hurt apart from a fright, but when he found his feet and the dust cloud began to settle, Arvinitis realised he was the first visitor to drop into this house since the holocaust. By an extraordinary coincidence an eminent Greek archaeologist, Professor Spyridon Marinatos, was on the island at that time looking for Thera and only a day or two before had spoken to Arvinitis of his search. Arvinitis hurried to the archaeologist to show him his entrance into the lost city of Thera and Marinatos went into the books as the discoverer.

After the Thera explosion the dust cloud hung like a blanket around the world, shutting out the sun and no crops could grow. An Egyptian poet of the day wrote, *'For nine days there was no exit from the palace and no one could see the face of his fellow. The Sun is covered and does not shine ... Life is no longer possible when the Sun is concealed behind the clouds. Ra has turned his face from mankind.'* Soon after that occasion, the Israelites made their exodus from Egypt.

So could it be that the tale of Moses pleading with the Pharaoh to 'Let my people go' was not quite accurate? Could be that they were told to leave because the land could no longer support immigrants, even though the Israelites had been there for 300 years. And could it be that the Egyptian chariots chasing the 'escapees' were coming, not to make them return, but to make sure they left. Whichever way it was, it is very likely that it was the Theran explosion that started Moses and his people on the road to Canaan.

By the time they arrived, their leader Moses, the statesman character of great charisma, was an old man and Joshua the warrior took over the leadership. So it came to pass that the Israelites set about claiming the land that had been promised them, the land that had belonged to the Canaanites for a thousand years and more. With great slaughter, which was the custom in those days, they captured much of the fertile land and many cities, including Jericho, said to be the oldest and lowest lying city on earth.

A hundred years or so later there was another invasion of people whose journey started due to the Thera eruption. They were to prove trouble to both the Canaanites and Israelites, particularly the latter.

*

Prior to 1628 BC the Minoans, the 'Sea People', were the greatest power in the ocean we call the Mediterranean. Their King Minos ruled from his Palace of Knossos, in ancient Crete. Their navy, the first known, ruled all of what was called in their day, the Minoan Sea. The Thera disaster virtually finished the Minoan empire. The islands' unity was destroyed, their populations disintegrated. Many went to Egypt where the culture was similar to their own. When they tried to land en masse they were repulsed. Nevertheless Pharaoh Thuthmosis III, who reigned at the time, together with his viziers considered "*the Cretans* (people from Crete) *civilised enough to be worthy of a name other than 'barbarians' or 'abominations against Ra',"* as, presumably, the Israelites had been known.

Many, including the majority of those still alive on Thera, eventually took to their boats and arrived at Canaan. They landed at Gaza and other ports and captured a considerable amount of land and towns. They settled mainly in the area surrounding what is now Tel Aviv and called that area Philistia, the land of the Philistines, the name by which they were known. They and the Israelites were always warring with each other.

An extremely interesting people the Philistines. Highly sophisticated and cultured, they were also known as strong, savage fighters. With their advanced technical knowledge their chariots and arms were superior to all others. Some credit them with the discovery of iron smelting. Whether or not they were the inventors, they were certainly in the van of the new Iron Age and collared the market in swords, ploughs and other utensils, which were harder, sharper and more efficient, but required more skill to produce, than the bronze items they replaced.

History gives two diametrically opposite views of the Philistines. The ancient hieroglyphics tell us that of all the many immigrant people to Egypt the Egyptians regarded the Philistines as the only ones they could regard as social equals, whereas the Bible gives the Israelites' view of the Philistines as everything that is bad. Indeed, 'Philistine' has come through to the English language as a derogatory word for any person regarded as devoid of principles, an uncultured person whose interests are purely material and selfish. How can a people be seen to be so opposite in character by different eyes?

The explanation may lie in the opposing religions and cultures of the two races. The Israelites, following Moses' dictate, worshipped one God and were inspired to live by the Ten Commandments, thwarting their baser instincts. The Philistines, on the other hand, had many gods, the main one being Dagon, a merman, half man/half fish, who, despite his shape, was considered an agricultural deity. They built a temple in his name at Gaza. They also worshipped Baal (male) and Astarte, the Goddess of Love, who was simply known and addressed as 'Lady'. To the Babylonians she was known as 'Ishtar' and to the early Greeks as 'Aphrodite' and to the Romans as 'Venus'. It is likely that our word 'tart' for a loose woman is derived from Astarte. Some words go back a long, long way.

Unlike the Israelites, bound by their Ten Commandments, the Philistine society, rather like that of our own today, enjoyed an extraordinary degree of personal freedom, of which the Israelites privately may have been intensely jealous although condemning their neighbours' behaviour as depraved and self-indulgent.

The Cretan/Philistine women were reputed to be particularly attractive. Like

432

the Ancient Egyptian ladies they were into cosmetics and hairstyling, unlike their Israelite counterparts. This sophistication, together with their sexual freedom, may have given them a confident poise that could send the men wild with desire. Whatever the attraction, it seems some Israelite men fell easily under their spell. Samson was one. He couldn't keep away from them, much to the chagrin of his mother. In the end this was his downfall, for Delilah was a Philistine who tarried with him a while before luring him into a trap set by her kinsfolk.

So what happened to the Philistines? Nothing really. They're still there, but greatly changed, like so many other people who were converted to Islam after the birth of that religion in 622 AD. 'Islam', the name in Arabic means *Surrender* or *Submission,* swept away all the Philistines' personal freedoms and especially those of the women. No more could they charm the passing males with their sophistication, make-up and body-talk. From now on they could never leave their houses unless swathed in loose, black robes and veil, must always be subservient to males and retire to the backrooms out of sight when a non-family male entered the home. Today, they are the Palestinians. Three thousand years after Solomon's time the Israelites/Israelis – versus – Philistines/ Palestinians bloody struggle still goes on and on and on: can it ever be ended by the stroke of a pen on some kind of agreement?

Not so lucky to still be around though, the Canaanites, or Phoenicians, as we know them, have disappeared, gone from this Earth completely. Once lords of all the land, by Solomon's time they were hemmed into that narrow coastal strip of land previously mentioned, never more than 7 miles wide, between the mountains and the sea. Now that they had lost their most fertile land they had to look more to the sea and foreign trading in order to barter wheat from the Israelites to sustain themselves.

When the Minoans had ruled the sea the Canaanites had had to creep round the shores cap-in-hand to them. After the Thera explosion and the destruction of the Minoans they now dominated the whole sea, free to go where they pleased. And this they did, to the ends of the known world and beyond.

They sailed and traded with Egypt and Cyprus, Italy and Spain and even with the wild tribesmen of the North African coast. They made colonies in Sardinia, and eventually crept through the end of the sea where the land on either side pinched the waters to a channel, the place the Greeks, 800 years later, would call the 'Gates of Hercules' and is now Gibraltar. Turning north they discovered and traded with lands there and later, brought back tin from a land almost lost in the mists at the very edge of the world, a land that more than 1700 years later would be called Angleland and later still, England. One captain named Hanno turned his ships left after passing through the gates at the end of the sea and went south to The Gulf of Guinea. Another circumnavigated the complete coast of Africa, nearly 3000 years before Vasco da Gama, and brought back tales of a place where there was gold to be had as cheap as dirt.

*

While the Phoenicians sailed to the very edge of the world to develop their foreign trade, the Israelites and Philistines fought each other. Despite the Israelites' prophesy it seemed God was in no hurry to smite the Cretan foe. As they increased in numbers the Philistines spread though the land and eventually the Israelites were fighting for their independence. Above all, it was the Philistines' leadership and organisation that made them successful over their Semitic rivals. These qualities had made them top-of-the-pile in the Mediterranean when they were there and now it was carrying them through in Canaan. Both sides had their successes in the endless war; young David slew the Philistine giant, Goliath, and later when grown up and as a captain in the army of Saul he never lost a battle against the permanent foe. The Philistines, in their turn, won a great battle in which they captured the Ark of the Covenant, which was believed to contain the tablets of the Ten Commandments given to Moses by God. The Ark was the Israelites' talisman against evil and oppression and its loss was indeed a bad omen for the Israelites. But the Philistines had such bad luck after they had taken it they gave it back to their enemy.

When in old age Saul lost his last battle and his life, together with two of his sons, in a battle against the Philistines, the great Hebrew god Yahweh let it be known through Samuel, the king-maker, that David was to be the next Chosen One even though he, David, had fought on the side of the Philistines in the battle when Saul was killed. For some years Saul had outlawed David because he had become jealous of his young protégé's talents and leadership.

It was David who really laid the foundations of the Hebrew nation. Under his brilliant leadership the Israelites recaptured most of the land of Canaan they had lost to the Philistines, including many of its cities. Of these he chose Jerusalem as his own and erected an altar on the outskirts to thank God for stopping a plague right there, saving the inhabitants, after it had ravished the country. In this altar he placed the Ark of the Covenant.

During this time, although they mainly followed the Mosaic, or Moses', laws, many Israelites dallied at times with their neighbours' and enemies' multi-god religions which were much more pleasurable. Saul had swung like a pendulum between the two ethics and even good King David was not without the sins of the flesh. And here we have the place in the great tapestry where the threads cross to weave the legend of Solomon's mines.

*

Once in royal David's city the king stepped on to the high, flat roof of his palace. The morning was young and the sun pleasantly warm before the sun's boiler stoked it up to the midday heat. Flexing his muscles to rid himself of the night he breathed deeply of the champagne air as he stepped over to the stone balustrade that surrounded the roof. He liked to survey the heart of his kingdom, this little conclave, this little cluster of houses round his palace where his closest viziers, generals and entourage lived. The sight that met his eyes, however, was not the usual one of the morning. Instead, this was a dream, the kind that every man has dreamed sometime in his life and wished it was real. Only, this one *was* real.

On another, lower roof a beautiful, naked young woman stood, sponge-bathing herself in the pale sunlight, her hand-maiden nearby with towel and robe at the ready. Immediately the mad god Desire captured David's soul.

Although married to Saul's daughter, Michal, and at the same time running a sizeable harem, David immediately made enquiries and found that the young lady's name was Bathsheba, the wife of Uriah, a Hittite mercenary officer in his army. The Hittite tribe was a branch of the Phoenicians. Uriah at that time was away at war with David's great general Joab, fighting the Ammonites. David then had the wife brought to him and '*he lay with her*' and '*the woman conceived*'.

With lust clouding his judgement David brought in a Canaanite scribe and had a message sent to Joab, under the strict secrecy of the royal seal, to place Uriah at the very thickest of the fighting. Uriah was killed and after the due period of mourning David married Bathsheba. The baby son died soon after birth and Samuel said that Yahweh told him that this was punishment for David's infidelity.

Nevertheless, David and Bathsheba had more children and their fourth child, a boy, was named Solomon. When David grew old there was great machiavellian scheming among his elder sons as to who would wear the crown on the demise of their father. There was no precedence of hereditary kingship with the Israelites but Samuel, the kingmaker, was long since gone and David's sons thought the crown was theirs for the taking.

Adonijah the eldest, with the backing of the great general, Joab, was the prime mover in the jockeying for position. But he reckoned without someone far craftier and astute than they: Bathsheba. She was by now the matriarch of the family and a force to be reckoned with. Whether it was through a special love for him or that she saw in him the wise ruler he became, Bathsheba was determined that Solomon would wear his father's crown. With his mother behind him he could not fail. Palace intrigue was overcome and Solomon was King. And as was the way of the day when politics was a deadly game, his first act was to have his half-brother, Adonijah, and the mighty Joab, now grey and grizzled, slain.

During Solomon's reign Israel reached heights of wealth and world acclaim that it had never known before nor since. His was the perfect leadership to follow his father's. David had been a warrior king and had expanded Israel's frontiers to Egypt in the west and to Syria in the east. Now with enough land to be self-sufficient in agricultural produce, Solomon's wisdom told him it was time to make peace not war. He set about consolidating what he had by making friends with his neighbours and trading with the world. With eyes set more on defence than war he bought the best state-of-the-art war chariots from Egypt at 600 shekels of silver each, and the finest horses from what is now southern Turkey at 150 shekels each. His aim was to create flying-squads to guard the frontiers and report any impending dangers. Having secured his borders he used his country's manpower for a purpose other than war, as had been the way since they came through Sinai.

He embarked on a massive building campaign and to do this he needed money, great amounts of it and this was completely alien to Israelite ethics. Moses had preached the evils of self-aggrandisement and his message was echoed down the centuries by the Hebrews and passed on to the world by Christ's parables

Living between the Philistines and the Phoenicians, who both valued the good things in life, fine clothes, pillared and porticoed houses, exquisite jewellery for the women and no enforced inhibitions, it was difficult for the Israelite churchmen to preach against all these abominations and expect the public to follow. Most of all, Solomon. He set a terrible example.

Throughout his reign he caused great displeasure and anguish among his devout people by his tolerance of heathen religions and his association with those who followed them, even allowing them to build their obscene temples in their midst. There were even those who said he tarried and seemed to be happier and more at ease in these places than he was in his own synagogues. There is a very good reason for this to be true, for Solomon was only half an Israelite.

Bathsheba, being Phoenician, continued to live in the gracious splendour and easy living of her people. Young Solomon would have learned at his mother's knee and that would explain why he was perhaps more drawn to Phoenician ways than to those of his father.

An insight into the different influences his father and mother had on Solomon may be gained by a study of the love of poetry and song that both father and son had. It is odd to think of David the warrior king having the poetic bent that produced the Psalms of David which, 3000 years later, are very much alive in Christian churches today. Whether he composed these personally or had his name put to them because they were his style or to his liking will never be known. That David had the ability to compose is evident from the fact that Solomon inherited a love of verse and music, presumably from his father.

His 'Song of Solomon' or 'Song of Songs' is possibly the most beautiful and evocative love song ever written, and here lies the difference between father and son. While David's Psalms are all full of righteousness to God, the 'Song of Solomon' dwells on ecstatic human pleasures of touch, taste, smell and detailed descriptions of male and female bodies. Solomon was obviously a man among men for it is said he had a thousand wives, or to be more exact, 300 wives and 700 concubines. One wonders how he found time to run his country!

But run it he did, better and more energetically than ever before. He introduced a civil service and ended rule by king alone, retaining only the final arbitration. He divided the country into twelve regions, each with its own local government responsible to the national one. Each region was required to supply one month's necessities to the king's coffers These salaried administrators created a higher or upper class as opposed to the lower, working class. The pastoral society, where a goatherd sat with the master, was finished. The whole purpose of this was to introduce and collect taxes, for Solomon wanted money, lots of it.

If Solomon inherited his poetic bent from his father it was from his mother he may have received his inspirations, delusions perhaps, of grandeur. Though as king he was the religious head of the Israelites, Solomon hankered after the Canaanite delight in creating grand buildings and Solomon craved to outdo even their finest edifices. He would build a temple like no other to house the Ark of the Covenant on the site of his father's one, and a palace beyond the dreams of anyone on earth. All this in the name of a people whose religion abhorred ostentation!

This then was the reason why Solomon had to send his legions to the land of Ophir. But to fulfil his dream he needed help, for the Israelites were neither sea people nor builders. There was someone he knew who could command both. Once he had been an enemy, but now he was courted as an ally and a possible business partner. He would go to the Phoenician, Hiram, King of Tyre, and make him an offer he couldn't refuse.

*

The land of the Phoenicians was made up of mainly autonomous city-states with little or no overall national coherence. At this time however, King Hiram of Tyre was an important piece on the chessboard of the Middle East. Once an enemy while the Israelites took away the Phoenicians' land, Hiram, obviously of phlegmatic disposition, had agreed to live and let live, join them when he couldn't beat them. He had become a firm friend of King David, and now David's son was to put to him a massive business proposition.

The Land of Ophir would be known at this time. Since the days of their great navigator, Hanno, adventurers would have come home with fabulous tales of a place where gold, silver and ivory were there for the taking. They would prove this with their own small fortunes. Now Solomon, like Rhodes of the day, planned to go into it big-time, to monopolise the trade as an industry for his personal use.

Solomon wanted Hiram to build him a port and a navy and have his men man the ships to go to Ophir and bring back treasures unlimited. All that was secondary though, the ways-and-means, so to speak. Primarily, Solomon wanted Hiram have his architects and builders build him a temple and a palace the like of which the world had never seen before. Hiram must have seen a new dawn breaking after the years of war his people had endured and lost: *'and there was peace between Hiram and Solomon; and the two of them made a treaty.'*

Solomon agreed to sell or give back twenty Phoenician towns Israel had captured. (This is also quoted, perhaps more authentically, as 'villages', and when Hiram went and saw them he was not very well pleased with them.) *'Hiram supplied Solomon with all the timber of cedar and cypress that he desired, while Solomon gave Hiram twenty thousand cors (125,000 bushels) of wheat as food for his household, and twenty thousand cors (over a million gallons) of beaten oil. Solomon gave this to Hiram year by year.'*

So Hiram built for Solomon a port and a navy at Ezion-geber (near the northern end of the Gulf of Aqaba) a site that would make easier and quicker access to the eastern coast of Africa as opposed to the long roundabout voyage that had been used since Hanno's day. And, using Israelite labourers, the Phoenicians built Solomon a temple and palace that even he could not have dreamed was possible. Before the work was finished forced labour, both Israelite and Phoenician, was being used for the construction gangs. The architects, being also trading sailors who gathered ideas from the countries they visited, were obviously greatly influenced by Egyptian style, but to that they added a softer, more flowing appreciation of their own. It has been said that the early Greek Doric columns were based on or originated from that of the Phoenicians. The walls were built of *'Phoenician-style masonry* (which) *was unexcelled. The squared, unmortared stones fit so perfectly that not even a knife blade could be inserted between them.'* Think of that when we return to Zimbabwe!

So Solomon's Jerusalem became a most splendid city to which people from afar came to look and wonder in awe. *'Thus King Solomon excelled all the kings of the earth in riches and in wisdom. And the whole earth sought the presence of Solomon to hear his wisdom, which God put into his mind. Every one of them brought him presents, articles of silver and gold, garments, myrrh, spices, horses and mules, so much year by year.'*

The most famous of all visitors, certainly the one most written about in the Bible and history, was Queen Balkis of Sheba. She stayed a year in Solomon's palace and to him she bore a son. The boy was named Menelik and he became the first king of Ethiopia. From his father, Solomon, Menelik was granted the title 'Lion of Judah'. Since then all kings of Ethiopia have tenaciously held on to that title and claim direct descendancy from King David.

Although Solomon had sympathies towards his mother's Baal religion, he appears to have been a good keeper of the Mosaic religion for it seems that he ensured that Menelik should follow the Judaism gospel and from Menelik there descended through nearly 3000 years a line of people in Ethiopia who followed the Hebrew religion. Perhaps it was because of these people that Christianity penetrated Africa so early in its history, even before it reached Europe. In those early days the Ethiopian Coptic Church was formed and remains the oldest non-Catholic Christian church in the world.

That there may be some truth in the Menelik-line is evident from the fact that in 1984–5 the Falasha tribe, the so-called 'Black Jews of Ethiopia', were recognised by the Israeli government and air-lifted en masse to safety in Israel, away from almost certain death due to famine and civil war.

There appears to be little doubt that Southern Arabia, Yemen in particular, and Ethiopia were united as the Land of Sheba in the time of Solomon. The question is which side of the Red Sea was the dominant one. To which side did the Queen belong? Was she by birth Semitic and therefore light-skinned as an Arab, or was she dark as a native of Ethiopia; or as some old soldier might have said, "Was she Black or Tan?" There is no direct reference that would clear this matter, but by assumption she has been linked with the Sabeans ('People of Sheba') a northern tribe of Yemen. The Sabeans were known as a warlike people and it is known that at different times in history there were incursions from one side of the Red Sea to the other. At the time of Sheba it would appear that the dominant side was in Yemen. Yet there is no evidence of any ruler of Saba going back beyond the 8th century BC. The few remarks we have of The Queen of Sheba all point to her coming from Yemen to Israel. A passage in Isaiah says, *'The multitude of camels will cover thee ...; all they from the Sheba will come; they shall bring gold and incense ...'* All references we have allude to the method of travel from Sheba to Israel being by camel. And it is generally accepted that the Queen lived in Mirib, Yemen. But since the land of Sheba spread over both sides of the Red Sea, from Yemen to Ethiopia, was she a native of Southern Arabia or an Ethiopian overlord, if we may use that word for a Queen.

Semitic or African, she must have had a town in Ethiopia, and a palace no doubt, for she brought up her son, Menelik, there. This evidence begins to point to her being African.

Whatever her colour or countenance, there is little doubt that she was indeed a beauty and that Solomon loved her for it, perhaps more than he did any other of his harem. One in a thousand she was, if we read the Song of Songs. Although she is not named, the dialogue would strongly appear to be between Queen Balkis of Sheba and King Solomon and if that is so she was an African. Hear now the 'Song of Solomon'! A little of it anyway.

The song of songs, which is Solomon's.
Let him kiss me with the kisses of the mouth: for thy love is better than wine.
Draw me ... the king has brought me to his chambers: we will be glad to rejoice in thee, we will remember thy love more than wine: the upright love thee.
I am black, but comely ... as the tents of Kedar, as the curtains of Solomon.
Look not upon me because I am black, because the sun has looked upon me.
I have compared thee, O my love, to a company of horses in the Pharaoh's chariots.
Thy cheeks are comely with rows of jewels, thy neck with chains of gold.
We will make thee borders of gold with studs of silver.
A bundle of myrrh is my well-beloved; he shall lie all night betwixt my breasts.
The beams of our house are cedar, and our rafters are of fir.
I am the rose of Sharon, and the lilies of the valleys.
I charge you, O ye daughters of Jerusalem, by the roes, and by the hinds of the field, that ye stir not up, nor awake my love, until he please.
My beloved spake, and said unto me, Rise up, my love, my fair one, and come away.
For, lo, the winter is past, the rain is over and gone.
Who is this that cometh out of the wilderness like pillars of smoke, perfumed with myrrh and frankincense, with all powders of the merchant.
Behold his bed, which is Solomon's; threescore valiant men are about it.
They all hold swords, being experts in war: every man hath his sword on his thigh because of fear of the night.
King Solomon made himself a chariot of the wood of the Lebanon.
He made the pillars thereof of silver, the bottom thereof of gold, the covering of purple, the midst thereof being paved with love for the daughters of Jerusalem.
Thou art beautiful, O my love.
Turn away thine eyes from me, for they have overcome me:
Thy hair is as a flock of goats ... thy teeth are like a flock of sheep.
How beautiful are thy feet with shoes, O prince's daughter!
The joints of thy thighs are like jewels, the work of a cunning workman.
Thy belly is like a heap of wheat set about with lilies.
There are threescore queens, and four score concubines, and virgins without number.
My dove, my undefiled, is but one.

Song of Solomon! But only a small part of it. I have trodden very carefully through the minefield of the most diaphanous innuendo and naked love-play, lest delicate ears might be offended. Yet it is there for anybody to read in the only book that is placed in the drawer by every hotel bed in the country for a good read at bedtime.

There is a literary reference by Professor Albright that might give a clue to Sheba's nationality and appearance. He said, "Ophir is the Hebrew name for Somaliland and neighbouring areas, while Punt was the Egyptian name for the same region." Somaliland, or Somalia as it is now known, was part of Ethiopia. So the Queen of Sheba, although often associated with Ethiopia, may have been Somali and therefore of fine countenance and features. I remember the Somalis in Berbera comporting themselves with haughty dignity, striking postures and with regal ways and wonder if something in their genes told them they once held the keys to the greatest treasure trove in the world and had the mightiest powers of the ancient world at their bidding. And there they were, still acting out the part 3000 years later as if nobody had told them that the show was all over.

Taking Professor Albright's remark further, if both the Egyptians and the Hebrews believed that Punt was the land of Ophir and there is no evidence of gold having been mined in Arabia and not much in Punt, it can only be that the Ethiopians or Somalis wanted their customers to believe that they brought the gold from their own land. That way they could hide the real access to the source and keep it to themselves. And there in Somaliland, by Hargiesa, lie the twin peaks of Sheba's Breasts that are said to mark the start of the overland route, the gates, to Solomon's Mines. Or, more accurately, did the twin peaks show the way to *Sheba's Mines*, for it would seem that the people of Sheba were operating the gold trade long before Solomon got wind of it.

There is now a strong opinion that the Queen of Sheba did not come to test Solomon's wisdom as the Bible has it. She may have done that too, but more likely she came to trade, or even more likely, to try to bargain or make a deal with Solomon so that her country did not lose out entirely to the new, wealthy entrepreneur who was horning in on the long established Sheba family business. From what we gather from their union she seems to have handled the situation remarkably well and got the very best that she could have hoped for her crown and country.

As he grew old, Solomon, who had always been tolerant of those who followed his mother, Bathsheba, in the worship of Baal and Astarte, moved closer to that religion himself. Many of his wives were from his mother's people and he built many pagan temples for their use. Unfortunately many Israelites were also drawn to these places and to the worship of those heathen gods. *'For when Solomon was old his wives turned away his heart after other gods; and his heart was not wholly true to the Lord his God. And the Lord was angry with Solomon ...'* This no doubt was the reason why God chose this time to break the Israelites asunder.

On his death Solomon's son, Jeroboam, returned from Egypt where he had been hiding following an attempt on his life by his father some years before. He inherited the crown but was an ineffectual ruler and soon the north broke away from the south and the two were at war with each other. Centuries later, having weakened themselves by their conflicts, the ten northern tribes of Israel fell as easy-meat to Nebuchadnezzar, king of Babylon, who smashed all that Solomon had created and took the people into captivity for over half a century. When the Babylonians in their turn were crushed by the Assyrians, the victors allowed the Israelites to return to their own land, but only comparatively few did so, most preferring to stay where they had been born and brought up. With the break-up of the Mosaic tribes the southern people were absorbed into the general population and Judah passed into history. But the name lives on in Ethiopia where, even today, the rulers are proud to be known as the Lion of Judah, two-and-a-half thousand years after Judah failed to exist.

Some time later the Phoenicians also passed out of history. Following great pressure from the Philistines to the south and Assyrians to the north they took to their boats and headed west. They made colonies all through the Mediterranean Sea as far as Spain and finally settled in what is now Tunisia where they built their great city Carthage and became known as the Carthaginians. Here they ruled as the most powerful nation at the dawn of our European history, traded with the earliest Greeks and watched a seedling nation called Rome grow into the mightiest power in the world. They fought wars with Rome. Hannibal, their greatest leader led his elephant army through Spain, over the Alps and almost to the gates of Rome before returning home. But in the end they were smashed by the Roman armies. Their great city was razed to the ground and like Judah, Carthage and the Phoenicians/Carthagians were no more.

Although nothing of their civilisation remains the Phoenicians left a priceless legacy to the world. From 'Phoenicians' we got the word 'phonetics'. The ancient Egyptians wrote in hieroglyphics, a picture-form type, and the Sumerians improved on this with their cuneiform (wedge) inscriptions. But it was the Phoenicians who gave us the first use of letters that represented sounds.

*

With the passing of Solomon and the Phoenicians and Hiram's ships, the bare granite walls of Great Zimbabwe must have rung silent. Silent as a tomb. A tombstone edifice of a long gone people and their way of life. No more mass prayers to the Sun God and Moon Goddess within the high, sculptured walls of the Temple. No eager eyes watching, marking the progress of the sun's beams creeping daily towards the aperture through which a ray would herald the new solstice. No more orgies to ensure procreation of life and fertility of the fields and animals. No more thanksgiving to the gods for providing. No more. Nothing. Centuries of time spread their mantle of darkness over the past, hiding it, cloaking it with an aura of mystery, doubts and make-believe.

*

After the Solomon era it would seem that the gold trade diminished but did not stop. Gold, copper and ivory were still being imported by Egypt, from the land they called Punt, right up to Roman times and later. It is likely that the merchandise came by the old, Sheba land route for there is little evidence of the Sabeans being long distance sailors. Later perhaps, but at that time it would appear they confined their ships to the Red Sea area, criss-crossing between Ethiopia and Arabia.

Then came the Persians and they were sailors par-excellence. They colonised the East African coast with city-states. After some centuries they left, whether by force or general decline when new dynasties back home lost interest in foreign colonies or from pressures within. Their place was taken by the Arabs from the Gulf and elsewhere. Both the Persians and the Arabs occupied only the coastal areas. Neither of them penetrated more than a few miles into the interior of the country.

Somewhere around the 12th and 13th centuries great changes were happening in that interior. The Bantu Africans had begun to drift in from the north to occupy and populate the land and great chieftain kingdoms were being formulated. Greatest of these was that of Monomotapa who made Great Zimbabwe his capital. He and his successors realised to some extent the importance of gold as a trading commodity.

No doubt there had always been a trickle of the precious metal reaching the coast for the Persians knew about it. But there had to be someone, some people, more worldly wise than the average African native of the interior to know the true worth of the natural wealth of the land. Someone of importance who came or, like Solomon, sent his legions to acquire that wealth. The name that comes through legend and history is Prester John of Ethiopia.

Had the stories of Sheba's mines lived on in her land for over a thousand years and he was out to make the legend live again? Whatever, archaeological evidence tells that about that time Zimbabwe began a new life and great amounts of gold were exported, either by the land trail or, more likely by this time, by sea, as in Solomon's time, nearly 2,200 years before.

Prester (from Presbyter) John was reputed to be a Nestorian Christian king and priest. The Nestorians, a sect that originated with the Syrian bishop Nestorius in the early 5th century, maintain that there were two natures (and even two persons) in the incarnate Christ, one divine and the other human.

At the end of the 15th century the Portuguese arrived and from that moment we enter into living, written history. Reports of gold from the interior arriving at Sofala for export to other city states began to be received back in Lisbon. It was obvious that the gold trade had been going on a long time before the arrival of the Portuguese. It also appeared that the natives put very little value on the precious metal. One report said, 'The land is rich in gold ... but the people are so lazy in seeking it, or covet it so little that one of these Negroes must be very hungry to dig for it.'

In 1516 Duarte Barbosa described how the heathens from the kingdom of Monomotapa came to the coast laden with gold which they thought so little of they did not bother to weigh it in exchange for cotton cloth and glass beads. The Moors of Sofala, he said, must make at least one-hundred-to-one profit. On the other hand, one can imagine the 'heathens' going back home cock-a-hoop on their business acumen that enabled them to con those stupid people by the great sea out of their wonderful cloth and jewellery for this worthless stuff they dug out of the ground for nothing.

In 1531 came a gem of information. Vicente Pegado, captain of Sofala, reported that he had been told of a great ruin, a square fortress of masonry, built of stones of marvellous size with no mortar joining them, that stood among the gold mines of the inland plains. So Zimbabwe was already a ruin by that time! If, that is, the building referred to was indeed the ruin we know in our modern times. There is one discrepancy in linking that report to what we know as Zimbabwe; there are no square buildings in Great Zimbabwe. But that could be an error of the uneducated native porters who presumably carried the tale, or merely a fault of translation during the conversation. Pegado's report goes on to mention some more interesting remarks. He mentions one tower of stone that was '12-fathoms high'. Taking a fathom as two yards or six feet this is rather more than the height of the stone tower existent at Great Zimbabwe. But then, travellers' tales tend to exaggerate.

In the same report Pegado states in reference to these stone buildings, 'The natives of the country call all these edifices Symbaoe, which according to their language means *court*.' So Zimbabwe is a derivative or modern pronunciation of Symbaoe! and the court can only be that of the great king Monomotapa. It would be more correct to refer to this person by the African term, Munhu Mutapa, but from Nyasaland south I had been picking up odd references to the legendary Monomotapa of ancient times and although this is obviously an Anglicised term, it is the one best known in my day and the one I feel more familiar in using.

Old maps have the name 'Kingdom of Monomotapa' spread over the land from what became known as Angola in the west to the coast of Mozambique in the east. It is evident that the name cannot refer to one person for it appears over centuries of the early, sketchy history of Africa. There must have been a long dynasty of many Monomotapas, like that of the Caesars and Napoleons. The reign seems to have begun in the early 15th century when it was at its zenith and petered out in the 19th. David Livingstone, navigator extraordinaire, botanist supreme and wizard of native languages and customs, has this to say about Monomotapa in 1852, exactly one hundred years before my time in that area:

On the 20th we came on Monina's village (close to the sand-river Tangwe, lat.16° 13' 38" S., long. 32° 32' E.). This man is very popular among the tribes on account of his liberality. Boroma, Nyampungo, Monina, Jira, Katolosa (Monomotapa), and Susa, all acknowledge the supremacy of one called Nyatewe, who is reported to decide all disputes respecting land. ... Katolosa is "the Emperor Monomotapa" of history, but he is a chief of no great power. ... The Portuguese formerly honoured Monomotapa with a guard, to fire off numbers of guns on the occasion of any funeral, and he was also partially subsidised. The only evidence of greatness possessed by his successor, is his having about a hundred wives. When he dies, a disputed succession and much fighting are expected. In reference to the term Monomotapa, it is to be remembered that Mono, Moene, Mona, Mana, or Morena, mean simply chief. Motape was chief of the Bambira, a tribe of the Bunyai, and is now represented in the person of Katalosa. ... The government of the Banyai is rather peculiar, being a sort of feudal republicanism. A chief is elected and they choose the son of the deceased chief's sister in preference to his own offspring. When dissatisfied with one candidate, they even go to a distant tribe for a successor, who is usually of the family of the late chief, a brother or a sister, or a sister's son, but never his own son or daughter.

Though he must have passed very near Great Zimbabwe Livingstone never saw it or even knew of its existence or he would surely have recorded it. However, if Monomotapa is the name so linked with Great Zimbabwe when at its zenith in the 15th century, has Livingstone left us a description of the titleship at its nadir and the reason why it disappeared entirely for, to the best of my knowledge, there was no kingship of that name when I was in that region? Did the expected dispute on the expiry of the Monomotapa he mentioned fragment the tribe so much no chief ever ruled over them again and were the people absorbed into the other tribes he mentioned?

While Livingstone may have given us a glimpse of the end of the Monomotapa dynasty it is to the beginning of that reign we have to go to try and fathom out the link, if any, with Great Zimbabwe and the legendary mines from whence came King Solomon's gold. There is little doubt that in the 14th and 15th centuries gold ore was being brought from mines in the surrounding lands to Great Zimbabwe for smelting and that the precious metal was then carried to the coast for sale.

There was some evidence to indicate that Great Zimbabwe became uninhabited even before the end of the Monomotapa rule. For a people who valued cattle even more than gold it would seem that the land surrounding Great Zimbabwe became over-grazed and barren so that *Symbaoe,* the court of Monomotapa, was moved to another location. This could explain why the gold porters to Sofala referred to Great Zimbabwe as a ruin even when the gold trade was still at its height. On the other hand, were some parts of Great Zimbabwe already in ruinous state long before Monomotapa ever appeared on the scene.

Here we have the crux of the ambivalence of the yes and no attitudes towards the Solomon's mines' theory that existed in Rhodesia in my days there and still vehemently exists today in Zimbabwe. The great question is, how old is Great Zimbabwe, when was it built? Even more important, much more, who built it? Were they indigenous Africans who laid stone on stone, or were they foreign people who came long before the Bantu arrived in the area?

Archaeologists appear very reluctant to guess beyond those dates, perhaps because the 12th or 13th century corresponds to the arrival of the Bantu people, of which the Rozwe/Shona tribal group was prominent then and 800 years later now form the main group in today's government.

The controversy of Zimbabwe being built purely by Bantu people is not new. That debate has been going on for over a century. During his excavations in 1891, Theodore Bent sashayed from one side to the other: was Zimbabwe built entirely by native African labour or by foreigners, or at least with their influence? At first he was very sceptical of the tales of white builders going back to Phoenician times. Writing of his arrival and early days he says he could not abide the early Boer and British visitors who came with their pre-conceived ideas, all taking for granted that Zimbabwe was the place of Gold Mines associated with King Solomon, Queen of Sheba and, later, Prester John. He needed to have an open mind. Had he been there when I wandered into the ruins I suppose he would have given me short shrift, for my head was filled with these old legends.

Theodore Bent, an eminent archaeologist, noted for his work in the Middle East, came in 1893 at the request of Cecil Rhodes to fathom the mystery of Zimbabwe, twenty-two years after its discovery by Mauch. His book, *The Ruined Cities of Mashonaland,* was published in 1895. When I came on it by chance on a bookstall I felt I had discovered a piece of pure Zimbabwean gold, a nugget buried in a heap of dross. When I read it I eagerly ran across the floor of the debating chamber and joined the '*I believe*'s'.

*

Monday 11th August, 1952. Zimbabwe Ruins.

Walked through the Valley of Ruins this morning to the Temple. It is a fascinating place. It consists of a huge elliptical shaped wall with three narrow entrances. Inside is a labyrinth of passages and separate enclosures. One place is known as the Sacred Enclosure and contains a huge, cone-shaped tower over 30ft. tall and 14ft. diameter at its base. Beside it in a broken-down condition is a small one. A passage connects this sacred enclosure with one of the entrances. Thus it is possible to reach this part without entering the Temple proper. Perhaps it was the entrance for the priests so they didn't need to go through the body of people to get to the altar. The second Enclosure is a narrow opening into another enclosure. In here are the remains of a raised stone platform or altar.

What strange cult was practised in these grey, lichen covered walls? There is no evidence that the place has ever been roofed. Were the people sun worshippers? Were they people from ancient Egypt who came and built this great temple to worship their mythical Sun God, 'Isis'?

*

Theodore Bent began his exploratory diggings at the Temple and everything he found there could be attributed to indigenous African manufacture or imported ware, some of which, such as Chinese glass beads and porcelain, would indicate the extent of the wide international trade of a people living so far into the interior of Africa. From his early excavations in and around the buildings on the low plain, Bent deduced from the depth of the topsoil and the debris and detritus below, that the buildings had been unused for a long time, but before they fell into disuse it was evident that people, corresponding to the Bantu, had inhabited the buildings for a long time in centuries gone by, perhaps around the 13th or 14th centuries. This would correspond to the era of the Monomotapa empire at its height. Bent found nothing at the Elliptical Building or Temple that would indicate earlier foreign inhabitants. If there had been evidence of earlier foreign habitation it had long since been destroyed or overlaid with the debris of centuries of African people who lived there, too deep for his excavations. With little more to go on he was then inclined to assume that the Bantu inhabitants could have been the builders.

447

From my diary:

Zimbabwe is a dead city. Built perhaps three thousand years ago. Nobody knows by whom or why they left. It's like Gedi, the place I visited near Mombasa. But here there is no style of architecture to give a clue to the builders or when it was built. The masonry is marvellous. The whole place is built of granite blocks and no cement has been used to keep them together. In places the walls vary between fifteen to twenty two feet thick at the base, tapering to seven or eight feet wide at the top.

I spent all day wandering about the Acropolis, the name given to the fortress built on the top of a 300 ft. kopje, or hill. Whoever built this place must have been first class military engineers. The hills form a natural fortress and have been made impregnable with mighty walls. The remains of a defensive wall with a nook for a sentry on either side guards the shoulder-width passage between unscaleable sides. Here one man could bar the passage of an army. Inside the fort at the top is a maze of various enclosures, many in ruins. From here one can command a view of the whole surrounding district, look over the Valley of Ruins and see the circular walls of the Elliptical Building or Temple.

It was when Bent excavated on top of the Acropolis or Hill Fortress, where giant single rocks, fifty feet high, silhouette the ridge, that he found evidence that made him change his mind regarding the possibility of Bantus being the builders of these ruins. Wonderful evidence.

Bent explains:

'As I have said, traces of a recent Kaffir habitation will account for the absence of objects in the lower buildings, but the upper ruin, sheltered from the sun and hidden by the trees and lofty buildings, was a spot repugnant to the warmth loving Kaffir, and to this fact do we owe the preservation of so many objects of interest belonging to the ancient inhabitants.'

Bent's continual reference to 'Kaffirs' may be distasteful to modern ears but words of a particular time cannot be ignored or replaced when dealing with that era. Shakespeare's works would not be the same if his contemporary words were changed to those more suited to modern times. Kaffir, (also spelled kaffer, kaffre or caffre) comes from the Arabic, kafir, meaning 'infidel' or 'nonbeliever', and in the early days of the Cape Dutch colony the whole of South Africa outside the pale was called Cafreria. In early times the pale, or paling, was a wooden stake fence erected round an area that was then reckoned to be safe or civilised. Anyone who went 'beyond the pale' was likely to be in danger.

Most important of all Bent's finds in the hilltop ruin were eight soapstone carved birds, six of which were over five feet tall, all on high carved pedestals. More broken pedestals with no birds were found and it was thought that at one time they must have perched on the wall round the Elliptical Temple. They were stylised birds and though each was different Bent believed that from their thick legs, long talons and a beak that was still intact that they were meant to be vultures. This bird has become the National Emblem of modern Zimbabwe.

At the feet of one of the birds on top of its pedestal was an incised chevron pattern similar to a much bigger one built into the great wall that surrounds the temple down on the plain. The chevron pattern has long been accepted as a symbol of fertility much used in prehistoric buildings and carried through into Christian times, as can be seen in the mighty columns of many 11th and 12th century great churches of Norman architecture in Britain.

But the chevron pattern was no confirmation that the builders were not Africans. In writing of my visit to the 'Temple' that day I emphasised that fact in my diary. *'Even today some of the native women wear belts or skins, or dresses bearing the chevron pattern during the dancing which generally accompanies their marriage. The emblem is said to be a lucky mascot so that they may be blessed with many children.'* Nevertheless, it is one thing to paint, weave or sew patterns on cloth or skin, it is something else to work the same design into stonework. To carve the birds and incise the pattern into the relatively soft soapstone was not beyond the Bantu natives, but to build lattice patterns into dry-stone, granite masonry is another consideration.

Looking for comparisons with the stone vultures, Bent, an authority on Ancient Egyptian and early Middle Eastern history, wrote that he had little doubt in stating that the Zimbabwean birds were closely akin to those found in Assyrian temples, where they were sacred to Astarte, goddess of love and fertility, among the Phoenicians. He also tells us that the Ancient Egyptians also held the vulture in profound veneration for its great maternal qualities. *'Horapollo tells us the vulture was emblematic of "Urania, a year, a mother".'*

Having, to his satisfaction, established a link with prehistory, Bent now returned to the Elliptical Building and looked at it with renewed interest. He studied the great, round, cone-shaped tower. Some of the topmost courses of stone had fallen or been removed, but from the increasing angle of the curvature to the non-existent peak he estimated that the height would have been 35 feet.

By digging at the base of each tower he established that they were both solid. Could his earlier ideas of the greater one being a phallic symbol now be borne out. *"If the stone vultures could be likened to Assyrian temples and the religion of Astarte, why not the towers?"*

He writes;

'The religious purport of these towers would seem to be conclusively proved by the numerous finds made in other parts of the ruins of a phallic nature and I think a quotation of Montfaucon's will give us a keynote of the worship, "The ancients assure us that all the Arabians worshipped a tower, which they called El Acara or Alquetila, which was built by their patriarch, Ishmael. Maximus of Tyre says they honoured as a great god a cut stone; this is apparently the same stone resembling Venus ... Allusions to these towers are constant in the Bible, and the Arabian historian El Mosoudi further tells us that this stone or tower was eight cubits (about 12½ ft.) high and was placed in an angle of the temple, which had no roof. (A cubit was the length of the forearm, from elbow to fingertips, 18 to 20 inches, about 50 centimetres.) *Turning to Phoenician temple construction, at Byblos, we have a good parallel to the ruins of the Great Zimbabwe as depicted on the coins, the tower or sacred cone is set up within the temple precincts and shut off in an enclosure.'* Chamber's Encyclopaedia gives this on the subject of Baal, *'His presence was symbolized by upright conical stones, erected in the open air and later in temples, which are supposed to have a phallic significance.'*

The Indian writer, Aubrey Menen, also gives details of ancient open-air temples with phallic towers and offering altars in Palestine and Carthage (Tunis) the Phoenician city that was razed by the Romans. From information gleaned from chiselled murals on stone he gives details of the temples and graphic descriptions of what offerings were made on the altars. These ranged from wild sexual rituals in times of peace to horrific human offerings in time of supreme national crisis. In the worst of these, babies were slaughtered and dismembered by their fathers as the ultimate sacrifice to Moloch, the severe side of Baal. The bones of these tragic offerings are still to be seen in the urns in which they were placed at the time of the offerings, preserved in a cellar in Tunis that survived the holocaust of Carthage.

Barbaric? Yes, but the Phoenician/Carthaginians were not the only people who made that sacrifice to appease their God. The Israelites certainly practised it too. Indeed they had a word for it, *'Aqedau'*, meaning 'binding'. We know this from the Genesis story of Abraham being told by God to sacrifice his son Isaac to show his obedience. Abraham binds his son and is about to slaughter him when God relents and allows Abraham to substitute a ram.

So Baal, the god of the Canaanites, and Yahweh, god of the Hebrews, demanded the same sacrifice of sons. Does that mean that all Gods were commercial entities, trading with their people – 'you give this (your butchered son, for instance, or your penance) and I will give you that or save you from the impending catastrophe'?

Was there really any difference between Baal and Yahweh? Both come through as cruel, demanding, unforgiving gods. Could there be but one god who was known by different names by different people? Can that cruel, unforgiving, Hebrew God of the Old Testament, the unchanging God, be the same one as we know today, completely about-faced after Christ's day, a gentle God, eternally forgiving to the contrite. Or should the oft-quoted Bible adage of God making man in His own likeness really be that 'Man makes God in his own likeness' so He changes as we change?

Theodore Bent wrote of seeing natives praying, as I had also seen many times, *'Here we saw sticks set in the ground with the bark peeled off and bound round the top ... They (the natives) set these things up whenever they came to new country; also on similar occasions they kneel before a tree and burn snuff, saying as they do so, "Muali", the native name for God.'* To non-understanding strangers the natives' sticks would be a mere fetish without seeing it was a medium, a direct-line to their god. But what would those same natives make of seeing strangers kneeling beside a wooden cross without knowing the meaning or symbolism attached it: would these natives also see the cross as a fetish, perhaps even see it as a poor one compared with one of God's living trees?

*

One of Theodore Bent's exploration party was the mathematician R.M.W. Swan who, after extensive examination of the two towers in Great Zimbabwe and other parts of the buildings, came to the conclusion that the cubit was the standard measure of the builders.

He wrote in his *Orientation*

And Measurements Of Zimbabwe Ruins – 'The diameter of the great tower at its base is 17.17feet or 10 cubits, and is exactly equal to the circumference of the little tower. This ratio of circumference to diameter and the above measure of 10 cubits seem together to have determined either the length of the radius or diameter, or halves of these, of all the circular curves on which many of the walls are built. For instance, the radius of the curve behind the great tower is 169 1/3feet, and this is equal to the diameter of the great tower multiplied by the square of the ratio of circumference to the diameter; or 17.17 x 3.14 (2). = 169.34. The well built partly circular enclosure to the north-west of the tower has a diameter 54 feet, and this is equal to 17.17x 3.14.' And further on, *'We hardly expect to find the same measure always applying to the building on the hill, for the form of these buildings is often controlled by the nature of the ground. Still they do apply, and the diameter of the curve on which the wall of the eastern temple is built is 84 1/2feet, which is equal to half 17.17 x 3.14 (2).'* And summing up, *'The towers when built were doubtless made complete in their mathematical form and were carried up to a point as we see in a coin of Byblos, where we have a similar tower represented with curved outlines.'*

He goes on to explain in mathematical terms how the curves of the towers of Zimbabwe measure up to those of the Byblos one depicted on the ancient Phoenician coin.

There follows many, many other examples of the continuation of the equations mentioned, no doubt to show that all the builders did had nothing to do with chance. Whoever they were, they were brilliant mathematicians and extremely skilled builders to follow such intricate plans.

Having realised the similarity of Zimbabwe with Phoenician and Ancient Egyptian open-air temples with tower and sacrificial altars, Swan then went on to study the mathematics, positions and angles of the openings in the elliptical wall and the positioning of the altar. All temples of this type had been built to the worship of the sun and the exact daily position of that deity with that of the stars made up the calendar.

On this Swan writes:
'Accordingly we find that at Zimbabwe means had been provided for ascertaining the time of the summer solstice, and that the side of the temple which faced the rising sun at this period of the year was adorned with a decoration symbolical of fertility.

'But the temples at Zimbabwe seem also to have served a more directly practical purpose than that of mere worship of the powers of nature, and while regulating the festivals held in honour of natural powers, to have provided the means of observing the passage of the seasons and of fixing the limits of a tropical year, and thus providing the elements of a calendar.'

Reading more into the positioning of Great Zimbabwe in relation to the stars Swan writes;
'It is remarkable that only the stars of the northern hemisphere seem to have been observed at Zimbabwe ... The positioning of the doorways

relatively to the altars or the centres of the arcs is of interest; and we find that every important doorway in the walls of the original period ... is placed true north of the centre of an arc or of an altar.'

There is much more of these instances that seem to bear out that the original builders' eyes and interests were always to the north from whence they came.

In the end, after such thorough detective work, Swan could only conclude that the builders were not African natives. In a quote he refers to there possibly being two ancient eras of Zimbabwe with considerable time in between. In the second, some of the walls had been repaired and extensions made. In the later period the craftsmanship was inferior to the first. In the original building the stone courses were as straight and regular as if string-lines or spirit-levels had been used, as bricklayers use today. The work done in the second period was not of the same standard. Stone courses were laid to the lie of the land and the irregularities carried on up the wall. On these different builders, Bent remarks:

'When the western wall was rebuilt at the great temple at Zimbabwe there was apparently a want of stones, and the rebuilders were too lazy (or too unskilled as masons to fashion square ashlars) *to procure more, so they probably shortened the wall by decreasing the size of the temple and also economised stones by making the new wall much less thick.'*

Further on this topic he declares, *'It is incredible that such a style of architecture as we have described, and such a civilisation as it signifies, could have originated and developed in South Africa, for such a development would have required a very long time, and would have implied at least a long and peaceful settlement in the country; and although the builders of Zimbabwe may long have possessed the place they never considered the country was their own.'*

In conclusion Swan writes:

'When the original builders are traced to their home, it will remain to discover who were their successors in Mashonaland that rebuilt the western wall of the great temple and some portions of other buildings, for this certainly was not done by any of the present negro races.

'There is nothing to show that even these walls do not belong to a now far distant time; for ... at Zimbabwe they might endure for an indefinite period, for there, in a clear atmosphere free from dust, and a tropical climate with its yearly torrential rains, no soil can accumulate among the stones to support vegetation which would destroy the walls.

'Besides, the present inhabitants do not use stone in any if their construction, and never trouble themselves to remove stones from existing

walls, so more stones have probably been disturbed during the two years of British occupation of the country than the Kaffirs would disturb in as many centuries; and under the old conditions the walls might endure for an indefinite time.'

*

So back to the 20th century when any idea of connecting Zimbabwe with Solomon's mines had been quashed twice and for all by two leading archaeologists of their day. If the work of Theodore Bent was known at all it was rubbished by the silence it was given in academic circles. If mentioned in encyclopaedias or other books of reference, he usually gets little more than a cursory note. Take for example, the following account of Zimbabwe in *Chambers Encyclopaedia* (1955 edition) in which the two who get credence are mentioned.

'The site was discovered in 1868 (there is some discrepancy with this date and that which I have recorded from other sources, 1871) *and for a long time it was thought to be of great antiquity and the work of Orientals. The first serious investigations were carried out by D. Randall MacIver in 1905. He concluded that no part of the site was of pre-mediaeval age, but continued doubts led to more test excavations in 1929 by Miss G. Caton Thompson. Her findings were that the earliest buildings of this type in Southern Rhodesia cannot be any earlier than the 10th century AD and may be much later, while the latest cannot be placed any earlier than the 12th century and are almost certainly as late as the 16th century. The site is typically African Bantu.'*

Note, not one word on the work of Theodore Bent or R.M.W. Swan, both eminent professionals in archaeology.

How can experts on a subject be so diametrically opposite in their findings? When I arrived at Zimbabwe, Caton Thompson's deliberation was the 'in' thing, as I mentioned earlier. Any mention of the site being anything to do with Solomon/ Sheba gold was ridiculed. I wondered at the time how these two eminent authorities could ignore or dismiss Bent's work. Remember, it was Bent who discovered the wonderful soapstone birds that are the emblem of modern Zimbabwe. The silence of no reference to such an important find and credit given to the finder is deafening. I got a clue perhaps to the reason for this, soon after my return from Africa, in a most unlikely place.

When visiting a castle in Scotland I was interested to read of the son of the family whose home it was, who had escaped from a German prisoner-of-war camp during the Second World War and made his way across occupied territory in the guise of a Russian officer, Major Baggeroff, as he called himself. Obviously a brave and resourceful young man. After the war he went into politics and eventually found himself in Parliament where he did very well until he hit a brick wall, metaphorically speaking. Suddenly he was getting nowhere and he laid the reason for this to his stating in public that he believed in the Loch Ness Monster. Following that he felt no one took him seriously. His credibility had gone.

There is another example of the devastating effect of this line of thought to professional people, one which is even more pertinent to my theory of why the early 20th century experts misled their public. For this we must go back to the Minoan empire at its peak, just before the Thera catastrophe, and also to the discovery of the ruins by Professor Marinatos.

By the time disaster struck, the Minoan people had created a society that was perhaps the most advanced on earth, exceeding even the Early Egyptians who were at their height. Of the many islands that made up the Minoan empire, Thera was likely the most advanced of all. Marinatos discovered that the people, ordinary workers, of Thera lived in considerable comfort in multi-storey buildings with running water and flush toilets that ran into buried sewers that net-worked under the whole city. Their art, furnishings and hanging gardens showed a people with highly developed tastes and advanced knowledge. Like all Minoans they would admire and covet physical fitness, indulge in dangerous athletic sports and comport themselves with dignity. We learn this from the mosaics and painted murals in the Palace of Knossos in Crete. There, plainly to see, is the Minoan version of the Running-the-Bulls game where lines of young, athletic and unarmed men and women stand to meet charging bulls. But unlike modern toreadors who side-step the animals, their Minoan early ancestors leapt and dived over the horns of the charging animal, did a lightning hand-flip on the back of the animal and landed on their feet at the fast disappearing tail. Not every one made it for there are scenes of gore there too.

In his assessment of the Thera people Professor Marinatos had a secret, a secret in the shape of a piece of quartz he carried in his pocket. Like a priceless gem or a hidden-treasure map he would show it to only his very closest friends and only with that very small and intimate cartel would he discuss its probabilities. Marinatos never published details of his secret. But now let Charles Pellegrino, author of *Return to Sodom and Gomorrah* tell us about it.

"Some of us who were to follow in Marinatos' footsteps could not avoid wondering; if the Minoans had not been living in the most dangerous place on Earth, might there have been television by the time of Christ? And might interstellar voyages be something we were actually doing today, ...? Marinatos himself could not avoid such thoughts, as he turned a rarely talked-about but much prized sliver of cut and polished quartz between

*thumb and forefinger. When reconstructed, the crystal, convex on both sides, hinted that someone on ancient Thera possessed a knowledge of lens cutting. Nothing short of an actual wood and quartz tube buried in one of the buildings would compel him later to **risk his reputation by publicly voicing his speculations about Minoan telescopes**, but lacking such proof, he allowed himself the luxury of private speculations among friends."* The emphasis highlighted is mine.

Could this also be why Theodore Bent and Robert Swan appear not to be taken seriously? Was this why MacIver and Caton-Thompson would not risk going into controversial realms of science, finding it safer and more professionally safe to stick to the known, acceptable path?

That would account for the knowing attitude of the 'well-informed' in the mid '50s. It also dealt an ace to post-colonial politics in the new Zimbabwe.

*

While I was at Zimbabwe I was told that a piece of wood, part of a lintel I believe, had recently been sent away somewhere for a new scientific test that confirmed Caton-Thompson's estimate that the buildings dated from the 13th century. These tests are quite likely to have been the process now familiarly known as 'Carbon Dating', or more accurately, 'Radiocarbon Dating', developed by the US physicist Willard F. Libby about 1946.

This is done by measuring the carbon-14 content in an object. Carbon-14 is continually formed in the Earth's atmosphere and is absorbed from the air by green plants and then passed on to animals through the food chain. Every living thing contains carbon-14, humans, animals, fish, trees, grass, etc. Radiocarbon decays slowly in a living organism and the amount lost is continually replenished as long as the organism takes in air or food. Once the organism dies, however, it ceases to absorb carbon-14, so that the amount of the radiocarbon in its tissues steadily decreases. Because carbon-14 decays at this constant rate, an estimate of the date at which an organism died can be made by measuring the amount of its residual radiocarbon. Carbon-14, therefore, can only tell the age of past living matter. It cannot tell the age of metal or stone, unless the stone is sedimentary, and as such might contains fossils. Since Zimbabwe was built entirely with granite the dating method could tell nothing of the age of the building.

Had mortar been used in its construction there would have been a chance that living organisms would have got in the mixture and these could have been dated. In the absence of mortar it could be wildly inaccurate and wrong to positively date buildings such as those of Zimbabwe on a piece of wood that could have been inserted at any time.

456

From Theodore Bent's evidence and other references it is evident that Zimbabwe had several lives with perhaps hundreds of years between. First the original buildings by the Phoenicians, perhaps on an earlier site used by people of the land of Sheba. Later, after the death of Solomon and the demise of the early Israelites or Jews and the Phoenicians, the Ethiopians, the people of the land the Egyptians call Punt, continued to bring gold by land route with which to trade with Egypt and others. There appears to have been a rise in the gold mining in the 12th century during which time the name of Prester John crops up. Solomon's Mines were now renamed in legend as those of the Ethiopian priest/king.

The Prester John period went on until the 14th century which ties up with age of the carbon-dated wood from Zimbabwe. This could also tie up with the arrival of the Bantu people in their drift south from East Africa and the rise of the Monomotapa Empire. It is very likely that the early Shona tribes found the long-standing ruins of an ancient past, patched them up where necessary, made it their capital and referred to it as Symbaoe, their 'court'. This would account for the inferior craftsmanship on the repairs and extensions to the walls at later dates. The stone-masonry of some of the Citadel is haphazard compared with wonderful craftsmanship displayed in the building of the Elliptical Enclosure or temple.

These later repairs, however, may not be wholly Bantu. And here we have a very interesting thread running through the tapestry, the very stuff of mystery and legend. These 'old folk tales' may be woolly and embellished but they rarely start from nothing. If we only accept scientific evidence, such as carbon dating, we would have little or no ancient history. Here in our trail to find King Solomon's Mines we touch on the hoary chestnut of 'The Lost Tribe of Israel'. There is a tribe in South Africa who believe they are that tribe and claim that they built Zimbabwe.

*

In 1893 Theodore Bent wrote of a tribe working on his site in the Zimbabwe ruins:

'The Makalanga are above the ordinary in intelligence ... they rapidly learned their work, and were very careful excavators, never passing over a thing of value. Some of them are decidedly handsome and not at all like Negroes except in skin; many have a distinctly Arab cast of countenance. There is certainly a drop of Semitic blood in their veins. In religion they are monotheists.'

Forty years before Bent's remark David Livingstone wrote the following note when dealing with the customs of the Bechuana tribe:

'There is no stated day of rest in this part of the country, except the day after the appearance of the new moon, and the people refrain only from going to their gardens. A curious custom, not to be found among the Bechuanas, prevails among the black tribes beyond them. They watch most eagerly for the first glimpse of the new moon, and when they perceive the faint outline after the sun has set deep in the west, they utter a loud shout of "Kua!" and vociferate prayers to it.'

Unfortunately Livingstone does not mention the name of that tribe, but there are other clues as to their identity.

Almost one hundred years to the day later after Bent's excavations Dr Tudor Parfitt, senior Lecturer in Hebrew and Jewish studies at of the School of Oriental and African Studies, University of London, came to South Africa and Zimbabwe at the request of the Lemba people to study their claim that they are a lost tribe of Israel. The Lemba is a tribe who were driven out of Zimbabwe by Mzilikazi and spread south through northern Transvaal, but a small number remained or have returned to that land. The Lemba claim that they were originally a Semitic tribe from Sena, in Israel, who came south and built several cities, all called Sena, along the way and, eventually, after long travel they built, or helped to build, Great Zimbabwe and many lesser ones in the land between the Rivers Limpopo and Zambezi. The Lemba of today are as black Africans but proudly call themselves 'black Jews' and claim they are as one with the Falashas, the Black Jews of Ethiopia, whom Israel recognised as Jews and evacuated to Israel by air in 1984 during the civil war in Sudan. The Lemba follow Jewish customs, do not eat pork from time immemorial, wear skull caps and swear that their noses are Jewish.

The interesting tie-up with the past is that Parfitt says the Lemba are part of the Makalanga tribe of whom Theodore Bent also remarked that their noses were evidence of Semitic blood. The Lemba claim to follow an ancient Jewish custom of shaving their heads at the first sight of the new moon. This, in a way, tallies with the remark made by Livingstone when giving details of the tribe who honoured the first arrival of the new moon. This would also indicate that these tribes had an intimate knowledge of the days of the month. They knew exactly which night to congregate to welcome the new moon. This practice is interesting when read in conjunction with R.M.W. Swan's orientation of Zimbabwe's apertures being aligned to the moon's annual perambulations.

There could be another tenuous link with the Lemba and the ancient Semites. I remembered while in the Hadramaut Wing-Commander Ferkard, when talking of the Queen of Sheba, saying that the Arabs, and perhaps all the Semites, preferred queens to kings to carry on a dynasty since one always knew who the mother was, while the identity of the father could be obscure. The Lemba and the Makalanga tribes have long histories of Queens and High Priestesses in charge, a fact that Rider Haggard once again drew on with his *She* and *Solomon's Mines*. To this day the Lemba have a Queen, the Rain Queen, whom the tribe claims to be a direct descendant of the Monomotapa. Dr Tudor Parfitt, in his book *Journey to the Vanished City*, published in 1992, describes his visit to the current one. She lived in a small village in Northern Transvaal. Remember that both tribes are said to have Semitic features and the Lemba claim to have come from Israel, follow Jewish customs and religion and wear skull-caps and cloaks embroidered with the Star of David.

One other possible tie-up with Parfitt's *Lost Tribe of Israel* springs to my mind, outlandish and very personal but nevertheless as feasible as these related by the Lemba tribe. When relating my time with the Masai in Kenya and Tanganyika (Chapter Nine) I quoted Sangai's oral history of his people that evening by my fire. He told of the way Lenana gained the leadership of the tribe by subterfuge over the head of his brother Sandoyo when their father Mbatian was dying and I drew attention to the similarity of the Masai tale to the Biblical one of how Isaac (Israel) stole the leadership of the tribe from his twin brother Esau. I marvelled at the 'coincidence' of the same tale being told by such diverse peoples when no Arabs or Christian missionaries ever penetrated into Masailand.

In Parfitt's exposition of the Lost Tribe of Israel making their way down through Africa and taking part in the building of Zimbabwe there may be an explanation of the enigma of the two tales occurring with such diverse peoples. When the Lost Jews were wandering ever southward in Africa they were very likely to have met with the Masai who were also gradually making their way in the same direction from the land of the Nile from whence they came. The Jews would quite likely be telling the history of their people to those they met and, if so, might not the Masai have 'borrowed' or absorbed that story into their own history, as assuredly the Hebrews borrowed heavily from the Babylonians past when writing their Bible.

So, who were the original builders of Zimbabwe? Were they Phoenicians, Jews or Bantu Africans? From the words of the Bible on which the whole theory of King Solomon's Mines hangs the builders were not Jews, Hebrews, or Israelites, depending on the era of history of which we speak.

'And King Solomon made a navy of ships at Ezion-geber ... and Hiram sent in the navy his servants and seamen ... and they came to Ophir.' Solomon *made* a navy of ships! But it is evident that like any business man who can't or does not want to do the work he has in mind, Solomon hired Hiram, the Phoenician, to build, equip and sail his ships, for the simple reason that the Israelites did not know how to build or sail ships. ... *'and Hiram sent in the navy his servants and seamen.'* And when they arrived at Ophir, did not Hiram's servants, the Phoenicians, build a city and other lesser towns in the manner and style to which

they were accustomed, replicas of those they had left in their homeland of Tyre? And were these towns not all built with altars and phallic edifices with which to honour their Sun God and Moon Goddess and pray for fertility of crops and human procreation? And were not all their temples open to the sky the better to see the sun and the moon during their times of worship? And were not the walls of their towns pierced with door openings that would allow sun and moon beams to enter precisely on the very day or night and time when the main seasonal rituals would fall?

The people who built Zimbabwe as we see from the ruins, were certainly not Jews. Even if they had been able to build in stone at that time they would not have built pagan temples to worship multiple gods. And if these ruins really mark the site of Ophir they were not built by Bantus because these people did not arrive in the area for well over 2000 years. That the walls could be ageless was summed up by the mathematician R.M. Swan and is worth repeating in part.

'There is nothing to show that even these walls do not belong to a now far distant time; for there, in a clear atmosphere free from dust, and a tropical climate with its yearly torrential rains, no soil can accumulate among the stones to support vegetation which would destroy the walls.

The perfectly fitting stone blocks, between which even a knife could not go, would also prevent soil from penetrating.

So, if the Lembas' claim to be Jews and builders of Zimbabwe is true, they must have done it long after Solomon's era. Perhaps after hundreds of years of association in working with Phoenicians they eventually absorbed the trade, at which time a group might have made their way down the land route via Ethiopia to Zimbabwe. This would tie in with the Falashas stopping off in Ethiopia and the Lemba carrying on south. That too could be the reason for the inferior repairs and additions to the Zimbabwe building at a later date to the original. They could have come with, or arrived at the same time as Monomotapa and the Bantu Shona people, found the ancient ruins and made the repairs to the walls where necessary. The 15th century gold-bearers arriving at Sofala on the coast told the Portuguese that Monomotapa's Court was on the site of old ruins. So Zimbabwe had been born a long time before then.

Who, then, of the professionals gives the most feasible answers. The MacIver/Caton-Thompson camp maintain that the ruins are relatively modern and because 14th century Bantu could smelt metal from ore with skin bellows and fire, were good craftsmen in iron and good sculptors of wood, there was no reason why they could not have built in stone. Against these suppositions the Bent/Swan duo gives facts and figures to establish that it is possible that the buildings could be the work of early people from the land of Canaan, the architectural details of which tally with their religion.

My own opinion, written in my diary after spending days among the ruins was that while Zimbabwe may not be Solomon's workshop or gold factory it certainly was not the work of Bantu Africans. I say this not in any racist way. Far from it. After the past years living very close to the ground with African natives, I had come to respect the wealth of their intelligence and ingenuity and it would give me great pleasure to acknowledge them as the builders. But, experience told me that Zimbabwe was never built by DIY triers. That term had not been coined at the time I was there, but it best sums up my conclusions there and then.

Stone erections such as Zimbabwe could not have been built by trial-and-error. The builders had to know what they were about. Plans and measurements had to be worked out before a stone was laid.

I could not believe that such a building could have been done by native Africans without assistance. Wrought iron and wood carving were Iron Age skills but they did not lead to building in stone. Iron Age Britons made the most exquisite jewellery of gold, silver and precious stones which is hardly equalled in modern times. But, apart from Pictish brochs in Orkney and Shetland, they never built a stone house. With all the skills that were necessary to make sprung chariots, with spoke wheels and sword projected axles, they still lived in thatched, wattle-and-daub houses akin to those of Africa.

I reasoned, how could a people with Iron Age skills suddenly learn to build with stone to such advanced levels; to design magnificent, complicated monuments, learn the geometry of cubes and squares, the calculations of foundations and width to height, to know how to hammer-harden iron to the degree of hardness that would chisel stones to flat faces with 3-dimensional, 90-degree corners; to work out the mathematics of the slope of a conical tower that changes pitch near the top and meets all round at a given height, and to cut stones to the angle necessary to make it. To do all that so accurately that the ashlars fitted together so precisely that they needed no mortar to hold the structure together, no matter how high the building, was beyond belief.

All that does not come in one generation. Not even in a century and more, perhaps many more, if starting from scratch without assistance. And once acquired, a people so skilled does not give up those skills or lose them easily or abruptly and go back to living in grass huts again.

In conclusion, there is an interesting point I should like to raise that could put strength to the theory that the Phoenicians built Great Zimbabwe. The Bible tells us that Hiram's fleet took three years to make the round voyage to Ophir and back to Israel. Professor Albright puts the time of the voyage more accurately as half-a-year / a whole year / and another half without explaining why the time was divided up in such a way. I can. Back in my time in Somaliland when Major Fry was sending me off on what was to be my voyage on a dhow to Zanzibar, he told me that the round journey from the Arabian Gulf to Zanzibar and back again, took a year. Zanzibar was as far as the sailing boats could go on the south-blowing *kazkazi* trade wind. The sailors had just enough time to do their trading, careen the hull and a make repairs before catching the north-blowing *kuzi* wind that took them home again.

If they had wanted to go further south than Zanzibar they would have had to wait another year for the south wind to take them to Sofala and there wait for the wind to turn north again to take them back to Zanzibar. They would not have been able to do the full journey from Sofala to Ezion-geber at the head of the Persian Gulf in one go. Their programme would read: Ezion-geber to Zanzibar = half-a-year, Zanzibar to Sofala and back to Zanzibar = one year, Zanzibar to Ezion-geber = half-a-year. '*... for the king had at sea a navy; ... once in three years came the navy ... bringing gold, and silver, ivory and apes, and peacocks.*'

Tuesday 12th August 1952. Zimbabwe ruins

Pottered around the ruins today. This place fascinates me. But to get the most benefit I want to see it at night, if possible to sleep in the Temple.

Wednesday 13th August 1952.

Last night I laid in a good stock of wood and browsed in front of the fire till the moon rose, trying to see in the flames the people who had built this place long, long ago. The moon was late in coming, between midnight and 1 a.m. and then it was only a thin crescent. A faint, shadowy fluorescence fell over the ruins. They looked so eerie, yet so inviting. I had no qualms about leaving my tent unattended. No Africans ever come to these ruins and at night they wouldn't dare.

I walked through the Valley of Ruins. Isolated parts of walls stood out against the moonlight like headstones. A cemetery silence hung over the place, still and heavy as a tomb. A fear which sent effervescent tingles through my body made the walk exciting. I reached the Temple and stepped through the narrow opening which serves as a doorway. Inside it was like a grave. The narrow passages which connect the various chambers were as dark as pitch. I had to feel my way along them. I arrived at the Sacred Enclosure and could faintly discern the shape of the huge cone shadowed by the tree which has grown up beside it. At the Platform Enclosure I climbed the pile of rocks and sat on the remains of the platform and looked up at the great cone that towered over me and tried to fathom its secret. Was it an idol or symbol of some king? I tried to visualise the scene as it may have been had this been in the year of Zimbabwe's heyday.

The Temple was filled with a crowd of chanting people. Burning torches lit up the scene. The air was heavy with incense – frankincense brought from the Hadramaut, in the land of the Queen of Sheba, the wife of King Solomon.

The scene changed in my mind like slides in a magic lantern. These were too numerous to note. Once it was the house of prayer; again it was the scene of a terrible orgy. Were they of a local race long since extinct and buried 'neath the stones of time? Or were they people from another land come to extract gold for the coffers of King Solomon? My imagination wandered through a maze of possibilities. I must have sat for an hour or more before I realised that I was cold.

I groped my way back to the doorway. Once outside, the darkness was not so intense. The Acropolis Hill and ruins stood out against the sky. It was easy for me now to imagine that I saw 'She – Who Must Be Obeyed' glide across the land with all her radiant beauty.

I reached the tent without incident, no spooks.

Chapter Twenty-One

ONE END OF THE RAINBOW

Wednesday 18th February 1953 – Cape Town
  Tonight I arrived in Cape Town. I have done what I set out to do.

The knot in my stomach tightened into a hard ball as the last few miles of Rhodesian road, twin strips of tarmac with rough grass in between, ran out from under the truck like the wake of a ship. Two days had gone by since I walked back to Fort Victoria from Great Zimbabwe, spent the night there, then in the morning, wonders upon wonders, got on the last lap of the road to South Africa. But that day turned out to be a poor 'hitching' one, as the extract from my evening write-up in my diary shows:

Once again I'm in the wilds without a clue as to my position. The trouble is, of all Southern Rhodesia this part is about the worst to walk through. Between Fort Victoria and Beit Bridge (at the border) is one of the few parts of this country that is still wild. Here lions and elephants still roam. However, it can't be any worse than some of the parts of Tanganyika I passed through.

  Many cars passed me during the day but none stopped. All will be Union bound and since it's a long day's drive few will be able or inclined to spare the time to stop to pick up passengers. I don't blame them. Maybe I'll have better luck tomorrow.

My philosophical bent bore fruit in the morning. I set out in the grey dawn and walked a couple of hours when a little pickup truck drew alongside. The driver, a slight man with an eager smile, was accompanied by his wife and two small children, all crammed into the cab. After he offered me a lift and I had accepted gratefully he apologised for not being able to give me a seat inside. He made room for me up the back among a pile of baggage on which his 'boy' had already made his niche. The African servant smiled diffidently when I climbed in but after I spoke as man-to-man he relaxed and we were companions during the journey. He spoke quite good English and, as far as I could tell, excellent Afrikaans to his boss.

All day we had watched the road unwind as we chatted or sat in silence. Now the day was on the wane when the hazy blue spectre of Beit Bridge hove into view. Across the Limpopo River lay South Africa and my dreams of conquest. Supposing I was not allowed in? A great deal of doubt had been aired whenever I had discussed the problem of entry to the Union all the way down from Blantyre. Unlike my rebuff at Northern Rhodesia, there was no way round this one should I be rejected. The tension rose as the bridge structure hardened into the middle distance.

At last we were there and I held my breath. The Rhodesian officials at their border allowed me to pass without trouble. We crossed Beit Bridge with the Limpopo swirling below and stopped at the South African barrier. This was the crisis point of my years of travelling. It was almost an anticlimax when the South African officials passed me over with hardly a word. My passport stamped, I declared my pistol and camera. They waved me away without even charging duty on them. They even wished me luck on my journey. I felt like dancing a jig when I left the office. All these tales of South Africa being so anti-British seemed greatly exaggerated.

Once into South Africa was like entering a strange new world. A Roman legion returning from a foray into old Caledonia must have felt the same on leaving that wild region behind when passing through a gate in Hadrian's Wall and entering the safe and orderly world of Roman Britain. The twin tarmac strips that were the Rhodesian road – and that had been an enormous improvement to the bare earth tracks of the more northern Africa – suddenly blossomed out to a full metalled road. At once there seemed to be an old, established feel about the place.

The car sped through Messina, the first and last town in the Union, where there are primitive mineshafts, ancient dry-stone walling and evidence of an old gold-mining culture. Onwards through Northern Transvaal, past a string of towns that spelt history, Louis Trichardt, Pietersburg, Potgietersrus, Nylstroom, Warm Baths, and others, each with their own tale to tell on the making of the country. Between the towns there was some wild country that had not yet lost all its raw, African look and atmosphere.

The name 'Transvaal' first appeared in 1836 when some Voortrekkers who had left the Cape Colony as part of the Great Trek, crossed the Vaal River and claimed the country to the north as far as the Limpopo as their own. It was not until 1852 that they declared full independence, one hundred years exactly from that year to this one when I crossed the river from the north.

Towards evening we crossed the mountain range that overlooks Pretoria where I was dropped off in the outskirts. I reached up and shook hands with my travelling companion who smiled enthusiastically, thanked and said goodbye to the driver and his wife. They wished me good luck. The children waved. Nice people.

I walked through the streets to the centre of the city where the first lights twinkled and street lamps bloomed like nocturnal flowers. The city was coming to life. The Saturday night air of gaiety was abroad and caught me up with it. As on similar occasions when entering a town during my journey, I decided to celebrate my entry into the Union with a meal at a restaurant.

I was enjoying the event when a young couple came over to my table. The man said he had recently been to Rhodesia where he had seen something in the papers there about a Scot who was wandering about the country and asked if I was the one. I said that unless there was someone else doing the same thing I supposed I might be the one in question. We introduced ourselves and they joined me. Although in civilian clothes the young man was in the Army – the British Army – a member of the British Military Mission to South Africa. His wife was South African and they had married only recently. We chatted. They asked where I was going to stay. I said I hadn't a clue. The soldier jumped to the rescue, eager to help. He said the single men of the Mission were billeted in a private hotel. There were only about a dozen of them and one was away on leave. I would be able to use his bed. So saying, off we went and sure enough I got fixed up with the BMM lads who wined and dined me as one of them. A great bunch of chaps. Perhaps it was just Lady Luck but I couldn't help feeling there was someone up there keeping an eye on me. Here I was fixed up in luxury, a tramp off the street now guest of the British Army … again!

Over the next couple of days I did the sights of Pretoria, the Voortrekkers' Monument, Paul Kruger's house, the Government Buildings and all that. When I had done the round I easily hitched a lift to Johannesburg. Only 36 miles separated the two cities.

South Africa's premier city amazed me. I could see why it was called Little New York. Practically every building in the centre was ten to twenty storeys tall and in 1952 these were skyscrapers. Today they may be small fry, but then they had my mouth open, metaphorically. The great buildings towered over the streets like opposing rock faces and made them look like mere passages, through which ran racing torrents of trams, trolley-buses and big, flashy, American cars plastered with chromium jewellery. The broad pavements thronged with smartly dressed, busy people going places. Brashy neon signs highlighted most shops while pulsating ones drew the young into glitzy cafes, each one the home of a gaudy juke-box that could be operated from each table. This was all 21st century, at least a hundred years ahead of anything I had seen at home. After the past years in the north where space was infinite I had a feeling of claustrophobia. I hardly expected this in Africa.

It was hard to realise that all this had happened less than sixty years before my arrival. In fact the real building of Johannesburg did not start until after the formation of the Union of South Africa in 1910, so what I was seeing on my entry to the city was some forty years of development from nothing. It had all started in 1886, on a Sunday morning in February, when two roaming gold-prospectors trudged across the Witwatersrand (White Waters Ridge) seeking their fortune when they came across a rare, in fact the only, surface gold-bearing outcrop on the ridge. George Harrison, an Australian and his friend George Walker had hit the jackpot, but unlike millions who followed them they never made their fortune from their find. Far from it, and not even their names were commemorated with the event. That distinction went to two officials of the mining authorities, Johann Rissik and Johannes Joubert, to whom the prospectors reported their discovery. From these two high office workers the name Johannesburg was formed for the city that rose out of the wild, tented towns that mushroomed with the gold rush that quickly followed. George Walker sold his claim for £350 within a few months. George Harrison didn't do so well. He sold his diggings for £10 within a year. Thereafter the two who gave South Africa the richest mines in history disappeared into oblivion.

These were wild days indeed. Living and working a claim in these ramshackle camps was hard, tough and dangerous. And it was not always the bullies and thieves who were the most dangerous. Some time later I spent many wonderful evenings with an old man, he must have been in his eighties, who had worked a claim on 'The Rand' in the early nineties. In the quiet of an evening we sat on his *stoep* (verandah) while he puffed his pipe and yarned of his gold-mining days. In reverie his slow voice quickened as he lived again exciting moments, such as when they found a nugget, and went almost silent when recalling times of terrible despair when it seemed the claim was running out and there was hardly enough money to exist. Between tales his pipe glowed red in the gathering darkness and the eloquent silences were full of excitement of those tales told and perhaps those to follow. He told the minutiae of working a small claim, two men, sometimes three and sometimes only him, that would be multiplied a thousand times and more over the field. He told of the back-breaking work, the danger, the evil of some men and the heart-warming, brotherly camaraderie that grew and saw them through thick and thin.

There were the times they struck the town, such as it was, the clapboard saloons and rutted roads where wagon wheels could sink near up to the axles and the oxen to their knees. The joy of going through the swing-doors into the yellow lantern-light where smoke clouds lifted from the tables and drifted. The noise, the ribald shouts and coarse laughter, the pungent smell of tobacco and liquor, the hard men crazed with the release from the mine-shaft, and the ... girls! Harder than the soft-hearted miners, they were the real gold-diggers. They were the ones who won. Many a time past midnight, my storyteller said, he had seen nude prostitutes standing or gyrating on a table, selling themselves to the highest bidder. And money was not always the currency. Men woke up in the cruel light of the morning to find they had signed away the rights to their claims, while their partners for the night smiled their thanks and supremacy from the tangled bed.

All this, from the first earth scraping to this mighty city that could stand against any in the world, in the same time as it has taken me to tell my tale.

At this moment, however, when I was wandering about the city in question like the proverbial country bumpkin on his first visit to town, quite awed by it all, I was accosted by a little man in light, American-style suit and flashy tie.

"You look as if you are travelling," he summed up. I said I was. He asked some details. I outlined briefly what I was doing. "Have the papers got hold of you yet?" he asked hurriedly. I said I didn't think so, whereupon I found myself whisked off to the office of the *Rand Daily Mail* to give an account of my journey for a write up in the next day's edition. Photographs were taken and the piece ran to a two-page spread when it appeared. The little man was what he looked like, a radio and stage compere and publicity man. He seemed to be quite a noise about town. His name I will give as Morry Abel. He lived by himself in a flat in the centre of the city where he invited me to stay with him for a few days. I thought it was very decent of him. Later I changed my opinion.

On that first day however, he was like manna from Heaven. I walk into a strange, new city and out of its million inhabitants I meet him and here I was ensconced in his airy flat with all mod. cons. and Sophie, his stout, African woman who 'did' for him in the mornings, coming in with a tray of tea and toast, giving me her polished-mahogany charm complete with broad, piano-keyboard smile.

In those early days I found living with Morry very interesting. He was quite garrulous, as would be expected, and an authority on all things political and current, which quickly gave me the vibes of general conversation in the South Africa of the day. He had a way of putting you at ease by being self-deprecating and by telling derogatory stories about Jews as only Jews would do.

"Did you know that Johannesburg is nicknamed Jewburg. There are so many of us here. It's the gold you know. Where else would you find so many Goldbergs? You know how all the streets run in straight lines, criss-crossing in a grid pattern. Well, they say that it was us Jews who planned the city and put in far more streets than were necessary so there would be smaller blocks and more corner shops because people pay more for them."

One late afternoon, when I had been with him for a few days, he was rattling on about current government affairs, very much the main topic of conversation wherever you went at that time.

"The place is not the same since the Nationalists took over," he lamented, referring to the 1949 General Election that had swept the Nationalist Party, mainly Afrikaans-speaking, into power for the first time in their existence, overturning the dominance of the mainly English-speaking United Party, who had ruled continuously for the past forty years. "They're heading for a republic, you know. They're hell-bent on severing the country from the British Crown. Still that won't affect the economy much. The United Party says the country will go bankrupt, that foreign investment will dry up. But that's bunkum. Big business doesn't bother about politics, provided it doesn't mean nationalisation. There's gold and diamonds and all kinds of minerals down there," he jerked his thumb to the floor with a grimace, "and they'll come running.

"But it isn't the same since Malan (the new Prime Minister) and his crew took over. You know, these Japies are rigging the constituencies, moving the boundaries so they'll be sure of future elections. They mean business," and he was right for the Nationalists held uninterrupted power for the next forty or more years until white politics ceased when black power took over.

I was interested to hear the political views of a resident of South Africa, to feel the heartbeat as it were. I had gained a fair knowledge of things while in Southern Rhodesia for the two countries were very close. But now it was interesting to hear what the South Africans themselves thought apart from what one read in the newspapers. The Afrikaans takeover of government, three years before I arrived, was the biggest political upheaval since the formation of the Union.

Many years before that event Dr Daniel Francois Malan had become a predikant (minister) of the staunch, Protestant, Dutch Reformed Church. Ten years later he abandoned his ministry and became the editor of *Die Burger*, the Nationalist newspaper. Following that he made politics his career and became a Member of Parliament on the side of the opposition. A crusty, austere man of profound convictions he quickly made his mark and climbed through his peers. He had an unwavering belief in White supremacy, maintaining that Blacks, as the children of Ham were condemned in the Bible to be forever 'hewers of wood and carriers of water' and he intended to see that penalty enforced.

The Boers, who later became known as Afrikaners, saw him as a back-veldt Moses and naturally accepted him as their leader. He it was, through his machinations, who had *Afrikaans* recognised as an official language. Prior to that the *Taal* had been regarded as a polyglot lingua of Dutch, bastardised English and other derivatives. He it was too, to his everlasting shame, coined the word *apartheid* and made it government official policy. The separation of Blacks, Whites and Coloured into their designated reservations earned South Africa worldwide condemnation and alienation and certainly hastened the Black revolution that ended White supremacy.

"They've got the makings of Nazis these people," Morry went ruefully on. "They're going to carve up the country into black and white areas. *'Apartheid'* they call it. The idea is to keep the Blacks 'in their place' so they won't interfere with White expansion. I can tell you, I'm scared. They're anti Semitic. When they've got the Blacks to 'heel' they'll come after us Jews. Then they'll go after the Catholics. At the same time they'll stifle all English-speaking people, keep them as second rate, reserving all the top jobs for the Taal (another name for Afrikaans). But the Niggers might stop them before then and if that happens, everybody will be up the spout. Do you want a woman tonight?"

Without waiting for an answer he went to the phone saying as he went, "Sorry about that. I should have thought of it before." He dialled a number while I was too dazed to reply, too bewildered to really take in what he had said. In the same breath when talking politics he'd come out with this. Was I hearing him correctly? When he spoke on the line it was obvious that I had.

"Barney? Can you arrange something for a friend of mine who's staying here for a few days? ... Cathie? Oh no, she's as dry as old rope and too small. This guy'd eat her up. He's big, strong. He's been living in the jungle for years ... Who? Rusty ... No, haven't met her ... All right, I'll take your word for it. Eightish then. OK. See you."

He put down the phone and immediately took up the thread of politics again. But I wasn't listening, couldn't comprehend the banalities he was talking about. This, the most important thing in life, just sandwiched between sentences. Was that how it worked here, in this kind of society? Was that all the importance it was given? Surely life could not be as mundane as all that?

In a whirl and not a little apprehensive, I cut into his continued tirade against Malan's takeover of the government and mumbled something about not being interested in prostitutes. "Prostitutes? Hell, no, these girls aren't whores. They don't do it for money. They just like a good time and if they take up with a fella for a time and he buys a few presents along the way then they're happy. Barney's a funny guy. He has this sort of quirk, he gets a kick out of bringing people together, seeing them going off happy together. He has a business down Rissik Street and when he shuts up shop he keeps open house in the back room in the evenings. You'd be surprised at the people who drop in there. Doesn't allow anything on the premises, you know. He'll throw in a few beers and even some of the hard stuff if you like, to make the party sociable. No charge. He could be had-up for running an illicit business if money was involved. Barney's just a great guy. I'll take you down there some time."

All through dinner Morry prattled on putting the country to rights while my mind was a tangle of desires and apprehensions. Around eight o'clock the doorbell rang like a bugle call to battle. I'm not sure what I expected, a hard-faced besom or a loose slut. The girl who walked in was nothing like either of these. Tall, film-starish, with shoulder-length, chestnut hair tied back into a fat sheep's-tail down her neck, she was stunning. In a close fitting dress that did everything for her without shouting she wore a stole draped round her back and through her elbows. The kind of girl you'd be proud to walk with into a cocktail lounge and poke the nose of any guy who was coarse or swore near her. In her short walk in she carried herself with poise and assurance and I thought that apart from the colour of her hair there was nothing rusty about her. I suddenly felt terribly gawky.

Morry broke the ice with introductions then said, very diplomatically I thought, he was going down to the off-licence for a few beers and went out leaving us to it. Nice guy, but I felt embarrassingly alone. How did one go about these things? She was so at ease while I was completely tongue-tied. I don't remember what I said, probably something about the weather or how nice she looked. No, not that, that would have been too personal. But I do remember the amused smile she wore while I stumbled with words.

Presently I excused myself, went to the bathroom and had a good look and talk to myself in the mirror, took a couple of minutes respite, braced my shoulders, and went back again. Rusty was sitting on the settee facing me, flipping through a magazine. As I entered she laid aside the paper and crossed her long legs, taking care it seemed to show a great deal of thigh in the process. Smiling, she patted the cushion beside her. Gingerly, but trying not to show it, I did as I was bid. That resolve I had made to myself in the mirror was evaporating fast.

"What do you do? You know, what's your line?" I asked.

She gave me a funny look and in retrospect I can see her stifling a laugh. She looked away, perhaps to hide her amusement and answered with off-hand confidence. "Oh, I model a bit and act a little. I manage." I was sure she did. Very well.

"You haven't met Morry before?" I was garrulous, the great conversationalist.

"No. I've heard him on radio and all that, but this is the first time I've met him. He's all right." The quick summing-up was said in a throwaway, flat voice.

Suddenly she took charge, stood up and flattened down her dress. "Let's have some music," she commanded, walking over to the gramophone. "What kind of records does he have?"

"Do you think he'll mind?"

"Nonsense. That's what it's there for, silly man."

She stopped in her tracks, turned back and stood right in front of me, put hands on my shoulders and looked up into my eyes. Something about the nearness of our bodies, the warmth of her, the scent of her hair, something about her smile, and I felt more tongue-tied than ever. "You're much younger than you look behind that beard, aren't you. You haven't been around much."

I thought I had been around a great deal. I tried to remember the little laddie who had started out from Torryburn, (how many years ago?) and thought I'd come a long way indeed. But then I came to the conclusion (such insight!) that we might be been thinking at cross-purposes.

"I'm sorry." I said painfully.

"Oh, don't apologise," she whooped, the laughter in her voice. "You're lovely. Such a breath of fresh air. I don't like *experienced* men. They all follow the same pattern. Say the same glib things. You're so different." Her hands moved from my shoulders and went round my neck. "Come on now. Relax. I'm not going to eat you."

With her touch my shy restraints loosened and I felt emboldened to put my arms round her. "That's more like it," she said, "I'm not such a ogre, am I?"

"I never thought you were. I mean … It's just …"

"I know. Don't try to explain," she comforted. Then to break the embarrassing moment she changed the subject, smiling, "Morry said you wear a kilt and all that."

"Yes. That's my travelling garb."

"Why didn't you keep it on? I'd loved to have seen you in it." Then with a teasing smile she added, "I would have plagued you to tell me what you wore underneath."

I felt myself blushing under my beard yet suddenly bold and devil-may-care, answering, "In that case I would have had to tell you, as the Highlander told the American woman who accosted him with the same question in Edinburgh," I added in a broad Scots burr, "Mam, there's nothing worn under the kilt. Everything is in guid working order."

She shrieked with delight, "Oh, I might have tested you on that score if you really had said that to me," and I curled my toes with shock and sweet anticipation.

"Come on," she turned and took my hand, "Let's see what he's got to dance to."

Together we chose a Sinatra number. I wound the handle, placed the head over the shiny, hard, bakelite 78-record, listened to the hiss of the needle and stood up. We were very close. Suddenly I felt suave, debonair, master of the situation. Frankie was singing 'Come Fly With Me' and I took Rusty in a firm, masterly hold and whirled her to the moon and through the stars that were all about the room. There was a new look on her face when I looked down and caught her eye. We both laughed aloud and twirled with outrageous abandon. I was turning on some diabolical steps and she was following like a feather. Mad fools, it couldn't last. On a backward sweep we cannoned against the arm of the sofa and went over in a welter of arms and legs to land in a heap, laughing and giggling in delight.

Then the music stopped with a CRASH, as is said in *The Shooting of Dan MacGrew*.

It was not so much a crash as a scraping of the key in the door lock, but it had the same sudden shock effect that froze us in mid-movement and stilled our voices on a note. The door opened and Morry walked in carrying some bottles.

He really had been to the off-licence! He never said a word but he took in an eyeful of Rusty's long legs before we untangled ourselves and stood up.

So we sat around for a while. Morry drank his beer, Rusty a gin-and-it and I a fruit juice. The conversation was more stilted and painful than even my early attempt at girl-talk. We were all waiting for something to happen. I could see Rusty getting agitated. As host, the ball was in Morry's court and after some time in making up his mind, he hit it.

Emptying his glass he went through to the kitchen, presumably for a refill though he didn't ask us if we wanted one. Seeing how well we had been getting on, he'd shout he was going out again and stay for a while. But he didn't. The doorbell rang and we heard him answer it.

"Yes, he's here. Just a minute." Then louder in our direction, "Jock, someone to see you."

Someone to see me! I didn't know a soul and who would know I was staying here? Bewildered, I stumbled through to the door where Morry quickly put my jacket under my arm, pushed a piece of paper into my hand and shoved me, none too gently, out to the landing and shut the door. There was nobody outside waiting but me. The paper said, 'Give me half-an-hour. I'll see how the wind blows.'

I wandered the streets in a daze, drinking coffees in cafes, listening to cruel records in the jukeboxes that only reminded me of what I had lost. 'See how the wind blows'! I knew how it blew. There was a gale brewing and I had been pushed into harbour out of harm's way while Morry Abel did his best to prove that he was able, to a girl half his age and twice his size.

I stayed out most of the evening and when I went back I listened some time at the door to make sure I wasn't interrupting anything before tapping. When he opened the door Morry did not look a happy man. There was no satisfied, smug smile on his face. No merry twinkle in his eye. He looked older, smaller, slouched, his bald pate even more shiny in the light. He muttered something about having had to send Rusty home early in a taxi, not well, wrong time of the month, it seemed. There was no conviction in his voice, nor was the excuse very convincing considering she had obviously come out prepared for battle. She had said to pass on her goodbyes to me when I got back, for which I was grateful. Not exactly 'a good time had by all'. More an all round disaster. Ah well, *c'est la vie*!

The next evening Morry took me along to the dress rehearsal of a grand show, 'The Parade of Nations Ball', which he was producing and which was to go on the next evening with the Governor General in attendance. He introduced me to Nicholas Monsarrat, who was based in South Africa at the time as a big noise in the UK Information Office. We spoke a little while then Morry asked him if I could have a copy of his best-selling new book, *The Cruel Sea*, which embarrassed me extremely. The author gave a rather noncommittal "We'll see," and I was glad when I heard no more about it.

I wrote in my diary that night, *'Morry has some publicity stunts in mind for me which I'm not altogether in favour of. Anyway we'll see how things pan out.'* They didn't.

He had it in mind to be my manager and had dreamed up all manner of stunts. Some were feasible, such as he taking me to some of the clothing and boot factories to advertise their wares in their catalogues. Others were downright daft. I saw myself as being some kind of stooge, the thought of which made my flesh creep. One of these schemes was to have me walking through the streets wearing my kilt and carrying my pack with a sandwich board over my shoulders advertising somebody's taxis. Something like "I have travelled Africa on foot, but if you want to travel in comfort go by Biggs taxi."

At this I drew the line and refused to co-operate. Up till then he had been the epitome of the warm-hearted, expansive friend. He would take me round to his friends, mostly Jewish business men, but latterly I had got the feeling he was showing me off as some prize animal he had captured. When he saw I was not going to play ball with his money-making schemes his attitude changed and I began to feel I was making a nuisance of myself. When I got a job I moved into the YMCA and then my erstwhile friend and benefactor played his last card. Before I had collected my first pay packet he sent me a hefty bill for my laundry that Sophie had done while I had been with him.

However, the piece that he instigated in the *Rand Daily Mail* brought enormous returns. First, a lady who said her maiden name was Yates from Low Valleyfield, a village only a mile away my own in Fife, rang to invite me to spend a weekend with her and her husband, which I did and enjoyed very much. Her father who lived with them still had his Scot's accent that was as broad as the Firth of Forth. What made this visit lucky for me was the fact that her husband worked at OK Bazaars, the biggest department store in the city, and when I said I would be looking for a job he told me to visit him in his office and he would see that I got one. He carried considerable clout for he was chief buyer for the business.

During my visit my host told an interesting little story that was poignant to that era so soon after World War II. To appreciate the gist it is necessary to explain that the man was very deaf and wore two hearing-aids that were of the primitive type of those times. He also used a walking stick sometimes. He had started a 'Hard of Hearing Club' in Johannesburg which was growing in membership. The day came when he was called to the manager's office to meet a new, important sales representative. When he entered he found a suave, bespectacled, Japanese gentleman smiling to meet him. My new friend exploded. All the nightmare memories of the Japanese prisoner-of-war camp flooded over him, the beating by the guards using their rifle-butts as he rolled on the ground vainly trying to avoid the blows, hearing the crack as his knee broke, felt again his fingers breaking as he tried to cover his head, the excruciating pain as his eardrums burst. Now, his eyes blazing and letting out a battle-cry roar like a first World War soldier leaping from the trenches on a bayonet-charge, he went for the salesman with murderous intent, his raised walking-stick flaying the air like a Samurai sword. The Oriental made it to the door, but only just. Rather strange to relate, he didn't do any business with OK Bazaars that day, nor did any more of his countrymen in all the time my friend worked there.

So I went to work in the warehouse of OK Bazaars for £30 a month and left Morry Abel's flat.

Another phone call passed on by the *Rand Daily Mail* was from a Mrs McLean whom I had met with her husband, Dr McLean, up in Zanzibar where they were holidaying while working for the Ground Nut Scheme, then on its very last legs. Dr McLean, an eye specialist, had told me he was going to West Africa soon but he had left the Government Service and set up practice on his own in Johannesburg. His consulting rooms were on the 11th storey of Manor Mansions so I got a fine view of the city.

They were a fine couple and I saw quite a lot of them during the couple of months I worked in the city. They invited me to the Caledonian Society Highland Games and Highland Ball at night and insisted that I wear my kilt for the occasions. It was grand, especially seeing the march of the massed Pipe Bands.

Other outings were also memorable. I remember most the African War Dances at the Crown Mines. Each Sunday morning they had these dances at one of the mines. There were over a dozen different tribes taking part, each having its own group to display their traditional dances. The Zulu tribe was by far the best and the most picturesque.

An interesting thing that followed the newspaper article was a visit from a representative of Springbok Radio who wanted to interview me on their programme next day. I was still staying with Morry then and when I mentioned with enthusiasm that I was going on the air he knocked me back when he asked me if I could manage to work something into the script to thank him for all he had done for me. That's when the acid drops fell into the mixture. I was most grateful for his hospitality and help, but for him to openly ask thanks ... and for me to broadcast it ...! Though taken aback, I reasoned it was all part of his job. Publicity was his lifeline. So I mentioned it to the scriptwriter but he said it couldn't be done. This was a commercial programme advertising General Tyres and no individual names other than the people who were involved could be mentioned. When I told Morry he took it with a scowl and things were never the same after that.

I enjoyed my first day at OK Bazaars warehouse. The work was hardly stimulating, mainly opening crates and stacking the merchandise, but after the time on my own the company and chatter was good. Like Richard Burton's traveller coming in from the desert I relished everyday chit-chat and banter. I knew that there would come a time when it would all seem inane and I would have to travel on to find new wonders and more worlds to conquer. But for now, I looked forward to going to work. After the first few days I seemed to have made the grade for they raised my wage from £30 to £35 per month without my asking for it.

More publicity came my way. Too much in fact. OK Bazaars had a programme on Springbok Radio called 'Pot of Gold' and I was invited to be a guest on one show. It went on 'live', no recording, and I found the experience quite a thrill. I was paid three guineas for about three minutes broadcasting. Also, Johannesburg's other paper *The Star* interviewed me for two columns and a photograph in their weekend edition.

With all that publicity life was hardly worth living. Two radio broadcasts and two newspaper reports puts you in the public eye. People would stop me on the street and there was even some finger pointing. To many that would be the spice of life but in my solitary way I felt I had lost my freedom. To escape, I shaved off my beard. This made quite a difference to my appearance and after that life returned to something like normal.

When I walked into the barbers one Saturday morning and said I wanted to have my beard shaved off the fellow looked in amazement. "You mean trimmed," he corrected. "No, off," I insisted. He just stood and looked and I thought he was going to refuse. Then he let go a blasphemy with great emphasis and said incredulously, "I'd give three years' holiday to have a beard like that," as he reluctantly threw the sheet round my shoulders.

In a way I was sorry to lose my ginger, doormat fuzz, but there were compensations for its loss too. On Monday morning when in the queue to clock-in at work I overheard from further back in the line a girl's hushed whisper to her friend, "Oh look, he's a *young* man!" Involuntarily I turned to see a dark-haired beauty blush from her neck to the top of her head in mortified embarrassment when she saw that I had heard. When I smiled she covered her face with her hand but her eyes were sparkling through her open fingers.

Her name, I soon learned, was Magda van den Berg and by strange coincidence we found ourselves, over the next few days, sometimes sitting at the same table at lunchtime in the canteen. I debated whether to ask her out but felt it was not fair to start a friendship that must end when I moved on. There came a day, however, when she hesitantly said that she had told her parents of me and they invited me home for dinner one evening. Would I come? Indeed I would, gratefully and pleased.

The invitation led to others, sometimes at the weekends, and these gave me an insight into a section of South African society that was quite unique, the pro-British, English-speaking, Afrikaans people.

After the Boer War ended in 1901 and all the states, Transvaal, Natal, Orange Free and Cape, were united into the Union of South Africa under British rule, not all the Afrikaners, were anti-British. When the Great War broke out in 1914 a great many joined the South African volunteer force that went to Europe and fought under the Union Jack. All the South Africans, Dutch and British shoulder-to-shoulder, were commanded by General Smuts, a redoubtable enemy commander during the South African war, now turned an equally powerful ally.

After that war and later, a good number of Afrikaners chose to follow the British way of life, speak English as a first language, and follow British habits and mannerisms. On my journey to the Cape I met many men who were over-the-top, English 'varsity types, sporting striped blazers on all occasions, slender pipe clenched between gleaming teeth, speaking the clipped, *pukka sahib* jargon, who turned out to be 100% Afrikaner, and proud of it.

But not all Afrikaners who followed British ways were caricatures. Most adopted the simple, family ways and dress of ordinary British people. And such were the van den Bergs. I felt perfectly at home with them … and yet there was a brittleness there. At times in mid-sentence a pregnant hiatus would drop and I would realise that what I had said could be misconstrued or taken as innuendo or a plain reference to their dual nationality and they so wanted their Britishness not to be in question. A rather amusing incident in this line happened a month or two later after I'd left OK Bazaars and Johannesburg and gone to Durban.

The beach there is not for the faint hearted or average swimmers. It is wild and rough and only the strongest swimmers can battle through the pounding waves. But if you are a surfboard fanatic, Durban beach is Mecca. Despite the stampeding white horses from the Antarctic which vie for supremacy with those tearing in from the Indian Ocean to crash on the beach, ordinary humans as well as water-gods come in their thousands to swim to their limit or frolic in the surf. This is the haven to which the residents of Jo'burg and other land-locked places love to go for holidays.

I was lying on the beach after enjoying my first sight of sea and a dip since Mombasa, apart from a mere glimpse but no swim at Beira. There were a few people scattered about but none where I was. None, that is, except one girl looking a dream in a black one-piece swimsuit, sitting in the sand with her legs curled demurely under her. Unbelievably, in one of those million-to-one coincidences, I recognised Magda and she me. Perhaps the coincidence of our meeting was not one of such great odds for everyone on holiday goes to the beach and everyone there had to settle between two safety flags and most people were on view, so a meeting was not such a miracle. Anyway, Magda's pensive mood suddenly came alive and my face must have shown surprise and pleasure. She wriggled to her feet and stood waiting for me, a beautiful, wonderful, figure. The scene was the stuff of dreams or fiction, but this one was true. But there was one awful fly in the ointment.

I mentioned that there was just one girl on that part of the beach. That was true though not quite accurate, in that she was not alone. In a deckchair facing away from the sea, so I didn't see until I arrived, was a rather hefty woman of large dimensions, wearing a sun hat. Magda welcomed me rather apprehensively and almost comically, offered her hand which I took awkwardly. She then introduced me to her aunt who had accompanied her on holiday, obviously as chaperon. Here was one old Victorian, Afrikaner custom which had not been shed in the metamorphous change to British ways. Aunt was obviously of the old stock who pronounced Magda in the guttural, Afrikaans way, "Machta".

Auntie was not so welcoming. She received my greeting with stoic reserve, as if she suspected that our meeting was a tryst, long since prearranged. Magda and I sat in the sand and talked, the frosty atmosphere gradually melting. We were like children at the seaside in the charge of an eagle-eyed guardian. At last I said how about a swim. Magda was keen and since auntie said nothing to curtail her she struggled to put on her swimming cap, making sure all her ringlets were tucked in.

Now comes the point of this little tale that shows that no matter how one tries to bury their ancestry, it is always there to jump out like a jack-in-the-box when a word touches the spring.

When Magda was finished fixing her cap I said in jest, "Are you ready for the fray?" Magda suddenly stiffened with shock and aunt shot up in her chair, her face purple with anger. A knife went through me and I wondered what I had said to produce such reaction. To bridge the void that had suddenly dropped in front of us I changed the mood and said in mock American, "OK then, let's go."

We ran down to the water and splashed in. When we were waist deep and well out of aunt's earshot Magda wiped the water off her still red face and asked, "Why did you say that?" "Say what?" I queried, astonished and baffled. "You know, that remark you made," unable to repeat my awful words. "What, I only joked about being ready for the fray. You know, ready for the battle, the fight. It's a common saying," I replied. Suddenly the tension in her faded and she smiled. "Oh, I'm sorry. That's not what it means in Afrikaans." We didn't dare mention the subject to aunt and I doubted if she would have been placated if we had tried. After that she watched us like a hawk, dialogue was stilted and the day ruined. We never met again and Magda van den Berg passed into memory.

Jo'burg was fun and very interesting. A strange town, very friendly but hard and ruthless and lawless too. Its crime wave resembled Chicago during the heyday of its badmen. Every Monday the weekend's crime list was given in the papers. After one run-down on murder, theft and mayhem that I read the police officer's summary reported, "Quite a normal weekend." I was advised to, and I did, carry my pistol wherever I went at night. It seemed quite melodramatic to walk about a town 'pistol-packing', but no more melodramatic than some of the things that happened on those streets at night, and even during the day some times.

I enjoyed my time there immensely, but when I felt I knew the place and had lined my pockets enough I screwed my dude clothes into my rucksack, donned my kilt and lit out for the wide open veldt. My prearranged destination, the end of my journey, was Cape Town and the nearness of my goal was exciting. The desire to make a beeline for it was a great temptation. The most direct route lay through the Orange Free State but I had heard so much of Natal, the province to the east, home of the Zulus and the place of the Drakensbergs (Dragons Mountains) that I decided to make my way there although it meant a considerable detour. So I struck out south, via Newcastle, Dundee, Glencoe and Estcourt.

There were very few lifts in spite of hundreds of cars that passed. Like the city the country was turning more lawless. There had been cases of drivers getting knocked on the head by people to whom they had given lifts so I did not blame drivers for being wary. Only two weeks before there had been a case of a man being murdered by a couple of men whom he had given a lift. These were not necessarily black against white affairs. The culprits were mostly 'poor whites', a breed that existed only in South Africa, white tramps (who was I to point a finger!) who, because of drink-addiction, laziness or ill-luck, lived a squalid existence often below that of the poorest natives. I did get some pick-ups but I did a lot of walking too. I camped at the side of the road, but warily, more on edge than I had been in most of my time in northern parts, aware that man is the most deadly animal.

*

The car drew up just like any one of the many that had stopped to give me lifts in the past couple of years. I was in the foothills of the Drakensberg mountains where I was heading to climb the lofty, rugged peaks. I had been walking a few hours and the going was a hard, upward slog, so was more than a little pleased when the vehicle drew up beside me and a middle aged man with smiling round face, took his pipe out of his mouth and asked if I would like a lift. This was to prove no ordinary lift, apart from the fact that in the back seat were three gorgeous girls. Mr Milne, the driver and father of the girls and his wife were to prove to be among the kindest people I was privileged to meet, and during my travels I received a great deal of kindness from a great number of people.

Andrew Milne, an ex-bank manager who had taken early retirement, now owned and ran a 600 acre guest farm on which he also ran some cattle, some 16 miles from Estcourt. 'Spitzberg', their farm, was on my way to the mountains and rather than just drop me off when we arrived there he invited me in to have lunch before going on my way. The girls seemed discreetly enthusiastic that I accept the offer and I was pleased and grateful to do so. From then on things, just got better and better. So began a life-long, family friendship that has passed down the generations.

Maureen, twenty-one, the eldest of the daughters, taught at a private school near Pietermaritzburg. Monica, two years younger, did clerical work in Durban and Pauline, seventeen, was in her last year at High School. They all lived away from home and dad had been to Estcourt to collect them and bring them home for their annual holidays.

Mum, Mrs Doris Milne, a lovely, elegant, warm-hearted lady, hurried out from the house with affectionate greetings for her family, after which I was introduced. From that moment I was no stranger. Mrs Milne took me to her heart and for the next forty years we corresponded and exchanged Christmas cards. Indeed, when she died I learned from her daughter that she always referred to me as 'the son she never had' and in all that time she kept my photograph on her shelf. It was the most touching, soul-warming compliment I had in all my life.

The mood during the meal was hilarious and I really did feel as one of the family. Mr and Mrs Milne with the girls bright-eyed around them plied me to stay on for a time and I was enjoying myself too much not to stay over for a night or two. This stretched to nearly a week and each day the parents thanked me for giving my time to make the girls' holiday so enjoyable and I felt so mean and selfish because the pleasure was all mine.

Near the end of the week when I said I must go they warmly invited me to return in two week's time when they planned to have a big *braai-vleis* (barbecue). On the day I left Mr Milne said he would drive me up as far as the road went. Indeed, all the family would go too and have a picnic before seeing me off.

So we all went to Bush Man's River and had a rare time picnicking, laughing, teasing, all enjoying the company, the banter and talk. It was hot and I stripped to my shorts and dived in the river for a swim and the girls did their best to keep me from getting out again, all ending up wetter than I was. Great fun. Then mum and dad rested while we four went looking for fossils. The place was rich with them. We found many pieces of fossilised wood with perfect grain markings, proving that the near bare landscape was once forested.

We then piled into the car and drove to a point below the great, castellated peaks of Champagne Castle and Cathkin, both soaring well over 10,000ft. into the clouds. This was where we parted and my hike began. The car journey had saved me nearly fifty miles of hard, uphill walking and moreover I had been able to leave most of my kit at Spitzberg farm and travel light with only tent and a few essentials in a little knapsack I always carried. When I knew I would not be carrying my full pack I decided to leave my boots behind and walk in my sandshoes. The boots were looking in a sorry state with one burst across the toecap and I thought I must preserve what life was still in them for the heavy walking in full pack down to the Cape.

We said our goodbyes and the girls each gave me a light, sisterly kiss on the cheek, all slightly embarrassed, perhaps because it was in front of their parents, and so was I. The car moved off, arms waving out of the open windows and I suddenly felt very lonely.

Next day, setting off very early, I climbed Champagne Castle which at almost 11,000ft. was thought for a long time to be the highest in the range. Later, with more accurate surveying several others were found to top it. The climb was strenuous but not too difficult. There was a path of sorts most of the way up and starting off from about 6000ft. it didn't take too long. Cathkin, relatively near and looking far more daunting with its sheer faces, was out of my league as a single climber. On top of the Castle I felt a wonderful elation from just being there. Away to the west and south, below the haze and cloud banks, lay Basutoland (Lesotho), part of the border of which was formed by the Drakensbergs. Basutoland, a British Colony administered from London, was like an island, completely surrounded by the land of South Africa.

Champagne Castle and champagne air. I could almost feel the fizz in my blood as I inhaled. Being all alone on the top of the world and near the end of my long journey was really intoxicating. Coming up I got a grand panoramic view of the low-lying country. There was a drought over the country, but up on the higher ground it rained occasionally and the land was greener and fresher. How cut up with soil erosion it looked down below. The ground was parched and yellow and the livestock was in a bad way. It was a general drought all over the country and up in the Northern Transvaal and in the Free State the cattle were dying by the hundreds.

After a few days pottering about in the Champagne region I set off for Giant's Castle, another massif some fifteen to twenty miles' walking away, I reckoned, depending on the terrain. But at the end of the day when I estimated I had covered more than all that distance I didn't seem to be any nearer to it.

That evening about the time I was thinking of camping for the night I saw a clump of trees some distance up the side of the mountain with a track, almost covered over, leading up to it. What luck! Firewood was as scarce as hens' teeth up here and to find trees just when required was indeed a godsend. When I got nearer my luck increased beyond bounds. I could hear a trickle of running water. What luxury. My bottle was more than half empty and to find a fresh running supply ... wow! But that was not all I found there.

As I approached I saw, near the trees, the scattered remains of what was once a house, now not much more than a pile of stones, and as I entered that little glade I found three headstones. There was another grave a little distance away from these others that had been built up with stones but there was no headstone there.

After the surprise, shock even, I took a closer look at those lonely graves away out there on the mountain slope. There was nothing unusual about them except that one bore the names of two people who had died one day after the other. The inscription read : *To the Memory of Martha and Joseph Wray. Died 9th and 10th July 1901.* What tragedy did that cover ... wartime casualties, double accident, extreme sorrow of the second partner too much to bear ... mayhem, murder?

A cemetery! A queer place to camp, but there was water and trees to get firewood. The water was only a mere trickle, just a few inches broad, and I had to dig away some clumps of earth to get at it, but it was bubbling merrily and seemed quite clean. I picked some dry sticks from the graves, thanking these long dead bodies and hoping they didn't mind me walking over them. How eerie these white headstones looked in the firelight. Still they were shelter from the wind that was blowing and promised to be cold during the night.

Next morning when I was preparing to strike camp a little pickup truck drove by on the dirt road below, the only vehicle I'd seen in days. Then it stopped, reversed and a man got out and climbed up the path to the graveyard. We passed the time of day and the usual greetings. He said this was his land I was on. His family owned all this side of the mountain, hundreds of acres. I thought he was complaining but that was not the reason for his approach. He asked if I'd slept the night there and when I said I had he asked, casually it seemed, if I had had a good night. When I assured him I had, he asked if I had seen or heard anything strange through the night. Feeling it was rather an odd question I asked what exactly he meant. "Ghosts," he said bluntly. I smiled and said no, I had not been disturbed. I thought he was joking and laughed.

Undeterred by my scepticism he went on, "Well, you see that pile of stones, that's the remains of my parents' house and these graves are those of a long line of previous owners, not one died a natural death." He went on to say that seven people had died in that house. Some had committed suicide. One man was reported to have died of rinderpest, an animal disease. That was long ago but they were still supposed to roam the place. When his parents bought it they were told it was haunted but they scoffed at the idea. However so many unnatural sounds and things happened there they had the house razed to the ground, believing that theirs might be the next headstones to join the formidable group in the glade, and built another dwelling on the farthest reaches of their land, where he now lived.

An interesting little cameo, and an interesting tail to it too. A few years later, after I had finally returned from Africa, I heard from Mrs Milne, with whom I corresponded regularly, that her daughter, Maureen, had married Peter Kerr, a man a bit older than she. Nearly forty years later when my wife, Maureen, and I visited South Africa we visited Maureen and Peter near Bergville, in the Drakensbergs, where they were caretaking at a holiday camp there. In conversation I mentioned my queer experience when camping near there all those years ago. Peter exploded, "Was that you? I was the one who came on you that morning. That pile of stones was my family home." Peter and Maureen, now live in Howick, Natal.

On that day when we met at the gravestones I told Peter I was heading for Giant's Castle. With a wild exclamation he said I was on the wrong track. No wonder I thought it was a long way. So apart from a long friendship, our meeting that morning was very fortunate. I may still have been wandering aimlessly around the Drakensbergs looking for the elusive Giant's Castle, by now of course a local legend like Peter's haunted house.

I was a wee bit mad at myself for having gone the wrong way. I had to retrace my steps to the Bushman's River, then go up the other way. I must have done thirty miles that day.

Just below Giant's Castle was a Government Rest Camp. I asked if I could camp in the grounds but the Keeper would not allow it. After my long jaunt that day – my pack, though depleted, was still about 40 pounds – I decided on the luxury of hiring a hut for 6/- a day and wallowed in the comfort of it. There was a kitchen with a fine stove in it so I decided to try baking some scones on it as a change from the ones I usually made in the ashes of the fire. I did a couple of girdle (*griddle* to non Scots) scones just by putting the dough on top of the stove. They were not so bad – at least I got my teeth through them. Next day I tried some oven scones, but they came out like bricks from a kiln. Even the edible ones were not exactly like mother used to make. The trouble was my flour and rice got mixed up a bit and all through the scones there were these hard pieces of rice. Still, I was quite proud of my first attempts.

After a day or two of such sumptuous comfort and *cordon bleu* fare I took to my gypsy ways again, laying my head down wherever the day's end happened to find me. On the days I made the main climbs I left my camp on trust, tying the door strings, assuming no thieves would venture up there, and going on my way. My trust was never broken. At the end of each day's expedition I returned 'home' to find it as I had left it.

I climbed Giant's Castle and other peaks and gazed down on the lower regions in the grip of a drought, parched land that had a yellow, jaundiced look. But up in the heights the grass was green and fresh and the air was moistened each morning with dew. Pensively I wandered through this aerial world, walking, meandering, climbing and soaking in its grandeur. The lofty, soft blue summits swirling with clouds and the green valleys between filled with morning mists had the hazy, dreamy appearance of a Chinese painting. It made me just want to lose myself among them.

I searched out and gazed wistfully at Bushman paintings that have been left on the overhanging rock walls of these mountains. Such artists! What wonderful skills they displayed. Such an eye for movement and animal form. So gifted to capture forever the grace of antelopes in flight, the subtlety of the hunters. Such silent eloquence from a people often regarded by both 'big' blacks and whites as almost sub-human. Grim reminders that this was once the home of those people who had owned and roamed this land from ocean to ocean, since time began.

Apart from the artistry displayed I was interested in the Bushman's technical ability to make paints. Paint essentially requires two components, a colouring matter and a binder. The colouring matter, or pigment, is usually made into a powder and the binder must be fluid enough to allow the mixture to be applied to the surface and thereafter dry and hold the film to the surface. Preferably, when painting on rock faces, even sheltered ones under overhanging slabs, the binder should give the paint some protection from the elements. The Bushmen knew this, no doubt through trial and error. There must have always been some genius among every group who saw the problem of paint longevity and came up with the answer.

For colour the early stone-age man made carbon black from crushed wood char, yellows, browns and reds from ochre clays and white from chalk. For binders they used blood, the whites of eggs and animal fats. To apply the paint they used sharp pointed sticks and twigs chewed to form a fibrous brush end. There is even evidence of coloured powder having been blown through a narrow, hollow bone on to a picture pre-painted with hot fat, the first form of spray-painting. If a civilisation may be measured by its art the Bushmen were a very advanced people.

But foolishly they had treated first the Bantus' and then white men's cattle like wild animals and killed them. It is likely too that because these intruders to their land were quickly killing off the wild game the Bushmen were driven through necessity to attack domestic animals. Whatever the reason, the little folk, the Bushmen, were classed as vermin and exterminated in the region. When cattle killing became rife in an area the farmers banded together to hunt the Bushmen down and shoot them, just as farmers in England would organise a combined weekend foxhunt. Later, I met some longtime residents who could remember, sixty years before, when the last Bushman was shot dead in the Drakensberg Mountains. Exterminated.

I was doleful as I returned to my camp from the paintings. I mused over the primitive art as I cooked and ate my meal, trying to imagine those people who had lived in this paradise before the strangers came, before there were such things as politics, land claims, power and greed: before those intruders brought with them the virus of self-possession and the right-to-own, a deadly disease to a people who had never known such selfish ideas nor could ever imagine such ways could exist and so had no defence against it. When I touched the paint in the overhang caves, perhaps thousands of years old, I felt that tingle of time-bridge that I later felt when I held an Ancient Egyptian brush in my fingers.

That evening as I sat with my back against a large boulder drinking my coffee, the fire told its story, culled no doubt from things read long ago, past conversations and ideas forged on the anvil of long, lonesome miles of tramping. A story so poignant and sad of the little people, the San, who had led an elf-like existence, hunting, playing, singing and painting, until they were surprised by the real people who had little or no imagination, and like all fairy people who are suddenly caught, they vanished.

The day came when I could dally no longer in the heady air of the high mountains. I rolled up my tent, raked my fire out and covered the ashes with earth scratched from between some rocks and headed for Bushmans River and Spitzberg farm. It was no easy walk. My sandshoes were now in tatters. Though tied with string they kept sliding to the side on the downhill slope. Some people were appalled at me setting out to walk such distances in sandshoes but in their good state I found them light and easy footware for roaming about the hills. But they came to an end one slippy step when the sole of one was ripped completely from the upper. The other was not much better, so I took them off and stuffed them into my knapsack to dispose of them at the first tidy bin I found when I reached habitation.

I had hoped to go further that day but the fifteen miles to Bushmans River took longer than anticipated. The river was low due to the drought but deep enough to have a much enjoyed dip. Lying on the bank to dry off I decided to make one more camp. Next day I did the seven miles to White Mountain Inn and went in for some tea. While I was enjoying that respite a traveller came in who was going to pass Spitzberg Farm. We chatted and when he learned that that was where I was heading he warmly offered to give me a lift there and so it saved me a twenty-mile hike in bare feet.

I was welcomed back into the fold of the Milne family as if I were a warrior home from the battle. What a pleasure it was to be there. My room had been prepared for me and on the table was a cardboard box with a card attached that said 'Welcome home'. In the box were my boots, newly repaired by a cobbler in Estcourt and a new pair of trousers, the size discreetly taken by Mrs Milne from my old flannels which she had noticed were looking very frayed. What wonderful people they were. I couldn't find words to thank them, but they knew I was moved. Deeply.

Next day, Saturday, great preparations were put into action for the *braai-vleis*. The native cook and staff had been working towards it and the sisters were sparkly eyed with anticipation. I dare say I was too. In the evening the guests arrived and under hanging lanterns the barbecue smoked and smelled delicious and we danced on the lawn. Country, Square and Scottish dancing all mixed up, and even, for those who knew how, a '*ticky draai*'.

'*Ticky*' was the Afrikaans word for the old threepenny bit, half an inch in diameter, and the dance got its name from the couples having to turn, whirl, in the space of that small coin, so to speak. It was the stuff of madness when *voortrekkers*' paths crossed and the occasion marked by a *nagtmaal*, a celebration of families meeting. Then there would be great community bonding, happiness of trysts kept and marriages confirmed and blessed, some overdue, others hastily arranged while the Predikant preacher was available.

When the girls went back after their holidays I became a farm assistant. During the first few weeks when the drought was at its height there was little that could be done bar helping with the milking supervision, repairing fences and other odd jobs.

The grass was like straw and the cattle were suffering, though not as bad as in some places. The future looked black. Early crops had long since died. The ground was baked hard as iron. Ploughing was long overdue but the blades could barely scratch the surface. Would the rains never come? Each day the sun did its round, staring more intensely than on the previous day from the dead pan sky. Each day the air became more brittle and charged with oppressive power. It was not that the heat was unbearable, it was just dry.

Chasing trespassers became my main occupation. The farm was bordered on one side by a native reserve and constant streams of people made short cuts across the farm, much to the detriment of crops when they were growing and to the ailing stubble at this particular time. But that was minor damage compared with the practice the natives had of breaking down the fences and driving their own herds into Mr Milne's land to graze. Grazing at any time was precious in this thirsty land, but with the drought its value was immeasurable, and even more important, over-grazing could cause the disaster of soil erosion.

Soil erosion is the scourge of Africa. It is the thin edge of the wedge that starts deserts. It happens when the vegetation has been removed, leaving the soil loose and unprotected so that it can be blown away as dust or washed away with the flood waters during the rains. Apart from over-grazing, which exposes the roots to be killed by the sun, it may be caused by the perpetual growing of similar crops on the same land year after year without putting back any nourishment, such as fertilisers into the soil, so that it becomes exhausted and unable to support life.

The finger of the dreaded disease had already touched Spitzberg. Flood water had sliced a fifty-foot deep gulch out of the unprotected subsoil on the side of a hill. From the Drakensberg I had seen many other open and deeper wounds, especially in the native lands where some areas had been carved into minor deserts. I was to see worse, much worse, further south in Pondaland. I was to hear over and over again the lament, "If only they (the natives) would keep just enough cattle for their food requirements the land could support them. But they won't listen. Cattle is their currency. So they build up their stocks till the Ark gets overloaded. If only we could get them completely converted to our monetary system the land would be healthy and so would the people."

Even this seemingly simple task of chasing trespassers had its complications in this troubled land. Mr Milne solemnly warned me that even if I were able to catch up with any of these fleet-footed people, I was on no account to lay hands on them.

"If you do," he said, "they will take you to court and fifty of their friends will testify that they saw you beat them. In cases like this the Africans are always given the benefit of the doubt and we will be heavily fined."

This was a revelation in a country where one had been led to believe that all the cards were stacked against the non-whites. That may have been true when later *apartheid* really got underway. But at this stage when British ways were still predominant, the natives had their rights and knew how to use them. As I chased the people I felt like Paddy, our old spaniel dog who, when chasing strange cats from the garden, used to bark ferociously so long as the cats ran from him. He never caught up with them, and if they ever turned and faced him up he would sit and scratch himself in a dither as to what to do next.

Our only chance, Mr Milne said, was to impound the cattle of the grazing rustlers. But this would be no easy task and all the time I was there I never caught any, nor even tried to. The chase was enough. The little boys, many of them under ten years of age, who herded the animals had a way with them. They could round up the herd quicker than could a pack of sheepdogs. Indeed, it seemed that the animals were wise to the game, for in answer to the herders' whistles and shouts they would all dash for the break in the fence and be through by the time I had run full tilt down the hill to them. Once on his own side the boy would stand and hurl abuse and taunts, as did all the trespassers.

Suddenly the rains came. Every day there were great showers. The ground held forth its cracked lips and eagerly gulped the water down till it could take no more. The river, which had been dry for months, was a rumbling roaring torrent that rose and fell rapidly like a fever temperature and had to be forded by anyone leaving or entering the farm. One night when all the family (the girls had come home for the weekend) returned from a dance at

Estcourt, the nearest town sixteen miles away, the river had risen too high for the car to cross. We waded over and walked the couple of miles home. Next morning the car was drawn across by a tractor.

Now rain was the main conversation topic. When farmer met farmer the opening gambit was always the same. "How much?" referring to the rain-gauge everyone had in their garden. "I had 1.8, but up the ridge they had 2.5." People talked, dreamed, blessed and cursed rain for it was the knife edge on which balanced success or failure.

But drought and rain and soil erosion were not the only concern of these farmers. There was hail. Hail so devastating it could do more damage in a few minutes than months of drought. Once when the rains had subsided and the mud dried out sufficiently to allow tractors to manoeuvre and ploughing had gone on from dawn till dusk and the first shoots were showing out of the ground, we watched a hail storm pass within a mile of the farm, a gun-metal blue cloud on a saturation bombing raid. Crops in its path were smashed. One farm was completely laid waste. But next day all the neighbours sent machines and labour in a crash attempt to re-till the land so that it might still catch the season. Such was the comradeship among the farmers.

In a way that man was lucky for had the storm come slightly later he might have been ruined. This was brought right home to the Milne family some years later when Monica and Denis Taylor, her newly-married husband, bought a small farm. Before they had found their feet a hailstorm laid waste their lucerne and eclipsed their business, making them sell up at a ruination price.

*

Mention of Denis Taylor brings a story to mind that I must recount. A powerful, wonderful story. It may be out of context for this happened forty years after my time with the family Milne, but it is the story of Africa and that is the main one I am telling.

When in 1990 my wife, Maureen, and I spent a holiday in South Africa we visited the three Milne sisters, each now with husband and grown-up family. It was an unhappy, dangerous time for all. Murder and mayhem were reaching a crescendo following the release from prison of Nelson Mandela after twenty-seven years of captivity. Every day the newspapers were filled with details of the latest robberies and burglaries with violence and killings. Everyone knew of someone close who had suffered or died. While we were there the best man of a son-in-law died violently in Johannesburg when a pick-axe was driven through the windscreen of his car and into his head. We, ourselves, had a terrible fright while driving on a lonely road in Zululand and in Pietermaritzburg we arrived only two days after a clash between the warriors of Inkatha, the followers of

Zulu Chief Buthelezi, and those of the ANC (African National Congress) ended with great slaughter in the streets. We wandered about, completely innocent of the tinderbox atmosphere until screamed at to get out. I mention all that to emphasise the background to the tale I am about to tell.

There were a dozen or so men at the Pinetown Rotary Club meeting. Denis Taylor, Immediate Past President, had invited me along as a guest. Apart from meeting his chums he thought I might be interested in the guest speaker.

It was a mixed group. The faces round the table included two blacks and a brown Indian one. Dennis during his year of office had opened the door to other races. Apartheid was breaking down in the most recluse circles.

There was a lot of banter and bonhomie before the business matters were dealt with. Then the Chairman introduced the speaker. He was a little man, not much more than five feet, and slight. His face was thin, his hair sparse. When he spoke his voice was quiet and carried a soft Irish lilt with it. He didn't look like a hero. Not a man to be noticed in any company except that he wore the collar of a Roman Catholic priest.

I didn't know it then but learned afterwards that Father O'Hara was a living legend. His parish was in a poor quarter of Durban where trouble was a daily occurrence and tales of his prowess as a mediator were told far and wide. At that time Durban was the second fastest growing city in the world, beaten only by Mexico City. As it rapidly expanded to accommodate the great drift of population from the tribal areas to the city, its rolling perimeter continually overshadowed those people still living more-or-less in their traditional ways in thatched huts and corrugated iron shacks.

This created tensions and trouble beyond the norm between Black and Black. In addition to the political wrangle between ANC and Inkatha there was the clear-cut division between the 'haves' and the 'have-nots', the townies and the country people, the fear of the people who saw their homes and lands sliding under the steam-rollering concrete towers.

In flashpoint areas a state of almost continuous civil war existed. Such was the place where Father O'Hara administered his church. In his quiet way, with little emphasis or elaboration of details, he told his story. A true story. And because it had happened only two days ago it seemed so real. We felt we were there. What he told had happened that weekend. It was now Tuesday.

Trouble had been smouldering over the week and suddenly erupted on Saturday night. Maybe it was the weekend drinking that was the final catalyst. Whatever, a sudden uproar announced the all too common bloodshed. But by the time the action erupted the number of followers on each side had built up to sizeable armies and a battle of considerable proportions took place.

Father O'Hara listened to the terrible noise and screams and saw flames rise from several houses. Suddenly the commotion streamed towards him and half the mob ran into the church and barricaded the door, followed by the other half determined to force their way in to commit unholy murder. Imagine the scene, the seething, blood thirsty mob, the light from the burning houses, the torches, lamps casting highlights and shadows on the contorted faces, the long panga knives, spears and sticks, the chilling, blood-curdling pandemonium. Going into that mob seemed a veritable act of suicide.

But into the mob Father O'Hara went. Pushing his way forward he forced himself in front of the door and faced the most savage of those trying to break their way in. He told them they must not desecrate the church. Such was the character of the man and his standing among the people the mob actually stopped and listened to him. He told them to go home, he remonstrated on their bad behaviour and, furthermore, he wanted them all in the church next morning to pray. The crowd dispersed.

Next morning they returned. They came self-consciously, eyeing each other with apprehension, the followers of one faction taking their places on the right of the aisle and those of the other on the left. The congregation was larger than Father O'Hara could remember. They sang and they listened, yet overall there was fear and hostility, a powder keg that needed only a spark to cause it to explode.

Then Father O'Hara lit some candles and put forward a novel idea. He asked for volunteers from both sides to come and take a candle and give it to someone on the opposite side of the aisle. Silence, no one moved. The atmosphere was charged. No one wanted to back down in front of his followers. No one would give in to the other.

At last one man hesitantly stepped forward, paused, then went forward and picked up a candle. Every eye was focused on him. There was not a sound other than his steps in broken shoes. Apprehensively he turned and looked for and found a face he knew in the opposition. The families had grown up together. Slowly he walked over to the other and gingerly offered the candle. The other man hesitated as if he would refuse, conscious of his neighbours. Then he took the candle, laid it down carefully, and threw his arms round the donor and hugged him like a brother, tears rolling down his cheeks. Then they sat down together.

The tension was broken. Others hurried to collect candles and deliver them. The traffic across the aisle increased and later when they sang it was in one voice, one people, one family. The trouble was over.

*

My time on the Milne farm was not long. But it was enough to give me an insight into the difficulties of farming in Africa and to make me appreciate even more than I had done the courage of the Voortrekkers who, knowing that success

490

hinged on such a fine balance of luck, went with such meagre resources to establish new farms in distant, unknown and hostile lands.

While on the farm I learned of some unusual and interesting animal husbandry which was practised there when the need arose. On many farms there grew the wild tulip, a very dangerous, poisonous plant if eaten by the cattle. Strangely enough, any cow which was born and brought up where the tulip grew would not touch it. But a strange cow, coming from a place where the flower did not grow, would avidly eat this wild tulip when introduced to it. The cure for a cow in this circumstance or even if it was new on the farm and the farmer wanted it to learn not to eat it, was unique: the petals of the wild tulip were burnt and the ashes fed to the animal. An animal which was suffering from this poisoning would be cured and it would not look at the tulip again.

Away from farm matters, another thing I thought interesting and amusing was the way I saw how an old man's age was assessed. Mr Milne realised that his old cook was well over the age for old age pension. The old man in his ignorance had never claimed it for he had no idea of his own age. In an attempt to assess this Mr Milne asked him how old he was at the time of ...? I missed the word used for the particular period in the 1890s referred to, but I think it was 'rinderpest' a terrible cattle disease of which there was a great plague at that time. The old man, squatting on the ground, native style, thought hard for some time. Then he said he was an *'umfaan'* – a boy – but he was past the age for leading cattle. Then Mr Milne asked him his age at the time of the Boer War. The old man knew that without thinking. He was a *"nsiswa"* – young man in his prime. Lastly, the elder Zulu was asked his age at the time of the great influenza epidemic of 1918–9 that swept the world and killed more people than the whole of the Great War that had just finished. He rubbed his chin thoughtfully as he recalled the "flunza". Then he remembered that by that time he was a *'keshla'* – an old man. Mr Milne assessed his age between seventy and seventy-five, a very old age for a native, especially a working native. He was supposed to have stopped work long ago but on hearing that the cook had left Spitzberg and that Mrs Milne was without one he had come back of his own accord "to look after them" until they got another one. What a grand old man he was, loyal to his bones and caring for his family.

Another little incident I watched with interest highlighted the growing sophistication of young native women of the time. Looked on nowadays it would perhaps mean nothing unusual, for now many African country women are as chic as their white neighbours, but fifty years ago this was a surprise, to say the least.

Maureen came home from the school for a weekend and was passing on some discarded clothes and shoes to the native women of the house. I was amazed how the ultra modern slang and latest fashion names had crept into the native vocabulary. One said she'd like the *'ama-* (that) *Jeep'* coat and another fancied the *'ama Jaeger'* jacket. Everything had gone except two pairs of shoes, a pair of high-heeled silver dance shoes and a pair of low-heeled walking ones. I thought the high-heeled ones were the last thing they would want, but I was wrong. In fact, two of them wanted them. They argued for a while then they decided that one would have the *'ama-Jive'* pair and the other the *'ama-Goluf'* (golf) ones. The image of African women of that era *jiving* or even knowing the term was a eye-opener.

Eventually my departure could be postponed no longer and typical of him Mr Milne drove me to Durban on the pretext of some business there. Mrs Milne came too. It was a moving moment when we said our goodbyes. But fate hadn't finished with us yet, as time will tell.

When I arrived in the city I put up in the YMCA and before long made a few friends amongst the chaps who were also staying there. It was a great place for meeting people. The housekeeper of the hostel had a nephew who was a head reporter on the *Natal Mercury* newspaper and mentioned me to him, with the result I met Denis Craig and struck up a good friendship with him. Denis filed a report on my journey and in no time the telephone in the YMCA started to get hot. Quite a number of people, most with Scottish connections, rang to invite me to dinner and various outings.

My time in Durban was like a holiday. Having my own lodgings I lived the life of a tourist and did all the tourist things. I made friends at the YM and more elsewhere through Denis's article. I did the town, going out to dinner, films – once to see *High Noon* the western classic starring Gary Cooper and Grace Kelly – and twice to the Criterion Theatre. But it is for the sea that people from inland places come to Durban, and I was no exception.

Seeing the sea on the south coast of Africa was a wonderful moment after all those inland miles. I felt I had cleared the last obstacle of the assault course and there only remained the final unhampered charge at the target. Blissfully I gave myself to the sparkling water and for days I was a pious sun-worshipper with the main congregation on South Beach and with smaller, but equally devout gatherings at lesser known places. These smaller beaches had their dangers for not many, if any, had life-savers on hand for any swimmer who got into difficulty. One day I saw a man drown at one such beach. I was just one of several who stood and watched as he was carried further and further out. Apparently he lost his footing when struck by the backwash and was carried away. None but the very strongest swimmers can compete with these seas. So we stood and watched the doomed man fade smaller and smaller. I heard later that a rubber lifeboat went out after him but it was too late. How terrible it is to see someone die before your eyes.

On one occasion I went with friends thirty miles up the Zululand coast to swim in the natural pool under Chaka's Rock, a sheer precipice where, legend has it, the terrible Zulu king made a regiment of his warriors march over the edge to their doom in order to prove their obedience to him. So the legend goes, but if it did happen I thought it would be because the regiment had not performed in battle as Chaka expected them to do. Whatever the reason it was chilling to look up and imagine how regimented, soldiers could passively throw themselves to death at the whim of one man. But as my research in Rhodesia had taught me, Chaka was no ordinary man. What is it that a man can have, what charisma, leadership we might call it, hypnotism maybe, that enables that person to bend thousands, millions even, of people to do their will? Hitler had it, Stalin too, perhaps, though his may have been sheer brutality rather than personal persuasion. Chaka certainly had that genius, that total military command that compelled his troops to do whatever he wanted of them.

We know that by 1820 he had 100,000 of the finest warriors in Africa under his command and with these he extended his rule over another half-million. He drilled them into such a well-disciplined army it was well nigh invincible. His impis foraged far and wide. The effect of their might was felt as far north as Lake Victoria. So powerful, fearless and ruthless were the Zulus that all southern Africa trembled when they were on the rampage. The softest whisper of a rumour that the impis were approaching sent whole tribes fleeing with terror into the bush.

Much later and further up Africa, I met an Englishman, a missionary in the Congo, who was an expert on the secret African drum languages that are used as bush telegraph to pass messages across the continent. He was quite likely the only white man in the world with that knowledge and I am very proud to have on my shelf to this day a copy of his drum-wireless 'manual' which he submitted as his PhD thesis. He told me that due to Chaka, drums, talking drums, went out of use in South Africa and never returned. Because they gave prior warning of his army's approach, he decreed that every man, woman and child of any place in which his warriors found a drum would die. His warning was heeded so much that all drums were destroyed even though his men were nowhere in the vicinity.

Chaka was murdered by his half-brother Dingaan who suffered a terrible defeat by the Boers at Blood River in 1838. This battle followed the treacherous killing of Piet Retief and his men, 70 in all including Retief's son, who had gone to negotiate land concessions with Dingaan. The Zulu king agreed to the concessions, then entertained the Boers for a day before having them seized and slaughtered.

The Zulu military power was finally smashed by the British in 1879. That year saw the lamentable massacre of nearly 2000 British and Bantu troops by the Zulus at Isandhlwana and the courageous stand of a small British force at

Rorke's Drift when eleven Victoria Crosses were awarded. Before that year was out a British force marched on Cetewayo, the reigning Zulu king, and engaged his forces in a decisive battle which finally put an end to the might of the Zulus. Considering the impression they made on history, the limelight of the Zulus was short, scarcely more than half a century. But in that time their fame became world wide.

At the time I was in Durban there was a group of mad, suicidal, swimmers who made a play at competing regularly with the fierce conditions of that south coast, risking their lives as if they were not worth a docken, all in the name of sport. I daresay their sons and even grandsons are still doing the same … and more. I met the mad band several times when I was there and always enjoyed hearing their tales of the deep. They were not lifesavers and no self-respecting lifesaver would go where they went. They met at weekends and went into the sea lying along long, narrow boards and paddled with their hands till they were a mile out. There they would grab a lift on a passing wave and, now standing on the board, would ride the great, mad, bucking comber right back onto the beach, if they were lucky. If they were not lucky, that was a different matter. They told tales of being chased by even greater waves than the one they were riding, great monsters thirty feet higher that curled over them with horrible, open mouths dripping white foam saliva.

These were the 'surfers', though this was before the term had been coined, or perhaps it was that I hadn't heard of it yet. The sea, however, was not the only danger with which those fanatical and skilful maritime dervishes had to contend. There were the sharks. A mile out to sea the swimmers were way beyond the net barrier that stopped those denizens from going near South Beach for their meals. The danger was highest when the surf riders were static out at sea, watching the incoming waves, waiting for the 'big one' to come. That was when the sharks were most likely to attack. The leader of the pack of surfers, certainly the most locally famous one, was a man known as Sharky Botha (*Bo 'ta*, in Afrikaans) who was reputed to have been bitten three times by sharks. Sharky's joke was that it was not true … the third one was a barracuda. He certainly had the marks to prove it. One of his thighs had a large concave dip in it covered with thin, shiny tissue where a shark had bitten out a lump.

Of all the people I met in Durban, two were to have a considerable effect on my future. Both men, Mr William Nagle and Dr Crawford Lundie, hailed from near my home in Fife.

Mr William Nagle was a noted public figure. A Member of the Natal Parliament in Durban and also of the Union Parliament in Cape Town. His name was seldom out of the papers. He had his ardent followers and also his critics, Denis Craig being one of them. His public work had culminated recently in his appointment as chairman of the special committee set up to streamline the work on the Umgeni Water Scheme, a mighty dam, a great engineering project, which had been completed in 1950, to lift Durban out of the rut of continual water shortage. As an appreciation of his services the main dam in the scheme had been named after him. Situated deep within the Valley of a Thousand Hills, a great saucer-like land depression where the floor had wrinkled up to form innumerable mountainous ridges, the colossal sweeping wall of the Nagle Dam gleamed white in the sunlight. Few men could have a greater and more useful tribute than this.

When the housekeeper of the YM said there was someone on the phone for me, the voice sounded as if the person had left Scotland only a year ago. After the introductions Mr Nagle said he had known my father well. They had worked together in Blairhall colliery and each in turn had been the Trade Union delegate for the mine, my father having taken over from Willie when he had migrated to South Africa during the general depression of 1926.

Since his arrival in South Africa Mr Nagle had combined a successful business in insurance with an even more successful career in politics. I was invited to the Nagle home many times and both Mr and Mrs Nagle took me to the Valley of a Thousand Hills to show me with pride the great edifice of the Nagle Dam and, I thought, well might they be proud of such an achievement.

William Nagle's contribution to my future was a .38 Smith and Wesson revolver. It had lain untouched on a shelf since a native burglar had tried to climb through the bedroom fanlight years before. On that night Mr Nagle suddenly found himself for the first time in his life armed with purposeful intent, determined to defend his home and family. At that time the gun was kept in the bedside drawer. They had wakened up to see the burglar, head and shoulders into the room. Mr Nagle, in pantomime, showed how he had got the gun from the drawer, his hands shaking like a leaf, to confront the intruder, but in his excitement the shot went off prematurely, the bullet ricocheting off a marble table and drilling holes in a pair of trousers hanging over a chair. The burglar fled. The incident was reported in the newspaper under the headline 'Nagle Shoots His Trousers'.

When I was offered the revolver and refused, saying I couldn't possibly accept it, Mrs Nagle said in high dudgeon, "Take it out of here. He's more dangerous with a gun in his hand than any burglar is ever likely to be. You'll be doing us all a favour if you take it away." So it was agreed. The gun was brought at arm's length, still wrapped up in a newspaper, untouched since that day. But the gift was not as easily made as that. We went to the police station for a licence but this was refused. The sergeant said he would not endorse the giving of the weapon to an itinerant traveller. I did not mention I already had one lest he took it away from me. The inspector was called but even Mr Nagle's status would not make him overrule the sergeant's decision.

Outside, Mr Nagle asked me when I thought I'd be in Cape Town. I said I didn't know, maybe a month, maybe two. This was now near the end of November. He said he was going down to the main Union Parliament in the early New Year and if we met there he would see that I got the gun and licence. Apparently things were easier in Cape Colony than in Natal and apart from that he would have the influence of a full Member of Parliament there. We agreed to keep in touch as I made my way down.

The other person in Durban who contributed to my future was Dr Crawford Lundie, an elderly, semi-retired General Practitioner. His daughter, a lovely person, came to the YMCA and extended an invitation from her father to visit the family. Dr Lundie was the son of the manse of Newmills, the neighbouring village to mine in Fife, where his father had been the Free Kirk minister there about the turn of the century. He was a tall, aesthetic man, with snow-white hair and gentle manner. Beth his wife and daughter had his ways and characteristics. A kindly, genteel family who made me feel so easily at home. I made several visits and enjoyed every minute of their company.

While I was there one day, wearing shorts and sitting with my legs crossed in an easy chair, Dr Lundie remarked that I had a varicose vein running across my leg, just below the knee. I said I was aware of it and I had watched it become more prominent lately. He asked whether I was going to go home when I reached the Cape or was I going to continue to walk further in Africa. I said I didn't know at that stage. My idea had always been to finish at Cape Town. But recently I had begun to wonder about that. There seemed an awful lot of Africa still to see. I was still considering the idea.

"In that case I think we should do something about that. We can't have you stopped by a burst tyre somewhere up in the wilds. That could be very serious. I think you need a retread if you are going to go on walking as you have done." He smiled with his little joke.

He came over, knelt down and looked closely at the vein and touched it gently. Without a word he went back to his chair, sat down and looked hard at my leg, passing his hand over his pursed lips, pondering. Suddenly decisive, he straightened and said, "Would you like me to fix it now?" A little surprised I tried to hide my sudden shock and said something like, yes, of course, if he didn't mind doing it. He replied that he didn't mind in the least and would be delighted to help.

So saying he went out of the room and was gone a little while. He returned and asked me through to the kitchen and told me to stand up on the table. He left me a moment then returned holding a charged syringe in one hand and an open bottle of surgical spirit and a swab in the other. He upended the bottle, put it down and wiped a place on my vein with the swab. He lowered the syringe to the spot and … stopped, the syringe quivering in his fingers. An awful moment followed, the doctor hesitant, perplexed and me wondering how he was going to hit the vein with his hand shaking like that.

After what seemed an age, a highly charged age, Dr Lundie lowered the syringe and said, somewhat dispirited, "No, I don't think I will. I'll see if I can get you into hospital. They have all the facilities there. Yes, I think that would be better." He seemed to have aged visibly in those few moments and I'm sure I had too.

True to his word, but with some difficulty in arranging it I gathered, I went into the main Durban hospital on 7th December 1952 for my op. next day. The doctor told me I would not be able to walk much for while after it and I wondered what I'd do.

In my diary that night I wrote:

I think I will go to one of the south coast places and camp and lie up and take it easy for a few days till I get my legs back into shape. There is no camping ground in Durban and I will not be able afford to stay at the YMCA.

But there was no need to do that. Wheels were turning and despite anything I may have written to the contrary, there is little doubt that someone up there was watching over me even if He made others do the work for Him. First, Denis Craig, who visited me in hospital, invited me to stay at his house for a few days while something longer could be worked out. When I was discharged he met me, complete with my rucksack and belongings which his aunt had allowed him to take from the YM. He and his wife made me feel so welcome at their home I couldn't thank them enough. In the meantime, and to this day I don't know how they learned of my problem – I think Denis may have had a hand in it, for I had spoken a lot to him about Spitzberg – a letter came saying I must 'come home'. A door-to-door 'lift' was arranged and I was welcomed back with Mr and Mrs Milne like a son.

I could not have wished for a better place to recuperate and kinder people to be with. I used the time to write some articles for magazines, one of which, 'Gedi; The Lost City', I sold to the *Outspan* for seven guineas, a tidy sum then.

The girls came home for the Christmas holidays and the fun started. I had been doing short walks, gradually lengthening them daily and by the time the family came together I was looking towards tackling 'the Berg'. This was the hill on the farm which gave it the name, about a mile from the house. It was probably about 1000ft. high. So some days we all went for a picnic so far up Spitz Berg, each time going a little higher. When we came back there was always the round, corrugated-iron swimming pool to jump into with the frogs to cool us down.

Christmas on the farm was marvellous. There were about twenty guests staying including a few children. There was a Christmas tree complete with tinsel and shining metal balls, crackers and presents and children with happy faces and wonderment and anticipation in their big eyes when the presents were cut off the tree. The dinner was everything a Christmas dinner should be with turkey and Christmas pudding and paper hats and crackers and even champagne. Oh! It was grand.

On Hogmanay we all went into Estcourt to a dance to bring in the New Year. It was a howling success and well made up for the previous two that I was not able to celebrate very well. A few days later the girls went away sadly, as we all were, and life in the new year settled down again to normal. My legs – I had actually had veins in both legs done – were much stronger now and I tackled some jobs about the farm, mending a fence here, supervising some drainage there, but chasing trespassers was out.

I now climbed the Berg daily and it was the *time* I took to complete the round journey that I was pushing to improve. Near the end I was taking my sleeping bag and some food and going off for a couple of days rambling about the hills on my own. This was mostly to get my legs fully fit again and really acclimatised to hard walking, but it was also a good excuse to get away for a bit. Because I really enjoyed living on the farm and the cheery company of all the family and guests I knew that being on my lonesome again was going to come hard, so it was better to get away for a wee while to learn to be myself once more. That I did when I tramped over the mountains with only the winds and the rain for company and curled up in my sleeping-bag beside a log fire at night and woke up in the morning to see the green hills, silver with dew, and viewed the blue mountains that pierced the grey cloud of mist that filled in the valleys.

When I said I would leave after a weekend Mr and Mrs Milne made no move to coax me to stay. They knew as I did that the time had come. At the end of the weekend both Mr and Mrs Milne drove me to Pietermaritzburg where we parted, all, I'm sure, with heavy hearts.

*

I camped outside Pietermaritzburg and next day got a lift as far as Kokstad, a sleepy kind of place, main town in Pondoland, or Mpondoland, which was part of Griqualand East. The land I had passed through was sick and ill-used and soil erosion was wide and deep set. Kokstad, named after Adam Kok, a freed slave and former cook to the Cape governors, was founded in 1877 by William Dower of the London Missionary Society. Kok amalgamated the wandering half-cast outcasts from the main surrounding tribes and gave them their own identity. At first they called themselves the 'Bastaards', but that gave way to the 'Griqua' people.

In Kokstad it was very evident that I had left Natal for here in the only café that I could see for a meal, there were Coloured waitresses, something not seen in Natal. Seeing the people known as Cape Coloureds also told me that I was now in that colony, a landmark indeed.

On the road again I soon got a lift to Umtata where I camped just outside the town. Umtata was capital of the self-governing native territory of Transkei. No whites were allowed to own land in Pondoland or Transkei.

With a combination of lifts and walking, quite a lot of the latter, I made my way to East London where I spent a couple of nights in the camping site by the beach and then went on to Port Elizabeth. A big town built right up the face of a mountain, PE had the steepest streets of any town I had come across in this part of the globe. There was a lot to see here so I camped two or three nights.

In long-ago time, before Sir Rufane Donkin, the acting governor, named the port and town after his wife, Elizabeth, who had died of fever two years earlier in India, great herds of elephant and buffalo roamed this land. Man and beast had lived on reasonably equal terms of kill-and-be-killed. All that ended when white settlers came along.

Diehard white farmers had been creeping across the land for a couple of centuries, but in 1820 twenty-six ships bringing 4000 family immigrants, most from English deprived areas, landed in Algoa Bay that forms the seafront of Port Elizabeth. The prime reason for their having been brought was to form a buffer zone between the farmers and the wild, harassing Xhosa people, but as time went by the 1820 immigrants grew to form the main English-speaking group in Eastern Cape and Natal and almost certainly helped to fashion the history of the country.

While the scattered early settlers had lived an ongoing fight, barely holding their own against the great animals to maintain their meagre holdings, the arrival of so many new people meant so much bigger communities and eventually towns. Rifles and settled agricultural land and brick towns did not mix with the old equation. Buffaloes were dangerous and good for eating so they disappeared. Elephants possessed valuable ivory and destroyed farmlands, so they too very nearly became extinct.

In 1919 Major Jan Pretorius, a noted big-game hunter, was commissioned to exterminate the herd of elephants that lived in the Addo forest, some twenty miles north of Port Elizabeth, because the animals were continually raiding the citrus groves by the Sundays River and breaking the trees to get at the fruit. That was the last herd of any size still alive in the south. I had read his book, the name of which I forget, some time before and at the time admired his courage and skill. He told how he had had a special suit made of the thickest leather, like mail, so he could pass through the terrible tangled, spiky undergrowth of the forest, the reason why the bandit herd had survived so long. Where others had failed, Pretorius was invincible and demonically successful. In a year he shot

120 elephants and, if my memory serves me right, claimed he had shot the last elephant in South Africa. If my memory is correct he was wrong, but only by a hair's breadth.

In 1931 a dozen elephants were found to be alive in the deepest part of the forest and the Addo Elephant National Park was declared, ensuring the future of that tiny herd, the last indigenous South African elephants outside the far north-east in that area known as the Kruger National Park and its environs. In 1990 I believe the herd then numbered 135 and so had recouped the losses of that terrible slaughter.

The wind always seems to blow at Port Elizabeth and in the end I was pleased to pull up stumps and get away from the mini-sandstorm that blew continually and filled the tent and plastered food to distraction.

With some walking and a series of lifts I was some miles off Knysna when a battered old pickup truck stopped and the driver asked where I was going. I told him I was making my way to Cape Town and he said he was not going far but I was welcome to go with him. His English was heavily accentuated with Afrikaans, but he was very friendly although he didn't say very much. Tall and gaunt with a black beard he looked like Abraham Lincoln, with the same serious, taciturn manner. He introduced himself as Van Eeden with no mention of a first name. He was a farmer. When he turned off the road for his house he said the day was late for more travelling and he invited me to spend the night at his home. I willingly accepted, thinking how wonderful hitchhiking was as a way to meet and get to know the people of a country. Driving in your own car you could travel the length and breadth of the world and never speak to the indigenes.

We drove through acres of soft fruit to the farmhouse, a low, roughly made affair in rather a dilapidated condition. The work on the farm obviously left little time for maintaining the house. Mrs Van Eeden, a big, buxom woman, surprisingly dressed in full nurse's uniform, quickly overcame her surprise and after some words from her husband in the Taal, cordially welcomed me into her home. She worked at the local health centre and had not long been home herself. She continued to wear her white uniform all evening, complete with headgear, although she was not 'on call'. The room to which I was shown was small with a creaking, shoulder-width door. The window was dark, always in deep shadow of the extended roof that formed the *stoep* (verandah*)*. All over the house the walls were covered with dark, floral wallpaper, so strange to see in Africa, and everywhere were photographs of stoic-faced people in ancient garb, glowering from dark or faded ovals surrounded by broad, yellowed-white margins in ornate frames.

About six o'clock father went to the back door and clanged a metal bar hung up as a bell for dinner. Almost immediately three ragged twelve/thirteenish boys raced in and went straight to the table. Father introduced me as a traveller to

500

whom they were giving hospitality for the night; at least that's what it sounded like. The boys gave me quick smiles but were more intent on getting their dinner. We all sat down on straight-backed chairs, the boys very still, obviously under rigid rule.

Mrs Van Eeden, still in her uniform, said grace which lasted ten minutes or more. At times she was at a loss what to say and there were long, awkward pauses until she thought up something. After such a build-up the meal was a surprise. A fried egg each then hunks of water melon. Great masses of the latter, but nothing else. I kept thinking this is a tremendous leader to the main course and it was some time before I realised that this was it, the only course. By that time I was lagging the field badly. The boys' plates were piled high with rind and their parents had built themselves formidable redoubts. Strange fare to feed lusty youths, I thought, but very grateful to be sharing it with them.

During the meal the conversation as usual got on to politics. 'Conversation' is not exactly accurate for Mrs Van Eeden, huffy and puffy, did nearly all the talking, while father sat solemn and immobile as a judge, only poking his nose in, judge-like, to rule out any extravagant claims or irrelevant issues.

She dissociated the family from the political upheaval that had erupted since the Nationalists had come into power. They never voted at any election, she said, because children of god should be above political squabbling. She nevertheless went on for nearly an hour extolling the virtues of Dr Malan's government and decrying the terrible way 'the other ones' had run the country. They 'had been weak tools of Britain bent on suppressing the Afrikaners nationality and depriving them of their rightful sovereignty'.

When we had squelched our way through as much melon as we could stomach mother said a five-minute thanks to God for the food we had eaten and we went off to potter around for an hour, father and two boys to work on the lorry, the other boy oiling a rifle, mother sewing and me writing my diary.

I was surprised when just after 8 p.m. van Eeden said he must go down to town to collect his daughter. I couldn't believe that she was still working. They owned a little shop where the vegetables and fruit from the farm were sold. The girl, who didn't look much older than sixteen when she came in, worked from 8 a.m. till 9 p.m. and sometimes later, she said. She walked the two miles to the shop every morning, six days a week. Thinking of the hard, humdrum life for a young girl to lead I could not help feeling bitter at the parents for expecting so much from their daughter. But then, I mused, this was their life, all of them; long hours of work and tedium with no time for leisure or pleasure, those pastimes being the very antithesis of what their world was all about.

When the girl (I don't know if I was ever told her name, nor those of the boys, for that matter) had finished her meal father called the family together and read a bible chapter, in English, to all of us before we retired to bed, the boys still grimy and dusty as they had come from the fields.

Next day was Sunday and although I rose early the others were all up and about, busy getting themselves ready for church. There was no sign of breakfast. Perhaps they did not eat until they returned. I went out onto the *stoep* feeling awkward, busying myself looking at the scenery. Presently van Eeden pushed the gauze door open a bit with his foot while tying his tie and said for me to go to the garden and help myself to any fruit I wanted. I picked a great, yellow-ripe water-melon and with my knife cut off as much as I could stomach, then threw the rest away. Then I did the same with a giant, luscious pineapple and finished with a few plump apricots and handfuls of juicy black grapes, big as plover's eggs.

By the time I had packed my things and carried my rucksack out the family was ready to go. What a picture they made. As a group they could have been acting a part in a film set of a hundred years before. It was pure Victorian. Father was dressed in top hat and black frock coat and he carried a heavy bible piously. Mother wore a black cloak with hood tied tight at her throat so it pulled the hood with white frill round her face. The girl and the boys were also in their Sunday best, the boys looking like cherubs with clean faces. I marvelled at seeing how much Victoriana still lingered in South Africa.

Strangely enough, it was a Scotsman, Alexander Murray, who started their Dutch Reform Church. In the days of the old voortrekkers there was no recognised church until Murray, a Scots Missionary, came along. He organised the religion. So it is understandable that the Dutch Reform Church has much in common with the Scottish Presbyterian Church, except that the DRC come down much heavier on the Old Testament, with its reference to 'the Children of Ham' than the Scots do.

Mr van Eeden said the church was on my way and they would drop me off there. He did not invite me to join them in worship. He no doubt would have been black-affronted (Scots' term) to take such an ill-dressed associate into their congregation. So I thanked them for their kindness and they wished me well on my journey. I was hardly a mile along the road when the full force of all that fruit on an unaccustomed stomach hit me. Now there was a sight to strike fear or mirth into the stoutest heart, a wild eyed, shaggy Scotsman, high-tailing it across the open veldt, kilt flying, rucksack bumping, desperately trying to reach cover, a clump of gorse, a large boulder, the merest bush, to shelter from passing eyes before it was too late. Oh, the price of folklore!

*

In today's tourist trade brochures the road from Port Elizabeth to Cape Town is known as the Garden Route. But, before tourism became big business, that title was reserved for a relatively short part of the route, that from Plettenberg Bay down to Mossel Bay. Of that stretch the part from Plettenberg past Knysna to

Wilderness has without doubt the most stunning beauty. I was so struck by the area I decided to camp and spend a few days just living in it.

I spent a couple of days in Knysna. Apart from the sea Knysna was near surrounded by a wonderful stinkwood forest where elephants roamed. Furniture making was the local industry and hard work it must have been for stinkwood and ironwood, another of the indigenous trees in the forest, are among the most dense woods in the world. Examples of furniture shown on a factory tour were of exceptional quality and design.

For sheer delight though, it is to the sea one looks at Knysna. The town curls round what must be one of the most fabulous lagoon harbours in the world. Completely surrounded except for a narrow natural gateway flanked by two great sandstone pillars, one sheer and other less-so, known as 'The Heads', each nearly 700ft. high, Knysna must have been a dream safe harbour for the ancient mariners who rounded the Cape. It might also have been a picture-book hideout for pirates, being almost invisible from the sea or land surrounds.

I have a wonderful memory of standing at the edge of Knysna lagoon and looking to the Heads at sunset. There was a most beautiful sky reflected in the smooth water, dusted over with an occasional cat's paw ripple. How easy it was to imagine a four-master with all sails furled and its skeleton-like rigging etched against the golden sky, creeping slowly into the lagoon. I could almost hear the high-pitched voice of the linesman singing out the fathoms as he pitched the lead, sounding the depth.

From Knysna I made my way slowly along the seventy miles or so to Wilderness, launching pad for so many marriages – the Torquay of South Africa. I was heading for George and the mountains to the north, but I was so enchanted by the beauty around Wilderness I decided to spend a few days there. My journey from Knysna was slow indeed and difficult too, but worth every bit of the effort it required. I travelled the 'Old Road' because a lift I got took me onto it and I carried on. Had I hugged the coast things might have been easier but not nearly so interesting. In places the road winds from high passes down in tortuous curves through incredible ravines to wild rivers, then up the other side in similar manner. Easy in a car, but what lifts I got were short and all too often I was pounding out the miles on foot.

Close to the ground as I was, I perhaps could appreciate more the hard work and rugged determination of the early settlers. That road had to be cut through dense forests of great, tangled, hardwood trees and across innumerable deep gorges that must have dismayed the first surveyors. But cross them they did by incredibly tortuous routes and drove their road through the awful forest using the simple tools of the day, axe, saw, shovel and hammer, and most important of all, strong minds and backs. Buried in the forest by the side of dirt roads were many picturesque little *dorps* and woodcutters' hamlets.

At Wilderness I looked down on a golden sand bay smoothed with cooling white rollers. Hot, sweaty and jaded from a long climb uphill, my shirt sticking to me, I looked down on paradise. I decided I must spend some time there.

Here was another lagoon in an area of outstanding beauty. I was invited to camp in the grounds of the hotel there and kindly given permission to use at will a rowing boat that was tied-up at a little jetty in the grounds. I pitched my tent by the river, a delightful spot, shady through the day, with plenty of firewood easy at hand. So I passed a few idyllic days rowing over the lagoon and up the river and hiking around this paradise, pausing as desired to light a fire, grill a meal and drum up some tea. Bliss.

Back on the road again, the town of George was a mere ten miles away. I walked half of them, which were quite steep, then got a lift. George is gem of a place, full of old Georgian architecture and blancmange Dutch gables, startling white against a stunning backdrop of the Outeniqua Mountains. It takes your breath away at first sight. The town started in 1788 as a forestry camp. As the trees were cleared the farmer settlers moved in. By 1811 they were a community fit to be designated a town which was called George after George III.

Less than three hundred miles separate George and Cape Town and the end of my journey. Once again the temptation was great to keep on straight to Cape Town by the coastal road and be there in a couple of days or so. But there were places to the north I had heard about and wanted to see before leaving this country. There were the Cango Caves and the Ostrich Farm near Oudtshoorn in the *Klein* or Little Karoo, and the great desert area north of there. People told me that unless I got a car to take me to these places the going would be very difficult. How right they were.

Tuesday 3rd February, 1953. Near Oudtshoorn
From George I hiked over the Outeniqua Mountains by way of the Montague Pass. What a magnificent pass, but what a climb with my pack! Then I got a lift to a farm about five miles from Oudtshoorn. After that it was all walking again. The Cango Caves are about 17 miles from Oudtshoorn. I walked till nearly sunset when I found a fine place beside the river to camp.

This place is in the area known as the 'Little Karoo'. The country changes completely once you cross the mountains from George. The coastal belt is so green and fresh. Here it is dry and dusty. Over the next range, the Swartberg (Black Mountains) lies the 'Karoo'.

Wednesday 4th February 1953. In the Swartberg Mountains.
Oh the noise from the baboons last night! I am camping right in a valley that is almost a ravine, the sides are so steep. All night baboons screamed

and barked and grunted. Sometimes the noise would be deafening when a whole army seemed to be fighting among themselves and tearing each other apart. And all this noise was magnified with the echoes. This valley has some of the best echo effects I have ever heard. Several times I was wakened up with the noises. Sometimes they were very close to the tent.

I decided to spend another night here. I hiked round about today to get the lie of the land.

There are many terse notes in my diary that belie the moment. Reading it now the moment comes back to me very clearly. I felt very lonely that night as Africa's night noises exploded all round me. '... *very close to the tent*' meant the baboons were thumping past me – and they do thump heavily – so close I expected them to crash through my guy-ropes and carry my tent with them or get tangled up in it and me. All this with the horrific screaming only three feet from my head.

Thursday 5th February 1953. In the Swartberg Mountains.
Today I visited the Cango caves. It is an experience I will never forget. I walked the ten miles from where I was camping up to the caves. The caves are quite a tourist attraction. About thirty people went down in the party I was in. A European guide was provided. Down below we penetrated over a mile through tunnels and caverns. The limestone is formed into fantastic shapes. Stalactites and stalagmites are everywhere. (I always had difficulty remembering which went which way until I saw a never-to-be-forgotten, naughty little statement that stamped the answer in my mind, 'Tites come down and mites go up.') Some have met to form huge columns, some of them fifty feet tall. Growing at the rate of an inch every four hundred years these columns have taken some time to make. My reckoning says 240,000 years just to meet, then to gain the thickness that they were would be infinite, undoubtedly at the very making of the world.

It is impossible to describe it. Truly, it is like another world. Like a stage setting for some 'Opera Fantasia' or a Walt Disney nightmare scene. Yet it is hardly like that either for no producer or art designer could compete with Nature's work.

Near the end there was a portion that had to be crawled along on the stomach. It was so low and narrow. Only four of the party went through that bit. There was also a chimney of just shoulder width that had to be climbed. Down there it seemed as if time was petrified.

One thing not mentioned in my diary when describing the biggest cave or cavern, for it could hold 40,000 people, was a great, flat slab of rock situated so it was a natural stage overlooking the vast hall. I believe concerts have been held there, though I'm not sure. If not, it is the perfect place for one because I can vouch that the acoustics are wonderful. In our visit to South Africa in 1990 I had to show Maureen, my wife, the Cango Caves. They were much more given to tourism than I remembered from my long-ago previous visit. We went down with a party and did the tour only this time I didn't do that last bit where you have to crawl through on your stomach! In the great hall we held back and listened to the voices gradually grow faint as the party ascended the steps until all was silent.

At this moment, with much prompting from me, Maureen, a life-long chorister, took centre-stage and sang 'Amazing Grace'. It was spell-binding. The acoustics, the resonance, were perfect and the audience in its entirety rose with spontaneous and unanimous applause, but despite rapturous cries of 'More,' 'More,' the soloist declined to give an encore. There was a record out at the time on which the hymn was sung to the accompaniment of a full pipe band. Now, that would have been something to hear in that great Cango Cave auditorium!

Friday 6th February 1953. In the Swartberg Mountains.

Near where I am camping there is a huge pool in the river. The river bed widens out into a great basin. On one side a precipice drops sheer into the water and disappears far below. It must be a great depth. I thought it a natural place for swimming. This afternoon I went for a plunge. I started out from this bank to swim across to the precipice and back. But somehow a strange sensation came over me. I could not bring myself to swim over the bottomless pit. The blackness seems so ominous. I don't know why I didn't want to go, yet I could have swum the distance ten times over. From what I know now I would say it was a 'sixth sense' yet perhaps I was more truthful this afternoon when I climbed out and cursed myself for a coward. Yet, whatever it was, 'sixth sense' or plain fear, it undoubtedly saved my life.

The river beside which I am camping irrigates six farms. Each farm has a separate day to take the water and each has a little water gate they swing open or shut as appropriate. This evening a farmer stopped by my tent. He was checking that no one was drawing water off the river because this was his day for irrigating. I invited him to join me in some coffee. He sat long into the darkness beside my fire chatting away. In the course of conversation I mentioned the big pool that was fine and handy for swimming. Suddenly, he became excited, "For God's sake, don't go in there. Countless people have been drowned there. It's a whirlpool." I explained how smooth and inviting the surface looked but he said that underneath is a terrible current that would pull an ox down. Somehow the coffee tasted awfully good after that!

Saturday 7th February 1953. The Swartberg Mountains

Last night it began to rain, heavy and consistently and it has continued in a drizzle all today. Funny, the farmer last night said they wouldn't get rain for another three months. This is the 'Little Karoo', he said 'We don't get rain.' Well, speak o' the devil!

However, it has shown up the flaws in the tent. I find the sun has bleached the proof from it and now it is quite porous. It stood up reasonably to the rain last night but with the continual, non-stop drizzle today it gave up the fight long ago and a fine rain comes through now damping everything. Won't be too healthy tonight because my sleeping bag is quite damp. All my equipment is showing the strain of the long journey. My tent needs reproofing. My rucksack has more patches than original canvas and still there are a few new tears that will have to be mended at Cape Town. My groundsheet-cum-cape also needs reproofing. Right now I'm feeling a bit travel worn myself.

Once again the moment comes back to me and I think of my feelings at the time. My tent measured six-feet-by-four, with six-inch walls and sides sloping up to three feet six inches high at the apex. Not bad for sleeping in when lying down. But spending days in it, living, moving about, preparing cold meals, eating and tidying up in those backbreaking, cramped conditions and all the time very conscious, painfully so, not to touch the canvas for to do so will let the water in like a spout, is hard and very, very trying. I can remember feeling very wearied indeed after a night and a day in those conditions. A fly-sheet or inner tent would have solved the problem, but that would have been equivalent of carrying two tents and one, with all my other gear, was enough on long trails.

Sunday 8th Feb. 1953 Prince Albert. The Karoo.

Last night I had a bit of a scare. (And how!) I was suddenly awakened by something heavy, cold and clammy crawling over my chest heading for my face. The sensation was terrifying. It was pitch dark and the rain was drumming a tattoo on the tent. At first in my half awakened senses I thought it was a snake, then realised it was too compact for that. A great spider! It was almost on my face. My blood froze. I could feel its many legs through the sleeping bag. Moribund, I realised there were more. I could feel them moving over my legs and scrabbling over the ground sheet. Galvanised with horror I pushed from underneath and the thing rolled off with a bump. Heavy spider! I struck a match and to my great relief, yet abject revulsion, I found it was a big crab, the size of my fist. Looking around I counted six more of them in my tent. Sickened, for they were clammy things to handle in bed, I loosened the door strings and threw them out.

Something about a noise I heard apart from the drumbeat of the rain made me fish for my torch and look out. A blood-creeping sight met my eye. As far as the light beam went the place was a moving mass of crabs. There must have been hundreds, perhaps thousands, without exaggeration. I have never seen such a sight in all my life. In the pools the rain had made they were huddled in clusters. Over the wet ground they crawled to and fro. Big ones and small ones ranging from grey to black and brown in colour.

With a little sense of home security I tied up the door tight and spread my kit, boots, pans and anything that would do, round the bottom of the walls to weight the ends down, in the hope that that would keep out the intruders. Then I lay down to lose myself in sleep.

It was a foolish thing to do. I had a hunch, a feeling, premonition maybe, that things were not right. The crabs were telling me something and I should be reading their signs. But rousing myself out of my relatively cosy nest in the middle of the night was not easy to think about. I paid the price.

It could not have been long afterwards, just time enough to get into a deep sleep, when the river rose above its banks and flooded the tent. I thought disaster had come because I knew that a mountain river never floods gently. There would be a sudden rush of water soon, very soon, and I had visions of seeing everything I possessed getting swept away. Already I could hear a dull rumbling noise rapidly drawing near and I knew what it was. I was worried. I thought I was going to lose everything. If that had been the case I would have been left with what I stood in and at that moment the only thing I wore was a worried look for the flood had literally caught me napping.

There was panic in my movements as I tore up the pegs and threw everything into a heap on my groundsheet. The water was several inches deep and a few light articles were already floating away. I grabbed the four corners of the ground sheet and making it like a bag I managed to haul the lot to higher ground. I was just in time. About three or four minutes later a solid wall of water about four feet high swept past. The rumbling was like thunder as it rolled huge boulders along the river bed. The wave took everything before it. Fallen were trees buffeted about like matches. I would not have stood a chance against that. As it is, I saved everything but a few odds and ends.

Everything was sodden. All through the night I just sat in the mud trying to doze off while the rain poured down. Occasionally I got up and took a brisk walk, or at least as brisk as possible in pitch darkness, to try and get some circulation into chilled bones. I thought the night would never end. I longed for daylight and sunshine. Dawn found me stiff and drenched and cold. But even with daylight I got no respite because it continued to rain.

So there was no chance of drying off. I put on some wet clothes and managed to get a small fire going and cooked some porridge and coffee and that stiffened my backbone again. However it was impossible to dry anything at the fire as the rain, although not heavy now, kept everything wet. It would not be any use putting up the tent because it would offer no protection until it was dry again.

However, a farmer motoring past must have summed up my predicament. He stopped and said he would take me over the mountains into the Karoo. He had come from there this morning and there hadn't been any rain. Although it was taking me away north out of my way and most likely I would have to walk back since this road is seldom used by motorists, I was delighted. I bundled my sodden kit into the car and in an hour and a half I was whirled over the mountain into glowing sunshine. It was like breaking surface after too long underwater. I don't think there is anything more depressing than living in continual rain without shelter.

Prince Albert is a quiet, Sunday town. There is not a soul about. Not a thing moves. As in these outlandish towns I suppose the population is almost 100% Afrikaans and nobody breaks the Sabbath. I walked down the dusty street and it was as if I was walking through a ghost town. I could almost hear my footsteps echoing. I found a hotel. An old rambling place with a creaking wooden verandah with a frayed rexine couch for the comfort of any probable visitors. My footsteps on this wooden platform boomed in the silence. When a sleepy eyed boy appeared I was almost drawn to whispering my request for a meal since full throated speech seemed almost sacrilege in such silence. The dining room was in Old Dutch style with straight, high backed chairs.

Once again the long-silent words evoke the moment in my memory, as visible as television, the smells, sounds, touch, ambience, as potent to my senses as at that moment. I remember well that meal, so welcome, so incongruous. Me sitting in solitary, silent, faded high dignity and, after the release from the past horrible experience, relishing every mouthful of the repast. And afterwards sitting in the glorious, comfortable, burst rexine couch with coffee at my elbow while writing up my diary account of the past day and night. Life doesn't come sweeter.

I didn't stay long in Prince Albert. I got out and found a place to camp, and scattered my kit around in the sun to dry. There was quite a breeze too so things were dry in no time. Next day I had to start back up the Swartberg Pass, a long, hard road that was the price of my escape from that watery hell.

I could have avoided the Pass by going north up the Prince Albert Road that meets the main road to Cape Town from Beaufort West. But that way was through the Great Karoo and if I didn't get lifts it would have been difficult, dangerous in fact, going through that desert terrain. So having dried out after the night near Prince Albert I set out to recross the Swartberg in order to go down to the Cape via the more populous coastal region. But Fate had one more high card to play in a last attempt to win the game of my getting there. It is nearly twenty miles from Prince Albert to the top of the Pass. The road climbs very steeply, writhing and twisting like a demented serpent up the almost perpendicular face of the ravine. It is a wonderful tribute to the surveying and engineering skills of the Victorian road-maker Thomas Bain who forged the way through the mountains using convict labour during the 1880s. What a climb it was over these mountains carrying my pack.

I've been walking all day and climbing all the time. This is a magnificent Pass and I've seen every inch of it. The road curls in great loops up the sides of the mountain. Sometimes it creeps away into great curved recesses or folds in the mountain face and other times there is just room for it to squeeze through between the mountains where they have merged together to form cleft-like valleys. High overhead the sides of these clefts seem to lean towards each other.

So near was the road where it went into these recesses and where it came out again you felt as if with a good run you could jump from one side to the other and save the long loop in and out again. On second thoughts, I didn't try.

Where the Pass flattened out on top I decided to spend the night. A strong wind sighed with its exertion of bending trees and I knew it would be cold when the sun dropped. Luckily I saw a cave some way up the mountain slope from the road and made for it to camp inside. The cave was large with a fairly flat floor and a high roof sloping far back into the rock. On arrival I was surprised to find I was not alone. This mountaintop hostelry already had guests. Round their fire at one end of the cave sat a native family, the husband, his wife and two children. The man was obviously a pedlar and his ramshackle cart carrying his odds and ends was pulled up near the fire. Looking round it was evident that the place was a recognised stop for wanderers going over this Pass. The roof of the cave was black and shiny with old smoke of long-time fires.

I said my hellos. The woman smiled, the children giggled and the man nodded and muttered something as he puffed his pipe. I went to the other end of the cave and made my own fire. It was all very homely and comforting. The red glow of two fires danced across the black ceiling, driving away the evening darkness. The meal over, I settled down to write up my diary by fire and candlelight. Across at the family end my interest was caught by the man's strange behaviour. He scraped a groove in the earthen floor and placed a stick in it. I later found it was a piece of cane or bamboo bored through to form a tube. The cane was cut at an angle at both ends. At one end he fixed a wooden pipe-bowl and at the other a short tube at a right angle to the longer one in the groove. He then pulled the earth over the piece along the ground and poured water on the mound. I realised he was making a kind of hookah or hubble-bubble for smoking *dagga* (hemp, pronounced *dacha*). It was the first time I had seen this native practice. He filled the bowl and lit the contents then lay along the ground puffing at the piece of tube sticking up from the buried stem. His pleasure when drawing in the water-cooled smoke was evident in his face.

I took my camera and went over to the group and signalled that I wanted to take a photograph. The woman seemed amused that I should be interested and waved me on with a swing of the wrist. The man seemed lost in his repose and made no move of complaint, though he did open an eye on me and I got the chilling feeling of malevolence in his look. Surprised, for dope smokers are usually in a lazy daze and seldom register emotions, I went back to my pitch. Earlier I had already taken on board that the man was an addict from his slow movements and vague manner. I had met many under the influence from the Hadramaut down to the Cape and never felt threatened by them. Nevertheless, that night I had a feeling, a shiver, that I might have to be on my guard.

The African lay by his fire smoking late into the evening, long after his family had bedded down. Before going to sleep I put my pistol under the jersey I used as a pillow. Melodramatic? Perhaps, but so was the atmosphere. At least I thought so. Although *dagga* smokers are usually lethargic deadbeats, the look in that man's eye prompted caution. I had no intention of shooting him dead whatever happened, but should he try anything a shot in the leg or arm would knock the mischief out of him I reckoned.

Don't ask me why I wakened. Perhaps a nervous alarm primed with foreboding goes off when the mere weight of a shadow presses on it. For that is what I saw. A huge black shadow of a man, a genie from a bottle, small at its source with the fire behind it but growing bigger, bigger, as it rose and spread across the rock ceiling, huge, the great head above me, leering grotesquely and fluttering. At its source beside the fire the African was poised with a three-legged cauldron of steaming water in his hand, as at the moment of decision. He paused only momentarily then crossed the floor towards me at a speed remarkable for a man stupid with dope.

I leapt up in one movement, sloughing my sleeping bag from me like a snakeskin. Did he really mean to scald me? This was not the action pattern of *dagga* smokers. Still he came on. At the flashpoint when the cauldron swung back I forgot all about the pistol and punched him hard on the chin, a real, right-handed wallop, and he crumpled like an empty sack. The pot went clattering out of the cave and rolled down among bushes. He lay very still and I tested his breathing. It seemed steady. I was no authority on such matters but somehow I knew he would be out for a long time. I covered him with his blanket and eventually went back to sleep. In the morning nothing was said. We both went about our business as if nothing had happened. Perhaps he was oblivious to what he had done, but I'm sure he must have wondered how he came to be lying near me with his chin sore and swollen. The look on his face when he searched for his pot and found it among the bushes was the perfect laugh-line to drop the curtain on the little scene.

The walk down the south side of the Swartberg Pass was enjoyable besides being long and tiring. It is said that the Swartberg Pass is the most awe-inspiring in South Africa and I could well believe it. I was more able to appreciate the beauty of the scenery and the wonder of the dizzy road that carried me down. I camped the night by the Grobelaars River near Oudtshoorn and next day visited Highgate Ostrich Farm.

Ostrich feathers were exported from South Africa as far back as 1838, but these were from wild birds. It was not until 1850 that some farmers managed to catch some wild chicks and tame them; this was the first ostrich farm. They had about 500 birds there and they showed the complete run of things from the egg till the feathers were plucked or the bird was killed and made into biltong.

In the days when a bush hat was not complete without a majestic feather and ladies' feather boas were all the rage across Europe and America ostrich feathers, weight for weight, were worth more than gold. When feathers went out of fashion the business went into some decline but had picked up again and Highgate was a thriving farm. Apart from the life cycle of the birds you could watch native men ride them like horses.

From Oudtshoorn I took the old Bain's road that swirled down through the wonderful Robertson Pass towards Mossel Bay. It was a long lonely road.

Friday 13th Feb. 1953. In the Little Karoo

Walked all day today. This Karoo is a desert. The road seems to lead endlessly on to nowhere. On and on you go with nothing in sight. A couple of cars passed but they didn't stop. I hope I get a lift tomorrow or come to some water. My water bottle is half empty although I rationed myself severely.

Tonight I will eat some biltong and a handful of raisins with a couple of sips of water.

Sat. 14th Feb. 1953. Little Karoo

Walked all day again. Three cars passed but didn't stop. I really don't blame them. There are so many hobos who are permanently drunk with cheap wine or cane spirit who cadge lifts in South Africa, few motorists will risk picking anybody up.

I have cut my ration of water to a mere drop every couple of hours. My lips are dry and cracked. My pack felt extra heavy today. I feel tired and terribly fatigued with the lack of water. The biltong tastes like a dry stick and it is hard to swallow when I haven't any saliva in my mouth. But I forced myself to eat it because it is only through strict self discipline that I will be able to conserve any strength and energy I have left and I'm determined that this Karoo will not beat me.

Sunday 15th Feb. '53, Little Karoo

This morning it was difficult to rise and when I had struck camp my pack felt like a ton weight. George, the town I am heading for, isn't very far away, but the Outeniqua Mountains which loomed up in front of me and which I must cross to get there seemed an impregnable barrier.

The trickle of water I had left was hot. About nine o'clock I came to a farm. A dream of a cool drink of water was running through my mind as I entered the gate. I think I must have looked even worse than I felt or else perhaps these Afrikaners just know what a man wants out here. I knocked at the door. When the woman came I spoke for the first time in three days. My voice must have sounded awful for she brought me a glass of water before I had time to ask for it. How good it tasted! I wish a connoisseur of wine could go three days on a couple of pints of water – that is walking across a desert I mean – and then taste some cool water. I'm sure it would rank as the prime drink.

As I was sitting drinking the water Mr Kaiser, the farmer, came in sombrely dressed in black. It was only when I saw him I realised it was Sunday. One day seems very like another when you are on your own in the desert.

Mr Kaiser made me feel very welcome and said I must stay for lunch. After the meal it was typical Afrikaans hospitality when he asked if I would like to stay overnight. I'm pleased of the rest after the past few days. In the afternoon he suggested I have a walk over the farm. How delicious it was to eat a bunch of choice Honeypoort grapes straight off the vine. Also I picked a couple of peaches and ate them too. These past few days seem far away now.

The room I have been allotted is a big spacious affair. This farm house is built in typical old Dutch style.

Mon 16th Feb. 1953. George.

This morning before I left the farm Mrs Kaiser asked me if I would skin and butcher a goat. The boy who usually does it was not there and Mr Kaiser had already gone to the fields. I haven't done any of that since crocodile hunting a year ago but it all came back. When it came to cutting up the meat it was more hacking than fine butchery. It must have been OK for she was very pleased. These Afrikaners seem to take it for granted that anybody can skin and butcher animals. I wonder what would have happened if I had been asked to do that when I started out three years ago.

Today I crossed the Outaniqua Mountains via the Old Road. That old road was cut out by hand with convict labour. The new road is a broad highway and from the old road it looks like a white streak across the opposite side of the glen. No doubt that is why I haven't been getting any lifts lately. I have been walking along the old road when most of the traffic goes by the new one. It was quite a hard day coming over these mountains.

Tuesday, 17th Feb. 1953. Nr. Mossel Bay.
Walked a bit this morning then got a lift to within five miles of Mossel Bay. I walked that last stretch arriving just as the shops were closing. I just had time to get in and buy some bread.

Mossel Bay lies a little bit off the National Road. To get back on again I had to climb a street that must be the steepest in any town. It is over half a mile long and lies at almost 45 degrees. I am camping for the night just by the side of the road. There is a tear in my tent and it's agonising seeing it stretch with the wind. I hope it holds out till I get to Cape Town.

Mossel Bay was a leading port when the feather trade was at its height and even now it was very much alive. I had thought that Port Elizabeth had the steepest street in South Africa but, as mentioned in my diary, Mossel Bay had it beaten. Now I was on the very last lap of my long journey to Cape Town, 240 miles away.

I crept my way down this exciting stage of my journey in bits and pieces, camping beside the road until I got the big one, the last 100 miles in one lift. The man who made this momentous moment for me was an English speaking South African whose family had been in Natal for many generations. A self-professed Afrikaner through and through he nevertheless referred to England as 'home' and although he had never been there he was deeply concerned about the possibility of the 'Dutchmen' creating a republic and severing associations with Britain. I found it interesting and not a little confusing, to find an Afrikaner of long Africaans heritage denouncing the 'Dutch' (the old 'Boer' stock) as a completely different people to himself. South Africans were indeed an amazing potpourri of people.

My chauffeur and new friend, by dress, mannerisms and speech was the archetypal English public school gentleman. Nevertheless, his criticism of Britain for trying to intervene in his country's internal politics was as vehement as any overt Afrikaner I had met. When I said I had travelled through Africa and might be going back home by ship if I could, he seemed to take this as an opportunity to give me a message to take with me to tell all the folks back there.

"Britain seems bent on destroying a couple of hundred years of progress in this country," he said with great feeling. "The blacks aren't ready for an integrated society yet and if forced on us the country will degenerate to Chaka-days again."

He went on to criticise the ill-informed and biased press reports written abroad about South Africa. "The impression seems to be that the whites have no damned right to be here at all. Yet few people seem to understand that the Europeans came here before the majority of Africans who constitute the black population. You could say that the Zulus, Xhosas and Basutos have no right here and had better go back where they came from away in the north of Africa. They took over the land from the Bushmen. How many generations must you be in a place before you can claim domicile? Would you put everyone with a French name out of England? It's the same thing. Colour doesn't come into it. The Zulus are as different from the Bushmen as we are. Second generation blacks in England are accepted as British citizens with the full rights of the country. Why not the same for the whites in Africa? If you say there is a difference between blacks in Europe to whites in Africa that is pure biased racialism. We who are born in this country from many generations also born here have nowhere else to go. This is our country as much as, and many cases moreso, many blacks, as I said about the Zulus. If you are going to shout 'whites go home' in Africa you must shout the reverse to blacks who came uninvited to England. Of course the whole thing is ridiculous. A third generation English black person dumped in Africa would be just as lost and unhappy as a similar white South African forced to live in England. The fact is, we here are all Africans, black and white, and unless we get our heads together on this, there is going to be an unholy mess. Trouble is, the new Dutch government is bent on division rather than gradual integration. I hate to think of the future. But one thing is certain, we don't need wise guys who know nothing about our country coming here and telling us, or telling the newspapers to tell us, what we should do and how we must do it."

Travelling companions are easy talkers and because of this hitch-hiking was a crash-course in acquiring an insight to the thoughts and emotions of the diverse people in this complex and troubled land. I should have liked to have had the black Africans' view too but the only one I spent close time with was the one in the cave and he didn't talk very much, but his actions were eloquent.

But now, with Cape Town approaching and Table Mountain actually beginning to materialise out of the haze I was in jubilant mood with little interest for other peoples' worries. My mind was blurred by the glare from the end of the rainbow. Soon buildings took shape and the road passed into streets with bustling traffic. Somewhere near the centre of the town my driver pulled in and said, "This is it."

It certainly was and I could not have put it more succinctly, more informatively nor more accurately. I will never be able to explain, to describe the feeling I had when I stepped out of that car. I had arrived. I had done what I set out to do.

*

First glances at Cape Town showed it to be old and kind of dirty, but to me it seemed grand. The YMCA was full up so I went to a benevolent Working Mens' Home and got in there. The name was something of a misnomer for very few of the residents worked. What a place! It was full of the dregs off the streets. Drunks mostly. I was put into a big dormitory where there was hardly space to walk between the beds. But I had no complaints. None at all. It was wonderful.

Next day I renewed an acquaintance with a Mr Walker, a man I met up in the Zimbabwe Ruins where he was on holiday. When we met he immediately took me along to the *Cape Times* newspaper office where the editor was a personal friend of his. So they took a story which appeared next day and from there, once again, the ball didn't stop rolling.

South African Broadcasting Company got onto me through the newspaper and commissioned me to write my own script and present four, seven minute broadcasts at two and a half guineas per broadcast Then *Die Landstem*, the Afrikaans newspaper, paid three guineas for a story of my journey. After that I was very pleased when I had an article accepted by the *Times* magazine section for which they paid £4.00. I also wrote and sent a number of articles abroad. My pen was seldom idle most of my time in the city and I was delighted to be earning my keep doing what I enjoyed most.

The Working Men's Home was really a wonderful institution. Without it 90% of the residents there would have been walking the streets. But it really was some place. All the hobos and drunks and dope artists found their way there. Most of them had drunk their last penny. They owned no more than they wore. Their shoes were burst and their shirts torn. Their faces permanently flushed with booze, their bodies had lost their backbone and had settled into an easy, comfortable slouch. Their lodging with one meal a day, which is all most of them had, ran at about 18/- per week. That, for South Africa, was dirt cheap. The cheapest boarding house was usually about £12.00 per month. How the most of these derelicts paid even the little that was asked of them was a mystery. I never asked, but I'm sure nobody was ever turned away. The food menu rarely changed and came into the term 'hash' rather than 'gourmet' but there was plenty of it.

At night the air was pretty foul when the brandy-soaks drifted back, cursing and swearing as they argued with each other. Sometimes three or four arguments would be going on at once and someone would be sitting on his bed singing away to himself, while another cursed fluently as he fought with his clothes to get them off. Now and again a fight would break out. Not much of a battle because they would be too drunk to see each other. Often I stopped a fight by pushing the two contestants so that they fell on to a bed. Generally, when they fell they forgot about their fight and just fell asleep: not always on their own bed and that would start another barney. Then there were the filthy ones who would urinate on the floor and sometimes over the beds. Even after they had all found a bed and gone to sleep the night was bedlam with their grunts and snores. I have to say, this being Africa, that all these men were white. No doubt there would be the same places for black men too, but if there were they would have been out of town.

After ten days or so I was moved into a little cubicle about six feet square, just room for a bed and not much else. I hadn't asked to be moved but no doubt the management must have noticed that I was the only one who didn't get drunk. The walls of the cubicle only went up about six feet so I was not cut off from the noise and smells, but at least I wasn't disturbed by people continually falling over my bed at night and I had space to myself where I could write in some kind of peace.

The hostel wasn't the Ritz, but I was grateful to have my bed there and how I admired the people who ran the place. They had to be very special people to work there. Their rough kindness and compassion was an example beyond words. I wished so much that I could have the strength to be like them. The hostel was not a nice place to stay but it was a godsend to many and wonderful place to study life from the sordid to the sublime.

But after I got some money in from the broadcasts I said goodbye to the merry band at the hostel and took a room up in Hatfield Street. If not so interesting it was certainly much quieter there and much better for writing, especially when I wanted to knock some articles together. But it was only a bare room with shared bathroom. There was not even the means to make tea and apart from the odd meal I could not afford to eat out, with the result I lived most of the time on bread and jam and fruit with water. Rather plain fare for weeks on end, but it was my own place, my home.

On one of the rare occasions I chose to dine out, I went to a hotel restaurant some levels up from the cafes I would normally frequent on those special nights. I took a table some way from the little dance floor. A quartet was playing soft music. I enjoyed the rare ambience even if it made me feel a little lonely. I was studying the menu when there was a sudden stop in the music and I, with everyone there, looked in surprise to the orchestra leader who stood by the microphone to speak to the now silent diners, "Ladies and gentlemen," he announced in senatorial voice, "We have just noticed we have in our presence the Scotsman who has walked all the way through Africa to be with us this evening. Mister David Lessels, will you please stand. Give him a big hand folks." In total amazement I struggled to my feet feeling myself blush to the roots of my hair. After the pause I managed to stammer, "Thank you so much for your welcome. I am really pleased to be here with you, for so many reasons and in so many ways. Thank you." As I sat down to another round of applause a waiter swept across to me and with great flourish laid down another menu, this one near covered with signatures. As he handed me a pen he said, "Would you please sign our special guests card." Rather stunned I glanced through the names and recognised quite a few. The one immediately before mine was Ivy Benson of the 'All ladies orchestra'. They must have had some eagle-eyed person who recognised faces from newspapers. I ate in some considerable shyness that night. But when I asked for my bill the manager himself came over and said with great charm, "Your presence with us is our pleasure," and shook hands. I expressed my thanks before walking away feeling ten-feet tall but very self-conscious.

Not long after that my wellbeing took a dramatic turn for the better. It all started with a knock on my room door one frugal day while I was writing at the table. The fellow who stood there, about my own age, introduced himself as Bob Gass. When he had established that I was the person he was looking for he said he had been sent to take me home. I smiled at this and said he'd better come in and explain this to me. So started another family friendship that has gone down the generations to this day. Bob said his father came from Burntisland, Fife, and when he had read the paper about my journey and learned I was also a 'Fifer' he couldn't wait till the morning before he had sent Bob out to search me out and bring me home. The fact that I may not have wanted to go had not entered his head. Bob was sent on a mission and there was no question of him not fulfilling it. As it was, I was quite happy to pay up my board and bundle myself into Bob's little car and be taken 'home'. Bob seemed mightily relieved.

So it was that I met Mr Gass and gentle, bird-like, Mrs Gass. Robert (Bert) Gass had come to South Africa as a fourteen-year-old at the start of the first World War and immediately joined-up after lying about his age. He fought throughout Africa and Flanders, was wounded, and was an old campaigner by the time he was demobbed at seventeen years of age. Since that day he had stood on his own feet (and others) and would never talk about his war. He was the most forthright and forceful man I ever met. Bert Gass carved his way through the world and woe betide anyone who did not do his bidding. It did not take me long to realise why Bob, Jr., looked so pleased when I came along with him so easily.

Yet inside that iron-hard exterior was a great big heart that picked up broken bodies and minds and put them together again and sent their owners on their way through life better, more able to cope, than they had ever been able to do

518

before. A hard taskmaster, tight jawed and iron-willed, he broke men in his path if they did not comply, as easily and assuredly as he repaired those he felt needed his help. He would do anything, *anything,* for a friend, but to those who crossed him he could be merciless. Everyone who knew him had a tale to tell of him. Needless to say he was a very successful businessman with his own factory making neon signs which he had built up from scratch. But he was just as likely to walk away from it if another challenge took his fancy, as he had done before.

Mrs Gass had learned to accept triumph and disaster at a moment's notice with complete equanimity. She told me of the day her husband had come home and said to pack a bag, they were going off to Johannesburg. She did as bid without a word. Bert put the key of the door under the mat and phoned a friend to say that it was all his, the house, the lot. She left with a tiny child, a canteen of cutlery and her blankets. Nothing else.

That little tale I think, was the most I heard her say in all the weeks I lived with them. Forty years later when we visited her in Port Alfred I found a completely different and delightful character. Bert Gass had died a year or two before and here was another person who chattered non-stop, took Maureen through her garden discussing, explaining every flower and plant. A vivacious character who delighted in her grandchildren and they in her, an out-going person who played the piano and sang beautifully. She was like a jackdaw who had hidden a treasure under a stone and rediscovered it to its great delight near the end of its life.

From the day we met until he died Mr Gass, 'Pudd' to all his family, and I got on famously. I say that although at first I didn't take to him. I felt he was too hard. But after I got to know him I found that he had a heart of gold and would move heaven and earth to do anything for you. Apart from that I just enjoyed his company. If anybody were to ask me my most unforgettable character I would say without doubt, Mr Bert Gass.

I'm sure he enjoyed my company too. He liked the bond I gave him with his birthplace. When with me he would revert to his Scots dialect and revel in the fact I understood him, though some words had grown hazy with the years. He would say sometimes "Davie, dae they still talk aboot a thing being a perfect 'scunner' at hame yet?" (*Scunner* = Loathsome; also an over surfeit, such as of food.) Or maybe he would ask if the boys still played 'bools' (marbles). Once I referred to a coloured man who was sitting crouched on his heels as sitting down on his 'currie hunkers' and he hooted "Man, I havni' heard that since I left Burntisland," and slapped his thigh with pleasure, while saying softly, but with emphasis, as an aside to himself, "Curry hunkers! oh, that's a guid yin." Many times he would shake his head and add, "Man, Davie, I like to hear you speak." (*currie* – a small, very low milking stool. So *currie-hunkers*- squatting down on one's heels as if on a very low stool.)

He and Mrs Gass and I went off in his motor-caravan at the weekends and visited places that would have been beyond my reach. He was a past officer in the army and territorials and took me to The Castle army barracks and made the quartermaster give me two new pairs of boots, one pair I posted to poste restante Nairobi, on the assumption that I might decide to walk back through Africa, although that final decision had not yet been made. He was a wonderful patron and friend and I enjoyed the privilege of his friendship.

During my time with the family I made good friends with Bob and his fiancée, Beryl, and with her younger sister, Caryl. Bob and Beryl married soon after I left and we have always kept good contact since. Caryl later married her husband Frances and they too remain very close with cards and visits.

Apart from the lifelong friends I made there, Cape Town has always remained very close to me. It was old and a bit dirty in places, but the surroundings are magnificent. No other town in Africa can compare with Cape Town's doorstep scenery. Table Mountain dominates the background like a piece of stage scenery and the town seems to nestle down in its curve like a kitten to its mother. Looking with your back to the sea over on the right is Lion's Head, a sharp pyramid-shaped mountain. There is nothing bonnier than to see Lion's Head and the Twelve Apostles, a range of twelve peaks just round the corner, at sunset.

I did quite a bit of swimming around the Cape. The beaches on the Atlantic side of the peninsula are treacherous because of the sudden shelving of the sand and the backwash and the water is cold. Clifton and Camps Bay are the main ones on that side. But over on the False Bay side of the peninsula the water is warmer and the beaches are lovely with little or no backwash. I went to Gordon's Bay and the Strand on a few occasions. But the best of all swimming was to be had at Fish Hoek. To get there you must pass Muizenburg with its two beaches, Christian Beach and the Snake Pit (the Jewish Mecca) both nicknames. At Fish Hoek, it was not so much that the beach was better than any place else in False Bay, but the fact that two huge ten-foot porpoises came in and played with the bathers. I had fun one afternoon diving and catching hold of the tail of one and being hauled along at great speed by it. They came right into about three feet of water and dived and leapt and frolicked among the people, playful as puppies. When they first started coming in the papers were full of them. At first they came only to look, keeping a fair distance away. Gradually they got bolder until first one, the male no doubt, then the other threw discretion to the winds and went overboard with the bathers. Some fishermen tried to catch them on the grounds that they kept smaller fish away but the people petitioned against them and then the fishermen not only agreed to leave them alone but to feed them now and again and so entice them to stay. They were a great boon to Fish Hoek's tourist trade. At first the bathers too were a bit apprehensive about their intentions. In fact they were mistaken for sharks at first. But now the porpoises were friends with everybody and great fun was had by all.

One of Cape Town's greatest attractions is the Table Mountain cableway. It was a queer and wonderful sensation swinging up the face of the mountain, especially when a wind blew up and the car started to swing, perilously it seemed. When strong winds blow, and that is quite often, the cableway is closed.

The curse of the Cape is the southeasters, the wind that springs up and blows at gale force for days and sometimes weeks on end. I experienced two or three during my stay here. During the worst one the gusts at times were so strong it was impossible to walk against them and I had to just stand and lean forward into the wind or be blown over.

The southeaster is known as the 'Cape Doctor' because it is supposed to blow all diseases out to sea. But the only thing I saw it blow about was sand. After it had played itself out the streets were littered with paper and rubbish and sand was everywhere. When a southeaster blows, Table Mountain dons its tablecloth – a white cloud which lies just on top of the mountain and hangs down the side like a cloth sometimes.

One of the most striking things I noticed at the Cape was the large number of 'Coloured' people. One rarely saw a truly black native, although there were a few. In the past, before white women came out, there must have been wholesale mixing of the black and white. Now Coloureds married among themselves and had made a completely new race, quite apart from either natives or Europeans.

In many ways Cape Town resembled any port in Europe. There were the same cheap pubs and drunken merchant seamen. There were the slum areas with women hanging about. There were the recognised tough areas; Hanover Street and District Six could have compared with the Gorbals of Glasgow at that time.

What was strange about Cape Town was the almost non-existence of the colour bar. Segregation did exist but in many ways it was very, very slack compared with the rest of South Africa. Blacks and Coloureds sat side by side with Europeans in the buses and even in the men's lavatories in the gardens I crossed daily from Hatfield, all stood shoulder to shoulder.

This was all part of the charm of Cape Town. There was a friendliness, a warmth there, that was not in any other place. Even the drunks, so alien to the rest of Africa, were reminiscent of some places in Scotland on a Saturday night. I particularly remember boarding a double-decker bus – even that; who would have thought of these in Africa – while a drunk hung onto the pole at the back platform singing 'Sweet Sixteen' in the sweetest tones he could muster. I hadn't seen anything like that since leaving Scotland. Even so he only got out the first two lines:

'When first I saw the love-light in your eyes
I dreamt the world held nought but joy for me,'

when he rolled round the pole and would have fallen out while the bus was picking up speed if his pal had not grabbed hold of him. The pal was so drunk too he nearly went with the singer. What the black Africans on board must have thought of that doesn't bear thinking about.

As if I had not seen enough of Bain's roads, I went up over Bains Kloof, the old road going north from the Cape to take in the grand scenery there. I visited Groot Constantia, the former residence of a past governor, Van Der Stel, and admired its typical old Dutch gabled architecture and fine collection of antiques. The slave dungeons and the wine cellar remained the same as they were in Van Der Stel's day. Here were grown the first grapes for the famous Constantia wines.

I think I covered most of the ground around the Cape and enjoyed every bit of it. My most memorable journey, undoubtedly, was down the peninsula to Sea Point. On the way I gazed in wonder at the view from Chapman's Peak looking down on Hout Bay. It was magnificent. The Atlantic had a peculiar metallic sheen from that height and the Bay looked like a sheet of polished copper.

Interesting and beautiful though that area was, these were not the reasons that made my journey down the peninsula so memorable. The reason, the main purpose of my going down there, was because that toe of land represented to me the most southerly point of the great continent I had set out to travel. I say 'to me' because geographically Cape Agulhas, (Needles), a hundred miles or so back easterly, claims the southernmost point of Africa. But my goal had always been Cape Town and the peninsula that leads out of the town and curls down and round Simon's Town and beyond, was the last part of my south-going journey through Africa. Going down the Cape of Good Hope to the final step at Cape Point where I sat with my feet dangling over the end of the continent, with nothing between me and Antarctica, was a dream come true.

I sat long and cast my mind back over the past two-and-a-half years, trying to remember the most salient, the most memorable, the worst and the best moments and pondered my future. For some time now I had been pretty sure I would return through Africa but I had reserved the final decision to this moment.

Indeed, the reason I had remained so long in Cape Town was to be there when Mr Nagle arrived from Durban with the revolver he had promised me. We had kept in touch and he had given me a date for his arrival. We met in the Houses of Parliament, that imposing, august building so steeped in the history of the country, and he gave me a bag with the gun, still wrapped in the newspaper of the day, with a box of bullets. Had this happened in today's world and the newspapers had got hold of it both our futures would have been ruined. As it was we went to a police office and the weapon was signed over to me with a licence, all with no more ado and perfectly legal.

Now was the final moment of decision. To look for a passage home, preferably by working it, or to look to the north and head that way back through Africa? My heart was split. I dearly wanted to go home and see my family and friends. After all, I had enough material to write the book I had always dreamed of, so why not? Somewhere in the back of my mind there was an intangible thing that nagged me. That indistinguishable something that was there, mostly in repose, but ready to jump out in moments of indecision. Grasso Stellario, the little Italian who had entered my life so early in my journey, was still there, posing his question "what is it you are looking for?" the answer to which, like the Scarlet Pimpernel, was still 'damned elusive'. I still remembered Grasso's words as he said I would.

Whatever it was, it didn't bother me anything like it had before I started out on my journey. So did that mean it had been nothing, or if it was something important, did it mean I was well along the way towards finding it? If so, perhaps I might be able to give Grasso the answer to his question by the time I got back.

There were other reasons too, much more tangible, for my wanting to go back through the country. Kenya was now in the grip of the Mau-Mau uprising and I desperately wanted to know what it was all about and to do my bit if I could for the country. Kenya was my first love of all Africa, the place that had drawn me to it, and it remained so. I had to go back.

But apart from Kenya I was aware that there was so much of Africa I wanted to visit, places I had heard so much about on the way down that whetted my appetite for more. Far from being tired of it all, I was raring to go on. There was so much more to see.

To 'see' was the operative word at that poignant moment for I had now passed my twenty-fifth birthday and my eye was healthy. The doctor's prognosis at the time when he removed my right eye was that I must wait until that birthday to learn if the eye had stabilised. Now I knew it had. The great day had been in Salisbury. It was not full strength, but for some time before the date I felt it was stable.

All the relief from those four, long, waiting years was focussed on that birthday morning. It was if a door had opened from my small, frightened world into one so big I couldn't see the end, one that was brighter, more colourful and infinitely more carefree. That morning when I went about the city the jacaranda trees that lined the pavements and carpeted the streets with their blue blossom looked more beautiful than they had ever been before, and that was saying a lot, for even in my old world their beauty was indescribable.

Yet I knew I could have lived in a kind of happiness even if these things had been suddenly excluded from me. Their memory was ever there. When I closed my eye I could see quite plainly the beauties of nature and that would always be so. It was peoples' faces I dreaded losing. I had come to realise that it is people who are the wonders of the world. I would have been destitute if I could not have witnessed the poetry of expression in faces, each one different, each one changing by the second; faces that told hearts' stories, young faces growing up, grown-up faces growing old, faces of people not yet met, children not yet born. These were the things I had passionately hoped would not be taken from me.

Such were my thoughts when I turned my face north to start the long way home.